ECONOMIC DECISIONS FOR CONSUMERS

ECONOMIC DECISIONS FOR CONSUMERS

SECOND EDITION

DON R. LEET

California State University, Fresno

JOANN DRIGGERS

Mount San Antonio College

MACMILLAN PUBLISHING COMPANY, New York

Editors: Julie Alexander and Helen McInnis
Production Supervisor: Eric Newman
Production Manager: Sandra E. Moore
Text Designer: Linda Fischer
Cover Designer: Robert Freese
Cover Art: Viqui Maggio
Illustrations: Hadel Studio

This book was set in Trump Medieval and Clarendon by Polyglot and printed and bound by R. R. Donnelley & Sons Company.
The cover was printed by Phoenix Color Corp.

Macmillan Publishing Company
866 Third Avenue, New York, New York 10022

Collier Macmillan Canada, Inc.

Library of Congress Cataloging-in-Publication Data

Leet, Don R.
    Economic decisions for consumers / Don R. Leet, Joann Driggers. —
2nd ed.
        p.   cm.
    Includes bibliographical references.
    ISBN 0-02-369491-2
    1. Consumer education.   I. Driggers, Joann.   II. Title.
TX335.L43   1990   89-12779
640'.73—dc20   CIP

Printing: 1 2 3 4 5 6 7   Year: 0 1 2 3 4 5 6

ACKNOWLEDGMENTS

Photo Credits: Vernon Gerety (pages 7, 31, 58, 71, 195, 224, 259, 425, 432, 486, 507); Ben Arikawa (pages 42 and 112); Jack Christensen and James Echols (pages 49, 125, 150, 237, 271, 295, 297, 315, 327, 386, 399, 401, 445, 482, 495, 509, 547, 558); Dirk van der Elst (page 66); *Fresno Bee* (pages 469 and 508); Jerri Booth (page 605); NASA (page 622).

(Acknowledgments continue on page 669, which constitutes a continuation of this copyright page.)

PREFACE

Our Rationale

We wrote this book specifically for college students taking a course that relates to consumer education. We designed the text to focus on consumer decision making throughout the life-cycle. Thus we deal with the real-world problems of goal setting, consumer redress, money management, financial planning, and buymanship for a demographically diverse set of consumers. As we say in Chapter 1, we are not trying to move mountains—rather, we are trying to help consumers survive in those mountains.

In this new edition we place added emphasis on consumer responsibilities. Consumers must become more informed about how their individual decisions affect others. We devote chapters to the environmental and energy problems that face us today. We explore the global interdependence issues of international trade, deforestation, and the greenhouse effect. We also put the importance of consumer decision making in a macroeconomic context by exploring alternative economic systems and discussing the causes of inflation and recession. In short, we have attempted to add a global citizenship dimension to consumer education without ignoring the real problems of day-to-day life.

To the Student

There is a definite need for consumer economics education. During the past two decades, Americans have experienced record high interest rates as well as double-digit inflation and high unemployment rates. The 1990s begin with a more stable economy, but one in which many individuals feel that they are losing ground. Although some consumers are experiencing real gains in income, others are in danger of falling below the poverty line. Consumers are feeling the impact of the global marketplace. They are concerned about their future as they plan for an extended retirement in a world with serious economic and environmental problems.

v

Perhaps your search for a way to cope with one or more of these problems has led you to enroll in this course. Let us assure you that there are many actions you can take to improve your personal economic situation and assist in solving some of the global problems we must also face. We believe that after reading this text you will be able to make better, more informed economic decisions. We also hope that your decisions will be tempered by an understanding of how they affect others.

The Plan of the Book

We begin our effort to improve your decision-making skills by exploring in Chapter 1 the forces that influence consumer choices, values, and goals. We also introduce a decision-making model that we apply throughout the book. Chapter 2 describes individual life-styles and family life-cycles as well as career choices. Chapter 3 is a primer on basic economic concepts and how economic systems work. With these chapters as a common background, you will be prepared to learn in Chapters 4, 5, and 6 about financial planning, budgeting, banking, and credit. Chapter 7 looks at the impact of advertising and information on consumer spending, and Chapter 8 addresses the problem of consumer law and redress. In Chapter 9 we introduce the process of comparison buying and apply it to clothing, household textiles, and consumer durables. Chapters 10 through 17 show you how to apply your decision-making skills to important consumer topics like food, housing, transportation, energy and the environment, health care, government services, taxes, investments, insurance, and retirement. We conclude with an overview of consumer economics from a global perspective.

Special Features

''Did you know?'' Every chapter begins with a list of interesting facts or concepts that are explored in the chapter and that are unknown to most consumers. By perusing this list you will get some idea of the information contained in the body of the chapter.

Introductions and summaries. Each chapter also starts with an overview that explains how the topics and subtopics of the chapter fit into a cohesive whole. The summaries tie up loose ends and stress the major topics within the chapter. We believe that it is important to have both an overview and a complete summary of each chapter so that students will have an overall grasp of the chapter. These parts of the chapter will be especially helpful in reviewing for examinations.

Key terms and glossary. The backbone of knowledge of a subject is vocabulary. Each chapter contains many key terms, all of which are in bold type when they first appear in the text. All are defined in the glossary for future reference; this is particularly important since many recur in other chapters. The glossary will also serve as a study aid. Some particularly important terms, usually of a conceptual nature, are also defined in the margin of the text where they first appear. This is a clue to the student of their importance.

Boxes and worksheets. There exists a wealth of material that can enrich a course that focuses on the many economic decisions facing consumers. Some of this material involves applying concepts and strategies to the specific personal problems that a consumer may encounter. Accordingly, in most chapters we have provided worksheets into which the reader can enter real-world data and then use to try some of the strategies for better decision-making success in the text. These interactive worksheets should make the chapter material come alive and be more relevant in the day-to-day world of the student-consumer. Boxes provide asides or additional details that may not be crucial to a particular section but that add depth and breadth of knowledge. These "enrichment" boxes may also serve to open discussion in the classroom. Many boxes are followed by discussion questions that will involve the reader in applying the boxed material.

End-of-chapter material. Each chapter ends with "Questions" and "References and Readings." The questions were selected to emphasize the most important points of the chapter and to allow the student to apply the concepts presented. The "References and Readings" lists serve the dual purpose of documenting specific citations within the chapter and providing the names of articles and books from which a student can gather data and additional information about subjects explored within the chapter.

Appendix. We have included in an appendix a list of resources because we view our textbook as a reference and want it to be helpful whenever the reader confronts a real-world problem.

Acknowledgments

We are indebted to many people who have helped us in completing our second edition. Our first debt of gratitude must go to our families and friends, who have shown us support and consideration throughout the long and tedious process of creating a revised and updated edition of our manuscript. Second, we thank Jeffry Seibert and Shirley Pennell for typing parts of the manuscript. Jeff also served as Professor Leet's administrative assistant in the CSU Fresno Center for Economic Education. In this capacity he performed a significant set of functions that varied from research to proofreading, and just about everything in between. Most of the photographs were done expressly for our book by Jack Christensen, James Echols, Vernon Gerety, Jerri Booth, and Ben Arikawa—all colleagues or former students. They deserve our appreciation for work above and beyond the call of duty. We also thank the staff at Macmillan, who have all been very supportive. The second edition began when Julie Alexander became our acquisitions editor. Later our production supervisor, Eric Newman, diligently edited the text in a thoughtful and constructive manner. We thank our subsequent editor, Helen McInnis, for her support.

The quality and direction of this book owe a great deal to our reviewers. In the first edition we received advice from Joseph E. Barr, Framingham State College; Howard K. Boone, Monterey Peninsula College; Genevieve H. Cory, Canada College; Joseph L. Craycraft, University of Cincinnati; Joanne Dempsey, Bradley University; Judy Farris, South Dakota State University; Vickie L. Hampton, University of Texas; Hilda Jo Jennings, Northern Arizona University; John Neal, Lake Sumter Community College; Clifford Pew, Gavilan College; Shirley Schecter, Queens College, CUNY; Peter R. Senn, Wright College; Elsie Takeguchi, Sacramento City College; and June Varner, Ohio University.

For the second edition we consulted Joanne Dempsey, Bradley University; Emilie Duggan, Grossmont Community College; Virginia A. Haldeman, University of Nevada, Reno; Joyce S. Harrison, Middle Tennessee State University; Suzanne Hilsinger, Syracuse University; Susan Nowakhtar, Queens College, CUNY; Mary E. Pritchard, Northern Illinois University; Grace L. Pyles, Kent State University; Shirley P. Reagan, Louisiana Tech University; June Varner, Ohio University; and Roberta W. Walsh, University of Vermont.

I offer special thanks to my colleagues Loy Bilderback, Jack Christensen, Jim Echols, Bill Fasse, and Izumi Taniguchi at California State University, Fresno, and Kathleen Mikitka at San Diego State University for their help and support during the project. I also acknowledge the technical and legal assistance that my brother, James L. Leet, Esq., rendered above and beyond the call of brotherly duty. Finally, I thank my wife, Vickie, and my children, Sara, Megan, and Andrew, for their special support and understanding.

D. L.

I offer special thanks for encouragement and criticism to Jeanne Erskine, Louise Mast, Craig Petersen, and Phyllis Specht at Mt. San Antonio College. I also thank JoAnn Crist Thomas for her continuing understanding and counseling and Steve Collier for his encouragement and love. Without these two people, this project would have been more stressful, less manageable, and not nearly as much fun. I also thank my niece, Lisa Portlock, who during a time of personal change was understanding of the amount of time and dedication this project took.

J. D.

BRIEF CONTENTS

DETAILED CONTENTS

Chapter One

DECISION MAKING: LEARNING TO CHOOSE

- ☐ The Need for Consumer Education
- ☐ Scarcity: The Mother of Decisions
- ☐ Consuming: More Than Just Buying
- ☐ Values and the Consumer
- ☐ Goals: Values in Action
- ☐ The Consumer Decision-Making Model

DID YOU KNOW THAT...

. . . a study completed for the U.S. Office of Education showed consumer economics to be the greatest area of difficulty for U.S. adults?

. . . on the average, an American household loses about $700 per year from some form of consumer fraud?

. . . consumer economics is very close to Aristotle's idea of what economics ought to be?

. . . learning how to make better decisions is at the heart of consumer economics?

. . . scarcity is the reason that decisions have to be made? If there was more than enough of everything, we wouldn't need good decision-making skills.

. . . there are some basic rules of good decision making that you can learn and then apply in many different situations?

consumer economics: the study of personal decision making or maximizing well-being through rational economic choices

James Duesenberry (1960), former chairman of the Harvard Economics Department, once wrote, "Economics is all about how people make choices. Sociology is all about why people don't have any choices to make." If that is the case, then **consumer economics** is all about how individuals can make better choices.

Good decision makers are *made*, not born. You must learn and practice decision-making skills if you are to cope with the hundreds of decisions that you will make in a lifetime. Decisions come in all sizes and shapes. Some, such as choosing a career or getting married, occur only infrequently. Some, such as having children or getting a college degree, are irreversible. Other choices are important but occur frequently enough to allow for some learning and reevaluation. Buying a car or a house and making an investment are examples of these kinds of decisions. Then, there are the more frequently made decisions of food shopping or obtaining credit. Life is riddled with decisions.

This chapter develops some tools for dealing with our world of decisions. We begin with the rationale for studying consumer economics—after all, your time is valuable and you should be informed early about the benefits of this course. But there are costs, too. One of the most fundamental principles of economics is that *you never get something for nothing.* Comparing the costs and benefits of alternatives can help you make better decisions. Then we look at consumption itself and discuss its objective: to increase happiness. This leads us to the question of values: what they are, where they come from, and how you can clarify your own. After discussing values clarification, we will discuss goals and standards and will follow with a discussion of some constraints on the decision-making process. Finally, we will present our decision-making model and apply it to a consumer problem.

THE NEED FOR CONSUMER EDUCATION

Have you ever bought something that you really didn't need or even want? Has one of your appliances ever broken down the week after the warranty expired? Or have you ever had an appliance break down and discovered that the problem was not covered by the warranty? Do you think that chemical additives in your food, drink, or clothing are harming you? Are you paying higher taxes than other people with similar incomes?

Most consumers would answer yes to some or all of these questions. Perhaps experiences like those described above have increased your interest in a college-level course focused on the consumer. Or you may be considering a career as a professional in the consumer relations field and realize that this course is designed to help you meet that goal. Whether you are taking this course to improve your own skills as a consumer or as a basis for seeking employment in the private, public, or nonprofit sector, you may be surprised to learn that your fellow consumers are generally ignorant on even the most basic consumer economics concepts.

A study completed for the U.S. Office of Education concluded: ''The greatest area of difficulty in general knowledge areas of adults appears to be consumer economics. Almost 30 percent (34.9 million) of American adults fall into the lowest level of competency, while another one-third (some 39 million) adult Americans function with difficulty'' (Wilcox, 1979, p. 29). For teenagers, the test results are not any more encouraging. On a national test of economic literacy U.S. high school students incorrectly answered almost 60 percent of the questions. Paul Volcker, former chairman of the Federal Reserve System, announced these dismal results at the annual meeting of the American Economic Association in December 1988. He said, ''The news is not good. A basic understanding of our economic system is important if this country is to be successful in what everyone realizes is a period of global competition'' (Carmody, 1988).

If a large portion of adults and high school students cannot pass tests designed by well-meaning educators, how are they to protect themselves against firms that engage in fraudulent practices? Short weights and measures (selling fifteen ounces of hamburger and charging for a pound or charging for ten gallons of gasoline when pumping only nine) have been estimated to cost the consumer as much as $10 billion per year. For example, a report issued by West Virginia inspectors found that 23 percent of all items inspected for weight or volume contained less than the amount stipulated. Such common items as milk, orange juice, and beer headed the lengthy list of fraudulently packaged items (Greer, 1987). Another form of consumer fraud is the sale of **counterfeit goods**. These are cheaply produced imitations of popular brand names like Gucci, Levis, Benetton, and Cartier that have been produced illegally and sold as if they were the original item. This form of consumer fraud has been estimated to cost an additional $16 to $18 billion annually (Greer, 1987). Other forms of consumer fraud swell the estimate of consumer loss to more than $60 billion per year. Ignorance may be bliss, but it is also very expensive. And few people can afford it.

counterfeit goods: cheaply produced imitations of popular brand names that have been produced illegally and sold as if they were the original items

Sometimes we may find statistics rather impersonal and therefore boring, as when we hear that $60 billion is lost by ''consumers'' every year. If this figure seems mind boggling, divide it by the number of American households—like yours—and you get an understandable figure. On the average, an American household loses almost $700 every year from consumer fraud—$700 that may be saved by studying consumer economics.

It would be incorrect, however, to assume that the number-one problem facing consumers today is identifying and punishing businesses whose major goal is to defraud the public. Although the amount of consumer loss through fraud and deception is high, so is the annual cost of shoplifting—an activity in which a few consumers victimize businesses (and their fellow consumers). The annual cost of shoplifting amounts to $33 billion annually, with surveys showing one consumer out of 15 committing this crime at least once in his or her life (Morton and Rezny, 1989).

Of course, just as most consumers never engage in shoplifting, neither do most businesses attempt to cheat their customers. It would also be incorrect to point an accusing finger at government and lay the blame for consumer ignorance, fraud, and high prices on its doorstep. However, most consumers do receive their formal education at public expense, and a poor consumer education program in the schools, coupled with a lackadaisical approach to enforcing consumer legislation, can lead to an increase in consumer misfortunes in the marketplace. Some observers have also noted that some government regulations, such as those governing automobile emissions and safety standards, push up prices and restrict consumer choice, thus lowering the level of consumer satisfaction.

If one were to identify the root of most consumer problems, it would not be an unsavory character selling stolen goods on a street corner. Neither would it be an overly zealous government bureaucrat creating costly regulations. Most consumer problems result from poorly made decisions based on insufficient or inaccurate information obtained in an unsystematic way. In other words, the fault often lies not in our stars but in ourselves. The responsibility for making more satisfying choices and thus becoming a better consumer cannot be shifted to someone else. Because you are the ultimate beneficiary, it is only right that you take charge and assume the role of a rational, knowledgeable decision maker. Studying consumer economics can help you achieve this goal.

What Is Consumer Economics?

To the famous Greek philosopher Aristotle (384–322 B.C.), the term *consumer economics* would have belonged in what some comedians call "the department of redundancy department." Translated literally from its Greek origins, the word *economics* means management of the household. Thus, according to the early Greeks, all economics was consumer economics.

In modern times, the study of economics encompasses more than household management. In fact, there was a time when few economists bothered to study the household because household behavior had already been described by making a few assumptions. There seemed little need to clutter up a neat theory with messy, real-world behavior. However, those times are past. Today, consumer economics is a legitimate field of study for economists, home economists, and business professors alike.

In order to understand the discipline of consumer economics, you must first appreciate its two components: consumerism and economics.

consumerism: a movement whose goal is to ensure that individuals who buy and use products and services get what they pay for—fair value

Consumerism is a movement whose goal is to ensure that individuals who buy and use products and services get fair value. **Economics** is not a social movement, but a field of study that looks at how people and societies cope with the fundamental problem of satisfying their unlimited wants with limited resources. Economists' attempts to cope with this dilemma have led some people to offer a shortcut definition of economics as the "science of choice."

Consumer economics, like economics itself, can be seen as the study of choice but with a more limited scope. Whereas economics deals with the problem of unlimited wants and limited resources on both a society (macro) and an individual (micro) level, consumer economics deals with the wants-versus-resources problem in the area of personal consumption. Consumer economics is personal economics, and in that sense is closer to the original Greek meaning of the term. And because it involves choice, we can then say that it is the study of personal economic decision making.

This does not mean that consumer economics is not concerned with the entire economy. It is, but usually only insofar as the behavior of the economy in general affects a particular consumer. Thus, when we talk about inflation in consumer economics, we are often less concerned with the causes of inflation than with strategies for consumers to cope with inflation. Consumer economics does not try to move mountains; instead we try to make consumers better able to survive in those mountains. Nevertheless, your survival may depend upon your understanding of the economic landscape. To sharpen your perspective, we will devote several chapters to outlining and analyzing the broader contours of your macroeconomic environment. It is important for you to see how your decisions play a role in national and global issues. But first, we will describe the personal side of improving your decision-making skills.

The Rewards of Good Decision Making

One of the best ways to ensure your continued survival as a consumer is to develop your decision-making skills. This requires some hard work and practice. An important question to consider at the outset of the course is whether the benefits of improving your decision-making skills and knowledge of consumer economics exceed the monetary and time costs involved. E. Scott Maynes (1969), chairman of the Department of Consumer Economics at Cornell University, lists five advantages to effective consumer decision making:

1. It increases your purchasing power by helping you select the least expensive product of equal quality.
2. The money saved in this process is untaxed and therefore understates the true saving, because an equivalent amount of additional income earned would be subject to federal and state income taxes.

3. Decision-making skills can be learned by anyone; thus, greater purchasing power does not depend on someone's getting a better job or having an unusual skill.
4. Good decision makers are less likely to become the victims of fraud or deception; thus, they will not have to bear an equal share of the $60 billion consumer loss caused by fraud.
5. The actions of good decision makers have a social payoff because those firms that offer better goods on better terms will be rewarded with business, whereas less efficient competitors will disappear. This serves as an incentive for all firms to offer more value to their customers.

In a more recent article Brenda J. Cude attempted to quantify the returns to good consumer decision making. Using the prices for over 900 products tested over a ten-year period by Consumers Union, Professor Cude found that consumers pay between 14 and 124 percent more for an item when a brand is selected randomly without a rational search process. As she states in her conclusion, "[T]here are dramatic returns possible to informed purchase decisions. In each of the 12 product classes the potential maximum loss to consumers from purchasing a worst choice rather than a best choice was great." (Cude, 1987, p. 94).

As you can see there are significant rewards for improving your decision-making skills. Recalling Cude's results, you can look forward to getting at least a 14 percent return on your expenditures if you make rational choices. The next section explores the basic root of all choices—scarcity.

SCARCITY: THE MOTHER OF DECISIONS

Everyone knows that we have to make choices in all areas of our lives. We can't be in two places at once; neither can we have our cake and eat it, too, as the old saying goes. The reason for this fact of life is that our resources are limited whereas the possible uses of those resources are unlimited. Money is an obvious example. At this moment, you have a limited amount of money. What could you do with this resource? "Spend it," you say. But spend it on what? A new cassette, lunch, a moped, a textbook (good choice), a gift, shoes—what? There is a whole range of choices open to you. You have to *decide* the best use of your money at this time, based on your wants, needs, and goals.

Money, then, is a **scarce resource**: It is limited; you only have so much of it. An example of an opposite of a scarce resource is air. You can take in as much air as you like and no one will be very concerned. Air is what economists call a **free good**—it is there for the asking. It is a "good" because we like to use it, and it is free because it is so abundant that there is no cost.

Opportunity Costs

opportunity costs: the value of whatever must be given up in order to get something else—that is, the value of all resources, including time

All scarce resources have costs associated with them. The cost is often expressed as a money cost. For example, if a new stereo system costs $800, you must give up $800 to get the stereophonic sound that you want. But the $800 does not represent the real cost of the system. The only way to evaluate the real cost is to know what else you might have done with that money. You could have gone on a vacation, added significantly to your wardrobe, or simply let the money draw interest in the bank. Of these alternatives let us say that the vacation is your next best choice. Economists say that you gave up the opportunity to take a vacation in order to buy a stereo. The opportunity cost of the stereo decision is the vacation because **opportunity cost** is the value of what you must give up in order to get something else. Opportunity costs are often referred to as **trade-offs** because they involve trading one thing for another. Our example involves a trade-off between buying a stereo and taking a vacation. It is incorrect to say that the opportunity costs of the stereo is the vacation plus the clothes you didn't buy plus the lost bank account interest, because the alternatives are mutually exclusive. Once you decide to do one of them, you can't do the others.

Decisions always involve tradeoffs and require some thoughtful investigation. The advertised price of this stereo is $799, but what is its opportunity cost to this consumer? The same money could have paid for a vacation.

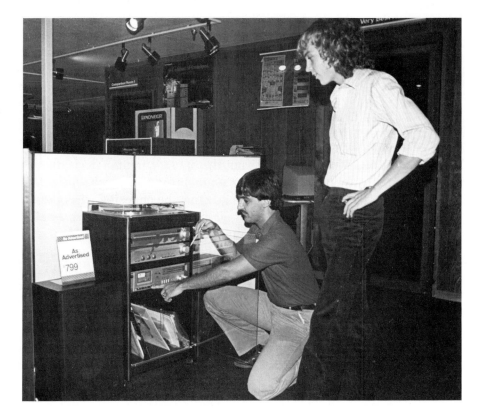

Opportunity costs are involved in every decision you make. Money is a fairly good measure of opportunity cost, as long as consumers understand the alternative uses of their money. If, on the other hand, consumers buy goods and services randomly, without thinking about alternatives, money does not serve as an accurate yardstick of the lost opportunities (opportunity cost).

The concepts of scarcity and opportunity cost are not tied to money alone, however. A person's time is also a valuable resource. Suppose, for example, that a good, but not great, student enrolls in a difficult math class. Assume that the student takes four other classes and works part-time. This consumer-student will have significant time problems by the end of the term. Eventually, a choice situation may evolve: In order to get a B in math, the student must run the risk of not studying for four other classes or cutting out the part-time job. The opportunity cost of the math class turns out to be very high. And that's where the importance of decision making becomes clear.

As a consumer—whether of education, ten-speed bicycles, or food—you need to be aware of the total cost of your decisions. The explicit money cost plus the implicit time cost should both be included in your opportunity cost calculation. If you underestimate these costs, your decisions will be based on faulty information and may lead to mistakes. These errors in judgment can be avoided if you develop good consumer decision-making skills and use them.

Understanding opportunity costs is an important first step in the process of learning to be a good decision maker, but you also need to be able to value the benefits of a choice. Once you can measure the costs and the benefits, you are well on your way to making a rational decision.

Benefits, Too

Cost is not the only element of decision making to consider. Benefits of a particular action must also play a role. The consumer-student in the math class example may be choosing wisely in taking such a time-consuming, high-cost class if the end result is favorable. Perhaps the professor is an outstanding teacher, or maybe the class will produce significant benefits. If, after talking to other students, sitting in on the class a few times, and seeing the professor during office hours, the student estimates that the benefits outweigh the costs, taking the course is an intelligent, rational decision. But it is not rational to take on four other classes and a part-time job! In general, to be a good decision maker you should remember these principles:

1. Your time and income are limited and both are valuable.
2. Total cost equals explicit (money) cost plus implicit (time) costs.

3. Decisions should be made only after weighing both the costs and benefits of alternative actions.

These basic principles form the core of the decision-making process. But before you can apply these principles to your personal situation, you must clarify your own wants and needs. This means examining your consumer life-style, the values that support it, and the forces that influence it. The remainder of this chapter helps you to do this and then to apply what you've learned to a full-fledged consumer decision-making model. But first, we need to clarify your view of consumption. Is more consumption always better than less, or are you concerned with the impact your consumption habits have on the world around you?

CONSUMING: MORE THAN JUST BUYING

Until recently, economists and most other people assumed, without necessarily saying so, that more is always better than less, bigger is always better than smaller, and too much is never enough. Most economists do believe that people are happier if they are able to consume more. When challenged, they might justify this judgment on the basis of observation: Would someone who just bought a modest two-bedroom home be willing to trade it for a larger, more comfortable one at no additional cost? Most would do so quickly and without hesitation. Thus, "more is better" seems to be based on reality.

But E. F. Schumacher, who wrote *Small Is Beautiful: Economics as If People Mattered* (1973), posed a new question. Would the family that moved to a larger house be happier there? How long would this happiness last? Would it change if someone built a bigger, more luxurious house across the street? The answers are far from obvious.

The elusive connection between more material possessions and human satisfaction has been the subject of a long debate. Many church leaders, political leaders, and humanists have argued against the view that more possessions bring greater happiness. Even Karl Marx (1933), the intellectual founder of communism, wrote pessimistically about the issue: "A house may be large or small; as long as surrounding houses are equally small it satisfies all social demands for a dwelling. But if a palace rises beside the little house, the little house shrinks into a hut."

Thorstein Veblen (1899), founder of the Institutionalist School of economic thought, was also fascinated by the transitory happiness that consumption brings. He coined the term **conspicuous consumption** to represent his observation that an individual's satisfaction from a good or service often depends on the number of goods and services consumed by other people. In other words, having more than you used to have is not

conspicuous consumption:
purchasing goods or services because of the status associated with them rather than for a specific need

enough. The important question is whether you have more than your neighbor. Conspicuous consumption leads people to buy goods or services because of the status associated with them rather than for a specific need. Suppose, for example, that your family has a well-running, but aging, family car. Let us further suppose that your next-door neighbor buys a beautiful new car. Suddenly your old car looks shabby and your family begins to wish they had a better one. Within a week or two your family buys a new car that is even more expensive than your neighbor's. You have engaged in conspicuous consumption, sometimes known as "keeping up with the Joneses." You don't need a new car, but you don't want your neighbors to think that you can't afford one. Neither do you want to appear to be a less-successful member of society.

values: strongly held, learned beliefs that tend to arouse strong emotional, physical, and intellectual responses when they are challenged

Is conspicuous consumption "bad"? This is a question of **values**, that is, learned beliefs that arouse strong emotional, as well as intellectual, responses when challenged. If your values include a high regard for individuality and concern about wasting society's resources, you may dislike conspicuous consumption because it leads to a society of spend-thrift conformity. This negative opinion is an outgrowth of your values and is often referred to as a **value judgment**. If, however, your values include a dislike for being different, you may want to practice conspicuous consumption and demonstrate by your consumption patterns that you do, indeed, belong to a group. In either case, if you understand and appreciate your values, your consumption patterns are more likely to lead you to a higher level of satisfaction. If you don't—if your consumer decisions are not built on known, well-defined values—you are not likely to be satisfied—or happy. Thus, the next section tries to help you clarify your values so you can set goals that will guide you in your consumer decision making.

VALUES AND THE CONSUMER

As we have implied, there are two reasons to examine values at this point in our study. First, you cannot make a logically consistent set of decisions without knowing what is important to you—without understanding your values. Second, you need a better perspective on the values of other consumers. We live in a multicultural society in which different people have different values. What might appear to be bizarre, uneconomic behavior to you may, in fact, be quite rational, given another person's value structure. A good motto is: Be slow to judge others, and regularly recheck your own value network.

Ronald Stampfl (1981), a professor at San Diego State University, has identified sets of values that underlie what he calls industrial-age, transitional-age, and post-industrial-age consumption patterns.

Following is a comparison of the two value clusters that are most opposed to one another, industrial-age and post-industrial-age (see Table 1-1).

TABLE 1.1.   Industrial-Age and Post-Industrial-Age Consumer Values

Industrial-Age Consumer Values	Post-Industrial-Age Consumer Values
Consuming as much as possible is desirable	Consuming only as much as necessary is desirable
Disposable products are desirable	Recycling is important
Convenience is more important than cost	Forgo convenience if benefit–cost ratio is low
Fashion and style are unrelated to function	Functional changes are more important than style or fashion
Ownership is important	Leasing is as acceptable as owning
Economic growth and the quantity of goods are important	Economic stability and the quality of goods are important
Environmental cost of consumption is not a major concern	Conservation is important
Consumer movement has limited impact and is unimportant	Consumer movement has great impact and is important

According to Professor Stampfl, American consumers who have **industrial-age values** reached adulthood between 1920 and 1960, when consumers believed "more was better, natural resources were all but inexhaustible, convenience was to be expected, and that every American was entitled to all the things that constituted the good life." Consumers with **post-industrial-age values** will reach adulthood after 1990, and they will be confronted by an era of "inflation, materials shortages, and environmental deterioration." Between these two eras are consumers with **transitional-age values**, who reached adulthood between 1960 and 1990. These consumers have been taught the industrial-age values but intellectually are moving toward post-industrial-age values. This change may lead to a conflict between consumption patterns and beliefs—between what consumers want and what consumers believe they ought to want. Worksheet 1.1 contains Dr. Stampfl's test designed to help you identify your values.

Sources of Values

As we said earlier, values are strongly held beliefs that tend to arouse strong emotional, physical, and intellectual responses when they are challenged. But where do we get our values? Generally speaking, the family is the most important transmitter of values. Often this transmission is more a product of osmosis than of conscious, well-planned instruction. As a child, you see and interact with your parents, and this contact tends to build a certain value framework for all of your future experiences.

A lack of respect for the environment is an example of an industrial-age value that can easily be transmitted from parent to child. For example, parents can (and often do) litter the highways with garbage hurled from

WORKSHEET 1.1   WHAT TYPE OF CONSUMER ARE YOU?

Place an X on the continuum that best represents your values—what you *believe*. Then reread the test and place a circle at a point that represents your *behavior* as a consumer.

I consume as much as I want, and I feel that . . . . more is generally better than less.	I consume only as much as I need, and I feel that more is not necessarily better.
When I am finished with a product or a . . . . package, I throw it in the trash.	When I am finished with a product, I try to pass it on to someone else who can use it. When I am finished with a package (bottle, can), I try to recycle it.
I always try to buy products and shop in stores . . . . that provide the most convenience for me.	I try to assess the cost of "convenience" when making product or store choices.
When I see a new model of a product I already . . . . own, I am anxious to trade in my old model.	When I see a new model of a product I already own, I don't care to have it unless it truly performs its function better than my old model.
I'd prefer to own my own home, car, ap- . . . . pliances, tools, recreational vehicles, and so forth rather than lease (rent) them.	As long as I can use a nice home, car, appliances, tools, recreational vehicles, and so forth, it doesn't matter to me whether I own, lease, or rent them.
I believe that government regulations to . . . . protect the environment and workers are a waste of my money if they increase the price I must pay for a product.	I believe that the government should fully protect the environment and the workplace even if I must pay more for the products I buy.
I believe that a good economy is continually . . . . growing and producing an increasing quantity of goods and services.	I believe that a good economy is stable (low inflation and unemployment) and provides a high quality of life for its citizens, rather than an increasing quantity of goods and services.
I believe that the consumer movement is a . . . . threat to jobs and adds unnecessary costs to products.	I believe that the consumer movement is an important force in protecting the rights of consumers in the marketplace and is, therefore, justified.

Analysis: If marks fall predominantly on the left-hand side of the test, you have industrial-age consumer values and behavior. If there is no real pattern or if most marks fall in the center, you are a transitional consumer. If the X's and circles are far apart, some conflict exists between what you believe and what you do. To check your accuracy, ask someone who knows you well to fill out his or her perception of your consumption pattern on this scale. The result could prove interesting.

Source: Ronald W. Stampfl, "What Type of Consumer Are You?" © 1981 J. C. Penney Company, Inc., Consumer Education Services, *Forum* (Spring/Summer 1981), pp. 3–5.

their cars and pickup trucks. They don't feel obliged to deposit trash in proper receptacles. Their children, who may be riding with them, in turn feel no compunction about littering the playground with candy wrappers and chewing gum. After all, they've learned by observing their parents.

On a more positive note, young consumers can and do learn values such as honesty and consumer responsibility by observing their parents' behavior. At the checkout line in a local market, for example, if a customer receives too much change or if the checker charges too little for an item, a responsible consumer calls this to the worker's attention. Such behavior reinforces the values of honesty and responsibility. It teaches young consumers by actions as well as by words.

After the family, the peer group generally exerts the greatest influence. Friends and acquaintances can affect the clothes you wear, the activities you engage in, and even your manner of speech. By now you can probably be objective enough to see the group influence on your values and your consumer behavior. But just in case you don't see the connection, think about the last article of clothing you bought, the last item related to sports you bought, or even the last novel you bought. Was your purchase influenced by a friend's opinion, either implicitly or explicitly? Did his or her values concerning beauty or competition or entertainment influence your values and thus your decision making? You would be a rare consumer if they played no role at all. And as long as you are aware of the influences that other consumers' values have on you and your consumption pattern, you are still in control of the decision-making process.

A third influential group consists of the people you admire or may wish to emulate. Their influence can vary greatly, but certainly rock music stars, athletes, comedians, and other media people affect our values far more than many of them realize.

Value Systems and Conflicts

An individual's values are generally quite complex and sometimes at odds with one another. The importance and sanctity of motherhood, for example, has been an important value in many societies, including our own. Anyone who challenges the importance of value of mothers had better be ready to defend that challenge against a storm of protest. Likewise, most of us accept the democratic value, as stated by the founders of our republic, that "all men are created equal." In the early 1960s, Betty Friedan's book *The Feminine Mystique* (1963) openly questioned whether adherence to the traditional motherhood value conflicted with the democratic value that all people, men and women, are created equal. The debate about an Equal Rights Amendment was born out of this controversy.

Clarifying Values

values clarification: the process of search and choice that helps one understand one's values

It is obvious that the values of a society, as well as those of an individual, can conflict, leaving one in a quandary. Resolving these conflicts and avoiding others can be achieved by frequently reviewing, evaluating, and revising one's values. The process of search and choice that helps you understand your values is called **values clarification**. It can take the form of a frank discussion with a counselor, a clergyman, or a good friend who can give you some insight into how your values have grown or changed. Or you can perform your own values clarification by reviewing your answers to the consumer values quiz in Worksheet 1.1. You might even keep a record of your opinions over time to see how your underlying values and your explicit consumer behavior have changed.

Many consumers are just too busy with their day-to-day activities to bother with the process of rechecking their values. The danger for such consumers is that, in a comparatively short time, they may discover that they are not enjoying their work or life-style or both. They may feel trapped or hooked into a set of roles that are not fulfilling. This is the stuff of which personal crises are made. You may read about the most extreme cases in the newspaper ("Mother of Five Abandons Children"), or you may hear of such disillusionment in stories of husbands who go out to get a pack of cigarettes and never return to their family or job. But the more common result of ignoring one's value structure is mental depression and a general state of unhappiness or boredom. If your life-style has not changed significantly over the past few years but your personal satisfaction index has plummeted, it is a good bet that your values have changed.

Part of this change could be the result of entering a new life cycle, of moving from adolescence to single adulthood or from being newly married to being a new parent. Chapter 2 discusses this process in detail. It could also be that your family, your peer group, or the media have led you to challenge and change values. Whatever the reason, the effect is the same: You no longer hold the values you once did; you no longer give a high priority to those beliefs that you once held sacred. And because your decision-making ability is founded on the assumption that you know what you believe and what you want, your decision about using your money, your time, and your energy will be haphazard. These decisions will not be satisfying or bring you the happiness that is the ultimate goal of all consumer behavior.

Even if you have a good grasp of your value structure, you will have difficulty in actualizing these values unless you set some goals for yourself based on your values. The next section outlines the goal-setting process and shows you how to measure your progress in achieving these goals.

GOALS: VALUES IN ACTION

Values are fairly abstract. They are not directly obtainable through a specific action. You cannot achieve a value. Goals, on the other hand, are

goal: a result toward which some effort is directed

specific and tangible. A **goal** is a result or an achievement toward which effort is directed. Values are the bases for goals. They are not the specific things sought, but they give meaning to the immediate objective. The goals that you pursue should reflect the values that you hold. If your external goals are not based on your internal values system, they will tend to be aimless and confused.

Setting Goals

As we discussed earlier, you must first clarify your values before you can expect to be a rational decision maker. Suppose, for example, that one of your most important values is to be independent. This value does not specify how you will become independent, but it could lead you to a specific goal, such as getting a good job. Such a job and its high income would certainly make you independent. But what kind of job can you (should you) get? You may need to break this overall goal into subgoals. For example, you might decide that the most likely avenue to a good career is a college degree. Thus, your subgoal is to get a higher education. The subgoal of that might be to get a degree in home economics.

We usually have many goals and subgoals, but given the ever-present problem of scarcity, we cannot work toward all of them at once. It is therefore necessary to choose a few that seem most important at a specific time and direct our resources toward achieving them by ranking goals in order of importance. In electing to pursue a particular goal or subgoal, keep in mind that this selection has an opportunity cost associated with it. The opportunity cost is the value of the next-most-preferred goal that must be postponed while you try to accomplish the higher-priority goal.

For example, if you decide to accept a full-time job, you may have to give up another important goal, such as completing your college education in four years. Or if you decide to get married and have a family, you must realize that this will have an impact on your career goals. By ranking your goals in order of importance, you can clarify your immediate course of action and thus simplify daily decision making.

It is important to set goals that are consistent with your values and to reevaluate those goals in light of the changes in your value system. For example, if being economically independent isn't so important anymore, the career goal may not be, either. Another part of evaluation involves considering whether these goals meet your values. For example, perhaps a college degree will not ensure a good career. Finally, you should realize that values and goals are interrelated and sometimes conflict. A strongly career-oriented person must adopt a different style of consumption and production from someone who places more emphasis on current income and employment. Getting ready for a good career may mean years of lowered consumption while you continue your studies. This describes the pattern of anyone who wants to practice medicine, for example. On the other hand, those who have both a strong need for immediate gratification and a strong desire for economic independence at a young age may be heading for a values clash and a mixed-up set of goals.

Evaluating Goals

You should review your goals and subgoals on a regular basis. It is becoming commonplace for firms to set up plans for the short run, the long run, and the very long run. The same should be true for households. They need to plan for the future. Can you imagine what you will be doing in one year? In five years? In ten years? If you have little or no idea, you are running the risk of drifting.

This is not to say that you must have a five-year plan with specific targets that cannot be changed. But a little planning review now can lead you to a more efficient allocation of your time in the future. And remember, your plans can change. You wouldn't want a seventeen-year-old running your life, would you? Then why stick to a decision that you made when you were seventeen?

In the sections that follow we will provide you with some tools to help you in your attempt to achieve your goals. First, we will discuss the establishment of standards, the most important technique in helping you discover how close you are to achieving your goals. Then we will discuss three other tools—the sunset clause, zero-based budgeting, and sunk costs—that can help you in the goal-setting and evaluation process.

Tool number 1: Standards. Once you have clarified your values and ranked your goals, you need to have some road signs to tell you how close you are to achieving those goals. These progress measures can be called **standards**. Standards are qualitative or quantitative measures of performance or achievement. In our career-oriented example, finishing one year of college might be a reasonable standard by which to gauge your progress toward the goal of economic independence. Finishing that year of education with better-than-average grades would give a quantitative, as well as a qualitative, index. Standards allow you to see, on a regular basis, your success (or lack of it) in attaining an overall goal.

Standards vary from person to person. As a general rule, it is good to stretch yourself somewhat, but not too much. In other words, don't set a standard that is so low and easy to reach that it invites sloth, but don't set the standard so high that you face continual frustration. Studies show that people do their best work when they are a bit uneasy about the likelihood of success. In such situations, they are just a bit on edge and get a small surge of adrenaline. If your standards for achievement are set at this level, you are challenging yourself in a coherent way. If your standards do not engender any stressful periods, you are probably not expecting enough from yourself.

standards: *qualitative or quantitative measures of performance that offer individuals a guidepost by which to measure progress toward a goal*

Tool number 2: The sunset clause. The **sunset clause** is a planning rule from government which states that any new agency or department will be terminated at the end of a specified period unless it can be proven that it should be kept. The sunset clause puts the burden of proof on the agency to prove its worth or else face automatic extinction. It is too bad that consumers haven't used this principle with respect to their values and goals. If a given value is simply cluttering up your life, supplying guilt and pain but little else, you should be able to purge it automatically.

Tool number 3: Sunk costs. A major objection to the sunset clause in goal setting comes from the fear of admitting that one is wrong. You may, for example, spend quite a bit of your time and resources pursuing the goal of an advanced degree, say a doctorate in history. Let us assume that your goal is to teach history at the college level and that a doctorate is essential. If new information comes to you that there are almost no openings in the history field now and there will be fewer in the future, your likelihood of success is nil. Should you continue to pursue your education in history? No. Continuing to pursue the unattainable simply because you are already devoting resources to the goal is foolish. Economists argue that you should ignore past costs and look only at the future costs and benefits. Past costs are called **sunk costs**; they are fixed and cannot be changed. They should be ignored in all current decisions.

sunk costs: expenditures of resources that cannot be reclaimed or salvaged; also called fixed costs

The principle of sunk costs is exemplified in our culture by two mottoes: "Let bygones by bygones" and "Don't throw good money after bad." Have you ever heard someone say, "I can't get rid of that car, it cost me too much to fix it"? Does this indicate an awareness of the doctrine of sunk costs?

Sunk costs apply to all decisions, whether they relate to consumer goods purchased or to goals you set and have spent time pursuing. It is uneconomical and just plain inefficient to throw good money after bad. Let bygones be bygones in your role as a goal setter, as well as in your role as consumer.

THE CONSUMER DECISION-MAKING MODEL

As we said at the beginning of this chapter, scarcity is the mother of decisions. If we did not live in a world where our wants exceed our resources, we would not have to be good decision makers. However, given that our resources are scarce, good decision-making skills help us to stretch those resources and thus get greater personal satisfaction out of the choices we make. Reaching our highest level of satisfaction entails learning about and using cost–benefit analysis so that we can evaluate alternative choices and rank them on the basis of their expected net benefits. In this way, higher-valued alternatives will always be selected before lower-valued ones.

Choices do not take place in a vacuum. Your choices are conditioned by your values and goals, as well as by those of others. Nevertheless, choices do exist. And if you are to be a better consumer, you should begin by studying a formal decision-making model. Throughout the remainder of this text we will apply this model wherever possible to clarify a choice-making situation. Our seven-step decision making model is summarized here, followed by an example to demonstrate how it might be used.

1. Define the problem and outline some potential solutions.
2. Determine how your values, goals, and standards may limit your choice.
3. Seek advice and collect information on the alternatives.
4. Weigh the costs and benefits of alternatives; include time as well as money costs.
5. Make a choice.
6. Evaluate and periodically review all major decisions.
7. Be responsible.

You are now prepared to use what you have read in this chapter in the context of this model. Perhaps the easiest way for you to pull all of that information together and put it into the model is to apply it to a common major consumer decision, such as providing yourself with transportation.

In step 1, you need to define the problem. Let us suppose that you are moving away from home and are going to college for the first time. You move into an off-campus apartment less than two miles from campus, but you have an off-campus part-time job on the other side of town. You will be commuting from home to school to work to home, five days a week. You need some form of transportation. After a brief brainstorming session, you identify several potential solutions: Buy a bus pass, a bicycle, a car, or a motorcycle or rely on hitchhiking. You also have the option of finding another solution. You don't want to be close-minded. (See Box 1.1 for a representation of this and the other stages of decision making.)

In step 2 you must clarify your values, goals, and standards concerning transportation. For example, you may be concerned with how your decision affects the environment and what effect it may have on your health and the health of others. On the other hand, you may value personal convenience and privacy more highly than the effect of your decision on the ecosystem. In either case, your values play a major part in your evaluation of alternative modes of transport.

In step 3, you seek input from knowledgeable sources. This may include talking to friends and acquaintances who may have already faced this situation and made a decision. It may also involve collecting some basic price information on the alternative forms of transportation. This process can be fairly long and involved, or it can be fairly brief. Remember, there are costs involved in finding information. For an important decision like

BOX 1.1   **AN EXAMPLE OF THE DECISION-MAKING MODEL**

1. Identify the problem.

   I need to decide what kind of transportation to use:

2. Determine which values, goals, and standards affect the problem:

a. Money	e. Privacy
b. Time	f. Ownership
c. Safety	g Other
d. Ecology	

3. Collect information:
   a. Books
   b. Magazines
   c. Telephone
   d. Personal interviews
   e. ?

4. Weigh costs and benefits of alternatives:

Values	Hitchhiking	Bicycle	Car	Bus	Motorcycle
Money	+ +	+ +	− −	+	−
Time	− −	−	+ +	−	+
Safety	− − −	−	+	+	−
Ecology	+	+ +	− −	+	−
Privacy	− −	+	+ +	−	+
Ownership	−	+	+	−	+
Other					

5. Make a choice.

6. Periodically evaluate and review.

7. Assume responsibility

finding basic transportation, higher search costs seem to be justified. In less important situations, such as deciding what to have for dinner or where to open a bank account, shorter searches are needed.

Once you make a good estimate of how much you can afford to pay for transportation and of the costs of the alternatives, you need to bring all this information together in a cost–benefit decision matrix (step 4). These cost—benefit calculations should include both the explicit monetary costs and the implicit time costs of all viable alternatives. Do not lose sight of the opportunity cost principle. Spending more money (or time) on transportation means spending less money (or time) on another area. If you decide to buy a car, you may not be able to afford a vacation. If you choose to buy a bicycle, you may spend more time commuting and therefore have less time to study.

Once you have established the advantages and disadvantages of your potential solutions, it is time to choose an alternative. In our example, hitchhiking is the least expensive in money terms, but it has significant time costs and is the least safe. If you are a bona fide "eco-freak," the bus and the bicycle get high marks because they are more socially responsible from an ecological point of view. The motorcycle falls somewhere between the bicycle and the car in money cost, but its safety rating is low and its cost in human energy is significantly higher than that of a car.

Now it's time for step 5, making a decision. If you have followed the procedure up to this point, one alternative should clearly be superior to the others. If there is no perfect solution, you have two options: Select the "least bad" alternative, or postpone a decision until you have more information. Both are viable options and should be considered if no clear choice emerges. But let us assume for the sake of our example that you choose to purchase a car. It offers the lowest time costs and more personal safety, and it fits well with your values of personal convenience and ownership. The increased cost means that you will not be able to take a skiing holiday, but that trade-off seems worth making, given the alternatives. You have made a rational decision, but, of course, this decision is only the beginning. Now you have to decide what kind of car to buy, whether to get a new or used one, and so on. We will return to this decision when we discuss transportation in a later chapter.

Once you get your car, you continue on your decision-making road by evaluating and periodically reviewing it. The experience you gain from your decisions should be used to make future decisions. You may discover, for example, that you don't use the car very much or that you underestimated the cost of owning a car. Gasoline prices and insurance costs, for example, have a way of exploding. Or your values, goals, and standards change; as a result, you may become dissatisfied with your decision. If this happens, you need to determine the cause of your dissatisfaction so that future decisions can lead to happier consequences.

The seventh point could simply be labeled "responsibility." You must take responsibility for your actions. Otherwise, it is too easy to blame others for your mistakes. If you are not enjoying the fruits of your labor because you feel cheated, take action. You can use this model to help you decide whether redress is worth fighting for.

Throughout the text we highlight this framework and suggest ways to use it in your multifaceted career as an American consumer.

SUMMARY

This is one of the most important chapters in this book. We have brought together the threads of the decision-making process in a way that we hope will be useful in the following chapters and for all your future major consumer decisions. Scarcity creates the need for decisions, and the attempt to maximize one's satisfaction while minimizing one's resource expenditure makes rational consumer decision making necessary. Understanding the reason for the scarcity dilemma is fairly easy, but learning to cope with it through good decision-making habits is not. Decision making is a skill that must be applied in order to be learned well. The following chapters refer to our decision-making model and use it to help you determine the most efficient course of consumer action. Keep in mind, however, that decisions are not made in a vacuum. As we have seen in this chapter, decisions are conditioned by personal values and goals. And they are constrained by a number of societywide factors. Nevertheless, we are more in tune with Professor Duesenberry's comment about economics (it is all about how people make choices) than we are with his comment about sociology (it is all about why people have no choices to make).

QUESTIONS

1. The Sentry Insurance Company recently commissioned Louis Harris to survey public attitudes on consumer issues. Harris found that 92 percent of those polled favored additional support for consumer education. What are the major societywide benefits to be obtained from better consumer decision making? What are the major personal benefits?
2. Opportunity costs are involved in almost all decisions consumers make. Use your understanding of this concept to explain the following behavior:
   a. Consumers often patronize the local convenience store even though it has higher prices and a more limited selection than the local supermarket.
   b. Most people choose Friday and Saturday to have a night on the town.
   c. People with active, physically demanding jobs are more likely to consume regular beer, whereas those with more sedentary occupations choose light beer.
   d. Television stations run public-service programs on Sunday morning rather than during prime time.
   e. Consumers take longer to decide where to live than where to bank.
3. If we lived in a place where all goods were abundant, would the concepts of scarcity and opportunity cost exist? Would decision making be important?
4. Does an increase in consumption lead to greater happiness? Give examples from your own experience in which it has and has not.
5. What is conspicuous consumption? Have you

ever engaged in it? Could the boom in merchandise made by such companies as Reebok, Guess, Benetton, and Esprit have been accelerated by conspicuous consumption? Can you think of other possible examples?

6. Take three important goals and measure your progress by a standard. Are you closer to meeting some goals than others? Do your standards result in stressful periods? Should they?

7. Have you ever heard someone say, "I can't quit now, I have too much invested"? This might relate to a business, a career, or a personal relationship. What kind of advice might you give such a person, based on your knowledge of the principle of sunk costs?

REFERENCES AND READINGS

Carmody, Deidre. "Many Students Fail Quiz on Basic Economics," *New York Times*, December 29, 1988.

Cude, Brenda J. "Estimating the Returns to Informed Decision-Making," *Journal of Consumer Affairs*, Summer 1987.

Duesenberry, James S. "Comment," in Universites—National Bureau Committee for Economic Research, *Demographic and Economic Change in Developed Countries*. Princeton: Princeton University Press, 1960.

Friedan, Betty. *The Feminine Mystique*. New York: Dell, 1963.

Galbraith, John Kenneth. *The New Industrial State*. Boston: Houghton Mifflin, 1967.

Greer, Douglas F. *Business, Government, and Society*. New York: Macmillan, 1987.

Marx, Karl. "Wage-Labor and Capital," in *Selected Works*, vol. 1. New York: International, 1933.

Maynes, E. Scott. "The Payoff for Intelligent Consumer Decision-Making." *Journal of Home Economics*, February 1969.

Morton, John S., and Rezny, Ronald R. *Economics for Consumers*. Boston: Houghton Mifflin, 1989.

Robinson, Jean R. "The Content of a College–University Course in Consumer Education," in E. Scott Maynes, ed., *The Frontier of Research in the Consumer Interest*. Columbia, Mo.: American Council on Consumer Interests, 1988.

Schumacher, E. F. *Small Is Beautiful: Economics as If People Mattered*. New York: Harper & Row, 1973.

Stampfl, Ronald W. "Consumer Values in Transition." *Forum*, Spring/Summer 1981.

Veblen, Thorstein. *The Theory of the Leisure Class: An Economic Study of Institutions*. New York: Macmillan, 1899.

Wilcox, Suzanne Dale. "The Educated Consumer: An Analysis of Curriculum Needs in Consumer Education." U.S. Office of Education, October 30, 1979.

Chapter Two

LIFE CYCLES, LIFE-STYLES, AND THE CONSUMER

- ☐ Income: Not Just a Paycheck
- ☐ Level of Income: Facts and Factors
- ☐ The Changing American Family
- ☐ Types of Households
- ☐ Special Problems in the Family Life Cycle
- ☐ Changing Family Roles: Money and Time

DID YOU KNOW THAT ...

. . . the biggest cost of employment is the time you give up in order to work?

. . . it won't matter how well you can do a job, you will not be able to find a job in your field if there is no demand for that skill or knowledge?

. . . one third of America's current population is a result of the "baby boom"?

. . . more than 50 percent of women with children under the age of 1 are in the work force?

. . . more than 40 percent of all single adults in America are women over age 55?

. . . two of every three marriages do *not* end in divorce?

. . . two of every five single-parent families live in poverty?

. . . remarried families represent 15 percent of all households?

. . . more than one-fourth of adults aged 18 to 34 live at home with their parents?

. . . husbands spend the same amount of time on household tasks, regardless of the employment status of wives?

Decision making doesn't take place in a vacuum. All that makes us who we are—our age, sex, education, income—affects the process and the results. In addition, most of us do not make decisions alone: 96 percent of us marry, and most of us have children. Family decisions change as a family grows up. Just as individuals go through a **life cycle** (that is, a series of identifiable stages that occur in a certain order from infancy through old age, as shown in Figure 2.1), so does a family. Decisions made during adolescence or during the early stages of the family life cycle stay with us for a long time and become increasingly difficult and expensive to change. Moreover, neither individuals nor families can meet their economic goals without considering the impact of decisions about careers, marriage, parenthood, and use of time that are made throughout the life cycle.

In this chapter we look at these factors as they affect us as consumers. In a sense, we are providing a context for much of what you will read about later in the book. Knowing what factors affect income, looking at the family and the family life cycle, and thinking about how we spend our time provide us with more information to use in decision making. Specifically, if we know how these forces and factors operate, we can better know what to anticipate, how to judge what happens to us, and how to make decisions, rather than feeling as though someone or something else

FIGURE 2.1
The individual life cycle begins with infancy and early childhood and progresses to the stages of adolescence, middle-age, adulthood, and older adulthood. The ages on the figure are approximate because people do not develop at the same rate. Percentages are based on a 75-year lifespan, although this too varies, particularly because women, on the average, live eight years longer than men. Each stage of the life cycle has distinct earning and spending patterns because needs and wants are partially affected by age.

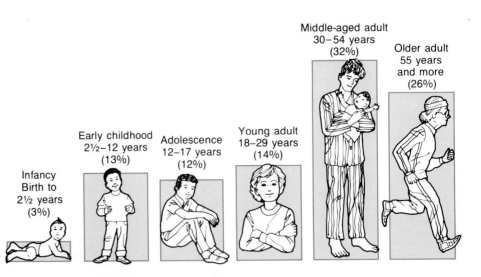

Middle-aged adult
30–54 years
(32%)

Older adult
55 years
and more
(26%)

Early childhood
2½–12 years
(13%)

Adolescence
12–17 years
(12%)

Young adult
18–29 years
(14%)

Infancy
Birth to
2½ years
(3%)

is controlling us. In addition, understanding these topics will be important when we get to other chapters, particularly those on budgeting, credit, transportation, and health care.

We begin this chapter with the basics of income: how we get it, how much we get, what factors affect our level of income, and how second incomes make a difference. Then we move to the family: its life cycle and how it affects consumer needs and decisions. From there we go on to time away from work. Although that may not seem part of consumer decision making, it definitely is part of personal economics because we spend 7 percent of our incomes, as well as much of our time, on recreation.

INCOME: NOT JUST A PAYCHECK

labor income: *the wage or salary paid to an individual in addition to paid benefits, such as pensions, medical and dental insurance, life insurance, paid vacation and sick days, and employers' Social Security contributions*

psychic income: *nonmonetary benefits of a job, such as feelings of satisfaction or pleasant working conditions*

The most obvious form of income is **labor income**, that is, the wage or salary paid to an individual, plus benefits, such as pensions, medical and dental insurance, life insurance, paid vacation and sick days, and employers' Social Security contributions. That is what we normally think of as income, but each job or career also has **psychic income**: the feelings of satisfaction, status, or prestige gained from the effort or the pleasure of working in certain surroundings. To most of us psychic income is also important.

The amount of psychic income that you want—and get—is determined in part by your values and standards. When you evaluate this aspect of a job, you have to look at psychic costs and benefits. For example, you have to weigh all the things you have to put up with—a long commute, disagreeable coworkers, a gloomy office, a restrictive dress code—against the things that make you feel good—your enjoyment in doing the work, the feeling of contributing, the freedom to set your own work hours. If you accept a different job at the same pay, the psychic income from your current job is negative or not enough. But if you stay on the job even with a cut in pay, the psychic income is positive.

As we saw in Chapter 1, time is a scarce resource that has to be spent wisely. When we spend a large portion of it to get labor income, we cannot use that same time for other purposes. Many people feel that they do not have enough time for everything they want to do. Time is a finite resource (168 hours per week), so the way we spend it is critical. If we do not work for income, we have more time, but we have less money. When we work for income, we often need to buy services that we ourselves have the capability to provide but no longer have time for, such as cleaning, gardening, child care, laundry, or cooking. Other chores or skills, such as carpentry, sewing, car repair, or fruit and vegetable canning, are even more time consuming (and may require special equipment); if you do not have the money to pay for them, you may have to take the time to do them yourself, or you may have to do without them entirely. When we take the time to save money and do home repairs and maintenance chores

WORKSHEET 2.1   LIFETIME GOALS

In his 1973 classic on time management, *How to Get Control of Your Time and Your Life*, Alan Lakein recommends setting lifetime goals in order to establish the balance you prefer between personal, family, social, career, financial, community, and spiritual goals. He recommends the following exercise to help you match your use of time with your priorities. You will need several pieces of paper, a pen or pencil, and a watch or clock.

1. Label the first paper "Lifetime Goals." Take *two minutes* to list on this paper as many goals for yourself as you can think of. Nothing is too far-out or outrageous to include. You are not required to reach these goals, so include everything that comes into your head.

2. Take a minute or so to review the list to see that it is complete.

3. Label a second paper "Five-Year Goals." Take *two minutes* to list all the things you would like to do in the next five years. This list will probably be more specific than the first one.

4. Take a minute to review the second list, being sure to include whatever else comes to mind.

5. Label a third paper "My Last Six Months." For a different perspective consider what you would do if you only had six months to live. Assume that matters relating to your death, such as a will, funeral, etc., are all taken care of. How would you spend your time? What would your goals be?

6. Spend a few minutes reviewing all three lists to make additions and clarifications.

7. Evaluate your results. Some people find that all three lists are similar, that lists 2 and 3 are extensions or elaborations of list 1. Other people find that list 3 is radically different from 1 and 2. There is no "correct" result, just an opportunity to learn about yourself. Ask yourself:

    a. What goals are on all three lists?

    b. What goals are only on one list?

    c. What does this result seem to indicate about my priorities?

8. Identify goal conflicts. Decide what is most important to you *at this time*. Your lists probably include more goals than there is time available, creating goal conflicts. You may have to give up one goal (like earning money) for another goal (like going to school). Recognize that both can be equally important to you, but that you may not be able to give them equal time at this point.

9. Set priorities.

    a. Select three goals from list 1 that are most important to you. Record them on the three blank lines under "List 1" below.

    b. Select your three most important goals from each of the other two lists, and also record them below.

List 1	List 2	List 3
_____	_____	_____
_____	_____	_____
_____	_____	_____

    c. Review these nine goals and choose the three long-term goals that are most important to you regardless of which list they come from. You now have a Lifetime Goal Statement, consisting of three top-priority goals and six goals of lesser importance at this time.

10. Use your Lifetime Goal Statement to evaluate situations in terms of what is important to you, for example:

    a. To evaluate a job

    b. To decide on job training or education

    c. To evaluate a potential marriage partner

    d. To decide to become a parent

    e. To decide to get involved in a professional, religious or community organization.

11. Update your Lifetime Goal Statement periodically, perhaps on your birthday. Your values and standards change, and so will your goals. You want to be alert to these changes, so you don't spend time on goals no longer important to you.

nonmarket home produc-
tion: household tasks that
include physical care for self,
family, and possessions

leisure forgone: the amount
of time one gives up in order
to work; time that is not now
available for leisure

ourselves, we engage in what is called **nonmarket home production**, which causes us to give up not only time that we could be working for income but time that we could be using for leisure. This sacrifice is called **leisure forgone**; if we give up leisure, it is income forgone.

Values and goals play an important part in making decisions about time and money. Some people choose a career or job that requires no overtime, has little additional responsibility, or has a short work week, so they can pursue hobbies and outside interests or perform more service tasks (gardening and cleaning, for example) themselves. Others may find the psychic income from their jobs so great that they are willing to work long hours and buy most of the services mentioned here. The important thing is to match your use of time with the priorities in your life. Worksheet 2.1 shows you a way to begin to do this.

LEVEL OF INCOME: FACTS AND FACTORS

''If you're so smart, why aren't you rich?'' This epithet has been hurled at more than one professor and it has a grain of truth to it. Intelligence—and by implication, education—do not automatically bring you fame and fortune. There are many factors that determine your income and consequently your ability to consume. In this section we outline these factors, beginning with education. Although your education level is strongly correlated with your income, other variables beyond your direct control can also affect your earning potential. The impersonal forces of supply and demand, along with your age, sex, race, and geographic location, can also play a role in the quantity of your income. By understanding the importance of these influences you can often adjust your goals, thus increasing your chances of personal success.

Education: Benefits and Costs

human capital: training or
skills (mental or physical)
that allow a person to per-
form services that he or she
could not otherwise do

Occupation, of course, determines labor income; training and education determine occupation. Although the gap in lifetime earnings between high school and college graduates has narrowed in recent years, college graduates still make more (see Table 2.1). This doesn't mean that schooling by itself makes money. It might be that only bright, goal-oriented people obtain college degrees and that they would make more money anyway. But an education does provide you with **human capital**, that is, training or skills that allow you to perform certain services that you could not otherwise do. You can increase your human capital by acquiring more skills or education, which makes you more valuable in the labor market.

Beside providing increased income, more education provides more job security. Generally, the unemployment rate for high school dropouts is four times higher than that for college graduates. During the 1980s there was a decreased demand for nontechnical workers such as machine

TABLE 2.1. Annual Median Earnings by Sex, Education, and Age[a]

Earner Categories	Male	Female
By Education		
Elementary	18,541	11,183
Some high school	20,003	12,267
High school graduate	24,701	15,947
Some college	28,025	18,516
College graduate	34,391	22,412
Postgraduate	39,592	27,279
By Age		
20–24	14,152	12,192
25–34	22,692	17,087
35–44	30,189	18,810
45–54	31,657	18,057
55–64	29,119	16,983
65 and over	27,326	17,180

[a] Full-time, year-round earnings of workers.

SOURCE: U.S. Bureau of the Census, "Money Income of Households, Families, and Persons in the United States: 1986," *Current Population Reports*, Series P–60, no. 159, June 1988.

operators, assemblers, and laborers, as much of this work was performed in other countries. Conversely, there was an increased demand for trained or educated workers. This trend continues in the 1990s.

More education may mean more income and better job security, but it also costs money and personal energy. For example, estimates of the direct costs of becoming a doctor (eight years of tuition, fees, and books) range from $75,000 to $140,000. This does not include room and board, even though it probably is necessary to move away from home to attend school; nor does it include long-distance travel between school and home for visits. A doctor achieves high income for one thing, then, because he or she has been willing to invest time, money, and effort in training.

Another cost of education is the lost labor income. Because it is usually not possible to work full time while in school, students have to give up income—and perhaps forgo other uses of their time. This opportunity cost is the highest single cost incurred for education.

A third, nonmonetary cost of investing in human capital is personal energy. Many people may not have the interest, abilities, or motivation to complete long-term training. Most educational programs contain at least a few courses that may be dull or distasteful to a specific student. Some courses may be too rigorous and require remedial training or additional effort. When all the monetary and nonmonetary costs are balanced, education may cost too much for some people. Fortunately, however, formal training is not the only answer. Neither is it the answer for everyone. You can learn on your own by reading and studying or through on-the-job training.

Supply and Demand

We have generalized that education can increase income, but the choice of occupation actually determines income. Some occupations are more in demand at some times than at others, which affects job availability and salaries. If few qualified individuals are available for an occupation, salaries in that field tend to rise. When other people become aware of the rise in salaries, they may enter the occupation, eventually leading to a surplus of job seekers, particularly if other factors contribute to a decline in demand. For example, between 1970 and 1984 annual wages for flight attendants rose 40 percent after adjustment for inflation. This attracted many job seekers, both male and female. But by the mid-1980s the effects of the recession of 1980–82 and deregulation of the airlines were felt: Many airlines cut back their personnel, and salaries stagnated.

Certainly, one aspect of evaluating a career is to weigh the amount of money you can expect to make in that career against the limitations it could impose on your needs and your preferred life-style. Although it is difficult to predict with certainty what the supply and demand conditions will be for a given occupation, estimates are available from the U.S. Department of Labor and from job market researchers, whose forecasts are published in periodicals and newspapers. Look for this information in your school library or placement office.

Age

Although you cannot do much about your age, it affects your income throughout your lifetime. When you are first employed, you are inexperienced and may need on-the-job training. As your skills and knowledge grow, thus increasing your **mental human capital**, your productivity and value to your employer also increase, and this value is reflected in a higher income that usually peaks between the ages of 45 and 55.

An exception to this is the person who develops **physical human capital**. Baseball players, ditch diggers, or welders find that their reflexes, strength, and senses begin to deteriorate after age 30 or 35. This means that they are less useful and productive for an employer, so their incomes peak earlier. The gradual rise in and leveling off or decreasing of an individual's income as he or she gets older is called an **age earning curve**. Figure 2.2 compares the age earning curves for someone who has mental human capital and someone who has physical human capital.

But this is not the whole picture. At this time, older people have (on the average) less education than younger ones because each successive

age earning curve: the gradual rise, leveling off, and perhaps reduction of income that occurs as a person ages

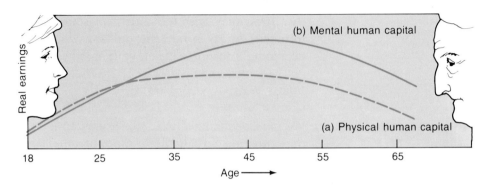

FIGURE 2.2
Age earning curve and human capital. Lifetime earnings partially depend
on human capital. Earnings are lowest when people start to work and
peak in mid-adult years. Those who use primarily physical human capital
(a) may find that their earnings peak between ages 30 and 35, when they
are most productive. Those who use primarily mental human capital
(b) may start with lower income while gaining education or training and
find that income peaks between ages 45 and 55. Income for both types of
individuals gradually decreases from the peak until retirement, around
age 65.

generation in America is better educated than the one before. As we saw earlier, those who have more human capital usually earn more. But remember, there must be a demand for workers in your field when you have finished training. Even if you are the best in your chosen career, if your skill is not needed by anyone, you will not be paid to use it.

Demography

demography: the science of vital and social statistics of a population—for example, of births, marriages, and deaths; the number of people of certain ages in a population

Demography—the number of people of certain ages in a population—also affects income. In the United States, individuals born between 1946 and 1964 are identified as members of the post–World War II "baby boom." This particular group of people—one third of our present population—has special employment problems, identified by Richard Easterlin in *Birth and Fortune* (1987). As a result of their large numbers, these people face stiff competition for jobs and have found lower salaries as a result. A larger proportion of this generation than of any previous generation has completed college, yet they can anticipate smaller raises, fewer promotions, and a flatter age earning curve. They have often accepted lower salaries than they had anticipated and settled for less than "college-level" positions. Between 1973 and 1986 the median real income of a typical young family headed by a person aged 25 to 30 fell by 26 percent (Irwin, 1988).

Gender

An individual's gender also affects labor income. The fact that women earn less money is apparent in Table 2.1. We will not explore the reasons in depth, but we would like to mention some of them. Women entered the work force in unprecedented numbers in the 1960s and the 1970s, often with few marketable skills. At the time, there was a large demand for workers in the expanding clerical and service fields. This made job hunting easier, but these jobs are traditionally low-paying and often dead-end positions. Because so many women were grouped in these low-paying

Although sex discrimination is still a problem, it is no longer unusual to find women in blue-collar occupations.

positions, the average yearly pay for women dropped from 72 percent of men's pay in 1956 to 59 percent by 1980.

During the same period, small numbers of men and women began to enter occupations previously more commonly held by the opposite sex. We are no longer surprised to find male bank tellers, nurses, phone operators, or flight attendants; neither is it strange to find female mail carriers, bank officers, truck drivers, or physicians. These options for both sexes of all races have been supported by the Civil Rights Act of 1964 and the women's liberation movement. Partially as a result of these changes and of developing mental human capital, by 1988 women's yearly pay had climbed back up to 68 percent of men's.

The often-cited 59 percent became a rallying point for feminists, and although the figure has been updated to 68 percent, activists feel frustration over the persistent wage gap. The reality is that these figures, based on yearly earnings for year-round work, including overtime, overstated the problem: Hourly earnings are a better measure. In one study in 1983, it was found that the typical woman working full time received an hourly wage that was 71 percent that of a man's (Tumulty, 1984). The gap narrows even more among younger workers. Using the data in Table 2.1, you can determine that the wages of women between the ages of 20 and 24 reached 75 percent of men's earnings in 1986. As women change their work patterns by interrupting their careers less often and for shorter periods of time for childbirth, and as they continue to invest in career skills, this gap will diminish further. (See Box 2.1 for more information on this topic.) It is important to note, however, that there is still a significant difference between the salaries paid to men and women in *identical* fields with virtually the same training and experience.

Box 2.1 **THE CORPORATE WOMAN: UP AGAINST THE GLASS CEILING**

As women have expanded their educations and increased their job skills they have entered less traditional fields, such as journalism, finance, sales, and computers. What can they look forward to, then, regarding their advancement and salaries? It seems that the struggles that occurred on the lower rungs of the career ladder in the 1970s and 1980s are destined to be repeated at the top of the corporate ladder in the 1990s.

Today, women fill one-third of all management positions, up from 19 percent in 1972. In most cases these women rise steadily, only to bump into an invisible barrier, a glass ceiling, that prevents them from occupying the executive suite. Reasons given for this include lack of mentors and sponsors, diversion by family concerns, and discomfort of male executives with whom they must work (*Wall Street Journal*, March 24, 1986).

As for salaries, the role of supply and demand seems to be the greatest factor in establishing compensation. In those fields where the influx of women has created a glut, salaries have declined. But in areas where the demand is high, women have held their own (Trost, 1986).

Almost all researchers agree that the main reason for the persistent gap between earnings of men and women is job segregation. About half of all women remain in the traditional women's occupations (those in which 70 percent or more of the work force is female). These positions include "pink-collar ghetto" jobs like secretarial work and waitressing, as well as the helping professions, such as teaching and nursing. In fields where women predominate, the wage scale is often lower than in those where men predominate, such as engineering. Efforts are now being directed to rectify this situation and achieve pay equity for workers.

comparable worth: the application of the concept that employers would pay workers equally for jobs that are comparable but not identical in responsibility and required skills and training

One method to achieve pay equity is the establishing of equal pay for **comparable worth**—paying workers equally for jobs that are comparable although not identical in responsibility and skill and training requirements. The comparable worth concept usually includes two parts: First, jobs that are different in content and demand on workers can be compared by objective criteria to determine worth or value to the employer; second, jobs of approximately comparable worth should be compensated equally by the employer. The first study of comparable compensation was commissioned in 1974 by the state of Washington on behalf of its employees. The results showed that women earned 20 percent less than men for comparable work. The study was updated in 1976, 1979, and 1980, each time with similar results. When the state took no action, the state employees' union filed suit, charging the state with violating state and federal antidiscrimination laws, including Title VII of the Civil Rights Act. Four months before the case was won in 1983, the state of Washington started correcting wage scales by passing legislation to achieve pay equity by 1993. Minnesota also exhibited leadership by establishing pay equity for state government workers in 1982 and then requiring cities, counties, and school districts to do the same by 1987 (Drennen and Makela, 1986). More than 100 states, cities, and school districts are now studying their wage scales to evaluate pay equity. Most of this action has been at the local level since the Reagan administration was opposed to comparable worth and in fact worked to overturn the Washington state ruling.

A major reason for the resistance to comparable worth is the direct cost of the increased wage scales. One congressman estimated that it could cost the federal government as much as $10 billion if comparable worth were adopted (*Los Angeles Times*, September 13, 1984). It is important to remember the dilemma of scarcity. Added income for one group, such as librarians, would mean less income for another group, i.e., taxpayers. If comparable worth were accepted voluntarily by the private sector, undoubtedly costs would be passed on to consumers. Proponents cite the benefits of added individual income, which would be achieved without incurring more costs for training or career changes. See Table 2.2 for other arguments for and against comparable worth.

TABLE 2.2 Major Arguments Against Comparable Worth and the Rebuttals

Argument	Rebuttal
Government should not determine the value of jobs.	A universal system of job worth has not been proposed; worth would be determined by each employer.
Equal pay is an adequate remedy.	After 20 years equal pay legislation has not reduced the pay gap significantly.
Equal access is an adequate remedy.	Occupational integration would result only if all occupations were equally attractive and suited to both men and women. Mid- and late-career persons are disadvantaged due to a need to retrain. Wages should not be the primary criterion for occupational choice.
Equal opportunity is an adequate remedy.	Limited access in the past precludes advancement for many workers.
Bringing compensation systems into compliance would involve large costs.	This argument assumes that implementation would be costlier than litigation and court-ordered back pay. It ignores the indirect benefits of added income, such as purchasing power and tax payments. Cities and states implementing comparable worth have costs of 3–8 percent of annual payroll during phase-in.
Comparable worth negates market supply and demand to determine the price of labor.	This argument assumes the labor market functions perfectly. Comparable worth strives for internal equity (to an employer) while allowing for external equity (market forces).
Job evaluation and the determination of worth are subjective.	The majority of workers are now in classification and/or evaluation systems. Current systems, including wage levels, have involved subjective decisions.

SOURCE: Nancy H. Drennen and Carole J. Makela, ''Comparable Worth: An Issue Demanding the Attention of Home Economics,'' *Journal of Home Economics*, Fall 1986.

Race

Another factor that affects income but that no one can control is racial background. Generally, nonwhites, such as blacks, Hispanics, and Native Americans, make less money than whites. For example, in 1986, when the median income for white males was $26,617 the median income for black males was $18,766, and for those of Hispanic origin it was $17,008. (Note that the figures in Table 2.1 included averages for all racial groups combined.) Unemployment rates for minorities are usually two to three times higher than for whites, contributing to the lower average income. As in the case of inequities for women, there are many complex socioeconomic causes for this situation, including a high dropout rate from high school and a high proportion of minority families headed by a single parent. The most important causes of lower income are lack of education and training, along with discrimination.

Studies indicate that members of minority groups with good educational credentials, work experience, and strong motivation are experiencing gains in professional, managerial, and skilled jobs. The problem for many members of minorities is being unable to afford an education. This is particularly true in the past decade, when educational costs have risen faster than the general cost of living. Generally, the higher the family income, the greater the probability that young people of all racial backgrounds will seek training beyond high school, because they can better afford the direct costs of tuition and books, as well as the opportunity cost of little or no income. Because of proportionately lower family incomes, children of minority families are less likely to receive job training beyond high school.

The second factor, discrimination, has been under federal regulation since the passage of the Civil Rights Act of 1964. Title VII of that act outlawed discrimination on the basis of race, color, sex, religion, or national origin in the areas of hiring, pay, and promotion. Preferential treatment in employment was mandated by Lyndon Johnson in 1965 in a presidential order requiring companies doing business with the federal government to take **affirmative action** to hire minorities and women. During the 1970s the Equal Employment Opportunity Commission, responsible for the enforcement of the Civil Rights Act, was given the power to initiate lawsuits on behalf of people who experienced discrimination in the job market. Companies who bypassed individuals for raises or promotions were required to compensate them with cash payments and advancements. These cases led to greater occupational upgrading for minorities in clerical, technical, and service jobs in government and education. Much slower expansion of job opportunities occurred in the corporate world, especially in management (National Urban League, 1980).

Progress toward the goal of equal economic opportunity for minorities and women was made sluggishly in the 1980s. Then in 1987, in *Johnson vs. Santa Clara County*, the Supreme Court ruled in favor of affirmative action plans, allowing an employer to create a temporary, flexible plan to increase participation of minorities or women in a company or job classification. It also protected the employer from reverse-discrimination suits. The decision did not support quotas or the promotion of unqualified workers, but it did encourage employers attempts to right the racial or sexual bias in employment.

Geographic Location

real income: the number of goods and services one can purchase with labor income

Besides education, age, gender, and race, your geographic choice of residence determines your **real income**, the amount of goods and services you can purchase with your labor income. For example, a $2,500-a-month income yields a lower real income in Boston, San Francisco, and Honolulu than it does in Atlanta or Spokane, primarily because of differences in the cost of housing. The cost of living varies by region because of differences in taxes, weather, union influences, and historic trends. For this reason, it is important to apply the decision-making process when evaluating jobs in various geographic regions. Your cost–benefit analysis should consider costs of food, housing, utilities, and transportation, as well as salary and psychic income.

Two-Income Households

Another important determinant of income is the number of people in a family who earn labor income. Most commonly in the American family today, both husband and wife are employed. In some families *more* than two members are employed, allowing more than 60 percent of the households in America to have two or more paychecks to budget and spend. In most families, the wife contributes the second paycheck prior to and following the birth of a child or children. In other cases, one spouse joins the other in the work force after completing career training or education. More often than in the past, one or more children are also employed and contribute to household expenses. This trend toward having more than one breadwinner has contributed greatly to the **level of living**, that is, the life-styles and types of possessions that the income levels of American families allow. As you can see in Figure 2.3, despite the low pay that many women received, by 1990 approximately 60 percent of those between the ages of 16 and 65 were employed, three-fourths of them at full-time jobs.

level of living: the life-style and types of possessions that an individual income makes possible

The most dramatic change in the female work force has been the increase in the number of employed mothers with young children. A woman no longer necessarily waits to see her youngest child off to school before entering or reentering the work force. In 1985 nearly 60 percent of all children under 18 had mothers in the work force, compared to less than 50 percent in 1975. Slightly more than one-half of this increase occurred among children under age 6 (*Family Economics Review*, 1986). Figure 2.4 shows the trend to rapid reentry into the labor force—as quickly as

FIGURE 2.3
The dramatic increases in the number of women of all ages in the work force, particularly in the number of married women (black broken line). The graph compares the number of working women by age group. The broken color line represents ages 16–24, the black solid line represents ages 25–44, and the solid color line represents ages 45–64. (SOURCE: U.S. Bureau of Labor Statistics.)

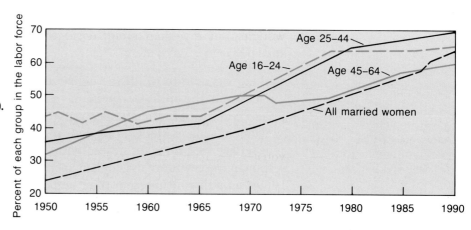

FIGURE 2.4
Percentage of women who had a child in the preceding 12 months and were in the labor force, by age. (SOURCE: U.S. Department of Commerce, Bureau of the Census, *Fertility of American Women, Current Population Reports: Population Profile of the United States*, Series P–20, no. 427, June 1987.)

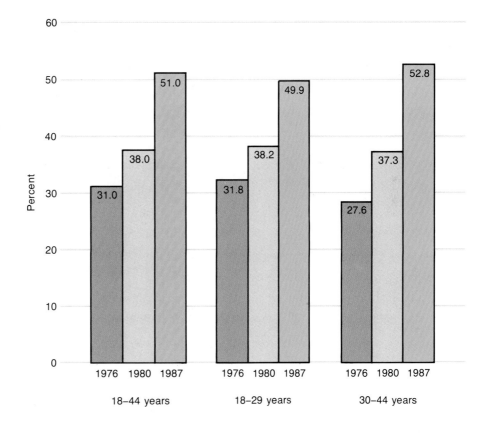

within the year of childbirth. Various factors led to the increased participation of women, and particularly mothers, in the labor force:

1. *The availability of jobs in a growing economy.* In the 1960s, the job market expanded to fulfill the demands of government-sponsored social services and the military spending related to the Vietnam war. This growth continued in the 1970s, primarily in jobs traditionally dominated by women, such as clerical positions in banks, government, and schools, and service positions in restaurants, retail sales, and personal care. Although the economy in general experienced a dramatic recession in the 1980s, growth continued in the number of jobs available in the service industries.

2. *Better birth control.* This gave women more choice about whether and when to have children. A Rand study in 1977 "decisively linked the decline in the birth rate of the 1960s and 1970s to the availability of jobs, rather than to the Pill" (Bird, 1979, p. 292). Although birth control is not the cause of increased employment, it does allow women to plan for education and careers.

3. *Rising college enrollments.* In 1958, women made up 35 percent of the college population. In the latter half of the 1970s, college after college across the nation reported that enrollments and graduation classes were composed of more women than men for the first time in history. This trend continues, and these female graduates set out, diplomas in hand, to meet the challenges of the world of work.

4. *Economic and social pressures.* Nearly two-thirds of all working women are single, widowed, divorced, or separated, or they have husbands who earn less than poverty-level income. Often a wife's earnings raise a family out of poverty. On the average, working married women contribute more than 25 percent of the total family income. For families in which the wife is employed full time, the median contribution is approximately 40 percent of the total income.

5. *Economic instability.* High inflation and high unemployment in 1974–75 and again in 1979–81, along with the 1980–82 recession, made bill paying very difficult for the average family. In those families in which two adults worked, the level of living was at least partially protected and there was the possibility that it might rise. The second paycheck served as security: About half the unemployed husbands in the country had wives who were working, which meant that, in many cases, the family could still make house and car payments and continue with insurance coverage.

All these factors have contributed to a general acceptance of a work force in large part female. As a result, the labor force participation of women has risen to approximately 60 percent. Concurrently, the labor force participation of men has been on the decline since World War II, reflecting a trend to early retirement, and is about 75 percent. That is, 75 percent of the men and 60 percent of the women aged 16 to 65 are employed.

What does the second income usually buy? For many families, it is the source of money for a second car. The next biggest spending difference between one- and two-income households is in regard to housing. Without a second income, many one-income families and single adults find it impossible to save money for a down payment or to have adequate income for mortgage and property tax payments, which combined are often higher than the cost of renting. Two-income families also spend more on furniture, household appliances, and housewares, as well as on clothing for all members of the family.

Up to this point, we have discussed the economic benefits of having two incomes. As you have probably guessed, nonmonetary factors also affect the choice to work for labor income. Box 2.2 provides the beginning of a cost–benefit analysis of two incomes. It is not meant to be complete. Can you think of additional costs or benefits of two incomes?

BOX 2.2   COST–BENEFIT ANALYSIS OF TWO INCOMES

The decision to spend time in acquiring labor income rather than in nonmarket home production involves a series of trade-offs. Here is the beginning of a list of monetary and nonmonetary costs and benefits of entering the labor force. Can you think of more?

Benefits

Monetary

More money to buy more or better shelter, household goods, transportation, and clothing.
Health and life insurance.
Pension plan or Social Security.
Family security in case of illness, unemployment of spouse, death, or divorce.

Nonmonetary

Self-fulfillment, good feelings about using abilities and skills.
Family members become more self-sufficient

Costs

Monetary

Increased need for transportation.
Increased wardrobe needs.
Increased need to buy services: childcare, housekeeping, and so forth.
Move to higher tax bracket.
Miscellaneous: dues, lunches, office gifts.

Nonmonetary

Having children later or having fewer children.
Less personal leisure time.
Less family time.
Guilt feelings over not being available for spouse or children.
Family members will need to share household tasks.
Increased stress caused by demands for time.

Managing two careers and a household is a tough job. Many who are now married do not have parents in this situation to serve as role models or examples, so they have few guidelines. Dual-earning couples consistently report having excessive stress and lack of personal time, particularly when both earners are concerned with career advancement. To survive these pressures, couples can benefit by applying the decision-making process described in Chapter 1 to identify and solve problems being flexible when looking for alternatives, and remembering that trade-offs are inevitable because time and energy are scarce resources.

So far, we have studied the many factors that affect an individual's level of income. Now let us look at the social and economic factors that affect how income is spent. We will look at the changes in the structure of the American family over the past two centuries and how they have affected the way families obtain necessities (such as food, clothing, and shelter) and protection during emergencies.

THE CHANGING AMERICAN FAMILY

The **nuclear family**, defined as a husband, a wife, and any dependent children, is one of a number of social groups that influence individual consumer decisions. Under normal circumstances, it is the first group an individual belongs to and the group an individual belongs to for the longest time. Approximately three-fourths of the nation's population currently lives in nuclear families, which are usually responsible for providing their members with food, clothing, shelter, other consumer goods, and protection during emergencies. Ideally, we are born into a family and remain with it during infancy, childhood, and, generally, adolescence. As we get older, we leave our nuclear family to live alone or to marry.

In this section, we briefly look at the economic functions of the family, both in the past and now. This gives us a basis for examining the economic needs and decisions a family makes through its life cycle. Understanding these concepts gives us, as family members and consumers, more information to help us make decisions to reach our financial goals.

Marriage and Family Patterns in the Past

In the marriage pattern of the lower and middle classes of eighteenth- and nineteenth-century Europe, a man could not marry until he had permission from community leaders to build a house or a cottage. In this home-production economy, productive property, such as a loom, carpentry tools, or bakery ovens, was mandatory. Men needed to show their ability to manage a productive enterprise, which indicated their capacity to support a family, before marriage was allowed; the oldest son, who inherited his father's farm or business, was luckier than his brothers in this respect. Women also made a financial contribution: a dowry of farm animals or household goods. When times were prosperous or the population small because of low birth rates and high death rates, more people could marry. When times were hard, people had to wait longer—sometimes marriage was impossible.

At the same time in America, land was plentiful and there was no limit on the number of businesses allowed in a community. Most families lived in rural communities where land was plentiful, and marriage was encouraged. Despite the well-known belief, there were few **extended families**—three generations living together—per se: There was adequate land for each family, and most people did not live long enough to become grandparents. On the other hand, aunts, uncles, sisters, brothers, or cousins might live very near each other. These blood relatives gave time and money to help during emergencies like fire, illness, drought, and death. In effect, they provided protection, insurance, and welfare for each other.

As technology increased in the late nineteenth century, fewer people were needed to produce a given amount of food on the farms. Technology simultaneously created new jobs in the cities and caused people to move from the farms to be near developing factories and businesses. As people relocated, they could no longer rely on their extended families; the nuclear family had to shoulder a greater responsibility for the economic welfare of its members.

Today's Marriage and Family Patterns

In a classic book focusing on decision making, Paolucci stated that "a major task of families is to prudently manage energy so all families exist above the level of mere survival" (Paolucci, Hall, and Axinn, 1977). As we become more conscious of our interconnectedness with individuals and families in other countries, prudent management of energy seems even more necessary. This energy includes the skills and strengths of family members to provide and produce goods and services for the family, such as food, clothing, shelter, and transportation. Families today usually purchase several forms of insurance to protect themselves in cases of accident, fire, theft, and death. This protection works in conjunction with government programs, such as Social Security, unemployment insurance, and welfare. In addition, both spouses are likely to be employed today in order to meet their obligations.

Perhaps as a result of increasing monetary and opportunity costs, a higher standard of living, and higher educational levels of women, family size has been decreasing. Following World War II, American fertility rates rose until they peaked at 3.8 births per woman in 1957. In 1962, the birth rate started its steep descent, reaching 1.7 in 1975. It has since stabilized at 1.8 (see Figure 2.5). Families are having fewer children and, in some cases, none.

As the cost of
childrearing rises,
couples are choosing to
have fewer babies.

FIGURE 2.5
U.S. total fertility rate,
1940–1988. This figure
shows the postwar
baby boom in graphic
format. At the end of
World War II (1945)
American women were
averaging a little more
than two children; by
the late 1950s, this
average had risen to
almost four children
per woman. Then, in the
1960s and 1970s the
fertility rate fell to less
than two. This is the
baby boom and bust.
During the 1980s the
fertility rate remained
fairly constant, at 1.8.
(SOURCE: U.S. Department
of Commerce, Bureau of
the Census, *Fertility of
American Women,
Current Population
Reports: Population
Profile of the United
States*, Series P–20,
no. 427, June 1988.)

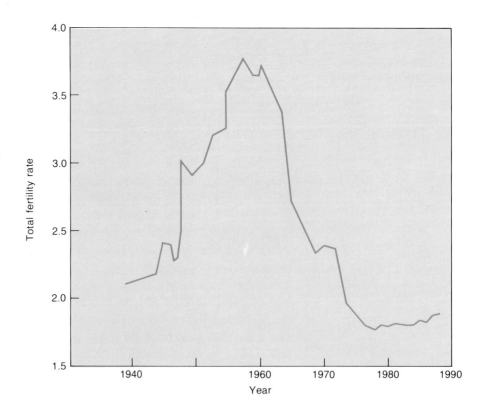

TYPES OF HOUSEHOLDS

The U.S. Bureau of the Census identifies three basic types of households: a married couple with or without children, one parent living with one or more children, and a person living alone. The remainder ("all other" category) includes nonrelated individuals of the same or opposite sex who live together: roommates in dormitories, sororities, fraternities, or apartments and nonmarried couples living together as husband and wife (cohabitants).

Single-Person Households

As shown in Figure 2.6, there has been a marked increase in single-person households, now totaling more than 20 million of the almost 90 million households in America. Part of the reason is that more young adults are marrying later, after having lived alone. Adults also form single-person households after marital separation, divorce, or the death of a spouse. Because of widowhood, two of every five persons living alone are women over the age of 55, the largest age-gender group of single-person households.

FIGURE 2.6
Household composition, 1970–1988. (SOURCE: U.S. Department of Commerce Bureau of the Census, "Household and Family Characteristics," Current Population Reports. Series P–20, no. 411, 1988.)

*Own children under 18

Single people are, of course, totally responsible for their own resources. They can decide how best to use their labor income, and they can choose the amount of nonmarket home production and leisure time they wish. But they must also support themselves and accept all household responsibilities, including establishing an independent household; purchasing furniture, appliances, and automobiles; and buying clothing, household linens, and consumer services, such as repairs, household maintenance, recreation, and entertainment. Because of their limited income, many single people cannot afford to purchase a home and find it necessary to rent shelter. Some adults may have a financial obligation to children of a previous marriage, or they may have to meet the challenge of living on limited resources (often the case for widows). Whatever their situation, they do it all on their own.

People are increasingly willing to live together as husband and wife without formal wedding ceremony. The number of cohabitating unmarried persons has doubled over the past 15 years and now exceeds 2 million. Although cohabitating may seem an easy way out or seem to provide more freedom, it does not eliminate the cost and obligations of marriage. This was dramatically demonstrated by the landmark case *Marvin vs. Marvin*, involving the movie actor Lee Marvin. When he and Michelle Marvin separated, she asserted that she should share the assets he had accumulated during the six years they lived together because she had given up her career to care for him and their home. This case established the right of nonmarried people to sue for community property, a right that exists in at least 31 states. Recognizing the legal factors involved, many unmarried cohabitants now write contracts to establish who owns what in case of separation.

Married-Couple Households and the Family Life Cycle

Approximately 58 percent of Americans live in married-couple families, about half of those having children under 18 years of age as part of the family. But the expectations for and the assumptions about the meaning of a married-couple family have changed radically. Changes in the past 50 years in family composition, in the standard of living, and in the roles of individual family members, particularly those related to work, both at home or in the labor force, have affected consumer decision making and spending patterns. As family members interact with the society around them, their goals and values change, which influences personal, economic, and social behavior. For example, most couples who married 15 or 20 years ago expected to follow the marriage pattern of their parents, with the man as the wage earner and the woman as the housewife. Many of these couples expected to live as well as their parents lived, but their standards conflicted with the reality of high inflation when prices rose faster than wages, making their economic goals difficult to reach.

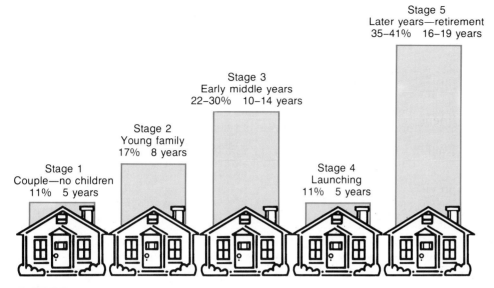

FIGURE 2.7
The five stages of the family life cycle, indicating the approximate years spent at each stage for an average couple with two or three children, married 46 years. Currently, two of every three couples have marriages that last until the death of one spouse, making the family life cycle relevant to most of us. If a couple has no children, they spend the first half of their marriage at stage 1 and the second half at stage 5. Note: Because of individual differences in the family life cycle and life expectancy, percentage may not total 100.

Simultaneously, it became easier for women to work outside the home because of changes in the society around them, such as the women's liberation movement, the increased availability of jobs, and access to the Pill. In the process of evaluating the possibility of employment for the woman, couples found that their individual values had changed. Sometimes, the newer value system of one spouse matched that of the other spouse, but other times it did not. Conflicts arose between spouses over the economic role the wife should fill, and unresolved conflicts occasionally resulted in divorce. In this section, we explore these issues as we identify the stages of the family life cycle and relate them to family composition; to decisions about family roles, economic goals, and spending; and to the economic effect of divorce and single-parenting on families.

Despite all the changes in family composition, Americans believe in marriage. As we have already noted, 96 percent of all men and 97 percent of all women marry at some point and begin the five stages of the **family life cycle** (Figure 2.7):

family life cycle: the identifiable stages that a family passes through, beginning with couples without children and progressing to the later years of retirement

1. Starting out, without children
2. Becoming a young family, with children of preschool age

3. Going through the early middle years, with children of school age
4. Launching (when children leave home)
5. Enjoying later years and retirement

Even with rising divorce rates, two of every three marriages remain intact until the death of a spouse. Some marriages go through all five stages, but others may experience only stages one and five if the couple has no children. The family life cycle may be disrupted by separation, divorce, or death. Divorced individuals may begin another family life cycle when they remarry. We will now look at the five stages and the economic decisions that go with them.

Couples without children. Young couples find that more goals related to career and income, family composition, and standard of living are formed during the first five years of marriage than at any later period (Deacon and Firebaugh, 1975). It is a time to shift from dependency on parents to responsibility for self and consideration of the welfare of a spouse. Decisions at this stage relate to the anticipated level of income and use of resources, such as skills and time. Will both partners have full-time labor income jobs? How will decisions be made about job transfers, especially in dual-earner families? Are children desired? If so, how many? Will the woman's career be interrupted or terminated when she has a child? How will the parenting and household responsibilities be distributed? All of these decisions are not entirely economic, but they affect family income.

Young families. Having children has always been viewed as one of the major functions—and obligations—of marriage. Becoming a parent should, however, involve conscious decision making, a process during which a couple discusses the pros and cons and realizes that having children implies a long-term commitment to create a positive economic, social, and moral environment for new family members.

There can be great joy in watching a child grow to adulthood. It can be ego gratifying to know that one is responsible for that growth. Although these benefits are difficult to put into monetary terms, many of the costs are easier to quantify. The total direct average cost of raising a child born in 1988 until age 18 on a moderate-cost budget is estimated to be $110,921. This does not include a college education. Table 2.3 compares these costs with those for a person born in 1960.

In addition to the monetary cost of children, the opportunity costs must be considered. Parents must give up their time to raise a child, particularly in the early years. If a parent chooses to stay home to care for a child rather than to be employed for, say, $22,000 a year, the opportunity cost of that child can be quite dramatic. In addition to the actual income loss, there is a

TABLE 2.3. Cost of Raising One Child[a]

Budget Item	1960s Child	1990s Child
Food	$ 8,766	$24,815
Clothing	3,662	6,862
Housing[b]	10,467	35,968
Medical care	1,602	8,028
Education	520	2,592
Transportation	5,267	16,432
Other[c]	3,990	16,224

[a] Comparison of the cost of raising one child from birth to age 18 in a husband–wife family with no more than five children. Data are for an urban setting at a moderate-cost level.

[b] Includes shelter, fuel, utilities, household operations, furnishings, and equipment.

[c] Includes personal care, recreation, reading, and miscellaneous expenditures.

SOURCE: *Family Economics Review,* ''Updated Estimates of the Cost of Raising a Child,'' 1988, no. 2.

growing recognition that responsibility for childcare, which rests primarily on women, is a significant barrier to equal opportunity for advancement.

The young-family stage merges two stages of the individual life cycle. The parents' adult needs, as well as the children's needs (special clothing, furniture, toys), must be met. Young families who often have a low or moderate income level feel these heavy demands on their budgets. Some families must choose between having children or purchasing a house, particularly because many families have only one income when children are infants. Growing family size increases spending for housing (shelter, furnishings, and utilities) and medical care. In order to keep budgets balanced, families usually reduce spending for clothing, recreation, and education and may have to forgo savings. These decisions are not made easily and may require difficult adjustments because couples become accustomed to a more generous spending pattern when they have smaller families. Young people beginning marriage are sometimes finishing their educations and beginning careers. All these goals are more difficult to achieve if a child is born soon after marriage or before marriage.

Early middle years. This stage of the family life cycle covers the time from when the youngest child starts school until he or she leaves home. By this stage, many family goals have been set and some have been reached, such as home ownership, career success, and financial stability. The percentage of income spent for housing and furnishings often declines because many families occupy homes they have owned for years. These are the years for Brownies, soccer games, and braces. Gail Sheehy, in *Passages*

(1976), describes this period as having an "in-turned focus on raising children" (p. 43).

As children mature and pass into adolescence, they begin to have money of their own to spend as they wish. Families with adolescents increase their spending for food, clothing, and recreation (cassettes, movies, sound equipment, sports). One of the highest expenses for this period is vocational training and education for maturing children. Parents themselves may decide to go back to school. Sometimes these same families are responsible for the care or partial support of grandparents. Even though these families may be at their peak of lifetime earnings, these simultaneous expenses can create a budgeting burden.

Launching children. As adolescents reach adulthood, become able to support themselves, and move to their own residences, the family gains new stability. This can be an exciting time for spouses, who now have more time together and more money to spend on themselves. Women can anticipate living with their husbands for an average of 13 years beyond the time when their last child leaves home (Barber, 1981). (Because many men die before their spouses, women find themselves single again in later years, as we will discuss shortly.)

Sometimes this period is called the empty-nest stage, referring to the decreased need for the woman to "mother" her children. Recent research indicates that this loss can have a negative effect on fathers as well as mothers (Barber, 1981). Also relevant to this stage is the potential need to house an adult child who returns home, often after a divorce and perhaps with children of his or her own.

The later years: Retirement. During this last stage, people face uncertainties in income and health and the eventual death of their spouse and themselves. Because of their reluctance to face these inevitable changes, some people enter this stage with inadequate planning for savings, investments, insurance, and protection of assets with a will. These issues are discussed in Chapters 16 and 17.

Retirement from employment changes established income and thus spending patterns. Money management is especially important if senior citizens depend on fixed incomes during a period of rising prices. Careful planning for this stage should begin earlier, at the young family stage, for example, to establish income from pension plans, Social Security, and investments. Most families find that their needs for housing and transportation have been met, so major expenses at this stage include travel, health care, and funerals.

This is a time to relax and maintain a slower pace, enjoying hobbies and the company of friends and relatives. For many, it is a time to fulfill long-

During the retirement stage of the life cycle, consumer decision making becomes more oriented toward hobbies and other leisure activities.

held goals for travel and recreation. Unfortunately, there may be too much leisure time for those who have few outside interests or hobbies.

The later years pose a special problem for women. There are more than one-third more elderly women in America than elderly men. More than half of these women are widowed or divorced; only one-fourth of the elderly men are in that situation. The reasons for this difference include the shorter life expectency of men, the fact that wives are usually younger than husbands, and the fact that when widowers remarry they often choose wives younger than themselves. The result is that many women spend their last years living alone, often on a poverty-level income. Decision making and planning in anticipation of this possibility can help ease financial difficulties, however, and make the later years a time for self-fulfillment.

SPECIAL PROBLEMS IN THE FAMILY LIFE CYCLE

The family life cycle, as we have viewed it so far, applied to couples who remain married until the death of one partner. As we have noted, this is the case for the majority of marriages, but certainly not for all. We will now look at the special economic circumstances that affect consumer decision making in families involved in divorce and remarriage. Then we will explore the financial stress placed on families that have experienced the return of young adults to the parental household, the need to care for an elderly family member, or both at the same time.

Divorce

During the 1970s the rising divorce rate was often cited as proof that the American family was dead; in fact, as we have seen, the family composition was just gradually changing. Divorce not only disrupts family composition, it also affects income and consumer decision making. The reasons for these trends have much to do with a changing society and its attitudes toward divorce. During the 1950s and early 1960s, changes were made in the law to eliminate the need to prove adultery, cruelty, desertion, fraud, insanity, or criminal acts in order to obtain a divorce. "Irreconcilable differences" is now an adequate reason for divorce in most states. Besides increasing the acceptable reasons for divorce, it also decreased the need for lengthy court battles, simultaneously decreasing legal costs. In addition, women have more education and marketable skills and fewer children than in previous generations, and their greater economic independence has given them the option to leave an unsatisfactory marriage. As more people seek divorce as a way out of an unfortunate situation, the stigma attached to it disappears in our society. Today, divorce is so common that the continuing pool of divorced adults comprises 10 percent of the population between the ages of 24 and 54.

This does not mean that divorce should be taken lightly. It is costly, both financially and emotionally. But it is a way to rectify what has turned out to be a bad decision. Remember, too, that the separation of marriage partners is not something new: Death has always been the disrupter of families. Because of improved medical care, more families have two parents today than in colonial times.

Single Parents

The prevalence of divorce has complicated economic relationships within the family. The children of a divorced couple may receive child support from a parent who is now a part of a second family that must now do without part of his or her income. This is difficult at best and probably plays a part in the fact that only about half of the parents without custody send the full amount of child support agreed upon, even if ordered by a court to do so (*Population Profile of the United States*). (Because of changes in the law in the 1980s, allowing the garnishment of federal tax refunds for child support, this rate has risen from 25 percent.) About one-fourth receive some money, but less than the expected amount, and the remaining one-fourth receive no money at all.

The number of single-parent families has risen in the past 20 years. In 1970, one of every nine families with children under 18 was maintained by a single parent. Today that figure is about one in four. Both divorce and birth out of wedlock are the main factors in this dramatic increase. For the wife, divorce generally means a loss of the primary wage earner, a decrease in income for the family, as she usually is awarded custody of the children, and establishment of a second household. The increased housing and transportation costs, coupled with lack of child support payments, account for the fact that two of every five single-parent families have incomes below the poverty level, compared to one in sixteen for two-parent families. Single-parent families account for about 11 percent of all households, and 90 percent are headed by women.

The Remarried Family

Approximately 15 percent of all households in the United States are made up of remarried couples. Today, remarriages occur early in the life cycle; within five years of a divorce at least 75 percent of spouses remarry. In our society, remarried families are also referred to as **blended families, reconstituted families**, or stepfamilies. The lack of agreement on a name is a clue to society's lack of agreement on how the family ought to function to meet its members' needs. Part of this ambiguity stems from the quantity of variations possible in a blended family. For example, there could be a divorced man–single woman combination or a divorced woman–widowed man. The relationships become more complex when children are in the picture.

Remarriage unites two adults with potentially different experiences in handling money, experiences gained from previous single life, a marriage, the individual's parent, or any combination of these. Therefore, "the process of determining how money should be spent, on whom, or from which source can be extremely difficult" (Dolan and Lown, 1985). As we mentioned when discussing single parents, it is difficult to predict accurately if child support payments will arrive. If the household contains children that are "his, hers, and ours," spouses may consciously or unconsciously resent payments being spent on members of the entire household. When income drops or financial needs increase it is difficult to set priorities on income allocation to two separate families.

A spouse's attitude toward money and its management can be symbolic of his or her commitment to the marriage. Past experiences may make an individual reluctant to disclose all of his or her financial resources to the new partner. As with cohabiting couples many involved in remarriage make prenuptial agreements to specify the disposal of assets if the relationship is dissolved. This is particularly important if the remarriage involves children.

The Empty Nest: Not So Empty

We previously identified two stages of the family life cycle: launching, when children leave home, and later years and retirement. These stages are now being affected by two recent social developments: the growing percentage of young people who are remaining in or returning to their parents' household and the significant increase in the elderly population. Because these developments affect the same household, perhaps

sandwich generation: refers to those currently in midlife who are caught between the needs of young adult children and those of elderly parents or relatives

simultaneously, this middle-aged group is sometimes referred to as the **sandwich generation**.

Families in this circumstance are caught between the needs of young adult children and the expectations of elderly parents or other relatives. The young seem reluctant or unable to find employment, even after job training or education. Sometimes they remain at home due to the high cost of housing or the trend to postpone marriage. At other times the young adult returns as a result of a divorce, bringing his or her own child/children too. The U.S. Bureau of the Census reports that 28 percent of all eighteen- to thirty-four-year-olds live at home with parents.

As for aging parents, living in their own home is usually the preferred solution. However, as health care extends lifespan, parental care becomes a part of the launching and later years stages more often than not. This may mean regular weekly visits to aging parents, or it may require more, such as assistance with household tasks, cooking, and transportation. Many members of the sandwich generation find that it is necessary also to contribute money for their parents' medical bills or an extended stay in a nursing home or residence. These expenses average $5,000 annually.

We can conclude that problems arise for families if their expectations for the last two stages are significantly mismatched with the reality, causing stress and frustration, especially if these stages are accompanied by financial strain. On the other hand, being forewarned can help individuals prepare.

CHANGING FAMILY ROLES: MONEY AND TIME

We have noted changes in family composition and level of living, particularly as a result of an increase in the number of dual-earner families. Concurrently, there have been changes in roles for men and women, both within families and within society as a whole. All of these changes are, of course, interrelated. These changing behavior patterns have involved Amercans in controversies ranging from who should open the car door to which partner is responsible for birth control to whether affirmative action plans are acceptable. The consumer issues that are affected include money management, buying decisions, and career and job choices, as well as management of household tasks and leisure time.

We will briefly look at how the Industrial Revolution defined work, created housework, and established values and standards related to household management—values and standards still held today. We will also see how twentieth-century technology has given us a new phenomenon—leisure time—and how its availability can affect our economic and physical well-being.

Work Roles

Before the Industrial Revolution it was necessary to work 12 to 14 hours a day, seven days a week, to eke out a living on a farm or in a small business.

By the early twentieth century, a typical work week had dropped to 50 or 55 hours, and many workers had weekends free because more goods could be produced in less time by fewer people. Specialization of family responsibilities developed. The man was employed outside the home on a specific job that provided money to purchase goods like food, furniture, a house, clothing, and, if the family was lucky, an automobile.

The woman's specialty was the home, and she provided services like childcare, housekeeping, cooking, laundry, and shopping. Many young women entered the job market for a few years in their teens while they waited for a marriage proposal; then they married and had children. Although it was possible to be an unmarried housewife, the majority of housewives were married. Ann Oakley wrote, in *Woman's Work* (1974), a perceptive analysis of the development of housewifery as an economically dependent occupation. She pointed out that the housewife's work was not and still is not appreciated for the time and energy it involves because housewives receive no salary. Because "work" is a place to which people go, and a "job" is a thing they do in exchange for money, the nonmarket home product performed by housewives is not work. In addition, because no money is paid for housework, housework is not valued.

Today, women are most often employed outside the home. Media coverage and the general "feel" of what is happening on the family scene reflect the American public's changing notion of what is appropriate sex-role behavior for women and men. More and more people are endorsing the need for equal division of labor at home because they recognize that a personal or a family decision to work more and have more income is also a decision to have less leisure time.

Housework

Several researchers have found that a full-time homemaker in the traditional pattern spends about eight hours a day, seven days a week on housework—nonmarket home production. This includes childcare, meal preparation, family shopping, cleaning, laundry, and outside errands. The home production of these goods (meals, clothing, and the like) and services (laundry, cleaning, and the like) is a direct contribution to the family level of living. Although the way the tasks are performed has changed, the amount of total time spent in maintaining a household has changed little over the past 75 years.

With an increasing number of women in the paid work force the amount of time women have available for housework has decreased. A woman working part time devotes approximately seven hours daily to household tasks, whereas a woman employed full time spends four hours daily. The decrease in time spent on household tasks by employed women is partially due to the smaller number of children in these households, as having children means more cooking and cleaning. A second factor is increased purchasing of services. Whether the wife is employed or not, studies consistently show that the amount of time spent by husbands on household tasks averages one and a half hours daily. Tasks are still gender stratified. Husbands tend to accept responsibility for tasks that can be deferred to a convenient time, such as car maintenance, yard work, or bill paying. Husbands may also help with grocery shopping, childcare, and meal preparation. However, the major responsibility is still the wife's. Children make even less of a contribution than husbands and are an untapped resource for nonmarket home production in most families (Lawhon, 1984).

We do not wish to blame men and children or imply that they refuse to help out. Deeply instilled role patterns are slow to change. Often, women desire to be all things to all people: They try to do the cooking, cleaning, and chores of the housekeeper as well as be a loving wife and mother and an effective employee. In short, some try to be "superwomen." Each individual needs to think over priorities and challenge rigid thinking about standards. Families need to determine what is desireable, appropriate, and manageable. Worksheet 2.2 gives some suggestions to help couples set priorities and improve their time management.

WORKSHEET 2.2 TIME MANAGEMENT AND HOUSEHOLD TASKS

Because the dual-earner family pattern is likely to continue, it is important that couples reassess the division of household tasks in terms of income, time, interests, skills, and physical capabilities in order to maximize life for all family members. It is a five-step process:

1. *Look for time wasters.* Check those that apply to you.

_____ Lack of objectives, priorities, and deadlines.
_____ Attempting to do too much at once, and underestimating the time it takes to do it.
_____ Involvement in routine and detail that should be delegated to others.
_____ Indecision and procrastination.
_____ Failure to set up clear lines of responsibility and authority for a job.
_____ Lack of or unclear communication and instruction.
_____ Lack of standards and progress reports.
_____ Crisis situations for which no plans are possible.

_____ Cluttered desk or work areas and personal disorganization.
_____ Telephone interruptions.
_____ Visitors dropping in unexpectedly.
_____ Meetings, both scheduled and unscheduled (including coffee klatsches).
_____ Inability to say no.
_____ Fatigue.

2. *Set priorities.* Alan Lakein, in *How to Get Control of Your Time and Your Life* (1973), suggests setting priorities for daily tasks by deciding whether tasks are: A's—highly important, must-do; B's—important but postponable; or C's—unimportant. By doing more A's and fewer C's you may have a greater feeling of accomplishment (although the A tasks may be more difficult or less enjoyable than the C's).

3. *Reevaluate your standards.* Time is wasted if standards for a specific task are unclear or inappropriate (too weak or too strict, for example). You need to identify standards for tasks that seem to

take too long or for tasks you do often, and then reevaluate them.

a. Identify standards

Draw a horizontal line on a piece of paper and write standards along the continuum to describe the task you are evaluating. For example, to evaluate your housekeeping, you might write:

Sloppy, disorganized	Moderately neat	Neat, well organized

Mark where you think you are on this continuum.

b. Reevaluate standards

Are you satisfied with your standards? Or should you change them? For example, valid reasons for wanting a neater, cleaner house might be to have a comfortable, attractive home where family members can enjoy living (disorder is inefficient, upsetting, fatiguing, embarrassing), to set a good example for children, to have a healthier, safer home (filth breeds bugs and germs, junk can be a fire hazard or can cause accidents), or to save money (grit wears out carpets and furnishings, redecorating costs a lot). Valid reasons for being less neat might be to save time and energy for more important matters or to provide a more comfortable, relaxed atmosphere. For best results, involve other family members in your evaluation. Have them use the same rating continuum you used to see whether their standards agree with yours.

By talking over the problems of differing standards and expectations you can often work out compromises, strengthen your relationships, and make your home a happier place for everyone. Such a discussion—if it is done calmly and cooperatively and not as a blaming confrontation—can help all family members see what their responsibilities are for the smooth functioning and operating of your home.

4. *Assign responsibilities*. Once you have identified time wasters, set priorities, and reevaluated standards, you are ready to assign responsibilities.

a. Identify the tasks that must be done to reach your goals.

b. Decide how often a task should be done—daily, weekly, monthly, yearly.

c. Decide, based on interests, abilities, and time, who will do the task.

You may want to have a rotating schedule of responsibilities, rather than having everyone do the same job all the time. Don't forget to include children of all ages in your plan—each according to his abilities.

5. *Work smarter—not harder*.

a. Save time for a purpose. Having your A-priority goals in mind will help.

b. Plan your schedule first thing in the morning and set priorities for the day. Make a daily to-do list and tick off important items first.

c. Eliminate nonessentials; practice "intelligent neglect" of C-priority items, and then don't waste time feeling guilty about what you don't get done.

d. Plan to eliminate tasks in the future: Replace "ironables" with permapress fabrics, light-colored floor coverings with darker colors, and so forth.

e. Set deadlines to help avoid procrastination; break down a dreaded task into smaller, more manageable tasks.

f. Use odd moments; put waiting time to good use; refer to your to-do list and ask, "What is the best use of my time right now?"

g. Delegate everything you possibly can to others.

h. Give yourself time off as a reward when you have accomplished important tasks.

i. Remind yourself that there is always enough time for the important things.

Making good use of time does not mean constantly trying to beat the clock or filling every waking moment with purposeful activity. Rest, relaxation, time to do nothing or to think or meditate are important, too.

SOURCE: Adapted from "Today's Homemaker" by Dorothy Wenck, Cooperative Extension, Orange County, California.

BOX 2.3   CHILDCARE: ASSESSING THE QUALITY

In millions of families across the nation children are left with caregivers as the parent goes off to work. In about half of these families the caregiver is also the child's parent or a relative (grandparent, aunt, etc.). But in the other half, the infant, toddler, or preschooler, must be placed in some form of day care. Parents can be assured that, as far as researchers can tell, decent day care does not impair a child's development. In fact, day care in a better-than-average facility may accelerate a child's development of social and intellectual skills because of the quantity and quality of activities that occur there. We will explore some of the childcare options for infants through extended day care, as well as methods of assessing their quality.

One of the first questions to ask of a caregiver regards **licensing**. Licensing provides minimum safety and health safeguards for a child, but does not evaluate the program or the staff. Licensing is usually regulated by the state department of social services. Licensed childcare facilities are divided into two basic types: *family day-care homes*, where care is provided in an individual's home for one to 12 children, and *day-care centers*, which can provide care for a number of children in a group setting. Although state laws vary, there is usually a minimum teacher–child ratio, such as one teacher for every 12 preschool children or one adult for every four infants. A list of licensed facilities in your area should be available from your state's department of social services, your local college child-development program, or perhaps the local YMCA or YWCA. Also look in your phone book for a childcare referral hotline.

After determining that a facility is licensed, use this list to assess the safety of the day-care setting:

Health and Safety

Floors, eating, and toilet areas are clean.
Adults do not smoke when with children.
Medicines, detergents, etc. are out of reach of children.
First-aid supplies are available.
Electrical outlets are covered with safety caps.

Toys and equipment are in good repair.
Heavy furniture (lockers, bookcases, etc.) is secure and stable.
Meals and snacks are nutritionally balanced.
The floor is warm in cold weather, and there is adequate ventilation.

If the facility meets these minimum safety standards you are now ready to ask questions to help you assess the physical facilities, care providers, and the program.

Physical Facilities

Is the center bright and cheerful?
Is there adequate space for indoor and outdoor activities?
Is there an appropriate storage space for each child's belongings?
Is there a space for naps?
Is there an "isolation area" for ill children?

Care Providers

Has the staff been trained in child development?
Is there adequate staff to supervise all the children?
Are the policies about child behavior consistent with your own?
Do the care providers relate warmly with the children?
Do the care providers encourage rather than reprimand?
What are the disciplinary policies?
Are the children treated as individuals?
Are parental visits, questions, and comments welcome?
Are the care providers enthusiastic about their responsibilities?

Educational Program

Does the facility have a written, planned program?
Is the program appropriate for each age group present in the facility?

Are activities planned to support and enhance the development of the total child: intellectual, physical, social, and emotional?

Are there age-appropriate materials and equipment to support this program and meet the needs of the total child?

If there is a television, how much time is spent watching it, and how is program selection monitored?

Do the planned activities indicate an acceptance of and respect for your family's cultural and religious values?

Once you have selected a setting for your child, it is important to continue to monitor its quality. Plan to drop in to observe your child engaged in the planned activities. Ask your child about what he or she does and how he or she is treated at the facility. Attend parents' meetings and programs.

Childcare

Childcare poses a special challenge to two-career and single-parent families. Although attitudes toward employment for women have gone from slight disapproval in the 1950s to total acceptance in the 1990s, considerable prejudice still remains toward employed mothers with very young children. No conclusive scientific or sociological evidence exists to prove that young children need their biological mothers around them all the time or that mothers are inherently better parents than fathers. Nonetheless, an employed mother who entrusts her child to a babysitter or to a day-care center may feel at least a twinge of guilt. Such guilt is unnecessary because most experts today agree that it is not the quantity of time spent on parenting, but the quality that counts. For suggestions on choosing childcare, see Box 2.3.

Career and Job Decisions

Job advancement is another area in which decisions about time need to be made. Part of the role of the traditional wife is to further her husband's career by giving him status, providing him with unpaid help to care for his home and children, and managing his social calender. Women have no such support system, and in fact, being a wife and mother can hold a woman back in the workplace. For example, because of commitments to husband and children, women are less available for out-of-town business trips and may not have time beyond the average work week to spend on extra job duties or entertainment. Single adults of both sexes face similar difficulties because they lack the services, such as household care, bookkeeping and banking, entertainment, and errand running, provided by a traditional wife.

To meet the challenge of combining a successful career with an involved family life, some new time-management role patterns are developing. Some two-career families decide to be less concerned about career advancement than families of the more traditional pattern and choose to turn down promotions and transfers that might result in a poor career move for the other partner. In other marriages, the woman's career may take precedence over the man's, and the man chooses more family involvement over career involvement. A third option is for both partners to choose jobs that allow for greater autonomy and flexibility of time schedules. Other options include remaining childless and maintaining separate residences in different geographic locations. Needless to say, these changes in marriage roles and in use of time involve far more than just a change in attitudes and behavior within the home. They call for sweeping reforms and changes on the part of employers, city planners, childcare providers, and society as a whole.

Leisure Time

Time not commited to income production or nonmarket home production is **leisure time**. Your time-management decisions determine how much leisure you have. Here, we want to discuss the role that leisure time plays in your mental, physical, and emotional health, because being healthy is essential to earning and spending. Leisure time used to refresh the mind, body, and spirit is **recreation**. The pressures of job and family can be put into perspective during moments of physical activity or quiet solitude, allowing us to be more effective members of family and society. An important part of recreation is exercise to help maintain proper weight and muscle tone and, at the same time, to reduce stress. Time spent for activities and play gives a pleasurable alternative to work.

Recreation for young families can be as simple as a day at the beach, but even here problems can arise.

Besides maintaining physical health, sports and hobbies provide an opportunity to develop our abilities and personalities. Recreation allows people who become narrowed by their jobs an opportunity to express themselves. For example, a computer programmer might choose to spend leisure time gardening or playing tennis. A carpenter might choose to collect stamps or practice yoga. As you can see, what is work to one person might be recreation to another. True recreation involves a free choice of activity, whether it be fishing, photography, dancing, sewing, or soccer. Such activities provide opportunities for relaxation, self-expression, and fulfillment.

Many jobs involve routine and rigid work, much of it done in isolation. Leisure time allows for a break in this seclusion. It might be spent interacting in club or fraternal organizations, in community volunteer work, or, more informally, in visiting with friends and family. It can provide one with personal support systems, as well as with a chance to get in touch with oneself.

Parkinson's law: a theory which states that the amount of time spent doing a job expands to fit the amount of time available

Some people "never have enough time" for recreation or leisure. In many cases **Parkinson's law** comes into play: Work expands to fit the time allowed. We need to remember that the counterpart of increased work time, whether market or nonmarket production, is decreased leisure time. Leisure forgone is the greatest cost of employment, particularly to single parents and those living alone, because these people are solely responsible for personal, family, and household care, in addition to employment responsibilities. A positive attitude toward time management needs to be applied in order to achieve a balance and allow for leisure time in busy schedules.

Retirement

Retirement provides full-time leisure, a time to be used however one wishes. The concept of retirement from work was born during the Depression as a way to create jobs for younger workers. For example, in 1900, three out of four males over age 65 were still working, compared to one out of five today. Thanks to exercise, modern medicine, improved diet, and decreased smoking, older Americans are healthier and more vigorous than ever before, which makes them physcially able to enjoy retirement.

Workers who retire today at age 65 expect an average of 14 years of retirement. By the year 2000 this figure is expected to increase to an average of 25 years. Because of increased health, economic need, and changing Social Security regulations, many people choose to postpone retirement, take part-time jobs, or start new businesses of their own. All these factors emphasize the need to apply the decision-making process to the use of leisure time during retirement. Retirement planning should map out the entire scope of this new phase of life and should focus on skills, values, and economic and psychic needs. One may choose to continue spending time in one's original field, such as sales, medicine, or accounting. On the other hand, this may be the time to explore a totally new field. In either case, one's skills might be used to earn money or might be given freely as a volunteer. The joy of retirement is that one's work is self-assigned, making it truly leisure.

SUMMARY

Most of us live much of our lives as members of at least one family. As a result, many of our consumer decisions are made jointly with family members. Key decisions regarding career, family composition, and family size can determine, to a great extent, the quantity of money and leisure time we have.

The career that a person chooses is a major factor in his or her present and future level of living. Generally, the more education one has, the higher one's salary and the greater one's job security. Other factors that affect individual income are age, sex, race, and location of residence. Family income depends on the earning capabilities of family members and on the number of members earning labor income.

A family is responsible for the economic welfare of its members. The ability to meet this responsibility often depends on family composition, size, life-cycle stage, and income level. In recent years there has been a marked increase of single-parent families, remarried families, and households composed of one individual. A fourth trend, a decreasing birth rate, has resulted in smaller families and a greater number of childless families.

Family spending patterns are a reflection of family composition, the stage of the family life cycle, the family income level, the number of family members who work, and values, goals, and standards. Any changes in these variables can cause changes in spending patterns.

We are constrained by time as well as by money. When we choose to spend our time earning income, we automatically decrease the time available for nonmarket home production or for leisure. The goal for individuals and families is to manage this time to allow for necessary household tasks and recreation. The challenge is to develop an equitable distribution of tasks so that all family members have sufficient leisure.

QUESTIONS

1. What is the difference between a nuclear family and an extended family?
2. What are the stages of the individual life cycle? Of the family life cycle?
3. There are differences in salaries between men and women who have similar education and experience. Why is this so? What has been done to rectify this situation?

4. What are the arguments involved in the demand for "comparable worth"?
5. Do you think there is a strong correlation between the time and money costs of an education and the salaries earned? Why?
6. What specific suggestions appear in the text to

improve time management? Which ones are particularly relevant for you?
7. From your own experience, identify some of the major expenses for each stage in the individual and family life cycles.

REFERENCES AND READINGS

"A Special Report: The Corporate Woman." *The Wall Street Journal*, March 24, 1986.

Barber, Clifton E. "Parental Responses to the Empty-Nest Transition." *Journal of Home Economics*, Summer 1981.

Bird, Caroline. *The Two-Paycheck Marriage*. New York: Rawson, Wade, 1979.

Blotnick, Srully. *Otherwise Engaged: The Personal Lives of Successful Career Women* New York: Facts on File, 1985.

"'Comparable Worth' Seen as Way to Increase Women's Salaries." *Los Angeles Times*, September 13, 1984.

Deacon, Ruth E., and Firebaugh, Fancille M. *Family Resource Management*. Boston: Allyn & Bacon, 1975.

Dolan, Elizabeth M., and Lown, Jean M. "The Remarried Family: Challenges and Opportunities." *Journal of Home Economics*, Fall 1985.

Drennen, Nancy H., and Makela, Carole J. "Comparable Worth: An Issue Demanding the Attention of Home Economics." *Journal of Home Economics*, Fall 1986.

Easterlin, Richard A. *Birth and Fortune*, 2nd ed. Chicago: University of Chicago Press, 1987.

Fabe, Marilyn, and Wikler, Norma. *Up Against the Clock*. New York: Random House, 1980.

Garfinkel, Perry. *In a Man's World: Father, Son, Brother, Friend, and Other Roles Men Play*. New York: New American Library, 1985.

Illinois Teacher of Home Economics: A Home Economics Response to the Evolving Family Structure. September/October, 1988. University of Illinois, Champaign, IL 61820.

Irwin, Don. "Those Under 30 Found to Be in Economic Bind." *Los Angeles Times*. September 5, 1988.

Lakein, Alan. *How To Get Control of Your Time and Your Life*. New York: Peter H. Wyden. 1973.

Lawhon, Tommie M. "Work and Stress in the Home: How Do You Help in the Family?" *Journal of Home Economics*, Winter, 1984.

Littwin, Susan. *The Postponed Generation*. Morrow, 1986.

"Mothers' Labor Force Activity." *Family Economics Review*, no. 4. Washington, D.C.: U.S. Department of Agriculture, 1986.

National Urban League. *The State of Black America 1980*. New York: The National Urban League, 1980.

Oakley, Ann. *Woman's Work*. New York: Pantheon, 1974.

Paolucci, Beatrice, Hall, Olive A., and Axinn, Nancy. *Family Decision Making: An Ecosystem Approach* New York: Wiley, 1977.

Shaevitz, Marjorie Hansen, and Shaevitz, Morton H. *Making It Together as a Two-Career Couple*. Boston: Houghton Mifflin, 1980.

Shaevitz, Morton. H. *Sexual Static: How Men Confuse the Women They Love*. Boston: Little, Brown, 1987.

Shank, Susan, "Women and the Labor Market: The Link Grows Stronger." *Monthly Labor Review*, no. 3, 1988.

Sheehy, Gail. *Passages*. New York: Dutton, 1976.

Shulman, Bernard, and Bermank, Raeann. *How to Survive Your Aging Parents—So You and They Can Enjoy Life*. Chicago: Surrey Books, 1988.

"The Children Who Get Cut Out." *US News and World Report*, October 12, 1987.

Trost, Cathy. "The New Majorities." *The Wall Street Journal*, March 24, 1986.

Tumulty, Karen. "Wage Gap: Women Still Second Sex." *Los Angeles Times*, September 13, 1984.

U.S. Bureau of the Census. "Money Income and Poverty Status of Families and Persons in the United States: 1986." *Current Population Reports*. Washington, D.C.: U.S. Government Printing Office, 1984.

U.S. Bureau of the Census. *Population Profile of the United States 1984/1985*. Washington, D.C.: U.S. Government Printing Office, 1986.

U.S. Bureau of the Census, "Money Income of Households, Families, and Persons in the United States: *1986: Current Population Reports*. Washington, D.C.: U.S. Government Printing Office, series P-60, no. 159, June 1988.

Chapter Three

BASIC ECONOMIC PRINCIPLES: BE PREPARED

☐ Economic Systems: Facing the Problem of Scarcity
☐ The Modern American Economic System: A Mixed Economy
☐ The Economy and You

DID YOU KNOW THAT ...

. . . there are only three pure types of economies in the world?

. . . consumers are the directors of market economies?

. . . the real cost of an item equals its price in time as well as money?

. . . the law of demand will never be repealed?

. . . the chief measure of inflation, the Consumer Price Index, surveys the prices of 400 items in 85 urban areas monthly?

. . . if inflation averages 7 percent per year, prices will double every decade?

. . . the biggest debtors are the ones who benefit most from inflation (and the U.S. government is the number one debtor in our economy)?

. . . business cycles have a major impact on your life-style?

. . . recessions often produce warning signs *before* they happen?

In this century Amercians have witnessed an unparalleled rise in consumer purchasing power. As a result, late-twentieth-century consumers have more decisions to make about how to use their income than any generation before. If you were to rewrite the Declaration of Independence from a modern consumer standpoint, it might read:

> We hold these truths to be self-evident, that all people are created equal, that they are endowed by their creator with certain inalienable rights, that among these are life, liberty, and the pursuit of happiness. This pursuit of happiness includes ownership of a home, a car, a home entertainment center, free health care, a prepaid retirement package, annual vacations and weekend escapes, as well as any consumer good owned by a typical television family.

As we said in Chapter 1, these economic wants can be insatiable. We could easily modify this list to include such yuppie amenities as a condo on Maui or a BMW automobile, but the point is that while our list of consumer wants grows exponentially, our ability to satisfy these wants is tempered by the ability of our economy to produce them and our environment to sustain them. We have had two centuries of success, but storm clouds are appearing on the horizon. Over the past two decades consumer incomes have begun to rise more slowly, interest and inflation rates have moved erratically, and the productivity of the labor force has actually declined in some sectors. Stock market averages have tumbled and risen in roller coaster fashion as investors have been whipsawed by two major emotions: fear and greed. Much of the blame for our two-decade-long doldrums has been placed on the federal government, which has not balanced its budget since 1969. It took our nation almost 200 years and two world wars to reach a trillion-dollar national debt, but in the 1980s the federal government doubled the national debt by borrowing an additional trillion dollars to finance its spending programs. Is it any wonder that many observers have turned pessimistic?

Modern critics argue that the gains of an earlier industrialized era are now behind us and the economy has stopped growing. If the pessimists are correct, then you will confront some very difficult economic, political, and social decisions in the very near future. Even if the pessimists are wrong and the economy begins to grow at its historical pace, you will still be faced with difficult choices. There will never be enough resources to satisfy everyone's wants, since income growth has always led consumers to want more. Thus, despite the fact that American consumers have entered the last decade of the twentieth century with more buying power than

scarcity: a situation in which we do not have enough resources to satisfy all our wants

they have ever possessed, they still are confronted with the problem of **scarcity**: not enough resources to satisfy all their wants.

The ever-present problem of scarcity highlights the need for understanding how our economy evolved, how it works, and the role you play in it. You need to be alerted to some basic economic principles and concepts. Once you have mastered these economic ideas, you will be better able to grasp the "big economic picture." which is called *macroeconomics.* Our ultimate objective is to arm you with enough knowledge to survive and prosper in bad economic times, as well as in good ones.

ECONOMIC SYSTEMS: FACING THE PROBLEM OF SCARCITY

If you were asked to list the basic consumer needs that everyone must fulfill, you would be hard pressed to come up with a better list than the traditional three: food, clothing, and shelter. These items are often called **needs**, or necessities, because without them, life could not go on. Consumers also have **wants** above and beyond their basic needs for survival. Television sets, stereos, and jewelry are all samples of things we could live without but want to have.

Resources are the things that satisfy our needs and wants. Money, for example, is a resource we use to purchase goods and services. Trees are the resources used to make the paper the money is printed on. Minerals from the ground are a resource used in manufacturing the goods we buy.

The fundamental dilemma we all face stems from the fact that our wants are unlimited, while our resources are limited, or scarce. As we saw in Chapter 1, scarcity is a major influence on our personal consumer decisions. On a broader level, it is a guiding force in the way the economy is structured.

economy: a system by which a society mobilizes its resources to address the problem of scarcity

An **economy** is a system by which a society addresses the problem of scarcity and attempts to answer three fundamental questions:

1. What goods and services are we going to produce?
2. How are we going to produce these goods and services?
3. Who will get these goods and services?

Just as a society must have a political system that formulates laws and governs acceptable, civilized behavior, so, too, it must develop an economic system that organizes its scarce resources to produce and distribute goods and services. Without some routine way of deciding what to produce, how to produce, and whom to distribute these products to, a society would not long survive. In a very real sense, then, an economy is society's life-support system. It is one of the most basic institutions in your life, and as such it deserves some study if you are to understand your role in it.

Three Theoretical Types of Economies: Traditional, Command, and Market

There is no single solution to the problem of scarcity. To clarify some of the common ways different societies have tackled the problem, economists have divided economic systems into three basic types: traditional, command, and market. Each is distinguished from the other by the way it answers the basic economic questions, What, How, and For Whom.

Traditional economy. A **traditional economy** is one in which the fundamental economic questions—What, How, and For Whom—are determined by age-old customs (tradition). Prior to the arrival of Europeans in North America, most Native American tribes would have been a good example, of societies with traditional economies. If you were to be magically transported to Lake Ontario in A.D. 1400 and you asked several Iroquois why they produced particular products or why they were in their particular occupations, they would simply answer that things had always been done that way or that their parents had been trained for particular occupations and had, in turn, trained them as successors. In short, it was *traditional* to do things a certain way or to enter a particular occupation. In such a society, individual decision making is highly limited, and for good reason. In a tradition-based economy, there is little margin for error. One mistake could lead to starvation.

Command economy. A **command economy** is an economic system in which the answers to the basic questions are predetermined by a central authority. The Soviet Union, China, and Cuba are run largely as command economies in which economic decision making is very centralized. In a command economy, consumers and producers have very limited choices and thus very little freedom in their day to day actions. No one can deny the effectiveness of such economies in achieving an increase in economic

Agriculture in a tradition based economy, depends on techniques that are centuries old.

activity. However, many would criticize their political and bureaucratic techniques, and some would argue that these repressive regimes must eventually allow for greater individual freedom or suffer an end to their economic progress. The recent *glasnost*, or "openness," in the Soviet system may signal some change in their command-style economy.

Market economy. Of the three basic types of economies, a market economy is the most difficult to understand. However, it comes closest to replicating the American experience and thus deserves detailed study.

In a **market economy** the basic economic questions are answered by individuals acting in their own interest in free markets. Unlike a command economy, a market economy is very decentralized, with no one person or small group clearly in charge. The absence of governmental control over the economy is called **laissez-faire**—the government "leaves the economy alone." If the government doesn't direct the economy, who does?

In a market economy consumers are the ultimate directors of what gets produced. If a business produces something that consumers don't want, consumers are free to refuse to buy it. In this case, the firm either produces something else or goes out of business. IBM PC*jr* computers, Premier smokeless cigarettes, Reggie candy bars, and Edsel automobiles are all examples of products consumers chose not to support with their dollars. In addition to producing goods that consumers want, business firms must also produce those goods and services as efficiently and cheaply as possible. Otherwise, they will be undersold by other, more competitive firms.

BOX 3.1 **THE MARKET SYSTEM IN A NUTSHELL**

The three crucial ingredients for a healthy market economy are (1) director, (2) motivator, and (3) regulator.

1. *Consumers are the directors.* Consumers act as the directors in a market economy. In fact, consumer acceptance is so crucial to producers that economists often refer to **consumer sovereignty**, which means that consumers are the rulers. Through their purchasing choices, they declare which products and producers will prosper and which will fail.

2. *Profit is the motivator.* Producers are willing to work hard to satisfy consumers' wishes because success is rewarded with sales revenue in excess of the costs of production. This reward is called **profit**. When profits are large, firms are motivated to produce more goods and services.

3. *Competition is the regulator.* Strong consumer demand and high profits will entice other firms into producing the desired good or service. As more firms enter the marketplace the supply increases. An increase in supply weakens the ability of producers to raise their prices. In essence, competition regulates and lessens the strength of any individual producer. The greater the competition among producers, the more sovereign the consumers.

Finally, who gets the output? Answer: whoever has the money to pay for it. You earn money in a market society by producing something someone else wants. The more efficient you are at supplying consumer wants, the more income you will earn and, in turn, the more buying power you will achieve.

The market economy system is described in more detail in Box 3.1.

THE MODERN AMERICAN ECONOMIC SYSTEM: A MIXED ECONOMY

mixed-market economy: an economic system that is predominantly market oriented but allows government to have a substantial role as a producer, consumer, and transfer agent

Very few societies today can be classified as having one type of economy. The Eskimo have electric lights and television, a large fraction of the fruits and vegetables in the Soviet Union are sold at market prices by individual farmers, and in the United States the federal government is the largest landowner. The United States has a **mixed-market economy**, an economic system that is predominantly market oriented but allows government a substantial role as a producer, consumer, and transfer agent. We will discuss the role of government in the economy at length throughout the text; here we just want to emphasize that government plays a central role in a mixed-market economy.

Government provides services, from national defense on the federal level to public education, parks, and police services on the state and local level. Government also consumes goods and services in the form of labor, building materials, and office supplies. A third role for government is to distribute income from those more able to pay taxes to those who are less able. This is generally done through **transfer payments**, which can be defined as payments to individuals that are unrelated to current productive activity. Unemployment compensation, old-age pensions, and welfare are all examples of transfer payments. Most of these government expenditures are financed by taxes; however, government can also finance these functions by borrowing.

In our economy, the "marketplace" is always in the forefront in our decision making. Government, custom, and tradition also play roles, but it is the dominance of the marketplace that characterizes the U.S. economy. In the sections that follow we will introduce the basic features of our modern economy.

The Circular Flow of Economic Activity in a Market Economy

To begin an examination of our mixed-market economy, we need an overall picture of how the economy works. Economists often use a **circular flow model** like the one in Figure 3.1 (page 70) to illustrate the flow of economic activity in a market economy. The model illustrates the dual roles we all play in a market economy, as both consumers *and* producers. It helps us to emphasize that production and consumption are interrelated. There can be no consumption without production, and production cannot be sustained without consumption.

The top half of the diagram shows the importance of consumer sovereignty in answering the question of what to produce. Households demand a wide variety of goods and services. The business firms that supply these needs and wants at competitive prices are rewarded with dollar payments. The flow of funds does not stop there, however, because firms must pay for the resources they use to create goods. These productive resources include human and natural resources, as well as man-made resources like tools and machinery. Economists call these resources the **factors of production** and they often label them **labor** (human resources), **land** (natural resources), and **capital** (man-made resources). The bottom half of the diagram shows that the owners of these resources must be paid if they are to be willing to let the firms use them. After all, there are very few of us in a market economy who would let some firm use our land or our labor without expecting some compensation. The lower half of Figure 3.1 illustrates this vital link. The payments we receive as resource owners are returned to firms in return for goods and service. In general, the more that firms want our services, the greater our incomes will be, and the more we will be able to influence what goods and services get produced.

factors of production: the general term for the productive resources of an economy; they are often called labor (human resources), land (natural resources), *and* capital (man-made resources)

Business firms. The block labeled Business Firms in Figure 3.1 may seem clear to you, but how would you define a business firm? A **business firm** is an organization that produces goods or services with the intention of earning a profit. There are more than 16 million American firms, ranging in size from General Motors, with more than 800,000 employees and more than a quarter of a million shareholders, to your local shoemaker who owns his or her shop and has no employees. Regardless of their size, all privately owned firms attempt to maximize their profits by organizing resources and producing the goods and services their customers are able and willing to pay for. Notice that in a market economy the ultimate ownership of all resources rests with households.

Households. Households compose the other major block in Figure 3.1. A **household** consists of any number of people voluntarily living together to form a decision-making unit. As we mentioned in Chapter 2, a family consisting of a husband, wife, and children would be classified as a household, and so would a single person living alone. Large or small, the objective of every household is still the same: to maximize its happiness by weighing the costs and benefits of consumption and then making rational decisions. Today, there are approximately 90 million households in the United States.

Factors in Household Consumption Patterns

A few key variables exert strong influences on household consumption activity: income, time costs, tastes, and prices. Each one shapes consumer demand for goods and services.

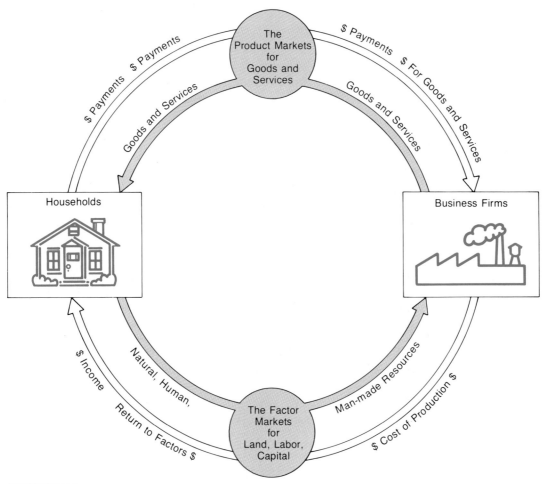

FIGURE 3.1
Circular flow diagram of a market economy. The top half of the diagram
illustrates the product markets. These are the markets where households
purchase goods and services from firms. If you bought a hamburger, rented an
apartment, or went to a movie, you actively participated in this part of the
circular flow. You received a good (hamburger) or a service (shelter,
entertainment) in return for money payments. Business firms compete for
consumers' demand by offering lower prices or better-quality products. The
lower half of the diagram shows the factor markets. Here, it is the households
that are the sellers, while the firms are the buyers. Households provide
productive resources like labor, land, or capital to firms in return for money
income. For example, if you work in a restaurant or own shares in a corporation
you actively participate in the factor markets.

Income. Income is the primary determinant of individual buying power
in the marketplace. In a market economy your income level determines
the strength of your voice. If you have high income, whenever you speak,
the market listens. If, on the other hand, your income is small relative to

Bus transportation is an example of an inferior good while airline travel is a normal good.

that of other consumers, you do not have much influence on what gets produced.

As your income increases relative to that of other consumers, your particular consumption pattern gains added weight in the society's economy. But something else happens as your income rises: Your consumption pattern changes. For example, if your income were to double over the next five years, would you buy twice as much of everything? Not likely, but you would spend somewhat more money on some goods and less on others.

Normal goods are those goods (and services) that we buy more of as our income rises. Most of the goods we buy are normal goods; that's why they are "normal." Furniture, life insurance, restaurant meals, new cars, private education, and foreign travel are example of these goods.

Goods purchased less often at higher incomes are called **inferior goods**. As a consumer's income rises, a smaller amount is spent on inferior goods. Public transit, generic brands, and used goods are generally in this category.

normal good: a commodity that consumers buy more of as consumer incomes rise

inferior goods: products or goods that are purchased less often by those with higher incomes than by those with lower incomes

To generalize from these observations, as a consumer's income rises, his or her budget will allow for more normal goods. New cars, diamond jewelry, large houses, and airline travel grow in relative importance, while the demand for used cars, costume jewelry, cramped apartments, and bus transportation declines. On the other hand, if a consumer's income falls, inferior goods command a larger portion of his or her budget.

Time. Time is another important determinant of our consumption pattern. As your income rises, so does the value of your time. In all societies there are, of course, the same number of hours in the day. But in highly productive, high-income societies, those hours are more precious because there are so many ways to use one's time.

For example, consider two female consumers. One is a highly skilled, highly paid attorney-at-law. The other is a semiskilled worker employed by a fast-food restaurant. Whose time is more valuable? Because the attorney is paid more for her time, we would say her time is more valuable. A less obvious observation is that the attorney's buying habits will also be affected by this difference—by what we call **time costs**. Time cost is the opportunity cost of using your time in one activity rather than in another.

All consumers are affected by time costs, but some are less aware of it than others. Have you ever waited for an hour at your doctor's office? Did that increase the cost of your visit? Of course, it did: You had to give up something in order to see the doctor. You gave up time as well as money. While you waited, you did not do something else you might have wanted or needed to do, such as working to earn money or having lunch with friends. Who is more likely to be willing to wait for the extra hour, the lawyer or the food server? Who has less to lose by waiting? The one with the lower time cost. Whenever you have to wait, visualize yourself as a taxicab driver with the meter running. A highly paid driver has a meter that runs faster and charges higher fares per hour. An unemployed cab driver has a meter that does not run at all

In general then, as an income rises, time becomes more precious, and it becomes more important for consumers to consider the cost of their time as well as the monetary cost of an item. Fast-food restaurants have boomed, while food prepared at home has become much less important in consumer budgets because of the time-cost factor (see Figure 3.2). Convenience food markets such as 7–11 and AM–PM Mini Markets prosper in spite of their higher food prices because they offer quicker service, longer hours, and more convenient locations than supermarkets. These characteristics help lower a consumer's time costs and thus the total cost of the loaf of bread he or she needs tomorrow morning.

Tastes: Consumer preferences revealed. Tastes, or consumer preferences, constitute another variable that influences consumer purchas-

FIGURE 3.2
The total cost of an item is equal to its monetary cost plus its time cost.

Homemade burger =
cost of hamburger + bun ($0.50)
+ preparation and cleanup time (20 minutes)

Big Mac = cost ($1.59) + waiting time
(5 minutes)

ing of items such as clothing, transportation, personal care, recreation, housing, and sometimes even food and drink. When designer jeans first became available, for example, teenage and adult consumers rushed to buy these name brands. Consumer tastes clearly changed from preferring ordinary-looking jeans to clothes that had more pronounced tailoring, with fancy stitching and a price to match. Thus, within a short period of time there were thousands of Americans wearing one or another of these fashion jeans. Another example of a change in consumer preferences can be seen in the popularity of wine. In the 1960s wine with a meal was rare in most households, but by the 1980s it was commonplace. In addition to developing a taste for the fruit of the vine, consumers exhibited a distinct preference for white wine. This led many wineries to produce a ''blush wine''—white wine from red varietal grapes. Although the causes of the change in consumer tastes for designer jeans and wine have never been fully explained, they had a real impact on what was produced.

Price. Certainly, income, time costs, and tastes influence what households buy, but the impact of price on our behavior is always given star billing by economists. Economists argue that as the price of an item rises, consumers find it worthwhile to buy less of that item, substituting other items when it is practical to do so. As noted earlier in this chapter, the relationship between a change in the price of a good and the subsequent change in the amount demanded by consumers is common—so common that the relationship has come to be called the **law of demand**. The law of demand holds that consumers will buy more at lower prices than at higher prices, assuming that income, time, and taste factors do not change. Sometimes the association between price and the quantity demanded is called an inverse relationship because the two variables always change in the opposite direction: As one goes up, the other goes down.

law of demand: the law which states that consumers will buy more of a given product at lower prices than at higher prices

The energy-related behavior of consumers provides an excellent real-world application of the law of demand. When the world price of crude oil rises, inevitably raising the price of fuel, the consumer remedy is to cut back on the use of oil and oil-related products. This means driving less, buying smaller, more fuel-efficient cars, insulating more, turning thermostats down in winter to save fuel, and keeping air conditioners off in the summer to save electricity. All these actions are in keeping with the law of demand.

Keeping the price constant but lowering the quality of an item has the same effect as raising the price. If a firm holds the price of its chocolate bars constant but begins to use imitation chocolate in the process, or if it shrinks the size of the candy bar to cut costs, the quality of the product has changed and so, too, has the real price. The law of demand says that consumers try to avoid higher prices whether they come in the form of bigger price tags or lower quality. However, this bargain-hunting attitude can be successfully implemented only when consumers have good information.

An ignorant consumer who always associates a higher price with higher-quality products will spend more than is necessary. For example, if one bottle of aspirin is twice as expensive as another, is it correct to assume that the more expensive brand is better?

THE ECONOMY AND YOU

macroeconomics: the study of problems that concern the entire economy

As the circular flow model illustrates, consumption and production are closely related. One cannot exist without the other. Your personal lifestyle and consumption pattern are influenced to a great extent by the general health of the economy. If the economy is strong and vibrant, there will be a wide variety of goods available at moderate prices. Jobs will be readily obtainable, with good wages and working conditions. Under such conditions consumption reinforces the productive spirit in all of us. Greater demand for goods and services leads firms to hire more workers to fulfill the demand. These additional workers earn income that they subsequently spend. Increased spending leads to greater production, more jobs, higher incomes, and eventually more consumption. These relationships are all part of what we call **macroeconomics**, the study of the economy as a whole.

A healthy economy is a prosperous one, but even the most dynamic market economy faces limits to its expansion. An economy has only a limited amount of land, labor, and capital goods: An economy's resources are finite. If most of the human, natural, and capital resources are employed, an increase in demand cannot bring about an increase in production, because firms will have a difficult time mobilizing the resources to produce more goods and services. Moreover, production can destroy some irreplaceable natural resources, such as oil or natural gas, and thus actually shrink the resource base of the economy.

The relationships between consumption, production, and the resource base of an economy are very complex. Nevertheless, a basic understanding of the interrelationships is a crucial part of your consumer education. These factors parallel the three major roles you yourself must assume in our society: consumer, producer, citizen.

A Diagnosis of the Economy's Health

No single measure can capture the state of your health. Your pulse rate, blood count, temperature, blood pressure, weight, and general attitude are all part of your health profile. In the same way, there are many indicators of an economy's well-being. The unemployment rate, inflation rate, and the stock market indexes are related to an economy's overall health. Nevertheless there is one measure that has the greatest ability to summarize the overall performance of the economy. It is called *gross national product.*

gross national product (GNP): the market value of an economy's annual output of final goods and services

Gross national product. The **gross national product (GNP)** represents the value of an economy's annual output of finished goods and services. The dollar value of every ton of grain exported, every visit made to a doctor, every gallon of gasoline bought, and every teacher's salary paid, plus every other final good or service produced in the calendar year, are added together to determine the value of the GNP for this year. The change in GNP from year to year (and even from quarter to quarter) gives us the most comprehensive view of the economy.

Figure 3.3 illustrates the growth in the productive power and health of the U.S. economy by illustrating our GNP from 1960 to 1990. As you can see from the solid line, by 1990 GNP is projected to be over ten times larger than 1960's GNP. The dotted line represents the annual value of all consumer expenditures from 1960, when consumers bought a little over

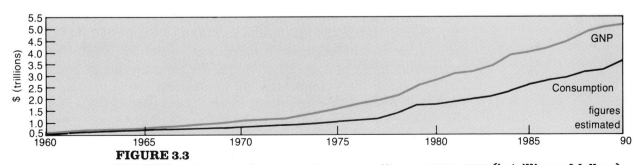

FIGURE 3.3
U.S. GNP and personal consumption expenditures, 1960–1990 (in trillions of dollars).
(SOURCES: *Economic Report of the President* [Washington, D.C.: U.S. Government Printing Office, 1989] and authors' estimates.)

$330 billion worth of goods and services, to 1990, when purchases exceed $3.5 trillion. This increase parallels the general rise in GNP.

Inflation in the Modern Economy

inflation: a sustained rise in the average level of prices

The tenfold growth in the health and wealth of our economy shown in Figure 3.3 fails to take inflation into account. This means it overstates the improvement in our well-being over this time period. **Inflation** can be defined as a persistent rise in the overall price level in an economy. This rise is a major problem, because it distorts the comparison of recent data on GNP with data from previous years. For example, one dollar in 1960 might have bought a little over three gallons of gasoline, four loaves of bread, or copies of both *Time* and *Newsweek* magazines. Today, you will probably be able to purchase only one gallon of gasoline, a single loaf of bread, or a couple of newspapers for a dollar. Neither *Time* nor *Newsweek* is available from a newsstand for a dollar. This example documents what we are all intuitively aware of: *prices have risen significantly over the past three decades.*

The consumer price index. How significantly have prices risen? Since consumers cannot possibly look at all prices at once, a government agency, the Bureau of Labor Statistics (BLS) has developed the Consumer Price Index to characterize the change in consumer prices. The **Consumer Price Index (CPI)** is a measure of the average change in the price paid by urban consumers for a fixed market basket of goods and services. Retail prices for a market basket of 400 items commonly purchased by 80 percent of American consumers are gathered monthly from 85 urban areas in the United States. In a given year, the BLS collects about 1.5 million price quotations on such common goods as food, housing, fuels, clothing, and medical services. The cost of these items is then totaled and divided by their cost during a preselected time period called the *base*. By comparing the cost of the same market basket of goods and services over time, the BLS is able to make some general statements about the change in consumer prices.

For example, if the cost of an identical market basket of goods and services was $30 in the base period and $45 five years later, the price of the basket rose by one-half, or 50 percent, over this period. The CPI summarizes price changes by arbitrarily assigning a value of 100 to the base period. In our example, the CPI would equal 100 in the base period and 150 (50 percent higher) five years later. The current CPI uses 1982–84 as the base and was calculated by the BLS at 119.0 in August 1988. This means it took $119 in 1988 to buy what $100 could have purchased, using average prices in the 1982–84 time period.

You can use the CPI for a variety of purposes, but one of its most important functions is to help you distinguish between nominal dollars and real dollars. **Nominal dollars** are measured by their face value. **Real**

BOX 3.2   INFLATION AND YOU: THE CASE OF THE $14 HAMBURGER

The power of inflation rates, like interest rates or population growth rates, is easy to underestimate. For example, if the price of a hamburger were to rise by 10 percent per year, how many years would it take for the price to double? Because doubling would equal a 100 percent increase, most students are inclined to divide 100 by the inflation rate (10 percent) and arrive at an answer of 10 years. But this is wrong, because in each succeeding year the 10 percent price increase is added to the increase for the previous year. This is known as **compounding**, and it makes it difficult to come up with the right answer to our question. Fortunately, there is a simple arithmetic rule for solving the question of how long it would take for something to double if it is growing at a specified rate compounded annually. It is called the **rule of 70**. Divide 70 by the inflation rate and you will discover the number of years it takes to double the price level. In our case, 70 divided by 10 equals 7 years to double the price of a hamburger; by 2004 it will double again, and by 2011, it will double yet again.

In tabular form, here is what it might cost you to go to McDonald's if prices rise at 10 percent per year.

Year	McDLT	French Fries	Medium Coke	Total
1990	$ 1.80	$0.75	$0.75	$ 3.30
1997	$ 3.60	$1.50	$1.50	$ 6.60
2004	$ 7.20	$3.00	$3.00	$13.20
2011	$14.40	$6.00	$6.00	$26.40

By the beginning of the twenty-first century, you could be lucky to get back some change from a $20 bill for a modest lunch.

---

dollars are nominal dollars adjusted for inflation. The *real* value of dollars equals the quantity of goods and services that they will buy at a given time. For example, a $100 bill printed in 1983 had a nominal value of $100, and if it was still in circulation in August 1988 it still had a nominal or "face value" of $100. But in *real* terms its purchasing power had declined because of inflation between 1983 and 1988. In 1983 that $100 bill could have bought more goods and services than it did in 1988.

The CPI helps us to measure the change in the real value of money. If we want to compare the real buying power of nominal dollars to base-year dollars, we simply divide the current nominal value of money by the price index. Using our previous example, an index of 119.0 in 1988 tells us that a 1988 dollar would be worth about 84 percent (100 ÷ 119.0 = 0.84) of its 1982–84 purchasing power. To return to our $100 bill example, it took $100 in 1988 to buy what you could have purchased for $84 in 1983.*

This decline in the value of money is caused by inflation. To see the impact of inflation on some rather common elements in the American lifestyle, read Box 3.2.

---

* The value of the CPI in 1983 was actually 99.6, since the base period incorporates prices from 1982 and 1984 as well as from 1983. A $100 bill in 1983 could actually purchase the equivalent of $100.40 worth of goods using the 1982–84 base, but this seems to complicate the calculations unnecessarily. In most cases you can simply use 1983 = 100, since 1983 is the midpoint of the base period.

The CPI and the cost of living. Many people believe that the CPI is an accurate measure of the cost of living, but it is not. In the first place, income and sales taxes are excluded from the CPI, despite the fact that they are an important component in our expenditures. Seond, the index assumes that consumers always buy the same mixture of goods and services. The current market basket mixture is based on mean expenditures derived from 1982–84 Consumer Expenditure Survey data. As prices of goods change, consumers will naturally respond by buying less of the more expensive items, such as veal, and more of the relatively cheaper items, such as chicken. Another problem inherent in using a fixed market basket of goods and services is a change in consumer expenditures stimulated by the introduction of new products. Videocassette recorders, smoke detectors, personal computers, and compact disc players are all examples of items that have become more important to consumers in recent years. The CPI market basket has difficulty adjusting to changes in the quantity and quality of these goods.

Despite its limitations, the CPI remains our number-one monitor of inflation. The question we want to address now is: What causes the CPI to increase?

The Causes of Inflation

Figure 3.4 shows the annual inflation rate in the U.S. economy from 1950 to 1988. Inflation of more than 4 percent per year was fairly rare before the 1970s. And such "high" rates were generally associated with periods of war. The Korean war inflation during 1950–52, and the Vietnam war inflation from 1968 to 1970 were associated with armed conflicts. Between these wars the inflation rates were generally well below 5 percent.

Demand–pull inflation. Why are wars generally associated with inflation? The answer lies in what the government does during a war. It demands more weapons and more people to use them. It often winds up paying for them with newly created money. If increased government demand is not offset by a decrease in the demand of the private sector, a classic case of "too much money chasing too few goods" exists. This is sometimes called **demand–pull inflation** because increases in demand *pull* the prices of products ever upward. This is essentially what happened in the United States during the Korean and Vietnam conflicts.

demand–pull inflation: a rise in the general level of prices caused by an increase in total demand; this kind of inflation can be characterized as too much money chasing too few goods

cost–push inflation: a rise in the general level of prices caused by an increase in the cost of doing business

Cost–push inflation. On the other hand, most economists agree that inflation can also be caused by a rise in the general cost of doing business. This is called **cost–push inflation**. The quadrupling of oil prices during the 1973–74 period is often indicated as the major culprit in that inflationary period. Energy is such a vital part of our economy that any sudden shift in price tends to boost the CPI unless other prices fall

FIGURE 3.4
The rate of inflation in the U.S. economy, 1950–1988 (percent change in the CPI). (SOURCE: *Economic Report of the President* [Washington, D.C.: U.S. Government Printing Office, 1989].)

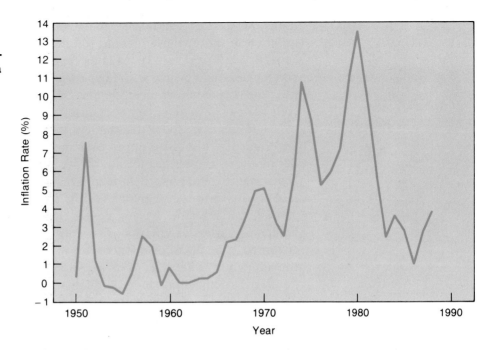

dramatically—a highly unlikely event. Thus, the rise in oil prices reverberates throughout the economy and brings inflation with it. The Iranian hostage crisis in 1979 and 1980 and the subsequent oil cutoff also set off a similar cost–push inflation, such that inflation averaged almost 8 percent from 1970 to 1981.

Although inflation rates fell during the latter part of the 1980s, they remained well above rates in the 1950s and 1960s. Moreover, 1980s rates persistently remained above historical levels even though there were no major wars involving U.S. troops and the price of oil actually fell as the Organization of Petroleum Exporting Countries (OPEC) found its members unable to restrict supply and maintain higher prices. Thus, it would probably be a mistake to conclude that inflation is dead. Should any one of a number of events occur (a crude oil price increase, a precipitous fall in the international value of the U.S. dollar, a major war), we could be facing double-digit inflation once again.

Inflation: Winners and Losers

At first glance it might seem that no one gains from inflation because, by its very nature, inflation eats away at the value of money and destroys people's willingness to accept money in exchange for goods and services. But there *are* winners in the inflation game: those who have more buying power at the end of an inflationary spiral than at the beginning. In general, the biggest losers are those whose incomes are fixed in dollar terms, for example, retired persons whose pensions are not adjusted for inflation or those whose income and net worth do not rise as fast as the general rise in prices. To be more specific, retirees, creditors, savers, bondholders, and people with large cash balances generally lose during an inflationary period, whereas debtors and those who hold real property or collectibles like gold, silver, and antiques tend to gain (Blinder, 1987).

It is ironic that one of the major culprits in most inflations—the U.S. government—also turns out to be a major beneficiary of inflation. Why? Because the biggest debtor in the American economy is the federal government. The federal debt is approximately $2.5 trillion. If the interest rate on this debt is less than the inflation rate, then the government is actually getting more buying power than it has borrowed for, and the lenders are losers to inflation. Consider this. Whenever someone buys a government bond, he or she gives up the use of that money in return for the assurance of getting his or her money back plus some extra money (interest) to compensate for lending that buying power to the government. The lender loses, however, if the principal plus the interest paid back to the bondholder in nominal dollars does not equal the real dollars (buying power) of the original loan. This happens if the rate of inflation is greater than the interest rate. The lender's loss is, of course, the borrower's gain. Some economists have argued that such a system rewards the government for encouraging inflation. Is it any wonder that investors are often concerned about inflation even when there appears to be no current basis for it?

The Business Cycle

business cycles: irregular but recurring patterns of fluctuations in real GNP

If you adjust the data on GNP for inflation, you will find periods of economic decline followed by periods of economic expansion. These irregular but recurring patterns of fluctuations in GNP are called **business cycles**. Figure 3.5 shows a stylized version of a modern business cycle.

Individual consumers have very little control over business cycles. Their wavelike form is reminiscent of ocean waves that inevitably crash upon the shore. Sometimes these waves can be fun, as they are for surfers. At other times these waves can be destructive. Like ocean waves, these cycles are always potentially perilous, and the average American consumer can only benefit from an understanding of their composition and character. In the sections that follow we will outline the major phases of the business cycle and analyze the methods for dealing with this cycle.

The phases of the business cycle. A business cycle has four parts: peak, recession, trough, and expansion. Periods of falling real GNP are called **recessions**. During recessions the economy is contracting, so employment, income, and investment are generally falling. With workers losing their jobs and businesses having difficulty selling their output at a profit, the

recession: a decline in real GNP that lasts for at least six months

**FIGURE 3.5
A stylized business cycle.**

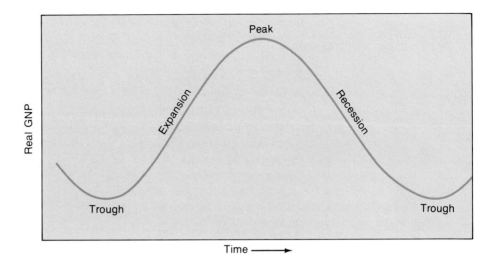

economy enters a downward spiral. Businesses lay off workers and reduce output to try to keep production more in line with sales. But by reducing the number of workers, businesses also reduce overall worker incomes, which means that consumption will also fall. A decline in consumption leads to further layoffs, followed by a deeper recession. A severe recession is sometimes called a **depression**.

Once economic conditions reach their lowest point, the business cycle is said to be at its *trough*. Unemployment rates have generally peaked at this point, and the economy is poised for a turnaround. The upturn phase is called the *expansion*, or recovery phase. During this portion of the business cycle, unemployment rates fall, investment and incomes rise, and the economy enters a growth spurt. Jobs become easier to find, and interest rates are lower than they were when the recession began. As this phase comes to a close, the cycle reaches the *peak*, or boom phase. At the peak of a business cycle, unemployment reaches its lowest rate. Prices and interest rates generally begin to rise significantly, and the ratio of consumer debt to income also peaks. Business firms and consumers generally become more pessimistic about their economic future and consequently postpone investments and purchases. A recession then follows, and the cycle begins anew. As you might suspect, consumers and investors who have some knowledge of the workings of this cycle can significantly improve their economic status. Borrowing or investing near the peak of a business cycle can have disastrous consequences. Worksheet 3.1 highlights some important questions to consider if you suspect a recession is near.

Length of the business cycle. Not all business cycles are created equal. In fact, even the lengths of the phases of the cycles differ. In general, the life

No economist possesses perfect foresight. Anyone who claims to be clairvoyant with regard to the economy should have his or her crystal ball impounded. Nevertheless, there are certain warning signals that the economy exhibits before it enters a recession. As an informed consumer, you would do well to keep a wary eye on the indicators listed below. If the answer to a majority of these questions is yes, then you would do well to postpone future purchases and additional long-term debt in antici-pation of an economic downturn in the business cycle.

1. Are interest rates rising?
2. Is the international value of the dollar falling?
3. Are the stock market indexes falling?
4. Is the unemployment rate low (near 5 percent)?
5. Is inflation increasing?
6. Is the Commerce Department's Index of Leading Indicators declining?

of a business cycle is measured either between troughs or peaks. If we use the trough-to-trough method, there have been eight complete business cycles in the United States since 1945. The average duration of the complete cycle has been five years. This includes a typical 48-month expansion followed by a 12-month recession. Thus, on the average, expansion lasts four times as long as contractions. Nevertheless, the adage ''What goes up, must come down'' is true for economies as well as baseballs.

Prescriptions for curing the business cycle. In the not too distant past several prominent economists proclaimed the death of the business cycle. These academicians believed that government policy could be ''fine-tuned'' to prevent recessions in much the same way that you fine-tune a radio or television if the signal becomes less clear. These economists believed that by decreasing taxes and/or increasing government expenditures, they could increase demand within the economy and thus end a recession. For example, they might avert a serious recession by setting up a large government program to build an interstate highway system. Such a program would create jobs, increase worker income, and stimulate the economy. Conversely, by raising taxes and/or reducing government expenditures, they could lower consumer demand and avoid the problems of inflation and high interest rates that ultimately carry a cycle past its peak.

The manipulation of demand within the economy is a legacy of John Maynard Keynes (1883–1946), a brilliant British economist whose followers are known as Keynesians. While there is certainly some validity to this theory, it is far from the panacea that some believed it would be. The manipulation of government economic policy involves political as well as economic forces that are far beyond the scope of a simple economic rule. For example, in the 1980s economists and politicians learned that it is much easier to cut taxes than to raise them. Similarly, it is much easier to increase government expenditures than to lower them. Since raising taxes and cutting government spending have proved to be difficult, the Keynesian prescription can only be followed in one direction: It can be used to fight recession, but not inflation.

A second group of economists emphasizes the importance of incentives and productivity in avoiding a recession. These policy makers are known as the supply-siders. Unlike the Keynesians, who stress the importance of demand to the health of the economy, the supply-siders argue that the economy will naturally avoid long recessions if the government will pursue a laissez-faire policy. Moreover, they say, the government should reduce its regulations and income taxes, which serve as disincentives to work and invest. Arthur Laffer, one of the chief economists in this school, once asked rhetorically, "What does the government do when you get a job? (Answer: Tax you). What do they do when you lose your job? (Answer: Pay you unemployment benefits). What is the government telling you by their actions? (Answer: Don't work!)." The economic program of the Reagan administration (1981–89) used this economic theory as its keystone.

SUMMARY

We promised that this chapter would help you in your roles as consumer, producer, and citizen. Now it's time to deliver.

As a consumer you would do well to review what you can do to insulate yourself from the vagaries of a market economy. As we mentioned at the beginning of this chapter, a market economy is only one way that society has to organize its resources to cope with the perennial problem of scarcity; economies based on tradition or command are viable alternatives. But you don't live in a tradition- or command-based economy, and as a result, your life is going to be filled with many more decisions than those in alternative systems have to face. You cannot simply expect to do what your ancestors have done, nor can you expect the government to decide on your best interests. In a market economy you are on your own. You must be an effective decision maker who can process information relatively quickly.

In the first part of this chapter we gave you the ground rules for market economies. These economies provide the most freedom, but they also require their citizens to be responsible for their livelihood and well-being. Individual economic decisions are summed just as political votes are added up to determine winners and losers. It is the interaction between consumers and producers that generates the circular flow of goods and services characterizing a successful market economy. As a consumer, you should be aware that your actions influence what is produced. As a producer, you must be alert to consumer signals and react in a cost-effective way to organize production. The households that are most productive will receive the greatest share of the output.

In the second half of this chapter we explored the world of macroeconomics, or the economy as a whole. We reviewed the meaning of gross national product and those macroeconomic indicators that influence it. We hope that you learned how prosperous our economy is. A fortyfold increase in GNP since World War II is quite an accomplishment. A five-trillion-dollar GNP ranks the U.S. as the largest economy in the world. But there have been and will continue to be macroeconomic problems that affect you. Inflation creates the appearance of prosperity when in reality only price, not the quantity of output, may be increasing. The business cycle, with its problems of unemployment and recession, persists, and economists are often at odds over methods to deal with these problems. As a citizen, you are going to be asked to decide which politician ascribes to the economic theories that make the most sense to you.

As John Maynard Keynes once wrote:

> The ideas of economists and political philosophers, both when they are right and when they are wrong, are more powerful than is commonly understood. Indeed the world is ruled by little else. Practical men, who believe themselves to be quite exempt from any intellectual influences, are usually the slaves of some defunct economist. Madmen in authority, who hear voices in the air, are distilling their frenzy from some academic scribbler of a few years back. (In Leet and Shaw, 1980)

This chapter has presented a perspective on the modern American economy and your role in it. When combined with the first two chapters, it serves as a foundation for the remainder of the text. This chapter may also help you to associate the "madmen in authority" with the "academic scribblers of a few years back."

QUESTIONS

1. Traditional, command, and market economies are ways of allocating resources. Given the list below, categorize the allocation mechanism as one of the three.
    a. Parking lot spaces on your campus
    b. Turkey dinner at Thanksgiving
    c. Income taxes
    d. A part-time or summer job
    e. Spending your recreation time
    f. The Selective Service system
    g. Leaving a tip in a restaurant

2. No two consumers have identical consumption patterns, partly because our incomes, time costs, and tastes are so diverse. Given the following

tasks:

- Housecleaning
- Preparing lunch
- Making clothes
- Childcare
- Cashing a check
- Repairing a leaky faucet
- Automobile tuneup

a. Evaluate the likelihood that members of the following groups will do these tasks for themselves:

- Lawyer
- College student
- Homemaker
- Physician
- Retired plumber

b. Are your predictions about the decisions of these people based on your estimates of income, time costs, and tastes? Explain how these factors might affect their choices.

3. Define inflation and discuss its impact on the following groups: retired people, college students, oil refinery workers, children, welfare recipients.

4. A senior vice-president of a large bank once wrote: '' There is nothing at all novel about what needs doing if inflation is to be restrained and avoided. All that is necessary is that the public authorities themselves adopt programs aimed at limiting the total of demand upon the economy to what the economy is able to produce without inflation.'' Do you agree? Is he speaking of demand–pull or cost–push inflation?

5. Describe the business cycle and graph it. What phase of the cycle are we currently in? What data support your answer?

6. Briefly describe the Keynesian and supply-side schools of economic thought. How would they each deal with a recession? What would each recommend to fight inflation? Which school do you feel most comfortable with?

REFERENCES AND READINGS

Armstrong, Fred C. *The Business of Economics*. St. Paul, Minn.: West, 1986.

Batra, Ravi. *The Great Depression of 1990*. New York: Simon & Schuster, 1987.

Blinder, Alan S. *Hard Heads, Soft Hearts: Tough Minded Economics for a Just Society*. Reading, Mass.: Addison-Wesley, 1987.

Board of Governors of the Federal Reserve System. *Historical Chart Book*. Washington, D.C.: Federal Reserve Board, 1989.

Economic Report of the President. Washington, D.C.: U.S. Government Printing Office, 1989.

Leet, Don R., and Shaw, John A. *Economics: Concepts, Themes, and Applications*. Belmont, Calif.: Wadsworth, 1980.

Malabre, Alfred, Jr. *Beyond Our Means*. New York: Random House, 1987.

Mason, Charles, and Butler, Clifford. ''New Basket of Goods and Services Being Priced in Revised CPI.'' *Monthly Labor Review*, January 1987.

Peterson, Peter G. ''The Morning After.'' *Atlantic Monthly*, October 1987.

Schwenk, Frankie N. ''Two Measures of Inflation: The Consumer Price Index and the Personal Consumption Expenditure Implicit Price Deflator.'' *Family Economics Review*, Winter 1981.

Sommers, Albert T. *The U.S. Economy Demystified* Lexington, Mass.: D. C. Heath, 1988.

Warden, Christopher. ''Power to the Consumer.'' *Consumers' Research*, June 1989.

Chapter Four

FINANCIAL PLANNING: GETTING IN CONTROL

- ☐ The Need for Financial Planning
- ☐ Income and Expenses
- ☐ Designing Your Financial Plan
- ☐ The Budgeting Process: How One Family Manages
- ☐ Net Worth
- ☐ Money and Emotions
- ☐ Collective Money Management Techniques
- ☐ Paying Bills

DID YOU KNOW THAT . . .

. . . a budget can help you get the things you really want?

. . . money management can help you control both your money and your life?

. . . food and housing account for about half of household spending?

. . . emergencies can and should be anticipated?

. . . money is a major source of arguments among couples, rivaled only by sex?

. . . spending helps people fulfill emotional as well as physical needs?

. . . traditional ways of handling money within a family are usually not effective in two-income families?

money management: a system of planning for spending based on expected income; also called budgeting

Have you ever wondered why one person with a certain income never seems to be able to pay his or her bills or handle a financial emergency, while another with the same income has no trouble with these obligations? The person who meets his or her financial obligations uses the process of **money management**, a system of planning for spending based on expected income. The basic tool used for money management is a **budget**, or spending plan, so the process is often called budgeting. The purpose of budgeting is to help people individually or as a household to achieve their goals. It cannot guarantee increased income, but it can ensure greater satisfaction with the results of spending. Financial planning is a direct application of the decision-making process discussed in Chapter 1.

This chapter provides you with the knowledge and skills necessary to plan a personal budget and the beginnings of a strong financial plan. You will need to analyze your goals and values, look at alternative uses for your money, and make decisions about priorities. You will then be prepared for the last half of this text, which deals with the purchase of consumer goods and services.

This chapter focuses on the reasons that money management is important in your life. We look at the spending patterns of average American families, which can be used as guides for personal budgeting. We include a five-step process for budgeting and apply the process directly to the needs of a typical family, the Tates. Then we provide an explanation of net worth and the pyramid approach to investing. Finally, we conclude our discussion with the emotional and practical aspects of budgeting.

Many factors affect financial decisions, including the external factors of advertising, social customs, and family background and personal factors, such as income level, family composition, and stage in the life cycle. When we discussed these factors in Chapters 1 and 2, we showed that one can control income level by one's career choice and by one's decision to use time for income production or leisure. As we showed in Chapter 3, the state of the economy impacts how much our income buys. Our use of credit, which also affects our economic choices, will be discussed in a later chapter.

THE NEED FOR FINANCIAL PLANNING

It takes money to get most of the things we want. Unfortunately, most of us do not seem to have enough money for all the things we want now. This is part of the scarcity discussed in Chapter 1 and 3. We were discussing this fact of life with an eight-year-old neice, Lisa Michelle. Lisa was in a toy store trying to decide which toy to buy with her $5. We explained that the choice is limited because $5 isn't very much money. Lisa suggested that we just go get more money. When asked where we would go to get it, she replied, "To the grocery store or bank." How simple it all seemed!

Most adults recognize, of course, that money is a scarce resource. If we choose to ignore the fact that we have a limited income, the result may be serious family arguments, job performance affected by anxiety about overdue bills, divorce, or any number of serious consequences. That's why money management is essential.

There are five basic reasons for financial planning:

1. *It helps you get what you really want.* It is very easy to spend money on items that will not supply much satisfaction. The American marketplace gives us an endless array of products. Unfortunately, many of our purchases end up unused in closets, basements, or garages. If you have a plan, however, you can apply the decision-making process rather than purchase haphazardly. Planning allows you to look at all of the options, consider what and when to buy, and make a rational choice. Planning provides you with an opportunity to express your own opinions and define your own life-style. For example, perhaps you like to travel, but cannot afford it. You could investigate sites that are close to home, inexpensive motels, or house-sharing and begin to set aside small amounts for the trip.

2. *It prevents you from spending beyond your income.* No matter how high one's income, one still must make choices, especially as one's income increases. Mass media can sometimes create needs and wants where none exists. There never is enough money to "buy it all." You need to apply the decision-making process, determine what your income is, decide what your goals are, and then set priorities. This requires compromise and even sacrifice. Nevertheless, it is always besst to make these decisions before spending money or signing a contract.

3. *It can help you maintain a harmonious home.* Studies repeatedly show that a major problem for households is failure to agree on a spending plan. Often, when counselors investigate a specific family's problems, they find that individual family members do not talk about their desires or wants. These problems can reach such proportions that they are often listed as a prime cause for divorce. Decisions about spending and saving for the future need to be a joint effort of all members of the household, based on values, goals, and standards.

4. *It can help keep track of expenditures.* Checking periodically to evaluate progress toward your goals is a part of planning that also helps in future planning. Budget records can also assist you in computing taxes and may minimize your tax bill. Such records are also useful when questions arise regarding warranties or product performance.

5. *It puts you in control and helps you stay there.* When consumers do not have enough money to pay cash for an item, they often borrow.

The cost of borrowing, that is, the interest charges, diminishes the amount of money available to a family. Too much debt can be disastrous. A system of disciplined spending is the key to avoiding financial disaster. Money management helps you control not only your money, but your life as well.

These five reasons for managing money make using a financial plan worth the effort. Following a plan allows a household to make rational economic decisions that reflect its values and help it achieve its goals. In this chapter, we will roll up our sleeves and learn how to create such a plan.

INCOME AND EXPENSES

net income: take-home pay; wage or salary minus deductions for income taxes, Social Security, retirement, and so forth; also called disposable income

gross income: the total of wages or salary before deductions for income taxes, Social Security, and so forth

The first step toward a sound financial plan is to get a clear picture of where you are now. This means looking at your **cash flow**, or typical monthly income and outgo. This will allow you to evaluate that cash flow and create a budget, or plan, for regular monthly expenses. It is useful to use budgets for the "average American family" as a guide for planning one's personal budget. Figure 4.1 shows how the average family spends its **net**, or **disposable income**. Net income is commonly called take-home pay, as opposed to **gross income**, which is total salary or wages before deductions. There are no categories for Social Security or income taxes because this money is primarily beyond the decision-making power of a household and usually is deducted before you get your paycheck.

Housing and transportation, the two largest budget categories, account for half of household spending. Housing and operations categories include rents or mortgages; utilities such as gas, electric, and telephone; furniture and appliances; household supplies; and purchased household services,

FIGURE 4.1
An average American family's budget for after-tax (disposable) income. (SOURCE: "Expenditures of Urban and Rural Households" *Family Economics Review*, Vol. I, no. 4, 1988, United States Department of Agriculture.)

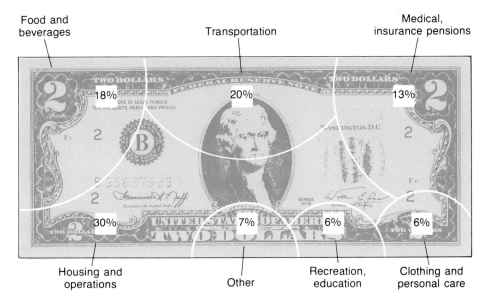

Food and beverages 18%

Transportation 20%

Medical, insurance pensions 13%

Housing and operations 30%

Other 7%

Recreation, education 6%

Clothing and personal care 6%

such as a housekeeper or a gardener. Transportation includes both personal and public transportation. Because this also includes the cost of energy, the percentage of money spent in this category has risen over the past decade.

The next largest expense is food. Included in this category is all food, regardless of whether it is eaten in or out of the home. Alcoholic beverages and tobacco also come under this category. The remaining categories include clothing and personal care, health care, and entertainment. The "other" category includes items such as savings, education, gifts, and contributions. Of all of these, health expenses put the most pressure on family budgets. (We will see why in Chapter 14.)

Charts like Figure 4.1 are useful only as guidelines. Differences in spending patterns occur according to the individual's or the family's stage of the life cycle, its size, and its geographic location, which involves both climate variations and setting, whether urban or rural. These differences create a wide variation in actual consumer spending patterns (Hefferan, 1987). The most obvious difference in spending patterns, however, relates to the household income level. Table 4.1 compares how an imaginary family of four in an urban setting might allocate its income, compared with a similar family in a rural setting.

TABLE 4.1 Comparison of Expenditures of Urban and Rural Households

Rural households account for approximately 15 percent of all U.S. households. Rural consumers are more likely to have household mortgages paid off, and they own more vehicles than urban consumers. They are slightly older than those in urban settings and are less likely to have employer-paid health insurance policies.

Component	Urban	Rural
Total family disposable income	$21,025	$17,953
Food	3,517	3,145
Housing	7,103	5,168
Transportation	4,566	4,850
Apparel and services	1,257	887
Personal care	216	145
Medical care	1,029	1,191
Entertainment	1,143	910
Reading and education	465	326
Tobacco	205	250
Cash contributions	887	538
Miscellaneous	365	211
Personal insurance and pensions	274	326

SOURCE: Adapted from John M. Rogers, "Research Summaries: Expenditures of Urban and Rural Consumers, 1972–73 to 1985." *Monthly Labor Review*. U.S. Department of Labor, Bureau of Statistics, 1988.

As noted, the amount of income available determines how much money is spent in each category. As incomes rise, families spend a smaller percentage of their money on food and a larger portion on housing. This is not too surprising. Although our appetite for more expensive food may increase with income, out stomach capacity does not. But our desire for larger and better-located housing generally outpaces the growth of our income.

Two less obvious differences are in health care and taxes. Although the nominal spending by low-income families on medical care would be similar to that of the intermediate- and high-budget families, low-income families spend twice as much on health care as a percentage of the total. And finally, it should be noted that personal income taxes increase as income increases. This is in part a function of our **progressive income tax** system: The more you make, up to a point, the greater the percentage of your income that goes for taxes.

Now that you know how an ''average'' family spends its income, you are ready to learn the specifics of money management. Keep in mind, however, that you need to tailor your budget to your family size, your life cycle, your life-style, your goals, and your values.

DESIGNING YOUR FINANCIAL PLAN

Creating a financial plan, or budget involves matching future income to future expenditures. As with other decisions, before making a budget you need to gather information. You need to know how you spend your money now, and you need an accurate estimate of your income. You can then evaluate your cash flow to see how it is or is not helping you reach your goals. It is very possible that you have never formally done this before. Recent research seems to indicate that one out of three families do not use a formal budget. However, those who do create one report that the effort was worthwhile in the long run because they really did reach long-term goals (Beutler and Mason, 1987).

The simplest way to begin is to record for one month how you and your family spend your money. Keep paper and pencil handy for each member to jot down daily how much money he or she spends. Keep a running total for each day, and round the amounts to the nearest dollar for simplicity. Grouping expenses into general categories simplifies record keeping. The food category, for example, can include the grocery bill, food eaten out, pet food, and alcoholic beverages. Transportation expenses include car payments, gasoline and oil costs, car maintenance and repair costs, and public transportation expenses.

Worksheet 4.1 is a form that you can use to group and record daily totals. The credit column provides a place to record the cost of using credit cards; you will find the monthly total on each bill. As you look at your own spending, you will gain insight to enable you to personalize the form by

WORKSHEET 4.1 RECORD OF DAILY EXPENSES

Our Family Income and Expenses for the Month of _____ 19 _____

Date	Income	Food	Clothing and Laundry	Housing (Rent)	Household Expenses	Utilities (Gas, Water, etc.)	Transportation	Insurance	Medical	Education	Recreation	Contributions and gifts	Credit Card Costs	Other	Savings	Daily Spending Total
1																
2																
3																
4																
5																
6																
7																
8																
9																
10																
11																
12																
13																
14																
15																
16																
17																
18																
19																
20																
21																
22																
23																
24																
25																
26																
27																
28																
29																
30																
31																
Amount Spent																
Amount Planned																

Income Grand Total   Spending Grand Total

FIGURE 4.2
The purpose of a financial plan is to cover your living expenses adequately, provide adequate emergency reserves, protect you and your family with insurance, and guide you in making investments to help you reach your goals. Included in the foundation of the pyramid are your checking and savings accounts, emergency fund, insurance (auto, property, health, life), and pension plans, including Social Security. This level also includes home ownership and low-risk investments, such as savings bonds and money market funds. After this foundation is in place, a medium amount of risk is in order to help establish funds for intermediate or long-term goals. Only after those needs have been adequately met are high-risk investments appropriate.

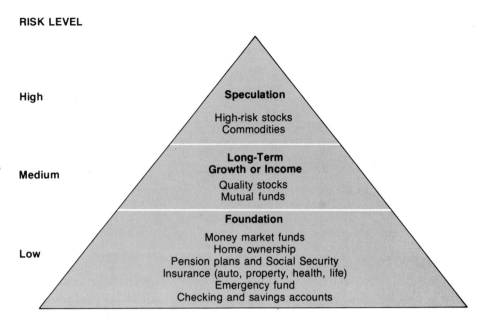

RISK LEVEL

High

Medium

Low

Speculation

High-risk stocks
Commodities

**Long-Term
Growth or Income**

Quality stocks
Mutual funds

Foundation

Money market funds
Home ownership
Pension plans and Social Security
Insurance (auto, property, health, life)
Emergency fund
Checking and savings accounts

adding categories like vacation, emergency fund, child-support payment, and so forth.

Next, *estimate your income* for a year. Those who earn a salary can refer to paycheck stubs to estimate income for the next 12 months. A second source of this information is last year's income tax return. Be realistic and do not include overtime, because it is not guaranteed. Be sure to account for recent raises, if appropriate. Add other cash income you expect, such as bonuses, veteran's benefits, Social Security payments, child-support payments, rents, investments, and interest on savings. Include money from all members of the household who depend on the unit for support. All of these figures should be added together and divided by 12 for a monthly budget or by 24 for a bimonthly budget.

Now you are ready to evaluate your current spending pattern and to decide how you want to spend in the next year, as well as further in the future. When the family meets together, each member should be informed in an uncritical manner of the result of the spending record. This is not a time to chastise a member of the family for past spending, which cannot be altered. Instead, this is the time for family members to share their short-term, intermediate, and long-term goals.

Short-term goals are those that need immediate attention or fulfill-ment, such as a new car or a vacation. Intermediate goals might include purchase of a house or paying for a college education. Long-term goals might relate to retirement. Overall, the purpose of the plan is to cover your living expenses adequately, provide adequate emergency reserves, protect yourself and your family with insurance, and to make investments to help you reach your goals. Figure 4.2 introduces this as the Pyramid

WORKSHEET 4.2   BUDGETING

Step 1: Calculate Income.

Income from jobs _____
Income from other sources _____
                    Total: _____

Step 2: Calculate Fixed Expenses.

Monthly
  House payment or rent _____
  Utilities _____
    Electric _____
    Gas _____
    Water _____
    Phone _____
  Installments
    _____
    _____
    _____
  Savings _____
  Other _____
Periodic
  Insurance
    Auto _____
    Health _____
    Household _____
    Life _____
    Mortgage _____

Auto license _____
Taxes _____
Other _____

**Step 3: Calculate Emergency Fund
Contribution** _____

Step 4: Calculate Flexible Living Expenses.

Food and beverages _____
Clothing _____
Personal care _____
Household expenses _____
Transportation _____
Entertainment, recreation _____
Gifts, contributions _____
Credit _____
Other _____
  _____

Step 5: Compare Income and Expenses.

Total all expenses _____
Compare with income _____
Re-adjust if necessay!

Investment Strategy. All family members should be involved so that their personal goals become known and contribute direction to the family's life. If all members are included in the decisions and involved in establishing goals, then all can be expected to cooperate to reach them. Every person should number his or her goals in order of importance. The family can then separate unrealistic dreams from goals and establish a financial plan to reach their goals by following the five steps outlined below and in Worksheet 4.2.

 1. *Record income information* that was previously gathered.

 2. *Calculate fixed expenses.* The spending record helps you distinguish fixed expenses from flexible ones. **Fixed expenses** are large, regular and predictable. They are fixed because you commit yourself to paying

fixed expenses: large, regular, and predictable expenses established by a contract or an agreement

them in a contract or agreement. There are two types of fixed expenses, monthly and periodic. *Monthly fixed expenses* occur on a regular basis and include rent or mortgage, installment payments, church contributions or tithes, and regular savings for family goals. Utilities are included here because you have agreed to pay for the service, and with the exception of a telephone, you would probably not consider eliminating them. However, the amount of these bills may vary monthly or seasonally.

Periodic fixed expenses occur quarterly, semiannually, or annually and include insurance payments, taxes, automobile license tax, and the like. Because periodic fixed expenses may not be reflected in the monthly spending record, you may need to consult checking and charge card records, as well as previous tax returns, for these figures. Once you know the annual cost of each periodic fixed expense, you can calculate how much money to set aside each pay day to meet the obligation without straining other budget categories or borrowing. For example, an auto insurance payment of $450 may be due twice a year. By setting aside $75 each month or $37.50 every two weeks in a special account, you will be sure to have the money, and you can stay within your budget. This procedure would be followed for each periodic fixed expense, and the monies could all be deposited in the same account, leaving you feeling more secure.

3. *Create an emergency fund.* Despite conventional wisdom, all individuals do not experience increasing prosperity during their lifetime. Particularly today, with divorce a common occurance and the job market changing, families must be prepared for change. An important longitudinal study from the University of Michigan indicates that most families can expect to experience unemployment and economic hard times. Few workers can expect continuous full-time employment (Lown, 1986). And, as Murphy's law holds, if something can go wrong, it will. It is normal for households to have unexpected expenses, such as those for illness or accident, unemployment, or the need to repair a car or broken appliance. Even more common is that all of these things happen at once! This is the most important step of the plan, yet most people skip it. Families who declare bankruptcy or lose their homes because of financial crisis often indicate that it was a "little emergency" that pushed them over the brink.

emergency fund: money reserved to pay unexpected bills or living expenses during unemployment

The amount of money you should set aside for an **emergency fund** depends upon the regularity of your employment, your job security, and your general income level. At minimum, an individual or family should have two months' income saved. The two months' income is above and beyond savings for periodic fixed expenses or savings set aside for a specific goal. For example, let's say that your net income is $2,000 each month and that you have calculated that you need to set aside $120 each month for periodic fixed expenses and already have $480 in an account for that purpose. You would need to have at least $4,000 additional funds in order to be protected from a financial crisis. If your employment is sporadic, as is the case with construction, for example, or has predictable periods of unemployment, as in teaching, then you may need to set more aside. Two months' income may seem like a lot of money, but just begin to save as much as you can. Box 4.1 provides suggestions on how to reach this goal. After you have established your full emergency fund, do not touch that amount, except for unexpected problems. When you do withdraw funds, they should be replaced as soon as possible by making cutbacks in your current budget and by following the techniques described in Box 4.1.

4. *Calculate flexible living expenses.* **Flexible expenses** include food, clothing, gasoline, routine medical care, entertainment, education, household expenses, and cost of using credit cards. They are considered flexible because consumers can control how much they spend, even to the point of choosing not to spend at all. Some of these expenses are paid for by **discretionary income**, the portion of income that is left after fixed expenses are paid and basic necessities purchased. Use your one-month spending record to determine the average amounts you spend on these items.

flexible expenses: daily living expenses that can be controlled by consumers, such as expenses for food, clothing, and entertainment

discretionary income: (1) buying power that does not have to be spent on basic, life-supporting goods or services; (2) the money left after fixed expenses have been paid and allotments have been made for basic necessities

---

BOX 4.1   EMERGENCY FUND: GETTING TO YOUR GOAL

How Much?

Your emergency fund should be enough to allow you and your family to withstand unemployment for approximately six months. Generally two to three times your monthly net income will be adequate. Consider:

1. Sources of support available to you, such as unemployment insurance, food stamps, or sick pay
2. Income from more than one salary
3. Sources of income other than salary
4. Possible cutbacks in the family budget
5. Current debt load
6. Frequency or likelihood of unemployment
7. Future dependents, such as custody of children or support of elderly family members
8. Plans for purchase of big-ticket items in the future

How to Save

1. Treat your emergency fund as a monthly fixed expense.
2. Have money deducted from your paycheck rather than making the decision every payday.
3. Deposit windfall money, such as tax refunds, bonuses, overtime pay, and the like.
4. Deposit the money earned from a pay raise rather than changing your budget.
5. Save "loose money" at the end of the day—all the quarters or single dollar bills—and watch them add up.
6. Have a "Rediscover Home Week" periodically: Spend no money on recreation, eating out, and so forth during the week, and deposit the savings.

5. *Compare income and expenses.* You and your family are now ready to compare expenditures with income. Total the monthly averages of the fixed expenses, the emergency fund, and flexible expenses, and compare them with your monthly income. If money is left over, it can be allocated to any goal or category you choose. However, if total expenses exceed income, you must adjust your budget. This is the time to make priority decisions. What can be changed? Which goals should the family strive for now, and which ones should be postponed? Is a vacation more important than weekends at the movies? Is it worth giving up new carpeting to get a new car? Since your income is limited, you and your family cannot have everything you want. This planning process involves compromise and requires sacrifices, but it results in satisfaction from reaching the most important family goals.

THE BUDGETING PROCESS: HOW ONE FAMILY MANAGES

Now that you are familiar with the budgeting process, it will be helpful to look at how one family applies and individualizes this process. Consider Bob and Cathy Tate—their experiences can be helpful to you, so let's take a closer look at how they create their plan.

Bob and Cathy have been married for eight years. Bob, 32, is a policeman, and Cathy, 29, is a secretary at a local elementary school and works ten months out of the year. They have two children, Jennifer, who is six, and Jason, who just turned four. They have always enjoyed family vacations, especially camping. When the children were very young, vacations were difficult to manage because of rising costs, increasing family needs, and having only one income. At that time Cathy began to sell cosmetics part time to supplement the family income. When Jason was almost three years old, Cathy began to work an eight-hour day during the school year. Her additional income allowed them to pay off some bills, add to their emergency fund, and afford a new car.

Recently, Cathy and Bob sat down to discuss their short-term and long-term goals. They dreamed of buying an RV and traveling the country in it with the children for a month. They have wanted a second car and thought that the RV might fulfill those needs. They also want to save for a down payment for their own house. As they talked, they set priorities and recognized that their dreams were a bit unrealistic. They decided to begin to save for a down payment on a house and a second car and for a ten-day camping trip in ten months. This meant that they needed a new budget to accommodate these goals. Before making their spending plan, they gathered the information they needed, which included the previous year's tax return, current check stubs, and receipts. They also kept a record of their spending for flexible expenses to get an up-to-date idea of where

their money was going. Cathy and Bob then followed the five steps we
have outlined. First, they *calculated their income:*

Net income from Bob's job	$25,880
Net income from Cathy's job	14,600
Income from savings	310
Total	$40,790
Divide by 12 monthly budget	$ 3,399

Bob and Cathy have rented their house for two years. It is a 15-year-old,
three-bedroom house, with one and a half baths. Now that the children are
older they would like to buy a larger house with a family room. They have
determined that they need to save around $12,000 for a down payment.
They recognize that this is a long-term goal, and that the only way to reach
this goal is to make a plan and follow it. They look forward to paying off
their refrigerator in two months and have 18 months of payments left on
the car. When the first car is paid off they intend to buy a new car and keep
the older one. In the meantime Cathy and Bob share rides with each other
and with friends, and sometimes Cathy walks the short distance to work.
They choose to view utilities as fixed expenses and have installed
conservation devices such as a water-heater blanket and water restrictors
in the shower. Their house was insulated to the recommended level by the
landlord several years before they moved in. With this information in
mind, they followed step 2 and *calculated their fixed expenses:*

Monthly fixed expenses	
Rent	$750
Utilities	
Electric	60
Gas	50
Water, trash	35
Phone	50
Installments	
Car payment	250
Refrigerator	50
Periodic fixed expenses	
Insurance	
Auto	50
Health (deducted from pay	—
Household (fire and theft)	20
Life	30
Auto license	15
Savings for vacation	45
	$1,405

Cathy and Bob have had an emergency fund since they first got married. Cathy was working full time before the children were born, so they were able to set aside $300 each month to build this fund. They still consider it very important, now that Cathy receives only ten paychecks in a year, since she works only when regular classes are in session. They know, moreover, that it would be difficult to pay all their bills and maintain their life-style without her paycheck. Therefore, they put $200 from each of her ten paychecks into a savings account through payroll deduction. This way they don't have to make the decision each month to save this money. Then, during the summer, when she does not get a paycheck, they have sufficient funds to maintain their life-style. In other words they spread her ten monthly paychecks over a twelve month period. Since these contributions are totally withdrawn in the summer, the Tates recognize that they are not contributing to the *growth* of the emergency fund. As a result they contributes $75 to the *emergency fund* for true emergencies or accidents (step 3):

Currently in the emergency fund	$6,000
Monthly allotments to the fund	75

They have used this fund many times for minor repairs and accidents. It was especially helpful after their second child was born. They had saved enough money for basic medical and baby expenses not covered by insurance, but then Cathy needed unexpected surgery. One time, Bob had to fly unexpectedly across country to visit his grandfather, who was ill. The monthly $75 allotment is used for household or major appliance repairs or emergency medical expenses, if necessary, during the month. If no emergencies occur, the money remains in the emergency fund savings account for future emergencies.

Their spending record provided Bob and Cathy with an estimate of their current spending for flexible items. The family eats out two or three times a week, usually at a coffee shop or cafe. They enjoy family movies and often rent videos. They have set aside at least one night each month for Bob and Cathy to go out alone for a special evening. They *calculated their flexible living expenses* (step 4):

Food and beverages	$600
Clothing and personal care	200
Household expenses	
Equipment, furnishings	75
Laundry and dry cleaning	25
Supplies and maintenance	25
Transportation	
Gasoline	100
Maintenance, repair	50

Entertainment, subscriptions	100
Gifts, contributions	95
Education	20
Routine medical	50
Childcare, dance lessons	400
	$1,740

After calculating their expenses and income, the Tates confirmed that they were not spending beyond their income. In following step 5 they *compared their expenses and their income*:

Total fixed expenses	$1,405
Emergency fund contribution	75
Total flexible expenses	1,740
Total monthly budget	$3,220
Total monthly income	3,390
	$170 left over

When they found that $170 was left unaccounted for, they felt pleased that their spending had not exceeded their income. The money provided a cushion or protection against emergencies. On the other hand, they realized that it would take a very long time to reach their goals if this was the only additional money they saved. With this in mind, they began to look closely at their budget for areas that could be adjusted to accommodate their plans for a vacation, a second car, and home ownership.

Cathy and Bob first set their goals. Their short-term goal was to have $1,000 for their vacation in ten months. They calculated their current savings budget would yield $450. They also wanted $2,000 for the car down payment in 18 months. And finally, for a long-term goal, they needed to save $12,000 for down payment on a house.

Next, Cathy and Bob looked at their flexible expenses—those they could personally control (Worksheet 4.3). The first area that the Tates decided to trim was the food and beverages. They felt that spending in this category had really gotten out of hand. So, beginning immediately, they cut down eating dinners out to one night a week. This sacrifice, combined with more careful menu planning and shopping, could, they felt, cut up to $125 from their past spending. They were already buying some of the children's clothes at thrift stores and felt that spending in the clothing category was all right. They resolved to be more thoughtful when considering purchases of household goods, and felt that they could decrease spending by about $20 there. They reevaluated their subscriptions and planned not to renew three of them. Combined with a more frugal attitude toward entertainment, the changes would net them another $20 monthly. Shopping for sales should cut the cost of gifts by $15.

The only item that had not been analyzed was the $400 for childcare

WORKSHEET 4.3 CATHY AND BOB TATE'S BUDGET

	First Budget	Adjusted Budget
Monthly fixed expenses		
Rent	$750	
Utilities		
Electric	60	
Gas	50	
Water, trash	35	
Phone	50	
Installments		
Car payment	250	pay off
Refrigerator	50	40
Savings for vacation	45	
Periodic fixed expenses		
Insurance		
Auto	50	
Health (deducted from pay)	—	
Household (fire and theft)	20	
Life	30	
Auto license	15	
Total fixed expenses	$1,405	$1,355
Flexible Living Expenses		
Food and beverages	$600	475
Clothing and personal care	200	
Household expenses		
Equipment, furnishings	75	55
Laundry and dry cleaning	25	
Supplies and maintenance	25	
Transportation		
Gasoline	100	
Maintenance, repair	50	
Entertainment, subscriptions	100	80
Gifts, contributions	95	80
Education	20	
Routine medical	50	
Childcare, dance lessons	400	325
Total flexible expenses	$1,740	$1,485

for both children and dance lessons for Jennifer. Usually, either Bob or Cathy drop the children off in the morning at Collier's Academy, a private preschool with an extended day school program. An hour later Collier's mini bus drives Jennifer to public school and later in the day picks her up and brings her back. Typically, the children are picked up around 5:00 or 6:00 P.M. at Collier's either by Bob or by Cathy. After much discussion, the Tates asked Bob's mother to watch the children on three afternoons a week. She agreed to pick up Jason from Collier's and then pick up Jennifer right after school. The Tates also decided to coordinate their schedules to aim for a 5:00 P.M. pickup the other two days of the week. As for the dance lessons, the Tates found group lessons in the community rather than the semiprivate ones Jennifer had been taking. These changes saved them about $75 each month.

Next, they looked at fixed expenses. The only expenditure they felt they could change was utilities. They were doing their best with everything except the phone. By making long-distance calls on weekends and by writing letters more often, they felt they could save $10. It wasn't much, but they felt that every little bit counted. The refrigerator would be paid off in two months and that would free up another $50. They decided to pay if off immediately since the interest rate on the loan was higher than on their savings.

The Tates then compared their new budget to their monthly income:

Total fixed expenses	$1,355
Emergency fund contribution	75
Total flexible expenses	1,485
Total monthly budget	$2,915
Total monthly income	3,390
	$475 left over for savings

The Tates were satisfied with these changes. They felt that the new plan would allow for an additional $550 for a vacation in ten months and a $2,000 down payment on a new car in a year and a half, plus a good beginning on funds for a house down payment. They recognized that they could live with the budget because it was flexible and allowed for emergencies. Therefore, they felt optimistic that they might even be able to save more, and vowed to save any extra or "found" money, such as overtime pay or bonuses. They also decided that it was time to learn more about investments, so that their savings funds would be kept in a secure place yet yield a satisfactory return (see Chapters 5 and 17).

The budget categories used by the Tates were personalized for their needs. You can create a plan for yourself to include your own needs and goals. For example, perhaps vacations aren't at all important to you. Maybe you would rather accumulate funds for a new large-screen TV or a computer. In either case, if you don't actually set money aside for your goals, you may never reach them.

Spending plans can be personalized in other ways, such as giving a separate clothing budget to each family member. Another good idea is to include a category of personal choice, or "mad money." This would be a small percentage of a budget (1 to 3 percent) but would allow each family member to spend without explaining or accounting to anyone else. It is important that a family periodically reevaluate its budget as the Tates did, considering changes in income, life-style, or the economy. At that time family goals should be clarified and prioritized in terms of values. Then families can reduce or eliminate spending for items that do not give them maximum satisfaction and add or increase spending on those that do.

NET WORTH

net worth: *the mathematical difference between assets and liabilities for a person or a business*

assets: *(1) something of value that can be sold to repay debt; (2) in financial terms, all forms of property owned by a person or a business*

Comparing actual spending to the budget you planned is one way to evaluate your financial position. In indicates your immediate progress but does not account for past spending patterns. For this you need a **net worth** statement, which shows the relationship between your **assets** and your **liabilities**. An asset is something you own; a liability is something you owe; the mathematical difference between assets and liabilities is net worth. In other words, net worth is what would be left if everything you own were sold and the money used to pay your debts.

An annual accounting of net worth will help you or your family keep track of your financial progress. Worksheet 4.4 is an example of a net worth statement. When using this form, record only the current cash value of each item. To find the cash value of a life insurance policy, locate the value table printed on the policy itself. Figures in the table are for each $1,000 of the face value (total amount of insurance) for each year of the

WORKSHEET 4.4 NET WORTH STATEMENT

Assets	Liabilities
Cash on hand	*Unpaid bills*
Checking account _____	Charge account _____
Savings account _____	Utilities _____
Investments _____	Other _____
Savings bonds _____	*Installment loans, secured*
Stocks and bonds _____	Automobile _____
Mutual funds _____	Other _____
Cash value of life insurance ___	*Installment loans, unsecured*
Cash value of annuities _____	_____
Home and property _____	*Mortgage loans* _____
Automobile _____	*Education loans* _____
Personal property (cameras,	*Other* _____
jewelry, and so forth) _____	
Total assets _____	Total liabilities _____

Net worth = assets minus liabilities.

policy's duration. The cash value of annuities can be determined the same way

Young people often have a low net worth or even a negative worth. If this is your case, do not be discouraged. You are in the process of obtaining education and establishing a career, and you can probably anticipate a higher-than-average future income. As individuals and families move through the life cycle, their net worth steadily increases. When retirement approaches and income slows or stops completely, net worth usually begins to fall as accumulated assets are used to pay for living expenses.

Once you have computed your net worth, you will want to consider questions the figures raise. Is your money helping you reach your goals? Is your emergency fund large enough to pay your bills for two or three months if you cannot work? Were your debts created to buy assets or to cover ordinary living expenses? What adjustments should you make in your spending to be sure you reach long-term goals five, ten, or 25 years from now? The net worth statement should be used to give focus to your budget. It should be updated annually to evaluate your progress.

Now you know what steps are involved in creating a spending plan. You may even have begun one. But a budget does not guarantee that you can manage your money successfully. The plan has to be followed consistently and revised when necessary. And that means regular family discussions about the way the budget is working. It means periodic reevaluation whenever there are changes in household income, family size, or family goals.

MONEY AND EMOTIONS

Throughout our budget discussion we have stressed the need for joint decision making. It is important for partners to work out these problems together, because money is a major source of arguments among couples, rivaled only by sex. Families that argue about money matters report that members do not feel free to communicate their opinions or desires. When we remember the contribution of both partners in labor and nonmarket home production, it is understandable that both partners want to be included in decisions. Older children, teenagers, and young adults living at home can also be involved in decisions related to the problem of scarcity; they should be able to understand the need for trade-offs.

It is important to realize that money discussions can be sensitive and can elicit strong emotional reactions, because spending often fulfills emotional as well as physical needs. Differences in values often become noisily apparent in budgeting discussions. People who pause to examine their own values will find it easier to plan cooperatively within the household. For example, we are all familiar with the individual who achieves status through spending. "Keeping up with the Joneses" can quickly put a hole in your budget. If this seems to be a problem, ask yourself if it is really your values that are creating your desire for a spa or a Caribbean cruise.

Sometimes individuals spend money to "get even" with others in the family. Consider the wife who buys a new dress because her husband stayed out late after work without calling her. To retaliate, the husband buys a new fishing rod. Both these people use money to repress anger. This does not solve their problem; it only creates a new, budgetary problem.

If one family member handles the money and withholds information regarding income or expenditures, he or she is using money to exert control. Other signs of this are the requirement that he or she be asked, even begged, for money or that he or she ridicules the wants and needs of other family members. Money can represent power to control decisions, life-styles, and life itself. Such a situation leads to resentment, lack of cooperation, and perhaps even rebellion.

All these attitudes and habits can sabotage family planning sessions and spending plans. They should be consciously avoided and eliminated. Being aware of these potential problems is part of the solution. Open and free discussions of individuals needs, goals, values, and feelings should be encouraged in your family.

COLLECTIVE MONEY MANAGEMENT TECHNIQUES

Even when everyone in a family is convinced that a plan is desirable and honestly wishes to cooperate, some partners cannot get through step one—determining income. They cannot agree how much of their income should be shared with the household and how much should be kept separate. Most of us grew up in a one-income family. We learned to handle money decisions within our families, so we tend to do as our parents did. Now that two-income families are becoming the norm, we need to devise new options.

We would like to present four methods that can be used to manage money collectively (Shaevitz and Shaevitz, 1980). One of these methods or a variation of it may help make you more comfortable with both the sharing of money and the sharing and delegating of power. The method you choose should clearly outline the financial responsibility of each family member and should be agreeable to him or her.

In the first option, *proportional contributions*, households determine their basic necessities, and then each individual contributes to basic expenses in proportion to his or her income. Let's say that a family needs $2,400 each month. If one member makes $2,400 and one makes $800, they would contribute $1,800 (three-quarters) and $600 (one-quarter) toward basic expenses, respectively. There is a degree of fairness in this method because both partners contribute to household maintenance, while both have a degree of freedom to spend as they wish. The obvious disadvantage is that the partner with the smaller income has less freedom because he or she has less money. This system is quite unfair if one partner makes little or no money.

A second option is to *split household expenses evenly*. In other words, if expenses are $3,000 per month, each contributes $1,500. Each person keeps separate checking and separate saving accounts. The advantages here are that each person contributes equally and each shares equally in any benefits derived from this system. Individuals would personally benefit from a raise; their income would increase but their contribution wouldn't. This method can be adapted easily to accommodate more than two people. It can be especially suitable for unrelated people sharing a household and has often been adopted by college students living away from home. Disadvantages exist with this system when there is a big difference in income; one individual ends up with considerably less discretionary income after contributing to the household.

In the third collective money management technique, household members *pool their income*. Under this arrangement all money is placed in joint savings and joint checking accounts. No one is penalized for earning less money, because all share equally. There is no distinction between contributions of time (household tasks) or money. All work is considered worthwhile regardless of where it is done (inside or outside the household) and without reference to the amount of money earned. This is one of the simplest methods and fits the traditional marriage pattern.

Pooling requires considerable trust and cooperation because both parties have access to all the money. This may be a real disadvantage if they do not agree about its distribution. Also, there is no money specifically available for independent use. It would be almost impossible to put money aside for a special purpose without the other partner knowing about it.

In the fourth option, couples pool most of their money but also create two small *independent fund accounts*. This system is similar to pooling, with one distinction: Each party withholds a specific amount of money available to spend as he or she wishes. The amount can be large or small, equal or unequal, but it is free from the influence or review of the other person.

To manage and control money you will need a plan or system. Discuss these four systems with your partner(s) before choosing one. You may find that you will create a totally different system from the ones presented here. What is important is that you talk over the advantages and disadvantages and find something that works for all of you. Consider how you feel, for example, about giving equal spending power to your partner(s). How will you feel about consulting your partner(s) before purchasing, rather than after the fact? Will the system provide adequate records and receipts for tax purposes and future planning? What are the annual expenses of maintaining more than one account? Experiment with a system, evaluate, and revise when necessary—to the satisfaction of all household members.

PAYING BILLS   Once you create a system, someone has to run it: You need to decide how the bills will get paid and who will pay them. Perhaps the person who most enjoys doing it should be appointed. Some people prefer to organize and control financial matters, whereas others feel uncomfortable with this task. One party may simply be better at keeping records and bank statements up to date. Remember to consider the time this individual spends in other household duties so as not to overload one partner.

You might decide to pay bills together. The advantage of sitting down once or twice a month to pay bills and discuss financial matters is that there are no "unknowns" for either partner. Each knows where the money is going and how much is left.

If no one really enjoys the details of record keeping and bill paying and doing it together seems tedious or unnecessary, one partner could take over the job for a specified time. After that, the task would rotate to the

---

BOX 4.2   PAYING THE BILLS: GET ORGANIZED!

Work Center

First you need a work center with

1. A place for writing
2. A place for supplies
3. A place for storing financial records

Usually, a desk, a drawer, and a small portable file fulfill these needs.

Work System

1. Have a definite place for incoming bills, notices, and so forth.
2. Stock this location with appropriate supples:
   Checkbook
   Account book
   Address book
   Writing supplies
   Postage
3. Create a filing system with accordian files or manila folders for
   Budget and financial records
   Salary statements
   Bills and debt notices, with dates of payment

   Sales slips, receipts, guarantees for major purchases
   Canceled checks and bank statements
   Investment records, including bankbooks
   Income tax records
   Property records, including insurance records
   Automobile records, including insurance records
   Credit card numbers, addresses, and phone numbers in case of loss
   Life insurance records
   Employment records
   Pension or Social Security records
4. Obtain a safe-deposit box for valuable papers:
   Stocks, bonds, negotiable securities
   Property records—deeds, mortgages, and so forth
   Record of insurance policies
   Birth certificate, passport
   Diplomas
   Marriage certificate, divorce papers
   Discharge papers from the armed forces
   Auto titles
   Wills, trust agreements
   Household inventory

other partner. This way, each partner would be familiar with the task and know the financial picture in general, but not always be responsible for it. In any event, both partners need to know and understand the details of family business matters and to be able to assume full responsibility for management and record keeping if the need arises. Many divorcees and widows have bemoaned the fact that they "knew nothing" about managing the family finances and as a result went though a difficult or costly adjustment period after a divorce or death of a spouse.

Box 4.2 provides some practical advice on how to set up a record-keeping system. Forms for recording spending have already been provided in this chapter, are available from some financial institutions, and can be purchased in stationary stores. Those who have personal computers are probably aware that record-keeping and financial-planning software are readily available. Some financial institutions offer computerized budget programs for a reasonable fee. A discussion of these services, as well as the mechanics of writing checks, is included in Chapter 5.

SUMMARY

Achieving consumer spending that provides maximum satisfaction depends on having a budget based on family goals and values. Budgeting is a direct application of the decision-making process. In this case, the "problem" is to create a budget that considers each person's needs, wants, and goals and that is realistically based on anticipated income. The next step is to gather information such as spending records, tax returns, and check stubs. Then the family weighs alternatives and prioritizes goals; analyzes current spending patterns and identifies financial commitments that result in fixed expenses. The family can then decide to readjust spending in areas they choose and select a method of managing money collectively, if appropriate. Budgeting also includes periodic evaluation of financial progress by using a net worth statement. Finally, it is important to realize that the decisions and discussions involved in creating and implementing the plan may become emotional, but all feelings should be listened to and fairly considered.

QUESTIONS

1. List five reasons for using a budget.
2. Why is it helpful to look at spending patterns of the "average American family"?
3. Planning a budget involves matching future income to future expenditures. What information must be gathered before a budget can be made? Where can you get this information?
4. What factors should individuals and families

consider when determining the size of an emergency fund? How much should *your* emergency fund be?

5. What is the purpose of a net worth statement?
6. Consider the four methods presented in the text for managing money collectively. Which one do you prefer, and why? Ask your spouse or close friend the same question. Is there a conflict of opinion? How could a compromise be reached?
7. Should children be included in budget-planning sessions? If so, at what age? How should teenagers be involved in planning the budget? Young adults who live at home with parents?
8. Some partners, most often wives, do not know how much money their spouse makes. What kind of problems could develop?

9. What types of information would a young adult need to know about the local cost of living before moving out of a parents' household into his or her own or into one that is shared with another person?
10. What should a young person who plans to marry know about a prospective spouse's attitudes and values about money and budgeting? Explain your answer.
11. What are some of the reasons that individuals and families cannot follow a spending plan?
12. What are some common emergencies that might force a family to dip into savings? Are all of these really unexpected? Defend your response.

REFERENCES AND READINGS

Abdel-Ghany, Mohamed, Bivens, Gordon E., Keeler, James P., and James, William L. "Windfall Income and the Permanent Income Hypothesis: New Evidence," *The Journal of Consumer Affairs*, Winter 1983.

Bailey, Anne Wisemaan. "Social and Economic Factors Affecting the Financial Well-being of Families," *Journal of Home Economics*, Summer 1987.

Beutler, Ivan F., and Mason, Jerald W., "Family Cash-Flow Budgeting," *Home Economics Research Journal*, September 1987.

Cole-Whittiaker, Terry, *How to Have More in a Have-Not World*. New York: Rawson Associates, 1983.

Hefferan, Colien, "Family Budget Guidelines, *Family Economics Review*, no. 4, 1987.

Hira, Tahira K. "Satisfaction with Money Management: Practices Among Dual-Earner Households," *Journal of Home Economics*, Summer 1987.

Lown, Jean M. "Family Financial Well-being: Guidance from Research," *Journal of Home Economics*, Winter 1986.

"Middle-Class Squeeze," *U.S. News & World Report*, August 18, 1986, page 36–43.

"1986 Revision of Poverty Income Guidelines," *Family Economics Review*, no. 3, 1986.

"The Principles of Managing Your Finances," U.S. Department of Agriculture Home and Garden Bulletin no. 245, Washington, D.C.: U.S. Government Printing Office, 1987.

Schiller, Margery K. "Personal Finance: A New Look at an Old Friend," *Illinois Teacher*, March/April 1986.

Shaevitz, Marjorie Hansen, and Shaevitz, Morton H. *Making It Together as a Two-Career Couple*. Boston: Houghton Mifflin, 1980

"Spending Patterns of Urban and Rural Populations: 1985," *Family Economics Review*, no 4, 1988.

Wall, Ronald W. "Aging and Economics: The Future Is Now," *Journal of Home Economics*, Winter 1986.

Chapter Five

MONEY AND BANKING: THE ALMIGHTY DOLLAR

- ☐ What Is Money, and How Does It Function?
- ☐ The American Monetary System
- ☐ The Federal Reserve System
- ☐ Financial Institutions
- ☐ Banking and Bill Paying

DID YOU KNOW THAT...

. . . there is no gold or silver backing our money system?

. . . if a creditor refuses to accept American paper currency in payment for a debt, then that debt is forgiven and can never be legally collected?

. . . the Federal Reserve is the name of our nation's central bank?

. . . banks, savings and loan associations, and credit unions have more similarities than differences?

. . . there may only be a matter of a few hours from the time you write a check at a business establishment to the time that it "clears" the bank?

Can you imagine a world without money? In a moneyless world every economic transaction would require people to use **barter**, i.e., the direct exchange of goods and services. If you wanted a hamburger, for example, you would have to find someone willing to trade one for something you owned—say, this textbook. Or perhaps you could offer to tutor your hamburger maker in exchange for lunch. In any event, you would be spending a significant portion of your day negotiating with others to get the goods and services you want. Since these negotiations would take a great deal of time and effort, you would quickly discover that it was simpler to do just about everything yourself. Economic specialization would be abandoned in favor of self-sufficiency and a lower level of living. Fortunately, we do not have to regress to a pre-money society to see the importance of this invention.

WHAT IS MONEY AND HOW DOES IT FUNCTION?

medium of exchange: something widely accepted for the payment of debt as well as the purchase of goods and services

Money is defined as something that is generally accepted as payment for goods and services, in other words, a **medium of exchange**. Money allows us to separate our consumption activity from our production activity. Using the example given for the barter system, money allows us to buy a hamburger without having to provide an immediate service to the person supplying the hamburger. We give money instead of tutoring services or a textbook.

In order for something to be classified as money, it must fulfill three basic functions:

1. Medium of exchange
2. Store of value
3. Unit of account

Savings bonds, gold, shares of stock, and credit cards are common examples of things that are *not* money in our society. Each of them fails to meet at least one of the criteria listed above. In order to understand the reasons for excluding these items, you need to become familiar with each specific function of money.

Criterion 1: Medium of Exchange

Something used as a medium of exchange must be widely accepted for the payment of debt as well as the purchase of goods and services. Savings bonds and gold are not money in our society because you cannot use them very easily in economic transactions. If you drive into your neighborhood gas station and pump ten gallons into your tank, you will be very disappointed if you expect to pay for the gas with a savings bond or gold. The station will refuse to accept them. However, you could probably use cash or a debit card that is tied to your checking account. You might also be able to use a credit card, but this invention is not money because it fails to fulfill other criteria.

All of these pieces of paper were once money because they fulfilled the most important monetary function — as a medium of exchange.

Criterion 2: Store of Value

store of value: the ability of a commodity to gather and put away the value of your productive activity, letting you spend it later

To separate your consumption and production activity, money must be a **store of value**: It must be able to store the value of your productive activity so that you can spend it later. For example, if you work in the campus bookstore, you will be paid in money that you can use at a later time. You will not be paid in books, and there is no expiration date on the money you receive. We should also reiterate a point we made in Chapter 3 about

inflation, the rise in the general level of prices. Rapid price inflation hampers the ability of money to serve as a store of value. To put this in the form of an analogy, inflation is to money as kryptonite is to Superman. Inflation makes money less powerful.

Credit cards are not considered money because they are not a store of value. They are a temporary extension of credit, a loan if you will, from a bank to a consumer. This loan must eventually be repaid in money, although some consumers seem to believe they can postpone the repayment of debt indefinitely. (This erroneous belief is reviewed in Chapter 6.)

Criterion 3: Unit of Account

unit of account: *an important characteristic of money that allows it to be used in a numbering system to count the size of wealth, debt, and everyday transactions*

Saying that money serves as a **unit of account** simply means that you can use it to measure the value of anything that can be purchased. In other words, it is a counting system that enables you to translate the value of all transactions into a single monetary unit. This is a great convenience for a modern economy. It allows us to compare apples and oranges in terms of a common unit, the dollar.

THE AMERICAN MONETARY SYSTEM

As an American consumer, you probably believe you are fairly familiar with our monetary system. Take this short quiz and answer each question either *true* or *false*:

1. Most American money is in the form of paper currency.
2. American money is backed by gold.
3. All one-dollar bills are identical.

The correct answer to all of these questions is *false*. Let's discover why, and what this information means to consumers.

The Different Kinds of American Money

National economic education tests indicate that most people believe the majority of American money is a piece of paper with a famous American's picture on it. George Washington, Abraham Lincoln, and Alexander Hamilton are some of the more familiar portraits that we carry in our wallets right next to pictures of our family and friends. If we measure the nation's money supply according to the three functions mentioned above, however, we will discover that only about 25 percent of our money is currently being held as paper currency. Coins are not very important in the total, either. The vast majority of American money is being held in checkable deposits. That is why we will discuss the management of checkable deposits later in this chapter.

What Determines the Value of Our Money?

Some people believe that the government has a vast storehouse of gold in Fort Knox and this is the ultimate source of the value of our money. This is simply wrong. Our money has no specific amount of gold or silver supporting its value. A dollar is worth just that, one dollar.

Our money has value for two reasons. First, and most importantly, because people are willing to accept it in exchange for goods and services. We have confidence that the money we accept as payment today can be used to purchase goods at some later time. Second, our confidence in the value of a dollar is bolstered by the fact that our federal government has declared U.S. currency to be **legal tender**. This puts the force of law behind the value of our currency. If something is declared legal tender, it must be accepted as payment for all debts. All U.S. paper currency bears this statement: "This note is legal tender for all debts, public and private." If an American creditor refuses to acccept our currency, then he or she legally forgoes the right to collect interest on that debt and forfeits the right to sue the debtor for nonpayment.

Most of the nations of the world have declared their money to be legal tender without any guarantee to redeem their currency for a certain amount of gold or silver. Such money is called **fiat money** because it is based on faith in the government rather than on precious metals.

Are All Dollar Bills Identical?

So now you know that most of our money is in checking accounts rather than currency. And you are also aware that our paper money is legal tender without a promise of gold or silver supporting it. But did you know that we actually have 12 different forms of each denomination of currency, from the one-dollar bill on up? If you look at a selection of American paper currency, you will discover that the seal to the left of the portrait bears a large capital letter that can be any letter from *A* to *L* (the first 12 letters of the alphabet). You will also find four prominent single-digit numbers associated with the letter in the seal and placed just inside the four corners of the bill. If you have a dollar bill with the letter *L* seal, for example, you will find four *12*s on the face of the bill. Figure 5.1 illustrates this, and more.

All paper currency is printed by the U.S. Treasury Department in Washington, D.C., but distribution is handled by the Federal Reserve System through one of its 12 regional banks, from Boston (*A*) to San Francisco (*L*). We will explore the structure and how these regions work a bit later, but first we will discuss the purpose of the Federal Reserve System.

1. The United States Government authorizes paper money—currency—of certain denominations and in some cases certain amounts. The authorized currency is legal tender. Basically, this means creditors may not refuse this money in payment for any debt expressed in terms of that money, assuring the United States of a single, reliable medium through which transactions can be conducted. However, this does not mean that a merchant must accept a dollar bill. If he or she feels the bill is counterfeit, for example, the merchant may demand some other form of payment.

2. Federal Reserve Notes. Most of our currency, over 99 percent, is Federal Reserve Notes. The government has authorized the 12 Federal Reserve banks to issue notes in denominations of $1, $2, $5, $10, $20, $50, and $100. Before 1945, notes were also printed in denominations of $500, $1,000, $5,000, and $10,000. These notes of larger denominations were issued until 1969. At that time, they were discontinued since there was little demand for them. After all, it is easier and safer to write a check for $5,000 than to use a $5,000 bill.

3. Take a look at a dollar bill; it probably is a Federal Reserve Note. To the left of the portrait is a seal of the Federal Reserve bank that issued that note. The seal bears the name and the code letter of that bank. Which Federal Reserve bank issued your currency?

Boston	A	Richmond	E	Minneapolis	I
New York	B	Atlanta	F	Kansas City	J
Philadelphia	C	Chicago	G	Dallas	K
Cleveland	D	St. Louis	H	San Francisco	L

4. To the right of the portrait is the Treasury seal, which is overprinted on the face of each note. This seal and the serial numbers are printed in green.

5. Serial Numbers. No two serial numbers are alike for two bills of the same denomination, type, or series of note. The serial numbers appear in the upper-right and lower-left corners of a bill. A prefix letter, eight numbers, and a suffix letter make up the serial number.

On Federal Reserve notes, the prefix letter corresponds to the issuing Federal Reserve bank's code letter. This is the letter in the Federal Reserve seal. The notes are numbered in lots of 100 million. The 100 millionth note is designated by a ☆. The suffix letter designates the run, A being the first, B the second, through Z. O is omitted because of its similarity to zero. So the first note of a denomination and series issued by the Federal Reserve Bank of Boston would have the serial number A 00000001 A. If the issuing bank was New York, the number would be B 00000001 A.

6. Faceplate Numbers and Letters. Other identifying numbers on a note are the faceplate numbers and letters. You can see these numbers in the lower-right and upper-left corners of a bill.

7. Series. The series identification shows the year that the design for the notes was first used. Small changes in the design, such as changes in the signatures of the treasurer of the United States or the secretary of the treasury, are designated by a letter below the series year. For example, Series 1969 D means the design was first used in 1969 and was slightly changed four times.

8. The portraits on our paper money are those of deceased American statesmen. On the reverse side are famous buildings, monuments, and ornate numerals. The uniform back designs were adopted in 1929. Portraits and emblems presently on our currency are as follows:

Denominations ($)	Portrait	Emblem
1	Washington	Great Seal of the United States
2	Jefferson	Signing of Declaration of Independence
5	Lincoln	Lincoln Memorial
10	Hamilton	U. S. Treasury Building
20	Jackson	White House
50	Grant	U. S. Capitol
100	Franklin	Independence Hall
500	McKinley	Ornate 500
1,000	Cleveland	Ornate 1,000
5,000	Madison	Ornate 5,000
10,000	Chase	Ornate 10,000

THE FEDERAL RESERVE SYSTEM

It is a sad comment on the economic literacy of the American public to publish some of the most common answers to the question, "What is the Federal Reserve?" These include "The national police force," "The land reserved for Native Americans," and "The National Park System." Most Americans are unaware of this institution, which is the chief monetary authority in the United States. The Federal Reserve System has a greater quantifiable influence on the quantity of money, the structure of interest rates, and the health of the economy than any other entity in the U.S.

Federal Reserve System (Fed): the central bank of the United States; it regulates the supply of money and credit in our economy

The **Federal Reserve System**, commonly called the **Fed**, is our nation's central bank. It was established by Congress in 1913 to help regulate the supply of money and credit in our economy. It was generally believed that a central bank could help the economy avoid what were then known as "panics," called recessions today (see Chapter 3.) The Fed has by-and-large fulfilled that function; however, there are some significant errors on its record—the Great Depression of the 1930s, for example. Nevertheless, the Fed remains a bulwark against economic recession and rapid inflation.

The Structure of the Federal Reserve

The Federal Reserve Act of 1913 has been amended many times, but the system maintains a vitality and relevance that few other institutions can match. The United States is divided into 12 Federal Reserve districts, each with a Federal Reserve bank that services and regulates the financial institutions in its district. These Federal Reserve banks and the cities containing their 25 branch banks are shown in Figure 5.2.

The 12 regional Federal Reserve banks are under the overall authority of the Board of Governors of the Federal Reserve System, whose headquarters are in Washington, D.C. The Board of Governors is composed of seven members who are appointed by the president and confirmed by the Senate. The appointments are for 14-year terms, with a new appointment slated every two years. Thus a president will appoint a minimum of two governors over a four-year presidential term. The idea behind these long terms is to insulate the members of the Board of Governors from political influence, so that economics, not politics, dominates motivation. The chairman of the Board of Governors is one of the most influential figures in world economic affairs, and yet most Americans are blissfully ignorant of his or her existence. Dr. Alan Greenspan is the current chairman of the Fed.

The Functions of the Fed

The Federal Reserve System performs a variety of functions, but none is more important than controlling the amount of money in the economy. Too much money can lead to inflation; too little money can lead to recession. The Fed influences the money supply by regulating the re-

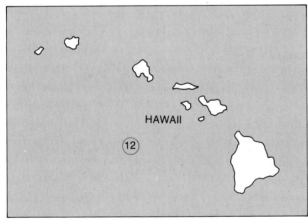
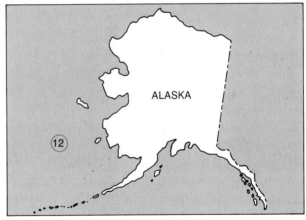

Legend

——— Boundaries of Federal Reserve Districts

——— Boundaries of Federal Reserve Branch Territories

✪ Board of Governors of the Federal Reserve System

◉ Federal Reserve Bank Cities

• Federal Reserve Branch Cities

· Federal Reserve Bank Facility

FIGURE 5.2
The Federal Reserve System: boundaries of Federal Reserve districts and their branch territories.
Approximately 22,000 individuals and $853.9 million in land, machinery, and buildings, with the
Board of Governors in Washington, D.C., 12 regional Federal Reserve banks, 25 branch banks, and 12
additional facilities (including check-clearing centers), add up to a large bureaucracy constituting
the world's most influential and powerful central bank, the Federal Reserve System. Additional
offices of these banks are located at Lewiston, Maine; Windsor Locks, Connecticut; Cranford, New
Jersey; Jericho, New York; Utica at Oriskany, New York; Columbus, Ohio; Columbia, South Carolina;
Charleston, West Virginia; Des Moines, Iowa; Indianapolis, Indiana; and Milwaukee, Wisconsin.
There is a communications and records center in Culpeper, Virginia. (SOURCE: *Federal Reserve Bulletin,*
August 1982, p. A78.)

serves held by the banking system. If it takes actions to increase those reserves, the banking system can lend more money and thus expand the money supply. If the Fed tightens reserves, the money supply will shrink as the banking system will have less money to lend. These actions have an impact on the cost of lending money, i.e., the interest rate charged by the banks for a loan.

The Fed performs many other important services in the economy. One of these is the provision of check-clearing services for banks. For example, if you live in Honolulu (Federal Reserve Bank of San Francisco District) and pay for your *Time* magazine subscription (Federal Reserve Bank of New York) with a check drawn on your bank, your check will probably be cleared by the Federal Reserve system. Another role for the Fed is banker to the federal government. The Fed maintains checking accounts for the federal government to assist in the collecting and spending of tax revenues. Finally, the Fed regulates all national banks and enforces many of the provisions of federal credit legislation.

FINANCIAL INSTITUTIONS

financial intermediary: a business that acts as a go-between, taking lenders' funds and making them available to borrowers

Now that you understand more about money and the American monetary system, you are ready to explore the financial institutions that link consumers to our monetary system. We will first look at depository institutions, such as commercial banks, thrifts, and credit unions. They are a common form of financial intermediary in the American economy. A **financial intermediary** is a business that acts as a middleman (intermediary) by taking the funds of lenders and making them available to borrowers. A financial intermediary makes a profit by charging its borrowers a higher rate of interest than it pays to its depositors.

Over the past decade, financial intermediaries have changed substantially. By exploring these changes you can better evaluate the services they provide when you pay bills, save, borrow, or invest. Some of these services will be familiar to you, while other, more recent developments, may offer novel avenues in your financial world. First, we provide guidelines on selecting a financial intermediary, and then we will look more closely at checking accounts. Other banking services will be covered in later chapters.

Financial Intermediaries

Once a person has an income and owes bills, he or she usually feels the need for financial services. Where will you keep the money that you have no current desire to spend? You could keep it in your bedroom drawer, under a mattress, or hidden in the cookie jar. Or you could keep it in a safe place where it will earn interest, such as a commercial bank or a credit union. And when your bills arrive, how will you pay them? You could make payments in cash, but for some large payments that would be neither convenient (because of the bulkiness of the cash) nor safe. It would also require personal delivery of the cash to each business, since it's never safe to send cash payments by mail.

For these reasons most people leave, or **deposit**, their money in a financial intermediary and pay their bills by check. A **check** is your authorization or approval to withdraw your money from the bank and give it to someone else. An account or record is kept of deposits, and withdrawals, providing a good financial record for budgeting and tax purposes. In order to explain the array of financial services and providers of those services, we will briefly consider the changes in the banking industry during the 1980s.

deregulation: the removal of rules and laws governing the operation of a business or type of business, such as banking or air travel

Deregulation and change. In the past there was a clear distinction between one type of financial institution, say, a bank, from another, say, a credit union. But with the passage of *The Depository Institutions Deregulation and Monetary Control Act of 1980*, which provided for the **deregulation** of the banking industry, government-controlled distinctions were greatly reduced (see Box 5.1). The 1980s saw the removal of limits on

---

BOX 5.1 **THE DEPOSITORY INSTITUTIONS DEREGULATION AND MONETARY CONTROL ACT**

In 1980 Congress passed the most far-reaching piece of financial legislation in almost 50 years: The Depository Institutions Deregulation and Monetary Control Act. There are many sections to this act and we cannot outline all of them here, but consumers should know some of the most important ones and a little history besides.

The Banking Act of 1935 made it illegal to pay interest on checking accounts and gave regulatory agencies the authority to impose ceilings on the interest that banks could pay on savings accounts and time deposits. In 1966, these regulations were extended to include almost all financial institutions and almost all forms of saving. These rates were quite low by recent standards, and when consumers realized that they could get higher interest by taking their money out of these saving accounts, banks and savings and loan associations began to lose reserves. The system was further complicated

by the appearance of negotiable order of withdrawal (NOW) accounts, which function like checking accounts but also pay interest. The combination of higher-interest opportunities and novel checking accounts led Congress to seek a complete reform of the system.

The Monetary Control Act (MCA) created a committee to oversee a gradual phasing out of all interest rate ceilings by April 1986. The first order of business was to allow all banking institutions, from commercial banks and savings and loan associations to credit unions, to offer interest on checkable deposits. Although there was an initial maximum of $5\frac{1}{4}$ percent allowed, all interest rate ceilings were eventually removed.

Because of these changes, consumers have to spend more time investigating the yields offered by competing financial institutions, but they will receive higher returns for this effort.

the **interest** (payment for lending consumer monies to the bank) that institutions could pay for savings; the creation of accounts that provide all-in-one services of checking, savings, and investing; and the removal of restrictions that prevented financial institutions other than commercial banks from offering accounts with check-writing privileges, among other innovations.

What all of this means to us today is that the financial industry is more competitive, offering more services and options to consumers. On the other hand, it means that consumers must be better informed and spend more time searching out the financial intermediary that is best for them. We will begin that search with a discussion of the different types of **depository intermediaries**, financial intermediaries that accept deposits from consumers and offer checking accounts.

Types of depository intermediaries. The most common type is the **commercial bank**; there are more than 15,000 in the United States. Many commercial banks are very small institutions, but the 50 largest control about one-third of all deposits made in America. Commercial banks offer a full gamut of services, including savings, checking, loans, mortgages, trust facilities, and safety deposits. Because of this they are often called full-service institutions. Commercial banks may be chartered by the state or the federal government to operate within a particular georgraphic region.

A **mutual savings bank** is state chartered. You will find this type of bank throughout New England, the Northeast, Ohio, Minnesota, Washington, and Oregon. Mutual savings banks were originally founded for the convenience of savers and for making loans on real property—mortgages and home-improvement loans. Deregulation has allowed mutual savings banks to expand their services to include checking accounts and a variety of consumer loans.

savings and loan associations: a financial intermediary that offers checking accounts, mortgages, and other loans; offers a dividend on savings rather than interest; also called thrifts

Like mutual savings banks, **savings and loan associations** (sometimes called **thrifts**) used to concentrate on savings and mortgages, but deregulation has allowed for the expansion of their services, too. Mutual savings banks and savings and loan associations have another thing in common: Most offer a dividend on savings, instead of interest. This means that the amount of money earned by depositors in any given quarter can vary, since the money is paid out of profits, and the dividend is not guaranteed.

Credit unions are playing an increasingly larger role in savings and lending in America. Credit unions are cooperative, not-for-profit organizations that are owned by their members, people who have a common bond such as the same occupation or employer. When you open an account in a credit union, your deposit is technically used to purchase shares of stock. The shares earn dividends and entitle you to a voice in how the credit union is run. They also make you eligible for low-cost consumer loans. Since deregulation, many credit unions offer a draft account, allowing checking services, and home equity loans. Some also offer free term life insurance protection and/or free loan protection. The former may yield up to $4,000 to a beneficiary upon death, while the latter could pay off an outstanding loan to the credit union upon death of the debtor.

Choosing a Financial Intermediary

A quick look at Table 5.1 shows that the most popular financial intermediary is the commercial bank. But following the crowd might not be the way to choose. There are four factors to consider when selecting a financial intermediary: *safety, services, convenience,* and *cost.* One important aspect of safety is the reputation and history of any financial institution, as well as the sound judgment of its executive management staff. But a second consideration for the depositor is insurance, should a bank fail. Deposits in commercial and mutual savings banks are insured by the **Federal Deposit Insurance Corporation (FDIC)** for up to $100,000 *per depositor* (see Box 5.2). Most savings and loan associations are insured by the **Federal Savings and Loan Insurance Corporation (FSLIC)**, which performs many of the same tasks as the FDIC. Although insurance on credit union accounts is available from the **National Credit Union Association (NCUA)**, many credit unions are not insured. In such a case, you are relying on the decision-making skills and knowledge of your credit union manager for the safety of your savings.

After you have considered safety, you can further evaluate a financial institution by available services, convenience and costs. As you read this section, consider what is important to you. Then search for a financial intermediary that will provide most of these services to you. But consider that since interest rates and fees vary from one institution to another, it might be smart to deal with two or three financial intermediaries, rather than just one. Then consider not only convenience of location, but also ease of use. In these days of computers it might not matter that your bank

TABLE 5.1 Number and Assets of Depository Intermediaries in the United States

	Number	**Total Assets (billions of dollars)**	**Percent of Total Assets**
Commercial banks	15,175	2,365.2	63.7
FSLIC-insured savings and loans	3,246	1,069.4	28.9
Mutual savings banks	364	157.4	4.2
Credit unions	15,045	119.7	3.2
Total	33,830	3,711.7	

SOURCE: *Statistical Abstract of the United States, 1987,* Tables 800 and 807.

BOX 5.2   HOW SAFE IS YOUR BANK?

If you have seen a documentary about the 1929 stock market crash and the Great Depression of the 1930s, you must have witnessed a scene in which huge crowds gathered outside a bank hoping to get their deposits out. This frightening scene was all too real in the early years of the Depression, and more than a few people lost lifetime savings. You can get a feel for the scale of this catastrophe if you realize that the number of banks in the United States shrank from 25,000 in 1929 to 15,000 by 1934. The fear, the uncertainty, and the grief that this banking contraction forced the public to bear left an indelible mark on this country. As a result, Congress established the Federal Deposit Insurance Corporation (FDIC) to insure accounts in commercial banks. The FDIC was followed by the Federal Savings and Loan Insurance Corporation (FSLIC), which insures savings and loan association deposits, and the National Credit Union Association (NCUA), which insures deposits in affiliated credit unions. Each association is independent of the government and is financed by association members. Nevertheless, if a broad-scale, 1930s-like situation ever developed, there is little doubt that the U.S. Treasury would come to the rescue, as evidenced by relief provided to the savings and loan industry in 1989.

But what about the health of individual financial institutions? The first questions to ask are, Is it insured, and if so with whom? Currently, an account can be insured for up to $100,000. If you happen to be in the enviable position of needing more than $100,000 in insurance, you can do one of two things: You can go to another insured institution and open a new account in your name, or you can open a second account at the same bank, but make it a joint account for you and a trustworthy partner (for example, your spouse). We provide a short checklist of other safe banking tips below:

1. Find out if your intermediary is a member of FDIC, FSLIC, or NCUA. If they are, they must display the appropriate seal prominently.
2. If your deposits exceed the federally insured maximum of $100,000, you may want to open another account with a different financial institution.
3. If an intermediary is offering unusually high interest rates to depositors, be wary. It could be making risky loans and may be headed for insolvency.
4. If you read or hear that state or federal bank regulators have instigated a management change at the bank, take this as a warning signal.
5. You can obtain a thorough analysis of your bank by contacting an independent research firm. Two examples are:

Sheshunoff & Company   Veribanc Inc.
505 Barton Springs Road   P.O. Box 2963
Austin, TX 78704   Woburn, MA 01888

Prices of these analyses will range from $10 to $75.

---

is in the next town, if it has all the services that you need and provides an easy check-cashing system. Finally, be sure to compare costs. Worksheet 5.1 provides a form that you might use to record data.

Services from Financial Intermediaries

As we have mentioned, since the Monetary Control Act of 1980 the selection of services available at financial intermediaries has expanded. We will identify what is available, so that you will be better prepared to select a financial intermediary.

WORKSHEET 5.1 CHOOSING A BANK

Given the deregulation of banking interest rates and the increasing competition for deposits, selecting a bank is becoming a more important task for many consumers. Convenience has always been an important criterion in choosing a bank, but the Monetary Control Act has made this less of a problem by allowing most financial institutions to provide checking as well as savings accounts. One way to choose a bank, then, is to select the one that is federally insured, close to home, is open at convenient hours, and has automatic tellers, statewide service, low charges, and high interest. Once again, no bank will come out the best in all departments, but you must set your personal range of acceptable trade-offs. You can use the following worksheet to evaluate various interest-bearing checking accounts. The form is adapted from a survey done by Professor Pat McDermott at Kansas State University to evaluate local options.

	Banks		Savings and Loan Associations		Credit Unions	

Yield
Annual percentage rate
Compounded
Annual percentage yield
Computed
		Sample
		5.25%
		Daily
		5.39%
		Day of
		  deposit
		  to day
		  of with-
		  drawal				

Costs Check printing (per check) Overdraft fee Stop-payment fee		$ 0.05 $15.00 $10.00				

Schedule of Fees
Balance
 	
Monthly account fee
Check charge (per check)
Balance for free checking
How is balance
  calculated?
		Under
		  $1,000
		$2.00
		$0.20
		$1,000
		Lowest
		  balance
		  for the
		  month				

Statements Frequency Checks included?		Monthly Yes				
Additional Services and **Costs for Use** Safe-deposit box Traveler's checks Automatic teller Saturday banking		$12.00 free No No				

SOURCE: Adapted from Richard Morse and Pat McDermott. "Now Accounts: Costs and Benefits for Consumers." Kansas State University.

Savings accounts. The purpose of a savings account is to provide a safe place to accumulate money over a long period of time. Since money accumulation implies investment, savings accounts will be dealt with in greater detail in Chapter 17. At this time, we only point out that savings accounts are available at most financial intermediaries and come in two basic forms: passbook accounts and savings certificates of deposit (CDs).

passbook account: a simple form of savings account that can be opened with a small amount of money and that pays low interest rates

Many people had a **passbook account** as children and so are familiar with them. Usually, a passbook account can be opened with a small amount of money, such as $25, and deposits and withdrawals can be made as desired. Today a nominal, monthly fee may be charged if the account balance remains below a minimum level. Since the intent is that the account remain relatively inactive, some financial intermediaries limit the number of withdrawals in a given time period and charge a fee if that limit is exceeded. Interest rates vary but are usually on the low end of the scale.

certificate of deposit (CD): an agreement between a financial institution and a depositor that the bank will pay a guaranteed rate of interest as long as the depositor promises to leave a certain sum of money in the bank for a specified time

Certificates of deposit (CDs) have grown in popularity over the past decade. A CD is a contractual agreement between the depositor and the institution. The depositor agrees to leave a certain sum of money with the institution for a specified time, anywhere from seven days to ten years. The institution agrees to pay a specific rate of interest over that time. The interest rate is usually higher than that for passbook accounts since the financial intermediary knows how long it will have the use of the depositor's money. If the depositor withdraws the money early, he or she incurs a penalty.

Since deregulation, there is no restriction on the interest rate that financial intermediaries can offer its customers, so the wise consumer will comparison shop.

Checking accounts. Three out of four American families have at least one checking account. Even though financial intermediaries market their accounts with fancy names, there really are only two types of checking accounts: a regular checking account or a special checking accunt. A **regular checking account** requires you to maintain a minimum balance; otherwise, the bank charges a service fee against your account. There may also be an additional fee charged after the number of checks you write exceeds a given number. Some of these accounts allow the customer to write checks for an amount greater than that in the account. This service, commonly called **overdraft protection** amounts to a personal loan. A fee is usually charged for each such check written, as well as interest on the amount itself. A **special checking account** requires no minimum deposit. The cost of this service usually includes a monthly maintenance fee plus a fee for each check written. This type of account is appropriate for a person who writes checks infrequently.

negotiable order of with-drawal (NOW): a checking account that pays interest

NOW accounts. A **NOW account** combines checking and savings into a single financial service. As a savings account, a NOW account earns interest. As a checking account, it allows you to write checks, or negotiable orders of withdrawal, against the funds in the account. The negotiable order of withdrawal looks and functions like a check. A minimum balance is usually required in order to avoid a monthly service fee, which is typically a few dollars each month. It may be profitable to transfer funds from a passbook account into the NOW account in order to maintain the required balance and avoid the fee. Even though the interest paid on NOW accounts is usually slightly less than a passbook account, the free checking service more than makes up the monetary difference.

A NOW account should not be confused with a share-draft account offered by credit unions. A share-draft account typically does not require a minimum balance, nor does it charge per-check fees.

Additional services. Financial intermediaries can meet other financial needs that you have. Installment, business, and mortgage loans are available at most, as well as major credit card. (In Chapter 6 we discuss getting and using loans and credit in detail, and in Chapter 11 we explore mortgages.) A safe-deposit box, available at most commerical banks, mutual savings banks, and savings and loan associations, is the best place to store documents that cannot be replaced or duplicated.

Most banks have automated teller machines (ATMs) that provide twenty-four-hour service.

*electronic funds transfer
(EFT):* use of automated
teller machines, telephones,
and computers for deposits,
withdrawals, loan payments,
and movement of money
from one account to another

Finally, most financial intermediaries offer **electronic funds transfer (EFT)**, using tools such as an automated teller machine, telephone, and computer. The most common form of this service is the **automated teller machine** (ATM), which allows for deposits, withdrawals, loan payments, and transfers from one account to another within a specific financial intermediary. For example, a person could go to the ATM at the financial institution or at a convenient location, such as a grocery store, shopping center, or airport, and deposit a payroll check, make a loan payment to the financial intermediary, as well as a credit card payment, and get some cash back. To use this service, which is available 24 hours a day, a customer need only insert a special **debit card** into the machine, enter a personal identification code, and then indicate the desired transaction. The debit card immediately deducts the money from the depositor's account.

BOX 5.3   THE 24-HOUR CONNECTION

"The stupid machine just ate my card!" In the early days of ATMs this was a very common problem. The plastic card got warped in pockets or wallets, and couldn't be removed from teller machines once inserted. Because of improvements in the system—such as needing to insert the cards only an inch or two, without letting go—and a better understanding on the part of consumers, ATMs are far more satisfactory.

What should you look for in an ATM system?

1. Find locations that have more than one machine; this will improve the odds that an ATM is operational when you need it at midnight.
2. Machines that look clean on the outside will probably be well maintained mechanically as well.
3. Can you get information at that location? Is there a service phone or interactive computer to provide assistance if you need help completing a transaction?
4. Is the location safe? Is there a service phone or video camera available to provide protection from theft?
5. What about fees? Are there charges for the transactions?

How can you protect yourself?

1. Select a personal identification number (PIN) different from your address, birth date, telephone number, or Social Security number, making it more difficult for a thief to use your card.
2. Never write your PIN on the card, or carry it with the card. Memorize it.
3. Never put your PIN on the outside of a deposit slip, envelope, or the like.
4. Examine all receipts and card statements as soon as possible.
5. Know where your card is at all times, and report its loss as soon as possible. Most card fraud occurs within 48 hours of loss.

If you report an ATM card missing before it is used without your permission, the card issuer cannot hold you responsible for unauthorized withdrawals. If you report the loss within two business days after you realize the card is missing, you will be responsible for only $50 at most for unauthorized use. If you wait longer, you could be held responsible for up to $500. And if you do not report an unauthorized use or transfer within 60 days after your statement is mailed to you, you risk unlimited loss.

The same debit card may be used to make purchases directly in some stores, eliminating the need to write a check. Box 5.3 provides more information about using an ATM card.

A newer version of EFT allows you to pay bills owed to companies other than the specific financial intermediary that services you, simply by calling the financial intermediary over the telephone and indicating from a previously composed list, which bills are to be paid and in what amounts—$50 to the phone company, $35 to ABC department store, etc. This eliminates the time and effort on your part to write the checks, and saves the institution the cost of clearing the checks. At the end of the month, your account statement lists all the telephone transactions made. Some people are accomplishing the same thing using personal computers or an ordinary television set with a special key pad. As more people become comfortable with EFT, the availability of these services will become more prevalent.

BANKING AND BILL PAYING

Once you have money in a checking, share draft, or NOW account, you will be given printed checks. These checks have your account number on them and will be numbered sequentially, or will have a space for you to do this. The numbers will help you sort the checks at a later date or identify a lost or stolen check. Most people have their name and address printed on the check as well, for further identification.

Check Processing

magnetic ink character recognition (MICR): a string of numbers or code printed in magnetic ink at the lower left bottom of a check, identifying your bank, branch, and account; it is used to debit your account

At the bottom of the check on the left-hand side, you will notice a line of code (see Figure 5.3). This is called **MICR** encoding, or **magnetic ink character recognition**. The numbers are printed in a magnetic ink in a shape that can be read by machine. The first number of the code indicates the branch of your bank, the second is the code for your financial intermediary itself, and the third is your account number. When your check is processed, electronic equipment scans the code, debits your account, and sorts the check for distribution, all in a matter of seconds. The data are used later to help create your **monthly statement**, or record of account transactions. The monthly statement must be verified for accuracy, and your records must be reconciled with it.

Millions of checks are written across the United States every day on bank accounts. Each check must be sent to the bank on which it was drawn for final payment. This process of making withdrawals, debits, and recording the transactions, is called *clearing*. This is done without actually moving money from one bank or one state to another. We will explain as simply as possible how this is done.

FIGURE 5.3
Check-writing tips.
Always initial any
changes, and do not
leave blank spaces
around the payee or the
amount.

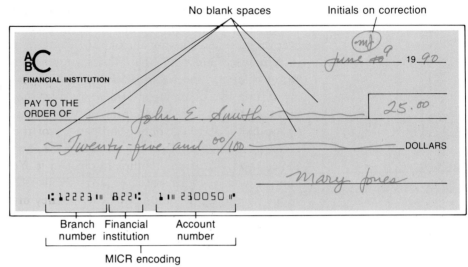

clearing house: in banking, a
central location responsible
for sorting checks and returning them to the appropriate
financial institution and
branch

At the end of a business day each branch of each financial intermediary
sorts the checks that have been deposited or cashed there that day. A tally
is made of their monetary value. The checks and tally are then sent to the
institution's main branch or head office. All are sorted and tallied again.
Any checks that are drawn on that financial institution are sent back to the
appropriate branch. All others are exchanged at a **clearing house**, so each
check eventually returns to the appropriate institution and branch. The
Fed serves as a clearing house for most interstate checks, but locally
deposited checks are often cleared by a local bank network. At that point
the check is sorted and money is deducted from the proper account. If
appropriate, the checks are filed to be returned to the drawer or depositor
with his or her monthly statement.

This is quite a process, isn't it? With so many steps, the process could
take one or two weeks to proceed from deposit to canceling. But today, on-
line computers considerably shorten the time. A check you write in the
afternoon may be cleared before you go to sleep that night. That's why it is
imperative to have sufficient funds to cover each check, to keep accurate
records in your checkbook, and to check your monthly account statement
as soon as it arrives. If you find any errors, correct the checkbook balance.
If you find an error in the statement, report it to the bank as soon as
possible.

You will want to reconcile your checkbook as soon as you receive your
statement. This will diminish the number of checks outstanding. It will
also facilitate matters if a mistake is found and may prevent you from
overdrawing the account.

**Other Ways to
Pay Bills**

Besides personal checks, you have several other types from which to choose. These include certified checks, money orders, drafts, telegraphic transfers, and travelers' checks.

A **certified check** is a personal check for which payment is guaranteed by the financial intermediary. To get this, take your completed check to a bank official, who will check that enough money is on deposit to cover the check and will then immediately deduct the amount from your account. The money then becomes the property of the bank until the check is presented for payment. The face of the check will be stamped "Certified" or "Accepted," and the official will sign it. You will then be charged a small fee for this service.

A second method of payment is a **money order**. This is used often by people who do not have a personal checking account. Although there are several types of money orders, all are checks made payable to a specific person for a specific amount of money. With any type of money order it is important to obtain a receipt or duplicate copy. If the money order is lost, the value will be refunded or a new money order will be issued upon presentation of the receipt.

When you travel away from your own community, it may be difficult to cash a personal check, but carrying large amounts of cash isn't safe either. There is a substitute for both, called **traveler's checks**. Traveler's checks can be purchased in denominations of $10, $20, $50, and $100. When you buy them, you will be required to sign each check in the presence of the issuing agent. When you cash a traveler's check, you must sign it a second time. The person cashing the check needs to verify that the signatures are identical.

The best thing about traveler's checks is that they can be replaced or totally refunded if they are lost or stolen. Like personal checks, each traveler's check is sequentially numbered. As with personal checks, after cashing each traveler's check, you will want to make a record of the transaction. When you purchase them, you will be given a list of these numbers for your own records. Be sure to keep this list separate from the checks themselves so that you can make a claim and be reimbursed if the checks are lost or stolen.

A **bank wire service** can transfer large amounts of money across the country or even to another country. Money can be electronically transferred to another financial institution, where a cashier's check is issued. The fee for this service varies.

A quick but expensive method to send money is the **telegraphic transfer**. This is an order from one telegraph office to another to pay a fixed amount of money to a specific individual or business. This transaction can take as little as two hours. To ensure that only the payee is paid, the drawer can include a question that only the payee could answer. This test question can relate to personal data, such as a maiden name, or a personal experience.

SUMMARY

We have presented a short explanation of the monetary system in America. You have learned that money is something that is accepted for payment of goods and services. And that money fulfills three basic functions: a medium of exchange, a store of value, and a unit of account. You have learned where our paper money comes from and why it has value. This value is partially protected by the Federal Reserve, the chief monetary authority in the United States. The Fed plays a very important role in our economy, the most important being to control the amount of money available at any time.

After our discussion of money, we explored financial intermediaries, the link between consumers and our monetary system. We discovered that the Monetary Control Act of 1980 provided for the deregulation of the banking industry, resulting in expanded banking options for consumers. When selecting a financial intermediary, consumers need to consider safety, services, convenience, and cost.

QUESTIONS

1. What is the significance of the Monetary Control Act of 1980?
2. What is the Federal Reserve System, and how does it function?
3. How does the Fed influence the money supply? Interest rates?
4. What are the factors to consider when selecting a financial intermediary?

REFERENCES AND READINGS

"Banking: A Three Part Series." *Consumer Reports.* July 1988.

Frantz, Douglas, and Furlong, Tom. "Contagion of Ailing S&Ls Poses Threat to Entire Thrift Industry." *Los Angeles Times*, January 3, 1988, part IV, p. 1.

Galbraith, John Kenneth. *Economics in Perspective: A Critical History.* Boston: Houghton Mifflin, 1987.

Hedberg, Augustin. "Ways to Get the Most from Your Bank," *Money*, March 1988, p. 96.

Klein, Robert, and the editors of *Money* magazine. *The Money Book of Money: Your Personal Financial Planner*. Boston: Little, Brown, 1987.

Morse, Richard L. D., and McDermott, Pat. *NOW Accounts: Cost and Benefits for Consumers.* Kansas State University, March 1981.

Sing, Bill. "More People Banking on Credit Unions." *Los Angeles Times*, July 12, 1987, part IV, p. 1.

Yeager, Robert C. "How Safe Is Your Bank?" *Reader's Digest*, March 1988.

Chapter Six

CREDIT: BUY NOW, PAY MORE LATER

☐ An Overview of Credit: How Big? How Much? How Important?
☐ The Benefits of Credit
☐ Costs of Consumer Credit
☐ Sources of Credit
☐ Applying for Credit
☐ The Equal Credit Opportunity Act
☐ The Fair Credit Billing Act
☐ How Much Credit Equals Too Much Debt?
☐ Bankruptcy: The Last Resort

DID YOU KNOW THAT . . .

. . . about one-third of all retail sales in the United States involve some form of credit?

. . . more than 75 percent of American families have at least one credit card?

. . . all lenders are required to disclose in writing both the absolute cost (finance charge) and the relative cost (annual percentage rate) to a prospective borrower before any agreement is signed?

. . . credit card accounts with identical interest rates can have widely different finance charges?

131

. . . if you are denied credit, you have the right to know why?

. . . if you receive damaged goods or poor-quality services purchased with a credit card, you can get a refund from your credit card company?

. . . bankruptcy allows you to retain some property but does not cancel all obligations?

credit: an arrangement to receive cash, goods, or services in the present in return for payment in the future

Few topics are closer to a consumer's heart than the availability and use of credit. Some commentators have argued that without the massive transformation of the way we buy goods and services, the age of high mass consumption would never have become a reality. Our economy would have had the ability to mass produce and mass market its products, but consumers would have had a difficult time purchasing them. Vast financial empires have been established in our economy to give consumers **credit**— an arrangement to receive cash, goods, or services in the present and pay for them in the future. Debt—the amount of money a consumer owes— has become a way of life for most Americans. In this chapter we deal at some length with the hows and whys of credit.

Before we begin, we should point out that we are not dealing with all types of loans or consumer debts. We are primarily concerned with consumer credit as it pertains to borrowing for noninvestment purposes. Installment debt and credit card charges are two examples of noninvestment borrowing. We are not talking about borrowing money to invest in the stock market or to buy a home; these purchases should produce a return in excess of the original purchase price and as such are not relevant here. (We deal with home mortgages and investment loans in Chapters 11 and 16, respectively.) The primary objective of consumer credit is the enjoyment we receive from consumption, not the increased income we get from wise investments.

After reading this chapter, you should have a better understanding of your credit rights and responsibilities, such that when you face credit problems, you will be in a better position to make informed decisions. To improve your credit decision-making skills, we have designed this chapter to cover specific problems as well as general topics. We begin with an overview of the role of credit in the American economy. Then we present some information on the benefits and costs of credit, so that when you come to the cost–benefit step of the decision-making model, you will be able to weigh all the factors *before* you make a choice. After the cost–benefit sections, we outline some of the major sources of credit, the application process, and steps to take if you have a credit problem. Finally, we offer some guidelines on self-disciplined credit limits and how to work your way out of credit problems, including the last resort: personal bankruptcy.

AN OVERVIEW OF CREDIT: HOW BIG? HOW MUCH? HOW IMPORTANT?

installment (closed-end) credit: loans that are set up to be repaid in set amounts at constant intervals over a period of time

In the not so distant past, *debt* was one of those four-letter words that was not used in public. Consumers were taught to be wary of debt and to avoid it at all costs. The maxim in *Hamlet*, "Neither a borrower, nor a lender be," was repeated and learned at a very tender age—for good reason. In Shakespeare's time, people were sent to debtor's prison if they were unable to pay their debts. Today, of course, these penalties have been erased, yet the sense of disapproval is ingrained, and some people still avoid debt out of fear of what might happen to them if they were unable to repay it. Consumer surveys continue to reveal a dread of credit among the general public. For example, a study conducted by the Survey Research Center at the University of Michigan showed that only a little more than 50 percent of those surveyed gave their unqualified approval to **installment (closed-end) credit**, that is, borrowing a certain amount of money and then repaying the debt with interest in equal monthly payments (installments) over a specific time period.

Despite their protests, however, consumers are using the vast credit network of banks, finance companies, credit unions, and other financial institutions to help them obtain goods and services in the present rather than in the future. As Figure 6.1 illustrates, consumer installment debt has been rising over the past 30 years, from less than $50 billion in 1958 to more than $650 billion in 1988. The burden of this debt on the average consumer's budget has also grown, as the percentages in Figure 6.1 show. In 1958, consumer installment debt represented about 11 percent of

FIGURE 6.1
The length of the bars expresses the amount of U.S. consumer installment debt in billions of dollars. The numbers in parentheses express consumer debt as a percentage of disposable income in ten-year increments, 1958 – 1988. (SOURCE: *Economic Report of the President* [Washington, D.C.: U.S. Government Printing Office, 1989].)

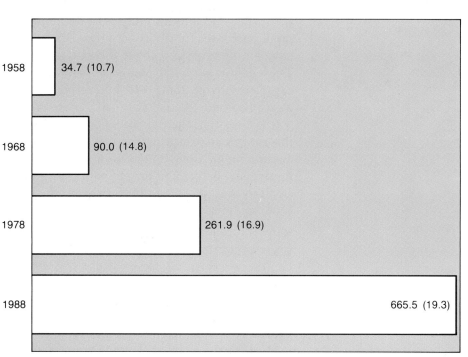

after-tax (disposable) income. This figure rose to almost 15 percent by 1968, and just under 17 percent by 1978. By 1988, consumer debt was more than 19 percent of consumer disposable income. As a nation of consumers, we are deeper in debt than ever before.

The rise in the amount of consumer installment debt and in the ratio of this debt to consumer income has led some credit executives to speak out on the subject. For example, Patricia Patterson, then legal counsel for the American Express Corporation, has warned us, "Credit can be sinister. Adults are like kids with their nose pressed up against the candy store window. You have to realize you have to stay within your means." Of course, it is difficult to heed this advice when at every turn we are being bombarded with invitations to join in the charge of the credit brigade. At the start of the 1990s, there were approximately 391 million credit cards worldwide, accounting for $450 billion in total spending. Even the Soviet Union has joined this capitalist crusade by agreeing to issue VISA cards to its citizens who travel abroad.

In the largest capitalist nation in the world, the United States, three out of every ten retail sales dollars are rung up with the help of credit. Is it any wonder, then, that the federal government has also gotten into the act? The Treasury Department has contracts with four major banks to process VISA and MasterCard transactions for more then 40 federal agencies, ranging from the Agriculture Department to the U.S. Customs Service (*Los Angeles Times*, October 12, 1987). This means that you can use your credit cards to pay for a wide range of federal services and even fines. They also issued special MasterCards to 350,000 federal employees who make small purchases for the government. Of course, our nation's leaders may have a different view about the size of purchases from one you'd hold: They define a "small purchase" as anything less than $25,000. They expect to charge about $19 billion per year on these credit cards. (*U.S. News*, February 29, 1988).

It is clear that the pressure, both on the seller to provide credit and on the consumer to use it, has reached monumental proportions. But this doesn't mean that everyone of us is destined for wild spending and insolvency. Before you turn in your credit cards and swear off installment credit forever, you ought to learn about the benefits of credit. There can be good, sound reasons for seeking and obtaining credit.

THE BENEFITS OF CREDIT

Credit, like most inventions, is neither all bad nor all good. Used wisely, credit can be much more a benefit than a burden.

The benefits of credit depend on a consumer's life-style, values, and needs. Few consumers will consider all of the following advantages relevant to their personal circumstances, and not all forms of credit offer

---

BOX 6.1   CREDIT: A SUMMARY OF POTENTIAL CONSUMER BENEFITS AND COSTS

Benefits

1. Help in synchronizing income with life-cycle expenses
2. Forced savings
3. Emergency buying power
4. Help in taking advantage of inflation
5. Record keeping
6. Identification

Costs

1. Risk of insolvency
2. Reduced budget flexibility
3. Higher prices
4. Finance charges

---

all of these benefits. Nevertheless, these advantages are legitimate reasons for seeking and obtaining credit. Whenever credit appears to be one of the potential solutions to a consumer problem you have identified, you would do well to review these benefits to see whether credit can indeed be of some help. (You do not want to ignore the costs of consumer credit, of course. We consider this topic in the section following this one.) Box 6.1 presents a thumbnail sketch of these benefits and costs.

Synchronizing Income with Expenses

Although people may earn their incomes hourly or daily, the shortest pay periods are generally once a week, twice a month, or sometimes once a month. A monthly paycheck makes it especially difficult for one to meet daily expenses or to take advantage of clearance sales or bargains. Credit can be a dollar stretcher because it gives the consumer buying power for items discounted for a limited time. Thus, credit can help us satisfy a primary goal of budgeting: synchronizing income with expenses.

We can apply this principle to the consumer's life cycle as well. As we discussed in Chapter 2, a household's income is generally low in the early years and then builds as workers age and gain experience. For most occupations, late middle age is the time of peak earnings. Yet the need for income to support a household is often highest when the household is producing and nurturing children. Figure 6.2 illustrates a typical pattern of lifetime income and expenditures. Notice that in the earliest stage, expenditures of young households exceed income, and couples have to draw on their savings to make up the difference. During the family formation years, expenses continue to rise more rapidly than income. In fact, income may actually decline if the wife or the husband decides to leave the workforce for a while to rear the children. During this stage,

FIGURE 6.2
Example of a life-cycle income and expenditure pattern. Credit allows consumers some leeway in matching their needs for goods and services to their ability to pay for these commodities with current income. Of course, the economic problem is always important. For most consumers, wants will always exceed limited resources; nevertheless, the burden of the economic problem is generally more severe for younger families. For them, the judicious use of credit can become an asset rather than a liability. The wise use of credit can help a family over the inevitable hump of rising expenses and lagging income.

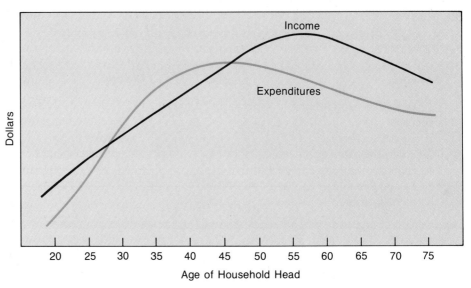

credit can play a crucial role in helping households cope with their needs. As the children grow up and establish households of their own, the life-cycle expenditure pattern levels off and may even decline. Meanwhile, the household is in its peak earning years. Both spouses may be working, and surplus income can then be used to repay old debts and establish a savings pool for the retirement years.

These patterns have been confirmed by studies at the University of Michigan's Survey Research Center. As part of their work on consumer finance, they interviewed a sample of families and then followed this cohort in later years. According to their findings, the best customers for consumer installment loans are householders in the 25-to-54 age group. While this age group comprises less than 40 percent of the population, it accounts for more than 80 percent of all consumer debt in the United States (Schwartz, 1988).

Forced Savings

Because many consumers find it difficult to set up a budget and save money, credit purchases can be a source of forced saving. Consumer researchers have found that many people borrow money to purchase something—a set of encyclopedias, for example—even though they have enough money in their savings account to purchase it outright. Since the interest rate on the loan is generally greater than the interest rate on savings, it seems illogical to choose to lose the difference. Why do consumers do this? The answer given most frequently is that they fear they wouldn't be able to build their savings back to the previous level. However, making room in one's budget to pay off a loan amounts to letting oneself be forced to save after the fact. (For the same reason, some workers choose to have an excess amount of taxes taken out of their paychecks. Even though they earn no interest on the money withheld, they find the procedure is a form of forced savings.) Obviously, planned savings are preferable to forced savings, but forced savings are better than no savings at all.

Emergency Fund

In Chapter 4 we stressed the importance of having a fund of ready cash for emergencies. If you are sick for a long time or lose your job, you may be forced into a financial bind. Credit should not be used in place of an emergency fund, but it can reinforce your savings. A good credit rating and a few closely supervised credit cards can help a household that is temporarily in distress. We cannot, however, overemphasize the importance of knowing the difference between a real emergency and a simple desire to consume more. Like the little boy who cried wolf once too often, if you use your credit in nonemergency situations, no one will be around to bail you out of a real emergency. If consumers exhaust their financial resources by transforming all their wants into needs and then paying for them with credit, they mortgage their future earning power. This can lead to financial disaster when something unexpected happens.

Inflation and Credit

real interest rate: the difference between the nominal rate of interest as stated on your loan and the inflation rate

In the late 1970s and early 1980s inflation reached such a high rate that it became advantageous for some consumers to buy on credit. You recall from Chapter 3 that inflation can be defined as either a rise in the general level of prices or a fall in the purchasing power of money. If the rate of inflation is higher than the interest rate and if your income is rising with the general rise in prices, it may make good sense to borrow to buy something you really want, because the loan's **real interest rate**, i.e., the interest rate adjusted for inflation, will be negative. In effect, you will be borrowing at a negative rate of interest, because the money you use to pay off the loan in the future will be worth less than the money you borrow today. This is a highly unusual circumstance (creditors generally figure on a reward for giving you the use of their money); nevertheless, it can happen.

The real interest rate on any loan can be calculated by subtracting the annual inflation rate from the nominal interest rate stated in the contract. A 5 percent nominal rate becomes a minus-2 percent when the inflation rate is 7 percent. Here is the formula:

$$\text{nominal interest rate} - \text{inflation rate} = \text{real interest rate}$$

In our example: $5\% - 7\% = -2\%$.

Lenders, of course, are also aware of the real rate of interest, and they try to take it into account. But sometimes they offer loans with very low interest rates to attract buyers. New car dealers often offer such incentives so that the real interest rate is actually negative. For example, a 1.9 percent loan rate amounts to a minus-3.1 percent real rate if inflation averages 5 percent over the loan term $(1.9\% - 5\% = -3.1\%)$. Of course these below-market loans are not such a bargain if they are available only on less desirable models.

Record Keeping, Identification, and the Cashless Society

Credit cards have three advantages that normal installment credit does not: They provide record keeping and identification and minimize cash transactions. Consumers make hundreds of transactions every month; purchasing food, buying gasoline, and paying rent are only a few of them. Many people find it advantageous to have a record of these transactions. Checking accounts can help; so can credit cards. Every month the credit card company sends a statement showing where you made a credit purchase and how much you paid. You also receive a receipt from the merchant when you make the purchase. Receipts from the merchant have a way of disappearing, but the monthly statement provides a valuable record of your purchases that can help you in establishing your budget and preparing your tax return or other records of expenses.

When you make a purchase by check, merchants frequently ask for some form of identification and some assurance that you are a good credit risk. Properly validated and up-to-date credit cards can provide this assurance. Credit cards can also limit the need to carry large amounts of cash, because you can use them in place of cash. The use of credit cards has become so commonplace in hotels and motels that it is difficult to check in without presenting one. Hotel keepers often run a blank charge on your card to ensure that you don't leave without paying for the room.

COSTS OF CONSUMER CREDIT

Now that we have outlined many of the benefits of obtaining credit, we will look at the other side of the coin: the costs to the consumer. As we emphasized in Chapter 1, only by weighing the costs and benefits of a particular action can you come to a rational decision. Credit is no exception to the decision-making rule.

The Risk of Insolvency

Whenever you apply for or use credit to purchase something, you should always keep this question in mind: "Can I afford it?" In this world of choices, decisions about *what* to buy can be so overwhelming that people don't pay enough attention to *how* they'll pay. This can become a real problem when a consumer discovers that, after paying creditors at the beginning of the month, there simply is not enough income to buy even the bare necessities. If what you owe exceeds what you make and if there is no way to pay off your debts, you end up in a condition called financial insolvency. We will discuss this problem in greater detail later in this chapter.

Budget Commitment and Flexibility

Warning signs do appear well before a consumer becomes financially insolvent. One of these warning signs is the degree of flexibility in the monthly budget. As consumers take on more installment debt, they begin to notice that they don't have as much discretionary income as they once had. Have you ever heard someone say, "Oh, we would like to do that, but it's the end of the month and we just can't afford it"? This kind of statement should be like a smoke alarm going off in the middle of the night: It should alert all the members of the household to the danger of impending bankruptcy. Loss of flexibility means that the household in question is walking a tightrope; one false move, one tiny slip, could cause disaster. As a rule of thumb, if one spends more than 20 percent of after-tax income to pay off short-term debt, one is on that tightrope and could be in danger of falling off.

Limited Choice and Higher Costs

Credit can also limit your options in deciding where to shop. This limitation is not as severe in the case of universal charge cards like VISA or MasterCard, but it may apply to individual store accounts: You can get locked into shopping at stores that have already given you a credit account. Of course, you might be able to take advantage of special sales and bargains at those stores, but you also might be less likely to shop around. No store has a monopoly on bargains. Hitching your credit wagon to only a few retailers limits your choice, and you may end up paying more for goods and services.

The problem of paying more is especially applicable to those with lower incomes who use credit as a form of forced saving. Some merchants even advertise "easy credit" to entice the unwary. In general, if a retailer is advertising his or her willingness to offer loans, it generally means that the prices of both the merchandise and the loans are higher than those of competitors.

Finance Charges

In the final analysis, you get credit by promising to pay in the future for something you receive in the present. For this service, the lender charges a fee to cover the costs of maintaining the credit staff, obtaining the money, providing for losses on unrepaid loans, and earning a profit for the company. The fee you pay for the conveniences of obtaining credit is called a finance charge.

annual percentage rate
(APR): the finance charge
over a full year expressed as
a percentage of the loan; the
APR must reflect all the costs
of the loan, as required by
the Truth in Lending Act

The **finance charge** is the total dollar amount you pay to use credit. It includes interest on the money borrowed, service charges for processing the loan, and even insurance premiums, if they are credit related and required by the lender. Under the Truth in Lending Act provisions of the Consumer Credit Protection Act of 1968, a creditor must tell the borrower, in writing and before any agreement is signed, the exact amount of the finance charge in dollars and cents.

In addition to informing the prospective borrower of the exact amount of the finance charge, the lender must also convert this charge to an **annual percentage rate (APR)**, the percentage cost or relative cost of credit per year. The higher the APR, the greater the cost of the loan to the consumer. The APRs for two loans of equal amounts from different lenders can vary, depending on service charges, interest rates, or even methods of structuring the repayment. When you are shopping for a loan, always compare finance charges and APRs.

Table 6.1 reinforces the idea that consumers can save money by comparing finance charges and APRs. It illustrates the total costs of a $2,000 loan for various interest rates and time periods. As you can see, the shorter the loan period, the smaller the finance charge. This makes sense, because the charge is calculated to compensate the lender for giving up the buying power of that money for a period of time. The longer the loan period, the greater the finance charge. For example, an 18 percent loan incurs a $200.32 finance charge on $2,000 repaid in one year, but it incurs a $602.80 finance charge if repayment is over a three-year-period. Finance charges are always lower on shorter-term loans when APRs are equal. Another advantage of a shorter-term loan is that if you choose to prepay the

TABLE 6.1 Monthly Payments, Finance Charges, and Total Cost of a $2,000 Loan, Various Repayment Periods and Annual Percentage Rates

APR (%)	Length of Loan (years)	Monthly Payment ($)	Total Finance Charge ($)	Total Cost ($)
12	1	177.70	132.40	2,132.40
12	2	94.15	259.60	2,259.60
12	3	66.43	391.48	2,391.48
15	1	180.52	166.24	2,166.24
15	2	96.98	327.52	2,327.52
15	3	69.34	496.24	2,496.24
18	1	183.36	200.32	2,200.32
18	2	99.84	396.16	2,396.16
18	3	72.30	602.80	2,602.80
22	1	187.18	246.16	2,246.16
22	2	103.75	490.00	2,490.00
22	3	76.38	749.68	2,749.68

BOX 6.2 **THE RULE OF 78: WHAT HAPPENS IF YOU PAY A LOAN OFF EARLY?**

The finance charge on an installment loan is smaller than you would suspect if you were to simply multiply the APR by the principal for only one month and then make monthly payments that would reduce the principal and pay the finance charge in equal amounts. The fact is, a larger portion of your monthly payment goes to pay interest in the early months of your loan than in later months. If you decide to pay off the loan early, your creditor will have to calculate how much of a finance charge you still owe.

On a one-year loan, creditors sometimes use the **rule of 78**. That is, they assign 78 parts to a finance charge for a 12 month loan, based on the fact that $1 + 2 + 3 + \cdots + 11 + 12 = 78$. The first month, you pay $\frac{12}{78}$ of the finance charge. The second month, you pay $\frac{11}{78}$ of the finance charge, and so on, until the twelfth month, when you pay only $\frac{1}{78}$ of the charge. The rule of 78 means that you will pay considerably more interest in the early months of your loan. For example, say you pay a 12-month loan off in six months. Common sense would argue that you owe only 50 percent of the finance charge, because six months is half of the loan period. However, according to the rule, you owe $\frac{57}{78}$ of the finance charge $(12 + 11 + 10 + 9 + 8 + 7 = 57)$, or about 73 percent. Applying the rule of 78 to the first loan in Table 6.1, if you decided to pay off your 12 percent loan after six months, you would have to pay $96.65 in finance charges $(0.73 \times \$132.40)$, not the $61.20 you might think you are supposed to pay.

For loans of two or three years, the rule of 78 does not apply because there are 24 or 36 payments instead of 12. But the basic principle of charging a higher portion of the finance charge earlier in the loan period does apply. For loans of 24 monthly installments, most financial institutions use the rule of 300, because $1 + 2 + 3 + 4 + \cdots + 23 + 24 = 300$.

For 36 monthly installments, the rule of 666 applies, because $1 + 2 + 3 + 4 + \cdots + 35 + 36 = 666$. If you choose to repay a three-year installment loan at the end of two months, you would owe $\frac{71}{666}$ of the finance charge $([35 + 36]/666)$ in addition to the principal.

Using Table 6.1 and the rule of 78, calculate how much you would owe in finance charges if you chose to pay off a 12-month, 22 percent, $2,000 loan in six months. How much would you owe if the creditor prorated the finance charge equally for all months?

Which rule would a creditor use to estimate the finance charge owed on an early payoff for a two-year loan that was to be repaid in 24 monthly installments?

loan, the finance charge is less. For further details on how finance charges are computed on early payoffs, see Box 6.2.

The finance charge also varies with the size of the APR. The higher the APR, the greater the finance charge. According to Table 6.1, a $2,000 loan for two years at 12 percent interest would cost the borrower $259.60 in finance charges. At 22 percent interest, the same loan's finance charge would almost double.

When looking at the APR and the associated finance charges in Table 6.1, notice another interesting feature of installment loans: The amount of the finance charge is not equal to the annual percentage rate times the size of the loan. For example, in line 1 of the table, the finance charge for a $2,000 loan at 12 percent APR, repayable in 12 monthly installments, is not $240 (12 percent of $2,000); it is only $132.40. The difference exists because the consumer does not have the use of the $2,000 for the entire year. Repayment of the loan begins the month after the loan was made, so the consumer has the full amount for only one month. Each payment further reduces the principal on which the interest is calculated.

As a shortcut method for converting the finance charge to an APR for a monthly installment loan, multiply the finance charge by 24 and then divide the product by the value of the loan times the number of payments plus 1:

$$\frac{24F}{L(n + 1)}$$

where F = the finance charge

   L = the value of the loan (the principal)

   n = the total number of monthly payments

For example, if you were to get a $500 loan that was to be repaid in 12 monthly installments and the finance charge was $100, you would pay $50 per month, or $600. This might seem like an APR of 20 percent, because $100 is 20 percent of $500. But if you plug these numbers into the formula, you discover:

$$\frac{24 \times 100}{500 \,(12 + 1)} = \frac{2,400}{6,500} = 36.9\% \text{ interest}$$

So the APR is almost double what it appears to be if you simply divide the finance charge by the amount of the loan. The difference exists, again, because the borrower has the use of the entire $500 only for the first month; thereafter, part of the principal is paid back. On the average for an installment loan, the borrower has the use of only one-half of the loan over the life of the contract. We will return to this fact later when we discuss borrowing from friends and relatives.

The Cost of Open-End Credit

The preceding discussion works well in determining the cost of closed-end (installment) loans, that is, loans that are set up to be repaid in set amounts at constant intervals over a fixed period of time. But a growing portion of consumer debt now takes the form of what was once called revolving charges or **revolving credit** and is now often termed **open-end credit**. Open-end credit can be used over and over as long as the consumer does not exceed a prearranged borrowing limit. Open-end credit includes bank credit cards, department store charge plates, and check overdraft accounts that allow you to write checks for more than your actual balance in the bank.

open-end credit: a line of credit that may be used repeatedly up to some specified limit. There is no preestablished payment schedule, although there often is a required monthly minimum payment. There is no definite period of time for repaying the entire loan.

The Truth-in-Lending Act applies to open-end credit just as it does to installment credit. But in addition to clearly detailing their finance charge and the annual percentage rate, these creditors must also tell you (a) when finance charges begin on your account and (b) the method of calculating the finance charge. The first requirement tells you how much time you have to pay your bill before a finance charge is levied. Some creditors, for example, may give you 30 days to pay your balance before imposing a finance charge. However, this free ride is rapidly becoming extinct, because it amounts to an interest-free loan from the creditor to the consumer that, in times of high inflation and high interest rates, are extremely costly to the lender.

Methods of calculating finance charges. The method of calculating the finance charge can affect the cost of credit to the consumer. The three most common methods are adjusted balance, previous balance, and average daily balance.

Under the **adjusted balance method**, creditors add finance charges only after subtracting all payments made during the billing period. This amounts to giving the consumers up to 30 days of free credit if they pay off their bills every month. To see how the adjusted balance method works, assume that a consumer owes $500 on a credit card on which the interest charge is 1.5 percent per month (18 percent APR). If the consumer makes a $400 payment to the company, the interest charge that appears on the next statement will be $1.50. The company will have calculated this $1.50 charge by subtracting the $400 payment from the $500 owed and then applying the 1.5 percent interest charge to the $100 outstanding balance.

According to a recent survey, about 39 percent of all credit card owners take advantage of the adjusted balance method by paying off the entire balance before the billing period is over (*Wall Street Journal*, March 7, 1988). This means that the consumer does not owe any interest on charges made during the previous 30 days. Since there is a cost of making 30-day, interest-free loans to consumers, many credit card companies now charge an annual fee so that the consumer pays for the privilege of carrying the card, regardless of the number of times it is used. Still other credit card companies are changing their interest computation procedures to the previous balance method.

The **previous balance method** gives no credit to consumers for payments made during the billing period. This means that even if you pay off your balance in full, you still owe interest on the charges you made during the month. It is as if you have borrowed a sum of money for an entire month regardless of any payments you make. For example, if a consumer pays $400 on a $500 outstanding balance to a company charging an 18 percent APR and using the previous balance method for computing

TABLE 6.2 Three Methods of Computing Finance Charges on Open-End (Revolving) Accounts

	Adjusted Balance	Previous Balance	Average Daily Balance
Monthly interest rate	1.5%	1.5%	1.5%
Previous balance	$400	$400	$400
Payments made on the fifteenth day	$300	$300	$300
Interest charge	$1.50	$6.00	$3.75
	($100 × 1.5%)	($400 × 1.5%)	(Average balance of $250 × 1.5%)

SOURCE: Board of Governors of the Federal Reserve System, *Consumer Handbook to Credit Protection Laws*, Washington, D.C.

finance charges, the consumer will owe $7.50 in interest for the month. This is five times the amount that would be owed if the credit card company used the adjusted balance method. The reason for the difference is that the previous balance method does not subtract any payments before computing the interest owed. Therefore, in our example, the 1.5 percent monthly interest rate is applied to the entire $500 balance 1.5% × $500 = $7.50).

A third plan for computing interest charges is called the **average daily balance method**. It requires creditors to compute the outstanding balance each day in the billing period by adding charges and subtracting payments on the day they are received. These daily balances are then totaled and divided by the number of days in the billing period to give an average daily balance. The APR is then applied to this balance. For example, if the previous balance is $500 and the monthly interest charge is 1.5 percent, and if the consumer pays $400 on the fifteenth day of a 30-day billing period during which no further purchases are made against the charge card, the interest would be $4.50 based on an average daily balance of $300 ([$500 × 15 days] + [$100 × 15 days] ÷ 30 days = $300).

Under this system, making your payment early in the cycle lowers your interest cost, whereas delaying payment increases it. If you do not pay until the last day of the cycle, this method amounts to the same cost as the previous balance method. With the average daily balance method, though, the interest cost is partly based on consumer decision making. A comparison of the three plans is made in Table 6.2.

Credit Cards: Cost and Convenience

If you are considering getting a credit card, you are not alone. Credit card balances were the fastest growing form of consumer debt in the 1980s. According to a study done by Federal Reserve economist Paul Watro

(1988), they were also the most profitable part of banks' loan portfolios: The annual pretax earnings on bank credit card balances averaged 3.6 percent, while in the same period banks earned only 2.4 percent on mortgages, and 1.4 percent on commercial loans. Watro finds that many

TABLE 6.3 The Major Credit Cards and How They Compare

	VISA	MasterCard	American Express	Discover
Issuer	More than 20,000 financial institutions affiliated with VISA USA, San Francisco, CA	More than 16,000 financial institutions affiliated with Interbank Card Association, New York, NY	American Express, New York, NY 10004	Greenwood Trust, Newark, DE
Approximate number of cardholders worldwide	165,000,000	144,000,000	29,000,000	25,000,000
Approximate number of retail merchants worldwide	5,741,000	5,945,000	2,200,000	800,000
Minimum income to get card	Set by issuing bank	Set by issuing bank	$24,000	Set on individual basis
Annual fee	Generally $15 to $25 when charged; sometimes free	Same as VISA	$45 for basic card	None
Average credit limit	About $2,500	About $2,500	No preset limit	About $2,500
Extended payments permitted?	Yes	Yes	Airline tickets only	Yes
Annual interest rate	Set by issuer; typically 17% to 19.8%, but some are variable	Same as VISA	None	19.8%
Cash advance	Generally from designated automated teller machines (ATMs)	Same as VISA	At designated ATMs and at Amexco offices	At designated ATMs and all Sears stores
Special features	Some donate part of fee to specific charity; others offer traveler's insurance and/or frequent-flyer miles	Same as VISA	Offers some insurance coverage	Cash-back bonus of up to 1% on annual purchases
Check-cashing privileges	No special privileges, but may be very helpful in establishing creditworthiness	Same as VISA	Up to $1,000 per week at Amexco offices; smaller amounts at hotels and airlines	Same as VISA and MasterCard

banks are targeting high-risk consumers and charging higher fees for their credit cards.

For a number of reasons, then, you would do well to read each credit card's disclosure statements. Look at their APRs, their computational methods, their annual fees, and their service charges. No federal law limits the annual percentage rate that a creditor can charge, but some states do have **usury laws**, which limit the maximum interest rate that banks can charge. Arkansas, for example, prohibits banks from charging more than five percentage points above the Federal Reserve's *discount rate*, the interest rate the Fed charges banks that wish to borrow directly from our nation's central bank. In 1989 the discount rate was 6.5 percent, so the maximum legal credit card rate in Arkansas was 11.5 percent, the lowest rate in the United States. Despite the differences in interest rates and fees, industry surveys indicate that 25 percent of credit card holders do not know their card rates, and 60 percent believe that most banks charge about the same rates (*Wall Street Journal*, March 19, 1987). One consumer, asked by a *Wall Street Journal* reporter to explain the rate she was paying for a credit card, said, "I have no idea how much my interest rate is. It doesn't say on here [the card]. Well, as long as I can buy things with it, who cares?"

For consumers who do care, the *Wall Street Journal* publishes a monthly table of selected bank credit card interest rates and annual fees. The table appears in the second week of each month and lists the 25 banks with the lowest VISA and MasterCard interest rates. It also shows the rates for the ten largest credit card issuers who solicit customers nationally with massive direct-mail compaigns.

Table 6.3 summarizes the major credit cards and compares their features and costs. Some credit cards are accepted at more places than others. Some have annual fees, credit limits, and extended payment plans. As a rational decision maker, you should treat the decision to seek credit as you would any other consumer problem:

1. *Identify the problem.* Why do you think you need credit? For example, you may find it difficult to check into a hotel without a card or to carry enough cash for a long trip.

2. *Determine how your values and goals may limit your options.* Do you have any reservations about owing money? Are you able to handle your debts in a responsible manner?

3. *Collect information about various credit cards.* How many and what kinds of retailers accept the card? Do you have enough income to qualify? What are the credit limits and fees associated with the card? What are the interest rates, and how are the finance charges computed? The information in Table 6.3 and the *Wall Street Journal* should help with some of these questions.

4. *Weigh the costs and the benefits of the various cards and match them to your needs.* For example, if you will use the card primarily for

---

usury laws: legal constraints on how much interest can be charged on a loan; these ceilings have a tendency to contract the amount of money available to borrowers and to restrict the number of people who qualify for loans

identification, try to find one without an annual fee. These cards usually charge higher rates of interest. Of course, if you often carry a balance from month to month, check the APRs carefully and make sure you understand how the finance charge is calculated.

5. *Make a decision and apply for your card.* If you get a card, monitor your behavior and that of the credit card company to see that you made the right decision. If you do not get the card, you have the right to know why. We will discuss these rights later in this chapter, but you will probably want to apply to a second or possibly a third credit card company. Knowing why the first company turned you down could be important information.

6. *Review and evaluate your decision.* Save your monthly credit statements and periodically review them. Has your outstanding balance shown a tendency to get larger? What goods and services are you charging on your card? Are these the uses you envisioned when you first applied for the card? If you are having difficulty handling credit, these questions may make the reason more obvious. Perhaps you should consider putting the card away for a while. Try a "creditless" month or two.

7. *Take responsibility for your actions.* Do not blame the credit card company or advertising if you find it difficult to control your credit behavior. On the other hand, you have certain rights under the law, and you should not be afraid to use them if there is a billing error or if you have received poor service.

The Hidden Costs of Credit

Although the Truth in Lending Act requires a full disclosure of the terms of a credit contract, it is still possible for consumers to be confused by the fine print of the contract. There are a number of clauses that seem to defy comprehension and yet can have serious effects. Box 6.3 presents some of these, with ordinary English translations. You should be especially leery of acceleration clauses, which are found in many loan contracts. An **acceleration clause** requires that the entire debt become payable in one lump sum if the consumer fails to meet a single payment. Obviously, if you miss a payment because of financial difficulties, you are not likely to be able to pay off the entire loan when the next payment is due. This may mean that whatever you purchased on credit will be repossessed. Furthermore, if the item cannot be sold for the amount you owe, you may be held liable for the difference.

SOURCES OF CREDIT

Now that you understand the costs as well as the benefits of credit, you may be interested in learning about the major sources of consumer credit. In the subsections that follow, we will list and evaluate where you can go in your search for credit. Table 6.4 lists the major holders of installment

BOX 6.3 DO YOU SPEAK CREDIT?

The following credit-language translations were done by the Federal Trade Commission Bureau of Consumer Protection. They transformed legal jargon into understandable English. Many standard-form contracts contain these provisions, but consumers frequently overlook their importance until the lender calls attention to them.

Acceleration Clause

Contract Language: Default in the payment of any installment of the principal balance or charges hereof or any part of either shall, at the option of the holder hereof, render the entire unpaid principal balance hereof and accrued charges thereon, at once due and payable.

Translation: If I miss a payment, you can make me repay the whole loan immediately.

Insecurity Clause

Contract Language: If the Debtor fails to pay any installment of any advance secured hereby or part thereof, or if there is a breach of any of the covenants, agreements, or warranties contained herein or in the credit agreement, or if the Secured Party shall feel insecure, all sums then owing under said credit agreement shall immediately become due and payable without demand or notice.

Translation: If you start to feel insecure about getting paid back, you can demand that I pay the entire amount at any time.

Late Fee Clause

Contract Language: In the event Debtor defaults for 15 days in making any of the aforementioned payments when the same becomes payable hereunder, creditor may charge the debtor a delinquency or collection charge of 5 percent of the amount of payments in default or the sum $5, whichever is less.

Translation: You can charge me a late fee if I'm 15 days late, and if I can't pay on time just once, my state law may let you charge me a late fee on all my other payments, too.

Right to Collect Deficiency Clause

Contract Language: The creditor may retain the goods as its property or may sell or otherwise dispose of the item pursuant to the (State) Uniform Commercial Code, whereupon Debtor shall be liable for and shall pay any deficiency on demand.

Translation: If you repossess what I bought from you and you do not get a good resale price for it, I'll still owe you the difference. (For example, if you take back a perfectly good $500 television and can get only $150 for it, I lose the TV and still owe you $350.)

TABLE 6.4 Major Holders of Consumer Installment Credit

Source	Dollars (billions)
Commercial Banks	302.0
Finance Companies	143.8
Credit Unions	85.5
Savings and Loans	68.2
Retailers	43.6
Other	3.7

SOURCE: *Federal Reserve Bulletin* (November 1988), p. A40.

credit in the United States, in the order of their importance. As you can see, there are a number of institutions that serve this consumer need. We will deal with them in the order of their importance, and add nonregulated sources as well. The object throughout is to provide more information, helping you make better decisions about where to seek credit.

Commercial Banks: Full-service Institutions

As we mentioned in Chapter 5, until the passage of the Depository Institutions Deregulation and Monetary Control Act of 1980, commercial banks were the only depository institutions permitted to offer all financial services, from personal and real estate loans to savings and checking accounts. Today, other financial intermediaries, such as savings and loan associations and credit unions, can offer many of these services, including a type of checking account. Nevertheless, as Table 6.4 shows, commercial banks continue to dominate the consumer credit market. They supply almost half of all installment loans and open-end credit.

secured loan: a loan agreement containing a provision that if the debt is not paid in full, certain pledged property may be claimed by the lender as payment

Loans from commercial banks generally take one of two forms: secured or unsecured loans. A **secured loan** is one for which the borrower must offer some guarantee beyond a simple promise to repay the loan. This guarantee usually takes the form of **collateral**, something of value pledged to assure loan repayment and subject to seizure if the borrower defaults. Collateral can be property owned by the borrower or money that is deposited in an account at the lending bank. Sometimes a loan can even be secured by the purchase itself. For example, automobile loans are generally considered secured loans because the bank's risk of loss is secured by its ability to repossess the car and sell it to pay off the loan. Since the bank's risk is less on a secured loan, the interest rate charged to the borrower will also be lower.

collateral: anything of value pledged to ensure loan repayment and subject to seizure on default

Home equity loans are becoming an increasingly popular form of secured loan. A **home equity loan** is a commitment by a financial institution to extend a certain amount of credit to a consumer with the understanding that failure to repay the loan may result in the seizure and sale of the borrower's home. The difference between the current market value of your home and the amount you currently owe on your mortgage is the dollar value, or **equity**, you currently have in your home. Home equity loans generally have lower interest rates than unsecured loans, and they can have certain tax advantages over other loans. For example, interest charges on home equity loans are in many cases tax deductible. This contrasts with the tax deductibility of interest charges on consumer installment loans and credit card debt, which will be completely phased out of federal tax law by 1991. Some banks have even begun to offer what amounts to a home equity credit card, allowing the homeowner to charge up to a prespecified amount, with the understanding that the credit is secured by the equity in the home.

While lower interest rates, easier access to the credit markets, and tax advantages may make secured loans very attractive, you should be wary of overextending yourself and thus running the risk of losing control of assets it may have taken years to acquire. This is especially important when considering the application for a home equity loan.

An **unsecured loan** requires only the consumer's promise to repay. It does not require the borrower to pledge any real property or other assets as collateral. Unsecured loans are generally offered for shorter periods and at higher interest rates than secured loans. There are many forms of unsecured loans, including cash advances on bank credit cards and overdraft advances that are automatically extended whenever you write a check for more than you have in your checking account. Some banks will also offer small, unsecured loans repayable in equal monthly installments, but this form of bank loan is not very popular with bank loan officers. Given the administrative costs involved and the small size of these loans, banks prefer to offer overdraft protection or cash advances on credit cards.

Credit Unions

Credit unions are important holders of consumer installment debt. As mentioned in Chapter 5, **credit unions** are cooperatively owned financial institutions that accept deposits from and offer loans only to their members. The most common way to join a credit union is to belong to a definable group, such as teachers, government employees, or union members. Because the members of a group are normally employed by a common organization and have similar jobs, the risk of loaning money is

People who belong to a particular group, like teachers, can join a credit union for educational employees.

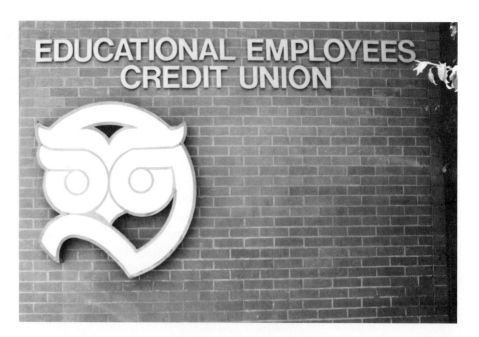

lessened. As a consequence, credit unions frequently have the lowest interest charges in the community. They also often have the advantages of being able to deduct loan payments directly from your paycheck. This can be very convenient for the consumer, and it also reduces the cost of administering the loan.

| **Consumer Finance Companies** | Some financial institutions specialize in small consumer loans. These **consumer finance companies**, usually listed in the yellow pages of the phone directory, often do business across the country, unlike local commercial banks. They sometimes advertise on national radio and television, and in general they try to make the business of borrowing money as appealing as possible. Because they specialize in small consumer loans, their rates are generally higher than those of commercial banks. On the other hand, their rules for qualifying are not as rigid as those of banks. |

Finance companies are often criticized for charging high interest rates on loans. As we mentioned earlier, some states have usury laws that limit the amount of interest a loan company can charge. These laws can interfere with a lender's ability and willingness to loan money. Such laws are particularly important to finance companies, because finance companies generally charge the highest rates. But before you say "good riddance" to such companies, remember that they do serve a consumer need. They are the financial institutions most willing to lend to high-risk, low-income consumers. If legislation forces finance companies and other lending institutions to lower their rates, finance companies will respond by tightening the qualifications consumers must meet to obtain loans. It is ironic that when usury laws are the most effective, they discriminate against low-income borrowers. So instead of getting a loan from a finance company at 24 percent interest, low-income borrowers must either forgo the loan entirely or borrow from a loan shark at exorbitant rates.

| **Savings and Loan Associations** | Until recently savings and loan associations were a very unimportant source for consumer credit. The reason for their low profile can be found in the reason for their initial founding: They were established to finance home construction. As a result, most of their loans were long-term mortgages for single-family residences or apartments and condominiums. In order to attract money for this form of lending, savings and loan associations were given the right to pay more interest on savings accounts, but they were prohibited from issuing checking accounts to their depositors. As we pointed out in Chapter 5, the passage of the Monetary Control Act of 1980 phased out these regulations, and the distinction between savings and loans and other depository institutions has become |

quite small. This means that savings and loan associations and commercial banks function in about the same way. Savings and loan associations offer consumer loans, grant check-overdraft protection, and issue bank-style credit cards. You can expect them to compete favorably in credit markets with their major competitors, the commercial banks.

Retail Outlets

Some retail outlets, such as department stores, furniture stores, and jewelers, were once almost as important in offering installment credit to consumers as banks and finance companies are today. As Figure 6.3 shows, they are still important, but over time they have fallen to a distant fourth in the race to provide consumer credit. Nationwide chain stores such as Sears, K mart, Montgomery-Ward, and J.C. Penney offer consumers both forms of short-term credit: installment credit and open-end credit.

As mentioned earlier, installment credit is closed-end credit in the sense that the loan has a specific amount and a specific repayment period. An example of such a debt might be the purchase of a $1,500 living room set from a local furniture company, with an agreement to pay back the amount in equal monthly installments over the next year.

Open-end (revolving) credit allows the consumer to buy store merchandise and then repay the loan in any amount each month, subject to a minimum payment. The credit revolves in the sense that, as the debt is repaid, the consumer can reuse the same credit line to purchase more goods. Most major retailers are emphasizing revolving credit plans because they tend to be more flexible and encourage their customers to make additional purchases.

FIGURE 6.3
The growth of installment credit, by source, 1950–1988.
(SOURCE: Board of Governors of the Federal Reserve System, *1988 Historical Chart Book* [Washington, D.C.: U.S. Government Printing Office, 1989].)

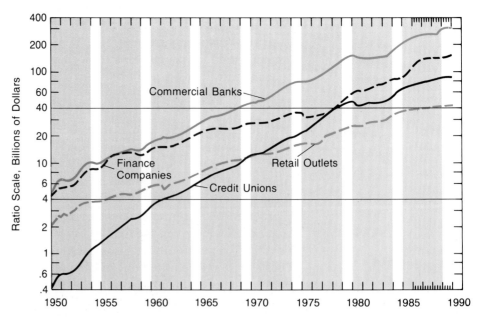

Family and Friends

Important sources of consumer loans that are not directly regulated by federal or state agencies are your immediate family and friends. We have no objective way of determining how large a portion of consumer debt is held by this group, but any discussion of the sources of consumer credit would be seriously lacking if it did not consider this alternative. Most of us have been on both ends of the borrower–lender relationship, and we know the advantages as well as the disadvantages of such loans. On the plus side, there are no applications to fill out or references to supply, and the decision to lend is generally made fairly quickly. The disadvantages can be great, however. If repayment is delayed, friendships can dissolve and family relationships can be strained. Often it is more difficult to repay such loans because they seldom fit easily into a budget. No monthly statement is issued, and borrowers are sometimes conveniently forgetful.

If you do decide to seek a loan from a friend or a relative, proceed in a businesslike manner. Draw up a contract stating the amount of the loan, the interest rate, and the repayment schedule. Be sure to consult the section on finance charges and the annual percentage rate in this chapter, because they can make a difference in the interest rate. For example, if you borrow $1,000 at 8 percent interest and begin to repay in 12 equal monthly installments, you should not pay $90 per month. This may seem correct ($90 × 12 months = $1,080, or 8 percent more than $1,000), but you do not have the use of the $1,000 for an entire year, since you begin to repay that money the month after the loan is made. The best approximation of an 8 percent APR in which you begin to repay by the following month and continue in equal installments for one year is to divide the loan in half ($1,000 ÷ 2 = $500) and compute the 8 percent interest charge on this average loan balance. This results in a finance charge of $40 (0.08 × $500) and a monthly payment of $86.67, rather than $90.00. On the other hand, you may decide to avoid the hassle and pay whatever interest rate your friendly lender wants to charge.

Pawnbrokers

Another source of consumer loans that can be used as a last resort is one of your local pawnbrokers. You will often find these folks near the municipal jail, surrounded by bail bondsmen, unseemly bars, and boarded-up stores. The characters who frequent such neighborhoods are not typical honor students. On the other hand, if you need a loan badly enough, you may want to consider this source.

Pawnbrokers specialize in loans secured by personal property. You must bring in some article of value, such as a guitar, a stereo, or a class ring, and the pawnbroker will take it as collateral for a loan that is generally about half the resale value. You generally have up to one year to reclaim your collateral by paying back the loan and the finance charge in one lump sum. Interest costs vary but are rarely less than 36 percent. If you do not reclaim your pawned article, the pawnbroker has the right to sell it. If the sale brings more revenue than the amount of the loan and the accumulated interest, you have a right to the excess. However, it is rare for such surpluses to exist, let alone to be repaid to the borrower.

Which Credit Source Is Best?

We have covered a bewildering array of credit sources in the past few pages. Which source is the best for you? As you might guess, there is not a simple answer to that question. The answer depends on your needs, values, goals,

TABLE 6.5   A Comparison of Different Credit Sources

Source	Interest Rate	Qualifications	General Remarks
Commercial banks	Average	Strict	Strict credit requirements make borrowing more difficult but allow more competitive rates
Credit unions	Below average	Strict; must be a member	Automatic payroll deductions; low default rate means lower interest rate
Finance companies	Higher than average	Relatively easy	Trade-off between interest rate and ease of obtaining credit; more aggressive collection practices; often buy loans from others
Retail stores	Higher than average	Relatively easy	Credit can only be used at approved stores; may require co-signer; may sell loans to others; some offer zero-interest accounts
Life insurance	Lower than average	Guaranteed if cash value policy owned by borrower	Must have a cash value policy; reduces insurance award in the event of death; actually only borrowing your own money
Family or friends	Varies, usually lower	Kinship or friendship	Personal knowledge of need and use of loan; can strain interpersonal relationships
Pawnbrokers	Much higher than average	Must own something of value	Must retain security for one year; very high APR; generally offer half of the resale value of your possessions

and circumstances. But Table 6.5 does integrate much of the information we presented. As you can see, each credit source has some advantages and some disadvantages. As we have said before, life is full of trade-offs, or opportunity costs. If you want a low-interest loan, you will probably have to go to a financial institution that requires more information from you and more of your time than a creditor who charges a higher interest rate. It's a question of how you value your time and your money. Similarly, if you shop around, you will certainly get a better deal than by simply taking the first loan offered to you. On the other hand, your time and patience have a value, too. How many credit contracts do you want to read before making up your mind? Table 6.5 will give you a better idea of where to go for your loan when the time comes. And if you are a typical consumer, the time is very near.

APPLYING FOR CREDIT

It has been said that only two things are certain, death and taxes, and not necessarily in that order. We might add a third item: consumer credit. The vast majority of Americans seek credit at some point in their lives. You may have already applied for a car loan, a credit card, or a department store charge plate. Whether you got the credit or not, you probably do not know why you did or did not get it. This section will provide you with that information, so that the next time you decide to apply for credit you will know what creditors are looking for.

The Three C's: What Creditors Are Looking For

Whenever a consumer applies for credit, whether it is for closed-end credit, such as an installment loan, or open-end credit, such as a credit card, the lender wants to know whether the prospective borrower has both the ability and the willingness to repay the debt. This overriding concern can be divided into the three *C*'s: capacity, character, and collateral.

Capacity. There are many questions on a credit application that refer to the ability of a consumer to repay a debt. Creditors ask for employment information: how much you earn, what you do, how long you have worked. They also want to know what your expenses are, so they ask questions about whether you have current loan payments, how many dependents you have, and whether you pay alimony or child support. These may seem to be personal questions (and they certainly are), but the reason for asking them is not simply idle curiosity; creditors want to know whether you have the ability and the budget flexibility to repay the loan.

Character. The consumer's willingness to repay the loan is a quality that is quite distinct from his or her ability to shoulder the debt. Stories of

BOX 6.4   QUALIFYING FOR CREDIT

Banks, oil companies, and major retailers are always looking for ways to reduce their losses on bad credit risks without turning down good customers. This search has led them to outside consultants who often tailor a score card system to meet the needs of a particular creditor. The following score card was developed by the Fair, Issac Companies of San Rafael, California, a consulting firm that has created more than 900 scoring systems. This particular score card is a two-step process. Step 1 assigns points to various responses that applicants make when they fill out a credit application. For example, homeowners get 25 points, renters 15 points, and someone living at home with parents would score only 10 points. Stability and white-collar jobs are

highly rated, as you can see from looking at the point totals for years at current address, occupation, and years on the job. In this score card, a major credit card like VISA or MasterCard gives more points than a department store card. And if one of your credit references is a finance company, you lose six points. The applicant's score is totaled at this point, and the creditor's scoring guidelines are applied. On this particular example, you would have to score 100 points to obtain credit, although the cutoff can be adjusted up or down depending on how much risk the creditor was willing to take. If you were a borderline case, the creditor would move to step 2 and seek additional information from a credit bureau. Take the test and see how you score.

Sample Score Card

STEP 1 - APPLICATION DATA							
Own/Rent	OWN	RENT	OTHER				
	25	15	10				
Years at Address	BELOW 0.5	0.5–2.49	2.5–6.49	6.5–10.49	over 10.49		
	12	10	15	19	23		
Occupation	PROF/EXEC	SEMIPROF.	MANAGER	OFFICE	BL. COLLAR	RETIRED	OTHER
	50	44	31	28	25	31	22
Years on Job	BELOW 0.5	0.5–1.49	1.5–2.49	2.5–5.49	5.5–12.49	12.5+	RETIRED
	2	8	19	25	30	39	43
Finance Co. Ref.	YES	NO					
	5	11					
Dept. Store/ Major C.C.	NONE GIVEN	DEPT. STR.	MAJ C. C.	BOTH			
	0	11	16	27			
Bank Reference	CHECKING	SAVINGS	CK & SV	OTHER REF			
	5	10	20	11			
Source	NEW CUST	PRES. CUST	FORM CUST				
	5	5	18				

Application Score _____   Final Score _____

STEP 2 - CREDIT BUREAU INFORMATION							
Number of Inquiries Where Credit was Denied	0	1	2	3	4	5–9	NO RECORD
	3	11	3	−7	−7	−20	0
Worst Reference	NO RECORD	ANY DER.	ANY SLOW	1 SATIS.	2 SATIS.	SATIS.	
	6	−29	−14	17	24	29	

SOURCE: The Fair, Issac Companies. Reproduced by permission.

prominent, affluent people who obtained large loans and then flew off to Tahiti never to be seen again are legion among bank loan officers. Of course, these are exceptional cases, but they do happen. Creditors want some assurance that consumers will repay the debt. This willingness, or character, is often demonstrated by your **credit history**, your track record of past borrowing activity. Creditors want to know who has given you credit in the past, how much credit you were given, and whether you repaid your bills on time and in full. They also look for signs of stability, asking, for example, how long you have lived at your present address, whether you own or rent, and whether (and for how much) you are insured.

Collateral. In this context, collateral serves as additional debt insurance for the creditor. Basically, the creditor wants to know whether you have any assets. An **asset** is anything of value that you own that could be used to pay off your loan in the event that you are unable or unwilling to do so. The assets part of the application asks you to list those physical assets— your house, your car, or other consumer items—that could be sold to repay the debt. Creditors may also want to know how much you have in your savings accounts, where your savings accounts are, and whether you have any investments in stocks, bonds, or real estate. All of this information may be used in processing your credit application.

The Creditor's Decision to Accept or Deny Applications

In the final analysis, the creditor can accept or refuse to extend credit. This decision hinges on the characteristics outlined in the preceding section, but the importance attached to each element of the three *C's* varies among creditors. Some creditors also employ scoring systems such as the one in Box 6.4 to help them decide which loan applications to pursue further and which ones to deny almost immediately. For the consumer who wants credit, such variations in the lending policies of creditors could well mean that one would accept and another would deny the same credit application. A person deemed an acceptable risk by one creditor may be immediately turned down by another. But there are certain guidelines that all creditors must follow, and all credit applicants have certain rights. These are discussed in the next sections.

THE EQUAL CREDIT OPPORTUNITY ACT

Whatever criteria creditors use, the Equal Credit Opportunity Act requires them to apply these criteria fairly, impartially, and without discrimination. This does not mean that everyone is guaranteed credit. It does mean that discrimination on the basis of age, sex, marital status, race, color, religion, national origin, or public assistance (welfare) is expressly forbidden. Discrimination can involve more than simply denying you a loan. You may also be discouraged from even applying for a loan, or you may apply and obtain a loan on terms different from those granted to others with similar incomes, expenses, collateral, and credit histories.

Credit Without Discrimination

There are three common types of discrimination prohibited by the Equal Credit Opportunity Act: age, sex, and receipt of public assistance discrimination.

Age discrimination. Many consumers complain about being denied credit solely on the basis of their age. This is especially true of retired persons and young consumers. The law states that a creditor may ask your age, but if you are old enough to sign a binding contract, a creditor may not

1. Deny credit solely because of your age.
2. Decrease credit because of age or retirement.
3. Deny credit because credit-related insurance is unavailable to persons of your age.
4. Ignore your retirement income in rating your application.

On the other hand, creditors may take your age into account if it has a bearing on your ability to repay the loan. For example, a creditor may ask when an applicant plans to retire, because a person's ability to repay a loan may be affected by retirement. A loan could legitimately be denied if it could be shown that age had a direct bearing on risk of default. An 80-year-old's right to a 30-year mortgage with a 10 percent downpayment is not guaranteed by the Act because such loans do not make good economic sense.

Sex discrimination. Both men and women are protected by law from discrimination based on sex and marital status, but the law is especially designed to prohibit practices that make it difficult for women to get credit. Before the Act was passed, many creditors refused to acknowledge a woman's participation in the family's credit history; they assumed that the family's credit was based solely on the *husband's* ability and willingness to pay. In the past, some creditors would automatically close a single woman's account when she married. Other creditors would cancel credit on learning of a divorce.

The law now states that creditors may not require a person to reapply for credit just because he or she has married, been widowed, or been divorced. A woman may also continue to use her maiden name or a combined last name on her credit accounts. In addition, creditors cannot ask for information about a husband or an ex-husband when a woman applies for her own credit. There are two exceptions to this rule: (1) when there is dependence on spousal support to qualify for the account or (2) when residence is in a community property state, where husband

and wife legally share all property and debts equally (these states are Arizona, California, Idaho, Louisiana, Nevada, New Mexico, Texas, and Washington).

Public assistance. The Equal Credit Opportunity Act also prohibits denial of credit to persons on Social Security, welfare, or any form of public assistance. In the past, these forms of assistance usually led to a quick dismissal of the applicant. Now these factors may affect a person's application only if they relate to creditworthiness. For example, a mother who receives money from Aid to Families with Dependent Children (AFDC) may have to disclose the number and ages of her children, because these benefits will terminate as the children reach a certain age.

What to Do If You Are Denied Credit

Credit is not a right; it is a privilege. Nevertheless, if you are denied credit, you have the right to know why. Under the Equal Credit Opportunity Act, your application must be acted on within 30 days. If you are turned down, the reasons must be stated or you must be told in writing how to obtain this information. The creditor must also tell you whether a credit report was used and give you information about how to contact the relevant credit bureau. If a creditor violates this law, you may sue for actual damages plus punitive damages of up to $10,000. But before you go off to find a lawyer, check your record at your local credit bureau.

credit bureau: a firm that assembles credit information about consumers and then sells this information to other businesses

Credit bureaus. A **credit bureau** is a firm that assembles credit information about consumers and then sells it to other businesses that are interested in a consumer's ability and willingness to repay loans. There are more than 2,500 credit bureaus in the United States, and they process more than 150 million credit reports per year.

Contrary to popular belief, the credit bureau does not make a value judgment about how good or bad a credit risk you are. Instead, it simply collects and stores information about you that banks, financial companies, retailers, and your employer are willing to give it. This information may include your repayment patterns on old loans, your occupation, records of any court proceedings against you, and even your marital history. This record is then furnished to prospective creditors for a fee, and the lender ultimately decides whether or not to extend you credit. If you are denied credit, a good place to begin your search for the cause of the denial is with your credit record at the local credit bureau.

If a prospective lender denies you credit because of an unfavorable credit report, you have the right to request the information directly from the credit-reporting agency. The Fair Credit Reporting Act is the legislation that ensures fairness and objectivity in a consumer's credit report. You may request in writing or in person a summary of your file from the credit bureau. If such a request is made within 30 days of a credit denial, the credit bureau is not allowed to charge you for this information. The summary must tell you the sources of the bureau's information, and it must list everyone who has received a copy of your report within the past six months.

If you find that the report contains false, incomplete, or obsolete data, you should challenge its accuracy and ask the credit bureau to recheck its information. If the bureau finds the information to be incorrect, it must change its report. The bureau must also notify (at no cost to you) those who have previously received your report. Any information in your report that is more than seven years old (ten years in the case of bankruptcy) must be deleted as being obsolete.

If you disagree with the credit bureau's findings and it refuses to change them, you have the right to file a 100-word statement that will be sent in all future reports. You may also request that this statement be mailed to anyone who has sought information about your credit rating in the past six months. If you believe the intent of the Fair Credit Reporting Act has been violated, you have the right to sue.

THE FAIR CREDIT BILLING ACT

Even if you have no difficulty obtaining credit, you may have some disagreement with your creditors (or their computers) over their billing procedures. Our modern credit network is so tied to computers and other electronic marvels, it is a wonder that humans can understand it. Most consumers have had or will have some problem with their credit statement. The Fair Credit Billing Act was passed to give consumers some clear and definable rights when they disagree with their creditors.

Correcting Billing Errors

A billing error may be as simple as an error in arithmetic, or it may be as complex as an unauthorized charge on your account. If you notice an incorrect charge on a credit account, the procedure to follow is straightforward:

1. Notify your creditor in writing within 60 days. Remember, a phone call is *not* sufficient for this purpose, because it will not legally preserve your rights.
2. Be sure to include your name, address, and account number, as well as the reason the bill is wrong.
3. Do not withhold payment on the portion of the bill you agree with.

The creditor is required to acknowledge your letter within 30 days and correct your account within two billing periods.

Stopping Payment for Defective Goods or Services

If you receive damaged goods or poor-quality services purchased with a credit card, The Fair Credit Billing Act can be invoked to stop payment. But first, you must attempt to resolve the dispute with the merchant. If the merchant refuses to cooperate, you have the right to withhold payment. The right is limited to a credit charged on a bank card or any card not issued by the merchant from whom you made the purchase. Thus, it does not apply to a retail store card, such as a J.C. Penney card, or to a gasoline credit card, such as a Mobil Oil card. In addition, the sale must amount to more than $50 and must have taken place in your home state or within 100 miles of your home. If you refuse to pay because the goods or services are defective, the merchant may sue you for payment. You have a legitimate defense, however, if the goods were defective.

Reporting Lost or Stolen Cards

If you lose a credit card, you must act quickly to avoid financial loss; however, the Truth in Lending Law limits your liability for unauthorized charges to $50 per credit card. The Electronic Fund Transfer Act extended this $50 limit to debit cards (the cards used in automated teller machines and the like), but only if you notify your card issuer within two days of the theft. Otherwise, you are personally liable for up to $500 per debit card.

A relatively easy way to protect yourself against these losses is to keep a list of the account numbers of all your credit and debit cards, along with the addressses of the issuers. Most cards have these addresses on the reverse side. And where debit cards are concerned, *never* carry your personal access code in the same place as your card.

HOW MUCH CREDIT EQUALS TOO MUCH DEBT?

There is no magic formula to determine how much debt a consumer can safely afford. The decision to take on additional debt depends on your stage in the life cycle, your current and potential income, and your values. For example, a newly married couple in which both the husband and wife borrow money to complete their medical school training could afford a significantly higher debt load than a newly retired couple trying to get along on Social Security and a company pension. The young couple can expect their income to grow dramatically over the next few decades, thus making the burden of their debt considerably lighter. The older couple can foresee no large increase in their incomes, and if health problems develop, their expenses could also rise. Thus, two couples with identical current incomes could come to quite different conclusions about how much debt they could afford.

Nevertheless, there are some general principles that you should consider before you enlarge your indebtedness. As a general rule, it is not a good idea to go into debt to pay for ordinary expenses like food, clothing, or rent. If you have to take a loan to go to the grocery store or to buy clothes, you are heading for trouble. These expenditures should be paid for with your normal income. For more expensive and less frequently purchased items, such as houses, automobiles, and major appliances, most consumers have good reason to seek loans.

But even here, one must be careful. Can you afford these loans? How many is it safe to have at one time? And where can you go and what rights do you have if you miscalculate your ability to repay these loans? The following sections answer these questions by offering you some guidelines for anticipating credit problems *before* they develop, as well as for handling these problems as they arise.

Some Guidelines for Establishing Credit Limits

There are several ways to establish a personal debt limitation. Some are fairly complex, whereas others can be calculated in a few minutes. But the important point to remember is that none is foolproof. A seemingly rational consumer can be caught in a credit squeeze even with the best laid plans. Having said this, we present three plans.

Debt ceiling. Set a ceiling on your total amount of short-term debt and compare it to your current debt load. Your income can support only a limited amount of debt. Once you go beyond this point, you will either be unable to pay or your life-style will have to be downgraded considerably before you are able to reduce the debts.

Most credit counselors use a formula to determine the ceiling that a consumer's income can support. Worksheet 6.1 presents three of the more common methods that money managers recommend to estimate what an installment loan ceiling should be, excluding home mortgage payments. Method A is the most generous formula in the sense that it allows the largest debt ceiling before sounding an alarm. It assumes that a consumer can handle a debt load equal to 20 percent of his or her annual take-home pay. For someone earning $2,000 a month after taxes, this amounts to a credit ceiling of $4,800.

Method B was derived from a rule that states that one should never owe more than he or she can pay off by devoting 10 percent of his or her monthly take-home pay to the repayment task for 18 months. This amounts to a debt ceiling of 15 percent. (You can verify this by using the data from our previous example: 10 percent of $2,000 times 18 months equals $3,600, or 15 percent of the consumer's income.)

Method C considers the importance of necessity expenditures in calculating a safe debt ceiling. If a consumer with a take-home pay of $2,000 a month spends $1,000 each month on food, clothing, and shelter, then the debt ceiling is $4,000. (This can be calculated as $24,000 minus a $12,000 necessities expenditures times $\times \frac{1}{3}$.)

WORKSHEET 6.1 THREE METHODS FOR ESTIMATING INSTALLMENT DEBT CEILING

Method A

Step 1   Enter annual after-tax income.   _____

Step 2   Multiply by 20 percent.   _____

Method B

Step 1   Enter monthly after-tax income.   _____

Step 2   Multiply by 18 months.   _____

Step 3   Multiply by 10 percent.   _____

Method C

Step 1   Enter annual after-tax income.   _____

Step 2   Subtract yearly expenditures for the necessities (food, clothing, shelter, and so forth).   _____

Step 3   Multiply by $33\frac{1}{3}$ percent.   _____

To compare debt ceiling to current debt:

1. Enter results:
   Method A   _____
   Method B   _____
   Method C   _____
2. Enter current short-term loans:
   a. Credit cards

      _____ $ _____
      _____   _____
      _____   _____
      _____   _____

   b. Installment loans

      _____   _____
      _____   _____

   c. Education loans

      _____   _____
      _____   _____

   d. Automobile loan

      _____   _____

   e. Other loans

      _____   _____
      _____   _____
                              Total loans $ _____
3. Subtract current debt load from the A, B, and C estimates of debt ceiling. A negative number indicates that you have overextended your debt ceiling.

Method C is a more accurate formula than methods A or B because it can take abnormally large (or small) expenditures on necessities into account when calculating a sustainable debt ceiling.

After you have filled out the top of Worksheet 6.1, compare your debt ceiling to your current debt load by totaling your outstanding debts, excluding your home mortgages. The list of loans should include your current balance in all closed-end loans, such as auto or personal loans, that have a definite repayment schedule, and all open-end loans, such as credit card balances, that require only a minimum payment. Don't be surprised if you have exceeded your debt ceiling. This is common, especially for young adults. But this should alert you to the dangers of overextending yourself.

Debt liquidation timetable. Establish a timetable for liquidating your consumer debt. This technique calls for you to pay off all your outstanding installment and credit card debts on a regular basis. This might mean resolving your debts once a year, or it could mean waiting as long as three years to clean your consumer debt slate. A timetable might suit a consumer whose income is steady but increases during certain seasons. A postal worker, for example, might be assured of getting overtime pay during the peak holiday season each year; this extra income might be used to pay off the consumer debts that accumulate during the year. A teacher whose paycheck is divided into 12 monthly installments might get extra pay for teaching summer school; this extra income could be used to clean up the debts that build up over a year or two.

This technique has two serious drawbacks, however. First, the job you were counting on to give you the extra income may not materialize. Second, you may develop the "mañana syndrome," allow yourself to go deeper and deeper into debt, postponing the liquidation of your debts to "a couple of years" in the future. Only a well-disciplined consumer should try to apply it.

Assessment of net worth. Set up a balance sheet with the value of what you own (assets) on one side and the value of what you owe (liabilities) on the other. This is considerably more involved than the first technique we cited, but it is similar to the process that commercial lenders go through before they approve or reject your loan application. The difference between your assets and liabilities is called your net worth—a concept discussed in Chapter 4. In general, loans are denied to people whose net worth is negative, that is, whose liabilities are greater than their assets. If you find that your net worth is very low or negative, you have probably reached your debt limit, and you would be ill advised to take on additional debt, even if someone is willing to loan you more money.

Credit Counseling

It is not unusual for consumers to overextend themselves financially, and it is easy to tell when this has happened. Being unable to make payments on time, getting delinquency notices, receiving letters from collection agencies, and seeking new loans to pay off old debts are all trouble signals. These situations call for help. One of the best approaches is to seek some form of credit counseling. Five out of six families in credit trouble can be helped by credit counselors. Without the counseling services that exist today, the number of consumers who declare personal bankruptcy would probably rise by 50 percent.

Credit counselors can be found in a number of institutions. Some universities provide these services in their home economics or business departments. Most credit unions and other creditors also provide help. One of the best places to seek counseling is a nonprofit community-based organization like the Consumer Credit Counselors Service. There is probably one in your community, and consumers who have overextended their credit would do well to contact it. Basically, credit counselors advise consumers on money management problems and assist in providing a commonsense plan for paying off debts. They will contact the relevant creditors if this seem advisable, and they will prepare a repayment plan that is acceptable to all parties.

Dealing with Debt Collectors

You do not have to be in serious financial trouble to cross paths with a debt collection agency, a firm that regularly collects debts owed to other businesses. Even a merchant error can lead a bill collector to get in touch with you. Often, your first notice will come in the form of a letter, frequently a friendly reminder. But if you ignore it, you could be in for a real war of words. In the past, correspondence from a debt collector to a consumer could verge on harassment. The collector could phone you at all hours of the night and even threaten you with lawsuits or the loss of your reputation.

In order to eliminate these abuses, the Fair Debt Collection Practices Act was passed. Under this Act, abusive, deceptive, and unfair debt collection practices are expressly forbidden. Debt collectors cannot phone you or visit you in person at inconvenient times—generally before 8:00 A.M. or after 9:00 P.M. Neither can they call you at work if your employer disapproves. In addition, they cannot

1. Use threats of violence
2. Use obscene language
3. Use telephone calls to annoy you
4. Make you accept a collect call or a telegram
5. Advertise your debt

If a debt collector violates this Act, you have the right to sue for "actual damages," that is, personal and financial costs sustained in the course of the transaction in question. You also may sue for $1,000 in "punitive damages," money sought to punish the wrongdoer. However, if you sue in bad faith or simply to harass a bill collector, you can be held liable for the court costs. Before you decide to sue, you might consult your state attorney general's office or write to the Federal Trade Commission, "Debt Collection," Washington, DC 20580.

Wage Garnishment

wage garnishment: *a court order that instructs an employer to set aside a portion of a consumer's wages until a debt is paid off*

If you are working but refuse to pay a debt, a creditor can, under some circumstances, get a court order that instructs your employer to set aside a portion of your wages until the debt is repaid. This is called **wage garnishment**, and it has been used by creditors for years. However, the Wage Garnishment Law (part of the Consumer Credit Protection Act) limits the amount an employer can deduct from an employee's salary to no more than 25 percent of take-home pay. Another section of the law prohibits an employer from firing employees because of wage garnishment. A violation of this provision can bring a $1,000 fine and/or a one-year prison term.

BANKRUPTCY: THE LAST RESORT

bankruptcy: *a court action freeing a person of debt because of his or her inability to pay; although most debts are discharged with this action, not all are dischargeable and the assets of the debtor, with some exceptions, are turned over to the creditor in lieu of payment*

In spite of all your efforts to avoid financial insolvency, you may find that you simply cannot pay off your debts. If you find yourself in such a predicament, bankruptcy may be your only alternative. In 1988 more than 800,000 Americans filed for bankruptcy, and many more gave it serious consideration. What is bankruptcy, and what are its advantages and limitations?

Bankruptcy is a court action that declares a person free of most debts because he or she is declared incapable of paying them. It is a serious matter, because it stays on one's credit record for ten years and seriously impairs one's ability to obtain credit well into the future. Once a person becomes bankrupt, he or she cannot file again for six more years. Nevertheless, all consumers have a legal right to declare bankruptcy, and the courts are likely to grant it unless fraud or dishonesty is involved.

Because bankruptcy proceedings can be very involved, it is generally a good idea to retain a lawyer. The procedure for starting a bankruptcy action consists of filing a petition with the bankruptcy court requesting that you be declared bankrupt. You will also be required to file a Statement of Affairs, which describes your personal background and financial history. You must also file a list of your creditors (Schedule A) and your assets (Schedule B). After you have filed your papers, the court clerk will inform your creditors, and a court appearance called the First Meeting of

Creditors will be scheduled. When you attend this meeting, you may be questioned about your case, and a trustee who represents the creditors will be appointed to sell your assets and distribute to the creditors the amount received.

Not all of your debts will be canceled by a successful bankruptcy proceeding. Some debts, such as taxes, alimony, child support, and loans that have nonbankrupt co-signers, will remain in force. For example, banks often get both the husband and the wife to sign for a loan. If the husband goes bankrupt, he need not repay the loan. However, the wife, who co-signed the loan, remains legally obligated to repay it. Thus, it is especially important for married couples to decide whether they should jointly file for bankruptcy. Joint filing has the added benefit of doubling the value of the assets one is allowed to keep after the bankruptcy is completed.

Bankruptcy law was not intended to encourage consumers to use it to get out of their debts, but neither was it intended to wipe them out financially. All states have laws governing what a bankrupt individual is allowed to keep. In California, for example, bankruptcy law exempts certain personal belongings, such as household furnishings, appliances, one piano, one radio, one television, a three-month supply of food, one shotgun, one rifle, and certain works of art. A Californian may also keep tools necessary for a trade, a cemetery lot, and an inexpensive automobile. He or she may even keep a maximum of $1,000 in a savings account. Other states have different rules.

In an effort to minimize the variability among state laws, The Federal Bankruptcy Code, Public Law 95–598, established federal exemptions effective October 1, 1979. This code is not mandatory for either the debtor or the state. Virginia, Ohio, and Florida have chosen to deny these exemptions, but in all other states the debtor may choose to use these federal exemptions or the ones issued by the relevant state.

According to the Federal Bankruptcy Code, a debtor is given the following exemptions:

1. $7,500 worth of equity in a home (commonly referred to as the homestead exemption).
2. A motor vehicle worth up to $1,200.
3. Items of household furnishings, goods, clothing, appliances, books, animals, crops, or musical instruments worth up to $200 each. The total of all such items cannot exceed $4,000.
4. Jewelry up to $500.
5. Other property worth up to $400 (including any unused portion of the homestead exemption).
6. Implements, professional books, or tools of the trade worth up to $750.

7. Dividends, interest, or loan value accrued on any unmatured life insurance contract worth up to $4,000.
8. Any unmatured life insurance contracts.
9. Professionally prescribed health aids.
10. Income from Social Security, unemployment, disability, public assistance benefits, alimony, and child-support payments.

The type of bankruptcy we have just described is technically known as a **Chapter 7 Bankruptcy**, or a **straight bankruptcy**. The Bankruptcy Act also contains a section that allows for the restructuring of a consumer's debt. This section is called **Chapter 13**, "Adjustments of Debts for Individuals with Regular Income." This chapter of the Act is often called the **wage-earner plan**, because it is aimed at the consumer who has a steady job but simply cannot repay debts on time. Under this plan, the debtor files a statement with the local bankruptcy court, agreeing to give a portion of his or her future earnings to a court-appointed trustee whose job is to repay the creditors in no more than five years. The filing of this plan halts all creditor action against the debtor. A hearing is held during which the creditors may object to the plan; however, as long as the creditors can expect to receive as much under this plan as they would if the debtor filed a straight bankruptcy, the plan will generally be approved.

Once the court accepts the plan, it orders the debtor's employer to garnish his or her wages and send the money to the court-appointed trustee. This plan binds the creditors as well as the debtor to the repayment schedule. On successful completion of the agreement, the court discharges the debtor of all debts. On the other hand, if the plan proves unworkable, the debtor can file for a straight bankruptcy.

A Chapter 13 wage-earner plan has a number of advantages over a Chapter 7 bankruptcy. The Chapter 13 plan allows the debtor to retain possession and control of his or her property and relinquish only future income. This means that the Chapter 13 debtor does not have to liquidate all assets, as would be the case in a regular bankruptcy. In effect, the debtor can hold the creditors in check until his or her check comes in. Unlike straight bankruptcy, a successful Chapter 13 proceeding also protects anyone who co-signed a note with the debtor.

Another benefit is that the demonstration of willingness to repay debts, albeit over a longer time period, is sometimes viewed as a good sign by future creditors. At least the debtor did not declare personal bankruptcy or simply refuse to pay the debt. By choosing the wage-earner plan, the debtor allowed the lenders to get back most of what was owed them. And finally, the wage-earner plan requires the consumer to follow a budget that is outlined with the help of the court. As a result, new spending habits can be created, which will help consumers to avoid future monetary crises.

SUMMARY

In this chapter we outlined the costs and benefits of consumer credit. Few of us can get along without any credit at all. Even fewer of us would prefer a creditless existence. The key is to use credit wisely to augment your buying power.

If you are going to use credit, however, you must understand the rules of the game. This includes knowing the principal sources of credit, how to apply for credit, your legal rights in the process, and what to do if an error is made on your credit account. Once you have established your credit, you need to continue to evaluate your credit and your credit behavior, and you need to guard against overextending yourself. If you do run into trouble that credit counseling cannot solve, you have two options: straight bankruptcy or the wage-earner plan. Neither plan is ideal, but bankruptcy may be the only way to achieve a new start.

We have covered a lot of material in this chapter, but because credit has become such an important part of our lives, we have to understand its role and how it works. A great deal of legislation has been passed in this area, from the Consumer Credit Protection Act to the revision of the Federal Bankruptcy Code. Consumer rights have never been as well established as they are today, and you would do well to learn about them. Responsibilities are equally important: Our vast credit network runs on trust, and all parties must make an honest effort to use and offer credit in a responsible manner. But if you get into financial difficulties, you do not give up your rights. And if you believe that you have been dealt with unfairly, there are a number of government agencies, including the court system, that are designed to help you.

QUESTIONS

1. How important is credit in the United States today? Give some examples that illustrate your point.
2. Make a list of the advantages and disadvantages of consumer credit. Given your current situation, should you seek credit? Explain.
3. If you borrowed $1,000 for one year on the installment plan at 12 percent APR, would you pay a finance charge of $120? Explain.
4. If you are considering opening a credit account, which method of calculating finance charges would you *least* prefer: adjusted balance, previous balance, or average daily balance?
5. What is the difference between a secured and an unsecured loan? Which one is likely to have a lower APR? Why?
6. What are usury laws, and how do they affect consumers?
7. Using the system in Box 6.4, estimate your ability to obtain a loan. Do you qualify?
8. If you believe that there has been an error in your billing statement, what should you do? What must the creditor do in response? What law guarantees these rights?
9. If you lose a credit card, what is your maximum liability? Describe the rules for personal liability on a debit card. How do they differ from credit card rules?
10. What does "garnishing wages" mean? What rights does a debtor have with respect to wage garnishment?

REFERENCES AND READINGS

Board of Governors of the Federal Reserve System. *Consumer Handbook to Credit Protection Laws.* Washington, D.C.

————. *Alice in Debitland: Consumer Protection and the Electronic Fund Transfer Act.* Washington, D.C.

Federal Reserve Bank of New York. *The Arithmetic of Interest Rates.* New York: Federal Reserve Bank, 1984.

Federal Trade Commission, "Fix Your Own Credit Problems and Save Money," *Facts for Consumers,* April 1987.

"Is There Life After Credit?" *Los Angeles Times,* October 12, 1987.

"New Risks in Consumer Credit," *Bankers Magazine,* January–February 1988.

"Playing Your Cards Right," *Consumer Reports,* January 1985.

"Plastic Battle: Big Credit Card War Seems Likely," *Wall Street Journal,* March 19, 1987.

Schwartz, Joe. "Who Will Borrow Tomorrow?" *American Demographics,* March 1988.

Sullivan, A. Charlene, and Drecnik, Debra A. "Social Efficiency of the Bankruptcy Reform Act of 1978 with Regard to Personal Bankruptcy," *Journal of Consumer Affairs,* Winter 1984.

"Take Control of Your Credit: Should You Pay for Credit Reports?" *Consumer Reports,* July 1987.

"Wall Street Journal to List Interest Rates of Bank Credit Cards," *Wall Street Journal,* March 7, 1988.

Watro, Paul R. "The Bank Credit-Card Boom: Some Explanations and Consequences," *Economic Commentary: Federal Reserve Bank of Cleveland,* March 1988.

Chapter Seven

ADVERTISING: INFORMATION OR MANIPULATION?

DID YOU KNOW THAT . . .

. . . U.S. firms spend more than $100 billion each year to advertise their products? This amounts to an expenditure of $400 for every consumer.

. . . advertising can actually result in lower prices to the consumer by providing valuable information and by stimulating competition among firms in an industry?

. . . some firms spend a third of their revenues on advertising?

. . . a typical consumer sees 20,000 television commercials a year during the 1,300 hours he or she spends watching TV?

. . . there are a half-dozen federal agencies with some jurisdiction over advertising practices?

. . . the Consumer Information Center was established to help distribute pamphlets and other useful publications developed by federal agencies for consumers?

. . . it is illegal for firms to use "bait and switch" tactics?

If you had to remember just one product that is currently being advertised, what would it be? If you are typical, it would probably be either Coca-Cola or Pepsi-Cola. Their commercials traditionally rank first and second among American consumers who are asked for their impressions of current advertisements. A host of surveys are constantly being taken by the advertising industry in their quest for success in the marketplace. Their goal is to leave you, the consumer, with a memorable message and a favorable image so that you will select their product rather than a competing one.

In many respects the advertising industry has succeeded. Many of us would find it easier to match imaginary advertising characters like Mr. Whipple, Mrs. Olson, or Spuds Mackenzie with their products (Charmin bathroom tissue, Folgers Coffee, and Budweiser beer) than to recall the political affiliations and terms of office of the American presidents Lyndon Johnson, Gerald Ford, and Ronald Reagan (Democrat, 1963–69; Republican, 1974–77; Republican, 1981–89, respectively) who served when the fictitious Whipples, Olsons, and MacKenzies of the world were created to hawk their wares. If you are concerned about the well-being of our society, you would be hard pressed to justify our ignorance of major political facts and our wealth of commercial trivia. Part of the answer lies in the fact that our nation spends almost as much on advertising as it does on elementary education in public schools. But we must also realize that consumers value information only insofar as it is relevant to them. Advertising is an important way that consumers receive information. And sometimes we are more interested in a good cup of coffee than we are in the political party of a presidential candidate.

This chapter focuses on advertising and related informational media that are an important part of one's everyday experience. As you saw in Chapter 1, good decisions are impossible without good information. Advertising at its best can provide this crucial input. At its worst, advertising can hinder your decision making by giving you false or misleading information that could lead you to make poor choices. But as you may already suspect, most advertising is neither all good nor all bad. There are some real benefits that can be attributed to advertising, along with some genuine costs to society as well as individuals.

On the benefit side, by providing consumers with information, advertising can promote competition among producers and thus help create lower prices for consumers. It is also true that firms that produce many brands and advertise heavily are investing in their name. This means they must maintain product quality or risk tarnishing their reputation. Procter & Gamble's swift action in removing Rely tampons from the marketplace as soon as danger to the consumer was suggested can be seen as an example of a large advertiser trying to protect its reputation and that of its other consumer-oriented products. Advertising also has some beneficial side-effects, for example, providing subsidies to other informational media, such as television, radio, magazines, and newspapers.

The negative aspects of advertising hinge on its ability to produce informational confusion among consumers so that their decision-making ability is impaired and they buy what they are told to buy. According to this view, firms advertise to create wants in the consumer rather than to satisfy consumer needs that already exist. Advertising can also be used to keep potential competitors out of a market by making it expensive to get the consumer's atttention. Small firms may find it impossible to spend millions of dollars just to become sufficiently well known for consumers to try their products. If smaller firms are intimidated by the huge advertising budgets of their larger rivals, advertising becomes a barrier to competition that can result in higher prices.

In this chapter we explore the pros and cons of advertising in greater detail, but our emphasis is not on deciding the merits of advertising. Instead, we want you to be able to distinguish information from manipulation. Then you can feed the information provided by advertising into your decision-making process and get more satisfaction out of your expenditures.

The first part of this chapter describes the development of the advertising industry and the firms that use it. The middle sections analyze the major types of advertisements and give you some ways to recognize them. The next sections deal with consumer benefits of advertising, and the final section extends the consumers' search for information from advertising to other readily available sources.

THE BIRTH OF THE ADVERTISING INDUSTRY

In the eighteenth and nineteenth centuries most of our labor force was on the farm. Consumer goods as we know them today were almost nonexistent because most products were made in the home. The biggest household expenditure was for the family stove, which often served the dual purpose of cooking and heating. As our economy industrialized in the late nineteenth century, people moved off the farm and into the cities to work for wages. By and large, this migration to industrial areas was accompanied by greater real income for most workers. Because urban residents could not produce most of their own goods and services, they exchanged their larger labor income for a variety of products. As consumers' incomes grew and their agrarian roots faded, American business provided more goods and services that were once homemade. Business firms discovered that large concentrations of people made the delivery of traditionally homemade products like soap and spices commercially profitable. Firms like Procter & Gamble (Ivory Soap) and H.J. Heinz (pickles, relishes, ketchup) began marketing their wares to city dwellers. Other firms established grand urban distribution networks such as department stores (John Wanamaker, Marshall Fields, and Macy's) and supermarkets (The Great Atlantic & Pacific Tea Co., known as A&P).

By the beginning of the twentieth century, consumers' needs were increasingly being met by the market system. An important part of that system was (and still is) *information*. Producers needed to let consumers know what they were willing to produce, and consumers wanted to know what was available and at what price. The time was ripe for the birth of the advertising industry.

Figure 7.1 illustrates the growth of advertising in the United States since 1890. You can see a gradual but steady growth in expenditures from 1890 to about 1930. This coincides with the entrance of the U.S. economy into an era of high mass consumption. The 1930s show a decline because of the Depression, a decade when unemployment rates soared to 25 percent and almost all industries experienced a decline in sales. Beginning in the 1940s and continuing to the present, we have seen a veritable explosion in advertising in the United States. In 1940 advertisers

FIGURE 7.1 Advertising expenditures in the United States, 1890–1990.

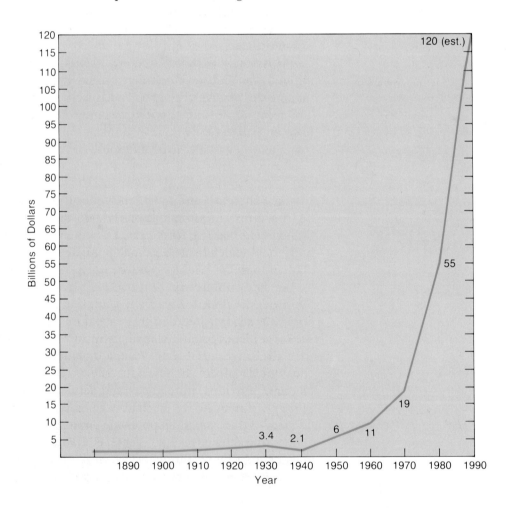

were spending about $2 billion. By 1950 advertising revenues were $6 billion. With the advent of commercial television, these expenditures tripled over the next 20 years. The 1970s and 1980s witnessed the growth of massive advertising campaigns and significant price inflation, such that by 1987 advertising passed the $100 billion mark. By the 1990s advertising expenditures should exceed $120 billion.

Because advertising is part of the cost of doing business, it is included in the price of the product. This means that by the 1990s, the average consumer will be contributing $400 to firms' advertising expenditures by buying their products. Thus, a typical four-person American household will pay for $1,600 worth of advertising annually through its purchases. In essence, these dollars pay for a vast information service that many consumers may not be using to their best advantage. Think about it. If you were paying $400 a year to subscribe to a buying information service, you would be very concerned with its usefulness. However, many consumers seem to take advertising for granted. They don't realize that it can supply helpful information that can be incorporated into their decisions. On the other hand, advertising can also send misleading signals that consumers should ignore or avoid. Throughout this chapter we want to help you distinguish between these two so that advertising is an aid in, not a hindrance to, your decision making. The next section gets you started by profiling the typical advertisers. Then we discuss the rationale for advertising, the types of ads, and finally, how you can benefit from advertisements.

WHO ARE THE MAJOR ADVERTISERS?

retailer: a firm that sells directly to the consumer

wholesaler: a firm that sells to other firms, rather than directly to consumers

Table 7.1 lists the top 30 advertisers in the U.S. economy. Take a look at the list to see how many names are familiar to you. Some of these companies, called **retailers** because they sell directly to the consumer, are well known. Sears, K mart, and J.C. Penney are good examples of retail firms. Other firms may be less familiar because they are largely **wholesalers**; that is, they sell in bulk to firms that either retail their merchandise or use it to produce other goods to be sold to the consumer. Another reason you may have difficulty recognizing some of these firms is that they may not advertise under their own name. These unfamiliar corporations frequently own a number of better-known and better-advertised firms. For example, Unilever owns Thomas J. Lipton, Inc., which produces a variety of consumer goods such as Lipton Soups and Lipton Tea. They also own Prince Matchabelli, which manufactures such fragrances as Wind Song, Aviance, and Elizabeth Taylor's Passion. Unilever recently acquired Chesebrough-Ponds the makers of Cutex, Ragu spaghetti sauces, and Vaseline Petroleum Jelly. Another big advertiser, Warner-Lambert, owns a plethora of familiar brands, such as Certs,

TABLE 7.1 The Top 30 Advertisers

Advertiser	**Advertising Dollars**
1. Procter & Gamble	$1,435,454,000
2. Philip Morris	1,364,472,000
3. Sears, Roebuck	1,004,708,000
4. RJR Nabisco	935,036,000
5. General Motors	839,000,000
6. Ford Motor	648,500,000
7. Anheuser-Busch	643,522,000
8. McDonald's	592,000,000
9. K mart	590,350,000
10. Pepsi-Cola	581,309,000
11. General Mills	551,561,000
12. Warner-Lambert	548,726,000
13. BCI Holdings	535,852,000
14. Unilever N.V.	517,746,000
15. J. C. Penney	496,241,000
16. Pillsbury	494,877,000
17. Ralston-Purina	478,031,000
18. American Telephone & Telegraph	439,919,000
19. Kraft	437,952,000
20. Chrysler	426,000,000
21. Johnson & Johnson	410,672,000
22. American Home Products	395,718,000
23. Kellogg	374,142,000
24. Coca-Cola	370,379,000
25. General Electric	354,250,000
26. Bristol-Meyers	330,997,000
27. Mars	312,607,000
28. Quaker Oats	309,239,000
29. U.S. Government	306,094,000
30. Nestlé	305,451,000

SOURCE: Reprinted with permission from the September 24, 1987, issue of *Advertising Age*. Copyright 1987 by Crain Communications, Inc.

Dentyne, Efferdent, Listerine, Rolaids, Sinutab, Schick shavers, and Trident. Unilever and Warner-Lambert are not exactly household words, but very few consumers are unaware of their products.

Most consumers have only a vague appreciation of the huge sums of money spent on advertising. A 30-second television commercial can cost over $1 million to produce and many times that amount to show on prime-time TV during the regular season. Why does Procter & Gamble, the largest advertiser in the American economy, spend more than $1 billion on such tactics? Its priorities may seem especially odd when you learn that their annual advertising budget is greater than the profits distributed to their shareholders. Why don't the shareholders unite, throw the advertising maniacs out, and double their dividends? At least part of the reason lies in the basic belief that advertising increases sales and gives the firm a competitive edge in the marketplace. In 1988 Pepsi, IBM, and McDonald's paid more than $600,000 for each 30-second spot during the Super Bowl; they calculated that reaching 50 million household in that time period was cheaper than using the U.S. mail system.

Clearly, there is more to advertising than simply trying to give consumers what they need. The objective of a profit-making firm's advertising is to benefit the corporation first. Often, this means satisfying the consumer; thus, both parties are better off with the advertising expenditures. It may seem odd that the advertising of some products actually competes with that of other products made by the same company. Procter & Gamble is the leader in this field (see Box 7.1 for details). P&G produces a dozen detergents, from Ivory Snow to Tide to Oxydol, all heavily advertised. It also produces both Mr. Clean and Spic & Span— products familiar to all soap-opera watchers. But Procter & Gamble is

---

BOX 7.1 INTRACORPORATE COMPETITION, PROCTER & GAMBLE STYLE

All brands listed below are produced by Procter & Gamble. Many of them compete against each other in a crowded, heavily advertised marketplace.

Product Line	Brand (Year First Marketed by Procter & Gamble)
Shortening and cooking oils	Crisco (1911), Crisco Corn Oil (1986), Crisco Oil (1960), Puritan (1976)
Detergents	Bold (1965), Cheer (1950), Dash (1954), Dreft (1933), Era (1972), Gain (1966), Ivory Snow (1930), Liquid Bold–3 (1985), Liquid Cheer (1986), Liquid Tide (1984), Oxydol (1927), Solo (1979), Tide (1949)
Dishwashing detergents	Cascade (1955), Dawn (1972), Ivory Liquid (1957), Joy (1949), Liquid Cascade (1986)
Cleaners and cleansers	Comet (1955), Comet Liquid (1976), Mr. Clean (1958), Spic & Span (1945), Spic & Span Pine Liquid (1983), Top Job (1963)
Bar soaps	Camay (1926), Coast (1974), Ivory (1879), Kirk's (1930), Lava (1927), Monchel (1982), Safeguard (1963), Zest (1952)
Toothpastes	Crest (1955), Denquel (1980), Gleem (1952)
Shampoos	Head & Shoulders (1961), Ivory (1983), Lilt (1985), Pert Plus (1979), Prell (1946)
Paper tissue products	Banner (1982), Charmin (1957), Puffs (1960), White Cloud (1958)
Disposable diapers	Luvs (1976), Pampers (1961)

SOURCE: "Team Strategy: As the Marketplace Changes, P&G Changes the Way It Develops and Sells Its Products," *Wall Street Journal*, August 11, 1987.

not alone in its intracorporate competitiveness. Ralston Purina has the distinction of producing the greatest variety of pet food brands. It makes Chuck Wagon, Dog Chow, Hi Pro, Kibbles & Chunks, Lucky Dog, and Puppy Chow for dogs, and Cat Chow, Tender Vittles, Meow Mix, Alley Cat, and Smart Cat for feline consumers. Parkay and Chiffon margarines are both trade names owned by Kraft. General Foods, a subsidiary of Philip Morris, advertises a wide variety of coffee: Maxim, Maxwell House, Sanka, Yuban, and Brim.

Critics of advertising say that this proliferation of brands and the heavy use of advertising is a way of limiting competition. After all, there is only so much space on supermarket shelves. If General Foods heavily advertises five different brands of coffee, there is less shelf space for the products of other firms. And the fact that there are so many brands gives the appearance of competition, when, in fact, only a few firms control the major portion of production. These leading producers are quick to point out that consumers' tastes differ. For example, not everyone likes the same coffee blend; by producing a variety of brands, firms are able to increase sales (and profits) by responding to demand in the marketplace. Moreover, how else can consumers learn about different blends unless the firm gives each a distinctive name and then informs consumers about its availability?

This debate cannot be resolved here. For our purposes, a more important question is one of cost. Who pays how much to whom?

Table 7.2 shows the advertising expenditures and sales revenues of representatives from the top 100 advertisers in the United States. The last column shows what proportion of each dollar earned from sales goes to pay for advertising. As you can see, many firms advertise a lot, but spend relatively little in percentage terms. The airline, automobile, chemical, and petroleum companies spend 3 percent or less of their sales revenue on advertising. So for every dollar spent on Mobil gasoline, for example, less than one penny went for advertising. But some corporations, especially those dealing with personal care items, such as cosmetics, spend relatively large amounts on ads. If you bought a $3.00 jar of Noxema (Noxell Corporation), almost 30 percent of the cost (about 90 cents) went to pay for their ad campaign. Warner-Lambert, the maker of a wide variety of heavily advertised products, such as Rolaids and Efferdent, tops the list with almost one-third of its revenues being spent to convince you to buy their products. If you have ever watched professional sports on television, it will come as no surprise that beer companies also spend significant amounts on advertising. Budweiser, Coors, and Strohs collectively spent almost 1 billion dollars trying to convince the American public that their beers are among the finest brewed anywhere in the world. But for every six-pack sold, 7 to 10 percent of the revenue went toward advertising, not ingredients.

TABLE 7.2 Advertising Expenditures as a Percentage of Total Sales
for Firms Selected from the Top 100 Advertisers

Primary Business	Ad Rank	Company	Advertising ($)	Sales ($)	Advertising as a Percent of Sales
Airlines	83	Delta	104,554,000	5,320,000,000	1.9
	60	Texas Air	132,287,000	4,406,897,000	3.0
Automobiles	20	Chrysler	426,000,000	20,489,000,000	2.1
	6	Ford	648,500,000	50,034,000,000	1.3
	5	General Motors	839,000,000	89,099,000,000	0.9
Beer	61	Adolph Coors	130,609,000	1,314,000,000	9.9
	7	Anheuser-Busch	643,522,000	8,402,000,000	7.6
	63	Stroh Brewery	123,690,000	1,499,000,000	8.5
Chemicals and Petroleum	70	Dow	119,508,000	5,165,000,000	2.3
	50	Mobil	167,777,000	18,717,000,000	0.6
Food	23	Kellogg	374,142,000	2,269,000,000	16.5
	16	Pillsbury	494,877,000	5,510,000,000	9.0
	4	RJR Nabisco	935,036,000	15,978,000,000	5.9
Gum and Candy	90	Wrigley	96,243,000	493,026,000	19.5
Restaurants	9	McDonald's	592,000,000	3,077,000,000	19.2
	81	Wendy's	110,001,000	1,140,000,000	9.6
Soaps and Cleaners	1	Procter & Gamble	1,435,454,000	17,000,000,000	8.4
	14	Unilever	517,746,000	4,842,000,000	10.7
Soft Drinks	24	Coca-Cola	370,379,000	4,650,000,000	8.0
	10	Pepsi-Cola	581,309,000	8,065,000,000	7.2
Toiletries and Cosmetics	79	Noxell	112,110,000	377,152,000	29.7
	12	Warner-Lambert	548,726,000	1,700,000,000	32.3

SOURCE: Reprinted with permission from the September 24, 1987, issue of *Advertising Age*. Copyright 1987 by Crain Communications, Inc.

TYPES OF ADVERTISING

As consumers, we are constantly exposed to advertising—while we're walking, driving, riding a bus, looking at a magazine or newspaper, even in our homes while watching TV. In fact, according to the most recent surveys, the average American logs 1,300 viewing hours each year, from the age of two on, more time than he or she spends in school. This means that a viewer sees 20,000 commercials a year.

TV and other forms of advertising create a situation that calls for consumers to know about and be prepared for this overwhelming amount of information. If we allow ourselves to be manipulated or persuaded to buy without thinking, we abandon our role as careful and conscious decision makers responsible for our choices. However, by analyzing advertisements, we can learn to use the information and disregard the rest, including the emotional or false and deceptive advertising that sometimes accomplishes a company's sales goals at the expense of our own.

In this section and the ones that follow, we present the major categories of advertising as outlined by the Federal Trade Commission (FTC). The FTC is the federal agency with the major responsibility for policing national advertising campaigns and ensuring that false or misleading claims are stopped. The FTC is not the only agency that regulates advertising. On the federal level, the Food and Drug Administration (FDA), the Federal Communication Commission (FCC), the U.S. Postal Service, and even the Securities and Exchange Commission (SEC) all have a hand in overseeing the advertising practices of some firms. Consumer protection agencies in various states and their respective attorney generals are also involved in advertising at the local level. And in recent years, the FTC has come under fire both from those who oppose government regulation in the economy and from those who feel government is doing too little to protect consumers from false advertising. In spite of this controversy, the FTC continues to be the most prominent government agency involved in advertising and national consumer protection matters.

The FTC classification is based on ad content. It lists ads as ''informative,'' ''puffing,'' or ''deceptive.'' We will adopt this framework for broad categories of ads but will break some of them down into more specific types so that you can see the kinds of appeals that producers make.

Informative Advertising

informative advertisement: an advertisement that provides the consumer with specific, understandable, and verifiable claims about a product or service

An **informative advertisement** provides the consumer with specific, understandable, and verifiable claims about the product or service. For a consumer, one of the most important pieces of information contained in any informational ad is the price. It is very important that the consumer know ahead of time just how much a good or a service will cost. Otherwise, the cost–benefit step in our decision-making framework becomes a ''guesstimate,'' or one is required to spend additional time searching for price information. Given the importance of price information, it seems odd that this particular item is often missing from the promotional pitch. Retail store ads are a notable exception. They frequently give specific price and product information. Even here, however, the modern trend seems to be to advertise the noninformative slogan ''We have the lowest prices in town.''

It is true that in the national advertising of brands, mentioning specific price information is often impossible because prices vary with different retailers. A pair of Levi's jeans, for instance, may sell for quite different prices, even in the same town. Even the price of an orange is affected by transportation costs, store overhead, and seasonal variation. So there are times when even the most avid consumer advocate has to admit that specific price information is not possible. Nevertheless, if advertising is to serve a valuable service to consumers, advertisers have an obligation to try to inform, not simply persuade, the public about their product.

Besides telling price, ads can include information on nutritional content, resistance to shrinkage, and fabric composition or practical tips on how to use the product. Recipe ads are informational because they tell the public how to prepare and use the product or how to combine it with other ingredients to fix a meal. Utility and oil company–sponsored energy ads are also examples of informational advertising if they actually inform the consumer about conserving energy. Changing the filter in your furnace, closing the drapes at night, and checking the air pressure in your tires are all tips on how to be more energy efficient and how to save money, too.

Informational advertising is the most valuable kind for consumer decision-making because it lessens the time that consumers must spend searching for information. It also aids consumers by specifying more clearly the costs and benefits associated with the good or service involved. This makes the cost–benefit calculation easier and more accurate in our decision-making model. And finally, informational ads are valuable because they give the consumer more options. A greater variety of options leads to more competition, better service, lower prices, and, ultimately, greater consumer satisfaction.

Only a small proportion of all ads are purely informational. Most contain some fluff, if only to retain consumer interest. The key to classifying and then analyzing an advertisement is looking at the major thrust of the ad. If you know a good deal more after seeing it than you did before, the ad was informational. If, on the other hand, your knowledge was only minimally increased or if you were misled, then the ad falls into another category.

Puffery Advertising: A Lot of Hot Air

puffery: *Advertising that provides only dubious or unverifiable assertions. Its major goal is to persuade rather than to inform the consumer. Appeals on the basis of emotion, trust, institutions, rigged comparisons with the competition, or half-truths are all forms of puffery.*

Puffery is an advertising category the FTC uses to describe ads that supply little or no constructive information about the product. After you read or hear a puffing ad, you do not know much more than you did before. Price information is always left out, and the claims in favor of using this product are laudatory but vague and not easily tested. There are many forms of puffery, but all aim to persuade rather than to inform. The advertiser wants the consumer to buy the product based on some unverifiable emotional belief rather than on hard, empirical evidence. The forms of puffery—testimonial, institutional, emotional, comparative, and truth to convey falsehood—are the most common advertising techniques. They can be combined in any number of ways to achieve the goal of getting you to buy. In many cases, they try to succeed by short-circuiting your decision-making process.

testimonial advertisement:
a positive recommendation
about a good or service, often
given by a famous person

Testimonial ads: Trust me. A **testimonial advertisement** is a positive recommendation about a good or a service. As consumers, we often ask our friends or relatives about the merits of a particular restaurant, movie, or appliance they have tried; we ask for opinions that we can weigh, and then we come to our own conclusions. The difference between testimonials and recommendations is that testimonial ads are always favorable. They glow with superlatives about the quality of the service or the longevity of the product or the whiteness of the wash. They are never balanced or objective, so it is important to weigh them carefully—and skeptically—when we use them as part of the information we need to make a decision.

Testimonials come in two varieties: celebrity endorsements and "typical consumer" endorsements. Celebrity endorsements are by far the older and more traditional type of endorsement. In your experience you must have seen or heard thousands of these ads from people like Bill Cosby for Jell-O, Arnold Palmer for Pennzoil, and football quarterback Jim McMahon for Honda and Taco Bell. All of these ads are puffery in the sense that they provide no specific verifiable claims. They amount to the classic line, "Trust me. Would I steer you wrong?"

In one of the most successful testimonial ads ever run, the late John Wayne made a pitch in his cowboy outfit for a bank in southern California. Millions of dollars were deposited in that bank because "the Duke" said it was all right. On the other hand, Pat Boone was sued when it was discovered that the acne remedy he and his family recommended simply did not work. And Karl Malden, the spokesman for American Express, was taken to court by an irate consumer who did not get an instant refund when her traveler's checks were stolen in Latin America. Even former Olympic hero Bruce Jenner was taken to task over his sponsorship of Wheaties breakfast cereal. The argument was that he did not eat them. The rules as laid out by the FTC state that the person giving the testimonial must use the product at least some of the time. Jenner was subsequently cleared when it was shown that he was a Wheaties consumer.

Partly because of some of the problems with the FTC rules and partly because of consumer skepticism about the sincerity of famous folk, advertisers have turned to common people to give an "honest" evaluation of their products. Sometimes this takes the form of unsolicited letters to the manufacturer, which are followed up and then reenacted for the television ad campaign. You have surely seen the all-American mother who got those dirty socks clean even though they were covered with grease, the watch that kept on ticking after it had been inadvertently left in a tire for six months, or the family that would never part with their *TV Guide*.

These ordinary testimonials may also be contrived by an advertising firm that tests hundreds of consumers with hidden cameras and then produces honest testimonials: "My headache is gone," "I didn't think he would like stuffing instead of potatoes," "It *is* cleaner," "My hands are younger looking," and so forth.

Institutional ads. Successful political campaigns often appeal to the underlying values held by the public. One of these appeals is to invoke a patriotic theme. Anyone who has ever traveled outside the United States knows that special feeling of seeing our flag in foreign lands. It reminds you of home. Similar appeals to underlying American values can be used by corporate advertisers to sell their products. An **institutional advertisement** tries to associate a product with ideas and institutions that are not only familiar, but generally very dear to the vast majority of the American public. The Chevrolet Motor Division of General Motors, for instance, did this very effectively with its "Heartbeat of America—Chevrolet" theme. The ad campaign began with television commercials that mixed a pulsating heartbeat sound with a memorable musical tune. All of this bore witness to a basically patriotic theme with red, white, and blue colors. The ads were a rousing success both with the public and the critics. Chevrolet's share of the car and truck market rose after several years of decline, and the ads were nominated for ten Clio Awards (the most prestigious ad prizes in the industry). It didn't seem to matter that some of the Chevrolets being advertised were not American at all—they were imported.

The nature of institutional advertising often promotes **stereotyping**, that is, a subtle form of discrimination that identifies people with certain roles and thereby restricts their behavior and image, both individually and as a group. Have you ever noticed how the elderly are depicted in television commercials? Old people wait for phone calls, care for their dentures, and find it unbelievable that lemonade can actually be made from a mix. They rarely drive a car or drink Coca-Cola, and they seldom wash their own hair. According to a study done at the University of Maryland, children's images of older people are a product of their television watching. Children reported that old people are sick, sad, tired, dirty, ugly, wrinkled, crippled, and toothless. When asked how they will be when they are old, the children denied that they will ever grow old (Adler, 1980). More recent research has indicated some change in the perception of seniors, but a content analysis of major network television advertising still indicates bias in the presentation of older Americans. According to Linda Swayne and Alan Greco (1987) seniors are underrepresented in ads, and when they are in commercials, they are likely to be in the background.

Stereotypes are part and parcel of institutional puffery because an institutional ad must rely on the common conceptions and feelings of

institutional advertisement: an advertisment that associates a product with ideas and institutions that are valued by a majority of the consuming public the masses. This means that such ads unwittingly reinforce these ideas and thus in some cases help to foster discrimination. For an interesting pictorial review of how ads have treated sex, race, health, diet, and even alcohol, read Robert Atwan's classic book on the subject, *Edsels, Luckies & Frigidaires* (1970).

emotional advertisement:
ads with the major focus of
persuading consumers to buy
a product for psychological
reasons, such as guilt, fear, or
snobbery

Emotional ads. An **emotional advertisement** is one whose major focus is to persuade a consumer to buy a product because it will satisfy a psychological rather than a physiological need. Thus, a producer of Scotch whiskey might stress that only a few consumers will be able to appreciate the exquisite taste of a limited bottling of its aged scotch. The ad intimates that if you buy the product, you are among an elite. It appeals to your self-image, your ego.

All consumers carry emotional baggage. Advertisers who use emotional ads attempt to open this pyschological bag. Advertising firms employ staffs of psychologists and sociologists, who apply their knowledge of human behavior and emotions to create a profitable ad campaign. Guilt and fear are two old standbys that can be highly effective tools in convincing consumers to pay more. For example, an ad asks, ''Doesn't your family deserve the best?'' Another encourages us to ''Reach out and touch someone.'' Cosmetics and vitamin manufacturers have appealed to vanity for decades. Even the federal government (the twenty-ninth largest U.S. advertiser) uses some psychological ploys when it promises adventure to navy recruits or status to marine recruits (''The Marines are looking for a few good men'') Taken as a whole, emotionally based puffery ads can make consumers feel dissatisfied, insecure, or downright miserable, unless they do as they are told. A better solution is to use the consumer skills you develop in this course to see through ads and block the unreasoning response. But not everyone has the benefit of a course like this one (see Box 7.2).

comparative advertising: an
advertising strategy that
compares the name-brand
competitor(s) of the product
being advertised

Comparative ads. Advertisers have for a long time used **comparative advertising**, pitting their brand against ''Brand X,'' an unnamed (and clearly inferior) competitor. Recently, however, actual brand-name competition has become common. Now we can see for ourselves that extra-strength Anacin has twice the pain reliever of its two major competitors, Bufferin and Bayer. Of course, the advertiser never mentions that the pain reliever is acetylsalicylic acid, commonly called aspirin. And no price comparison is made (often it would be cheaper to take two tablets of aspirin rather than one tablet of extra-strength Anacin).

The failure to mention price is what turns comparative advertising into puffery. Some comparative advertising could be classified as informative if useful price comparisons were made, but that has proved hazardous in

BOX 7.2 KIDS AND THE TUBE

It was Saturday morning in the Clemo household, and Sara, eight, Megan Ann, five, and Andrew, two, were gathered before their color television set watching early-morning cartoons. The attention of the two smaller children occasionally wandered, but generally their eyes were riveted on the electronic marvel in their living room. Practically every show was interspersed with short, incisive, and often entertaining tidbits about the wondrous world of cereal, snack foods, candy, and soft drinks. Characters similar to their cartoon "friends" slyly tempted the children to try sugar-frosted this or sweet, crispy that. By the time their parents awoke and herded the children to the breakfast table, it was obvious that a meal of juice, eggs, and bacon was not at the top of their list.

"Why don't we ever have anything good to eat?" asked Sara, who was the most articulate spokesperson in the group. "We never get chocolate-covered Sugar Sparkles," she went on.

"I like Tony the Tiger," Megan Ann interrupted, affirming her loyalty to the cartoon huckster most closely associated with one of those sugar-based confections labeled "cereal" by its producers.

"Me, too. Mmm, good," burbled the youngest Clemo, Andrew.

"Don't you want me to make you bacon and eggs?" asked Vickie, their mother.

"No!" was the resounding chorus as the children wiggled and jiggled in their seats. "We want Tony! We want Tony!" was the watchword of the day.

"All right, all right, we'll buy some of that at the store next time. I promise," said the weary homemaker. And so she did.

1. Is this a farfetched example? Have you ever witnessed a scene in which children requested (or perhaps demanded) an advertised brand?

2. Studies conducted on the influence children aged six to eleven have on their parents' purchases indicate that a large percentage of them believe they have a major impact on their parents buying decision with regard to children's clothes (80%), toys (80%), cereal (72%), soft drinks (55%), and toothpaste (30%) (Stipp, 1988). Do these percentages seem correct in your experience?

3. As the influence of children becomes more obvious, advertisers will appeal more directly to them. Do you believe advertising aimed at children should be more closely regulated than general advertising? Why or why not?

some cases. Bristol-Myers used one of the earliest comparative advertising blitzes to introduce Datril, a nonaspirin pain reliever (acetaminophen), which competed with the number-one seller, Tylenol. Datril's manufacturer decided to undercut Tylenol's price and advertise the price difference. After the ad campaign was set, the commercials made, and time and space purchased, Tylenol cut its price dramatically. The result was a misleading ad campaign in which Datril claimed to be just as effective (true) and cheaper (true when the commercials were made, but false when they were run). The makers of Tylenol sued Bristol-Myers and all the newspapers, magazines, and networks involved, creating a messy situation that almost brought back "Brand X." It was a warning to other competitors, who rarely advertise comparative prices, to avoid doing what Datril did unless they are sure that there will be no retaliation.

Truth to convey falsehood. When advertisers tell the truth but make it sound as if they have a competitive edge when in fact they don't they are using **truth to convey falsehood**. For example, some automobile manufacturers advertise the fact that a car or pickup can go farther than its competitor can on a tank of gas. The fact is, the cruising range is higher because the gas tank is bigger, not because the car gets better mileage. The oil industry is not immune to this type of advertising, either. Back when oil companies aggressively tried to lure customers from a competitor's brand to their own, Shell Oil Company made a television commercial in which two cars with identical amounts of gasoline drove around an auto race track. They erected a paper barrier on the track to indicate where the first car ran out of gas and where the second car dramatically crashed through because it had fueled with Shell gasoline, which contained the high-mileage additive called platformate. What they didn't say was that almost all gasoline sold in the United States contained a similar additive. Shell told the truth but conveyed a false impression about its competitive advantage.

truth to convey falsehood: an ad that tells the truth but makes a product or service appear decidedly better than its competitors

Deceptive Advertising: An Attempt to Mislead the Consumer

deceptive advertising: any conscious attempt by a firm to mislead a consumer, this may take the form of false claims, free goods, high pressure, contests, or bait-and-switch tactics

Truth to convey falsehold and all other forms of puffery have their faults, but none involves outright lying. Whereas puffery-style advertising tries to direct (or misdirect) the consumer's attention gently—to blur his or her vision a bit—**deceptive advertising** is a conscious attempt to trick and mislead the consumer. In less serious cases, firms exceed the bounds of acceptable puffery and stray into an area in which, according to the FTC, the average consumer cannot separate fact from fiction. In more extreme cases, outright fraud may be involved if the firm tries to gyp the consumer. In case of fraud, legal action involving fines or imprisonment may be imposed on the offender. Box 7.3 lists some of the commonly used phrases in deceptive advertising. In the sections that follow, we describe some of the more common forms of deception that involve these catch phrases: false claims, free goods, now or never, contests, and bait and switch.

False claims. In the latter part of the nineteenth century it was common to see individuals peddling medicinal tonics that promised to cure ills from rheumatism and arthritis to cancer. With the founding of the Food and Drug Administration in 1906 and the Federal Trade Commission in 1914, such claims had to be substantiated. Quack remedies were gradually removed from the highways and byways of the American economy, but false claims have not entirely disappeared.

In 1987 the FTC challenged Kraft Cheese Slices advertisements that implied that each slice of the advertised cheese contained as much calcium as five ounces of milk. The FTC claimed this misrepresented the food value of the product. Geritol was another well-known name that indulged

---

BOX 7.3   THE WATCHWORDS OF DECEPTIVE ADVERTISING

The Department of Justice of the State of California developed the following list of gimmicks that characterize deceptive advertising. If you hear these words, be careful—you may be cheated.

1. "You have won a free gift." You will usually end up paying more than the gift is worth.

2. "I am not a salesman," or "I'm the advertising manager." No matter what they tell you, a person who tries to get money from you or your name on a contract is trying to sell you something.

3. "Only a few people are getting this special deal." You can be sure that the company is selling to you at or above the regular price.

4. "This is your last chance—I will not be in the neighborhood again." Before you spend a lot of money on anything, think it over; compare prices elsewhere. Don't be rushed. And if the salesperson won't be in the neighborhood, how will you return a faulty product?

5. "This low-priced advertised special is not for you—you want the expensive one." If the salesper-son doesn't recommend the advertised product, walk away before you're subjected to the "bait and switch" technique.

6. "Not only do you get these books, but you also get . . ." Be careful when a person sells you more than one thing. You may not want or need all these items. And you must realize that you are paying for *all* of them.

7. "It will cost you only 50 cents a day." On a three-year contract that comes to more than $500.

8. "This is a great item—it is guaranteed for life." In most cases, if the company goes out of business, if you can't find the company, or if it is not reliable, your guarantee is worthless. If you read a guarantee carefully, you will often find that it is filled with mention of things the company will not do rather than with details of repairs and replace-ments it will make.

9. "I am in a contest—one more order and I will win." Most of these sales pitches are phony. Do not buy from anyone unless you want what the person is selling and are willing to pay the price.

---

in false claims. For years Geritol was advertised as a cure for iron deficiency anemia, or "tired blood." What the advertising didn't report was that almost no one in the United States suffered from the malady and, further, that it was not caused by a lack of iron in the diet. Geritol finally removed the ads after a decade of litigation with the FTC.

The FTC has been reprimanded by some consumer advocates for being too slow to act and too lenient when it does pursue false claims. Partly as a response to this charge, the FTC has sometimes demanded **corrective advertising** as part of the retribution for wrongdoing. Three cases of corrective advertising have involved Profile diet bread, Ocean Spray cranberry juice, and Listerine mouthwash. Profile's claim that its bread had fewer calories per slice was true, but only because the slices were thinner: there was no difference in the caloric count of the loaf itself. Profile was required to advertise the discrepancy and thus inform consumers of its misleading claim. Ocean Spray advertised that its cranberry juice gave the consumer more energy than orange juice. What did that mean? It meant that cranberry juice has more calories, a fact that the FTC made the company advertise correctively. The Listerine case was

corrective advertising: ad-vertising that a company must undertake when the FTC rules that the firm's past advertising was false and misleading

more blatant because for years the company had claimed that Listerine killed germs by the millions and prevented colds and the flu. These claims were false, and a portion of the advertising had to be devoted to correcting a false image that still lingers in the mind of many consumers.

Free goods. Economists are fond of saying that there is no such thing as a free lunch. All goods and services must be paid for by someone. In the early 1900s you could go to the local bar at lunchtime, buy a beer, and get a sandwich "free." That was the proverbial free lunch, but of course the price of the beer covered the meal, too, so it really wasn't free. Today, some firms pretend to give the consumers certain goods or services "free" if they purchase a product. Strange as this may seem, some consumers still believe they are getting something for nothing.

The free-goods sales strategy is common among door-to-door salespeople, country fair hucksters, in late-night television ads and record- or book-of-the-month clubs. Record club ads offer ten records or tapes for $1.00; the only obligation is that you join the record club and agree to buy a certain number of monthly selections at the regular "low" prices. Like the free-lunch cost included in the price of the beer, the free-album or free-tape cost is included in the "low" regular price of the additional records that must be bought to fulfill the agreement. This pitch is not illegal. All the conditions are advertised, but many consumers do not take the time to see them. The advertiser preys on the consumer's desire for a bargain, and this ploy must work some of the time, because "free goods" continue to be offered. This technique is often combined with a high-pressure sales idea: It's now or never.

Now or never: A once-in-a-lifetime offer. Often used in conjunction with the "free goods" technique, the now-or-never offer generally tries to get the consumer to act on impulse, to forget the adage "look before you leap," and to think only that "he who hesitates is lost." This kind of advertising is especially deceptive because it preys on people's fears of being bad consumers, of missing an opportunity to save money and stretch their budget. Door-to-door salespeople have been known to use this technique effectively to push a consumer from a "let me think it over" position to a "where do I sign" view. The typical situation is familiar: The salesperson looks perplexed at the consumer's unwillingness to sign up immediately for a set of encyclopedias, a life insurance policy, or a new car; then suddenly, an idea occurs to the salesperson, who offers to lower the price or throw in some "free" goods, but only if the consumer agrees to buy right away. Of course, no reputable firm withdraws a legitimate offer to sell if you refuse to commit yourself on the spot. After all, the heart of the decision-making process is evaluation. It is often difficult to evaluate your options rationally while the salesperson is staring at you with a once-in-a-lifetime deal.

The now-or-never pressure is even more difficult to escape when the sales pitch is made in your own home. A consumer can walk out of an automobile showroom or a furniture store; you may feel intimidated by a salesperson in your home, however, and find it difficult to get him or her to leave. Recognizing this difficulty, the FTC has placed a three-day **cooling-off provision** on door-to-door sales of $25 or more. If you sign an installment contract after talking with a door-to-door salesperson, you have three business days to change your mind and void the contract. You can cancel the contract either by sending a written notice to the seller within three days or by completing and returning the form that the salesperson is legally bound to give you at the time of purchase. Notice, however, that this law applies only when you are to repay the debt in installments, that is, when credit is involved. Door-to-door sales such as Avon and Amway, in which the consumer orders and pays on delivery, are not included.

Contests: Everyone is a winner. Another scheme to gyp and defraud consumers is the contest in which everyone is a winner. The contest could be carried out by mail, by telephone, or sometimes in person. In some cases, you never even enter the contest; you are informed by mail or telephone that you have won a prize and all you need to do is come to the store and pick it up. In other schemes, you may be asked a series of questions that result in your winning a "valuable gift," you may be asked to participate in a survey and earn a "valuable gift," or you may be asked to fill in a coupon with your name and address and later learn that you have won a "valuable gift." All of these roads lead to the same place, a merchant's place of business, where you will be given the opportunity to spend your money to buy something to go along with your prize. A common prize is a sitting at a photography studio and an "8 × 10" photograph. Once you go in, you discover that several poses are taken, and then a magnificent array of photos are available for you to purchase, If children are involved, especially grandchildren, it is often nearly impossible to walk away from the offer with your single "free" photograph. Photographers are not the only contest runners; dance studios, health clubs, real estate agents, sewing machine shops, solar energy firms, and cookware and meat companies have all been known to use these schemes.

Bait and switch. Bait and switch is one of the oldest and most successful ways to defraud consumers. However, it is an illegal tactic that is punishable by fine or imprisonment under federal law. Like many other forms of deception, bait and switch involves the consumer's natural urge to get a bargain, to get something of value for a low price. The low-priced

---

cooling-off provision: a time period (3 business days under an FTC ruling) during which a consumer is allowed to cancel a door-to-door installment sales contract

bait and switch: an illegal sales technique in which a merchant offers a product at a low price but then refuses to sell it and attempts to switch the consumer to a high-priced item

item is the "bait." It lures the "fish" (consumers) by its appealing low price and apparent high quality. Once the consumer has been attracted to the store, the sales staff tries to get him or her hooked on another more expensive model. This is called the switch. During the switch, the salesperson carefully and forcefully convinces the prospective buyer that the advertised bait is inadequate for his or her needs and that the consumer should buy (switch to) a more expensive model. In a variation on this sales technique, the merchant is supposedly out of the advertised item but sells the consumer a much better model at a slightly higher price. Home appliances such as washers, dryers, vacuum cleaners, and sewing machines are the favorites of bait-and-switch artists because they are expensive enough to provide the salesperson with a commission on each sale, and they are complicated enough to make it difficult for the consumer to compare quality and performance of different models at the time of sale.

The best defense against bait and switch is a strong background in consumer education and a history of dealing with longstanding, reputable businesses. However, even a reputable firm can be found guilty of this technique. In the 1970s, Sears, Roebuck & Company was said to have practiced this time-honored technique in some of its stores. The original complaint alleged that a Sears ad offered a $58 sewing machine that could do buttonholes and zig-zag stitches and could operate in reverse. But if a customer tried to buy the machine, a salesperson said that the machine really could not perform as well as advertised and that it was noisy, lacked a standard guarantee, and required a lengthy wait for delivery. A more expensive model was then suggested—a classic example of bait and switch.

It is important to realize that not all merchants are on the wrong side of the law. Most are decent, law-abiding citizens who abhor the techniques described under the "false claims" section. We now explore the positive side of advertising to see how advertising can benefit the consumer and the economy.

THE BENEFITS OF ADVERTISING

A few years ago when X-rated movies were the objects of local indignation and filmmakers were periodically hauled into court for producing pornographic acts on celluloid and distributing them to the public as "art," the courts were asked to weigh the traditional right of free speech versus the public's right to decency. The judges, after considerable discussions, research, and viewing of the films, handed down a doctrine that generally absolved the filmmakers of any wrongdoing as long as they could demonstrate that the films potentially had some redeeming social value. In other words, the judges asked whether there was anything in the film that provided some benefit to society. A similar question might be put to the advertising community. Consumers are perpetually bombarded with ads that run the gamut from impugning one's ability to select the correct after-shave to intimating that one's temperament and bodily functions can both be improved by using a laxative. Are there any socially redeeming qualities to advertising?

Information: More Than You Ever Wanted to Know

The initial defense of advertising has been made and will continue to be made on the basis of the consumer's need for information. In other words, advertising alerts consumers to the availability of a particular product. As one advertising executive put it, familiarizing the consumer with a product "is the absolutely basic value created in advertising, the one underlying all the others" (Commanor and Wilson, 1979, p. 472).

A more traditional view of the producer–consumer dichotomy argues that if someone were to build a better mousetrap, the world would beat a path to his or her door. We know that is not true in our economy today. A new consumer product has to have tremendous promotion and field study before it will be allowed on the store shelf, because an unwanted product can mean large losses for a firm.

Of course, you should not conclude that massive advertising outlays and a skilled public relations campaign automatically result in a profitable product. On the contrary, the marketplace is littered with new, improved brands that never made it or were profitable for a while and have since been discontinued. Ipana toothpaste, Billy Beer, Osborne computers, Premier smokeless cigarettes, Edsel automobiles, and Micrin mouthwash are just a few of the thousands that have disappeared despite heavy advertising. Advertising may be a necessary, but certainly not a sufficient, condition to ensure success among consumers.

Supporters of advertising as an informational medium are not terribly concerned with the FTC's categories. The advertising message may provide some useful information regarding product characteristics and price, or it may simply call attention to the existence of the product, or it may even be entertaining. The point, as far as these supporters are concerned, is that you, the consumer, become aware of their product. If they make the product a household word, they consider their job successfully completed. See Box 7.4 for some examples of successful brand-name and item identification.

Advertising and Competition: Lower Prices

Some studies have shown that advertising can result in greater competition among firms and lower prices for consumers. This seems to be especially true when the public is dealing with a professional group whose services are fairly standardized—physicians, pharmacists, lawyers, and

---

BOX 7.4   **ADVERTISING AND BRAND-NAME IDENTIFICATION**

"I have a cut, Mommy. Can I have a Band-Aid?"

This request is honored in millions of homes throughout America. Very few children—or adults, for that matter—ask for "adhesive plastic bandage strips." This is an example of a marketing executive's dream: succeeding so completely that even the competition is willing to accept your brand's name as ideal. There are a number of products that have so overwhelmed the competition that their trade name has become the accepted term for all products of that type. Many of us ask for a Kleenex when we mean a tissue, Jell-O when we want a gelatin dessert, or Vaseline when referring to petroleum jelly. Some product names actually become verbs, as in the phrase "Xerox it" rather than "photocopy it." This kind of success is not the result of advertising alone, but it is seldom achieved without advertising.

---

dentists, for example. The original discovery of the correlation between advertising and lower prices was reported by Lee Benham (1972) in "The Effect of Advertising on the Price of Eyeglasses." According to Benham, those states that prohibited opticians from advertising had significantly higher prices than those areas where advertising was permitted. In fact, the average pair of glasses cost more then twice as much in the restrictive states.

Since Benham's pioneering study, the FTC has conducted more studies to determine the effect of advertising on the cost and quality of eyeglasses and examinations provided by optometrists. The FTC reported that the average cost of an eye examination and glasses in cities with the fewest restrictions on advertising was $71.91, compared with $94.58 in the most restrictive cities. The FTC report concluded:

1. The existence of advertising and commercial practice by some optometrists in a market does not result in a lowering of the quality of examinations available to consumers.
2. The existence of price advertising and commercial practice by some optometrists does result in lower prices. The prices of both less and more thorough examinations and eyeglasses were significantly lower in the least restrictive cities than in the most restrictive cities (*Consumers' Research*, 1981).

Given the results of its investigation on eye examinations, the FTC has fought to eliminate bans on most professional advertising. Professional associations such as the American Medical Association (AMA) and the American Bar Association (ABA) attempted to limit this avenue of competition because abuses might creep in. The possibility that a physician or a lawyer would appear in a television commercial to drum up new business was, to the AMA and the ABA, unprofessional at best and unprofitable at worst. Nevertheless, the ban on professional advertising was overturned in the 1980s and as a result consumers now benefit from more informational advertising.

Brand Names and Quality Control

Poet Gertrude Stein wrote, "A rose is a rose is a rose." And Romeo said, "A rose by any other name would smell as sweet." But many consumers simply do not believe this—and they show it in their behavior. They continue to buy nationally advertised brands, while similar, lower-priced products are conveniently located on the adjoining shelf of the local supermarket. Despite its higher price, the heavily advertised brand of peaches or pudding often outsells its lesser-known counterpart by as much as ten to one. Is it collective brainwashing that prevents the consumer from buying the nonadvertised product? Advocates of brand names frequently argue that it is something else, namely, quality assurance.

If a firm spends millions of dollars on advertising its products, it is doing more than simply informing the consumer about a particular product. It is investing in a reputation. Multiproduct firms like General Motors, General Electric, and Procter & Gamble are well aware that their advertising does more than sell cars or toasters or shampoo; it says something about the advertiser. Once they put their brand on an item, they are implying that their reputation stands behind it. Consumers are aware of the unwritten guarantee of brand names and are often willing to pay a premium price for the uniform quality and performance implied by large advertising budgets.

A large advertising investment must be safeguarded, and one way to do so is to produce a good product and then stand behind it. Nothing can be more damaging than a bad reputation or a company "trading on its name." Procter & Gamble's handling of the Rely tampon problem is a good example of how a large advertiser with a good reputation of quality deals with a potentially damaging situation. In 1980, reports of a new disease called toxic shock syndrome began to appear in the news media. This disease seemed to strike women who used tampons, especialy Procter & Gamble's brand, Rely. Although the evidence linking toxic shock syndrome to Rely tampons was far from conclusive, Procter & Gamble elected to remove them from the marketplace rather than run the risk of harming anyone and ruining their reputation. If Rely tampons had been produced by a small manufacturer, the chances are slim that they would have been recalled voluntarily. A smaller firm would have been bankrupted by such an incident; besides it would have had a considerably smaller advertising investment in its reputation to protect.

The ability to discriminate among competitors on the basis of brand names is considered a luxury that socialistic countries often decide to avoid. However, even the Soviet Union is beginning to change in this regard. It has begun to require labeling of some consumer products so that the particular factory of origin is obvious. The reasoning is similar to that of the supporters of brand-name ádvertising. Brand labeling is a defense against shoddy workmanship. Imagine one Russian saying to another, "I only buy vodka made of People's Factory Number 5. I know it's of good quality."

Positive Side Effects of Advertising

spillover effects (externalities): unintended impacts of production or consumption on third parties

Sometimes an economic transaction between two parties has an unintended impact on a third party. This third-party impact is called a **spillover effect**, or **externality**. Spillover effects can be either negative or positive. For example, if you bought some rose bushes for your garden and planted them in your front yard, you would have beautified not just your house, but the neighborhood as well. You and the owner of the nursery who sold you those plants are satisfied with the transaction; you both gained from the sale of the roses. And your neighbors gained, too. They now have a more pleasant-looking neighborhood.

Democratic societies gain information media as a side-effect of advertising, because revenues from ads support newspapers, magazines, radio broadcasts, and television news departments. None of these media could survive as we know them today without advertising revenues. Advertisers, who provide more than two-thirds of the gross revenues of newspapers and magazines, use the media to inform the public about their products. Indirectly, however, such expenditures allow the press to gather general news and to produce special stories that inform, enlighten, and entertain the public. As Sean MacBride, winner of the Nobel Peace Prize, wrote in his UNESCO book on communication, "[S]ince the advertising revenue of a newspaper or a broadcaster comes from multiple sources, it fosters economic health and independence, enabling the enterprise to defy pressure from any single economic interest or from political authorities" (1980, p. 110). Without advertising it would be difficult to imagine us having as many hard-charging political correspondents as we currently support. Thus, advertising is an example of a good that has some significant spillover benefits, such as strengthening political democracy.

On the other hand, there are clearly negative side-effects, or externalities, from the proliferation of ads. Outdoor billboards are often a form of visual pollution, marring our landscape. All must endure them, even those of us to whom they are not directed. There is also a possible externality that is more insidious: whether a significant advertiser doesn't sometimes have the clout to squelch the coverage of an unfavorable story. These are two of the potentially negative side-effects of advertising that must be weighed against the positive side-effects if we are to achieve a balanced view of advertising's political impact.

MAJOR SOURCES OF CONSUMER INFORMATION

Advertising is certainly not the only source of consumer information. In fact, given the main purpose of advertising, namely to persuade the consumer to favor a certain good or service, it is a wonder that ads have as much information in them as they do. Nevertheless, there are other ways that consumers can obtain unbiased information. Some involve the communications media like magazines and newspapers, others involve institutions like testing laboratories and government. All can help you when you are making a decision.

Obtaining Information from the Media: Just the Facts, Please

Given that advertising revenues support our newspeople, where can consumers get straight talk? One way is by reading some of the major consumer-oriented magazines in the library or by subscribing to them. One magazine that accepts no advertising and threatens to sue companies that use its names in promotional literature is *Consumer Reports*. It publishes an annual buyer's guide in addition to a monthly magazine. Consumer products are purchased and rated in competitive tests by experts. The ratings are then published, giving consumers objective data on the relative strengths and weaknesses of a particular brand. This magazine is

A wide variety of consumer magazines provides information on consumer products.

especially helpful for expensive, in frequently purchased items, such as clothes dryers, automobiles, and room air conditioners. But even here, you may find that you disagree with the "experts." For years, *Consumer Reports* rated the Volkswagen sedan an unsafe car that should not be purchased. However, millions were sold, not out of ignorance, but because in the minds of consumers the other features of the VW bug—mileage, performance, durability, and price—outweighed the safety factor. As with all information, only you can be the final judge. But at least with *Consumer Reports*, you know that potential advertising revenue loss (or gain) is never a factor in the ratings.

Other consumer-oriented periodicals like *Money, Changing Times, Consumers' Research,* and *Consumer's Digest* contain good consumer information. Periodicals that focus on family living, such as *Better Homes and Gardens, Family Circle,* and *Sunset,* frequently have articles on consumer interests: among others, energy, food, banking, appliances, and personal inflation strategies. Still other magazines narrow their focus to one type of consumer good, such as automobiles. Thus, you may want to look at *Road & Track, Motor Trend,* or *Car and Driver* to get more information about a particular car, or you may turn to *Stereo Review* to find out about a certain sound system. But you must be wary of the evaluations and recommendations of the commercial magazines, especially those that cater to a particular industry. Advertising pays a large portion of their bills, and they don't want to upset a big account by criticizing its products.

You might also look more closely at your local media for sources of consumer information. It is a rare local newspaper that does not contain at least one consumer column, and many local television and radio stations are hopping on the consumer bandwagon by featuring consumer advocates.

Government-Sponsored Sources of Consumer Information

Consumers do not have to rely solely on the private sector for important product information. Many federal agencies provide consumers with materials that are helpful and educational at little or no charge. One of these sources of information, the Federal Trade Commission, was mentioned earlier in this chapter. Other agencies like the Food and Drug Administration, the Consumer Product Safety Commission, and the U.S. Department of Agriculture will be outlined in more detail in later chapters. For an overall view of government-generated consumer information, you should be familiar with the Consumer Information Center, which was established in 1970 to help federal agencies distribute informative pamphlets produced with tax dollars. In addition to serving as a clearinghouse for consumer publications produced by other federal offices, the Consumer Information Center (CIC) publishes a quarterly *Consumer*

Information Catalog. Every three months, the CIC updates its list of publications and reviews new federal pamphlets relevant to consumers. Most of the titles in this catalog are either free or available at a nominal charge. You can obtain a copy of the most recent catalog by writing to the Consumer Information Center, P.O. Box 100, Pueblo, CO 81002.

Person-to-Person Information

There are many sources of consumer information that do not directly relate to advertising. Nationally oriented consumer magazines, buying guides, general periodicals, and local media are only a few. You may also rely on the experiences of friends, relatives, and even casual acquaintances to fill in some gaps in your knowledge about particular brands or products. It is a common practice to ask someone who has just bought a new appliance or a car, "How do you like it?" This natural inquiry is not simply idle curiosity; it is a request for information that can be used in a later decision.

Of course, as we stressed in our decision-making model, options must always be conditioned by personal values and goals. If you ask someone's opinion and his or her values do not coincide with yours, the opinion should be weighted accordingly. In the Volkswagen example given above, one of the reasons consumers continued to buy VW bugs despite their dismal ratings in *Consumer Reports* was that the values held by the rating experts were different from those held by the consumers. The experts clearly valued safety above all else. And crash tests showed that the lightweight, compact, rear-engine Volkswagen was no match for the heavier, full-size, front-engine V-8s produced in Detroit. But consumers by the millions were not as concerned with safety as with dependability and economy, values that the magazine gave secondary consideration.

Similar examples can be drawn from conversations about most consumer items. A family that values convenience may be happy with a huge frost-free refrigerator-freezer because it stores large amounts of food and dispenses water and ice right through the door. A neighbor who is a post-industrial-age consumer (see Chapter 1) and who values convenience less might be happier with a smaller, less resource-intensive unit. Information received from convenience-minded consumers would not help their post-industrial-age neighbor make a wise decision.

Weighing the Time Costs of Seeking Information

Besides accounting for possible differences in values, you must also consider the cost of seeking information in your decision-making process. Remember, the cost of anything equals the explicit monetary cost plus the implicit time costs. Sometimes you can get a trade-off between these two kinds of costs when you consider information costs. For example, if you pay for a subscription to a consumer magazine, you save time by not having to go to the library to read it, but the dollar cost is, of course, higher. If you realize that getting information involves both explicit and implicit costs, you also know that it is possible to spend too much time or money obtaining information about a purchase. In general, the information costs you are willing to incur should be directly proportional to the amount of income you spend on the item. In other words, you should be more willing to spend time and money on gathering information about getting a place to live than you do on buying a pair of pants because the impact on your budget of a bad choice in homes is more devastating than the impact of buying the wrong apparel. As our cost–benefit rule suggested, limited resources should be spent on the highest-benefit items first. It is interesting that most consumer magazines have the same opinion about how much space to devote to various consumer items. They spend more time on big-ticket items like cars, stereos, and refrigerators than they do on toothbrushes or clothing.

Goods and services that you purchase frequently, such as gasoline, food, and clothing, have fairly low information costs if you pay attention to the feedback you get after consuming them. For such repeat-purchase items, there is little need to spend much time or money on obtaining information for the early steps of the decision-making framework. The key to good decision making with these items is in step 6, review and evaluation. This is where you allow your experience to provide information. For example, suppose you plan to purchase a cake mix. Perhaps you normally purchase a certain brand, but you see that the store has a sale on a competitor that you never tried before. The overall cost of either brand is small, but the sale difference amounts to perhaps 20 percent of the price. Because this is a repeat-purchase item that takes a small portion of your budget, it does not justify a lengthy information search about the merits of the less-expensive brand. A quick cost–benefit analysis will probably lead you to choose the sale item because it is cheaper. Once you have tried it, you should mentally review and evaluate it according to step 6 of our model. If it is as good as your old brand, you have widened your choices by obtaining some experience-based information at little cost. If you judge it to be inferior to your old brand, you still have more information, and you can buy it again if you want to bake a cake for someone with less finicky tastes.

SUMMARY

The consumer's search for information is an integral part of the decision-making process. The advertising industry has grown, at least partly, because it is able to fill this need. Firms spend more than $100 billion each year to advertise their products and inform consumers about the benefits of their brands. Some of the information they provide is of genuine service to consumers, who need input before making a decision. And as we have shown, advertising provides benefits besides information. Ads sometimes promote competition and thus lower retail prices. They can create an image of product quality that firms do not want tarnished. This emphasis on a good reputation leads larger firms to act responsibly, maintaining quality and even removing potentially hazardous products before they are required to do so. Advertising expenditures subsidize much of our news media, with significant spillover benefits in a democratic society. On the other hand, advertising can mislead or even manipulate and deceive consumers. Such advertising can be an unproductive but harmless expenditure, or it can be fraudulent activity punishable by fine or imprisonment. Fraudulent advertising, puffery, and stereotyping are some of the major criticisms leveled at the advertising industry by critics who feel that advertising is not simply a helpful information-providing system.

Of course, advertising is not the only way to obtain product information. Consumer demand for information is large enough to have stimulated a number of other sources. Magazines, newspapers, and radio and television newscasts furnish the consumer with information on a regular basis. Contacting the Consumer Information Center is another way you can obtain updated news about a variety of topics that have been investigated by various federal agencies. Finally, your information network extends beyond the media, to friends, family members, and acquaintances. Apply economic theory to your information gathering. Remember that the search for information has a significant opportunity cost and should not be prolonged beyond the point where the additional search cost exceeds the expected future benefit.

QUESTIONS

1. Figure 7.1 shows the growth in advertising revenues in the United States from 1890 to 1990. How do you explain advertising's early growth, its decline in the 1930s, and its subsequent boom?

2. List and then briefly explain ways that advertising can benefit consumers. Give some real-world examples.

3. What are the three major categories of advertising according to the FTC? Classify the following according to FTC categories:
   a. Weekly grocery store ads
   b. A ridiculously low advertised price for a color television
   c. A famous ballplayer extolling the virtues of a new yogurt
   d. An ad for expensive automobile tires in which young children are shown swinging in a tire with nothing on but their diapers
   e. A television commercial in which several headache remedies are shown side by side, but only one has more of the pain reliever "doctor's recommend most"

5. If you agree to buy a set of encyclopedias on a time payment plan from a door-to-door salesperson, how long can you legally wait before canceling the sale? What is this period called?

6. Explain the bait-and-switch advertising technique. How can you recognize it?

7. Not all items that we purchase are worthy of the same degree of information search.

    a. Rate the following items in order of the time you would be willing to spend on seeking information about them; list the item you would spend the most time on researching first, and the one you would give the least time, last:

toothpaste, denim jeans, new car, rental apartment, stereo system.

    b. Why did you rank them in a specific order? Did price play a major role?

    c. Beside each item, list where you would seek information about it. Did advertising play a role?

REFERENCES AND READINGS

Adler, Richard P. *The Effects of Television Advertising on Children*. Lexington, Mass.: Heath, 1980.

Advertising Age. Annual Special Edition of the 100 Leading National Advertisers, September, 24, 1987.

Atwan, Robert, et al. *Edsels, Luckies & Frigidaires*. New York: Dell, 1979.

Benham, Lee. "The Effect of Advertising on the Price of Eyeglasses." *Journal of Law and Economics*, October 1972.

Commanor, William S., and Wilson, Thomas A. "Advertising and Competition: A Survey." *Journal of Economic Literature*, June 1979.

"How Advertising Affects Price and Quality." *Consumers' Research*, April 1981.

Leffler, Keith B. "Persuasion or Information: The Economics of Prescription Drug Advertising," *Journal of Law and Economics*, April 1981.

MacBride, Sean. *Many Voices, One World*. New York: UNESCO, 1980.

McNeal, James U. *Children as Consumers: Insights and Applications*. Lexington, Mass.: Heath, 1987.

Miracle, Gordon. *Voluntary Regulation of Advertising: A Comparative Analysis of the United Kingdom and the United States*. Lexington, Mass.: Lexington Books, 1987.

Pollay, Richhard W. "The Distorted Mirror: Reflections on the Unintended Consequences of Advertising." *Journal of Marketing*, April 1986.

Stipp, Horst H. "Children as Consumers." *American Demographics*, February 1988.

Swayne, Linda E., and Greco, Alan J. "The Portrayal of Older Americans in Television Commercials." *Journal of Advertising*, 1, 1987.

Chapter Eight

CONSUMER PROTECTION AND REDRESS: DOING UNTO OTHERS AS THEY DO UNTO YOU

- ☐ Caveat Emptor: An Outdated Concept
- ☐ The Informed Consumer: An Ounce of Prevention
- ☐ The Beginning of Consumer Legislation
- ☐ The Modern Consumer Protection Movement
- ☐ The Costs and Benefits of Government Regulation
- ☐ Consumer Redress: Types and Levels of Consumer Protection
- ☐ Consumer Rights and Responsibilities
- ☐ Enforcing Your Rights: A Practical Problem
- ☐ Consumer Protection in the 1990s

DID YOU KNOW THAT...

. . . consumer protection regulations date back to early Greek and Roman law?

. . . muckracking journalists are responsible for creating public awareness of the need for pure food and drug laws?

. . . before 1938 drugs were not tested for safety before marketing?

. . . most accidents with consumer products are caused by consumer error or recklessness rather than by faulty product manufacture or design?

. . . there is a Federal Information Center to help answer consumer questions or put you in touch with experts who can?

As noted in Chapters 1 and 2, American life-styles have changed dramatically in this century. The simple life of the eighteenth-century farm family has gone the way of the pterodactyl. We drink low-calorie liquids containing nonnutritive sweeteners that, according to some studies, cause cancer. Our medicine chests are generally crammed with an assortment of over-the-counter and prescription drugs whose ingredients and their side-effects test the understanding even of physicians. Our normal life routine so depends on energy that an oil shortage or an electrical blackout would give us problems ranging in severity from not being able to get to work to sleeping in a cold, unheated waterbed. And, of course, we pay for our wide range of consumer goods with a financial system so complex that it can be managed only by computers.

Given this exceedingly complex level of living, it is little wonder that consumers seek, need, and expect help. This chapter explores the help available to consumers. It begins with the historical progression of consumer legislation from primarily providing information to providing protection and safety. It shows the transition from consumers having total responsibility for their economic and physical well-being in the marketplace to the sharing of that responsibility by industry and government. This chapter also provides specific suggestions for seeking help with consumer complaints, including information about consumer rights and the responsibilities that accompany those rights. Included are procedures for complaint handling, beginning at the local level, progressing to state and federal agencies, and concluding with small claims court.

The vast majority of businesspeople are reputable and want to provide the best possible goods and services; it is in their best interest, enabling them to retain loyal customers and get repeat business. However, some unscrupulous businesspeople do exist, and mistakes do happen. This chapter offers guidance for dealing with fraud and error.

CAVEAT EMPTOR: AN OUTDATED CONCEPT

People have been involved in the exchange of goods since prehistoric times. With the passing of centuries, buyers and sellers have become more skillful at exchanging goods. **Caveat emptor** is a Latin phrase that means "let the buyer beware": The buyer is responsible for not being cheated. According to this doctrine, if you happen to buy something that breaks after a few uses or that turns out to be less suitable than you expected, you should not expect any sympathy from the merchant or society. In the classic caveat emptor scenario, a visitor to New York (or Paris or Portland) is approached by a street vendor selling $400 watches for $50. Obviously, these watches have been obtained illegally, but the prospective consumer is caught up in the idea of getting such a bargain. A few days later, the consumer finds out that the watch is a cheap imitation of a more expensive brand and is not even worth $10. Many of us would blame and want to punish the seller, but the buyer's greed is also at fault. The buyer who fails to beware has little recourse. There is simply no way to report the fraud without incriminating the buyer as well as the seller.

The caveat emptor doctrine resulted from increased specialization and technology compounded by a complex marketing system. As technology advanced and individuals became more mobile, the likelihood that purchased goods were produced by a stranger rather than by a friend or a relative increased. In the nineteenth century the roots of our mass-marketing and distribution system began to develop as railroads were built, mail-order chain stores were founded, and department stores opened in downtowns across the nation. According to anthropologist Marvin Harris (1981), the social relationship between producers and consumers is a major factor that determines whether a product is well made and safe. A man is not likely to chisel a blunt arrowhead for himself; neither is a woman likely to weave her own basket out of rotted straw. In contrast, when the product has been made by a stranger and sold by another stranger, as is typical in industrial societies, the buyer indeed must be wary. In this impersonal relationship, caution is often not enough.

THE INFORMED CONSUMER: AN OUNCE OF PREVENTION

Of course, it has never been good business to bilk the public repeatedly, especially if one has competitors. Consumers will then *vote* for one's competition by buying *their* products. The decision to buy from one producer rather than from another, however, depends on knowledge of the existence of a better-quality or lower-priced good or service.

In societies less complex than ours, sufficient information can be acquired through personal experience with a product. Consider a society in which the diet is simply rice, fresh fruit, and occasional bits of chicken; in which food is cooked in an iron pot over an open fire; in which transportation is by foot or ox cart; in which clothes are simple flat fabrics wrapped around the body, and houses are made of bamboo. Members of this society can easily judge the quality of the few consumer goods they purchase.

In contrast, the number of consumer goods in our society seems to approach infinity, and their complexity can be overwhelming. In our complex environment a cautious attitude is not adequate protection against consumer disappointment or fraud. Product information is essential to decide whether an item should be purchased and, if so, with what features and from whom.

Additionally, an ignorant or misinformed consumer is of concern to a legitimate business and to society as a whole. Ignorant consumers do not follow rational, logical rules of consumption. They fall prey to criminals who pretend to offer goods or services that are comparable with those

fraud: deceit or trickery used
to gain an unfair advantage

available from reputable local businesses. They listen to falsehoods told by a seller whose intent is to make a sale by misleading the buyer (Eiler, 1984). Such **fraud** tarnishes the reputations of businesses in general and literally steals money from the honest firms. If money is spent on a cheap watch that breaks after one winding or a television that turns out to be worthless, it cannot be spent for legitimate goods at reputable businesses. As a result, it is in the interest of consumers, businesses, and governments alike to inform and protect consumers.

THE BEGINNING OF CONSUMER LEGISLATION

Regulations to protect consumers are not a new idea. Societies have had to deal for a long time with the problem of short-weighting and adulterated food. The standardization of measures for ale, wine, and corn in England was set by King John in the Magna Carta (A.D. 1215). In an earlier era, Greek and Roman law specifically prohibited selling wine that had been diluted with water; offenses were punishable by death. Even in Colonial America, consumer protection was an issue. Records of the Massachusetts Bay Colony indicate that in 1630, Nicholas Knopf was sentenced to pay a fine or be whipped in the town square for selling "a water of no worth nor value" as a cure for scurvy (a vitamin C—deficiency disease). For another example, see Box 8.1.

It is clear from this brief digression into history that government involvement in consumer protection is not just a twentieth-century phenomenon. In the next few sections we outline the early role that our federal government played in establishing weights and measures and the beginnings of its more recent attempts to regulate food and drugs.

Weights and Measures: Information

In its broadest form, consumer protection as a part of economic activity has been a governmental responsibility since the earliest days of our country. The Constitution of the United States gave Congress the power "To regulate Commerce with foreign Nations, and among the several States" and to "fix the Standard of Weights and Measures." Congress provides national **weights and measures standards** that are used today in buying and selling goods, in judging environmental quality, and in ensuring consumer and product safety. It provides consumers with product information necessary for comparison shopping and decision making.

Despite its power to do so, Congress has never enacted an all-inclusive weights-and-measures law; instead, it has chosen to pass occasional laws that regulate specific products. The responsibility for comprehensive weights-and-measures legislation has instead rested with state governments, which are responsible for inspecting businesses and policing the laws.

BOX 8.1   THE ROOTS OF CONSUMER PROTECTION

We have reproduced below the first general prohibition in the United States against all forms of food adulteration. This Massachusetts law, passed in 1785, shows early concern for legislating consumer protection.

An Act againſt ſelling unwholeſome Proviſions.

WHEREAS ſome evilly diſpoſed perſons, from motives of avarice and filthy lucre, have been induced to ſoll diſeaſed, corrupted, contagious or unwholeſome proviſions, to the great nuiſance of public health and peace :

Be it therefore enacted by the Senate and Houſe of Repreſentatives, in General Court aſſembled, and by the authority of the ſame, That if any perſon ſhall ſell any ſuch diſeaſed, corrupted, contagious or unwholeſome proviſions, whether for meat or drink, knowing the ſame without making it known to the buyer, and being thereof convicted before the Juſtices of the General Seſſions of the Peace, in the county where ſuch offence ſhall be committed, or the Juſtices of the Supreme Judicial Court, he ſhall be puniſhed by fine, impriſonment, ſtanding in the pillory, and binding to the good behaviour, or one or more of theſe puniſhments, to be inflicted according to the degree and aggravation of the offence.

[This act paſſed *March* 8, 1785.]

SOURCE: ''The U.S. Food and Drug Law: How It Came, How It Works,'' FDA 79–1054 (1979).

As consumers, we often take weights and measures for granted. But they are among the most important protection that consumers have, because they provide information as well as protection in the form of inspection and penalties for violations. If no one periodically inspected gasoline pumps, how long would it be before some stations altered the rate at which gasoline flows through the nozzle? How long before a liter bottle of cola contained less than a liter? Even with inspections, it is estimated that consumers in the United States lose $8 to $10 billion per year because of short-weights or -counts, as the expense of hiring more inspectors to check more products more frequently is prohibitive.

Historically, weights and measures standards were initiated by the business community because producers were concerned about the marketing of short-weight goods. In the dairy industry, for example, one dairy was cited for selling milk by the gallon in a container that could not hold a gallon of liquid. A toothpick manufacturer put 400 toothpicks in boxes labeled 750. A butcher sold meat by the pound, but in his store a pound equaled only $14\frac{1}{2}$ ounces. In all these cases, not only were customers cheated, but the firms' competitors were injured by unfair competition. Misinformed consumers, seeking to stretch their budgets, bought these "cheaper" products, and the legitimate firms lost customers.

Food Safety: Protection

Until the late nineteenth century, American consumer protection resulted incidentally from government intervention as it established standardized weights and measures. As 1900 approached, the dangers of consuming grew apace with urbanization and industrialization. When families left their farms and moved to the city, fewer and fewer people could raise their own food. As a consequence, a large wholesale and retail food industry blossomed. The development of refrigeration and the use of preservatives led for the first time to national food distribution. Names such as Armour, Heinz, and Swift grew to be household words. These companies were instrumental in supplying the urban consumer with the staples of life.

Unknown to the consumer, however, conditions in some food-processing and packaging companies were dusty, dirty, and germ ridden. In the absence of standards (and paid leave for illness), sick workers often handled food in a filthy environment. Worse yet, food products were not always what they seemed to be. For example, rancid butter was disguised by using flavorings or was extended by oleomargarine, wheat flour was mixed with flour from cheaper grains, and diseased swine and cattle were slaughtered and sold for human consumption. Much of this adulteration was not visible, so some producers represented the food as high quality but sold it for lower than market prices, making a generous profit.

Not surprisingly, the earliest pressure for regulation came from farmers whose markets were invaded by these inferior products. In states where farming was a major industry, demands by farmers caused the creation of state departments of agriculture. Food chemists in these departments organized the National Association of State Dairy and Food Departments and began lobbying for regulations against adulterated food and farm products. Many reformers, particularly Harvey W. Wiley (then chief chemist for the United States Department of Agriculture), added their voices to the call for a Pure Food and Drug Act.

The proposed regulations had little support until the publication of Upton Sinclair's *The Jungle* in 1906. The work was an exposé of the deplorable conditions in the Chicago meatpacking houses at the turn of the century. Sinclair described, for example, the problems that the meatpackers had with rats. The meatpackers solved the problem by placing poisoned bread around the plant to kill the rodents. That seemed fine except that the employees threw the dead rats and poisoned bread into the vats where sausage and salami were being made. It was clear from Sinclair's study that the federal government needed to protect consumers' physical safety as well as their economic well-being.

The Jungle shocked the Congress and President Theodore Roosevelt into taking some action specifically to ensure the safety of consumers. Before this time, consumer protection had been a side-effect of government regulations, rather than its main purpose. The resulting action was the Pure Food and Drug Act of 1906, which established the Pure Food and Drug Administration (today called the FDA). The Meat Inspection Act was passed in the same year, specifically to rectify the problems described in *The Jungle*.

Public opinion played a strong role in the passage of these first two acts of consumer protection. Credit for public awareness goes to muckraking journalists of the time, whose major themes included the purity and safety of foods and drugs. Muckrakers worked for mass-market, inexpensive magazines that specialized in exposing fraud and corruption in business and politics. This early push for protective legislation should be viewed within a larger social, intellectual, and political development of the time: progressivism. In its broadest form, the progressive spirit was seen as a struggle of "the people" against special-interest groups.

In 1914 the Federal Trade Commission Act was passed and the Federal Trade Commission (FTC) was created. Although its prime function was to help maintain competition and prevent monopolies, it was also given responsibility for policing unfair or deceptive trade practices. (In 1938, this latter function was interpreted and amended to include advertising.)

Vigorous consumer protection activity died with the onset of World War I and the business orientation of the 1920s. In the interim, court cases had limited the powers of the FDA so much that by the 1930s it played only a minor role in consumer affairs. Once again, it took publication—in this case, of two books—to inspire a major outcry against firms that marketed unsafe products. Arthur Kallet and F.J. Schlink's *100,000,000 Guinea Pigs* (1932) pointed out that many goods came to the market untested and untried. If they were harmful, the public found out the hard way. Ruth de Forest Lamb's *American Chambre of Horrors* (1936) described cases of horrible disfigurements, blindness, poisoning, and death caused by some unregulated drugs and cosmetics.

Corrective legislation was proposed and public hearings were held, but there were strong objections from the patent-drug industry. Business in general opposed the advertising regulations contained in the proposed bill. In 1938 a compromise was made, and the latter issue was resolved. A separate bill, the Wheeler–Lea amendment to the Federal Trade Act, assigned responsibility for regulating advertising to the more lenient Federal Trade Commission rather than to the FDA.

A tragedy was the final impetus necessary to force passage of a strengthened Pure Food and Drug law. A new liquid sulfa drug called Elixir

Sulfanilamide came on the market in 1938. Sulfa drugs were called wonder drugs in those days because they cured so many serious diseases. This particular drug, however, had never been tested for safety, and over a hundred people died from using it. When it was learned that the 1906 law allowed the FDA to act only after the fact, a great deal of public pressure was generated.

Shortly after this tragedy the Food, Drug, and Cosmetic Act was passed, and on June 30, 1938, the modern Food and Drug Administration was created to enforce the law. The new law sought to prevent problems by establishing a product's safety before it got on the market and included regulation of cosmetics as well as food and drugs. Major provisions were that new drugs be proven safe before marketing, the definition of food adulteration be expanded, and the FDA be given the power to prevent the sale of products found hazardous.

THE MODERN CONSUMER PROTECTION MOVEMENT

Interest in consumer protection was a casualty of World War II. From the late 1940s through the 1950s, the only consistent voice of consumer interests was *Consumer Reports* (Nader, 1965), a magazine published by Consumers Union, a private nonprofit organization (discussed later in this chapter).

Increasing Consumer Awareness

In the 1960s Americans began to develop greater awareness and a willingness to question existing conditions and to make changes in all areas of their lives. Studies like Rachel Carson's *Silent Spring* (1962), which alerted us to the dangers of pesticides and others forms of environmental pollution, and Ralph Nader's investigation of the automobile industry, *Unsafe at Any Speed: The Designed-in Dangers of the American Automobile* (1965), woke consumers to specific threats to human health and safety.

The consumer movement found support from legislators as well as from ordinary citizens. As a result of hearings on the prescription drug industry held by Senator Estes Kefauver's Antitrust and Monopoly Subcommittee, Americans learned that they had narrowly missed another tragedy. Thalidomide, a drug that produced birth defects when taken by pregnant women, had been approved for mass marketing in the United States. Luckily, slow production and the persistence of a Food and Drug Administration employee kept thalidomide off the market in the United States until reports of children born without limbs surfaced in Europe and triggered a ban of the product in the United States. Public emotion created by the issue caused a demand for drug amendments to require more stringent testing. The amendments became law in 1962.

In the opinion of many consumer activists, the "breakthrough" issue that brought consumer protection permanently to the front page was auto safety. Between 1962 and 1964 Congress passed three auto safety bills as a result of congressional hearings held between 1956 and 1964. Public attention focused again on this issue with the publication of *Unsafe at Any Speed*, resulting in demand for additional safety regulations.

These auto safety laws, coupled with the drug amendments, indicated a trend toward providing consumers with protection as well as information. Consumers need information for comparitive shopping and prudent decision making. **Informative legislation** requires that businesses supply consumers with product specifics. In contrast, **protective legislation** forces producers to alter the features or quality of their product or in some cases to discontinue its production altogether. It is based on the principle that consumers are unable or unwilling to rationally choose a specific product. An example of informative legislation is the Federal Cigarette Labeling and Advertising Act of 1966, amended in 1983. It requires a statement on cigarette packages and advertisements similar to this: "Warning: The Surgeon General Has Determined That Cigarette Smoking Is Dangerous to Your Health." Protective legislation might take the form of banning the sale of cigarettes.

protective legislation: regulations that force producers to alter the features or quality of their products or in some cases to discontinue production altogether

Presidential Support for Consumers

The successful passage of federal legislation often depends on the position taken on the issue by the president. The first presidential support for consumer issues came from President John F. Kennedy. In the first Consumer Bill of Rights to Congress in 1962, he outlined four consumer rights: (1) the right to safety, (2) the right to be informed, (3) the right to choose, and (4) the right to be heard. A significant result of Kennedy's speech and support for consumer issues, and similar thinking by the president who followed him, Lyndon Johnson, was the creation of the office of Special Assistant to the President for Consumer Affairs in 1964. This position was created to expand and institutionalize consumers' "right to be heard." It was Johnson who was first during this period to adopt a set of legislative consumer protection proposals and work actively toward their passage.

By 1965, consumer protection was high on public and government agendas. Spurred by the increasing availability of complex consumer goods, the introduction of bank credit cards, general increase in the use of consumer credit, and the rise of computerized billing, Congress responded with consumer legislation. The most notable was the Consumer Credit Protection Act, commonly called the Truth-in-Lending Act, which requires full disclosure to consumers of all interest costs and terms when borrowing (see Chapter 6). At a time when involvement in the Vietnam war was being questioned and the poverty and civil rights issues were becoming subject to tension, support of consumer protection was just good politics! Furthermore, the costs of consumer protection were extremely low for government compared to the costs of other legislation of the period, such as pollution control, or social programs, such as Medicare or subsidized housing. As a result, this was a strong consumer period. More than twice as many federal consumer protection laws were passed between 1965 and 1980 than in the previous 100 years.

The 1970s saw the passage of the Equal Credit Opportunity Act and the Fair Credit Reporting Act (both discussed in Chapter 6), the expansion of food- and textile-labeling laws, and in 1973, the creation of the Consumer Product Safety Commission (CPSC). This federal agency has authority to set standards for a wide variety of nonfood products, and it has the power to ban any consumer product outright if it feels it is hazardous to consumers. Also in the 1970s, the use of **recalls**—the power to reclaim and eliminate hazardous products from the market—was used extensively by the CPSC, as well as by the FDA, the FTC, and the Environmental Protection Agency (EPA), which is responsible for policing the Clean Air Act. In 1975 the Magnuson–Moss Warranty Act (described later in this chapter) clarified product guarantees for consumers, and in 1978 debt collection procedures were deliniated by the Fair Debt Collection Practices Act. This brought to a close a decade that saw passage of many consumer protection laws establishing a strong foundation of consumer rights.

Inflation and a tax cut were major issues in the political campaigns that elected President Ronald Reagan and fellow conservative legislators in 1980. It was a time to rethink government regulation as well as government spending. Government and industry struggled to fine-tune regulations, recognizing that regulations may interfere with individual freedom for some, while expanding freedom for others. By the end of the decade, many Americans for the first time began to feel what it is like to live with scarce resources. Consumers began to reevaluate their spending and to look critically at government spending, including the direct and indirect costs of regulation.

THE COSTS AND BENEFITS OF GOVERNMENT REGULATION

We have described the tremendous increase in consumer information and protective legislation in the past 30 years. Not everyone, however, agrees that increased federal regulation and consumer information or protection are worth the benefits we get from them. Murray L. Weidenbaum (1980), the first chairman of President Reagan's Council of Economic Advisors, once estimated that if the direct and indirect costs of the 55 federal regulatory agencies that dealt with consumer activities at that time were to be totaled for one year, the bill would amount to $96 billion: $4.5 billion for

FIGURE 8.1
The hamburger, staple of the quick, inexpensive meal, is the subject of 41,000 federal and state regulations, many of those stemming from 200 laws and 111,000 precedent-setting court cases. Together, they add an estimated 8 to 11 cents per pound to the cost of a hamburger. This illustration gives just sampling of the rules and regulations governing the burger you buy at the corner sandwich stand.
(SOURCE: Copyright Feb. 11, 1980, *U.S. News & World Report.*)

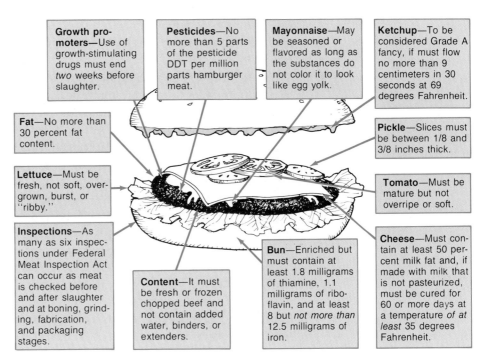

Growth promoters—Use of growth-stimulating drugs must end *two* weeks before slaughter.

Pesticides—No more than 5 parts of the pesticide DDT per million parts hamburger meat.

Mayonnaise—May be seasoned or flavored as long as the substances do not color it to look like egg yolk.

Ketchup—To be considered Grade A fancy, if must flow no more than 9 centimeters in 30 seconds at 69 degrees Fahrenheit.

Fat—No more than 30 percent fat content.

Pickle—Slices must be between 1/8 and 3/8 inches thick.

Lettuce—Must be fresh, not soft, overgrown, burst, or "ribby."

Tomato—Must be mature but not overripe or soft.

Inspections—As many as six inspections under Federal Meat Inspection Act can occur as meat is checked before and after slaughter and at boning, grinding, fabrication, and packaging stages.

Content—It must be fresh or frozen chopped beef and not contain added water, binders, or extenders.

Bun—Enriched but must contain at least 1.8 milligrams of thiamine, 1.1 milligrams of riboflavin, and at least 8 but *not more than* 12.5 milligrams of iron.

Cheese—Must contain at least 50 percent milk fat and, if made with milk that is not pasteurized, must be cured for 60 or more days at a temperature *of at least* 35 degrees Fahrenheit.

government to run the agencies and $91.5 billion for private firms and individuals to comply with the regulations. According to Weidenbaum, the average house was $2,000 more expensive, the average hospital bill was $22 larger, and the price of hamburger was 7 cents higher per pound because of regulations (see Figure 8.1) at that time. Ten years later, *Consumers' Research* estimated that "regulatory overkill . . . still costs the consumer from $60 billion to $100 billion a year." One major industry is subjected to 5,000 regulations imposed by 27 different government agencies. (Schlink, 1988). The concern over the costs of regulation resulted in an emphasis on voluntary control by industry rather than regulations by government during the 1980s.

Costs May Outweigh Benefits

Consumers pay for consumer protection in two ways. They pay government costs with tax dollars and industry costs with purchasing dollars. Examples of regulations that increase costs are housing insulation standards, detailed hospital billing procedures necessary for Medicare, and strict regulations on the fat and water content of hamburger, which include labeling and record keeping. The general activities required by regulations include product development and testing to meet government standards, consumer and business surveys, public hearings, and enforcement. These regulations may prevent consumers, particularly those with low incomes, from purchasing some products, because of their higher costs.

Besides increasing product costs, regulations often restrict product design. Automobiles underwent many design changes in the 1970s and 1980s to incorporate required safety and pollution-control standards. In the 1980s home appliance design was affected by energy-efficiency standards. For example, refrigerators have greater insulation but proportionately smaller usable interior space. New automatic clothes washers achieve energy efficiency by using less hot water in wash cycles and by eliminating warm rinse cycles. Changes have also occurred in electric ranges, room air conditioners, and freezers. In the late 1980s all-terrain vehicles (ATVs) with only three wheels were totally removed from the marketplace as a result of an agreement between federal agencies, ATV manufacturers, and consumer activists (*Consumers' Research*, February 1988). The initial cost of these changes, which individual consumers may or may not want, is passed on to those who purchase new products. The result may be that families choose to keep and repair older products or completely do without the newly designed items that no longer fit their needs or budget.

Economists like Murray L. Weidenbaum and Rose and Milton Friedman worry about the lack of choice that regulation creates, as well as the cost increases. The Friedmans, in their book *Free to Choose* (1980), attack federal regulation on this ground. Besides being forced to change current products, businesses must channel their resources away from product development in order to comply with regulations. Thus, they have fewer resources and less flexibility to meet changing consumer needs and demands. Red tape and bureaucracy can slow down or totally discourage the introduction of new products (see Box 8.2). The issue is one of choice and economic freedom for businesses to offer products in a competitive market and for consumers to choose based on rational decision making and product information.

For example, the FDA standards for new drugs are so strict that a company must do extensive testing before it can bring a drug to the market. When one drug firm wanted to put a skeletal muscle relaxant on the market, the documentation for safety and effectiveness consisted of 456 volumes, weighed more than a ton, and would have stood higher than an eight-story building. Such red tape, these experts argue, has hindered innovations in the United States, whereas in other countries new drugs find their way to market much more quickly. In the mid-1980s individuals smuggled in zidovudine, commonly called AZT or trade-named Retrovir, from Mexico or Switzerland for the treatment of acquired immune deficiency syndrome (AIDS) before it became available here (D'Adesky, 1987). Currently, drugs available for the treatment of certain types of cancer are available but banned in the United States pending fur-

---

BOX 8.2 **DISAPPEARING AND CHANGING PRODUCTS**

What have the Copper 7 IUD (intrauterine contraceptive device), Wyeth Laboratories DTP (diphtheria, tetanus, and pertussis) vaccine, three-wheel all terrain vehicles (ATVs), Rely tampons, and football helmets have in common? These are all products that have ceased being manufactured or have seen the number of manufacturers decrease dramatically. The first four products are no longer on the market due to **product liability**, the threat of lawsuits by users who claim to have been injured or died as a result of product use. Although we all know that football helmets are still available, over a half-dozen companies have left the field to two giants, Bike Athletic Co., owned by Colgate-Palmolive, and Riddell, part of MacGregor Sporting Goods. The latter makes helmets for the pros, but was found liable in the case of a high school football player who broke his neck in a scrimmage. The jury decided a warning sticker should have been on the helmet cautioning players about the danger of butting opponents with it. Riddell is appealing (Brody, 1986; Riley, 1986).

Everyone recognizes that the costs of product liability will be passed on to the purchaser. As the number of product liability suits climbed in the 1980s, along with the total dollars paid out in damage awards and out-of-court settlements, businesses saw the cost of liability insurance skyrocket. Many resorted to a variety of tags and stickers warning against specific product misuse. A few tried more traditional ways of user education. Some redesigned products and/or raised prices. Some companies have left the market as a result, while still others went into bankruptcy. Fear of litigation is behind it all, the specter that a consumer will be injured or killed.

The business community and consumer activists encourage a closer look at the state and federal product liability laws and recommend negotiation and compromise. Some features of our laws to consider include, first, the fact that American manufacturers remain liable for the product as long as it is in use. Second, other governments bear some of the costs of liability within their countries. Third, perhaps a no-fault claims system could be set up for victims in lieu of suing. Business groups recommend that any award cover actual damages, not punitive damages. Although some consumer groups disagree with that opinion, industry, consumers, and the legal community do agree that there is much that needs to be done to simplify and facilitate product liability issues.

---

product liability: threat of lawsuits by users who claim to have been injured or died as a result of product use

ther testing. This extensive testing may cost some Americans suffering, pain, and perhaps even their lives.

Sometimes regulations are created in response to a risk, large or small, real or imagined. Scholars cite the fact that claims of risk are exaggerated out of proportion by certain experts on one side of an issue, only to have these risks discounted by equally credible experts, confusing the public. These distortions are a natural result of professional organizations, researchers, and government agencies competing for scarce dollars to support their individual causes, and they are fed by the media's need for a new story (Sapolsky, 1986).

Consider the various groups on either side of the tobacco issue. First, there are those who do not smoke for health, moral, or aesthetic reasons, along with the major disease associations, such as The American Cancer

Society, the American Heart Association, and the American Lung Association and antismoking groups like GASP (Group Against Smokers' Pollution). On the opposing side are the major manufacturers of cigarettes and all of their employees. Then there are the American farmers who grow tobacco. And, although the percentage of adults over 18 who smoke has decreased in the past decade, the sheer number of smokers is still significant. Add this group to those involved in the growing and manufacturing of tobacco products and the sides are drawn. But we cannot forget the United States government. Every U.S. Surgeon General since 1964 has come out against smoking, while at the same time, the government has provided subsidies to tobacco growers. We require a warning about the danger of cigarettes on each package, yet pay for the results of cigarette usage through Medicare. Complex situations like this one make it difficult for consumers to put risks into perspective.

Finally, on the matter of product safety, we must note that accidents are most often caused by consumer errors or recklessness rather than by inherent faulty product design. For example, mattresses are required to be flame retardant because people fall asleep while smoking in bed, not because the mattresses are inherently dangerous. Automobile accidents are caused more often by driving under the influence of alcohol and/or at unsafe speeds than by product design. "Zero-risk," or the total elimination of risk, cannot generally be achieved by product design or by government intervention. Consumers themselves must accept some responsibility for their own safety.

Regulations Provide Safety

In defense of existing regulatory bodies, consumer advocates remind us that consumer protection legislation reduces suffering and saves lives. In the late 1970s the CPSC, for example, estimated that its actions saved approximately 300 lives a year (Kirkland, 1981). Its regulations have practically eliminated crib deaths caused by strangling. The regulatory agency ruled that all cribs manufactured after 1975 must have bars closer together so that infants cannot put their heads through, get caught, and perhaps strangle. Before 1975, not one manufacturer had used the idea on a voluntary basis, partly because it costs more. Before the CPSC took action against three-wheel ATVs 700 people had died from 1982 to 1987 and 298,000 had been injured (Shapiro and Golden, 1987). The CPSC eliminated three-wheel vehicles, which over-turned easily. Here are examples of improved designs and safety that consumers may have wanted but that no producer felt confident enough to offer because it increases the consumer's costs.

The automobile industry also resisted safety change, claiming that safety features do not appreciably add to the salability of their cars and only increase prices. The government finally intervened to require model changes, not just for appearance, but to make cars safer for people during a collision. These changes included the addition not only of seatbelts, but of redesigned dashboards, bumpers, and seats and the addition of airbags.

And recently the FDA worked closely with the manufacturer of zidovudine, brand name Retrovir, the first drug approved for the treatment of AIDS. According to the FDA, it gave experimental treatments for this disease a top priority and approved the drug within just four months after receiving the application for its use (*FDA Consumer*, October, 1987).

Cost—Benefit Analysis

We have seen that some consumer legislation provides information that allows people to make rational point-of-purchase decisions. Other consumer legislation provides protection when consumers are unable to evaluate the quality of a product on their own. The latter occurs most often in food, drug, and related health issues, since consumers find it difficult to determine or evaluate what has been put into food or dumped into oceans. The result of consumer legislation in most cases is economic saving and physical well-being and safety. The debate between those who see increased regulation as a terrible injustice and those who feel it is necessary will undoubtedly continue, since choice is what we cherish. In the final analysis, you and the political community as a whole will decide whether to increase, decrease, or maintain regulation at current levels. An **economic impact statement** might be one way to judge the merits of a proposed agency or regulation.

Such a statement weighs the social costs of the agency or regulations against the expected social benefits. In the case of the baby crib regulation, all babies using cribs marketed before 1975 were in danger of death by strangulation. There seems little doubt that the saving of innocent lives far outweighs the costs. What parent wouldn't pay a few extra dollars for the elimination of this hazard? In another instance, the Occupational Safety and Health Administration (OSHA) banned oval toilet seats in the workplace and now requires, because of sanitation reasons, that only the horseshoe-shaped seat be used. In this case the costs of collecting data, identifying hazards, setting standards, publicizing regulations, and prosecuting those who fail to comply may not be worth the benefits of increased sanitation. When social costs exceed their benefits, there is **overregulation**.

As consumers, we are required ultimately to bear the cost of governmentally mandated programs to clean the air and water, increase product safety, and provide us with product information. We pay with taxes, increased product costs, and often with decreased freedom of choice. A decision to support consumer information and protection should be made only after carefully comparing the costs to the benefits for society as a whole.

**CONSUMER
REDRESS: TYPES
AND LEVELS OF
CONSUMER
PROTECTION**

As a result of legislation at the federal, state, and local levels, there are hundreds of agencies and thousands of regulations that give consumers information and protection when they make buying decisions. Of course, passing a law does not guarantee information or improved safety; it is only the first step in the process. Consumer advocates often cite three factors that result in consumer legislation providing less than anticipated protection: inadequate enforcement, insufficient budget allotments, and a close relationship between regulators and business that is detrimental to consumer interests. Enforcement procedures should clearly outline the consequences for noncompliance: a fine, withdrawal of a business license, or removal of the product from the market until the violation is corrected. Adequate money must be alloted for inspection and the prosecution of violators. Critics of consumer legislation point out that these ideal conditions do not usually exist.

The Geritol case mentioned in Chapter 7 is often cited by consumer advocates as an example of inadequate enforcement complicated by a ''pro-business'' attitude. In 1962 the FTC issued a complaint against the makers of Geritol, the J.B. Williams Company, for falsely advertising that the product would keep people young. The company made no changes in its advertising, so finally in 1965 the FTC issued a cease-and-desist order that formally required the Williams Company to change its ads. The order was challenged by Williams but affirmed by the U.S. Court of Appeals in 1967. In 1969 the FTC found that the Williams Company was still violating the law, but it did not ask the Justice Department to take action until the end of that year. It took the FTC over eight years to stop one business from advertising falsely.

In a more recent example, consider the link between toxic shock syndrome (TSS) and newly designed and formulated, superabsorbent tampons introduced in the late 1970s. The illness received little attention until the winter of 1979–80, when public health departments began receiving reports of young women becoming unexplainably, violently ill, many of them dying. By 1980 doctors at the Federal Centers for Disease Control (CDC) in Atlanta established a strict case definition of toxic shock syndrome (''syndrome'' being used for an illness that has a consistent collection of clinical symptoms but no proven cause), and began to conduct studies. By June 1980 the CDC, in conjunction with the FDA, held a conference with representatives of all U.S. tampon manufacturers to inform them of the association of tampon use and TSS. It took two and a half years of research for the FDA to require *any* sort of warning about TSS on tampon packages. Superabsorbent tampons made with *synthetic* fibers (use of which is a major factor in TSS) were finally withdrawn from the market in 1985 (Riley, 1986). By early 1988 manufacturers had failed to agree with the FDA on a voluntary labeling program despite recent studies by the CDC confirming the link of high absorbency tampons to TSS. The most recent report has the FDA still working to get a mandatory absorbency labeling standard to make informed choice easier for consumers. (*Consumers' Research*, October 1987). It should be noted that tampons are one of 1,800 medical devices assigned to the FDA as a result of the 1976 Medical Devices Act. Items range from tongue depressors and tampons to pace makers and dialysis machines. And like many governmental agencies designed to assist consumers and tax payers, the annual budget of this agency has been drastically cut. Considering the scope of responsibilities of this one important agency and its limited resources, we conclude that consumers cannot depend solely upon their government for protection.

Besides indicating inadequate and tardy enforcement of the law, critics of governmental agencies often point to the fact that agency regulators are often former employees of the industries they oversee. Certainly, this increases their understanding of the industry, but could it result in a bias toward the manufacturer rather than the consumer? Consumer advocates think so and thus have often criticized this close association between regulator and industry. Their fear is that the regulator can too easily lose sight of his or her primary concern, the consumer's interest.

Since the Geritol case and the rise of the consumer movement in the 1960s, pressure has been applied to federal and state agencies to set priorities and to increase consumer participation in policy decision making. Consumers have also begun to recognize their responsibility to participate actively in their own protection by being informed, by choosing safe products, and by reporting hazardous ones to appropriate agencies by telephone, by letter, or in person at public hearings.

Public hearings regarding consumer and industry reactions to a proposed or current regulation are usually held in major cities across the nation. Participating in public hearings away from home can place a strain on a family budget. In order to encourage and facilitate consumer participation, a few federal agencies now provide reimbursement for expenses incurred when participating in agency and court proceedings. Potential recipients of these funds must usually show that they represent a group that would be substantially affected by the proceedings, would not otherwise be adequately represented, and could not be represented without financial assistance. A goal of consumer advocates today is to pass federal and state legislation to sustain and advance reimbursement and tax credit policies for individual consumers who participate in public hearings. The reasoning is that travel costs for lawyers, public relations personnel, and researchers for industry are passed on to consumers in the price of goods and services, that government specialists are paid for by taxes, but that consumers do not have such support or such representation. An example of industry's ability to support its position can be found in the first wrongful death case to come to trial against Procter & Gamble's Rely tampon. In preparation P&G's legal defense team hired individuals to act as jurors, and conducted three separate, consecutive *mock trials* of the Kehm case in order to perfect its positions and strategies. The trials included appearances of the witnesses for the defense, and enactments of probable testimony for the plaintiff. After each mock trial, the defense witnesses and attorney's would modify their presentations according to the critiques of the jurors (Riley, 1986). Consumers face this level of preparation when they speak out for their rights.

To facilitate problem solving and increase your feedback to consumer agencies, we will identify channels of communication available to you at the federal, state, and local levels, commonly called the **public sector**, as well as in the **private**, or **business, sector**. You should be aware, however, that many government agencies can only act on behalf of large numbers of consumers and will not be able to force a company to replace a product or refund money to one individual, no matter how strong the case. We also recommend that you order *Consumer's Resource Handbook*, an indispensable reference that lists names and addresses of many large corporate consumer affairs offices for airlines, food products, appliance manufacturers, insurance companies, national retailers, and the like. It also lists trade associations, state and county consumer protection offices, state regulatory offices, and local offices of many federal agencies. Request your *free* copy from the Consumer Information Center, Pueblo, CO 81002. For a list of common consumer problems and the appropriate agencies to assist you, consult the appendix (page 633).

Federal Protection

At the federal level, 40 agencies and 400 bureaus and subagencies are responsible for running almost 1,000 consumer programs. We will briefly identify seven major agencies here and include a description of each agency's responsibility. The *Consumer's Resource Handbook* mentioned above contains a more complete list.

Federal Information Center (FIC). The FIC helps consumers find needed information or the right federal, state, or local agency to help with problems. They can be reached only by telephone, but they have toll-free numbers and are located in major cities throughout the United States. For the number closest to you order a free copy of "Federal Information Centers," publication 637H, from Consumer Information Center, Department Z, Pueblo, CO 81002.

Consumer Product Safety Commission. The CPSC protects consumers against unreasonable risks from consumer products used in and around the home, in schools, and in recreation areas, and it assists consumers in evaluating product safety. The CPSC develops uniform safety standards for consumer products, promotes research, and investigates product-related deaths, injuries, and illnesses. The CPSC has the authority to ban hazardous products, set mandatory safety standards, and seek court action to have products declared hazardous.

By law, a manufacturer that learns about a defect must notify the CPSC. If necessary, CPSC may order a recall. Most recalls are voluntary, with manufacturers offering either repair, replacement, or refund. Occasionally, CPSC takes a manufacturer to court to obtain a recall.

It has the authority to administer the Hazardous Substance Act, the Child Protection and Toy Safety Act, the Poison Packaging Act, the Flammable Fabrics Act, and the Refrigerator Safety Act.

CPSC has a toll-free hotline to take reports from consumers about product-safety hazards and to provide information on product recalls. The Commission provides sample copies of approximately 200 fact sheets and pamphlets on most products used in and around the home. These consumer information-education materials cover fire safety, electrical safety, poison prevention, toy safety, recreation equipment safety, power equipment safety, and household structure safety. Write to the Director, Office of Communications, Consumer Product Safety Commission, Washington, DC 20207. Call 1–800–638–CPSC, 1–800–492–8104 (in Maryland), or 1–800–638–8270 (Telecommunications Device for the Deaf [TDD]).

Environmental Protection Agency. The EPA is charged by Congress to protect the nation's land, air, and water systems. Under a mandate of national environmental laws, the EPA's programs focus on air, noise, radiation, water quality, drinking water, solid waste, hazardous waste, toxic substances, and pesticides. It establishes and monitors pollution requirements, tests automobiles for gas mileage performance, and publishes a booklet that lists EPA mileage figures. The EPA also conducts studies on the effectiveness of water purifiers and sets standards for home and farm use of pesticides.

Many of the EPA's programs include congressional mandates to develop and enforce regulations, provide technical assistance, provide information and grants, and require public participation in its decision-making processes. The EPA is highly decentralized; its regional offices work closely with state agencies to implement environmental laws.

The EPA's goal is to achieve a compatible balance between human activities and the natural systems that support and nurture life. Write to Consumer Complaints, Public Information Center, Environmental Protection Agency, Washington, DC 20460. Call 1–202–382–2080, or call the Inspector General's Whistle Blower Hotline to register violations: 1–800–424–4000.

Food and Drug Administration. The FDA assures that all food (other than meat and poultry), food additives, and cosmetics are safe, pure, and wholesome and honestly and informatively packaged and labeled. It also assures that drugs and medical devices are properly labeled, safe, and effective for intended use. If these products do not meet FDA standards, they cannot be marketed in the United States. The FDA determines whether a drug should be a prescription drug, obtainable only with a doctor's order, or sold over the counter, readily available in any quantity to anyone.

Unsanitary or mislabeled food, drugs, or cosmetics or injuries or adverse reactions caused by food, drugs, or cosmetics should be reported to the FDA, which will investigate and take corrective action as necessary. The FDA is particularly interested in seeing the container or the food, cosmetic, or drug that has caused the problem, because the product can then be traced to its location of manufacture or packaging. Write to the Director, Consumer Affairs and Information, Food and Drug Administration, Department of Health and Human Services, 5600 Fishers Lane, Rockville, MD 20857. Call 1–301–443–4166.

Federal Trade Commission. The FTC is responsible for preventing the use of unfair, false, or deceptive advertisements of consumer products. This includes television, radio, and printed ads. This agency enforces laws related to the use of credit: the Truth-in-Lending Act, the Fair Credit Reporting Act, and the Fair Debt Collection Practices Act (discussed in Chapter 6). It administers the Magnuson–Moss Warranty Act, explained later in this chapter, plus the Textile Labeling Law and the Energy Efficiency Ratings (ERR) for major household appliances (discussed in Chapters 9 and 13 respectively). Although the FTC does not investigate individual complaints, it can act when it receives a large number of specific advertising complaints involving substantial consumer harm. Write to the correspondence branch, Federal Trade Commission, Washington, DC 20580 for complaints. Call 1–202–326–2222 for publications only.

National Highway Traffic Safety Administration (NHTSA). The NHTSA works to reduce highway deaths, injuries, and property losses by writing and enforcing Federal Motor Vehicle Safety Standards (FMVSS) for vehicles and vehicle equipment. NHTSA investigates reports of safety-related defects and substantial equipment failures, and it enforces laws requiring recall and remedy.

Recalls may be done voluntarily by a manufacturer when it discovers a safety problem through its own testing or from other sources. Recalls may also be ordered by NHTSA when a vehicle or its equipment has a safety-related defect, when the manufacturer fails to comply with FMVSS, or when the problem is common to a group of vehicles or items of equipment of the same make, model, and year.

Whether a recall is voluntary or ordered by NHTSA, the manufacturer must supply NHTSA with information on how the recall will be conducted and what actions will be taken. Manufacturers must also notify all owners by mail, and the defect must be corrected at no charge.

NHTSA establishes average fuel economy standards for manufacturers of passenger cars and light trucks. It does not have jurisdiction over actual gas mileage performance of individual vehicles. Write to National Highway Traffic Safety Administration, Department of Transportation, Washington, DC 20590. Call Auto Safety Hotline: 1–800–424–9393 or 1–800–424–9153 (TDD).

U.S. Department of Agriculture (USDA). The USDA supervises the Food Safety and Inspection Service (FSIS) Agency, which assures that meat and poultry—and products made from them—are safe, wholesome, and truthfully labeled. In packing, housing, and processing plants, the FSIS inspects meat and poultry products for sanitation, accurate labeling, and proper use of food additives. The FSIS also monitors meat and poultry to detect potentially hazardous residues above the levels set by the FDA. In the case of suspected food poisoning from meat or poultry, the FSIS recommends contacting a doctor or a local public health authority who will contact USDA's Meatborn Hazard Control Center.

The FSIS also provides voluntary grading services and develops grade standards for meat, poultry, eggs, dairy products, and fresh or processed fruits and vegetables. In addition, egg products are inspected for freshness and quality. The FSIS investigates individual complaints concerning the freshness and quality of egg products and the grading of dairy products, eggs, poultry, or meat. Write to Food Safety and Inspection Service, Department of Agriculture, Washington, DC 20250. Call: 1–202–447–3333 or 1–800–535–4555 (TDD).

The Food and Nutrition Service (FNS) of the USDA administers programs that make food assistance, including food stamps and the National Lunch and School Breakfast programs, available to the needy.

USDA also serves as the national office for the U.S. Cooperative Extension System, a three-way partnership including the state land-grant universities, the Department of Agriculture, and the county government. Extension home economists provide information on new and useful ideas for life management and family living. Their educational programs focus on family-related concerns, such as nutrition and food; housing; consumer education on use of money, credit, and other resources; development of healthy human and family relationships; and clothing for function, utility, and economy. Look in your telephone directory under "County Government'' for the Extension System or write to Department of Agriculture, Washington, DC 20250.

State and Local Protection

There is also a great deal of consumer protection at the state and local levels. State and local governments generally have the freedom to establish laws that are more stringent than federal laws. As a result, many state laws have served as models or pilot cases for national legislation. State and local governments are responsible for setting standards for marketing behavior in the areas of advertising, labeling, and weights and measures; defining fraud; maintaining wholesomeness and sanitation in public and institutional eating and medical facilities; and ensuring contract rights of both buyers and sellers. These laws can be enforced locally by city or county officials or by the state attorney general's office.

In addition, each state has a collection of commissions, boards, and departments that regulate the operation of specific professional or occupational services. Their purpose is to maintain standards by protecting the public from incompetence and fraud. These state boards either license or register professions and occupations—doctors, nurses, accountants, attorneys, funeral directors, plumbers, and collection agents, among many others. To be licensed, a professional must have a certain amount of education and experience and must pass a test that measures qualifications. Registrants do not have to pass a test; they are simply granted a legal right to do business under the laws and regulations that apply to their trade.

State boards set licensing standards; set rules and regulations; prepare and conduct examinations; issue, deny, or revoke licenses; bring disciplinary actions; and handle consumer complaints. Say that you have a complaint against an accountant. First, you would check your local phone book under state government offices or professional listings in order to contact the licensing board. After hearing your complaint, the board would conduct an investigation. If necessary, the board would take disciplinary action against the licensee in the form of probation, license suspension, or license revocation. Many boards also have consumer education materials to help you to select a professional or a tradesperson.

In addition to licensing and registering boards, there are state and local consumer affairs offices to provide further assistance. Local consumer offices can be particularly helpful because they can be easily contacted by phone or in person. These offices will either help you with a problem directly or refer you to the proper agency for assistance. If you have a consumer problem with a business outside the state where you live, you should contact the consumers affairs office in the state where you made the purchase. Consult your phone directory for the appropriate office address and phone number.

Private-Sector Activity

Private industry has played an important role in consumer protection in the past 50 years. Some organizations in the private sector, or business world, are primarily interested in consumers. These organizations may offer information, assistance with complaints, or actual protection from faulty products. On the other hand, some are offices of consumer affairs or public relations within or representing businesses for profit and so have the company's best interest in mind. That interest might, however, be to make the consumer happy, even if it does cost money. Many have arbitration or dispute resolution boards, a panel of business and consumer representatives who hear both sides of the problem and recommend a solution. **Arbitration** is a way to settle a dispute by having an impartial person or board decide the outcome of the dispute. In arbitration, parties are bound by the decision, and it can be enforced by the courts. Do not enter into arbitration lightly, because you must follow the decision that is made.

Trade associations. Many industries have an established method of helping resolve problems between their member companies and consumers that could not be solved at the point of purchase. Depending on the industry, this responsibility may lie with a consumer action panel (CAP), a trade association, or a service council. Examples of these trade associations include the American Society of Travel Agents, Inc., for travel agents, the Direct Marketing Association for those who market goods and services directly to consumers by mail, and the Major Appliance Consumer Action Panel, which arbitrates problems between consumers and appliance manufacturers.

Before contacting a dispute resolution program, consumers need to attempt to solve the problem with the place of purchase and if that is not successful, directly with the manufacturer. A list of manufacturers and dispute resolution programs is found in the *Consumer's Resource Handbook* mentioned earlier in this chapter. Or ask at your local library for *Consumer Sourcebook* (Gill and Wilson, 1988) a directory of 6,200 agencies, organizations, and panels. If that is not available, consult the National Trade and Professional Associations of the United States for the address of an appropriate resolution program. If the problem is still not resolved after contacting the manufacturer, you may wish to seek help through a dispute resolution program. Be sure to ask for a copy of the arbitration rules before you file your complaint. This will reveal if the decision of the mediators is binding on both parties, binding only on the business, binding only on the consumer, or not binding on either party.

Better Business Bureau (BBB). Perhaps the best-known nongovernment organization related to consumer problems is the Better Business Bureau.

The Better Business Bureau is the best-known private-sector consumer protection organization. Businesses that are members will prominently display their emblem as a sign of good business practice.

Originally organized in New York in 1911 to combat "badvertising" and business dishonesty, this group has branches in most major cities. The bureaus are organized locally, are totally sponsored by private businesses, and collect membership dues; therefore, they must be careful not to antagonize members lest they withdraw their support. The BBB has no policing authority and depends on voluntary compliance and peer pressure from other businesses. Its influence is primarily over its members. Thus, it is not always effective, particularly in communities in which membership is small.

In response to consumerism, the BBB has increased its arbitration program to include the areas of auto repair, dry cleaning, home improvement, television repair, and household appliances. Although it was created to benefit business, it can be helpful to consumers as well. You will find the BBB in the white pages of your phone directory.

Seals and ratings. Consumers are increasingly concerned in this era of high-technology and computers about how well products work. In some cases, the presence of a seal indicates that the product has met certain standards of performance. Perhaps best known is the UL seal, which stands for a nonprofit testing organization, Underwriters' Laboratories. This seal applies only to the electrical parts of the appliance to which it is attached, usually the cord. For gas appliances such as ranges, clothes dryers, and outdoor grills, the Blue Star indicates that the product has met defined standards for safety, durability, and performance.

The National Association of Furniture Manufacturers Seal of Integrity may be attached to any manufacturer's furniture that meets the minimum warranty. This furniture is supposed to be free from defects in workmanship, material, and construction for a reasonable period of time, but for not less than 12 months' time from the date of delivery to the customer. Other types of seals (see Figure 8.2) exist for a variety of electrical or gas, steel, or aluminum products. They indicate that a product meets industry standards.

The Energy Efficiency Rating (EER), mandated by the federal government to appear on major household appliances, including air conditioners, refrigerators, and washing machines, is useful in comparing the cost of energy use for different brands of major appliances. Details of the EER are discussed in Chapter 13.

Another seal that indicates the level of confidence that a third party has in a product is the so-called seal of approval, such as those issued by *Good Housekeeping* magazine and *Parents* magazine. Many consumer educators are skeptical of these seals for several reasons. First, the only products that qualify for such seals are those that advertise in the magazines. This generally means that a company buys a minimum of two-thirds of a page of advertising per year at an approximate cost of $40,000. Second, the standards for testing the product are seldom revealed. Third, there is a basic conflict of interest, because the higher the standards for testing, the smaller the number of potential advertisers, which lowers the magazine's potential gross income. Finally, neither magazine will disclose the number of cases in which replacements or refunds are made to consumers, in effect refusing to be accountable for their guarantees of quality.

warranty: an assurance given by the seller that a product is in good working order and will provide good service for a period of time

Warranties. The private sector has another device, a **warranty**, to reassure consumers regarding the future performance of products. A warranty, in simple terms, is a guarantee that a product is in working order and that it will give good service for a reasonable period of time. Most of us are familiar with statements such as "money-back guarantee" or "life-time guarantee." These statements are virtually worthless. Whose lifetime do they mean? The product's? The consumer's? Is the guarantee transferable if you sell the product?

The Magnuson–Moss Warranty Act of 1975 was established to eliminate such confusion. It provides comparison-shopping information by setting regulations for warranty provisions, and it leaves the decision to offer or not to offer a written warranty to the manufacturer. It does require that any product that costs $15 or more and that offers a written warranty must clearly provide the following information:

1. Name and address of warrantor
2. What is covered and for how much
3. Procedure for placing a claim
4. Procedure for settling disputes over the claim
5. Warranty duration

FIGURE 8.2   What is in a seal? Many different companies manufacture the same appliance, equipment, or merchandise you buy. It is often difficult to make a wise decision about the brand you want to purchase. One way to decide is to see if the product has a seal. This seal means the product meets specified standards, regardless of its cost, that are important to you, the buyer, but that you cannot easily measure or verify yourself. The seal should be one of the criteria you use to decide which product to buy.

The Seal	What It Means	Where to Find It
Air-Conditioning and Refrigeration Institute "Sound Certification" Seal	Equipment has been sound rated according to stringent industry-wide standards.	Found on outdoor condenser units of "split" cooling systems and on "single package" systems.
American Gas Association Certification Seal	Products have been tested by AGA and conform to standards of the U.S.A. Standards Institute. They are factory inspected at least once a year to insure continued conformity.	Found on gas appliances and/or accessories such as clothes dryers and ranges.
American Institute of Laundering Certification Seal	Products have passed original and periodic AIL tests for color and sun-fastness, shrinkage, fiber strength, launderability of zippers, buttons and snaps, appearance after laundering and other tests related to product performance during or after laundering.	Found on labels attached to ready-made merchandise such as bedding, clothing, and draperies.
Architectural Aluminium Manufacturers Association Certification Seal	Products have passed tests for such factors as air infiltration, windload, strength of members, and water resistance.	Found on prime windows, sliding glass doors, and aluminum combination storm windows and doors.
Association of Home Appliance Manufacturers Certification Seal	Nameplate capacity ratings on products have been tested according to nationally recognized standards.	Found on portable electric heaters, room air conditioners, humidifiers, dehumidifiers, refrigerators, freezers, and home laundry appliances.
Better Light Better Sight Bureau "Seal of Approval"	Lamps have met a set of conditions including the "Lighting Performance Recommendations for Portable Study Lamps" of the Illuminating Engineering Society, standards of mechanical and electrical safety.	Found on study lamps.
"Steelmark" Seal	Products are made of steel and have the qualities of steel.	Found on anything made of steel such as washers, dryers, manicure scissors, mobile homes.
Underwriters' Laboratories Inc. Certification Seal	Products have passed original and laboratory tests and periodic examination according to UL standards for safety.	Found on all equipment, appliances, and materials that could be fire, electric, or accident hazards or used to stop the spread of fire.

SOURCE: "What's in a Seal?" *What's New in Home Economics*, September 1974, p. 87.

This act also prevents manufacturers from requiring that the buyer of the product use it in conjunction with a specific brand-name product or service. For example, the maker of a washing machine cannot require you to use only Tide detergent for the warranty to be effective.

There are two types of **expressed warranties** (written warranties): full and limited. The difference between the two lies in consumers' rights regarding repairs or replacement.

expressed warranty: a written guarantee from the manufacturer that itemizes the rights and responsibilities of both the consumer and the manufacturer regarding product repair or replacement

Under a **full warranty**, the warrantor must fix the product within reasonable time without any charge. In fact, the warantor must pay for incidental expenses (food, lodging, rental fees) caused by unreasonable delays. Say that you buy a heating system that does not function properly, despite many repairs. If you needed to move to a hotel because of extreme cold weather while the heater was being repaired, the cost of your lodging might be covered by the warranty. (Refer to Chapter 12 for a discussion of automobile warranties.)

full warranty: a warranty that guarantees a consumer's right to full repair of a product in a timely manner at no cost to the consumer; may pay for incidental expenses incurred as a result of product breakdown

The Magnuson–Moss Act gives the FTC the power to limit the number of unsuccessful repair attempts possible under a full warranty. If repeated attempts at repair are futile, the consumer can choose between replacement or refund. Replacement must be free. If the consumer opts for a refund, the warrantor can deduct a sum for depreciation; that is, the warrantor can subtract a reasonable amount of money based on the actual use or age of the product. All rights given to consumers by full warranties can be transferred to the new owner if the product is sold during the warranty period.

If a warranty does not include free repair or replacement and compensation for inconvenience, it is a **limited warranty**. This limited status must be explicitly stated, along with all other conditions or exceptions. For example, if the motor on a power lawnmower burns out within one month of purchase, a limited warranty might indicate that the consumer must pay for the labor to repair it but that the parts must be replaced free.

limited warranty: a written guarantee in which the costs for product repair are shared with the consumer

So far we have discussed expressed warranties, those guarantees explained on product labels, in instruction booklets, or in advertisements. A product also carries an **implied warranty**. This means that the manufacturer implicitly states that the product is usable and will not fall apart or break down under normal use. This implied protection can often last beyond the limited-warranty period. Twenty-five states have some explicit provisions for implied warranty protection. Every state except Louisiana has adopted Section 2–719 of the Uniform Commercial Code, which states, ''where circumstances cause an exclusive or limited remedy (warranty) to fail of its essential purpose, remedy may be had as provided in this Act.'' For example, say that you buy a raft that does not have a warranty, and when you take it home and pump it with air, it does not stay inflated. The implied warranty protects you and guarantees replacement or refund.

implied warranty: an automatic guarantee by the producer that a product is usable and will not fall apart or break down under normal use

The Uniform Commercial Code, which governs sales of items in the United States, includes two categories of implied warranties: one of merchantability and the other of fitness. An *implied warranty of merchantability* arises every time a merchant sells a good in which he or she specializes. Retailers of waterbeds give an implied warranty of merchantability whenever they sell a waterbed, but an individual who sells a waterbed through an advertisement in the newspaper does not.

Products that are merchantable are "fit for the ordinary purpose for which such goods are used." They must do what they are created to do. Examples of nonmerchantable goods include inflatable air mattresses that do not remain inflated, clothes dryers that do not get hot, flame-proof fabrics that burn, and electric lawnmowers that give a shock when turned on. The implied warranty of merchantability places absolute liability for product safety on the merchant.

There is also an *implied warranty of fitness* whenever a seller, whether merchant or nonmerchant, knows the particular purpose for which a buyer will use the product. This warranty of fitness takes effect when the seller knows that the buyer relied on the seller's skills or judgment to select suitable products. For example, say that you need a room air conditioner. You take the measurements of your family room and purchase an air conditioner to cool that space on the advice of the salesperson. When you get it home and install it, however, you find that it does not have the power to cool the room adequately. Under the implied warranty of fitness, the product is returnable.

A contract can include both a warranty for merchantability and a warranty for fitness. For example, a seller recommends a particular food blender knowing that a customer wishes to mix beverages, chop foods, and crush ice. The buyer, relying on the seller's judgment, purchases the blender and then finds that the blender mixes and chops but will not crush ice. The seller has met the warranty for merchantability but has breached the warranty of fitness for the buyer's particular purpose.

Consumers should study warranties and instructions carefully before choosing products, in order to avoid disappointment later. Obviously, a full warranty provides more recourse than a limited warranty, but limited warranties are far more common.

recalls: the power to eliminate hazardous products from the marketplace

Recalls. Sometimes, product defects are not easily or immediately observable by consumers, even though the defect may pose a safety hazard. No doubt you are or have been the owner of a recalled product. If you don't think so, it might interest you to know that in a typical year the Consumer Product Safety Commission recalls over 50 million products. Such products have included electric hair dryers that expelled asbestos and baby cribs that could strangle infants. These figures do not include the 10 million or more cars, trucks, and motorcycles and 2 million items of vehicle equipment, such as jacks and fuel filters, recalled by the NHTSA.

If a recall becomes necessary, the CPSC issues a press release giving details of the hazard and including the number of people likely to be affected. The notice is then picked up at the discretion of media personnel and included in radio and television newscasts and in the newspaper. Companies that make the unsafe or defective products also have a responsibility to alert the public to the problem. They often create advertisements offering a refund or an exchange. In the case of automobile recalls, the NHTSA sends written notification to every owner. Despite these efforts, CPSC and NHTSA estimate that only half the products are returned for repair or replacement.

Consumer publications. Product information is essential for rational decision making. There is one private-sector organization in the United States that publishes objective product information on a wide variety of consumer goods, and that is Consumers Union (CU). It was chartered in 1936 in the state of New York, and it publishes *Consumer Reports* (available by subscription or at newsstands). Since the magazine's inception, it has included articles on the merits and relative costs of consumer goods ranging from toys to breakfast cereals to videocassette recorders and ATVs. It also includes advice on purchasing services such as legal assistance, home insulation, and medical care. *Consumer Reports* contains no advertising, so it is not susceptible to influence by businesses. Moreover, it strongly defends its prohibition against use of its name or product ratings in advertisements or for any other commercial purpose (*Consumer Reports*, September 1987). Products featured for review are purchased by Consumers Union in the open market and are usually tested in their own laboratory and research facility. CU is particularly known for annual testing of automobiles. It publishes a *Buying Guide* as its December issue, with summaries of recent product test results.

Consumer's Research is published by Consumers' Research, Inc., and contains general consumer information and advice, as well as product test results. *Consumers' Research* finances its publication through subscriptions and newsstand sales and only accepts non-product advertising. Other noteworthy consumer publications (too numerous to mention) specialize in a particular category of product, such as automobiles, audio equipment, computers, and the like. They can be found on newsstands and in the public library.

CONSUMER RIGHTS AND RESPONSIBILITIES

Although consumers are quick to point out the shortcomings of the business world and complain loudly if their rights have been violated, they often ignore their own responsibilities. A supermarket chain in Los Angeles experimented with this issue. It purposely shortchanged 20 customers and gave 20 customers too much change. Can you predict which group reported the error more often? Most of the people who were shortchanged noticed the error, whereas only a few of those who received too much change "noticed." This example reminds us that consumers have the responsibility to see that they do not cheat merchants, just as the merchants have the responsibility to see that they do not cheat customers. Without consumer responsibilities, consumer rights are worthless.

As mentioned earlier in the chapter, President John F. Kennedy presented the first Consumer Bill of Rights to Congress in 1962. With these consumer rights come corresponding consumer responsibilities, listed below. In the social relationship between buyer and seller, you, as the buyer, need to use the decision-making process. It is the fundamental tool for consuming and the ultimate antidote for caveat emptor.

1. The right to saftey
   a. Examine the safety features of merchandise before buying.
   b. Study warranties and labels.
   c. Read and follow care or use labels carefully and in detail.
   d. Keep receipts in case of product failure.
   e. Use the merchandise with reasonable caution and care.
   f. Contact the appropriate seller, manufacturer, agency, or legislator if a product proves unsafe.

2. The right to be informed
   a. Collect accurate information about goods and services.
   b. Study or evaluate product performance claims carefully.
   c. Question retailers about products, and pursue answers if necessary.
   d. Expand your understanding of the American marketing system.
   e. Let the appropriate manufacturers, legislators, or policy makers know that you need specific information.

3. The right to choose
   a. Understand consumer motivation and persuasive selling techniques.
   b. Expand your perception of alternatives.
   c. Apply the decision-making process to the selection of goods and services.
   d. Compare the cost of time, money, and other resources necessary to obtain a product.
   e. Assume personal responsibility for your choice.

4. The right to be heard.
   a. Assertively state your rights when you find dangers or poor quality of goods or services.

b. Be familiar with consumer protection agencies and know how to get redress.

c. Inform merchants about poor selling techniques or practices, and praise good ones.

d. Actively support changes in laws and policies when necessary.

e. Suggest improvements to manufacturers.

ENFORCING YOUR RIGHTS: A PRACTICAL PROBLEM

Even with government and private regulation and personal acceptance of responsibilities, problems still arise for consumers. You may take the appropriate steps to avoid a problem, yet your car brakes may squeal, the picture on your television may roll, a toy may break on its first use, or your microwave oven may not cook food. Before you do anything else, find out whether the problem is a simple one. For example, check to see that the item is plugged into the wall socket or that it is turned on and properly adjusted. (A high percentage of "repairs" involve only these basics!) Check care labels, warranties, instruction books, and the like.

If these first-line remedies fail and you are sure that a problem exists, you have two choices: be passive or be active. Being passive means choosing to ignore the problem. In some cases, this may be defensible if you determine through the decision-making process that the costs of asserting your rights are greater than the benefits. Your costs are time, money, energy, and possibly some personal unpleasantness. Your benefits are a product that works, value for your money, and perhaps some personal satisfaction in receiving redress. This text can lower the costs of pursuing the active solution because it lets you *know* what to do and whom to see about the problem. You will spend less time on solving the problem, and you will be more efficient and presumably more successful.

Having decided to respond actively to the problem, what should you do next?

1. *Identify the problem.* Prepare yourself to describe the problem clearly and concisely to a stranger. When stating your complaint, be factual, specific, and as brief as possible. Do not be sarcastic or emotional.

2. *Explain what you expect the firm to do about it.* Do you want the product replaced, or would you settle for a repair? Or do you want your money back?

3. *Support your request.* Supply proof of purchase and warranty, and include receipts, charge slips, canceled checks, service invoices, hang tags, and any other documents to support the accuracy of your request. Make copies of these douments to show to the business firm or manufacturer, but save the originals for your records. Keep in mind that some stores will not make adjustments or give cash refunds without a sales receipt.

To provide an example of this process, assume that you buy a waterbed mattress that begins to leak.

1. *Identify the problem.* "I recently purchased a waterbed mattress, style H349. After one week of use, the water bag sprang a leak."

2. *Explain what you expect.* "I have decided that I would like a different style, one that is stronger. I would like to exchange this waterbed mattress for style H549 and apply the credit toward that purchase."

3. *Support your request with proof.* "I have the sales charge slip and the one-year warranty that promises repair or replacement."

Now that you have accomplished this, where do you go to complain?

The Local Level: The Place to Voice Your Problem

Start the complaint procedure at the local level. Go back to or telephone the business or individual that sold the service or product and explain why you are displeased. More than likely, the problem will be solved right there. Occasionally, a salesperson may not have the authority to help you. Simply ask the clerk to tell you who does have the authority and talk with that person. Nearly every business of any size has a person or office set up to handle consumer complaints.

If you cannot get satisfaction by telephone or in person, your next step is to write to the merchant or dealer with whom you have the problem. This indicates that you are a serious complainer, and it provides a record for purposes of legal action, if necessary later. A sample complaint letter is provided in Figure 8.3. Your letter should include the following:

1. Your name, address, and home and work phone numbers
2. The name of the product with style and serial number or identification of the unsatisfactory service that was performed
3. The date and location of purchase
4. The reason for the complaint
5. What you have already done
6. A request for action within a reasonable time
7. Copies of all documents to support your request

Keep a copy of this letter for your records.

The Manufacturer

If for some reason you do not get satisfactory action at the retail level, the next step is to write to the manufacturer of the product in care of the consumer relations department. Names and addresses of manufacturing firms can be found on product hang tags, product packaging, warranties, and instruction booklets. If you cannot find it through these sources, look up the manufacturer's address in *Thomas' Register of Manufacturers* or *Standard and Poor's Register of Corporations*, available at the public

Your Address
Your city, state, ZIP
Date

Appropriate Person
Company Name
Street Address
City, State, ZIP

Dear Sir or Madam:

The purpose of this letter is to inform you of my dissatisfaction with
[name the product with serial number or the service performed], which I
purchased [state the date and location of the purchase].

My complaint concerns [state the reasons for your complaint]. In order to
solve the problem, I [state what you have already done]. Because the
problem still exists, I would like [state the specific action you desire
for satisfaction].

I look forward to your reply and a resolution to my complaint, and I will
allow two weeks before referring it to the appropriate consumer agency.
Write to me at the above address or contact me by phone at [your home
and office phone numbers].

Sincerely,

Your name

Enclosures: [Include copies, *not* originals, of all related records]

library. Your letter should follow the format shown in Figure 8.3, and it
should include a description of the efforts you have already made to
remedy the problem.

As mentioned earlier, industries have organized consumer action panels
or dispute resolution programs to facilitate consumer disputes. If your
problem has not been solved by a local dealer or manufacturer, write to the
appropriate dispute resolution board for assistance. Refer to *Consumer's
Resource Handbook* for a full listing of such panels. Here is a list of names
and addresses of some of these panels:

Automotive Consumer Action Program (AUTOCAP)
8400 Westpark Drive
McLean, VA 22102
1-703-821-7000

Direct Selling Association
1776 K Street, N.W., Suite 600
Washington, DC 20006
1–202–293–5760

Major Appliance Consumer Action Panel (MACAP)
20 North Wacker Drive
Chicago, IL 60606
1–312–984–5858

Toy Manufacturers of America
200 Fifth Avenue, Room 740
New York, NY 10010
1–212–675–1141

State and Federal Agencies

If efforts to resolve the problem at the local level fail, assistance is available from state agencies. Many states have departments of consumer affairs that are involved in legislation, research, advertisement substantiation, and protective lawsuits. Such agencies also provide consumer education and can refer you to the proper state or federal agency for your problem. Some maintain branch offices at locations throughout the state. Many have assembled directories that contain names and addresses of complaint-handing agencies. Ask to see these directories at your local consumer affairs office or at the public library.

As mentioned earlier, there are dozens of licensing or registering commissions in each state. One of their functions is to resolve consumer complaints. Each agency is responsible for the honest and orderly conduct of professionals or tradespersons. To register a complaint, locate the proper agency, either through a local consumer affairs office or in the telephone book. You should find a complete list under "Consumer Complaint and Protection Coordinators." When filing a complaint, write a letter stating all the facts as shown in Figure 8.3.

As you have already discovered in this chapter, numerous federal agencies deal with consumer issues. Sometimes a single issue may be shared by more than one agency or office. Appendix I and the *Consumer's Resource Handbook* provide lists to help you identify the agency most appropriate for your problem. The *Consumer's Resource Handbook* includes guidelines for making complaints, lists of regional offices of federal agencies, and a directory of state and local consumer affairs and protection offices.

If your search for an appropriate regulatory agency is not successful, telephone the FIC. This agency is operated by the General Services Administration and has offices in major cities across the country. FICs have been organized to answer questions or put individuals in touch with experts who can. We urge your patience with the speed at which these agencies respond, however, as they have undergone budgetary and staff cutbacks. Consult your local phone directory.

The Courts and Legal Assistance

If you have a complaint that you have not been able to resolve through other channels, it may be necessary to get legal advice or to take legal action. Legal advice is available from attorneys or legal clinics or through prepaid legal plans. It is, however, a rare individual who files a lawsuit for his or her rights as a consumer; the costs of attorney and filing fees are too high. The most practical alternative is small claims court, which was created to provide low-cost litigation (a landlord–tenant dispute over a security deposit, for example).

Legal assistance. Fear of high costs for legal advice often keeps people from pursuing their rights. One popular lower-cost alternative is the **legal clinic**. In this setup, several lawyers share office space and equipment. They standardize procedures and forms and select common case types (uncontested divorces, traffic citations, etc.), trying to conduct a high-volume business in these categories. Highly trained paraprofessionals assist the lawyers in routine work that does not involve actual law practice, such as completing forms or filing forms with the court. All of these adaptations allow the attorneys to set fees 25 to 50 percent less than what a regular law firm might charge. As you might expect, legal clinics usually do not take cases involving extensive litigation.

legal clinic: a group of lawyers who offer their services at reduced fees by using paraprofessionals and standardized forms, and by concentrating on common case types such as uncontested divorces and traffic citations

The availability and visibility of legal clinics has increased tremendously in the past 15 years, largely because of two Supreme Court decisions. In 1975, the U.S. Supreme Court ruled that lawyers' associations should not be allowed to dictate "minimum fee schedules." For example, all the lawyers in a geographic region cannot decide to charge a minimum of $1,000 for an uncontested divorce. In the 1977 case, *Bates* vs. *State Bar of Arizona*, the Supreme court ruled that lawyers' rights to advertise were guaranteed in the Constitution (right to free speech). Since then, lawyers have begun to be more price competitive and consumers have begun to comparison shop for legal services on the basis of price as well as quality. As a result, prices for services have declined, and we have grown accustomed to seeing advertisements for legal services on television. Today, you can find lawyers and legal clinics listed with prices and descriptions of services in the yellow pages of telephone directories.

Perhaps legal clinics are becoming more common because the number of lawyers has doubled in the last decade. Each year around 30,000 lawyers are admitted to the bar, but only about 16,000 positions open annually in law offices and public service. The strong competition has made lawyers more innovative and service oriented. Besides creating clinics, lawyers have developed two new alternatives to benefit consumers: prepaid legal plans and advice by telephone.

Prepaid legal plans function much like medical insurance and are available through independent agents or from some employers. Often, the sponsors of these plans are labor unions, credit unions, business organizations, and school systems. Most plans cover everyday legal problems, such as wills and estates, divorces and separations, and consumer debt. The plans stipulate what services are offered, whether the lawyer will be from the legal staff of the employer, and whether the employee is free to choose his or her own attorney. Fees for the plan are typically $15 to $20 per month for family coverage. They depend on the nature and amount of services offered, how many members of the group actually use the services, and how the lawyers are chosen. If staff lawyers from the place of employment are used, expenses are less than if a private attorney is consulted.

Information about prepaid legal plans as well as legal clinic locations, is available from the National Resource Center for Consumers of Legal Services, 1302 18th Street N.W., Washington, DC 20036, or from the American Prepaid Legal Services Institute, 1155 E. 60th Street, Chicago, Illinois 60637.

In an effort to encourage consumers to seek legal advice as soon as a problem arises, rather than waiting until a formal lawsuit is filed against them, many bar associations now sponsor a service commonly called Tele-law. For a small fee (around $15) billed to a bank credit card, consumers can call and briefly speak to an attorney to seek advice. Or they can call and listen to *free* recorded messages on consumer topics like auto repair, landlord–tenant problems, credit, and wills.

Alternative sources of assistance for some people are Legal Aid and Legal Services. These programs are financed by federal, state, or local funding to provide legal assistance to people who cannot afford to hire private lawyers. There are more than 1,000 of these offices around the country, staffed by lawyers, paralegals (people who have taken courses in legal assistance), and law students. All offer free legal services to those who meet the financial eligibility requirements based on income and family size that are set by each office. People living on fixed incomes (Social Security Disability, Supplemental Security Income, general welfare, Aid to Families with Dependent Children, unemployment, and some retirement incomes) are often considered automatically eligible.

Eligibility is usually determined as soon as you contact the office, because problems often require immediate help. These offices give legal assistance with noncriminal problems, such as landlord–tenant disputes, credit problems, problems with utilities, and with family issues, such as divorce and adoption. In the past few years these programs have experienced deep budget cuts, so the availability of these services may be limited in your area. For more information, look under ''Legal Aid'' or ''Legal Services'' in your local phone book, or phone your local consumer office or courthouse. Even if you are not eligible or if the office involved cannot help with your problem for some other reason, you will be referred, if possible, to other sources of affordable help (Gallagher, 1987).

Small claims court. After pursuing all complaint channels and perhaps seeking legal advice, you may decide to file a legal claim. **Small claims court** was established in all states to provide a simple, economical system for individuals to obtain help in cases involving small amounts of money, usually less than 2,000. It has many advantages, including a small filing fee (around $20), informal atmosphere, no need for attorney representation, and prompt settlement of the issue. Recently, some courts have scheduled evening and weekend sessions to better accommodate the needs of those employed during the daytime. The two major problems cited with respect to small claims court are the difficulty in collecting your judgment (the money requested) if you win and the possibility that the defendant will ask to have the case transferred to a civil court where you, the plaintiff, will also need an attorney. Worksheet 8.1 outlines the entire process

small claims court: a court that handles disagreements between parties in which the sum involved is small— generally less than $2,000— and for which legal counsel is not necessary

Asserting your rights as a consumer may not be easy. You may ultimately have to go to small claims court.

Using Small Claims Court

Follow this checklist for success in small claims court.

_____ 1. *Identify your opponent (the defendant).* Use the legal name of the business, which can usually be found on certificates or licenses posted to be visible to the public.

_____ 2. *Send a warning letter to the defendant.* This may encourage a quick settlement without going to court. State your claim unemotionally. Include dates, dollar amounts, and how much you expect to be paid. Indicate that you will go to court if there is no reply within a certain time, say, 14 days. Send the letter by certified mail so you will have a receipt.

_____ 3. *Find the court.* It may be listed in the phone directory under "Small Claims Court" or under the name of the parent court, usually a city or county civil or trial court.

_____ 4. *File a claim.* Be prepared to give your name and address, the defendant's name and address, a short description of the problem, and how much, in dollars, you expect to receive. After paying the filing fee and the summons fee (less than $20), the clerk will schedule a hearing, most often within two or three weeks. The clerk is your best source of up-to-date information on how to use the court.

_____ 5. *Notify the defendant.* The court will make the first attempt to notify the defendant, usually by certified mail. If this is unsuccessful, you can have the notice delivered by a marshal or a sheriff.

_____ 6. *Gather the evidence.* Gather as much evidence to support your claim as possible. Include contracts, warranty statements, receipts, canceled checks, repair estimates, correspondence, and photographs showing the problem. If the evidence is verbal rather than written, take a witness with you. If your witness will not come voluntarily, the court can order (subpoena) him or her to appear.

_____ 7. *Consider settling out of court.* When the defendant realizes that you are serious, he or she may decide to settle out of court. If so, write down the terms of the settlement on paper. Each of you should sign it, date it, and keep a copy.

_____ 8. *Present your case.* Typically, both the plaintiff (you) and the defendant will be sworn to tell the truth. Then each presents his or her side of the case, including all documents and witnesses. The judge may choose to ask questions during the procedure. Then each party can ask questions or challenge the other's evidence. The judge may immediately announce the decision, or he or she may choose to notify each party by mail within a few days.

_____ 9. *Winning by default.* If the defendant does not appear, the judge will still ask to hear your evidence. If he or she is convinced by your testimony, he or she may award a "default" judgment, and you win the case.

Collecting a Small Claims Judgment

It is common for successful plaintiffs to have trouble collecting their judgments, that is, the money. If you do have trouble, contact the small claims clerk and ask what steps you can follow to collect. Some possible actions follow:

_____ 1. *Revocation of a business license.* After giving a business seven days to pay the judgment, call and say that you expect to receive a check in five days. If you do not receive it, say that you will take a copy of the judgment to the business license bureau and ask them to revoke the license. This procedure is usually effective. If not, use one of the other techniques described here.

_____ 2. *Garnishment of wages.* If the defendant is employed and you know where, you can request that the sheriff or marshal arrange to have deductions made from the defendant's wages. Garnishment has some restrictions, but the clerk can help you with the procedure.

_____ 3. *Deductions from bank accounts.* For a fee, a sheriff or a marshal can take the money owed to you from the defendant's savings or checking account. You must first find out which bank the defendant uses (if you paid by check, look at the back of the canceled check for the bank name). The sheriff's fee for this service can also be collected from the defendant's account.

_____ 4. *Liens on real estate.* You can put a lien, or claim, on any real estate the defendant owns. When there is a lien on property, it cannot be sold until the debt is paid off. Again, check with the clerk for details.

of pursuing a complaint in small claims court. It is essentially an easy process, but it requires planning on your part to build your case and gather proof of your claim.

CONSUMER PROTECTION IN THE 1990s

As we have noted, the direction of consumer protection often depends on the position taken by the U.S. president. As Ralph Nader noted in the Foreword to *Consumer Sourcebook* (Gill and Wilson, 1988), during the 1980s there was "a major decline in regulatory standards and enforcement for consumer protection." For example the CPSC issued no product safety regulations during the four-year time period between 1984 and 1988. During that time, consumer activists were concerned with disposable cigarette lighters, swimming pool covers, bunk beds, lawn dart games, and baby pacifiers (Shapiro, 1987). As we begin the 1990s, faced with an increasingly complex marketplace and economic challenges to our country, it is difficult to know what direction consumer protection will take.

We do note a trend toward consumers banding together in grassroots efforts for group purchasing and to negotiate consumer protection and redress. For example, a growing number of cooperative buying organizations allow consumers, who contribute a limited time and receive fewer amenities by shopping in a warehouse setting, to benefit from volume buying. Perhaps the strongest example of grassroots effort for consumer protection is the loose national network which developed in the 1980s to deal with the AIDS crisis. Individuals with AIDS were frustrated by the failure of the U.S. health system to care for their needs. With the support of their friends and loved ones, and aided by a telephone and computer network, they gathered research information and discovered ways to procure alternative therapies. In 1987 they also filed the first civil class-action lawsuit against federal health agencies, including the National Institutes of Health, the FDA, and the Department of Health and Human Services for deliberately delaying the development of appropriate treatment.

The challenges of the 1990s require consumers to have knowledge of their rights and be cognizant of the features of existing protective legislation. Consumers must also accept the responsibilities that correspond to their four consumer rights. It is more important than ever that they exercise these rights and responsibilities to ensure continuing information and protection.

SUMMARY

We have briefly shown the transition of consumer legislation from providing information to giving consumers protection. At the same time we have looked at some of the public sector agencies and regulations that give us this information and protection. We have shown that the private sector also provides agencies, seals and ratings, warranties, and publications that can be useful to consumers.

Consumers have a responsibility to seek out and use product information and to apply the decision-making model in order to avoid disappointment in consumer choices. Despite all this, consumers still encounter problems with products and services. As a result, they must return to the place of purchase and request assistance. When this recourse is ineffective, consumers need to contact local, state, or federal consumer affairs agencies or they may need to file a claim in small claims court.

QUESTIONS

1. What are the two types of consumer legislation? Give examples of each.
2. What are the two types of expressed warranties and what are their features?
3. What are the four consumer rights identified by John F. Kennedy? What consumer responsibilities accompany each right?
4. What reasons can you give for being easily taken in by deceptive manufacturers and dishonest sellers?
5. What seal of approval or rating do you trust? Why?
6. Considering both costs and benefits, do you think it is valuable to have and enforce weights-and-measures laws? Defend your opinion.
7. What did you do the last time you were dissatisfied with the performance of a relatively new purchase? What would you do now if you had the same experience?
8. What position has the president of the United States taken concerning consumer protection in the last two or three years?
9. What sources of information do you generally use when choosing a product?
10. What consumer services do you want and expect from your local government?

11. Do you think the federal government should financially assist private citizens so that they can testify at hearings or special meetings that represent a consumer viewpoint? Does the government help business in any way when they testify? Why or why not?
12. It has been said that an intelligent and alert consumer does not need help from the government in consumer matters. Do you agree? Why or why not?
13. Economist George Stigler (1980) once said, "No method of displaying one's public spiritedness is more popular than to notice a small problem and pass a law. It combines ease, the warmth of benevolence, and a suitable disrespect for a less enlightened era . . . [but] I urge you to attempt the more difficult task of exercising your critical intelligence in an appraisal of the comfortable wishfulness of contemporary policy." Does this statement fit the history of the consumer protection movement? Have we sometimes simply passed laws to end "small" problems?

REFERENCES AND READINGS

"The American Consumer." *Current History*, May 1981.

Brody, Michael. "When Products Turn." *Fortune*, March 3, 1986.

Carson Rachel. *Silent Spring*. New York: Houghton Mifflin, 1962.

"The Consumers' Observation Post." *Consumers' Research*, October 1987.

"CU Wins a Round in Fight to Stay out of Advertising." *Consumer Reports*, September 1987.

D'Adesky, Anne-Christine. "Breaking the F.D.A. Drugjam." *The Nation*, October 17, 1987.

"Dateline Washington." *Consumers' Research*, February 1988.

Eiler, Andrew. *The Consumer Protection Manual*. New York: Facts on File, 1984.

"Fast-Tracking the First AIDS Drug." *FDA Consumer*, October 1987.

Friedman, Milton, and Friedman, Rose. *Free to Choose*. New York: Harcourt Brace Jovanovich, 1980.

Gallagher, Michael S. "The Future (?) of Legal Services for the Poor." *America*, May 16, 1987.

Gill, Kay, and Wilson, Robert, eds. *Consumer Sourcebook*, 5th ed. Detroit: Gale Research, 1988.

Grigg, William. "The Making of a Milestone in Consumer Protection: 1938–1988," Parts I, II, III. *FDA Consumer*, October–November 1988; December–January 1989.

Harris, Marvin. "Why It's Not the Same Old America." *Psychology Today*, 1981.

Kallett, Arthur, and Schlink, F. J. *100,000,000 Guinea Pigs*. New York: Vanguard, 1932.

Kirkland, Richard I., Jr. "Hazardous Times for Product-Safety Cars." *Fortune*, June 15, 1981.

Lamb, Ruth de Forest. *American Chambre of Horrors*. New York: Farrar & Rinehart, 1936.

Nader, Ralph. *Unsafe at Any Speed*. New York: Simon & Schuster, 1965.

Pertschuk, Michael. *Giant Killers*. New York: Norton, 1986.

———. "The Role of Public Interest Groups in Setting the Public Agenda for the '90s." *The Journal of Consumer Affairs*, Winter 1987.

Riley, Tom. *The Price of a Life*. Bethesda, Md.: Adler & Adler, 1986.

Sapolsky, Harvey M., ed. *Consuming Fears: The Politics of Product Risks*. New York: Basic Books, 1986.

Schlink, F.J. "Who Serves the Consumer?" *Consumers Research*, January 1988.

Shapiro, Joseph P., and Golden, Sharon. "Crossing Swords over Consumer Safety." *U.S. News & World Report*, October, 26, 1987.

Silber, Norman Isaac. *Test and Protest: The Influence of Consumers Union*. New York: Holmes & Meier, 1983.

Stigler, George. "The Government of the Economy." In Robert C. Puth, ed. *Current Issues in the American Economy*. Lexington, Mass.: Heath, 1980.

Weidenbaum, Murray. "Time to Control Runaway Regulation." In Robert C. Puth. ed., *Current Issues in the American Economy*. Lexington, Mass.: Heath, 1980.

"When Consumer Reports Talks, Buyers Listen—And So Do Companies." *Business Week*, June 8, 1987.

Young, Frank. "A Golden Anniversary of Consumer Protection." *FDA Consumer*, June 1988.

Chapter Nine

COMPARISON BUYING IN FASHIONABLE AMERICA: THE BUYING-PROCESS MODEL

- ☐ Fashion, Style, and Fads
- ☐ The Buying Process
- ☐ The Buying Process: Textiles
- ☐ The Buying Process: Household Durables

DID YOU KNOW THAT . . .

. . . current fashion influences our choices of all sorts of consumer goods, from tennis shoes to televisions?

. . . our choice of certain fashions tells other people about our values, standards, and goals?

. . . the *process* used to evaluate the purchase of a shirt and a sound system is the same?

. . . the word *textiles* refers to products like carpeting, draperies, sheets, shirts, pants, and jackets, which are made of fibers and fabrics?

. . . you should analyze your needs and your budget before going shopping?

. . . using the buying process described in this chapter will increase your satisfaction with your purchasing decisions?

A strong force affects every aspect of our lives. It influences our choice of carpeting and cabinetry, refrigerators and recreation, automobiles and art. It encourages manufacturers to sell and consumers to purchase. This force is **fashion**, which has been defined by fashion authority Paul Nystrom as ''the prevailing style at a given time.'' Few consumers understand the impact that fashion has on buying decisions of all kinds. Fashion explains the popularity of exaggerated tailfins on cars in the 1950s and of the European-style moderate-sized, rounded-edged aerodynamic sedans of the 1980s. It explains the color of towels we favor at a given time, the style of furniture we prefer, the type of window coverings we select for our homes, and where we take our vacations. Fashion, however, is constantly changing, and its inconstancy can become uneconomical if consumers do not understand its impact on decision making. This chapter explores fashion's impact and provides guidelines for comparison shopping and decision making in the areas most affected by fashion: clothing, household textiles, and consumer durables such as furniture and appliances.

fashion: the prevailing or accepted style at a given time; the code language of status

We will define fashion, see how it enhances our lives, and explore how styles become fashionable and influence choices available to consumers. We introduce the **buying-process model**, which shows you how to analyze your needs, your budget, and your options; how to narrow your choices; and how to make purchasing decisions. We apply the buying process throughout the rest of the text, usually focusing on one category or area of the family budget. In this chapter we first apply the buying process model to clothing and household textiles. We combine clothing and household textiles like bedding, towels, carpet, draperies, and upholstered furniture because they are made of the same materials—fibers and fabrics—and so can be investigated and evaluated in much the same way. Then we apply the buying process to the purchase of other household goods, such as wood furniture, kitchen appliances, and audio and video systems. Rather than supplying buying information for every household product, we provide a basic buying process that can be applied to all household goods and illustrate the buying process with specific examples. Our intention is to teach you how to analyze your individual needs and budget, how to find necessary information, and how to weigh the costs and benefits of the alternatives so that you will be able to make wise buying decisions.

buying-process model: a variation of the decision-making model; a step-by-step process that can be applied to the purchase of any consumer good

FASHION, STYLE, AND FADS

Fashion plays a major role in our selection of food, housing, transportation, and recreation. It describes both the prevailing or preferred way of dressing, writing, behaving, or buying at a particular time and the effect that such behavior has on others as a signal of social standing or status. For example, a BMW or a Porsche might be considered an elite car in the United States; if you drive one of these cars, you are ''in fashion'' and are demonstrating that you have the money and status that goes with it. Not everyone who drives a BMW is wealthy, of course, just as not everyone who drives a battered Volkswagen is needy. Similarly, not everyone who wears designer clothing is as rich as the price tags imply. The point is that we use fashion to enhance ourselves and to make ourselves and our homes more attractive.

Fashion has several specific characteristics in addition to signaling status:

1. *Fashion is constantly changing.* It reflects a need for novelty and a desire for change. Fashion changes in apparel are the most recognized, but fashion changes cut across a wide spectrum of goods, even items as utilitarian as a telephone and a tea kettle (Jarnow, Guerreiro, and Judelle, 1987). The torn and tattered, off-the-shoulder look inspired by the film *Flashdance* in the early 1980s, the popularity of Reebok athletic shoes, and the mass appeal of merchandise featuring the California Dancing Raisins and Batman—all are examples of changing fashion.

2. *Fashion cannot exist in isolation.* Fashion "is the code language of status" (Konig, 1973), and as such allows us rapidly and nonverbally to share information about ourselves with others. It requires an audience that is aware of what a fashion signals. A BMW has much more status now than it did in 1970, when more people preferred the bigger, more extravagant American cars. We plan and produce goods with a specific purpose, but also with an eye to attractiveness. We create beauty in our environment through fashion. We adorn our bodies to please ourselves and to attract others. The reaction of other people to our appearance and possessions helps us form our self-esteem. We like to be admired. To have other people imitate us builds our ego and increases our status.

3. *Fashion is followed.* Fashion deals in trends and cycles. People adopt a fashion for a while, then abandon it and adopt a newer fashion in order to be more up to date, special, and distinctive. These trends can be charted for all aspects of one's life-style. Groups of people within a community or nation develop a life-style establishing "patterns of family, housing, eating, speaking, working, playing, governing, and dressing" suitable to the place and time (Kefgen and Touchie-Specht, 1986). For example, the dominant colors in the late 1960s for household goods, from refrigerators to carpeting to bath towels, were avocado green and gold. These colors gave way to earth tones in the 1970s. The mauves, grays, and blues that were found appealing in the 1980s have in turn yielded to newer choices. Clearly, nothing forces a consumer to purchase fashionable goods. There is, however, subtle peer pressure to look and act in ways that reflect the group as a whole. What parent has not heard a child complain "If I wear that, the other kids will laugh at me"? Or who among us has never asked

"What are *you* going to wear?" when planning to attend a particular event? Although the sanctions that fashion imposes are vague, their power should not be underestimated.

style: a particular design or line having characteristics that do not change

4. *Fashion is not style.* A **style** is a particular design or line, such as a turtleneck sweater, a French Provincial settee, or a hatchback car. Its design characteristics never change. To become a fashion, a specific style must be accepted (purchased and used) by the majority of a group. For example, English and American nineteenth-century oak furniture became increasingly fashionable in the past decade. This popularity gave rise to reproductions and to the manufacture of household accessories that complement them. Styles that endure—that change little and are continuously accepted over a long period of time—are called **classics**. They include tuxedos, Rolls Royces, and ladderback chairs. A short-lived fashion is called a **fad**. Fads are usually adopted by small groups of people and can quickly come and go, often in a matter of a few months (see Figure 9.1). Do you remember "mood" rings or yellow, diamond-shaped signs that hung in car windows? Because home furnishings are more expensive, most people do not buy faddish furniture; it would be out of fashion before it wore out.

classics: styles that endure and that are accepted over a long period of time

fad: a short-lived fashion, often more popular with smaller groups than those that adopt fashions

5. *Fashion follows a cycle.* The fashion cycle (see Figure 9.2) begins when a small group of fashion leaders starts to use an innovative product that, in the beginning, is experimental and expensive. If the product proves satisfactory, more people purchase it. Soon it is copied and imitated, often using less-expensive materials or production methods. As it is sold to an increasing number of people, it achieves peak acceptance. Then fashion leaders begin to search for something new. The original fashion tends to be offered at reduced prices in specialty stores at the same time that lower-priced discount stores introduce it. As the first fashion declines, a new one emerges. In the final phase, consumers cannot be

FIGURE 9.1
Whether a style becomes a fad, a fashion, or a classic depends on sales volume over a period of time.

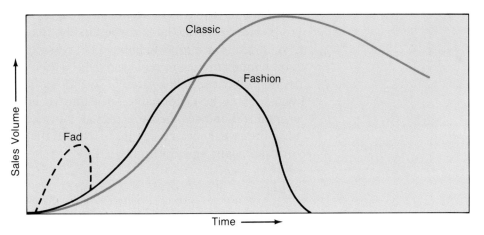

**FIGURE 9.2
Merchandise
acceptance curve, or
fashion cycle.**

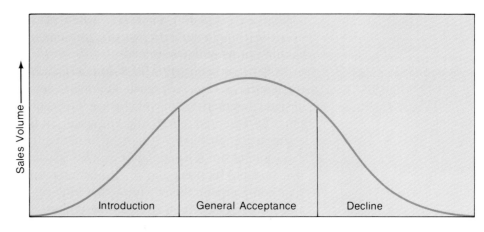

*merchandise acceptance
curve: the graphic repre-
sentation of a typical
fashion cycle*

enticed to purchase the first fashion, and it becomes obsolete, that is, no longer current. Obviously, sales measure a product's acceptance—and decline.

An example of the **merchandise acceptance curve** can be found in the yellow yield signs previously mentioned. The cautionary ''Child on Board'' was originally printed on a yellow diamond-shaped sign and hung in car windows so that other drivers would know that the driver of the car with such a sign might be distracted by children and therefore might not be as alert to problems on the road. It also was a warning that in case of an accident, to look for a small child trapped in the car. The idea caught on quickly and signs with variations of the original message, such as ''Baby on Board,'' were produced. Soon the slogan took a humorous turn (''Mother-in-Law in Trunk''); eventually, any message might be offered, as long as it was short. By then, the color choices of the diamonds had expanded to match car exteriors; the signs were available in any variety store, and their price had dropped to less than half that of the original.

6. *Fashion is a luxury*. Following style trends requires that consumers have enough money to replace or add to their possessions. In other words, fashion merchandise is often a ''want'' rather than a ''need.'' For those who wish to be fashionable on a limited budget, classics are the most economical choices, because they do not become dated and can be used until they wear out. This helps to explain the popularity of classic looks in furniture, cars, and clothing.

Influences on Fashion

Now that you understand that fashion is an integral, constantly changing part of your life, it is time to explore the causes of fashion changes to understand the role they play in consumer decision making. A number of elements influence fashion: politics, technological developments, social attitudes, religious beliefs, economic conditions, and government decrees. Fashions mirror the times by reflecting values, goals, and standards, and so are influenced by many of the same factors that influence values (see Chapter 1). For example, the effects of politics and current events can be seen in the availability of silk fibers for clothing since travel to and trade with China were renewed in the late 1970s. An example of fashion influenced by social attitudes can be found in the selection of classic suits by career-oriented women in the 1980s. These women were trying to meet the wardrobe standards set in a predominantly male business world, indicating the seriousness of their career goals. An example of the economic impact on fashion is the renewed interest in remodeling and room additions triggered by the high cost of housing in many areas of the country.

For political, technological, social, religious and economic developments of an era to influence fashion, there must be a leader to introduce a style. Today's fashion leaders may be movie or recording stars, television personalities, sports figures, politicians, or campus or community leaders. They can be influential locally, nationally, or internationally.

Fashion Dictators?   A common misconception is that designers dictate fashion and offer only what they like. A close examination of the dynamics of fashion shows that this is not the case. Designers of consumer goods such as apparel, furniture, appliances, automobiles, and houses have thousands of ideas each year. From these, manufacturers choose to produce only those products that they think will sell. Then retailers select some of the manufacturers' offerings, based on market research and previous sales records. Consumers make the ultimate decision about what or whether to buy. When many consumers make the same choices, a product is declared fashionable. Fashion is not a function of opinion, but of sales and is measured at the cash register. Even strong sales promotions cannot change the direction in which a fashion is moving. Consider the mid-thigh-length skirts marketed to career women in 1988. Most women rejected this length skirt for work apparel, although some bought shorter lengths in after-five dresses. When asked why they made these choices, women indicated the shorter lengths were not appropriate on-the-job, much to the chagrin of retailers who suffered heavy financial losses. Perhaps the most well-known example is the "New Coke" recently offered to consumers by the Coca-Cola Company. Despite marketing research before introduction and a heavy advertising campaign, the product experienced such poor sales that the original product, now called Coca-Cola Classic, had to be returned to the shelves. In the final analysis, consumers decide what is fashionable and whether fashion is worth the price.

THE BUYING PROCESS

consumer durable goods: items that provide satisfaction to their owners over a longer period of time and, because of high cost, are often purchased with installment credit

In Chapter 1 we introduced the concept of a decision-making model, a way of sorting out purchasing and other consumer decisions to achieve maximum satisfaction from investments of both time and money. This model is particularly important when it comes to buying **consumer durable goods**, such as computers, television sets, carpeting, washing machines, and refrigerators. Consumer durables have several characteristics: (1) They are expected to last for several years, (2) they are often bought with credit, (3) they wear out and depreciate, or lose value, (4) they must be repaired or maintained, and (5) they may be insured for loss or damage.

When applying the decision-making model to the purchase of items requiring a major expenditure, it is particularly important to account for fashion, as well as for personal values and goals. Each makes a difference in the ultimate decision you make—and perhaps in the amount of rational thought you put into the buying process.

In this section we apply a variation of the decision-making model, called the *buying-process model*, to two kinds of purchasing decisions: decisions about textiles/clothing and decisions about household consumer durables. Some of these items are purchased often, whereas others are seldom purchased. You buy socks more often than you buy a new refrigerator; in your lifetime you may spend almost as much to keep your feet warm as you do to keep your food cold. Nevertheless, in both cases comparison shopping is essential. Acquiring the habit of comparing and shopping around as part of the buying process not only makes you a wiser consumer but may also save you money; it helps you invest your time more wisely and ensures that you will be more satisfied with what you buy. But before going on to look at some buying decisions, we will compare the decision-making model developed in Chapter 1 to the buying-process model used here.

Decision-Making Model	Buying-Process Model
1. Define or identify the problem.	1. Determine what you need.
2. Determine how your values, goals, and standards may limit your choice.	2. Review your budget in terms of your values, goals, and standards.
3. Seek advice and collect information on alternatives.	3. Investigate options.
4. Weigh the costs and benefits of alternatives	4. Narrow your choices
5. Make a choice.	5. Make a choice.
6. Evaluate your choice.	6. Evaluate your choice.
7. Be responsible.	7. Accept responsibility of ownership.

As you can see each step in the decision-making model matches one in the buying-process model. Students of this course have indicated that this buying process model was one of the most important concepts they learned, and they have reported that its application really makes a difference in their lives. Some have fondly dubbed it DRINMEA, for the initials of the first word in each step of the model. We will now take a closer look at each step.

Determine What You Need

The first step is like the first step of the decision-making model, *define or identify the problem*. Determine your physical and psychological needs and wants in relation to the purchase. Be sure to gather input from every family member affected by the decision, so everyone's needs will be identified as precisely as possible by asking:

1. Who will use the product?
2. What should the product do?
3. What physical needs ought to be met?
4. What role does fashion play in this choice? How important is fashion in this purchase?
5. Will the product be used daily, weekly, or only occasionally?
6. Is the appearance of the product as important as its performance?
7. What size or quantity will give the most satisfaction for the money?
8. How long can the product be expected to last?
9. How does the cost of product care affect selection?
10. Will owning the product require the purchase of other products, accessories, or services?
11. Will the purchase save me or my family time?

Review Your Budget

Decide approximately how much money you can be spent for the product in light of your values, goals, and standards. Decide who will do the buying and look at the overall budget to make sure it can accommodate the purchase. (See Chapter 4 for help in setting budgetary priorities and making trade-offs.) Ask:

1. If the item is purchased, what are the trade-offs?
2. How does the purchase fit relevant goals, values, and standards?
3. How important is fashion in this purchase? How can the merchandise acceptance curve be most economically applied? (See Box 9.1.)
4. Can cash be used for the product without using money from an emergency fund?

**BOX 9.1   MERCHANDISE ACCEPTANCE CURVE:
AN APPLICATION**

Consumers who wish to have fashionable cloth- ing, household goods, or other durable goods can chart the progress of a particular look or trend. They can then purchase as early in the merchandise ac- ceptance curve (see Figure 9.2) as they can afford to. For the fashion conscious, purchases made at the decline stage may actually prove to be relatively expensive. For example, let's say that Bob and Bill, equally interested in wearing fashionable clothing, see a new-style sportswear jacket. Bob decides to buy it in the introductory stage for $140, but Bill decides to wait until it is less expensive. One year later, Bill buys a jacket similar in quality and style to Bob's for $90. Both men quit wearing their jackets at approximately the same time, because the style is declining in fashion. In this example, Bill wears his jacket for three years at an annual cost of $30.00, whereas Bob wears his for four years at an annual cost of $35.00. For this little extra money each year, Bob has the satisfaction of having the new style sooner. Understanding and applying the merchandise acceptance curve, and remembering that fads are very short-lived, can increase consumer satisfaction with buying de- cisions, particularly for those who want to be fashionable.

5. If cash isn't available, how will the product be paid for?
6. If a loan is needed, how will the payment plan fit into the budget? (See Chapter 6 for help in selecting a loan.)
7. Will the loan extend for longer than the usable life of the product?

Investigate Options

As in step 3 of the decision-making model, you should seek advice and collect information about variations in product features, appearance, and durability. Sometimes, personal experience or a friend's experience can be a good source of information. Because it is relatively inexpensive to test a new brand of canned peaches, personal experience is a good source of information when buying such a product. Even if you do not like the peaches, you lose little money. But it can be costly to use the same technique with a durable good like a personal computer. Professional purchasing agents and retail buyers would not think of making a decision without first gathering technical preshopping data. You, as a consumer, should do the same. (See Chapter 8 for sources of technical information available to consumers.) The number of sources you consult and the amount of time you devote to research should be proportional to the amount of the expenditure involved. It would be irrational to spend weeks to investigate a new brand of peaches, for example. By planning ahead, you can integrate the search for information into your daily routine: conversa- tions with friends, reading the paper, and the like.

Products marked "seconds" or "irregulars" sell at lower prices. They may have minor flaws, primarily in appearance, that do no affect their performance. Clothing, household linens, furniture, and appliances are often in this condition. The flaw might be crooked stitching in clothing or a scratched finish in durable goods. Evaluate your needs and standards and consider these products, because purchasing irregulars can save money.

Do not overlook the savings possible by purchasing used rather than new products. Retailers often have used appliances for sale at substantially lower prices. In addition to standard retail outlets (see Box 9.2), newspaper classifieds, swapmeets, garage sales, auctions, and second-hand stores may yield the bargain you are looking for.

Sometimes you can get what you want without spending any money. For example, you may be able to use barter, which is an exchange of goods or services between two parties in which money is not used. It is essentially a swap. You probably engaged in barter as a child. Remember when you traded cards or swapped marbles? Today, many Americans are resorting to barter because it gives them more spending power and it's fun. For example, you might trade your old personal computer for a motorcycle, or if you can repair engines, you could trade your skill for legal assistance from an attorney. Almost anything can be bartered, from time to talent to merchandise. Bartering can help you decrease the impact of depreciation, because you can get rid of what you don't want before it is valueless and get something else in return.

As you focus on product features and benefits, on whether to buy new or used, and whether to pay cash or barter, ask yourself:

1. What do I know about the features and the durability of the product from previously using it?
2. What do technical magazines or books say about the features, the appearance, the durability, and the care of the brands and models available?
3. What are the opinions of friends who have used the product?
4. At what stage of the merchandise acceptance curve should I purchase?
5. What are the complaint or repair histories of the various brands or models?
6. What are the time and energy costs of using various brands or models?
7. Is the product a fad, or will it have lasting appeal for me?
8. Should I purchase the product new or used?
9. Is it appropriate to purchase this item from a conventional retailer or from a classified ad, at a second-hand store, by mail order (see Box 9.3), or by bartering?

Finally, you might consider the do-it-yourself option. Granted, it is difficult to do-it-yourself for many goods and services (not many of us can build our own cars or create our own carpeting), but you may be able to

BOX 9.2   WHERE TO BUY?

There are many types of stores that serve consumers. The type you choose depends on your budget, the time you have available for shopping, and your preference regarding personal service.

Chain store. A chain store is an organization of stores managed from a regional or national headquarters. It may specialize in one product, such as food or shoes, or it may carry everything from hats to hardware. Chain-store prices tend to be lower than those of independently owned stores because the chain can buy and sell in larger quantities. Larger chains may have their own brands of merchandise. Customer service and sales personnel are available but may be limited.

Independent store. An independent store is a family business, usually with only one location. It may offer telephone ordering, delivery, credit, and special ordering at the customer's request. These services and the smaller volume of sales may cause prices to be slightly higher than those of chain stores.

Department store. A department store usually carries clothing and household goods. If it is part of a chain, it may offer slightly lower prices than an independently owned store. Some department stores that cater to middle- or upper-income families may offer customer services such as ordering special merchandise, free gift wrapping, attractive decor, and special consultants to help in product selection. The cost of these services is included in the prices of all the store merchandise.

Discount store. A discount store is a retail store that attracts customers by offering lower prices than those charged by competitiors. This is done by eliminating customer services, such as gift wrapping, valet parking, and store restaurants; by mini-mizing sales staff; by streamlining store decor; and by using as much floor space as possible for selling purposes.

Mail-order service. Mail-order services originally developed because people lived far from retail stores. This method of selling has boomed in the past decade. Catalogs feature accurate descriptions of products, and they usually include photos. Customers who shop at home save time and gasoline, and they can shop at their own convenience.

Manufacturer's outlet. A manufacturer's outlet is often located near the place of manufacturing. Merchandise usually costs half its retail price or less and is available because a surplus was not purchased by retail stores. Some merchandise may be irregulars or seconds, so look for flaws. To locate outlets in your community, look in the telephone directory, check with the chamber of commerce, read local newspapers, or ask friends.

Off-price store. An off-price store attracts customers with designer and/or brand name products at prices lower than those charged by competitors. Merchandise is purchased from manufacturers at the end of the season or in broken lots. Products are first quality, but may be in less fashionable colors or styles.

Warehouse club. A warehouse club is a cash-and-carry operation, sometimes limited to small business owners, government employees, credit union members, or members of other approved organizations. The no-frills warehouses are usually located on the outskirts of town, often resemble airplane hangars in size, and have spartan interiors. Products are offered in bulk at prices much lower than conventional stores.

make clothes and furniture or attempt minor plumbing repairs. Even preparing a meal at home may be considered part of the do-it-yourself trend when you consider that the alternative is buying a restaurant meal. Obviously, it takes time to do the labor yourself. Many of us buy goods and services that we could have provided for ourselves, because we simply

BOX 9.3 MAIL ORDER: TIME SAVER OR HEADACHE?

Ordering merchandise by mail can be fun, it can let you buy things that you cannot find in your local stores, and it can save you time and even money. There are also no parking problems or time constraints. This helps explain its growing popularity. Today, the typical household receives catalogs from more than 50 sources annually. Since many companies send several editions a year, this means crowded mailboxes filled with enticing appeals. Selection of products varies from classic clothing from L. L. Bean, to Figi's gourmet food, to electronics, gifts, and gadgets from Sharper Image. The methods used to sell these products vary from straightforward product descriptions to testimonials to the enactment of a romantic fantasy on the catalog pages. However, can these companies deliver the goods and meet consumer expectations?

Generally, the answer is "yes." Most mail-order dealers rely on repeat business and are eager to provide good service. Computerization of ordering in conjunction with credit cards has eliminated the time lag associated with shopping by catalog and is making "mail order" a misnomer. Today, more than half of catalog orders are placed over the phone, often utilizing a toll-free number and a 24-hour answering service. If you pay with a credit card, computerized inventory and regional distribution centers make shipment possible within a day or two. (If you pay by check, most mail-order companies will wait until the check clears, delaying shipment for up to two weeks.) Clothing is the largest product category sold by mail, so when ordering it, be aware that the color of items shown in catalog photos may vary slightly from the actual garment.

If you follow these guidelines when ordering catalog merchandise you will save time and avoid a headache.

Comparison Shop

1. Comparison shop for product features and benefits as if you were purchasing from a retail store.

2. Consider shipping expenses when comparing costs. Some companies charge a flat fee, a fee per item, or fee according to weight.

3. Consider state sales tax when comparing costs. You are exempt from paying state sales tax if the company does not have a retail store in the state in which you're ordering. Sales tax may be charged on handling and shipping.

4. Check the return policy before ordering and know the time limitations.

5. Fill out the order forms carefully and keep a copy of the catalog you ordered from.

Know Your Rights

1. You have the right to know when you can expect your merchandise to be shipped. If no date is stated by the seller, it must be shipped within 30 days of order. (The 30-day rule doesn't apply to telephone orders unless you mail in the payment immediately.)

2. You have the right to cancel your order and get your money back if the seller can't ship to you in the stated time.

3. You have the right to get all your money back if you cancel the order.

How to Complain

1. If you have a problem with an order, first, write a letter to the company explaining the situation (see Chapter 8).

2. If you do not receive a satisfactory response within 30 days, contact the Direct Marketing Association (6 East 43rd Street, New York, NY 10017) and your local consumer protection agencies.

One concern that catalog shoppers have is that their names will be placed on national mailing and phone solicitation lists, and they will be inundated by catalogs and telemarketing compaigns. Consumers not wishing to receive "junk mail" can send their name and address to Mail Preference Service of the Direct Marketing Association listed above. This organization then circulates this information to its subscribers who are obligated to remove these names from their mailing lists. To avoid "junk phone calls" contact the Telephone Preference Service at the same address.

choose not to invest time in creating the product or performing the task. After all, no one places a zero value on the opportunity cost of his or her time. But if it is possible to create products and do tasks yourself, you can often substantially raise your level of living.

Narrow Your Choice

As a result of the research you did in step 3 of the buying process, you should have selected one or two specific product models or styles. As in step 4 of the decision-making model, you should weigh the costs and benefits of the styles you chose. You can begin to shop around at various types of stores (see Box 9.2). Since your time is valuable, integrate comparison shopping into other planned shopping trips or while doing errands. When at the store, ask questions to verify and expand your knowledge of the product. Read all printed, point-of-sale product information such as labels, hangtags, and warranties. Do not rely on the claims of sales people. Ask yourself:

1. Which brand or model will best meet the needs I determined in step 1 of the buying process?
2. What are the monetary and time costs of selecting various brands or models?
3. How does the warranty for one brand or model compare to the warranty for other brands or models? (See Chapter 8 for a discussion on warranties.)
4. Are repair facilities available if I need them? What is the reputation of the company?
5. If durability is important, which product is the best buy?

Make a Choice

As in step 5 of the decision-making model, select the product that will give you the greatest satisfaction in light of your comparison shopping. If one product is not clearly superior, consider choosing the one with the fewest negative characteristics, or postpone the purchase until an acceptable alternative becomes available.

Evaluate Your Choice

As in step 6 of the decision-making model, you need to evaluate your purchase periodically to see how it is withstanding consumer use and maintenance. This increases your product knowledge and leads to a higher level of personal satisfaction with buying decisions. Ask yourself:

1. Does the product perform as I expected it to? If not, why not?
2. Did I buy the right size? (Whether you are buying a refrigerator or a pair of shoes, size is always important.)

3. Will the product last as long as I expected it would? If not, why not?
4. Does the product require more costs (money and time) for care and maintenance than I expected it to?
5. What characteristics does the product have that I want to avoid in a future purchase?
6. What characteristics does the product lack that I want in a future purchase?
7. Did I purchase at a stage in the merchandise acceptance curve that was right for me?

Accept Responsibility of Ownership

Product ownership entails not only rights, but responsibilities. As we discussed in Chapter 8, a buyer can assure satisfaction and good performance by doing certain things both before and after purchase. Moreover, because the costs of processing returned merchandise are passed on to the consumer, it is in everyone's interest to be a responsible buyer. When you have purchased a good or a service, don't forget to ask yourself:

1. Did I file the sales slips, the warranty information, the instruction booklets, and the other information in a place where I can find them if I need them?
2. Do I know how to use the product properly so that I can prolong its working life? If not, do I have the information I need to learn to use it properly?
3. Do I know the procedures for lodging a complaint?
4. Did I ask all necessary questions about the product? Did I compare what the salespeople told me to information from other sources?
5. Did I follow all the steps in the buying-process model to ensure my satisfaction with the purchase?

You have just reviewed the buying-process model based on the decision-making model. As we apply the buying process throughout the remainder of this text, you will see that the information you seek and the questions you ask will vary from product to product. As you study the use of the buying-process model, you will become adept at inventing your own questions about a purchase. The rest of this chapter applies the buying process to the purchase of clothing and household textiles and to household consumer durables, such as wood furniture, kitchen appliances, and audio-video systems. We explore the purchase of clothing and household textiles in depth because a large share of the average family's budget is spent on textile products. Our second example reinforces the process and offers suggestions for sources of product information.

THE BUYING PROCESS: TEXTILES

textiles: fabrics that are constructed out of fibers or yarns, generally by means of weaving or knitting

Textiles are fabrics that are woven or knitted. Textiles, in the form of clothing, account for 8 to 9 percent of a typical family's expenditures. Textiles are also used for floor coverings such as wall-to-wall carpeting and indoor–outdoor carpeting; for window coverings such as draperies and blinds; for upholstery on sofas and chairs; and for household linens, such as blankets, sheets, bedspreads, and towels. All these uses account for 11 to 12 percent of a family's budget expenditures, certainly a substantial part.

Determine What You Need

When choosing clothing and household textiles, you should consider your physical needs as well as your psychological needs for fashion and performance. For example, sheets with colorful designs may give pleasure, yet white or pastel sheets are available at one-third the cost, and they perform just as well. Only you can decide which will fulfill your needs best, but the questions outlined in step 1 of the buying process and the information in the following sections should put you on the right track.

Household textiles. Household textiles fulfill physical needs, such as keeping the floor warm or a room dark. They also fulfill psychological needs, such as providing attractive surroundings or indicating status. Some household textiles last a relatively short time, whereas others are durable goods. Because of the diversity of household textiles, you should identify personal needs for each purchase. In addition to asking the questions in step 1 of the buying-process model, ask yourself:

1. Which is most important to me—appearance or durability?
2. How much wear and tear must this product withstand?
3. Is deterioration or fading from sunlight a consideration?
4. Is anyone in the household allergic to a specific fiber?
5. Do I want this product to be washable?

Clothing. Most of us buy clothing more frequently than we buy other types of textiles. Americans have more clothing than they need for physical protection, indicating that the psychological needs for status and self-esteem are being met with fashionable clothing purchases.

The best way to determine clothing needs is to take an inventory of what you already own. Worksheet 9.1 provides a simple inventory format that can be adapted to anyone's needs. Taking stock of your present wardrobe alerts you to your clothing needs based on your job, your leisure-time activities, your current wardrobe, your values, and your standards. Analyze the inventory results by asking yourself:

1. Do you have appropriate clothing to keep you physically comfortable? If not, what additional items are needed?

WORKSHEET 9.1 **WARDROBE INVENTORY**

	Coordinates
	suits
	women—dresses
		Separates
		pants
		sweaters
		jackets
		women—
		    skirts,
		    blouses
		men—shirts
			Coats
			jackets
			topcoats
			raincoats
			poncho
				Accessories
				shoes
				ties
				belts
				hats
				jewelry
				gloves
					Miscellaneous
					or special
					activity items

Leisure or work active sports, work at home					
Casual school, relaxing, spectator sports					
Business/tailored school, work, dates, travel					
Semidress or formal entertaining, parties, formal occasions					

2. Do you have appropriate clothing for your job and leisure activities? If not, what is lacking?
3. Have you met your fashion standards?
4. Do your separates (pants, sweaters, and so forth) work well together? Which ones can be worn with several other items? Are there any that you cannot coordinate with anything else in your wardrobe?
5. Are there some items that you are not currently wearing that could be altered, restyled, or worn in combination with other items?
6. Do you have one or two predominant colors in your wardrobe? If so, your clothing will be more interchangeable, and you will require fewer shoes, coats, and so forth.
7. Do your accessories (shoes, belts, and so forth) coordinate with the rest of your wardrobe? Do you need any key accessories in order to wear certain items in your wardrobe?
8. Is it more important that you have many lesser-quality clothes or fewer better-quality clothes?

When you have answered both sets of questions, you have begun to identify your clothing and household textile needs. You may even have discovered that you have fewer needs than you thought. The next step is to see how much you can afford to spend to meet these needs.

Review Your Budget   Review your budget, and clarify values, goals, and standards in reference to clothing and household textiles. Although prices have increased somewhat in the past few years, overall, consumers have found that retail apparel and textiles have remained among the most stable categories in the Consumer Price Index over the past 15 years. Three basic factors are responsible for this stability: First, the textile and apparel industry consists primarily of small, highly competitive firms. Second, consumers have put up more resistance to price hikes in clothing than to similar increases in the costs of other goods. Many consumers value a tank of gas or a week's worth of groceries more highly than they do a new bedspread, and they therefore "make do" with the textile products they already own when there is a squeeze on their pocketbook. And finally, a growing percentage of textile products are imported at lower prices. To help you make a decision about purchasing a textile product, ask yourself the questions outlined in step 2 of the buying process. Then consider:

1. How does the initial cost of the item fit into the family budget?
2. Will the item have to be dry-cleaned? If so, how often can I afford to have that done?
3. How much will I use the item? (A shirt purchased for $25 and worn only twice is much more expensive than one purchased for $40 and worn 35 times.)

Investigate Options

Investigating options and information about features, appearance, durability, and care of textiles and clothing means learning about fiber content, fabric construction, coloring methods, finishes, and product construction.

Fiber content. The **fiber content** of a textile is its basic ingredient. It may consist of natural fibers, such as cotton and wool, or of synthetic fibers, such as rayon, nylon, and polyester. The 1958 Textile Labeling Act, which regulates the labeling of apparel, floor coverings, draperies, bedding, and other household goods, is enforced by the FTC. Labels must include the percentages of all fibers used in the product in order of their predominance. The ''generic,'' or family, name (cotton or nylon, for example) of the fiber must be stated, although including trade names (Supima or Dacron, for example) is optional. The fiber content is not a complete indication of performance, but it can help consumers who understand the characteristics of various materials to choose between products made of different fibers. Table 9.1 includes the generic names, some common brand (trade) names, performance characteristics, and

Spending some time checking labels and reading hangtags on clothing can reduce your chances of making a poor decision about wearing apparel.

TABLE 9.1   A Guide to Fibers Used in Clothing

Generic Name	**Trademarks**	**Characteristics**	**Suggestions for Care**
Acetate	Acele Estron Chromspun	Moth and mildew resistant; high luster; colors sensitive to fading from atmospheric gases if not solution dyed; dissolves in acetone and nail polish remover.	Dry cleaning may be preferred; remove oily stains before washing; heat in washing, drying, or pressing may set stains permanently; use low temperature in laundering and ironing.
Acrylic	Acrilan Creslan Orlon Zefran	Soft, warm, lightweight, non-allergenic; quick drying; resistant to sun rotting.	Can be dry-cleaned; is machine washable and is dryable at moderate temperature (check label).
Cotton Flax (linen)	Supima None	Cool, comfortable to wear, strong, durable. Wrinkles easily unless treated with wrinkle-resistant finish; subject to damage by mildew.	Bleach only if label indicates it is safe; remove oily stains before washing; heat in washing, drying, and pressing may set stains permanently. Can be dry-cleaned (check care label).
Glass	Betaglas Fiberglas Fiber Glass	Does not shrink or burn; limited resistance to abrasion; resists moths and mildew; most resistant of all fibers to sun rotting; resistant to soil and stains.	Wash by hand unless label lists other methods; do not iron; do not mix with other items in washing; dry cleaning is recommended; remove soil by soaking; do not rub, twist, or wring.
Modacrylic	Dynel SEP Verel	Used in children's sleepwear because it is flame retardant; resistant to sunlight; soft, quick drying.	For washable items, use warm water and low heat in dryer; dry cleaning or fur cleaning suggested for furlike items.
Nylon	Antron Cantrece Qiana Vivana	Strong fiber; low in moisture absorbency; develops static electricity unless treated.	Machine washable; dries at low temperatures; scavenges color (wash whites separately).
Olefin	Durel Herculon	Does not absorb water; soil and stain resistant; strong, except on long exposure to sunlight.	If washable, use low wash and dry temperatures; do not iron 100% olefin fabrics; may be dry-cleaned.
Polyester	Dacron Encron Fortrel Kodel Quintess Trevira	Strong, quick drying, wrinkle resistant; retains heat-set creases and pleats; resistant to sunlight; has a tendency to pill; develops static electricity unless treated.	Launder in warm water; dry in low heat; fabric softener will prevent static; may be dry-cleaned, with the exception of pigment prints.
Rayon	Bemberg	Absorbent; comfortable to wear; weak when wet.	May be dry-cleaned; pretreat oil spots before washing; iron on wrong side to prevent shine.
	Avril	Stronger than regular rayon when wet.	May be washed and ironed without special care.

TABLE 9.1 *Continued*

Generic Name	Trademarks	Characteristics	Suggestions for Care
Silk	None	Strong, luxurious fiber; may tend to water spot; subject to static electricity; white silk may yellow with age; low resistance to sun rotting.	Dry cleaning is usually preferred; if washable, use moderate temperatures in washing, drying, and pressing; use a mild soap or detergent.
Spandex	Elura Lycra Monvelle (Spandex + nylon)	Good elasticity and recovery; resistant to perspiration, body oils, and detergents; lightweight.	Avoid constant overstretching (give garments a rest); do not use chlorine bleach; machine wash in warm water; dry at lowest heat, shortest cycle.
Triacetate	Arnel	Holds permanent pleats; mildew resistant; white may be chlorine bleached; burns and melts.	Can take higher pressing temperatures than acetate; can be laundered or dry-cleaned.
Wool *Virgin wool:* fiber never used before. *Reprocessed:* reworked from fabric never used by consumer. *Reused:* reclaimed from products that have been used.		Resilient, springs back into shape; has excellent insulating properties; subject to damage by clothes moths and carpet beetles; burns slowly.	Dry cleaning is usually preferred. If washable, use moderate temperatures in washing, drying, and pressing; use mild soap or detergent and use as little agitation as possible. To press, use a press cloth and moist heat (steam iron or damp press cloth).

SOURCE: Adapted from Madelyn C. Williams, ''A Consumer's Guide to Fibers, Fabrics and Finishes'' (California Department of Consumer Affairs).

suggestions for care. The table applies to household textiles used for carpeting, upholstery, draperies, bedding, and clothing.

Fiber content is the major determinant of the method of product care. As a result of the Permanent Care Labeling Act of 1972 (expanded in 1981), most clothing and household textiles must have a permanent, legible, easily understood care label that has appropriate instructions for washing, bleaching, drying, ironing, and/or dry cleaning. Such labels provide preshopping information, and they reduce confusion regarding garment care (see Box 9.4). When choosing fiber content:

1. Check labels and hangtags for product care.
2. Determine the resiliency of the fiber by crushing the fabric in your hand and observing its appearance when it is released.
3. Rub two pieces of the fabric together to check for static cling. If they stick together, they may stick to you as you wear them, or they may attract dirt when they are used in the home.
4. Fabrics that are susceptible to static cling absorb less body moisture, so they are less comfortable to wear.

BOX 9.4   **INTERNATIONAL CARE LABELS**

Clothing in America must have permanent-care labels. They are easy to understand when written in English, but can you decipher the instructions when they are written in French or German, as is the case with clothing imported from Europe? Learning to ''read'' the symbols is the key, as you can see here. An *X* through any symbol means *do not do it.*

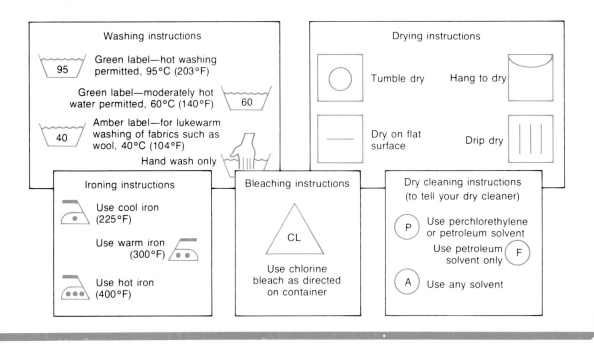

5. Check Table 9.1 for specific problems with mildew, moths, sun rotting, and so forth.

Fabric construction. Fabric construction is of three basic types: *woven,* yarn interlaced to form a fabric (basketweave, twill); *knit,* yarn looped to form a fabric (jersey knit, doubleknit); and *nonwoven,* loose fibers bonded or adhered to form a fabric (felt). To evaluate the future performance and durability of a fabric:

1. Pull the fabric in all directions. A stable fabric should not pull off-grain. This is particularly important for draperies, because unstable fabrics hang unevenly.
2. Do the thumb test: Grip two edges of the fabric with one hand and press down on the fabric with the thumb of your other hand. A durable fabric does not ''give'' or show slipping or separating of

yarns. A single knit, or jersey knit, will show some stretching, but it should gradually return to its original shape.

3. Rub the fabric surfaces together. The fabric should not look rubbed, and there should not be any pills (tiny balls of fiber).

Coloring methods. Coloring methods are numerous, and they often depend on fiber content. As a consumer, your main goal is to determine the permanence of the solid color or printed design:

1. Check labels for descriptions like "solution dyed" or "color fast"; they indicate good color stability.
2. Hold the fabric up to the light. Does the dye go through the fabric or just sit on the surface?
3. Slightly dampen the fabric and rub the surfaces together, or better yet, against a white fabric. Does the color come off?
4. Scratch printed fabrics with your fingernail to see whether the color comes off.
5. If possible, examine the color in natural, fluorescent, and incandescent lighting. The color may appear different under different lights.

Finishes. Finishes are chemicals applied to fabrics to improve their durability, the ease of care, their appearance, or their feeling. You may have noticed that washable clothing often is wrinkle resistant, that carpets are frequently soil resistant, and that tents are usually water repellent. Finishing processes may be listed on labels or hangtags, allowing consumers to choose products with or without these features. Your decision should be based on your need and your budget, because the use of finishes slightly increases product cost.

Product construction. Product construction is the final factor that affects performance. There are four aspects of construction to consider: style (the design or line of the upholstered furniture, carpet, suit, or whatever); supportive materials (chair stuffing, carpet backing, or suit collar interfacing); construction details (stitch length, placement of textile design); and finishing details (such as lining and trims).

A style, as we have seen, can be faddish, fashionable, classic, or totally out of fashion. The most important consideration is whether you like it—whether it suits your personal taste.

Supportive materials add shape or stability. They are found in collars, cuffs, front button plackets, and waistbands of clothing. They help stiffen and pleat the top few inches of draperies, they give stability to rugs and carpets, and they provide cushioning in chairs, sofas, mattresses, and pillows. To evaluate supportive materials, ask:

1. Do the supportive materials wrinkle or distort the outer fabric?
2. Are they securely sewn or bonded (specially treated with heat or chemicals) to the product?
3. Can the supportive materials be cared for as easily as the outer fabric? Will they last as long as the rest of the product?
4. Is the cushioning of sofas, mattresses, and so forth free of lumps? Does it provide adequate padding for the furniture frame or springs? Is its quality equal to that of the outer fabric?

Construction details include stitch length, seam finishes, hem appearance, comfort or fullness, and matching of the design. The following checklist offers an effective way to determine the quality of product construction.

1. Is the machine stitch short enough to be durable (tug on the seams to check for pulling) without causing a pucker seam?
2. Are the seams stitched, turned, or enclosed to prevent raveling?
3. Are the seams pressed flat, particularly where one seam crosses another?
4. Are hems invisible from the right side? They should be, unless a visible hem is a design feature (for example, a top-stitched hem).
5. Is there adequate fullness in the material to allow for pleats and gathers if they are part of the design? This is a consideration in buying items such as pants, dresses, jackets, draperies, and upholstered furniture.
6. Is the design matched? Do the stripes, plaids, floral geometric, or pictorial prints come together to create a balanced appearance?

Inspect clothing to see whether:

1. The sleeves are set into garments without tucks or puckers (unless these are design features).
2. The collar is set onto the garment so that both sides are symmetrical.
3. The cuffs button properly, with the buttonhole on the upper portion of the cuff.

For household textiles:

1. Does upholstered furniture "creak" when you sit on it? (It shouldn't.) Do cushions fit snugly? (Zippers are put in to give a neat fit, not to ensure ease of removal when cleaning.)
2. Do cushioning materials in sofas and chairs provide adequate back support?

3. Does upholstered furniture pass the "tipability" test? Place your knee on a cushion and put your full weight against the chair or sofa back. The chair or sofa should not tip over.
4. Check upholstered furniture to see that tacks, staples, or nails used to secure fabrics to wood frames are firmly attached and will not catch clothing or scratch people.
5. Are chair or sofa cushions reversible? Are sofa cushions the same size, so that they are interchangeable?
6. Are pleats in draperies securely stitched?
7. For carpets, the deeper and denser, the better. Compare identical styles (one plush to another plush, for example) by bending the carpet back on your hand to reveal the length and density of the yarn.

Finishing details include items such as linings, buttons, buttonholes, zippers, and trims. Let's use a checklist to help evaluate quality:

1. Are buttons securely fastened? In furniture, they should be hand-sewn through the filling. This is especially important for sofas, chairs, and pillows in households with children.
2. Are buttonholes properly spaced and sized correctly to accommodate buttons?
3. Do zippers zip smoothly? The zipper should be well covered by the outer fabric, unless otherwise indicated by design.
4. Trims such as welt cording, braid, and so forth should be straight. Stand back and look at the product from several angles to spot "wavy" or irregular trim application.
5. Linings should hang smoothly and evenly without causing distortion. Coats and jackets should have their linings firmly attached at the shoulders and sleeve caps to prevent pulling or showing at the sleeve hem. Drapery linings should be 1 inch shorter than the draperies themselves.

So far, we have provided basic preshopping information. Your decision to seek more technical information at the library should depend on your experience with the product and its cost. You may decide that you have enough information to buy a tailored suit, for example, but that you want more information on carpet construction techniques before making a carpet purchase.

With a more critical eye and with increased knowledge of textiles, you are now ready to plan your shopping trip.

When to purchase. You can get more for your money by knowing when and where to buy clothing and household textiles. Taking advantage of sales is an ideal way to save money, particularly on clothing. If apparel has not sold within three or four weeks, most stores will reduce the price (that is, mark it down) by 20 percent. Additional reductions of 50 to 60 percent are often made in subsequent weeks to speed sales and to make space for newer merchandise. Because apparel usually appears in stores several weeks in advance of its season, markdown prices may occur during the season of use. For example, bathing suits are first marked down at the end of May. This coincides with the beginning of summer, the peak of swimwear use. Table 9.2 provides a more complete calendar for obtaining price savings.

Recently, sales have become a way of creating a demand for a fashion. Fashion apparel, sheets, towels, and bedspreads are on sale *before* the season, particularly in stores that are fashion leaders. Sales are usually promoted in newspapers, and the advertisements indicate that a product is selling at preseason reduced prices.

A word of caution: Do not buy an item only because it is on sale. If it doesn't fit into your current household or wardrobe and suit your life-style and your budget, it is not a bargain, regardless of the price.

Most consumers purchase clothing and household textiles at department or specialty stores. With some research, greater savings on clothing, bedding, table linens, and curtains can be found at manufacturer's outlets, off-price stores, Salvation Army or Goodwill stores, second-hand stores, swapmeets, or garage sales. Consumers who shop for bargains must be armed with information on textiles, and they must be able to judge quality construction. Those who are prepared stand a good chance of finding a real bargain.

Narrow Your Choice and Choose

As a result of your investigation, you should have a clear picture of the product features, appearance, durability, and care that you and your family want in clothing and household textiles. You should also have a clear picture of the price you can afford. Applying your knowledge of the fashion cycle and the merchandise acceptance curve will be helpful, too. For most consumers, the general acceptance stage of an item is probably the best time to buy, because individuality of style and quality of materials and construction will be available for a reasonable price. Purchases made earlier will be more expensive, whereas purchases made later may be made of lower-quality materials and have a shorter time "in fashion." Fads, of course, have the shortest life of all. Applying this information can be particularly important for purchasing textile products with several years of use in mind (carpeting, draperies, or upholstered furniture, for example); you want to be happy with the decision as long as you use the product.

Clothing and household goods are often purchased primarily for their appearance. People make choices based on personal *taste*, their judgment

TABLE 9.2 Shopping Calendar for Textile Savings

January
Bedspreads
Carpeting
Dresses
Furs
Handbags
Infant wear
Lingerie
Men's clothing, especially shirts and coats
Sheets
Shoes
Sportswear
Suits
Towels

February
Curtains and draperies
Dresses
Men's shirts
Rugs
Sportswear
Women's hats

March
Children's shoes
Hosiery
Infant wear
Spring clothes for all groups
Winter coats

April
Dresses
Infant wear
Lingerie
Men's and boys' suits
Women's and children's coats

May
Bathing suits
Handbags
Lingerie
Sheets
Sportswear
Towels

June
Boys' clothing
Dresses
Summer clothing

July
Bathing suits
Children's clothing
Dresses
Handbags
Infant wear
Lingerie
Men's shirts
Shoes
Sportswear
Summer fabrics

August
Back-to-school clothes
Bathing suits
Coats
Curtains and draperies
Fall fashions
Furs
Men's clothing, especially coats
Rugs
Sheets
Towels
Bedspreads

September
Back-to-school clothing
Children's clothing

October
Back-to-school clothing
Hosiery
Lingerie

November
Automobile seat covers
Children's clothing
Children's and women's coats
Dresses
Fabrics
Men's and boys' shoes
Men's and boys' suits

December
Carpeting
Children's clothing
Men's and women's shoes
Men's and boys' suits
Winter clothing
Women's and children's coats

of what is attractive or beautiful. Taste is an individual matter, because the standards for evaluating beauty are a result of family, cultural, social, and educational experiences.

When comparison shopping for apparel and household textiles:

1. Take a list of correct sizes and measurements. Try clothing on, because standard sizing does not exist.
2. Take color swatches and compare them in natural, fluorescent, and incandescent light.
3. Read labels and hangtags for fiber content, textile information, product guarantees, and so forth.

4. Compare the quality of materials and workmanship as described in step 3 of the textile-buying process.
5. Look for permanent-care labels on clothing and household textiles.
6. Consider current fashion trends and personal tastes.

Make a choice, or postpone the decision until you have found a product that meets your needs.

Evaluate Your Choice

To increase your knowledge and skill as a textile or clothing buyer, pay attention to product performance:

1. Do you use the product a little or a lot? Can you figure out why?
2. Did you choose the correct color and size?
3. Would a lesser-quality or a higher-quality product suit your purpose better?
4. What do you like most about the fiber content? What do you like least?
5. Does the fabric construction keep its shape? Is it heavy enough or dense enough for your purpose?
6. Is the product fading, pilling, or hard to keep clean?

Accept Responsibility of Ownership

Once you have made your clothing and textile purchases, your responsibilities as a consumer revolve around proper use and care of the items. This includes following use and care directions as precisely as possible. Do not assume, for example, that an item labeled "hand wash" can be safely machine washed or dry-cleaned. Make sure that your washer and dryer function properly, that you use appropriate wash additives (detergent, bleach, and so forth), that you use correct washing and drying temperatures, and that you launder or dry-clean textiles before you store them away for a season or longer. Some problems with clothing or household textiles are not apparent until after the articles have been used or cleaned. Occasionally, the fabric shrinks excessively, buttons disintegrate, bonded fabrics separate, or artificial suedes lose their nap or texture. If problems do become apparent, immediately return the product to the place of purchase. Most retailers will gladly exchange faulty merchandise. However, you should be aware that a merchant has *no* obligation to give an exchange or a refund just because you change your mind.

It is important to choose a good dry-cleaner. Look for someone who has been certified by a state licensing board. Ask friends and neighbors for recommendations.

If problems occur after dry-cleaning, go to the cleaning establishment first. If textile damage is the dry-cleaner's fault, attempt to resolve the problem with him or her. Sometimes, the fault lies with the manufacturer, who may have mistakenly mislabeled the garment or made a poor choice when combining fabrics and notions (buttons, trims, and the like). For example, say that you take in slip covers for dry-cleaning, according to label instructions. When you pick them up, you find that the welt cording has shrunk and looks puckered. This is the manufacturer's fault, not the dry-cleaner's, so return the slip covers to the place of purchase.

If the retailer, the consumer, and the dry-cleaner cannot agree on who is at fault, the textile product can be sent to the International Fabricare Institute in Joliet, Illinois. Its laboratory can perform tests to determine the cause of the problem. Another way to obtain redress is to report the problem to the Better Business Bureau (BBB) in your area. Many metropolitan BBBs have a dry cleaning arbitration panel that will listen to all the facts, study the evidence, and recommend a solution.

THE BUYING PROCESS: HOUSEHOLD DURABLES

Every year, Americans spend more than $200 billion on consumer durable goods (television sets, radios, stereos, furniture, washing machines, refrigerators, and so forth). Because durable goods are purchased less often than nondurable goods (food and clothing, for example), consumers may have difficulty in recognizing quality. Some products, such as videocassette players or personal computers, are relative newcomers in the marketplace, so we may lack personal experience with them. And because durable goods are expensive, it is important for consumers to make rational and careful buying decisions. We will now apply the buying-process model to household durable goods.

Determine What You Need

depreciation: (1) a lessening of the value of a product because of age or use; (2) the decline in the market value of an asset

Because consumer durable goods last a long time, it is crucial to spend time to define needs. Choices made on the basis of only a few factors may lead to future problems and dissatisfaction. For example, a single person living alone may feel that a small refrigerator is more than adequate for his or her needs. But if that person were to marry, his or her life-style would change dramatically. If children arrive, the small refrigerator would be woefully inadequate. Of course, the "almost new" refrigerator could be sold, but consumer durable goods do not hold their value. In other words, they **depreciate** quickly. A three-year-old refrigerator that cost $700 new might sell for as little as $150. This is bad news for the consumer who does not forecast his or her life-style well, but it is good news for the consumer who buys the used item. If you are not sure of your future plans, consider buying used consumer durables that have more than half their expected lifetime ahead of them. The lifespan of an appliance or piece of electrical equipment depends on its complexity, its workmanship, and the care it receives.

Determine what tasks you want the appliance to perform in addition to its one or two major tasks. For example, some refrigerator/freezers are equipped with an optional cold water dispenser. List both the features that you and your family expect the product to have (needs) and those that you would like it to have (wants). Then prioritize these features by considering their costs and benefits. You will be able to refine and adjust this list during product investigation (step 3). Besides the questions from step 1 of the buying process, ask yourself:

1. How much floor or wall space is available for the product?
2. What work capacity does my family need from the product?
3. What special features do we need? What features do we want?
4. What are the current fashion trends for the product, and how do they fit my values, standards, and goals?
5. Is my house adequately equipped with energy (gas, electricity, and water) to operate the product?

Review Your Budget

Examine your budget to see how much you can afford to spend for an item, once you have determined that you need it. In calculating the total cost of an appliance or a new piece of furniture, consider the purchase price as well as the costs of interest, operation, maintenance, repair, and depreciation.

Purchase price. Say that you are considering buying a new, larger-screen television. The purchase price you can afford is $2,000, and you expect to use the TV for 15 years. Do you have the cash? Have you considered the opportunity cost of being unable to buy other goods? If you decide to finance the TV, can you afford the payment? (At 12 percent interest for three years, $2,000 equals a monthly payment of approximately $68, and more at higher rates.)

Interest. A further cost of owning a durable good is the interest on the purchase price. Consumers may be charged 10 to 18 percent or more if they borrow part or all of the cost of the item (see Chapter 6). If $2,000 were financed for three years at 12 percent, interest, the explicit interest charges would be $400. When you pay cash, the implicit interest that is, the interest you could have had if you had left your money in savings, must be calculated. If $2,000 were left in savings at 8 percent interest and compounded annually, it would earn $264 in interest in three years. So consumers have an interest cost whether they finance the purchase (explicit interest) or pay cash (implicit interest). In our example, the annual interest costs of borrowing average $26.67 ($400 divided by 15 years).

Buying a durable good involves more than just the purchase price. The consumer must also consider the costs of operation and maintenance, as well as depreciation.

Operation. Most consumer durables require energy (electricity, gas, batteries, or water) for operation. Chapter 13 discusses energy costs and the efficiency of various durable goods in detail. Generally, operation costs are based on product brand, quantity of usage, and local utility costs. In our example, we estimate that the annual cost of electricity for the TV will be $100.

Maintenance and repair. This expense is usually smaller the first few years of ownership for products covered by warranties (see Chapter 8). The TV maintenance and repair might be minimal. However, consumers should anticipate some repairs over the lifetime of a product, and they should set money aside for this purpose (see "Emergency Fund," Chapter 4). The TV is not a high repair item, so we estimate maintenance and repair to average $40 a year for the 15-year life expectancy.

Actual costs for three years. The out-of-pocket costs of consumer durables is highest in the first years of ownership, whether cash or credit is used to pay for the product. Actual costs for the TV are $79.66 monthly or $955.92 annually for three years.

	Monthly	**Annually**
Purchase price plus interest	68.00	816.00
Operation	8.33	99.96
Maintenance/repairs	3.33	39.96
	$79.66	$955.92

But because consumer durables are expected to last many years and because we "consume" only a portion of the good each year, we need to analyze the dollar cost of the depreciation and service flow of the purchase or investment.

Depreciation. Depreciation, or lessening of value, occurs most in the first year of product ownership, because most consumers prefer to buy new things. To see how this works, consider that the average annual depreciation of the TV is $132 (purchase price of $2,000 divided by life expectancy of 15 years). But it would be impossible to sell the TV for $1,868 ($2,000 minus $132) after one year. Despite this disparity, if a consumer intends to use a durable good for several years, the average depreciation figure should be used to determine the annual cost of the investment. This method of cost analysis recognizes the **service flow**, the amount of usage during the entire lifespan of the item, rather than only in the first few years of ownership. For the TV, then, the total average annual cost above the purchase price is $298.59.

service flow: the amount of usage that a consumer receives from the entire lifespan of a product

Depreciation	$132.00 ($2,000 ÷ 15 years)
Interest	26.67 ($400 ÷ 15 years)
Operation	99.96
Maintenance and repairs	39.96
Annual average cost	298.59

By determining annual average costs, consumers can better evaluate whether they should purchase, rent, or lease the product, in light of family needs and anticipated amount of product use. For example, you may decide that owning a TV is worth the investment, but when you analyze the annual average cost of snow skis, you might decide to rent the equipment. Determining monetary costs, however, is only half the process of reviewing your budget or making a cost-benefit analysis.

Benefits. The benefits of investing in durables can be both monetary and nonmonetary. There are few if any monetary benefits in owning a TV. On the other hand, the monetary benefits of purchasing a food freezer might include reduced food bills, less food spoilage, and less time (opportunity cost) and gas spent for grocery shopping. Monetary benefits should be estimated and compared to the annual average cost of product ownership to see whether benefits equal or exceed costs. The nonmonetary benefits of a purchase might include convenience, better service, improved decor, and pleasure or comfort. A TV provides many such benefits. A freezer provides convenience and better service by providing adequate space to store a large quantity of food. The food is available for use at any time, and it can be purchased in fewer shopping trips, both of which save time.

When you do a cost–benefit analysis, remember that you have to live with your choice for a long time, so it is a good idea to buy the best quality you can afford. If you choose to buy a poorly made product that is used often, you may find that the flaws produce disappointment and irritation that can build over time.

After you have determined that you can afford to buy a product, consider the timing of the purchase. The prices of many consumer durables are reduced during August and September, when newer models are being introduced. January and February are also clearance months, because retailers are trying to reduce their inventory tax obligation (see Table 9.3). Purchasing a sale item can save you 20 to 25 percent of the product price.

Investigate Options

After identifying your needs and analyzing your budget, gather information about the product in general, as well as data about appearance, features, durability, operating costs, and repair records for specific brands and models.

It is not our intention to tell you how to select every durable good that you might purchase in your lifetime. The selection of durable goods is potentially infinite, and technological developments change the standards that are used to judge quality. The main point here is that product information is available to help you evaluate quality and make a choice. For example, say that you want to buy bedroom furniture: a low chest of drawers, a high chest of drawers, and a headboard. You should go to the library and investigate the general features of *case goods*, furniture made entirely or almost entirely out of wood. Box 9.5 provides a sample checklist for evaluating case goods, but applying it requires knowledge of wood and wood finishes (1, 13, and 14) and furniture construction (5, 6, and 9). Checklists of this type, as well as information about wood, wood finishes, and furniture construction techniques, can be found in reference books on furniture selection and in periodicals like *Better Homes & Gardens*.

You can find general information and brand and model comparisons in two periodicals, *Consumer Reports* and *Consumers' Research*. If you

TABLE 9.3 Shopping Calendar for Household Goods

January
Small electrical appliances
Sporting goods
Water heaters

February
Air conditioners
Clothes dryers
Furniture
Pianos
Typewriters

March
Luggage
Winter sporting goods

April
Kitchen ranges
Microwave ovens
Outdoor furniture
Paint, wallpaper
Vacuum cleaners

May
Furniture
Housewares
Televisions
Outdoor furniture

June
Cameras and accessories
Furniture
Typewriters

July
Air conditioners
Camping equipment
Refrigerators, freezers
Woodburning stoves

August
Camping equipment
Freezers
Patio furniture

September
China
Dishwashers
Furniture
Glassware
Hunting equipment

October
Bicycles
Clothes dryers
Fishing equipment
Furniture
Kitchen ranges
Microwave ovens
Washers

November
China
Furniture
Glassware
Radios
Silverware
Televisions

December
Winter sporting goods equipment
Post-Christmas clearance on everything

want to buy a washer, for example, you can get information to answer questions like these: Will a front-loading or a top-loading washer be best for my family? What washer capacity do I need (12, 16, or 20 pounds)? Do I want bleach and fabric softener dispensers? How many washing cycles do I want? How many temperature combinations do I want? How does one brand compare to another in removing sand or clay from fabrics?

Once you have this information, you can compare it to your needs. Consumer guides can't tell you what to do, nor should they be followed blindly. But they can help you find out what factors to consider in a decision.

Recent research indicates that a primary source of information for consumers is salespeople (Wilkie and Dickson, 1985). The recommendations of salespeople should not be followed blindly any more than those of consumer publications. Unlike consumer publications, of course, salespeople have a vested interest in your choice. Many salespeople make a commission, that is, earn a percentage of each sale they make, or receive a bonus based on their sales volume. Although they also have a vested interest in pleasing the customer, in anticipation of repeat business, sometimes the short-term gain of commission can cause a salesperson to be

BOX 9.5 SHOPPING FOR CASE GOODS

The major difference between high-quality and low-quality furniture is in the type of wood used. The belief that solid wood furniture is superior to veneered wood furniture (made of two or more layers) is quite common, but it is often invalid. Furniture of low, medium, and high quality may be made of solid wood, veneered wood, or a combination of the two.

Solid wood furniture is easily repaired or refinished, its edges show no layers, and there is no chance that the surface may become loosened. Veneer is strong and lightweight, and its surface resists warping, cracking, and swelling.

Checklist for Shopping for Case Goods

1. Is the article made from soft wood or hard wood? Is it kiln dried?
2. Do doors shut tightly without sticking?
3. Are doors held shut with magnetic catches?
4. Are doors and drawers flush with openings?
5. Have corner blocks been used for reinforcement?
6. Has dovetail construction been used on drawers?
7. Are dust panels provided between drawers?
8. Do drawers slide easily on guide strips or ball bearings?
9. Are legs attached with mortise and tenon or dowel joints?
10. Do legs stand squarely on the floor?
11. Have insides of drawers, backs of chests, and undersides of tables and chairs been sanded and finished?
12. Are surfaces free from defects when viewed in good light and touched with fingertips?
13. Are exterior surfaces solid, veneered, or wood-finish stain?
14. Has a protective plastic coating been used on surfaces that will receive hard wear?
15. Is the hardware attractive and securely attached?
16. Will the furniture piece fulfill your requirements for use, style, color, and size?
17. Is the piece of furniture within your planned budget?

SOURCE: Courtesy of JoAnn Crist, Creative Interior Design Lecture Series.

overly supportive of a particular product choice. For additional thoughts on this subject see Box 9.6.

The information-gathering process should include determining the importance of financial factors like service, design, operating costs, and, of course, price. Table 9.4 shows the degree of importance of these factors, that is, the degree of variation among brands and styles, for ten major appliances. Clearly, service and operating costs are both important for air conditioners, whereas for a freezer, operating costs are important, but service is not. Price and design features for both of these items are of moderate importance.

By recognizing and investigating various factors in shopping for appliances, consumers can minimize their true annual cost of ownership. The federal government has begun to help consumers to compare operating costs by testing major household appliances in laboratories that simulate home use. In 1980, the Energy Policy and Conservation Act

BOX 9.6   SEARCHING, SEARCHING

Despite repeated suggestions from consumer educators delivered in classrooms, newspapers and magazine articles, and consumer action television programs, it appears that many consumers do very little investigation of options. Research indicates that a large number of consumers visit only one store and consider only one brand before buying consumer durable goods (Wilkie and Dickson, 1985). Although this might be expected from people who neeed to replace a broken, worn-out appliance quickly, it seems to occur as frequently with those who have planned on and controlled the timing of the purchase. Wilkie and Dickson's research also indicates that once consumers are in a given store they are more likely to focus on a single brand rather than to comparison shop. Perhaps the most astonishing fact to consumer educators and marketers alike is that two out of five people in Wilkie and Dickson's national survey said the salesperson was the *most* useful source of information. Clearly, educators and consumers must focus on the role of salespeople in product selection.

Wilkie and Dickson suggest that salespeople perform three significant functions. First, they help consumers clarify their needs and wants, based on what is available in the marketplace and the particular consumer's budget. Second, they facilitate decision making, particularly joint decision making. Third, they provide an impetus toward closure by asking for a decision, arranging for delivery, credit, and so forth. It is this last function that needs to be noted well. If a saleperson can convince a consumer through a cost–benefit analysis that it is not worth the time and energy to investigate further at another store, a sale more than likely will be made.

The decision to stop searching and purchase immediately depends upon a belief by the consumer that a better product will not be found and/or that a better value will not be found. It is frequently the salesperson's assurances that convinces the consumer of this, rather than the consumer's previous research. Wise consumers use their personal goals, values, and standards to do their own cost–benefit analysis, instead of being unduly influenced by a salesperson.

TABLE 9.4 Factors in Shopping for Appliances

| | | | Importance of: | |
| | | | | |
Appliance	**Service**	**Price**	**Design Features**	**Operating Costs**
Air conditioner	Yes	Moderate	Moderate	Yes
Television	Yes	Yes	Yes	No
Range	No	Yes	Yes	No
Refrigerator	No	Moderate	Yes	Yes
Freezer	No	Moderate	Moderate	Yes
Dishwasher	Moderate	Moderate	Yes	Moderate
Clothes washer	Yes	Moderate	Moderate	No
Dryer	Moderate	Moderate	Moderate	Moderate

SOURCE: From *Personal Money Management* by Thomas E. Bailard, David L. Biehl, and Ronald W. Kaiser. © 1986, 1980, 1977, 1973, 1969 Science Research Associates, Inc. Reprinted by permission of the publisher.

mandated that all new air conditioners, dishwashers, water heaters, humidifiers, ovens and ranges, and heating equipment other than furnaces be accompanied by estimates of their annual energy cost. As we will see in Chapter 13, these energy cost ratings are important.

Narrow Your Choice

Now that you have focused on your needs, reviewed your budget, and gathered the necessary information, you are ready to choose a particular piece of furniture or equipment or an appliance. By this stage, you should have been able to compare and evaluate products from several manufacturers and you should have chosen two or three brands that might be suitable. Now you are ready to go to the stores. Find out the brands a merchant carries and the services he or she offers; get acquainted with the dealers to see who can offer you the best deal. Browse through the store; ask questions. If you are considering a TV, listen to it, try the dials, test whether it is easy to adjust the color and picture. If you are shopping for furniture, try it on for size. Sit on chairs for 10 to 15 minutes to check for comfort. Lie on beds or sofa beds. Check drawers, doors, or other movable parts of cabinets and chests to test for convenience and performance. Look carefully at the insides of refrigerators to check for number and flexible positioning of shelves, the location of the drawers, and the keepers for meat, eggs, and dairy products. Examine the setup and the features of range-ovens. Read labels carefully. It is illegal to deceive a buyer about the composition of a product, so plastic must be labeled as such, and wood must be identified as solid, veneer, wood product, or simulated wood grain.

This is also the time to apply your knowledge of the fashion cycle. If one criterion for this purchase is fashion, select a product that is moving toward general acceptance rather than away from it.

Be sure to compare warranties (see Chapter 5). Occasionally, stores offer more extensive warranties than manufacturers' warranties at no additional cost. This competitive device encourages consumers to buy from them rather than from other dealers. Store warranties are valuable only from well-established businesses that are likely to be around to honor the extended warranty. Be sure to get it in writing. Box 9.7 offers other suggestions for negotiating the best deal in the store.

Make a Choice

Now that you are armed with comparison-shopping information, you are ready to choose. You should anticipate that you may not be able to buy the best brand or model available because of budget constraints. You will, however, have the satisfaction of knowing that you have selected the product that best meets your needs without exceeding your budget.

BOX 9.7 **IN THE STORE: GETTING THE BEST DEAL —
AND WHAT YOU WANT**

People who sell durable goods often earn commissions. They are, therefore, highly motivated to sell the highest-priced model and to close the sale as soon as possible. Be sure that in dealings with salespeople that you take adequate time to consider all the alternatives. Leave the store, if necessary, to think it over.

In some stores and with some products, consumers can negotiate a price reduction. The way to do this is to ask for a reduction in the list or sticker price. This is particularly common during the purchase of a stereo or an automobile. Consumers who gather information on brands and models from consumer periodicals are familiar with typical markups and selling prices and know what price reduction is reasonable.

Another way to save is to bargain for a larger trade-in allowance. A considerable leeway is available when trading in automobiles, typewriters, vacuum cleaners, refrigerators, or sewing machines. If you are naive, you may receive only part of the anticipated allowance, but if you are informed and patient, you can bargain for the full amount.

You can get an indirect price reduction by negotiating for extra features or services (no extra cost for an appliance in a decorator color, free delivery or installation, or no billing for 30, 60, or 90 days). When shopping around, consider the total cost of the deal: product price, trade-in allowance, delivery and installation costs, billing procedure, availability of free extended warranties, and convenience of servicing if repairs are needed.

Evaluate Your Choice

As a result of using the buying process, you should get many years of consumer satisfaction from your purchases. Using a product will give you knowledge of materials and features that can be applied in buying other consumer goods. Consider the questions posed in the buying process model.

Accept Responsibility of Ownership

Once you have purchased a consumer durable, your responsibilities revolve around the proper installation, use, and care of the product. This means carefully following the instruction book, the hangtags, and the labels. Store this information with the purchase receipt in a handy place. Take advantage of the free lessons that often come with items like a microwave oven, personal computer, or sewing machine. This will help you get maximum use and satisfaction from the purchase.

service contract: a contract that covers the repair and servicing of consumer durables for a specific time period and for a flat fee when the warranty runs out

More than likely, at the time of purchase or as the end of the warranty approaches, you will be asked to purchase a **service contract**. This is appliance repair insurance. You pay a predetermined amount of money each year in order to get specific repairs or servicing without charge. Service contracts are available for all major household appliances, televisions, and stereo equipment. Because these contracts entail sales costs, commission costs, and a profit for the seller, they are rarely a bargain for consumers. Base your decision about whether to buy a service contract on the first year's performance of the appliance. If the appliance does not seem like a "lemon," put half of the monthly cost of the service contract into a special repair fund. (See Chapter 4 on budgeting for emergencies.) If repairs are needed, you will be prepared. In the meantime, your money is earning interest.

If you do have problems with an appliance, be responsible for checking the instruction book before you schedule a repair appointment. Approximately 25 percent of repair calls could be avoided if people checked that a "defective" item was plugged in, turned on, and properly connected. Keep receipts of all repair work done, whether covered by warranty or not. These receipts may be needed to prove that the product should be replaced because of excessive repairs. A growing number of Americans are trying to save time and money by doing their own repairs. One major appliance manufacturer, General Electric, is making that easier. It now sells repair manuals and 94 common replacement parts, and it provides detailed advice on how to fix problems with five major appliances. The GE program, dubbed the "Quick-Fix System," covers washers, dryers, refrigerators, dishwashers, and ranges. Because of safety considerations, it does not apply to televisions, air conditioners, or microwave ovens. Manuals and replacement parts are sold by GE dealers. See Chapter 8 for a more complete discussion of the complaint process.

SUMMARY

A fashion is a style accepted by a large group of people at a given time. There are fashions in clothing, household goods, food, automobiles, housing, and entertainment; fashion affects all areas of our lives. Fashion is the result of economic, social, political, and technological factors, and it is transmitted through fashion leaders. Politicians, entertainers, and community or campus trend setters all may be fashion leaders. Consumers who understand fashion and the merchandise acceptance curve can make rational, economical buying decisions. By applying the decision-making model to the buying process, a consumer can determine needs, analyze his or her budget, investigate options, and narrow choices. After choosing a product, a consumer needs to evaluate the purchase decision and accept responsibility for ownership. The buying process can be applied to any consumer purchase. The amount of time spent on the process should be in proportion to the product cost; a poor choice in buying an expensive product will be a psychological and financial disappointment.

This chapter applied the buying process first to clothing and household textiles, then to household goods such as kitchen appliances, televisions, stereos, and case goods. Physical needs for comfort and protection as well as psychological needs for status, beautiful surroundings, and self-esteem of all family members should be considered in the buying process for all such items.

In this chapter we also discussed budget review, which includes determining *costs* (purchase price, interest, operation, maintenance and repair, and depreciation) and *benefits* of purchase (convenience, better service, improved decor, and pleasure or comfort). We stressed the need to investigate options thoroughly, take adequate time to narrow choices, and choose the product that best suits needs and budgets. Taking responsibility of ownership of consumer durables includes ensuring proper installation, use, and care of the product.

QUESTIONS

1. What are the seven steps of the buying process?
2. What are the differences between a style, a fashion, a fad, and a classic? Give an example of each.
3. Identify fashion trends that have occurred in the past two decades for refrigerators, carpeting, ovens and ranges, automobiles, and beds.
4. Fashion is truly a luxury from a personal economic viewpoint. Discuss the contributions and costs of fashion changes to society.
5. What factors affect the performance of textile products in general? What special factors should you look for when purchasing household textiles?
6. What factors should be considered when reviewing a budget during the buying process for consumer durables?
7. Name four magazines that often have articles on product information that is useful during the buying process. How can you locate additional information?

REFERENCES AND READINGS

Ackerman, Norleen M., and Windley, Leona K. "Predictors of Search Time for Mattress Purchase." *American Council on Consumer Interests—Proceedings*. Columbia, Mo., 1987.

Bailard, Thomas E., Biehl, David L., and Kaiser, Ronald W. *Personal Money Management*, 5th ed. Chicago: Science Research Associates, 1986.

Consumer Information Center. *Consumer Information Catalog*. Pueblo, Colo. 81002: CIC, issued quarterly.

Courtless, Joan C. "Recent Trends in Clothing and Textiles." *Family Economics Review*, 1987, no. 1.

Dardis, Rachel. "International Textile Trade: The Consumer's Stake." *Family Economics Review*, 1987, no. 2.

Jarnow, Jeannette A., Guerreiro, Miriam, and Judelle, Beatrice. *Inside the Fashion Business*, 4th ed. New York: Macmillan, 1987.

Kefgen, Mary, and Touchie-Specht, Phyllis. *Indi-*

viduality in Clothing Selection and Personal Appearance, 4th ed. New York: Macmillan, 1986.

Konig, Rene. *A la Mode.* New York: Seabury 1973.

Lovingood, Rebecca P., and McCullough, Jane L. "Appliance Ownership and Household Work Time." *Home Economics Research Journal,* March 1986.

Moore, Carolyn, and Gurel, Lois M. "Fabric Defect Tolerances in First Quality Piece Goods." *Journal of Home Economics,* Summer 1987.

Steinhaus, Nancy H., and Lapitsky, Mary. "Fashion Model's Age as an Infuence on Consumer Attitudes and Purchase Intent." *Home Economics Research Journal,* March 1986.

Smallwood, Victoria A. "Fashion by Mail: Implications for Home Economists." *Journal of Home Economics,* Spring 1986.

Wagner, Janet. "Expenditures for Household Textiles and Textile Home Furnishings: An Engel Curve Analysis." *Home Economics Research Journal,* September 1986.

Wilkie, William L., and Dickson, Peter R. "Shopping for Appliances: Consumer's Strategies and Patterns of Information Search," Report no. 85–108. Cambridge, Mass.: Marketing Science Institute, 1985.

Williams, Madelyn C. *A Consumer's Guide to Fibers, Fabrics, and Finishes.* Sacramento: California Department of Consumer Affairs.

Yeager, Jan. *Textiles for Residential and Commercial Interiors.* New York: Harper & Row, 1988.

Chapter Ten

FOOD: MORE THAN A MATTER OF TASTE

- ☐ Food for Thought, Fuel, and Fat
- ☐ Guides to Good Nutrition
- ☐ Government Labeling
- ☐ Safety and Quality
- ☐ Codes: Prices and Dates
- ☐ Hazards to Food Safety
- ☐ Make It Light and Natural: Health Claims and Vitamins
- ☐ Getting Good Nutrition at Reasonable Prices

DID YOU KNOW THAT...

. . . many Americans suffer from malnutrition, which is almost as common among the rich as among the poor?

. . . food expenditures account for 15 to 20 percent of American family budgets?

. . . bread, pasta, rice, and other grain products are not more fattening than foods like milk or fruit?

. . . good health depends on the consumption of a wide variety of foods from the Four Food Groups?

. . . food labels can reveal the major ingredients in packaged foods and therefore aid in comparison shopping?

. . . the two most frequently used food additives are sugar and salt?

. . . substances that are poisonous in food may occur naturally?

nutrition: the process by which we take in and use the nutrients essential for good health

nutrients: substances contained in food that are essential for good health, specifically from six categories: carbohydrates, proteins, fats, vitamins, minerals, and water

obese: twenty percent or more above ideal body weight

Although we may not think of it when we look at people around us, the biggest health problem in America is malnutrition. Most of us think of a starving child with big, dark eyes when we hear the word *malnutrition*. But if we think of **nutrition** as the process by which we take in and use the **nutrients** (food substances) essential for good health, and understand that the prefix *mal-* means poor, then **malnutrition** can also mean eating too much or eating too little as well as eating insufficient amounts of the foods needed to maintain good health.

Americans, it seems, are preoccupied with food—buying it, eating it, and getting rid of its after effects. Although some of us are exercising more and are more conscious of our health, studies by the U.S. Department of Agriculture (USDA) repeatedly show that at least one in four adult Americans is **obese**, that is, 20 percent or more above ideal body weight. In addition to the more than $400 billion we spend each year on food, we spend more than $100 million on reducing pills or special diets to lose weight.

Aside from its pervasive effects on our culture, food is expensive. Food expenditures account for 15 to 20 percent of family budgets. In Chapter 4 we explored the need to budget for our needs and wants. In this chapter we look at food as nutrition, a matter for government regulation, the source of some consumer misunderstanding, a consumer good that might be misrepresented, and an especially important topic for applying decision-making skills. By the end of this chapter, you should have a better idea of some of the issues and forces that affect your food choices, as well as the way the government protects and regulates the quality of food. More important, however, you will have specific skills for enhancing your nutrition and stretching your food dollars. Readers who have already taken a course in nutrition will recognize the important role nutritional information plays in food selection. For uninformed readers, we briefly present some nutrition basics.

FOOD FOR THOUGHT, FUEL, AND FAT

calories: measurement of food energy, or heat, produced as a by-product of the utilization of food

Everyone knows that we need food to provide ourselves with energy to keep our hearts pumping blood, our lungs breathing, and our bodies functioning in a normal, healthy way. The energy that food supplies is measured in **calories**, the amount of heat produced as a by-product of the utilization of food. Normally, if we take in fewer calories than we need to meet our energy requirements, we lose weight. The reverse, as so many people have found, is also true.

Factors That Affect
Calorie Needs

Four major factors affect how many calories we need to function normally at a healthy weight:

1. *Activity level.* Running obviously requires more energy, and thus more calories, than watching television. As shown in Table 10.1, the more active you are, the more calories you need. The less active a person, the more likely he or she is to take in more calories than he or she can burn off.
2. *Age.* Younger people burn more calories than older people, primarily because growth and a higher activity level add to their energy needs.
3. *Size.* A bigger person (in basic bone and muscle structure needs more calories to function and maintain body size.
4. *Gender.* Because, overall, men are larger than women, men need

TABLE 10.1 Calories Expended in Various Types of Activities

Type of Activity	Examples	Calories Used per Hour
Sedentary	Reading, writing, eating, watching television or movies, listening to the radio, sewing, playing cards, typing, nonstrenuous office work, and other activities done while sitting that require little or no arm movement	80–100
Light	Preparing and cooking food, doing dishes, dusting, hand washing small articles of clothing, ironing, walking slowly, performing personal care, doing office work and other activities that require some arm movement while standing, and rapidly typing and doing other activities more strenuous while sitting	110–160
Moderate	Making beds, mopping and scrubbing, sweeping, light polishing and waxing, laundering by machine, light gardening and carpentry work, walking moderately fast, doing activities while standing that require moderate arm movement, and doing activities while sitting that require more vigorous arm movement	170–240
Vigorous	Heavy scrubbing and waxing, hand washing large articles of clothing, hanging out clothes, stripping beds, walking fast, bowling, golfing, and gardening	250–350
Strenuous	Swimming, playing tennis, running, bicycling, dancing, skiing, and playing football	350 or more

SOURCE: U.S. Department of Agriculture, Agricultural Research Service, *Food and Your Weight.* Home and Garden Bulletin No. 74. Washington, D.C. (1977), p. 4.

more calories than women do. Men also have a higher basal metabolic rate, which means they require more calories just to sustain life (pumping blood, inflating the lungs, and so forth). But women, when pregnant or nursing an infant, for example, may need extra calories, too.

Table 10.2 shows how many calories it takes to maintain the desirable weights of women or men of various heights (sizes) and ages. Height, weight, age, and calorie intake are important, but you can change only one of them: calorie intake. If you are overweight and would like to change, you have two choices. You can increase your activity level or decrease your calorie intake. Each decrease of 3,500 calories causes a weight loss of one pound. In other words, by making no other changes, you could lose one pound a week by consuming 500 calories a day less than you usually consume or by dancing your socks off for two hours every night of the week.

Factors That Affect Food Choices

Making decisions about the food we eat requires more than counting calories. Food choices are often emotional rather than logical. Habits developed in childhood ("Clean your plate—or else . . ."), along with the psychological dimensions of eating (comfort, security, relief from boredom, reward, or status), can affect our choices throughout our lives. In America it is not unusual to eat for reasons other than hunger. For instance, food—and hearty eating—plays a major role in traditional

TABLE 10.2 Daily Calorie Allowance Based on Desirable Weight for Height[a]

Women					Men				
		Age					Age		
Height (in.)	Weight (lb.)	22	45	65	Height (in.)	Weight (lb.)	22	45	65
60	109 ± 9	1,700	1,550	1,450	64	133 ± 11	2,500	2,300	2,100
62	115 ± 9	1,800	1,650	1,500	66	142 ± 12	2,650	2,400	2,200
64	122 ± 10	1,950	1,800	1,650	68	151 ± 14	2,800	2,600	2,400
66	129 ± 10	2,000	1,850	1,700	70	159 ± 14	2,875	2,650	2,450
68	136 ± 10	2,050	1,900	1,700	72	167 ± 15	2,950	2,700	2,500
70	144 ± 11	2,200	2,000	1,850	74	175 ± 15	3,050	2,800	2,600
72	152 ± 12	2,300	2,100	1,950	76	182 ± 16	3,125	2,875	2,650

[a] Weights and heights without shoes or outer clothing

SOURCE: Adapted from National Academy of Sciences, National Research Council, Food and Nutrition Board. *Recommended Dietary Allowances*, 9th ed. Washington DC (1980).

BOX 10.1   DIETING AND EATING DISORDERS

Although it is appropriate to be concerned about maintaining a healthy weight level, some people go to extremes in order to become or remain thin. More than $30 billion is spent annually in this country on diet foods, diet pills, and the like. In addition there are the wraps, creams, and gadgets to "melt fat away." We do not have sufficient space to explain why these gadgets and diets are doomed to failure and costly both in terms of money and as a threat to your health and your life. We suggest that you attend a nutrition class or consult a reputable nutrition textbook in this chapter's References and Readings list. We can just briefly analyze a few common diets. As you review the following table, remember that the most effective diets require a decrease in calories, with an average minimum of 1,200 calories per day to ensure nutritional adequacy, and an increase in physical activity. And anyone who decides to diet to lose more than a few pounds, should first consult a physician.

Type of Diet	Composition	Considerations	Possible Dangers[g]
1,000 to 1,200 calories	High nutrient density[b]	Available, economical, familiar	None
900 calories	Liquid formula	Boring, expensive	None, if medically supervised
Low carbohydrate	Low carbohydrate high fat, high protein	High meat intake, expensive	Ketosis,[c] fluid loss, high saturated fat, high cholesterol, kidney failure or kidney stones
High protein	Protein oriented	High meat intake, expensive	High saturated fat, high cholesterol
Single food	Grapefruit, egg, rice, etc.	Boring	Low in minerals and vitamins
Very low calorie: 300–600 calories	Protein or protein-carbohydrate formula	Boring, expensive	Ketosis, nausea, diarrhea, weakness

[a] Adapted from Vincent Hegarty, "Types of Weight-Loss Diets," *Decisions in Nutrition* (St. Louis: Times Mirror/Mosby College, 1988), p. 310.

[b] See Box 10.2 for further explanation of high nutrient density.

[c] Ketosis: When carbohydrates are not available in enough quantity, fats are broken down incompletely to ketones. The presence of high levels of ketones in the blood and urine, known as ketosis, can be a precursor to kidney stones.

Occasionally, when the desire to be thin becomes an obsession, some people, particularly teenage girls, resort to self-induced denial of food (**anorexia nervosa**). Others binge on food, consuming as much as 10,000 calories, and purge their bodies by vomiting or using laxatives (**bulimia**). Binging is apparently triggered by stress and depression, and so is clearly tied to emotions. Both anorexia nervosa and bulimia cause life-threatening physical effects, such as irregular heart rate, kidney stones, and anemia. Bulimia can also cause dehydration, hemorrhage from the esophagus, dental enamel erosion, and ulcers. Some researchers believe that in a college population one in five females is bulimic.

Because eating disorders encompass psychological and nutritional aspects of a life-style, professional treatment should be sought. Treatment might include the administration of nutrients intravenously, along with counseling for the emotional problems that caused the destructive behavior. Emphasis needs to be placed on building the individual's self-esteem.

family and social events and holidays. The Thanksgiving turkey and pumpkin pie, the Fourth of July barbecue or picnic, the Halloween trick-or-treat candy, and the wedding feasts and cakes are all part of the values and ceremonies we associate with food—values we may seldom question.

One's life-style can also affect food choices. If one is busy and in a hurry, one may skip breakfast, grab something quick and available for lunch, and eat snacks for dinner, rather than plan a nutritious meal. Such a person is not making decisions: He or she is haphazardly taking in food, without much thought to its nutritional benefits. Perhaps the saved time is not worth the lower-quality health.

Poor food choices can result in increased susceptibility to illness, high blood pressure, and depression, as well as greater risk of death from coronary artery disease, stroke, kidney disease, and diabetes. Poor choices deprive the body of adequate vitamins and minerals for maintaining its functions. Obese people have an increased risk during surgery, pregnancy, and childbirth, because excess body weight places a strain on internal organs, particularly the heart and the circulatory system. There are also negative aspects to keeping oneself thin, despite popular belief (see Box 10.1). Research continues both on the causes of overweight and obesity and on the effects of these conditions on health.

GUIDES TO GOOD NUTRITION

Four Food Groups (Four Food Group Plan): a guide for wise food selection consisting of four food categories: milk and dairy foods, meat and other protein goods, fruits and vegetables, and bread and cereals

Recommended Dietary Allowances (RDAs): the adequate levels of intake of essential nutrients—such as vitamins, minerals, and protein—that meet the known nutritional needs of most healthy people in America

How can you tell whether you are making good food choices? In order to help consumers make wise selections, the USDA has divided food into categories, creating the Four Food Group Plan. You probably learned about the plan in school; it is still the simplest and most effective way to remember how to select food.

As Figure 10.1 shows that the **Four Food Groups** consist of meat (or other protein sources), dairy products (milk and cheese), fruits and vegetables, and cereal and grain products. By eating at least the recommended quantities, staying within appropriate calorie levels, and choosing a variety of foods, you will get adequate amounts of all the necessary nutrients.

The Four Food Group Plan is a simple and effective guide for consumers. Nutritionists and dietitians, however, most often evaluate the quality of a diet in a more detailed way. They compute the nutrient content of foods using sophisticated chemical analysis. The resulting research provides us with **Recommended Dietary Allowances (RDAs)**, which are levels of intake of essential nutrients that are adequate for the known nutritional needs of almost all healthy people in America. As with the need for calories, the amount of each nutrient needed varies according

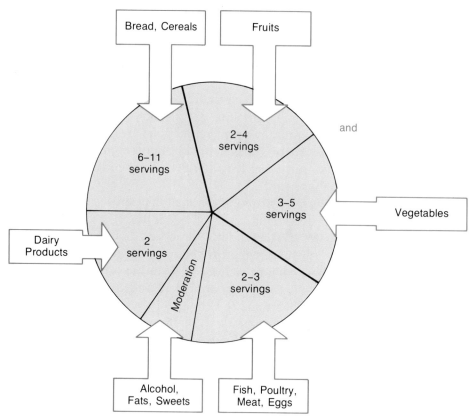

FIGURE 10.1
Four Food Group Plan (fruits and vegetables; bread and cereals; dairy products; fish, poultry, meat, eggs). Recommended servings per day for an adult.

to age, size, and gender. The recommended quantity of each essential nutrient is expressed in a unit of measure (see Table 10.3).

RDAs are recommendations, *not* average requirements, for groups of average, healthy people. To allow for individual needs and for a margin of safety, the RDA exceeds the requirement of most individuals, so that the needs of at least 95 percent of the people in each age-gender group are met.

More than likely, your RDA needs will be met if you eat a variety of foods from each of the food groups and if your caloric intake is adequate. Nutrition experts in the USDA Agriculture Research Service have analyzed more than 900 common foods for their nutritional values. Examples are shown in Box 10.2. An inexpensive publication called *Composition of Foods*, available from the U.S. Government Printing Office, contains the results of their research, which may be helpful in analyzing your specific diet. Classes in nutrition offered at most colleges

TABLE 10.3 Recommended Daily Dietary Allowances (RDA), 1980[a]

	Age (years)	Weight (kg)	Weight (lb)	Height (cm)	Height (in)	Protein (g)	Vitamin A (µg RE)[b]	Vitamin D (µg)[c]	Vitamin E (mg α-TE)[d]	Vitamin C (mg)	Thiamin (mg)	Riboflavin (mg)	Niacin (mg NE)[e]	Vitamin B-6 (mg)	Folacin (µg)[f]	Vitamin B-12 (µg)	Calcium (mg)	Phosphorus (mg)	Magnesium (mg)	Iron (mg)	Zinc (mg)	Iodine (µg)
							Fat-Soluble Vitamins			**Water-Soluble Vitamins**							**Minerals**					
Infants	0.0–0.5	6	13	60	24	kg × 2.2	420	10	3	35	0.3	0.4	6	0.3	30	0.5[g]	360	240	50	10	3	40
	0.5–1.0	9	20	71	28	kg × 2.0	400	10	4	35	0.5	0.6	8	0.6	45	1.5	540	360	70	15	5	50
Children	1–3	13	29	90	35	23	400	10	5	45	0.7	0.8	9	0.9	100	2.0	800	800	150	15	10	70
	4–6	20	44	112	44	30	500	10	6	45	0.9	1.0	11	1.3	200	2.5	800	800	200	10	10	90
	7–10	28	62	132	52	34	700	10	7	45	1.2	1.4	16	1.6	300	3.0	800	800	250	10	10	120
Males	11–14	45	99	157	62	45	1000	10	8	50	1.4	1.6	18	1.8	400	3.0	1200	1200	350	18	15	150
	15–18	66	145	176	69	56	1000	10	10	60	1.4	1.7	18	2.0	400	3.0	1200	1200	400	18	15	150
	19–22	70	154	177	70	56	1000	7.5	10	60	1.5	1.7	19	2.2	400	3.0	800	800	350	10	15	150
	23–50	70	154	178	70	56	1000	5	10	60	1.4	1.6	18	2.2	400	3.0	800	800	350	10	15	150
	51+	70	154	178	70	56	1000	5	10	60	1.2	1.4	16	2.2	400	3.0	800	800	350	10	15	150
Females	11–14	46	101	157	62	46	800	10	8	50	1.1	1.3	15	1.8	400	3.0	1200	1200	300	18	15	150
	15–18	55	120	163	64	46	800	10	8	60	1.1	1.3	14	2.0	400	3.0	1200	1200	300	18	15	150
	19–22	55	120	163	64	44	800	7.5	8	60	1.1	1.3	14	2.0	400	3.0	800	800	300	18	15	150
	23–50	55	120	163	64	44	800	5	8	60	1.0	1.2	13	2.0	400	3.0	800	800	300	18	15	150
	51+	55	120	163	64	44	800	5	8	60	1.0	1.2	13	2.0	400	3.0	800	800	300	10	15	150
Pregnant						+30	+200	+5	+2	+20	+0.4	+0.3	+2	+0.6	+400	+1.0	+400	+400	+150	h	+5	+25
Lactating						+20	+400	+5	+3	+40	+0.5	+0.5	+5	+0.5	+100	+1.0	+400	+400	+150	h	+10	+50

[a] The allowances are intended to provide for individual variations among most normal persons as they live in the United States under usual environmental stresses. Diets should be based on a variety of common foods in order to provide other nutrients for which human requirements have been less well defined. See text for detailed discussion of allowances and of nutrients not tabulated. See Table 1 (p. 20) for weights and heights by individual year of age. See Table 3 (p. 23) for suggested average energy intakes.

[b] Retinol equivalents. 1 retinol equivalent = 1 µg retinol or 6 µg β carotene. See text for calculation of vitamin A activity of diets as retinol equivalents.

[c] As cholecalciferol. 10 µg cholecalciferol = 400 ιυ of vitamin D.

[d] α-tocopherol equivalents. 1 mg d-α tocopherol = 1 α-TE. See text for variation in allowances and calculation of vitamin E activity of the diet as α-tocopherol equivalents.

[e] 1 NE (niacin equivalent) is equal to 1 mg of niacin or 60 mg of dietary tryptophan.

[f] The folacin allowances refer to dietary sources as determined by Lactobacillus casei assay after treatment with enzymes (conjugases) to make polyglutamyl forms of the vitamin available to the test organism.

[g] The recommended dietary allowance for vitamin B-12 in infants is based on average concentration of the vitamin in human milk. The allowances after weaning are based on energy intake (as recommended by the American Academy of Pediatrics) and consideration of other factors, such as intestinal absorption; see text.

[h] The increased requirement during pregnancy cannot be met by the iron content of habitual American diets nor by the existing iron stores of many women; therefore the use of 30–60 mg of supplemental iron is recommended. Iron needs during lactation are not substantially different from those of nonpregnant women, but continued supplementation of the mother for 2–3 months after parturition is advisable in order to replenish stores depleted by pregnancy.

SOURCE: National Academy of Sciences, Recommended Dietary Allowances, 9th ed. Washington, D.C.: NAS, 1980.

BOX 10.2 COMPARE NUTRIENT LEVELS

Some foods that we eat supply very few nutrients compared to the number of calories they supply. We sometimes say that these foods have "empty calories." Candy, soft drinks, some snack foods, and alcoholic beverages fall into this group. Foods high in calories and low in other nutrients are described by nutritionists as having a **low nutrient density**. Foods low in calories and rich in other nutrients (many vegetables and fish) have a **high nutrient density**. Listed below are some examples of each. Which are the low-nutrient-density foods? Place a check next to each one that is low in nutrients compared to its calorie content.

Food	Food energy (cal.)	Pro-tein (gm)	Fat (gm)	Vitamin A (IU)	Vitamin C (mg)	Thia-min (mg)	Ribo-flavin (mg)	Niacin (gm)	Cal-cium (mg)	Iron (mg)	Sodium (mg)
				Vitamins					**Minerals**		
1 cake doughnut	125	1	6	30	trace	0.05	0.05	0.4	13	0.4	200
2 slices whole-wheat bread	120	6	2	trace	trace	0.12	0.06	1.4	50	1.6	250
8 oz. orange juice	120	2	trace	550	120	0.22	0.02	1.0	25	0.2	3
8 oz. cola	96	0	0	0	0	0	0	0	0	0	54
10 potato chips	115	1	8	trace	3	0.04	0.01	0.01	8	0.4	100
2 cups popcorn with oil and salt	80	2	4	0	0	0	0.02	0	2	0.4	100
1 oz. gumdrops	100	trace	trace	0	0	0	trace	trace	2	0.1	0
1 medium banana	100	1	trace	230	12	0.06	0.07	0.8	10	0.8	0
1 cup broccoli	40	5	1	3,880	140	0.14	0.31	1.2	136	1.2	24

Were you surpised at the lack of nutrients in the cola drink? Probably not—but how about the data on the doughnut and the potato chips? Cola drinks and gumdrops are excellent examples of foods with empty calories.

SOURCE: Adapted from Agricultural Research Service, *Composition of Foods* (Washington, D.C.: U.S. Government Printing Office).

also help you analyze your nutritional status, often with the help of computers.

During the 1970s and 1980s, information grew about the elements of a healthy diet, culminating in the 1988 Surgeon General's report on food and diet, citing more than 2,000 scientific studies. Compiled with the advice of more than 200 health and diet experts, the report concludes that eating patterns can influence long-term health prospects. It establishes that modifying dietary choices to reduce saturated fat, and therefore **cholesterol** (fatlike substances in foods of animal origin that, when consumed in excess, increase the risk of heart disease), restrict sodium intake; and an increase in fiber can reduce risk of three major life-threatening diseases: heart disease (stroke and atherosclerosis), high blood pressure, and cancer. (It is estimated that in the United States, heart attacks account for 500,000 deaths and $50 billion in health costs annually.) The Surgeon General's report also recommends cutting down on sugar and alcohol, as well as generally decreasing caloric intake. In place of fatty or empty calories, the report suggests increasing intake of whole grains, fruits, and vegetables.

Consumers would be wise to keep up to date regarding nutrition and to use this information when making food selections. To help consumers make decisions, the federal government requires manufacturers to print the contents of some essential nutrients on many food packages. In the following section we will discuss this regulation and those that require the disclosure of ingredient content information.

GOVERNMENT LABELING

On a typical trip to a supermarket, we choose from more than 25,000 items, from fresh foods to canned goods to packaged snacks to frozen products of all kinds. Six thousand new and improved products come each year from an increasingly sophisticated food-processing and -producing industry. At the same time, hundreds of products that were new and improved last year are discontinued. Some of the new products and some of those already on the shelves are a complex mixture of food and chemicals that do everything from enhancing or replacing flavor to preventing spoilage. In addition, foods are packaged or canned, so we can't actually see the product. Product changes and the use of advanced food technology and packaging create the need for new, often unprecedented, decisions relying on up-to-date product information. Labels tell us what the food is, what has been added to it, and what nutritional value we can expect from it.

Nutritional Labeling

enriched (fortified): foods that have had small amounts of nutrients added to increase their nutritional level

A 1975 regulation requires any food that is **enriched**, or **fortified**, with nutrients (such as vitamin C) or makes a nutritional or dietetic claim ("high protein," "low calorie," and so forth) to have a nutritional label. This allows consumers to compare and evaluate the need for, as well as the cost of, the enrichment. Nutritional labeling on other products is voluntary. A 1985 amendment to this law requires sodium content information on packaged foods that include other nutritional information. Manufacturers may voluntarily disclose the amount of sodium in a product. Slightly more than half of all packaged foods carry nutritional labeling, many of them voluntarily. All labels must use a standard format (see Figure 10.2):

FIGURE 10.2
Required label format.

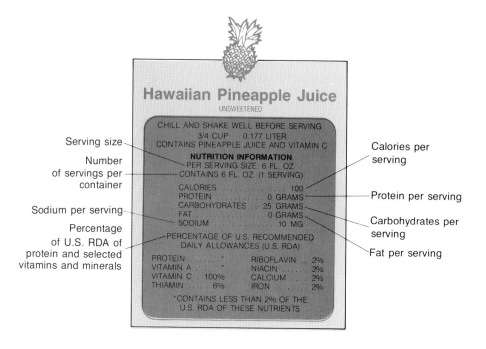

1. Serving size
2. Number of servings per container
3. Calories per serving
4. Protein per serving (in grams)
5. Carbohydrates per serving (in grams)
6. Fat per serving (in grams)
7. Sodium per serving (in milligrams)
8. Percent of U.S. RDA of protein and selected vitamins and minerals

U.S. Recommended Daily Allowances (U.S. RDAs): designed for use as a standard on food labels; expressed in a percentage, rather than as a unit of measurement, and applies to one serving size of a food product

Notice this last item carefully. **U.S. RDA** stands for **U.S. Recommended Daily Allowances**, and is based on but not identical to Recommended Dietary Allowances (RDA). The U.S. RDA (the *D* indicating *daily* need) was designed for use as a standard on labels. The U.S. RDA is a number expressed as a percentage, rather than a unit of measurement, and applies to one serving size of the food product. Since this labeling is based on the RDA for the group with the highest need (usually teenage boys), the percentages do not reflect what all people need. Most people do not need 100 percent of each nutrient, so meals should be planned for the needs of various ages. According to Table 10.4, a seven-year-old child needs only two-thirds as much protein (55 percent of the U.S. RDA) as a woman (75 percent of the U.S. RDA). But if a woman is nursing an infant, she needs twice as much protein (75 percent plus 35 percent) as a seven-year-old.

TABLE 10.4 Calories, Protein, Vitamins, and Minerals Needed to Meet U.S. RDA, for Children, Men and Women of Various Ages

Age	Calories[a]	Protein[b] (% of U.S. RDA)	Vitamins (% of U.S. RDA)					Minerals (% of U.S. RDA)	
			A	C	Thiamin	Riboflavin	Niacin[c]	Calcium	Iron
Children									
1–3	1,300	35	40	70	50	50	30	80	85
7–10	2,400	55	70	70	80	75	50	80	60
Men									
15–18	3,000	85	100	75	100	110	55	120	100
23–50	2,700	90	100	75	95	95	45	80	60
51+	2,400	90	100	75	80	90	35	80	60
Women									
15–18	2,100	75	80	75	75	85	30	120	100
23–50	2,000	75	80	75	70	75	30	80	100
51+	1,800	75	80	75	70	65	25	80	60
Pregnant	+300[d]	+50[d]	100	100	+20[d]	+20[d]	35	120	100[d]
Nursing	+500[d]	+35[d]	120	135	+20[d]	+30[d]	35	120	100

[a] Calorie needs differ depending on body composition and size, age, and activity level.

[b] U.S. RDA of 65 grams is used for this table. In labeling, a U.S. RDA of 45 grams is used for foods providing high-quality protein, such as milk, meat, and eggs.

[c] Will provide RDA for niacin if RDA for protein is met. Some niacin is derived from tryptophan, an amino acid present in protein.

[d] Add to allowance for appropriate age.

SOURCE: B. Peterkin, J. Nicholas, and C. Cromwell. "Nutrition Labeling: Tools for Its Use." Agricultural Information Bulletin No. 382, U.S. Department of Agriculture (Washington, D.C.: U.S. Government Printing Office, April 1975), p. 47.

It is important to remember that one food need not supply a whole day's worth of nutrients. Breakfast cereal, for example, is just one part of a meal, one nutrient source. The accumulation of total nutrients consumed during meals and snacks is what is significant. Box 10.2 provided information on how to compare the nutritional quality of foods.

Fair Packaging and Labeling Act

In addition to nutritional information, consumers need to know about the quantity and quality of the food they buy. Since the 1950s there has been a tremendous growth in the number of canned, packaged, and frozen goods, from fruits and vegetables to dinner and breakfast entrees to snacks and desserts. At first, consumers found product comparison difficult because standard product descriptions or information about container size were not required. As a result of the Fair Packaging and Labeling Act (FPLA) of

1966, this information is given on most food products sold nationally:

1. Name of the product and its form ("fruit cocktail in heavy syrup")
2. Net contents (weight or fluid volume)
3. Portion size, if number of servings is stated
4. Name and address of processor, distributor, or packer
5. List of ingredients in order of decreasing weight or order of concentration

Figure 10.3 illustrates how one company has met these requirements. But what happens if a manufacturer fails to comply with these regulations or does not tell the truth? Then, the FDA has the authority to investigate and prosecute, if necessary. A dramatic example of this involved Beech-Nut Nutrition Corporation, the nation's second-largest baby food manufacturer when, in 1986, a federal grand jury charged it with misleading consumers and indicted the corporation, its president, vice president, and distributors for marketing a drink that was only sugar water and a blend of chemicals simulating the taste and appearance of apple juice. This fraudulent product was distributed between 1978 and 1983 in 19 states and 5 foreign countries. The corporation was fined $2.18 million dollars, the largest fine paid under the Food, Drug, and Cosmetic Act by at least sixfold. In addition, individual executives were fined, and given prison sentences because they were aware of the fraud. Shipping an adulterated product is a misdemeanor. To do so with full knowledge is a felony.

The Fair Packaging and Labeling Act improved a bad situation. Besides requiring the information mentioned above, it required the food industry to establish guidelines for standardizing the way net contents are listed. Before 1966, one juice manufacturer might have measured only in ounces and another measured in quarts and ounces. As a result, comparison shopping was more difficult. Now, all manufacturers of similar products

**FIGURE 10.3
Required product
information.**

The Fair Packaging and Labeling Act requires that products come in just a few standardized sizes, but with rebates, coupons, and discounts it still is often difficult to find the best buy.

slack fill: the practice of accepting empty space in a food container to allow for product settling

use the same unit of measurement. Canned or bottled juices, for example, are measured and labeled in fluid ounces (say, 48 fl. oz.), then in quarts ($1\frac{1}{2}$ qt.), and then in liters (1.42 L.). The FPLA also required individual industries to set standards to clarify adjectives like *small* or *giant* and to standardize package sizes; now, for example, there are five toothpaste sizes, rather than 57. Finally, the FPLA required industry to set standards to prevent excessive **slack fill**, the practice of not filling a box completely and letting customers assume that the contents had settled. Consumers who judged the quantity by the box size were often fooled. Although some settling of cereals or snack chips, for example, is understandable, the industry now controls how much slack fill is allowed after settling, generally, 10 percent.

Despite the help FPLA has given, consumers still lack some information necessary for decision making. For example, on about 300 specific food products, including ice cream, peanut butter, and mayonnaise, there may be no list of ingredients. The federal government has decided that these foods fall under an **identity standard**; that is, their ingredients are so standard and well known that they require no labeling. Considering that more than 125 separate ingredients, in any combination, have been approved for ice cream, this seems illogical at the very least. Yet as long as a standard of identity exists, ingredient labeling is not required. Believing that this omission in the FPLA is not acceptable, many states have passed laws requiring ingredient labels on *all* food products sold, and many manufacturers voluntarily include such labels.

Need for Other Kinds of Labeling

Besides more complete labeling of ingredients, consumers could use more specific information regarding weight, contents, and ingredient origin. Currently, "net contents" includes both the food and the liquid in a can or package. So a ten-ounce can of green beans may contain seven ounces of beans and three ounces of liquid, whereas a competitor may offer eight ounces of beans and two ounces of liquid. The problem is more complicated when trying to compare canned products packed in liquid with frozen competitors. Listing the drained weight, or dry weight, would make price comparison more accurate.

It becomes even more difficult to determine the contents of a food package when the product is complex, as is the case with many convenience foods. If you have ever wondered how much beef is in a pot pie or how many apples are in an apple pie, you were wondering about the **characterizing ingredient**, that is, the main ingredient that gives a product its identity. Because the amount of an ingredient can vary from one brand to another, it would be useful to know the percentages of the ingredients in each brand of food when comparison shopping.

characterizing ingredient: the main ingredient of a food product, such as cherries in a cherry pie

The origins of ingredients would be useful information for people with allergies, chronic heart disease, or other ailments. In 1987, for example, the FDA banned the use of sulfites on most fresh fruits and vegetables and now requires disclosure of this preservative on food and alcoholic beverage labels. These restrictions were prompted by the fact that more than 1 million people in the nation, mostly asthmatics, are sensitive to sulfites. Reactions can range from hives, nausea, and diarrhea to shortness of breath and shock, ultimately causing death. Obviously, most additives or preservatives are not life threatening, but because they can cause mild allergic reactions, some people would like to avoid them. Other consumers, in an effort to reduce dietary cholesterol, would like to identify whether the cooking oil used is saturated or unsaturated, corn or cottonseed, palm or coconut oil. Identifying specific spices, flavorings, and colorings and the food source of fats and oils in food products would help consumers by eliminating some of the worry and guesswork caused by lack of information. Some manufacturers provide some of this information voluntarily.

The heart of the consumer decision-making process depends on complete and accurate product information. Such information can be obtained from package labels or as a result of product use. The costs of more detailed labeling would be passed on to consumers, who in turn would need to be more informed in order to use the information.

Consumers who want this information, recognizing that minuscule price increases may result, should tell manufacturers their wishes.

SAFETY AND QUALITY

In addition to providing nutrition and content labeling, the government provides consumers with other kinds of information about food appearance and flavor. Through inspection of meats and poultry, milk and milk products, eggs, and fresh produce, the government gives us a sense of the relative quality of these foods, Within each category, some grades (categories that indicate degrees of physical quality) are better than others—and usually cost more. If there were no inspection and grading, consumers could be deceived about the quality of what they buy. Inspection also provides a measure of the safety of the food, that is, its freedom from disease and contaminants. In this section we look at the specific kinds of information we receive through inspection and grading. Keep in mind, however, that no food is graded for nutritional quality (high nutrient density). You will have to make that judgment yourself.

Meat and Fish Inspection and Grading

Because meat quickly spoils and is the most expensive part of the family food budget, it was the first food to be inspected and regulated to ensure safety and quality. Federal standards for the cleanliness of both the product and the plant were set in 1906 and strengthened as a result of the Wholesome Meat Act of 1967 and the Wholesome Poultry Act of 1968.

Consumers have a wide variety of fresh produce in their supermarkets, but how do we know it is safe?

All states must meet minimum sanitation requirements for meat and meat products (sandwich meats, sausage, and so forth). The USDA inspects fresh and processed meat products sold locally or nationally. Although inspection is required, USDA *grading* is done only at the manufacturer's request.

Beef is graded U.S. Prime (available primarily to restaurants), U.S. Choice, U.S. Select (these two found in grocery stores), U.S. Good, U.S. Standard, U.S. Commercial, or U.S. Utility. Veal, mutton, and lamb are graded U.S. Choice (available to restaurants and consumers alike), U.S. Select, U.S. Standard, U.S. Utility, or U.S. Cull. Pork is not usually graded; all cuts are considered tender. Consumers generally find only USDA Grade A poultry in the market. Lesser grades of meat and poultry are usually used in processed foods, such as canned soups and sandwich meats.

Meat grades are determined partly by the quantity of fat found in muscle tissue. More fat is found in certain muscles because the animal moves these muscles less. More exercise means meat that is less tender. So, fat content, muscle location, and the age of the animal are criteria for determining grading and price.

Since, in an effort to improve the quality of our diet, many of us are consuming less red meat and more fish, it should be noted that the United States does not require inspection or grading of fish or shellfish. Even though inspection by the Department of Commerce is available on a voluntary basis for a fee, only about 15 percent of fresh or processed fish is protected by inspection. Many fishing boats lack refrigerated storage facilities, and some processing plants would not meet minimum standards.

The National Marine Fisheries Service, in conjunction with the National Academy of Sciences, is currently studying the risks associated with fish and shellfish contaminated with chemical residues from water pollution or with harmful bacteria or parasites. Fish that are eaten raw or minimally cooked are the major source of problems, which may involve mild stomach discomfort or cramps (see Box 10.3, pages 304–305). The joint study will determine what corrective measures could be initiated. In the meantime, it is important to purchase fish and shellfish from reputable firms, to learn to judge the freshness of fish, and to cook fish adequately before eating.

The Rest of Your Diet

After meat, milk and milk products take the largest chunk out of the average food dollar. The U.S. Public Health Service grades milk for freshness and indicates how long milk has been stored and under what conditions. There are three grades of fluid milk: A, B, and C. Generally, consumers find only grade A in their dairy cases.

Varieties and prices of fluid milk are based on butterfat content. Whole milk usually has 5 percent butterfat. Lowfat or nonfat fluid milk may be 5 to 8 cents less per quart because some of the fat has been removed to make butter. The fat content of cream can vary from 20 percent for light table cream to 37 percent for heavy whipping cream. Evaporated milk has only about one-half the water content of whole milk and may be less expensive to use because shipping costs decrease when the water is extracted. The same may be true for powdered milk. By using evaporated or powdered milk in a reconstituted form (with water added) for cooking or drinking, families can decrease food expenditures.

Eggs are available in six sizes, ranging from "jumbo" (30 ounces minimum per dozen) to "pee-wee" (15 ounces minimum per dozen). Standards for sizes and grades are regulated by the USDA. Eggs are graded U.S. Grade AA ("Fancy Fresh"), U.S. Grade A, or U.S. Grade B. Grade AA and Grade A are the best quality for frying, because the yolks are large and

TABLE 10.5   USDA Grades for Some Fruits and Vegetables

Product	Top Grade	Second Grade	Third Grade	Fourth Grade
Apples (all states but Washington)	U.S. Extra Fancy	U.S. Fancy	U.S. No. 1	U.S. Utility
Apples (Washington)	Washington Extra Fancy	Washington Fancy		
Broccoli (Italian sprouting)	U.S. Fancy	U.S. No. 1	U.S. No. 2	
Celery	U.S. Extra No. 1	U.S. No. 1	U.S. No. 2	
Corn (husked, on the cob)	U.S. Fancy	U.S. No. 1	U.S. No. 2	
Grapefruit (all states but Arizona, California, and Florida)	U.S. Fancy	U.S. No. 1	U.S. No. 1 Bright	U.S. No. 1 Bronze
Grapefruit (Arizona and California)	U.S. Fancy	U.S. No. 1	U.S. No. 1	U.S. Combination
Grapefruit (Florida)	U.S. Fancy	U.S. No. 1	U.S. No. 1 Bright	U.S. No. 1 Golden
Lima beans	U.S. Extra No. 1	U.S. No. 1	U.S. No.2	
Oranges (all states but Arizona, California, and Florida)	U.S. Fancy	U.S. No. 1	U.S. No. 1 Bright	U.S. No. 1 Bronze
Oranges (Arizona and California)	U.S. Fancy	U.S. No. 1	U.S. Combination	U.S. No. 2
Oranges (Florida)	U.S. Fancy	U.S. No. 1 Bright	U.S. No. 1 Bright	U.S. No. 1 Golden
Turnips	U.S. No. 1	U.S. No. 2		

round and the whites are firm and stiff. Grade B eggs have the same nutritional value but a thinner consistency. The color of the eggshell (white or brown) reflects the breed of hen and not the quality or nutritional value of the egg.

As with seafoods, the grading of fruits and vegetables is voluntary. Grades are based on shape, color, maturity, size, and absence of blemishes. As Table 10.5 shows, the symbols and terms used do not allow consumers to distinguish top from second or third quality easily, because the terminology is not uniform for all fruits and vegetables.

If, after this discussion of grading, you want to throw in the towel, you are not alone. Because of consumer complaints across the nation, the USDA began public hearings on the grading issue in the 1980s. But as we go to press no simplified plan has been selected to replace the grading muddle.

CODES: PRICES AND DATES

As we have seen, information on food packages is essential in decision making. Besides the labeling information, most packages today include two additional pieces of data: a product code and a date. Both practices have received extensive consumer attention. When introduced, the product code was the topic of an angry interchange between consumers and the food-packaging and -distributing industries.

Universal Product Code

Universal Product Code (UPC): a grid of lines and bars, printed on a product, that can be read by an electronic scanner and that indicates the type of product, the size, and the manufacturer

The **Universal Product Code (UPC)** is the grid of lines, bars, and numbers that appears on most products sold in grocery and drug stores and in some general merchandise stores. When read by a light scanner, the UPC indicates the brand or manufacturer of the product (for example, Hunt-Wesson), the specific product (for example, tomato catsup), and the product size (for example, 15 ounces). It appears on more than 90 percent of the packaged products typically sold in grocery stores. The UPC is designed for use by electronic cash registers and scanners at the checkout stand. When the checker moves the item over the scanner, the UPC triggers the machine to charge a customer the amount of money the machine has been programmed by the store to charge. The code carries no price information per se, only product identification. The transactions are flashed on an electronic readout panel visible to the consumer and the checker and are, at the same time, printed on the register receipt.

The introduction of the UPC and electronic scanners was controversial in the early 1980s. The UPC and scanners provide retailers with accurate, up-to-date inventory counts, allowing them to order and stock more efficiently to meet customer demand, and the system can speed up the checkout procedure and reduce checker error. These seem to benefit consumers. However, the system does not require that prices be marked on

product pricing: marking a product price on a package or product so that it is clearly visible to a consumer—a process required by many city and state laws.

individual items, and that is a source of contention. If a can of peas didn't have a price marked on it, would you remember its price when you looked at frozen or fresh green peas? A price comparison would be difficult, especially with a shopping cart full of groceries! In response, consumer activists have been instrumental in the passage of city and state laws that require **product pricing**, that is, laws that require most or all packaged products to be individually priced.

Unit Pricing

unit pricing: calculation of the price of a small unit of a food product, such as 1 ounce or 1 gram; usually appears on a shelf tag

With the vast assortment of products in supermarkets, and with more demands on time and money, selecting suitable, delectable, *and* economical packaged products can be a challenge. But take a closer look at the shelf tag and you will discover **unit pricing**, the cost calculation for a small unit of measure, such as an ounce, a gram, or a pound. This information is often provided on the shelf tag along with the price for the entire item. Figure 10.4 shows how to calculate the unit price. Using unit pricing allows you to make price comparison among product brands and product sizes without spending the whole day in the grocery store, calculator in hand.

Fresh, Aged, or Stale?

The last time you purchased milk, yogurt, or cottage cheese, did you notice the date stamped on the bottom of the container? The practice of

FIGURE 10.4
Unit pricing. For most canned or packaged goods, the unit price is the price per pound. Small items and personal-care products will often show the price per ounce. Most liquids are priced per pint. Other items may be priced per 100 square feet or per 100 count.

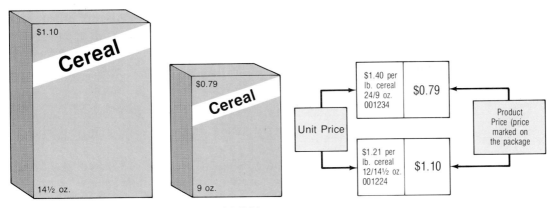

To determine which is the best buy, you could divide:
$0.79 by 9 oz. (8.8 cents per lb.)
and $1.10 by 14½ oz. (7.6 cents per lb.)
or
You could look for the unit price on the shelf tag.

putting a **sell-by (pull) date** on perishable foods is common for major manufacturers. This date indicates when a product should be sold or removed from the shelf. It does not mean that the product will spoil by that date, because it allows the consumer time for home storage and eventual use. Because pull dates are actual dates (for example, June 29) rather than codes, the practice is referred to as *open dating*.

If you look at other packaged goods, such as canned vegetables or a frozen entree, you will probably find a date on these packages as well. But it may not look like a date, because it is most often in code. The date hidden within the codes tell one of three things: expiration date, packaging date, or date of manufacture. Some codes indicate an **expiration (use-by) date**, that is, the last day that the product can be used with proper performance or safety. Expiration, or use-by, dates are commonly found on sandwich meats and spreads or on bread-dough products in the refrigerated section of the store. Some manufacturers also record the pull date in code on items like peanut butter, mayonnaise, and snack foods.

For products with somewhat longer shelf life, two more methods of dating are often used. The **pack (packaging) date** indicates when products as diverse as pasta, nuts, breakfast cereals, and tea have been placed in the containers that we see on grocery shelves. The date of manufacture indicates when the ingredients were all mixed together and processed to form the product. This date is often used by canners of fruits, vegetables, and soups. The shelf life of a product may vary from six months to several years from the date of manufacturing or packaging. So even if these dates were decoded (open), they would not be helpful to consumers without the corresponding recommended shelf life.

Many consumer specialists advocate a uniform system of open dating for packaged foods. Some major cities, such as New York, and a few states now require this. When shoppers in New York were polled, 75 percent of them used open dates to judge freshness, indicating the usefulness of this information. Open dating has also made it possible for store personnel to rotate stock properly and thereby substantially cut losses caused by waste.

HAZARDS TO FOOD SAFETY

Besides regulating food labels and grading standards, the federal government inspects food for safety. Food inspectors look for substances unintentionally added to food. Such contaminants may enter food during growth, harvest, transport, processing, packaging, or storage. Food technologists rank hazards to food safety in order of importance:

1. Microbiological (food poisoning cause by bacteria)
2. Nutritional (inadequate or excessive nutrients)
3. Environmental (heavy metals, such as lead, plastics)
4. Natural toxicants (such as oxalates in rhubarb and spinach)

5. Pesticide residues (such as malathion on fruit)
6. Food additives (those that cause disease, particularly cancer)

Consumers seem to worry most about the more visible or controversial contaminants, such as food additives and preservatives, pesticide residues, and "filth" (small stones, rodent hairs, and insect parts). It may surprise you to learn that the FDA has set allowable levels of filth; if the levels are above what is permitted, the food cannot be sold. Although these levels are low, critics have argued that they are too lenient. Yet a standard of zero contaminants would be unrealistic. Completely uncontaminated food would be very expensive, and enforcing the law would be virtually impossible.

In the home, insects are frequent and troublesome contaminants. With the exception of cockroaches, however, they are seldom health hazards. If you find weevils or pantry beetles in foods such as cereals, pasta, crackers, dried fruit, nuts, or spices, you can save the food. First, check all packages. If food is contaminated, either throw it away or kill the bugs by freezing the product for at least two days or by placing it in a warm (130-degree) oven for two hours (stirring to ensure heat penetration.) The food will then be safe to eat.

Box 10.3 illustrates seriousnesss of microbiological hazards in homes. But since most consumer controversy and regulation has centered around the last two hazards, pesticide residue and food additives, we will focus on these two matters for economic and consumer decision makers.

Pesticide Residue

Pesticides are used to prevent damage and destruction of crops. Even with pesticide use however, U.S. farmers sometimes lose as much as one-third of their crops to pest destruction. The high loss is partly attributable to the high standards we have for how food should look. We allow for little visible evidence of insect damage, even if the food remains wholesome. Who wants to share his or her apple with a worm? Probably no one. But does it really matter if a snail ate part of a lettuce leaf?

The increased bounty of fresh fruits and vegetables in our markets is due, in part, to increased and extensive use of chemical fertilizers and pesticides. A recent study shows that the crops with the most frequent incidence of pesticide residue include strawberries, peaches, celery, cherries, and cucumbers (Mott and Snyder, 1988). Of course, pesticides in high enough doses could be harmful to humans. So the EPA establishes tolerance levels, based on the toxicity of a pesticide, for those who work with the pesticide, and it establishes residue levels for crops that receive the pesticide in the United States. (There are no standards for imported fruits and vegetables.) The USDA and FDA assist in monitoring inspections of the harvest.

BOX 10.3 SALLY AND SALMONELLA

Early in the morning on a warm summer day, Sally cut up a chicken on her cutting board. She wiped the board with a damp sponge and cooked the chicken. After the chicken had cooled, she deboned it and cut it up on the cutting board. She also chopped celery and onion on the board. She mixed these ingredients with mayonnaise and put the salad in a covered bowl. A while later she put the salad in an ice chest and took it to a picnic. The ice chest sat in partial sun on the picnic table until afternoon, and when opened, the ice had melted. The chicken salad was served and remained on the picnic table for a couple of hours before all of it was eaten.

The next day, people who ate the chicken salad got sick with varying degrees of vomiting, diarrhea, abdominal cramps, fever, and headache. An elderly woman became critically ill and diagnostic tests showed she had salmonellosis—a gastrointestinal infection caused by salmonella bacteria. The chicken salad was identified as the source.

What did Sally do wrong?

1. *The cutting board*. Raw chicken (and other poultry, meat, and fish) may carry salmonella bacteria. The bacteria contaminated the cutting board; the board was not thoroughly washed. Salmonella bacteria grew on it, then contaminated the cooked chicken when it was cut on the board. (Cooking destroyed the salmonella that were present in the raw chicken.)

2. *The chicken salad*. Moist protein foods are especially good places for bacteria to grow. The mayonnaise made the chicken more moist and vulnerable. The mayonnaise was not the source of the bacteria, however—it was the raw chicken.

3. *The temperature*. The contaminated chicken salad might not have made anyone sick if it had been eaten fresh or kept very cold. But it was not chilled in the refrigerator before it went in the ice chest. The ice melted in the chest so the temperature was not cold enough to keep bacteria from growing. Later the salad was left on the warm picnic table where the temperature was ideal for rapid multiplication of the bacteria.

4. *The time*. Enough total time elapsed (4 or more hours) when the chicken salad wasn't cold to give the salmonella bacteria time to multiply to unsafe levels. Everyone who ate the chicken salad was infected by the bacteria, which multiplied in their intestinal tracts. Older people are especially vulnerable to attacks by salmonella.

Sally should have:

1. Thoroughly washed and rinsed her cutting board immediately after using it for raw chicken, using hot water, detergent, a brush, and even diluted chlorine bleach.

2. Thoroughly chilled the salad in the refrigerator—overnight, for example—before taking it to the picnic.

3. Used enough ice in the chest, or replenished it, to keep the foods good and cold (below 40 degrees F). Putting the ice chest in the shade—even covered with a blanket—would have helped.

4. Served the chicken salad immediately and returned it to the ice chest rather than letting it stand on the warm picnic table.

5. Better yet, not taken a vulnerable food like chicken salad on an all-day picnic. As an alternative, she could have taken cans of chicken, a jar of mayonnaise, and the chopped vegetables, and mixed the chicken salad just before serving time.

Remember These Facts

• Most incidents of food poisoning occur because food handlers do not follow good sanitation and health practices.

• Food poisoning bacteria need food, water, a temperature between 60–120 degrees F, and time to grow. At cold temperatures—below 40 degrees F—bacterial growth is very slow. At temperatures above 165 degrees F, bacteria are destroyed.

• The most vulnerable foods are low-acid, moist protein foods—eggs, meat, poultry, fish, beans and peas, dairy products, puddings, custards, salads of potato, macaroni. Least vulnerable are fresh fruits and vegetables; acid foods—canned fruit, pickles, fruit salad; and dry foods—breads, cereals, cakes, cookies.

To prevent food poisoning, vulnerable foods should be protected from contamination, and kept very cold or very hot until eaten. Leftovers should be chilled quickly in the refrigerator (spread out large quantities in shallow pans to speed the process). Vulnerable foods should not stand at room temperature for longer than a total of 4 hours, including preparation time.

SOURCE: Dorothy Wenck, ''True Life Stories of Salmonella and Staph,'' *Today's Homemaker* (Cooperative Extension Service, University of California), July/August 1981.

There has, however, been criticism of the effectiveness of the monitoring programs, as accidents have occurred and products have found their way to our table containing illegal amounts of pesticides. Examples include heptachlor in Hawaiian milk, Temik in California watermelons, and daminozide in apple juice. In all cases, the products were withdrawn from the market when the problem was discovered. Of equal concern is the safety of individuals who work in the manufacture or application of pesticides. Croplands are spread throughout our country, from border to border and from ocean to ocean, making inspection and enforcement prohibitively expensive.

To remedy these problems, some people call for reform of the Federal Insecticide, Fungicide and Rodenticide Act (FIFRA) to establish the testing, or retesting, of all pesticides being used now and to reevaluate tolerance levels for workers and for food. Research continues on the potential hazards of pesticides and on alternative ways to control pests. Biological control has been used; for example, a nondestructive insect, such as a ladybug, is introduced into the environment to feed on destructive pests, such as aphids. Perhaps we should also reconsider the standards of appearance that we require for fresh produce. Must fruit be picture pretty?

Food Additives

food additive: a substance added to food as a result of processing, production, or packaging

Saccharin, red dyes, salt, sodium nitrate, and sulfides became conversation topics among health-conscious consumers over the past 10 to 15 years. Each of these is a **food additive**, a substance or combination of substances found in food as a result of processing, production, or packaging to (1) make foods more appealing by improving flavor, color, and texture, (2) increase nutritional value, (3) prevent spoilage and increase shelf life, or (4) improve performance or ease of preparation. In short the approximately 3,000 additives put in our food are designed to increase our satisfaction with the products. So why all the concern? In a word: safety.

Additives like sugar, salt, and vinegar have been used for centuries to improve flavor and prevent spoilage. Sugar and salt are the primary additives today, accounting for 93 percent of the 140-plus pounds of

FIGURE 10.5
Common food additives other than sugar and salt. The ones shown here constitute 6.4 percent of all additives, or 10 pounds per person per year. The remaining 0.6 percent, or 1 pound per person per year, includes 2,900 other additives. (SOURCE: Adapted from *Nutrition Today* magazine, Williams and Wilkins, 428 East Preston Street, Baltimore, MD 21202 © July/August 1973, with permission.)

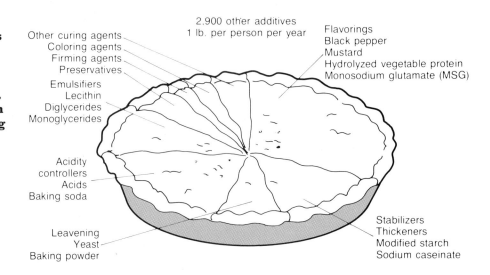

Other curing agents
Coloring agents
Firming agents
Preservatives
Emulsifiers
Lecithin
Diglycerides
Monoglycerides

2,900 other additives
1 lb. per person per year

Flavorings
Black pepper
Mustard
Hydrolyzed vegetable protein
Monosodium glutamate (MSG)

Acidity controllers
Acids
Baking soda

Leavening
Yeast
Baking powder

Stabilizers
Thickeners
Modified starch
Sodium caseinate

Delaney Clause: a section of the 1958 Food Additives Amendments that prohibits the use of any chemical linked to cancer in people or animals

additives that each of us consumes annually. Sugar is used in various forms, including honey, corn syrup and dextrose, accounting for approximately 83 percent of annual additive consumption. Salt (sodium chloride) is the largest single source of sodium in the diet, being about 40 percent sodium; it accounts for 10 percent of the additives we consume. The remaining 7 percent, which includes more than 2,900 different additives, has been the focus of negative comments by consumers. Figure 10.5 shows the purpose of the most common food additives. You might be most familiar with the largest category of additives, *flavorings*, which includes all herbs and spices. *Thickeners* and *stabilizers* improve and maintain the texture of foods. *Leavening* causes foods to increase in volume. *Acidity controllers* neutralize or alter sourness; *emulsifiers* enable oil to stay dispersed in water; *preservatives* prevent the growth of microorganisms, such as mold; *firming agents* prevent foods from becoming mushy; *coloring agents* improve appearance (make cherry pop red, for example); and *curing agents* prevent discoloring and rancidity or spoiling.

Many people question the use of additives, because additives seem mysterious. Additives, as a rule, do not have simple, common names, nor are they ordinarily used in home cooking, which is consumed shortly after it is prepared.

Since the passage of the Food, Drug, and Cosmetic Act of 1938, the FDA has been regulating the use of food additives. Initially, its responsibility was only for labeling, but in 1958 the Food Additives Amendment was made to the 1938 regulation. The **Delaney Clause**, one section of the new regulation, required that the safety of a new food additive be established by the manufacturer and approved by the FDA before it was put into common usage. But what of the hundreds of food additives already in common usage by 1958? The FDA drew up a list of the additives and solicited the

Generally Recognized As
Safe (GRAS): designates food
additives that have been in
use for a long time with no
previous problems; before
1968 many of these food additives had not been tested
for safety

opinion of several hundred experts regarding their safety. From the original list, 415 additives were then placed on a **Generally Recognized As Safe (GRAS)** list, because they had been in use with no previous problems. In the next decade a few additives on the GRAS list *were* found to be potentially hazardous, so in 1969 the FDA was directed by Congress to test all GRAS substances. As a result, some additives, such as red dye number 2, were removed from food. For increased safety, since 1976 all food additives undergo periodic review.

The Delaney Clause specifically prohibited the use of any additive that had been linked under any circumstances to cancer in people or animals. The amendment was absolute, allowing for no special circumstances. Between 1958 and 1986 the FDA used this amendment to ban nine food additives. For example, in the late 1960s cyclamate, an artificial sweetener, was shown to cause cancer in rats, so it was banned from food. In order to reach the level of cyclamate intake found to cause cancer in rats, a person would have had to drink at least 138 twelve-ounce bottles of cyclamate-sweetened soft drinks daily (Clydesdale, 1979). Although consuming 138 bottles seems impossible, the product was banned because of its carcinogenic effects.

Some scientists believe that the 1958 Delaney Clause is too rigid, since it requires that additives be banned even when the dosages are hundreds or thousands of times greater than the typical consumption. It should be noted that the Delaney Clause eliminated only the carcinogens that are purposely added to food; carcinogens may also occur naturally in food. Coffee has caffeine, cabbage contains thiourea, and flour and orange juice contain patulin; all can cause cancer when consumed in large enough doses and therefore cannot meet the standard required for food additives.

As a result, in 1985 the FDA instituted a more liberal interpretation of the clause, allowing known carcinogens in foods if the risks to humans seem negligible. The first additive approved under this approach was saccharin, a sugar substitute used initially by diabetics. Its usage expanded to diet foods in the 1950s and 1960s. In 1977 the FDA banned its use because studies showed it caused bladder cancer in test animals, but Congress placed a moratorium on the ban to allow for more study. Research confirmed that in high doses—the equivalent of consuming 875 twelve-ounce bottles of saccharin-sweetened soft drinks daily—saccharin is carcinogenic (Clydesdale, 1979). In 1987 Congress extended the moratorium on the ban for another five years, leaving the product on the market to provide a choice for diabetics and others whose health may be endangered by sugar consumption. Products that contain saccharin bear a warning like "Use of this product may be hazardous to your health. This product contains saccharin, which has been determined to cause cancer in laboratory animals." A similar arrangement has been proposed for cyclamate.

Costs and Benefits of Safety

The food safety controversy centers on the costs and benefits of creating a risk-free food supply, compared to those of accepting a minimal risk as determined by specialists in toxic substances. Some consumers have called for the elimination of all food additives, but as we saw in the decision-making model in Chapter 1, decisions involve opportunity costs, or trade-offs. So we will do a cost-benefit analysis of the effect on consumers of eliminating additives from our food. Because consumers usually accept sugar, salt, herbs, spices, and leavening agents, we will exclude these additives from our analysis.

The elimination of some additives may result in *higher ingredient costs*. Saccharin and aspartame (the most commonly used sugar substitute in diet beverages; some toxicologists believe it may occasionally cause brain seizures in humans) are less expensive than sugar. And, of course, they are lower in calories, a desirable feature to many consumers. If sugar or honey were all that could be used as sweeteners, the prices of foods now using saccharin and aspartame would rise. Because the overall demand for sugar and honey would also increase, foods that now contain these ingredients would increase in price.

Distribution costs, along with ingredient costs, determine product cost. Anyone who has shopped for bread knows that whole-wheat breads without additives can be as much as 25 percent more costly than white bread with additives. The additive-free bread requires daily distribution because it becomes stale quickly, which increases its cost. Distribution costs of bacon and processed meats would probably increase if the preservative sodium nitrite were banned. It is this chemical that allows safe storage for several days of these normally highly perishable products.

Food that spoils at home due to inappropriate storage increases family food costs and might endanger family safety; people might consume food that is not visibly spoiled, but spoiled nonetheless. And a multisyllabic chemical name does not necessarily indicate a harmful substance. Calcium propionate, a mildew retardant used to prolong bread shelf life, might sound terrible, but it occurs naturally in Swiss cheese and raisins. Without it, bread may grow an invisible but toxic mold.

Without additives, we would need to accept that *some foods would change appearance*. Coloring is responsible for the appearance of soft drinks and the reddish color of sandwich meats and frankfurters, for example. Certainly, we could become accustomed to these changes, but *food selection* would also change. Staples like margarine or other convenience foods, for example, would change drastically or leave the market entirely. The decreased selection of frozen, canned, and packaged foods could be a blow to families for which time for food preparation is scarce.

If we choose, then, to eliminate additives from our food supply, we might incur higher food costs, shortened time for safe food storage, health risks, changed appearance and selection of food, and increased time spent on food shopping and preparation. In exchange we would receive the benefit of zero risk of illness from food additives. In light of this, the federal government has chosen to ban only carcinogenic food additives. The decision to consume food additives and in what quantity is up to the individual consumer, who must do his or her own cost–benefit analysis.

MAKE IT LIGHT AND NATURAL: HEALTH CLAIMS AND VITAMINS

During the past two decades, as a result of concern about the safety and usefulness of food additives, some individuals began to purchase more fresh fruits, vegetables, and whole-grain food products grown without chemicals and processed without preservatives. Most recently, nutritionists have recommended decreasing saturated fat and sodium consumption and have alerted women to the need to include adequate calcium in their diets. These trends have given rise to specialty stores, restaurants, and food processors catering to the health-conscious consumer.

Health Foods: Natural and Organic

Health foods have been heavily promoted as a cure-all, a remedy for everything from lack of energy to the common cold. They are supposed to taste better or be more wholesome. But what are health foods? *Health food* is such a vague term that it has no nationally accepted legal definition. The FTC, whose job, in part, is to monitor deceptive advertising has said that the term "'health food' is undefined, indefinable, and inherently deceptive." But it continues to be widely used because of a persistent belief by many consumers that the term indicates better quality.

Specialty food producers generally agree that health foods can include foods for special diets, such as those for vegetarians, or foods used as nutrient supplements, such as brewer's yeast. These foods are not necessarily free of chemical additives, nor are they grown without pesticides, yet they may cost up to 70 percent more than their supermarket rivals.

Natural food is another vague category that has no nationally accepted legal description. Generally, a **natural food** is one that does not contain artificial preservatives to increase shelf life, emulsifiers to prevent separation of the ingredients, or artificial flavorings or colors to enhance taste or appearance. This label may also mean that the food has been minimally processed, as in the case of whole-wheat flour as opposed to white, refined flour. However, neither the federal government, nor many states have incorporated this definition into law. And even if there were a regulation, there would be nothing to prohibit a manufacturer of a granola cereal product from identifying that product as ''natural,'' even though it contained three times the sugar and four times the fat of an ''unnatural'' rival. ''Natural'' does not necessarily mean that the food is free of all additives or that it is the best nutritionally.

organic food: *food grown without artificial fertilizers or chemical pesticides*

Another confusing term is **organic food**, which refers to food grown with organic fertilizers, such as compost and manure, and untreated with chemical pesticides. Technically, ''organically grown'' is a more accurate label, because all food is organic (that is, derived from living organisms). It is difficult for the consumer to be satisfied that organic growing techniques have been used, however, since adjoining farms may not be using them. For example, what if one farmer grows tomatoes organically and the surrounding farmers spray their tomato fields with pesticides? The spray is likely to drift across the organically grown tomatoes. At any rate, it is impossible to prove that food was grown organically once it has gone to market. The buyer has only the seller's word on the matter. Consumers who are trying to improve the quality of their diets by eliminating pesticide residues, therefore, end up paying more for food without any guarantee that they are getting what they want. Moreover, although many consumers prefer organically grown foods because they believe such foods are more nutritious and have a higher vitamin content, research shows that organically grown food has neither more nor fewer nutrients.

The issue of buying organically grown food is, however, separate from using organic growing techniques in your own garden. Tomatoes grown commercially and then shipped and stored for several days cannot compare to tomatoes picked fresh off the vine at their peak of ripeness. And you can, of course, eliminate the need for pesticides by picking the hornworms off your tomato plants, a process that would not be economical for commercial growers with hundreds of acres.

Light or "Lite"?

In searching for a more healthful diet, some people are cutting down on calories as well as chemicals. What help can labels give us here? To be labeled **low caloric**, food must contain no more than 40 calories in a serving, and the number of calories must be stated. **Reduced calorie** foods must be at least one-third lower in calorie content than when normally prepared. And foods labeled as **diet** or **dietetic** must meet the requirements for low- or reduced-calorie foods or must be clearly described as being useful for a special dietary purpose other than for maintaining or reducing body weight. However, ''light'' and ''lite'' can mean light in color, light in sodium, light in taste and texture, or light in calories. As we go to press, however, legislation has been introduced to clarify these terms when used in labeling.

As we've discussed, sodium content is included on the nutritional label of many packaged foods. Since an excessive amount of sodium has been linked to hypertension (high blood pressure), the food industry has responded with innovative products to meet market demands. In turn, the FDA has established labeling guidelines for these products. First, two terms make reference to the food processing method but say nothing of the sodium content of the food itself: "Unsalted" refers to foods that are processed without salt but are normally processed with added salt: "reduced sodium" indicates usage of only 25 percent of the amount of sodium usually used in processing. Three other terms refer to the sodium content *per serving*: "Low sodium" applies to any product with 140 milligrams of sodium or less, "very low sodium" indicates 35 milligrams of sodium or less, while "sodium-free" indicates a food containing less than 5 milligrams of sodium per serving. Awareness of these labels and use of this information will assist the more than 60 million of us suffering from high blood pressure.

Dietary Supplements

vitamins: nutrients from food that are necessary for normal growth and health
mineral: an inorganic substance necessary for a healthy diet, such as iron and calcium

Because many people feel that they aren't eating properly or getting good nutrition through their diets, they often use various kinds of supplements to try to make up for the deficiencies. Others feel that if a little supplementing is good, a lot will be even better and will help them achieve "supernutrition." **Vitamins** and **minerals** (substances that are necessary in small amounts for normal growth and health) are probably the most common supplements. Others, such as seaweed and brewer's yeast, are taken to supply other nutrients as well as vitamins and minerals. In fact, more than $3 billion is spent in this country annually on vitamin pills.

The fact is, a good diet should supply most of the vitamins and minerals a person needs. There has been some controversy over the need for high doses of some vitamins. Generally, however, it is wise to take large doses of a vitamin only on your physician's or dietician's advice. Some vitamins, such as vitamins A and D, can make you ill if you take too much.

When you do have to shop for vitamin supplements, how should you choose among the many brands? Should you take natural vitamins? Are they worth the extra cost? By law, all vitamins must have the same chemical composition, so those that are made synthetically (made out of chemical compounds) are the same as natural vitamins that are extracted from foods. In addition, research shows that our bodies cannot tell the difference between "natural" and synthetic vitamins.

Because one company manufactures 60 to 70 percent of all the vitamins sold in the United States and packages them under different labels, the only real differences among brands are in dose size (500 milligrams, 250 milligrams) and price. When shopping for vitamins, then, buy the least expensive brand available in moderate doses, using the U.S. RDA as a guide. Or better yet, avoid the expense by eating a balanced and nutritious diet.

Food: More Than a Matter of Taste

Now that you know about the Four Food Groups, the U.S. RDAs for essential nutrients, and food labeling and grading policies, you are ready to make specific purchases. Because of the regularity of purchases, increases in food prices may be more noticeable than increases in the prices of most other budget items. And due to budget constraints, some consumers feel that nutritious foods like eggs, milk, meat, poultry, fruits, whole grains, and vegetables are just too expensive.

Is it possible to eat well on a low or moderate income? The answer is yes, if the principles of decision making and good buying habits are applied. Over the past 25 years the USDA has sponsored research on national food consumption to determine the relationship between income level and the quality of diets. As might be expected, research shows that as income levels rose, so did the amount of money spent on food.* Research also showed that the proportion of people who had diets rated good or fair increased as income increased. But 37 percent of the families with low incomes also had diets rated good, proving that it is possible to eat well on a small budget.

The research compared the consumption of key nutrients of low-income and high-income families (Table 10.6). In each case, the low-income families got more nutrients for their money. They did this by avoiding low-density foods like soft drinks, snack foods, "gourmet" convenience foods, and high-cost meats. Instead they ate poultry, eggs, liver, dry beans, nuts, and enriched cereals, rice and pasta.

TABLE 10.6 Nutrient Return per Dollar

		Household Income	
Nutrient	Unit	Low Income	High Income
Protein	gm	45.0	41.0
Calcium	mg	470.0	440.0
Iron	mg	9.1	7.7
Vitamin A	IU	3,720.0	2,930.0
Thiamin	mg	0.89	0.72
Riboflavin	mg	1.2	1.0
Vitamin C	mg	61.0	56.0

SOURCE: U.S. Department of Agriculture, *Family Economic Review*, no. 1, 1988.

* We must add that the proportion of income spent on food declines as income rises. According to the Bureau of Labor Statistics, in 1987 families of four that earned less than $18,500 yearly spent at least 28 percent of their gross income on food, whereas those with incomes of more than $41,600 spent 17 percent.

Planning, Spending, Eating — and Decision Making

Good nutrition on a budget does not happen automatically. It takes careful planning and decision making, and as you may now perceive, it is a complex task. Even though many foods will have the labels we discussed, and some of the stores will have unit pricing, this is obviously not true for all. And use of available information will take time and energy, which may be in short supply. The payoff, however, will be enhanced nutrition and wise use of your resources. Using the buying-process model (see Chapter 9) should give you a rational approach to the problem and a way of solving it to your satisfaction:

Step 1. Define the Problem. You want to have a nutritious diet on your current income, getting the best and most for your food dollar.

Step 2. Clarify Values, Goals, and Standards. Consider how your values, goals, and standards limit your food choices. For example, you may be willing to pay a higher price for convenience (a value); you may have decided to avoid food additives as much as possible (goal); you may think that taste is the main criterion for food selection rather than price (standard).

Step 3. Seek Advice and Information. Keep track of the money you spend on each food category for a month (Worksheet 10.1), using electronic cash-register receipts as an aid if available. Determine which category you are spending too much on. The USDA found that families who get the best diets for their money divide their budgets according to the pattern shown in Figure 10.6.

Reexamine your spending patterns:

1. Are you getting most of your protein from beef and pork? If so, you might consider replacing them to some extent with poultry, liver, and heart, which are high in protein but cost much less. And you might use more plant protein in the form of dried beans and peas, soy protein, peanut butter, and cereals. Plant proteins can also extend small quantities of meat in soups, casseroles, and salads, while providing necessary levels of protein. Oriental, Latin, and Italian dishes, for example, often use little or no meat but can be nutritionally balanced.

2. Lower the amount of meat per serving. Two-ounce or three-ounce servings provide sufficient protein, costs less, and are lower in saturated fat and cholesterol.

3. Choose simpler, cheaper foods for snacks. Processed snacks such as potato chips, pretzels, or candy, are expensive and low in nutrients. Other foods such as home-popped popcorn, fresh fruit, raw vegetables spread with peanut butter or cheese, and homemade juice bars are more nutritious and less expensive.

4. Monitor beverage consumption. Do the beverages you and your family drink make a positive contribution to your health? Soft drinks,

WORKSHEET 10.1 RECORD OF SPENDING FOR GROCERIES

	Dairy products: milk, cheese, yogurt, ice cream, and so forth.	Meat: meat, poultry, fish, eggs, dried beans, peanut butter, and so forth.	Fruits and vegetables: fresh, frozen, and canned (all varieties).	Breads and cereals: bread, cereal, pasta, rice, tortillas, and so forth.	Other items: fats, sugars, beverages (colas, alcohol), seasonings, dressings, and so forth.	Paper goods: towels, napkins, toilet paper, foil, and so forth.	Personal care items: toothpaste, shampoo, deodorant, and so forth.	Miscellaneous items: toys, magazines, cooking utensils, and so forth.
					Nonfood items can account for 20 to 30 percent of spending in grocery stores.			
1.								
2.								
3.								
4.								
5.								
6.								
7.								
8.								
9.								
10.								
11.								
12.								
13.								
14.								
15.								
16.								
17.								
18.								
19.								
20.								
21.								
22.								
23.								
24.								
25.								
26.								
27.								
28.								
29.								
30.								
31.								

**FIGURE 10.6
Optimal division of the consumer's food dollar. Note that these costs are for food *only*. Nonfood items, such as paper goods, cleaning supplies, magazines, and household accessories, average 20 to 30 percent of a typical grocery bill.**

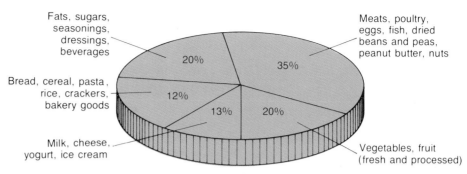

Fats, sugars, seasonings, dressings, beverages — 20%

Meats, poultry, eggs, fish, dried beans and peas, peanut butter, nuts — 35%

Bread, cereal, pasta, rice, crackers, bakery goods — 12%

Milk, cheese, yogurt, ice cream — 13%

Vegetables, fruit (fresh and processed) — 20%

flavored bottled waters, and alcoholic beverages are expensive and are low in nutrients. Use fruit juices as a substitute. Or use water with a slice of lemon, which is much less expensive, more flavorful, and low in calories too.

Study more closely the information in this chapter that you are most willing to implement. Look for other ways to sharpen your planning and buying skills:

1. To eliminate waste, make sure that family members like and eat the foods you buy.

Clipping and using coupons can save you money, but you must consider the time costs as well as the dollar outlay.

2. Keep track of what you throw away. Adjust your buying habits so that you purchase and prepare less of some foods or dishes that always seem to be tossed out (or fed to the dog).

3. Plan a weekly menu of all meals and snacks and compare it with recipes. Make a list of the items you need to purchase to prepare the meals on the menu.

4. Plan meals around weekly advertised specials, which are usually cheaper.

5. Plan to use cents-off coupons judiciously, only for items and brands that you would normally purchase (see Box 10.4).

6. Place a notepad, chalk board, or such in a prominent place so that household members can help create a running shopping list of necessary foods and supplies.

7. Take a shopping list with you to the store, organized by food categories and store layout if possible. Resist buying anything that is not on the list. In particular avoid impulse purchases of high-priced items like gourmet prepared entrees, snack foods, or out-of-season fruits and vegetables.

8. Make only one trip to the store each week. Extra trips can mean extra impulse purchases that you probably don't need.

9. Shop only when you have a full stomach. Studies indicate that shopping on a full stomach can cut your food bill.

10. Buy in quantity, if your budget and your storage space permit you to do so. Use unit pricing or your calculator to determine that bulk purchases are indeed lower in cost per ounce or per pound or in cost per serving.

11. Shop around. A grocery store that operates on a self-service, no-frills, no-games-or-contests basis and that is open a limited number of hours daily may have prices up to 30 percent lower than a 24-hour, full-service grocery store or a corner convenience store.

12. Buy store or house brands; they can save you 20 to 40 percent of the cost of each item, and they are just as nutritious and wholesome as brand-name products. They often are processed by brand-name manufacturers.

Keep your eyes open for articles in popular magazines on food buying. Check the local newspaper for articles on food and nutrition. They can give you recipes, food-buying tips, and more information about areas of consumer concern. Use the federal government's pamphlets as sources of information about food (write to Consumer Product Information, Pueblo, CO 81002). Look for cookbooks written by the American Heart Association, the American Cancer Association, or similar groups. You might also want to enroll in a nutrition or meal-planning class at your college or adult-education facility.

Step 4. Weigh the Costs and Benefits of Information and Planning.

BOX 10.4 **USE GOOD SENSE WITH CENTS-OFF**

Cents-off coupons are big business. In 1970, 16 billion coupons were issued. This number grew to 91 billion by 1979, and is well over 200 billion today. This explains why more than 80 percent of households in the United States redeem coupons at the market. Who ultimately pays for coupons? Do coupons really save the consumer money?

The answer to the first question, as you might expect, is that the cost of the coupon is passed on to consumers in the price of the product. Coupons are designed and printed and then distributed via newspapers (primarily the Sunday edition) and magazines and by mail. Only about 5 percent of the issued coupons are redeemed, many of them fraudulently by people who did not buy the product or who used an expired coupon. Redeemed coupons are sorted and counted at the store or by a clearinghouse, at an average handling cost of seven cents per coupon. The total cost of this process may exceed the actual value of the coupon and is considered an advertising expenditure. The non-user of coupons, therefore, pays the cost without receiving any benefits.

And what are the benefits? According to one study (Newman and Dubno, 1986), a typical savings of 13 percent, along with additional incentives of contests, sweepstakes, free items, and the like in the case of 25 percent of issued coupons.

How, then, is a consumer to evaluate the use of coupons?

1. *Is the coupon offered for a product or brand you would normally purchase?* Approximately one-third of all coupons are for nonfood items, such as paper goods and personal care items. Another 5 to 9 percent are for pet supplies. Are these items and brands products that you are already purchasing, or are they for the higher-cost brands?

2. *Will the coupon help you get the best nutrition for your dollar?* Approximately 20 percent of issued coupons are for beverages, snacks, sugars, oils, and condiments. Are these primarily low-density foods really what you want to purchase?

3. *Will the coupon help you improve your diet?* Most food coupons are for highly or moderately processed foods that may contain high amounts of sodium, sugar, and saturated fat.

4. *Is collecting and redeeming coupons worth the time and energy?* It very well may be if you could answer "yes" to the above three questions, particularly if stores in your community offer "double coupons" (give you twice the face value of the coupon).

In final analysis, coupon use is a matter of applying the decision-making model, and only you can decide if cents-off makes good sense.

Costs of information gathering might include (1) time spent reading food labels, unit-pricing shelf tags, and food-buying and nutrition articles and (2) increased food prices, if manufacturers are required to provide more information on packages and if stores are required to mark items individually. Benefits might include (1) increased knowledge of food buying and nutrition, (2) lower family food and health costs, and (3) better diet and better health.

Costs of planning might include time necessary to (1) analyze diet, (2) choose menus in advance and make shopping lists, and (3) change food preparation habits and try new recipes. Benefits might include (1) saving fuel and time by making fewer trips to the store, (2) less food waste, (3) better diet and better health, and (4) lower family food costs.

Step 5. Make a Decision. By applying the techniques you have learned, you should get a higher level of satisfaction from your food-buying decisions.

Step 6. Evaluate Choices and Review Decisions. Periodically review the strategies you have implemented, and begin to use others as well. As your income increases or decreases or as your family size and composition change, use the decision-making process we have outlined to sharpen and review your food and nutrition decisions. Train others in your family who are doing the shopping as well. This is increasingly important, as 50 percent of females ages 12 to 19 and 25 percent of males shop weekly for their families (Farrington, 1988). We must all recognize money and time as scarce resources.

Convenience Foods: Get It Quick

Our ability to get good nutrition at reasonable prices has been affected by the growing array of convenience foods, those foods that require less work or the addition of fewer ingredients than their home-prepared counterparts. These range from frozen orange juice and green beans, to frozen pizza and other entrees, to foods made mostly of artificial ingredients, such as Tang and Cool Whip. Because there are so many kinds of convenience foods and because they are so widely used, they deserve discussion here. Why do we choose these foods, and how can we be sure we are getting the most for our convenience-food dollar?

We select convenience foods because they save time. As families get smaller, as more people live alone, and as growing numbers of women seek paid employment, time becomes more precious. We are willing to pay other people to shell the peas, bake the meat pie, assemble the enchilada, and fill the egg roll. Convenience foods eliminate the need for special pans, utensils, or exotic spices or culinary expertise; all that's needed is an oven for heating. For the 60 percent of households that have a microwave oven, the process is even faster. And when we're finished, cleanup is a snap.

The trade-off of saving time is increased price and, in some cases, loss of nutritional quality. Approximately two-thirds of commonly purchased convenience foods cost more money than their home-prepared or fresh counterparts. (Notable exceptions include frozen orange juice and frozen French fries.) Sometimes you pay double or triple the cost of preparing the food at home. Is it worth it? That depends on what your time is worth to you and how you would use the time you save by using convenience foods.

Despite their higher costs, convenience foods often give lower nutritional value when compared to homemade foods. The main dishes or entrees usually contain less meat. The sugar, sodium, fat and cholesterol content are often higher than in home-prepared or fresh foods, and convenience foods often contain preservatives and other additives.

TABLE 10.7 Fast-Food Meals and U.S. RDAs

Food	Serving Size (oz.)	Calories	Fat (gm)	Carbohy-drates (gm)	Choles-terol (gm)	Sodium (mg)	Protein (gm)	Vita-min A	Cal-cium	Phos-phorus	Iron
								| Percentage U.S. RDA[a] |			
Burger King Whopper	9	626	38	42	94	842	57	12	8	29	27
Jack-in-the-Box Jumbo Jack	$8\frac{1}{4}$	485	26	38	64	905	56	7	6	29	39
McDonald's Big Mac	$7\frac{1}{2}$	570	35	78	166	979	50	8	20	44	27
Wendy's Old Fash-ioned Hamburger	$6\frac{1}{2}$	350	18	27	65	410	30	8	4	24	25
Roy Roger's Roast Beef Sandwich	$5\frac{1}{2}$	353	12	32	39	590	40	0	8	28	20
Hardee's Roast Beef Sandwich	$4\frac{1}{2}$	312	17	30	—[b]	826	35	2	9	29	18
Arby's Roast Beef Sandwich	$5\frac{1}{4}$	317	15	29	55	785	52	2	9	35	23
Arthur Treacher's Fish Sandwich	$5\frac{1}{4}$	439	24	39	42	836	46	2	9	32	3
McDonald's Filet-O-Fish	$4\frac{1}{2}$	435	26	36	47	799	25	3	13	27	14
Burger King Whaler	7	488	27	45	84	592	35	3	5	50	12
Domino's Cheese Pizza (2 slices)	$5\frac{1}{2}$	340	15	52	10	660	35	4	30	46	20
Jack-in-the-Box Tacos (2)	$5\frac{1}{2}$	382	26	32	42	812	24	25	20	33	12

[a] Recommended Daily Allowance for an adult woman as set by the National Academy of Sciences National Research Council.
[b] Not available.

SOURCE: Adapted from Michael F. Jacobson and Sarah Fritschner, *The Fast-Food Guide* (New York: Workman, 1986).

Besides the time-saving benefits they offer, convenience foods expand our food choices by making seasonal fruits and vegetables available year round. Freezing preserves the appearance, texture, and nutritional value of most foods. So we can have corn on the cob in December.

A different type of convenience food is available at fast-food restaurants. If we want a hamburger, a taco, pizza, or chicken, it is quickly ready. Many people purchase a third of their meals in fast-food restaurants. Table 10.7 shows the nutritional values of some of the best-known fast-food items. Notice that fat and sodium levels are often quite high, as are calories. Of all the items listed, which are the most nutritious?

As a rule, convenience foods are neither good nor bad. You will need to judge them individually on the basis of their costs, their time and money benefits, and their nutritional values.

SUMMARY

Because food expenditures account for 15 to 20 percent of a family budget, it is a subject that interests consumers and merits study. Wise food selection should be based on the Four Food Groups, individual calorie needs, and Recommended Daily Allowances. Food package information can be extremely useful to consumers when they search for nutritional value. Labels usually include product content information and sometimes nutritional data and inspection and grading designations. Consumers may find additional information and codes on food packages, including the Universal Product Code (UPC) and dates that indicate freshness.

Consumers are interested in food safety, particularly as it relates to pesticide residue and food additives. The federal government has provided consumers with protection in this area via the Delaney Clause. Some consumers provide themselves with further protection by avoiding highly processed foods. Others choose natural or organic foods. Both *natural* and *organic* are vague terms that are of dubious value to consumers.

The challenge for consumers, then, is to apply the decision-making process and comparison-shopping techniques to obtain a nutritious diet and keep their food budgets balanced.

QUESTIONS

1. What basic functions does food fulfill? What factors affect our specific food choices? Do people in other countries eat foods that we would not eat? Do you think the reverse is true?
2. What are the four general groups of foods that serve as the basis of an adequate diet? What factors sometimes stand in the way of changing poor eating habits?
3. What is the difference between bulimia and anorexia nervosa? What section of the population is most afflicted with these illnesses? What seems to be major causes of these illnesses? Can

these illnesses be life threatening? What types of treatment are recommended?

4. What information is required on food packages and labels? Have you ever used the information to make food choices? Do you know other people who have? Do you need other information that is not currently required?

5. What is the Delaney Clause, and what does it require? Name one additive that has been used differently because of this regulation. What impact has the new interpretation of this regulation had on available food choices?

6. What percentage of the RDAs do you need for calories, protein, vitamin A, vitamin C, calcium, iron, and sodium? In other words, what is your U.S. RDA for these nutrients?

7. What do the words *natural* and *health food* imply to consumers? Do you think consumers are getting their money's worth when they buy these foods? Explain your answer.

8. Consider all of the buying suggestions recommended in this chapter. Which would have the most effect in reducing *your* food budget and why? Which would take the least amount of time and offer the best results?

9. What two types of convenience foods are discussed in the chapter? What are the costs and benefits of using convenience foods?

REFERENCES AND READINGS

Ames, Bruce N., Magaw, Renae, and Gold, Lois Swirsky. "Ranking Possible Carcinogenic Hazards." *Science*, April 17, 1987.

Burros, Marian. "In the Jungle of Food Regulations." *The New York Times*, June 17, 1987, p. C1.

———. "U.S. Food Regulation." *The New York Times*, June 10, 1987, p. C1.

Clydesdale, Ferfus. *Food Science and Nutrition: Current Issues and Answers*. Englewood Cliffs, N. J.: Prentice-Hall, 1979.

Farrington, Jan. "Crusing the Aisles: Food Shopping Strategies." *Current Consumer & Lifestudies*, February 1988.

"Fast Food: A Survival Guide to the Greasy Kid Stuff." *Consumers Reports*, June 1988.

Friedman, Monroe, and Rees, Jennifer. "A Behavioral Science Assessment of Selected Principles of Consumer Education." Presented at American Council of Consumer Interests, Chicago, April 1988.

Ford, Barbara. *Future Food: Alternate Protein for the Year 2000*. New York: Morrow, 1978.

Hefferan, Colien. "Family Budget Guidelines." *Family Economics Review*, no. 4, 1987.

Hegarty, Vincent. *Decisions in Nutrition*. St. Louis: Times Mirror/Mosby College, 1988.

Hodges, Patricia A. M., Hertzler, Ann A., and Holder, Sandra Lynn. "Bulimia: A Coping Response to Societal Pressures." *Journal of Home Economics*, Fall 1985.

"How to Save $2500 a Year in the Supermarket." *Consumer Reports*, March 1988.

"It's Natural! It's Organic! Or Is It? *Consumer Reports*, July 1980.

Jacobson, Michael F., and Fritschner, Sarah. *The Fast-Food Guide*. New York: Workman, 1986.

Lappé, Frances Moore. *Diet for a Small Planet*. New York: Ballantine Books, 1971.

Lecos, Chris W. "'An Order of Fries—Hold the Sulfites.'" *FDA Consumer*, March 1988.

———. "Food Labels: Test Your Food Label Knowledge." *FDA Consumer*, March 1988.

———. "We're Getting the Message About Diet–Disease Links." *FDA Consumer*, May 1988.

Lehman, Phyllis. "More Than You Ever Thought You Would Know About Food Additives." Parts I, II, III. *FDA Consumer*, April, May, June 1979.

Lerza, Catherine, and Jacobson, Michael. *Food for People, Not for Profit*. New York: Ballantine Books, 1975.

Lindsay, Anne, and Fink, Diane J. *The American Cancer Society Cookbook*. New York: Hearst Books, 1988.

Modeland, Vern. "Juiceless Baby Juice Leads to Full-Strength Justice." *FDA Consumer*, June, 1988.

Mott, Lawrie, and Snyder, Karen. *Pesticide Alert: A Guide to Pesticides in Fruits and Vegetables.* San Francisco: Sierra Club Books, 1988.

Morgan, Karen J. "Socioeconomic Factors and Food Usage Patterns." *Family Economics Review,* no. 1, 1988.

Morgan, Karen J., Peterkin, Betty B., Johnson, S. R., and Goungetas, Basile. "Food Usage Patterns as Related to Nutritional Quality of Household Food Supplies." *Home Economics Research Journal,* December 1986.

Newman, Jacqueline M., and Dubno, Susan. "Coupon Use: Is Cents-off Sense or Nonsense?" *Journal of Home Economics,* Winter 1986.

Rudd, Joel. "Aiding Consumer Nutrition Decisions with the Simple Graphic Label Format." *Home Economics Research Journal,* March 1986.

Schein, Jeff. "The Sodium–Hypertension Connection." *Consumers Research,* October 1987.

Stephenson, Marilyn. "Meeting America's 1990 Nutrition Goals: We'll Need a Strong Finish." *FDA Consumer,* September 1987.

Surgeon General's Report—1988. Washington, D.C.: U.S. Government Printing Office, 1988.

Wilson, R., and Crouch, E. A. C. "Risk Assessment and Comparisons: An Introduction." *Science,* April 17, 1987.

Chapter Eleven

HOUSING: HOME SWEET HOME

- ☐ To Rent or to Buy?
- ☐ The First Step: Determining Your Housing Needs
- ☐ The Second Step: Estimating How Much You Can Afford
- ☐ The Third Step: Exploring Housing Options
- ☐ The Fourth Step: Choosing Your Housing
- ☐ The Fifth Step: Moving
- ☐ The Sixth Step: Evaluating Your Choice
- ☐ The Seventh Step: Accepting Responsibility

DID YOU KNOW THAT . . .

. . . the choice of whether to buy or rent depends on more than personal preferences?

. . . the cost of housing accounts for 25 to 50 percent of a family's budget?

. . . in most American cities landlords can raise rents as often and as much as the market allows?

. . . approximately one-third of all new homes being built today are mobile homes, often called manufactured homes by the industry?

. . . renters should carefully read month-to-month rental agreements or leases to see whether such agreements or leases prohibit subleasing, changing the color of interior paint, or having overnight guests?

. . . home equity loans may have attractive interest rates, but since the home is used for collateral, they should be used with caution?

. . . the federal government regulates movers of household goods and has given consumers protection when they buy this service?

. . . the supply of rental units is at a 35-year low, and the costs of home ownership are escalating?

Whether to buy or rent a home, apartment, condominium, cooperative, or manufactured home is an important decision—one not made very often in most cases and becoming more and more of a problem for many of us. In recent times the middle-class American dream was to own a single-family suburban home, and the booming economy of the 1960s led a growing population to believe that home ownership was a right. Today, as you will see, achieving this goal is becoming increasingly difficult, particularly for those under age 35. But as you are probably aware, not everyone prefers to be a homeowner in suburbia. Many people choose to rent apartments, particularly in big cities, not just for financial reasons but because they want to avoid the work and responsibilities that go with home ownership. Many renters have begun to assert their rights and realize that they are not completely at a disadvantage with their landlords, making renting a more attractive choice.

Today, for most people the choice of whether to buy or rent depends mostly on personal economics. Our national economy has been characterized by rising housing costs, including both rental and purchase. For example, in 1949 the average 30-year-old home buyer allocated 14 percent of monthly income to mortgage payments. By 1988 that figure had risen to more than 45 percent and was still climbing. Rental costs have risen as well and now typically account for about 30 percent of income. The reasons for what some people call a housing crisis are varied. Among the factors is the steadily increasing demand for new housing as a result of a population reaching the marriageable and childbearing stages of the life-cycle, along with more single-person households. Simultaneously, there has been an equally steady decline in the building and availability of new housing, particularly as a result of changing federal policies during the 1980s. This situation, coupled with inflation, fluctuating and historically high real interest rates on home loans, and the requirement of a large down payment, has forced some people to rent, who in years past would have bought.

Because housing accounts for 25 to 50 percent of a family's budget, it is important to consider housing decisions carefully. The consumer has many factors, both personal and economic, to keep in mind. These factors include determining whether to rent or buy, choosing a living space, establishing good relations with a landlord, and obtaining the best financing for a home. In this chapter we will help you apply the buying-process model to the selection of housing, giving you tools for making satisfactory housing decisions.

TO RENT OR TO BUY?

At first glance, the decision whether to buy or rent seems easy. If consumers do not have the money for a down payment and/or the income to support the monthly payments, they rent. This reasoning is based on old assumptions, though: It doesn't consider factors like one's values, goals, family size, life-style, stage in the life cycle, or career. Examining the roles of these factors and the advantages and disadvantages of both buying and renting gives us a starting point for later discussions of the types of housing and other aspects of the two sides of the housing coin.

Advantages of Renting

Most people rent housing at some point in their lives. The first time is usually when a young adult moves out of his or her parents' home and becomes self-supporting. Renting has also become common for single adults, students, couples without children, people with little interest in or time for homeowner chores, retired people, and those who have to move often because of their jobs.

Perhaps the major advantage of renting is that it doesn't require major cash outlays. A renter may have to pay the equivalent of two or three months' rent for deposits, but that is a relatively small amount compared to the down payment required of a buyer.

Renting also allows flexibility. Even when a renter has a **lease**, a written agreement with the owner about the amount of rent to be charged for a specific length of time, as well as about other aspects of their relationship, he or she can usually move more easily and cheaply than a homeowner. A tenant can relocate because of job transfers or changes, an increase in family size or income, the desire for a better or more convenient location, and so on.

Rentals may also have attractive facilities. Recreational facilities, such as game rooms, swimming pools, and health clubs, provide places for relaxation and meeting others. Some major appliances, such as an oven and a refrigerator, may also be furnished. Laundry facilities also make it possible for renters to avoid having to buy their own appliances or visit a laundromat.

Finally, for many people, renting means freedom from home repairs, gardening, maintenance, worry, and drudgery—and from responsibility for them. Even if they pay a monthly fee for this freedom, most renters find this opportunity cost a small price to pay for the savings in time. Many retired people, for instance, are ecstatic to be rid of a lifetime of homeowner chores, expenses, and responsibilities. Renters of all ages have realized that renting is the best situation for them—that they would rather have the flexibility that renting affords.

Disadvantages of Renting

Although renters are free from responsibilities, they cannot claim any rights to the property. They may be restricted or prohibited from making inside or outside changes to suit their own preferences, and they are governed by the needs and desires of the owner. If there is no lease or no rent control, an owner can raise rent at his or her own discretion and as high as the market will allow. Owners can ask tenants to leave, refuse to make improvements, let the property deteriorate, or make tenants unhappy in many other ways. Renters do have recourse, but uncertainty and lack of control are always factors.

equity: the dollar difference between the selling price and the mortgage payoff of real property

Another major disadvantage of renting is that tenants get no financial breaks. Renters help cover the owner's payments on the property, taxes, insurance, maintenance, and repairs, even though they receive no benefits for their contributions. Although the owner is accumulating **equity**, the increasing money value of the property over and above what he or she owes on it, the tenant gets nothing. Whereas the owner gets several kinds of tax credits and deductions, most tenants get no tax benefits.

Advantages of Buying

In addition to the financial benefits we have just listed, many of the advantages of owning one's own living space involve the feelings one has about one's property. The feelings of pride and independence are satisfying. People can live as they want, decorate according to their personal needs and tastes, and have more privacy than in a rental unit. They don't have to answer to anyone else or worry about being asked to leave. For many people, the feelings of security and responsibility in home ownership are very important.

Owning a home is usually a good financial investment too. Because of inflation and rising demand, most homes increase in value, especially when compared to the prices of other goods and services and compared to wages. Specifically, when the figures have been adjusted for inflation we find that since 1974 the value of the typical house has increased 4.3 percent annually, while wages have risen only about 3 percent each year. In some metropolitan areas, such as Boston, New York, San Francisco, and Los Angeles, the value of houses has increased as much as 10 to 15 percent annually. Although the increase in housing values probably will not be that spectacular in most areas in the early 1990s, some geographic areas may continue to experience rapid rises. Because of the tendency for homes to keep pace with consumer prices, they have been a traditional hedge against inflation for middle-class families.

Another financial advantage of home ownership (and a disadvantage of renting) is that, starting in 1990, interest on home loans is the only form of interest that is deductible on federal income tax returns, as well as on many state returns. Although the lower marginal rates as a result of tax reform in the 1980s make tax deductions less valuable, this is still a consideration. Property taxes are also deductible, and homeowners are able to defer or exclude capital gains when they sell their homes. (Cushing N. Dolbeare [1986] reported on a 1985 study by the National League of Cities that estimates these housing-related tax benefits to be worth $45.6 billion).

Disadvantages of Buying

With the advantages, of course, come the disadvantages. Recently, perhaps the most significant is the opportunity cost of saving for the down payment. Families who purchased homes in the past generation often used federal programs that encouraged home ownership by allowing for a small down payment, sometimes as little as a few hundred dollars. In the early 1980s, a 10 percent down payment was typical. Today the standard is 20 to 25 percent, which might translate into $30,000 or more. Saving this much money will certainly limit spending in other budget categories. (As we go to press, legislation is being introduced to allow first-time buyers to

Buying a new house is still the dream of many young families, but it is not always the best choice among all the alternatives.

use funds from Individual Retirement Accounts (IRAs) or 401(k) retirement plans for a down payment. This would go a long way toward assisting young people to attain homeownership, if that is their goal.)

Homeowners sometimes face budgeting hardships due to fluctuations in financial obligations. They have to pay taxes, loan payments, and insurance, and all three expenses may increase faster than income after

---

BOX 11. 1   BUYING DOESN'T ALWAYS PAY

Homeownership has long been a major part of the American Dream. But times change, as do economic conditions, and now many experts believe that renting is a better investment. The key to this change is the slowdown in most regions in the meteoric rise of home prices. The opportunity to take a small down payment and leverage it into a quick profit are gone for the most part. Moreover, *real* interest rates on mortgages remain high, making other investments more attractive.

If you are willing to take the time, you can evaluate whether renting or buying is for you. Keep in mind that monthly outlay for rent is not directly comparable to the cost of home ownership, because with ownership there are annual tax deductions of loan interest and possible profits when the house sells. The breakeven point of the buying-versus-renting dilemma depends on the tax bracket of the prospective owner or owners, as well as on how long they expect to live in the house. Generally, the higher one's income and the longer one intends to stay in one place, the more advantageous it is to buy.

So, to begin, estimate how long you might live in the home, for example, five years. Then calculate all the costs of ownership, including mortgage payments, taxes, insurance, utilities, association fees, and repairs during this time. Now estimate the tax savings gained from deducting the mortgage interest and property taxes. Subtract this from the ownership costs. This gives you the adjusted ownership costs (see below). Next, estimate how much you could get for the house in five years, subtracting broker and closing costs (which could total 5 to 9 percent of the selling price). From this

amount, subtract the adjusted ownership costs, and you have identified the real cost or profit of ownership. (If you do not intend to buy another house at that time, be sure to subtract capital-gains taxes as well).

Costs of ownership *minus* tax savings
= adjusted ownership costs

Estimated selling price in five years *minus* broker fees, closing costs, and adjusted ownership costs
= real cost or profit of owning

Now, calculate the cost of renting a similar space over the same five years, including rent and utilities. Be sure to allow for probable rent increases. To this add the cost of forgone interest on security or rental deposits. Since a down payment was not required, we assume that money is invested in another way. Therefore, estimate the after-tax income on the money you did not need to use for a down payment. Subtract this from the cost of renting.

Rent *plus* utilities *plus* forgone interest on deposits
= cost of renting

Cost of renting *minus* investment income
= real cost or profit of renting

Using this analysis, you can determine which is more expensive, renting or buying. Remember, this is just an economic cost–benefit analysis and does not take into consideration the psychic benefits of either option.

home purchase. In recent years state property taxes increased at such a quick pace that they set off a "homeowner's revolt," causing many states to pass measures controlling tax increases (and concomitantly controlling state-provided services). Loans that have an interest rate that fluctuates with changes in the economy have become quite popular since the 1980s. These loans have made it possible for many people to purchase homes, since they are often offered at a lower rate than fixed-rate loans. However, because the fluctuations in interest rates can increase the payment as much as several hundred dollars each month, budgeting may be difficult, as many borrowers can attest.

Upkeep on a house can take a lot of money—and time. Repairs are often expensive and unexpected, and postponing them can damage or decrease the value of the property (not to mention one's enjoyment in living). And all the time spent gardening, repairing, and working on a house is time that can't be spent doing anything else; it is leisure forgone. For many new homeowners, the feeling of not having time for other activities is sometimes overwhelming. In addition, money spent on the house cannot be spent on anything else; homeowners sometimes have to forgo vacations, new cars, furniture, and many other purchases, both big and small. Thus, the opportunity costs of home ownership are considerable.

Home ownership also restricts mobility. If consumers need to or want to move, they must sell their property, which involves getting a reasonable price, a good buyer, and possibly a real estate agent. Then they must put up with the one-to three-month wait it takes to process the sale.

Listing the advantages and disadvantages of buying and renting obviously doesn't get one very far in decision making. It gives only the basic information needed to begin thinking about a choice. If you want to do a rent-versus-buy analysis for financial considerations only, Box 11.1 will interest you. In the rest of the chapter, we follow both the renting and buying options through the decision-making model presented in Chapter 1.

THE FIRST STEP: DETERMINING YOUR HOUSING NEEDS

Whether you rent or buy, your first step in choosing housing is to determine what you need and expect from your living space. Here are some of the questions that have to be answered before you can choose among the available housing options:

1. How many bedrooms do you need?
2. How many bathrooms?
3. How large a kitchen is needed? Will you eat in the kitchen, or do you prefer a separate dining area? How many people will that area normally have to accommodate?

4. Do you need a separate room for recreational activities (such as watching TV and videos), or will the living room be fine?
5. What other special-purpose rooms are needed (for example, laundry room/area, sewing/crafts room, and so forth)?
6. How much and what types of storage space are needed?
7. How much outside private space do you need for pets, play, patio, garden, and various activities?
8. What kind of garage or parking facilities do you need? Will this space also be used for storage, woodshop, or the like?

Be sure to consult everyone in the family when making these decisions, because everyone has to live in the housing that's chosen—maybe for a relatively long period of time. It is important to ensure that housing supplies living space, protection from the elements, utilities, and convenience. Many forms of shelter might meet these needs, including single-family houses, multifamily dwellings, and manufactured homes. We will look at each of these in detail, but first let us consider budget.

THE SECOND STEP: ESTIMATING HOW MUCH YOU CAN AFFORD

Once you have identified the needs and goals of your household, the next step is to study your budget to estimate how much you can afford to pay initially for deposits or down payments and monthly for loans or rent. This will help you decide which form of shelter you can and should choose. It will also save you time and frustration, because you will not be tempted to look at places you cannot afford.

Down Payments/ Deposits

closing costs: fees for services that effect the formal transfer of ownership of real property from seller to buyer

Besides determining income and expenses, you will need to determine how much cash you have available for housing. When you buy housing, you have to pay a cash **down payment**, which may occasionally be as low as 3 percent or as high as 25 percent, although 10 to 20 percent is typical. In addition, there will be **closing costs** (discussed later in this chapter), which vary according to geographic location and are 3 percent or more of the selling price. Because these expenses can total $15,000 to $25,000 or even much more, many buyers are kept out of the housing market. This is particularly true of hopeful, first-time buyers who lack equity from the sale of another house. In order to overcome this problem, some people find a friend or relative willing to invest in the home, providing some or all of the down-payment money. (This money would be returned, with interest, upon sale of the house. A contract of this sort should be written for both parties by an attorney.) Others find friends who are willing to share the house both as an investor and a roommate.

Renters also have an initial cash outlay, although a modest one compared to what is required for purchase. It is common to require renters to pay the first month's rent in advance, plus a **deposit**, which could include the last month's rent and additional fees for cleaning, security, and the like. Some states set maximum limits on such deposits, but even these limits might allow the deposit to total three month's rent. If a space rents for $400, one could pay $1,200 in advance of moving. Deposits for utilities are also required in many locations. For most people, this means creating a savings plan in advance in order not to deplete funds set aside for emergencies.

Monthly Payments

The amount of money you can spend for housing depends on your present monthly income, your expenses for needs other than housing, and the amount of cash you have available. Use Worksheet 11.1 to estimate these figures. Calculate your current regular monthly net pay, and be realistic. Do not include overtime pay or future raises that are not a certainty. Add any other reliable income to that amount, such as Social Security payments, stock dividends, and so forth, to find the total of your present monthly income.

Next, determine monthly expenses for all spending, excluding housing expenses (rent or mortgage and utilities). Be sure to calculate annual and semiannual payments (for auto insurance, life insurance, and the like) in the monthly averages. By subtracting the nonhousing monthly expenses from your net income you have an estimate of how much you can afford for rent or housing payments. In the example in Worksheet 11.1, the family's total net income is estimated as $2,800 and the monthly housing expenses are $1,820, leaving $980 for housing. In many regions of the United States, this would be a generous amount to cover rent and utilities, but it might not be enough for ownerships costs such as mortgage payments, property taxes, homeowner's insurance, and household repairs.

A second guideline often used by financial counselors to determine a "safe" housing budget is to spend no more than 25 percent of one's budget for annual **recurring costs**, such as rent or loan payment, taxes, insurance, utilities, and maintenance. In our example, the family would find that it should spend $700, rather than $980, on housing, following this guideline.

The largest portion of money spent for ownership goes for the loan payment. This portion will vary according to geographic location, initial cost of the house, and the size of the down payment. As a rough guide, you can estimate that two-thirds of your monthly housing costs will go for the loan payments only. The remainder will be spent on real estate taxes, insurance, utilities, repairs, maintenance, and association fees (for maintenance of facilities used by all tenants or owners within a housing complex). Applying this guide to our first example, only two-thirds of the $980, or $657, should be spend on a mortgage payment. Using our second guideline, only $470 of the $700 allotted for housing should

WORKSHEET 11.1   ESTIMATING WHAT YOU CAN AFFORD TO PAY FOR A HOUSE

STEP 1

Figure out regular monthly net pay after deductions for taxes, Social Security, pension, union dues, and so forth. (Include only what you can definitely count on.)

	Your estimate	*Example*
Sources of income		
Wages (after deductions)	$ _____	$ ___1,785___
Social Security, disability or pension benefits, etc.	$ _____	$ ___0___
Alimony, child support	$ _____	$ ___0___
Interest on savings accounts	$ _____	$ ___21___
Stock dividends, bond income, etc.	$ _____	$ ___0___
Other income (such as from a second job)	$ _____	$ ___994___
Total net income	$ _____	$ ___2,800___

STEP 2

Figure out regular monthly expenses (excluding rent and utilities).

Expenses		
Education	$ _____	$ ___28___
Food (groceries, eating out, etc.)	$ _____	$ ___490___
Clothes (new clothes, laundry, etc.)	$ _____	$ ___140___
Personal care (cosmetics, hair care, personal hygiene)	$ _____	$ ___70___
Medical or dental bills (plus prescriptions)	$ _____	$ ___63___
Home furnishings and expenses	$ _____	$ ___84___
Recreation (movies, vacations)	$ _____	$ ___84___
Gifts (for birthdays, holidays)	$ _____	$ ___77___
Car expenses (auto loan, insurance, gas, oil, maintenance, etc.)	$ _____	$ ___357___
Life and health insurance	$ _____	$ ___70___
Childcare expenses	$ _____	$ ___140___
Installment loans (charge accounts, credit cards)	$ _____	$ ___70___

Regular savings	$ _____	$ ____105____
All other miscellaneous expenses	$ _____	$ ____42____
Total (nonhousing) expenses	$ _____	$ ___1,820___

STEP 3
Subtract the total in Step 1 from the total in Step 2 to get the amount available for housing expenses.

Total available for housing	$ _____	$ ____980____

SOURCE: Adapted from U.S. Department of Housing and Urban Development, *Home Buyers' Information Package: A Guide for Buying and Owning a Home* (Washington, D.C.: U.S. Government Printing Office, 1979).

be used for the mortgage. In many places in the United States, a family would find it impossible to buy a house with a $470 monthly mortgage.

Although all guidelines do not produce identical advice, it helps to know about them in order to avoid being "house poor" (that is, having a house and nothing else). It also helps consumers to evaluate loans proposed by lenders who may be more focused on the short-term profit of the loan than on the long-term ability of the borrower to make the payments. With that in mind, consider one more rule of thumb: A family can afford a house that costs 2.5 times its annual net income. This is called the affordability ratio. If we apply this to our example, the family would be able to afford a house costing $84,000.

$$\$2,800 \times 12 \text{ months} \times 2.5 = \$84,000$$

High prices and interest rates, and the strong desire for home ownership have caused many families to ignore these guides. In the late 1980s the national affordability ratio was not 2 or 2.5 but averaging 4.2. In our example above, this means a $141,120 house. Could you find a house that meets your needs and budget near your place of employment for $67,300? For $84,000? Or would that type of housing be closer to $141,120? Should you take a chance and buy a home that costs too much by these guidelines?

For decisions about your personal housing budget, you should apply all these guides realistically. It may be wise to select a more conservative housing budget if (a) you have heavy debts, car payments, or college tuition, (b) your income is irregular each month because you are in sales, construction, or another occupation for which income varies, (c) you may have future financial obligations for parents or other relatives. The point is not to overextend yourself in order to buy a dream house. Remember, the goal is housing that will meet determined needs and fulfill a reasonable level of wants. Trade-offs are to be expected and should be planned and evaluated in a rational manner by all family members.

By this time, you should have a rough estimate of how much of a deposit or down payment you could make. And you know your monthly budget for recurring costs. A perusal of local classified newspaper advertisements will help you draw some conclusions about your financial ability to rent or purchase shelter in your area. It is also important to be familiar with specific locations in order to assess distance to and from work, proximity to schools and shopping, neighborhood safety, and the like.

THE THIRD STEP: EXPLORING HOUSING OPTIONS

Whether you choose to rent or buy, you will find three basic types of shelter: single-family homes; one-unit living spaces in multiunit dwellings, such as apartments, cooperatives, or condominiums; and manufactured, or mobile, homes. Each type has distinct characteristics that appeal to a variety of needs.

Single-Family Homes

By far the preferred choice of housing in America is a single-family detached home on a large lot. What we are seeking is more privacy and freedom than is available in other housing choices. There is more physical space between houses and more interior space than is found in a typical apartment. The overall population density in neighborhoods is less, which can mean less noise and pollution.

Relatively new houses have open, free-flowing floor plans and lots of amenities, including a fireplace, skylights, bay windows, French doors, a master bedroom suite, often with an adjacent oversized bathroom featuring a whirlpool bath. Is it any wonder that the national median price for a new home is more than $100,000, or that it is more than $175,000 in the East Coast corridor and California? If these prices are beyond your budget, consider a resale home. It may not have a whirlpool bath but will probably be well constructed, have kitchen cabinets made of solid wood, may have hardwood floors, and may be large enough for today's smaller families. They are in greater supply and were originally built for moderate budgets, so they are usually offered at prices lower than those for new homes.

Lot size, in contrast to house size, has been decreasing. Today in a heavily populated area an acre might contain eight new houses, rather than the four of three decades ago. As the price of land and the demand for single-family housing have risen, builders have had to put more houses on the land they acquire. This pleases some of today's buyers, namely those who need little space for children to play and those who want to minimize yard maintenance.

Multiunit Housing Complexes

Some multiunit housing is designed specifically for rentals, whereas other multiunit housing may be purchased or rented, for example, cooperatives or condominiums. Apartments, which are always rentals, offer a broad selection of living arrangements. They may consist of one unit (an efficiency apartment) above a garage or in a remodeled basement, or there may be a small number of units clustered around a common garden or yard as in a duplex (two units) or a fourplex (four units). Two- or three-story apartment buildings with private patios or balconies are common in the Southwest and West. High-rise apartment buildings in cities may provide closeness to jobs, shopping, and cultural events. Luxury high-rises may include spectacular views and recreational facilities like handball courts, swimming pools, and health spas.

A **cooperative** is an apartment building or a group of dwellings owned by a nonprofit corporation that holds legal right to the building or dwellings. The residents of the building are the stockholders, and they own a share of the corporation proportionate to the living space they occupy. For example, if an apartment contains 2 percent of the living space of a dwelling, the occupant has a 2 percent ownership share. He or she has the right to occupy that space for as long as he or she owns the stock, and the occupant also has the right to sell the stock. Apartments are sometimes converted to cooperatives, providing an opportunity for ownership. Because cooperatives are nonprofit, unlike apartments, and because cooperative members have a personal interest in the maintenance of the property, residing in a cooperative costs about 20 percent less than comparable landlord-owned apartments.

The residents elect a board of directors to operate the cooperative. The board makes decisions regarding maintenance, upkeep, insurance, subletting, and rules of conduct for owners and their guests (parking, noise, and so forth). This board also determines the amount of monthly fee or lease payment that will be charged for the right to live there (for loan payments, maintenance, insurance, and so forth.) One may need to apply to this board if one plans extensive remodeling or wants approval to lease or sell the space to someone else.

A **condominium** is a group of housing units that may be either built to be sold as separate units or converted from apartment buildings. They may be stacked side by side or one on top of another. A condominium owner holds title to the living quarters plus a proportionate interest in common areas, such as lobbies, corridors, grounds, and recreational facilities. The homeowners either elect a board of directors for the association or hire a management firm (or a combination of both) to make decisions and take care of landscaping, upkeep, and repair or common area. Buyers arrange their own loans, pay their own tax bills, and pay a fee to the association for exterior maintenance and perhaps some services, such as security. Owners may refinance or sell their units or rent the property as they see fit.

Condominiums are growing in popularity in many areas because they offer all the financial advantages of buying a single-family home, often cost less money (because they are smaller, usually have common walls between units, and have a higher population density), and provide some of the benefits of renting, such as freedom from direct responsibility for exterior maintenance and upkeep.

Mobile Homes

A classic comedy film of the 1950s, *The Long, Long Trailer*, featured Lucille Ball and Desi Arnaz in escapades related to life in a cramped, mobile travel trailer, smaller than many of today's motor homes. Shortly thereafter, the concept of the travel trailer was transformed, yielding a mobile home that contained 700 to 800 square feet. Gradually, the styles of mobile homes have changed, and the size has continued to grow, such that in the 1990s this form of housing is no longer mobile and is often called instead a manufactured home. Typically "double-wide" (as wide as two traffic lanes, perhaps 22 to 28 feet) and containing all the amenities possible in 1,200 to 1,800 square feet, mobile homes offer a low-cost, minimum-upkeep housing alternative.

The cost savings of a mobile home result from the fact that it is built in a factory in sections, towed to the home site, and joined together. This eliminates work slow-down due to inclement weather and allows for mass production, as well as cost savings in materials and construction techniques. These differences account for the fact that the cost per square foot of mobile housing is about half that of conventional housing and usually includes kitchen appliances and some furniture (buffet, chest of drawers, and the like).

The quality of construction is an important consideration in selecting a mobile home. Since 1976, all mobile homes have been constructed to meet the National Manufactured Home Construction and Safety Standards. This code regulates design and construction, strength and durability, fire resistance, and energy efficiency. It also prescribes minimum standards for heating, plumbing, air conditioning, and electrical systems. Buyers should avoid mobile homes with (a) floors that sag, buckle, or squeak, (b) roofs that show evidence of leaking and are not insulated, (c) roofs and walls that are too flimsy for the weather in your area, and (d) doors and windows that do not allow exit in case of fire. Before purchasing, ask to see manufacturer warranties.

Prospective buyers of mobile homes must find a suitable place to park their home. Once installed, these homes are difficult and expensive to relocate, explaining why 95 percent of them are mobile only once, when they are transported from the factory to a lot, space, or pad. In most cases, one must rent a pad in a park designated by mobile homes. Rental fees include property taxes, grounds maintenance, recreational and laundry facilities, and perhaps some utilities.

Those who are seriously considering this modestly priced form of housing would benefit from reading *How to Buy a Manufactured Home*, available from the Consumer Information Center, P.O. Box 100, Pueblo, CO 81002. It discusses selection, placement, warranties, installation and inspection.

Until the mid-1980s most mobile homes were purchased with personal property loans, as is done with automobiles. This was due to their mobility, relative low cost, and tendency to depreciate, or diminish in value over time. Since today's mobile homes are larger and difficult to move, as well as more costly, they are usually purchased with loans just like conventional houses. Good quality, well-maintained mobile homes in prime locations can and do appreciate, or increase, in value.

New or Old

Decision making about a type of housing must include a consideration of the age of the dwelling. Recently constructed houses, condominiums, and apartments may be more energy efficient, make better use of space, and have more up-to-date style features (appliances, counter tile, skylights, and so forth). But they also may have less space for the money and higher prices or rents, they may lack the charm or interest of older homes or apartments, and they may require, if one is buying, an investment of several thousand dollars for landscaping, fencing, window coverings, and other decorator features.

Perhaps because of these factors, a large percentage of buyers choose older resale homes. First-time buyers like the lower prices of resale homes, despite the fact that, depending on age, such homes require more repair and maintenance and may be in less desirable neighborhoods. In addition, personal tastes may influence renters and buyers; many people prefer the look and feel of older homes and apartments, and they may even enjoy renovating them.

Whether Renting or Buying, Investigate

Besides deciding to rent or buy and choosing a particular type of shelter, consumers need to consider the geographic location and the construction features of the structure.

Geographic location. Between 1950 and 1975, record numbers of families moved away from the cities and into the suburbs, regions they perceived as having cleaner air, fewer people, and little crime. Gradually, small businesses, major department stores, office complexes, and even industry followed, diminishing many of the qualities consumers sought in suburbia. As a result of these changes and as a result of higher housing costs in the suburbs, during the past decade many consumers moved back

WORKSHEET 11.2 NEIGHBORHOOD INSPECTION CHECKLIST

Neighborhood Quality	Yes	No	Not important
1. Are the homes well cared for?	☐	☐	☐
2. Are there good public services (police and fire departments)?	☐	☐	☐
3. Are roads paved?	☐	☐	☐
4. Are there sidewalks?	☐	☐	☐
5. Is street lighting adequate?	☐	☐	☐
6. Is there a city sewer system?	☐	☐	☐
7. Is there a safe public water supply?	☐	☐	☐
8. Are the public schools good?	☐	☐	☐

Neighborhood Convenience			
1. Will you be near your work?	☐	☐	☐
2. Are schools nearby?	☐	☐	☐
3. Are shopping centers nearby?	☐	☐	☐
4. Is public transportation available?	☐	☐	☐
5. Will you be near childcare services?	☐	☐	☐
6. Are hospitals, clinics, or doctors close by?	☐	☐	☐
7. Is a park or playground nearby?	☐	☐	☐

Neighbors			
1. Will you be near friends or relatives?	☐	☐	☐
2. Will you be near other children of the same ages as your children?	☐	☐	☐
3. Will you feel comfortable with the neighbors?	☐	☐	☐
4. Is there an active community group?	☐	☐	☐

Does the Neighborhood Have:			
1. Increasing real estate taxes?	☐	☐	☐
2. Decreasing sales prices of homes?	☐	☐	☐
3. Lots of families moving away?	☐	☐	☐
4. Heavy traffic or noise?	☐	☐	☐

	Yes	No	Not important
5. Litter or pollution?	☐	☐	☐
6. Factories or heavy industry?	☐	☐	☐
7. Businesses closing down?	☐	☐	☐
8. Vacant houses or buildings?	☐	☐	☐
9. Increasing crime or vandalism?	☐	☐	☐

	Good	Fair	Poor
What is your overall rating of the neighborhood?	☐	☐	☐

SOURCE: Adapted from U.S. Department of Housing and Urban Development, *Home Buyers' Information Package: A Guide for Buying and Owning a Home* (Washington, D.C.: U.S. Government Printing Office, 1979).

into the cities, often to newly constructed apartments or condominiums. The choice of city, suburban, or country living is often dictated by one's job. But when deciding on geographic location, consider:

1. The cost of transportation to work, school, place of worship, shopping, and entertainment
2. Whether property taxes are likely to increase drastically
3. The quality of the schools (which sometimes has a direct relationship to property taxes): Are schools suitable, or will you feel the need to pay for a private school?
4. Air, water, or noise pollution (this may affect your health) from factories, airports, highways
5. Crime (statistics are available from the police department)
6. Zoning and development: What are the long-range plans for the area in terms of industry, airports, highways, and other housing?

To obtain this type of information, talk with friends, relatives, and neighborhood residents, read local newspapers, and visit real estate offices, the planning department of the city, the school board, and the local police department.

Physical construction. Once you have chosen a location, you need to investigate specific neighborhoods and houses. Worksheet 11.2 provides a checklist that will help you evaluate the quality and convenience of each neighborhood. By acquainting yourself with neighborhood characteristics and features, you can determine which neighborhoods do not meet your needs and standards and save time by excluding them from your search.

WORKSHEET 11.3   HOUSE INSPECTION: INSIDE THE HOUSE — STRUCTURE AND SYSTEMS

Inspection item	Condition		Item under warranty?	Additional comments
	Adequate— not a problem	Inadequate— needs repair or replacement		

1. Structure of house
   support posts
      (basement)
   floor beams
      (basement)				

2. Floors				
3. Stairs (treads, handrails)				

4. Plumbing system (check for cracks and leaks)
   water pipes OK?
   sewer pipes OK?
   water pressure OK?
   toilets work?
   sinks and faucets?
   drains work?
				Cost of water bills last year $

5. Heating system
   what type?
   how old?
   kind of fuel?
   when serviced last?
   adequate for
      size of house?
				Cost of heat last year $

6. Hot water heater
   how old?
   capacity or
      recovery rate?
   gas or electric?				

7. Electrical system
   how old?
   copper or aluminium wire?
   fuses or circuit
      breaker?
   no. of volts or amps?
   do fuses blow
      frequently?
				Cost of electricity last year $

8. Cooling/
   air conditioning
   evaporative
      or cooling?
   how old?
   when serviced last?
				Cost to use last year $

9. General room layout (traffic patterns)				

10. Kitchen size of kitchen stove/oven refrigerator dishwasher disposal/sink counter space cabinets/shelves electrical outlets floor condition windows/ventilation				

11. Bathrooms
no. of bathrooms
toilets, showers,
  tubs OK?
tiles and floors?
lighting and
  ventilation?				

12. Living room/
  dining room
size OK?
shape adaptable
  to needs?
adequate wall
  space?
do open doors
  affect space?
fireplace?				

13. Bedrooms no. and size closets adequate? windows? do open doors affect space?				
14. Storage space adequate? convenient? appropriate shape?				
15. Windows in house				
16. Doors in house				
17. Walls and ceilings				
18. Basement leaks or dampness? lighting OK?				
19. Attic signs of leaks? insulation? signs of rodents?				How much insulation?

SOURCE: Adapted from U.S. Department of Housing and Urban Development *Home Buyers' Information Package: A Guide for Buying and Owning a Home* (Washington, D.C.: U.S. Government Printing Office, 1979).

After selecting several neighborhoods, you should be prepared to evaluate a particular house or apartment. Use Worksheet 11.3 as a checklist during inspection and for comparing one choice to another. Information about warranties, cost of utilities, insulation, and the like is available from the landlord, owner, or real estate agent.

To use Worksheet 11.3 most effectively, adapt it to your personal needs with sketches or notes. For example, because first impressions are important, consider the front entrance of each dwelling. Is it pleasant and clean, with easy access? Are there more stairs than you can handle on a daily basis? Is there enough space inside the house? Is the floor plan logical and convenient for your needs? Room size is often deceiving, so measure your furniture and each room to ensure that your belongings will fit in the available space.

Layouts of kitchens and bathrooms can be critical in time management. Consider lighting, storage, continuous counter space, and ventilation in terms of your needs and your family size. Make sure all appliances and fixtures work. Is there enough space in the bathroom for two people to use the mirror? Does the kitchen have room for a table and chairs? Awareness of these factors and those shown in Worksheet 11.3 will prepare you to make a specific renting or buying choice.

Prospective buyers should be aware that **new-home warranties** are now available from the National Association of Home Builders. The coverage is transferable, so subsequent homeowners are also protected. During the first year of ownership, the builder guarantees the materials, structure, and quality of workmanship. During the second year, heating, air conditioning, wiring, plumbing, and structural flaws continue to be covered. And during the following eight years, the owner is insured against major structural defects. This coverage is offered as a ''feature'' with some new homes and, of course, is included in the purchase price. At approximately $4 per $1,000 of selling price (for example, $480 on a $120,000 home), it is a bargain for homeowners. Warranties for resale homes are also available in some locales. Companies that issue these warranties do not do inspections, but they issue coverage on the basis of written disclosures and home inspections that are standard during home resale transactions. Thus, if the seller is dishonest, or a problem is not uncovered during routine inspection, the home warranty company generally will not make repairs, since these were preexisting conditions.

Those who have decided to buy should also be aware of the real estate adage that it is better to buy an attractive, well-maintained home similar in value to others in the neighborhood than to buy the most expensive home in a lesser neighborhood. Remember, home ownership provides an investment as well as shelter, and the value of a home is tied to the quality and value of neighboring homes.

THE FOURTH STEP: CHOOSING YOUR HOUSING

Although you have done all the groundwork for a housing decision, you need one more important piece of information before you place your signature on a rental or purchase agreement: your rights and responsibilities. The Federal Fair Housing Law, Title VIII of the Civil Rights Act of 1968, updated in 1974, makes it illegal for anyone to discriminate on the basis of race, religion, sex, color, or national origin. In many states, other forms of discrimination (such as those based on marital status, sexual preference, or presence of children) may also be illegal. Discrimination in housing may be subtle, but as a result of it you may be denied the chance to look at housing in a particular neighborhood, you may be denied the chance to look at a specific dwelling, or you may be pessured into paying more than others would for rent or a house. Box 11.2 describes illegal discriminatory practices and tells how to contact your local office of the U.S. Department of Housing and Urban Development (HUD) if you feel you have been a victim of discrimination.

Renting

rental agreement: an agreement that outlines the terms for renting living space, either from month to month or with a longer-term lease.

Besides the features on the housing checklist, there are a few unique considerations for renters concerning security, convenience, and personal preferences. Are children allowed? If so, are there any restrictions? Are there local regulations that prohibit a landlord from refusing to rent to those with children? Are pets allowed, and if so, are there special rules regarding their care? If you are renting in a multiunit dwelling, will there be a manager or a superintendent on the premises at all times? If not, will someone be readily available to solve problems? What specific security measures are available in the parking facility, in the corridors, and so forth? Are there safe and clearly marked fire exits? Some of these factors may be included in **rental agreements** or in contracts that identify the rules of conduct and the payment required of the tenant. Contracts and rental agreements may also list the services that the landlord agrees to provide, and such contracts are signed by both tenant and landlord.

month-to-month rental agreement: a contract between a tenant and a landlord that identifies the amount of money charged to rent a living space for 1 month

Rental agreement. Basically, there are two kinds of rental agreements: month-to-month agreements and leases. With a **month-to-month rental agreement**, the rent can be raised monthly, although this is not likely. Payment of each month's rent is usually assumed to indicate that the renter continues to accept the terms of the agreement. In addition, the landlord can evict the tenant and change the terms of the agreement (rental fees, responsibility for expenses, and restrictions). A **lease**, however, fixes the rent payment and conditions of the rental for a period of time, usually a year. In times of high inflation, this provides renters with more budgetary security.

BOX 11.2   DEALING WITH DISCRIMINATION IN HOUSING

How discrimination may affect you:

1. You may be denied a chance to look at or buy a particular home in a particular neighborhood.
2. You may be "steered" by real estate brokers into looking at houses only in certain neighborhoods.
3. You may be pressured into paying more for a house than others would.
4. You may become so discouraged that you decide not to buy at all.

Discrimination is sometimes hard to detect. Some of the ways it is practiced include:

1. You are told the house is sold when it is not.
2. You are told that there are other offers or that there is no one to show you the house.
3. You are asked to leave your phone number, and if the exchange is for a minority area, no one calls you back.
4. You are told the seller has decided not to sell or has raised the price.
5. The broker says he or she has nothing available in your price range and refuses to show you the listing of houses for sale.
6. You can't get an appointment or the broker cancels appointments.
7. You are told that the house is not what you want, is too expensive, or is not desirable.
8. The owner is out, sick, sleeping, or whatever.

If you think you have been discriminated against, write down a few notes about how you think discrimination was practiced:

1. The names of the real estate agency, the seller, or other persons you think discriminated against you.
2. The date, time, and place it occurred.
3. How you think you were discriminated against.
4. The names of any witnesses who were with you when the discrimination occurred.

Call the people who can help. Get in touch with your local civil rights organization or the local office of the U.S. Department of Housing and Urban Development (HUD). The steps they take on your behalf usually include:

1. Taking down the facts of your case.
2. Sending out an investigator ("tester") to check whether your rights were denied in any way.
3. If they agree that you were discriminated against, contacting the seller, the real estate broker, or other persons involved to work out an agreement.
4. If they cannot work out an agreement or if the person denies having discriminated, beginning the legal process for filing a formal complaint before the state civil rights commission or the state or federal courts.

Remember, if you think you have been discriminated against, you can and should do something about it.

SOURCE: U.S. Department of Housing and Urban Development, *Home Buyers' Information Package: A Guide for Buying and Owning a Home* (Washington, D.C.: U.S. Government Printing Office, 1979).

The majority of rental agreements and leases are written to protect the landlord. Often, standard forms such as those purchased in stationery stores have clauses that may be illegal in the state where one lives. The forms may misstate current laws or fail to inform tenants of their rights. Such agreements or leases, although legally unsound, may frighten tenants into complying with the terms or discourage tenants from demanding the protections provided by state law. Uninformed landlords may also believe these forms to be legal and may operate accordingly.

In deciding whether to sign an agreement or a lease, you should examine its provisions carefully and weigh what you are getting against what you are giving away. To check on local and state laws affecting housing rights, get in touch with your state consumer affairs agency, a local consumer affairs agency, the local city hall, or a tenant's rights organization. Both a month-to-month agreement and a lease should indicate:

1. The amount of the monthly fee and the day of the month it is due. If a prepayment of the last month's rent is required, it should be so stated.
2. The amount of the penalty, if any, for late payment of monthly rent.
3. The amount of any required deposit and the conditions under which part or all of it will be returned.
4. Who pays for utilities, repairs, replacements, insurance, and the like.

In addition, a lease should state how it will be renewed when it expires, whether on a month-to-month basis, at a renegotiated rental rate and time period, or automatically extended with the same terms.

You should personalize the rental agreement or lease to include everything you have been promised. For example, if you have been told that the dwelling comes with appliances or furniture, make sure each item is specified. If the landlord has promised to paint the interior, make repairs, and so forth before you move in, have this written into the contract. If you have been promised use of common recreational or laundry facilities, be sure that this use is included, as well as the cost, if any, for such use.

Most rental agreements or leases list the landlord's policies regarding overnight guests, children, pets, noise, and so forth. Failure to comply may result in eviction or a canceled lease. This probably sounds reasonable, but consider that some leases include clauses that prohibit immoral behavior—judged by the landlord, naturally. Another common restriction may prohibit having overnight guests, requiring that the dwelling be occupied only by the tenant and the tenant's immediate family. Leases may prohibit subleasing, changing the color of interior paint, or hanging pictures on the wall. Be cautious of other clauses that make you liable for all repairs, that allow the landlord to enter the premises even when you are not there (except for emergencies, of course), or that require you to follow regulations that have not yet been written. If you disagree with any of the stipulations and convince the landlord that they should be changed, write these changes into the contract. If the landlord does not agree to changes that you feel are essential, you have two choices. You can sign the contract and hope that problem doesn't arise, or you can look for another place to rent. Naturally, if you choose the first, you need to be prepared to accept the consequences, which may include the possibility of eviction.

Most landlords require a deposit to cover the cost of cleaning, breakage, or loss when a tenant moves out. This "refundable" deposit can equal from one to three months' rent, and it is supposed to be returned if the dwelling is left clean and in good condition. A cleaning charge is commonly assessed against this deposit, however, regardless of how clean you leave the house or apartment, and the final judgment usually rests with the landlord. In order to protect your interests:

1. Make a list of all damage that already exists. It is best to do so on a "walk through" with the manager or owner. Sign the list immediately, and have the manager do the same. Make several copies of this list, and provide one to the manager and one to the owner.
2. Take photographs that show the condition and contents of the dwelling and the yard on the day you move in, and repeat the process on the day you move out. Have them developed by a company that puts a date on their pictures.
3. Save copies of all bills for maintenance, cleaning, repairs, or improvements you make.
4. Investigate state and local laws that regulate security deposits and refunds, so that you know your rights and responsibilities. When you move out, discuss the refund with the owner or manager, keeping these regulations in mind. If you encounter resistance to returning most of your refundable deposit, showing the owner the pictures and other documents will usually prove your point. If not, you can go to small claims court (see Chapter 8).

implied warranty of habitability: a warranty that requires rental units to conform to building, safety, and sanitation codes

Landlord–tenant relations. Considering the number of tenants in the United States, it is logical to assume that some landlord–tenant disagreements may arise. Many such disputes focus on a landlord's failure to provide necessary repairs or livable dwellings. Even though there is no federal landlord–tenant law covering privately owned housing, in recent years most state courts have extended rights to tenants by the application of an **implied warranty of habitability**, to ensure that landlords provide decent conditions. This warranty requires that rentals conform to building, safety, and sanitation codes. At the very least, this means that there are no roof leaks, broken windows, or broken doors; that plumbing works, including access to hot and cold water and a working sewer or septic tank connection; that the heater, lights, and wiring work safely; that the floors, stairways, and railings are in good condition; that the property is clean and free of pests when it is rented; and that there are enough covered garbage cans. Box 11.3 presents a case study involving the landlord's responsibility to provide habitable housing and problems that can arise.

In some states, tenants have the legal right to withhold part or all of the rent to force landlords to make repairs. Approximately half of the states

---

BOX 11.3 LANDLORD—TENANT RELATIONS: A CASE STUDY

"Hey, Tony," Nanette called out. "We've received a registered letter."

Tony came into the room as Nanette tore open the envelope. The look on her face indicated shock. "We're being sued!" she exclaimed.

"You're kidding! Who would do that?" Tony asked.

"Well, it says here that it's Robert Jensen, our past landlord from the house on Columbia Avenue. He claims that we caused damage to the draperies, carpet, plumbing, and backyard. He's suing us for $8,000 to cover damages, lawyer's fees, and two months' rent for the time the house was empty during repairs."

"I can't believe this. We moved from there because he wouldn't fix the plumbing. Remember how the shower leaked and kept the bedroom carpet soggy? We waited three months for him to fix that before we gave up and moved out. Those damages aren't our fault."

Nanette nodded in agreement. "Well, what do you think he means about the draperies?" she asked. "They weren't in very good condition when we first moved in—they were faded and had snags. It's true that our cat did climb on them once in a while, but they weren't really much worse than when we moved in."

"And I fixed the backyard before we moved out, remember?" Tony asked. "Snoopy dug those holes, but I filled them back up. There never was much of a lawn back there anyway."

"We just can't afford this," Nanette moaned. "What should we do?"

1. What can this couple do to protect themselves? Where can they go to get accurate advice?

2. What are the laws in your state that might provide legal protection for this couple?

3. What could this couple do to avoid being in this situation in the future?

---

allow tenants to deduct repairs from the rent, and each of these states has specific procedures and restrictions for this process. Some states limit the portion of a month's rent that can be used or specify how often this can be done. Many states also have specific legal procedures for rent strikes. Unfortunately, if tenants exercise any of these options, the landlord may ask them to move. Such "retaliatory eviction" is prohibited in certain circumstances, but it is often difficult to establish in court.

The future of renting. More than one-third of the households in America are renters. Renters make up over half the households in cities like New York, Boston, San Francisco, and Los Angeles, which are also among the most expensive cities in terms of home ownership. As costs of owning increase, and with houses and condominiums as well as apartments available for rent, more people are choosing the renting option. However, as we've already noted, rents have been rising faster than wages, albeit at a slower rate than home prices. This has put a particular stress on low-income consumers. In addition there were drastic cuts in the housing-assistance budget during the 1980s. Finally the revisions in the income tax code during the same time made it less profitable to invest in multifamily

BOX 11.4   RENT CONTROL: A PROBLEM OR A SOLUTION?

In the late 1970s many apartment owners raised their rents in an effort to keep up with the costs of taxes, energy, and maintenance. When the increases seemed excessive, angry tenants responded with picket lines and rent strikes. When rents continued to escalate, apartment dwellers in many regions developed enough clout to convince local governments to initiate **rent control**, regulations that state the conditions under which rent can be increased and the percent increase allowable. Currently, nine states, along with major cities like Boston, Los Angeles, San Francisco, and Washington, D.C., have instituted rent control, affecting 12 percent of the nation's housing (Fleetwood and Eichenwald, 1986). With costs of housing still on the rise and energy prices unpredictable, this is a critical issue for the 1990s.

Confusion and inequities have been the hallmarks of rent-control legislation ever since it was imposed nationally during World War II. Critics of rent control usually cite New York City as an example of the negative effect of such measures. This city, which has had rent control since 1943,

has lost more than 500,000 rental units since 1951, about half of the current stock of private regulated rentals (Fleetwood and Eichenwald, 1986). Mortgage money for new rent-controlled apartments virtually vanished during the same time. Since there is a consensus that rent-controlled apartments are not as profitable as other forms of real estate or investment, little new apartment construction has occurred.

Those who favor rent control point out that most measures exempt new construction. In addition, most measures usually allow increases to ensure that landlords usually get a "just and reasonable" return on their investment, usually tying new allowable increases to the Consumer Price Index.

When local regulations are being formulated, consumers have a responsibility to evaluate both long-term and short-term costs and benefits for tenants and landlords. The trade-off of lower rents for some people in the short term may not be worthwhile if it results in inadequate rental housing for consumers in the long term.

dwellings, slowing construction of this much needed housing. In this decade almost 2 million privately owned, low-income apartments built with federal aid could lose their subsidized status and convert to market-rate apartments or condominiums (Dreier et al., 1988). These issues ensure that landlord–tenant relations as well as rent control will be controversial throughout this decade. (see Box 11.4).

Buying a Home

You may have come to the conclusion that your family's financial and personal circumstances warrant purchasing a home. Besides your budget and your personal situation, two factors in the housing market will affect your chances of making a purchase. The first is supply and demand of housing and the second is the cost of the loan.

TABLE 11.1 Impact of Rising Interest Rates on Monthly Mortgage Payments[a]

Loan Amount	18%	16%	14%	12%	10%
$ 60,000	$ 904	$ 807	$ 711	$ 617	527
80,000	1,205	1,076	948	823	702
100,000	1,507	1,345	1,185	1,029	878
125,000	1,884	1,681	1,481	1,286	1,098
150,000	2,261	2,017	1,778	1,543	1,317
175,000	2,637	2,353	2,074	1,801	1,537
200,000	3,014	2,690	2,370	2,058	1,756

[a] Estimated monthly payments for principal and interest only on a 30-year loan, allowances for taxes, insurance, and other impounds not included.

SOURCE: California Federal Savings and Loan Association.

Supply and demand. If there are only a few buyers and many sellers in your community, you will be able to negotiate a reasonable price for your home. This "buyer's market" might occur in places where winters have been excessively cold several years in a row, where population has declined, or where building of housing units have exceeded the demands of a region. On the other hand, if you have to compete with other home buyers for a limited number of homes, you are in a "seller's market" and may have to pay more. As a result of decreased housing starts nationally over the past decade and strong demand, more and more shoppers may be facing sellers' markets.

Cost of the loan. A second factor affecting your housing purchase is the cost of financing a loan. This has two components: the nominal interest rate and the real interest rate. As we saw in Chapter 8, nominal rates refer to the number, or actual percentage, say 10 percent. As nominal interest rates rise, the cost of financing increases dramatically. For example, at nominal interest rates of 10 percent, a family that could afford a house payment of $878 a month, and 20 percent down payment could buy a $100,000 house. But at a 17 percent rate, they could only afford a $60,000 house. Table 11.1 shows more completely the impact of rising interest rates. Because the national median price of existing homes is more than $100,000 in many areas of the country, it is not surprising that fewer families purchase homes when interest rates soar.

Real interest rate (the nominal interest rate minus the inflation rate) plays a part here as well. For example, if the nominal interest rate is 10 percent and inflation is 4 percent, the real interest rate is 6 percent. This tended to be the situation in the housing market in the late 1980s. On the other hand, in the late 1970s the nominal interest rate was 12 percent and the inflation rate was 12 percent, so the real interest rate was zero. Given this equation, the cost of borrowing was zero, making housing or any loan a smart choice, particularly when the dollar cost of the mortgage was tax deductible.

Finding your dream home. All of the factors we considered when searching for a rental apply to looking for a home to purchase. Do not be pressured into buying the first house you see. Refer to Worksheet 11.3, and ask questions. Take a flashlight with you so you can see into those dark corners. Worksheet 11.4 provides a more detailed checklist for evaluating the structural condition of the building and grounds. Be sure to bring and consult other members of the household. Because you may be living in the house for a long time, it is important that the rest of the family be happy with the choice.

The two most common sources of homes for sale are owners and real estate brokers. You can learn about homes, condominiums, and manufactured homes for sale by owners by checking the classified ads in the newspaper, reading bulletin boards in stores and other locations, asking friends, and looking for signs on lawns and streets. But not every seller wants to put up with the trouble of advertising, showing the property, or dealing with the paperwork of selling. This is where **real estate brokers** come in handy. A broker, usually through his or her agents, handles all the ins and outs of selling the home for the seller, and he or she may take care of the buyer's side of the deal, too. Real estate agents and brokers are licensed by the state to perform these services (the legal responsibilities and extent of their work vary from state to state) for a **commission**, that is, a percentage of the sales price of the property.

real estate broker: someone who has been licensed to sell real estate by the state as a result of passing a qualifying exam and as a result of job performance

Real estate brokers and agents have several main functions:

1. They acquire listings of properties, for which they act as agents. In some states, such as California, brokers cooperate and compile all listings into a computerized book (the *Multiple Listing* book) that shows all the houses available in a given area. Thus, a buyer can go to a broker and find out about many more properties than the ones that the broker has in his or her office. There is no restriction on the buyer from purchasing a property from another broker, but the two brokers (and their agents, if any are involved) split the commission.

2. They negotiate the highest price that the buyer will pay and the lowest price that the owner will accept.

3. They show the property to prospective buyers, usually without charge, because they expect to be paid when they sell a house. If you are new to a region, a real estate agent or broker can be particularly helpful in showing you areas and houses you may be interested in, which can save you time. As a result, you may feel obligated to that person, but you are not legally bound to buy anything.

**WORKSHEET 11.4   HOME INSPECTION: OUTSIDE THE
HOUSE — STRUCTURE AND GROUNDS**

Inspection Item	Recent Repairs? (in past 2 years)	Condition		Item under warranty?	Additional comments
		Adequate— not a Problem	Inadequate— needs Repair or Replacement		
1. Foundation					
2. Brickwork					
3. Siding					
4. Exterior paint					
5. Porch(es)					
6. Windows and screens					
7. Storm windows					
8. Roof					
9. Gutters and downspouts					
10. Chimney(s)					
11. Walls and fences					
12. Garage					
13. Driveway and walks					
14. Grounds and landscaping					
15. Drainage and septic systems					
16. Other items outside the house					

SOURCE: U.S. Department of Housing and Urban Development *Home Buyers' Information Package: A Guide for Buying and Owning a Home* (Washington, D.C.: U.S. Government Printing Office, 1979).

Before you choose a broker or a real estate agent, try to research the person's reputation. Ask your friends or workmates for recommendations, talk to the person to see whether you like her or him, and check with the Better Business Bureau to see whether there have been any complaints. But remember, the broker or agent is actually hired by the seller, so don't give her or him information unnecessarily. The broker is obligated to tell the seller about your situation, whether you are in a hurry to move, what your absolute top price is, etc.

Most brokerage societies or real estate boards (that is, groups of brokers) have rules against price competition and have instituted a standard fee for services of 6 to 7 percent of the selling price. As you well know, the price of housing has increased faster than the prices of many other commodities over the past two decades, giving brokers an automatic and substantial raise. As a result, many homeowners sell their homes themselves or go to cut-rate or alternative brokers. These brokers provide advertising, signs, and flags; they line up prospective buyers; and provide advice to owners. Basically, they do everything except show the house to prospective buyers, a job left to the seller. Most alternative brokers will not be able to list houses in the computerized *Multiple Listing* book used by conventional brokers, but they may offer a similar service on a smaller scale. For these services, they charge 1 to 4 percent. Consumers should feel free to negotiate a broker's commission, because rising housing prices and competition by alternative brokers has created more fee flexibility. If there is no commission or a reduced commission, there will be a lower selling price, making the property more attractive to a buyer.

Another alternative for potential home buyers is to hire a **buyer's broker**. Ask at the local real estate board or look in the Yellow Pages of your phone book under "Real Estate Agents" to determine if this new breed of real estate agent resides in your community. A buyer's broker is an advocate for the buyer and can negotiate terms and price on the buyer's behalf. As a result, this service may actually cost you nothing, since he or she may be able to get the house price lower than you could. It is also possible for the seller's agent to split the sales commission (the 6 percent, for example) with your broker. In this case although the commission fee stays the same, you have had an advocate during the negotiations.

When you decide to buy. From looking at comparable homes in similar neighborhoods, you should be able to decide what a fair sales price is for a specific dwelling. Do not be deceived by quick cosmetic fixes (such as a cheap paint job on the front door or poor-quality carpeting or fancy wallpaper that hides defects) or by the owner's furniture and appliances. Look for the real value in the house: quality construction inside and outside, lot size and landscaping, the size of the house and the number of rooms, structural improvements, and the convenience and quality of the neighborhood.

If you are seriously considering a dwelling, it may be wise to pay an expert to explore the home for problems with structure, wiring, termites, plumbing, and the like before you sign a contract. Since only Texas licenses inspectors, if you live in any other state, be sure to ask for references when selecting an inspector. Select a member of the American Society of Home Inspectors, since they must be trained and experienced in order to have this affiliation. Inspection is particularly useful for a home 10 years old or older. It usually costs about 0.1 percent of the home selling price, with a minimum of about $150. For a newer home, for which the risks are fewer, you might want to postpone inspection until after you have made an offer for the home, but make the offer contingent on the satisfactory results of the inspection. This information can save you hundreds, perhaps thousands, of dollars and may serve as a bargaining point. That is, you can ask the seller for repairs or for an appropriate price reduction.

Also ask about easements for the property at this time. An **easement** is the right of an individual, business, or government to have access through or over the property. For example, a city might have the right to cross your property to clean out a flood-control channel. You will want to know about all conditions and restrictions of this sort.

After you are familiar with the house and its problems, as well as its charms, investigate the seller's situation. Sellers almost always ask for more money than they are willing to accept. But look, too, for other factors. If the house has been on the market for a long time, the owner may be eager to sell and may accept a lower price. Negotiation is expected, and under most situations, you should offer less than the seller's asking price. Your first offer should be below your safe budgetary limit. You can expect the seller to accept or reject it quickly, within a day or two. The seller might reject your offer and make a counter offer, with another price or different terms. You, of course, can do the same in turn.

If and when you and the seller agree on price, you will need to put up a deposit, often called **earnest money**. This deposit is evidence of the seriousness of your intention, and it is usually applied to the down payment later. The amount varies by geographical location but is usually 1 to 2 percent of the selling price, which could be $1,500 to $3,000 on a $150,000 house. At the same time, you will draw up an **earnest agreement**, or **binder**, a written offer to buy the home at a given price. The binder should contain a clause like "contingent upon the buyer's obtaining financing," and both you and the seller need to sign and date it. The advantages of a binder to the buyer are that it fixes the price of the house and provides proof that the offer has been accepted; thus, it is

earnest agreement (binder): a written offer to buy real property at a given price important to get the seller to sign the binder as soon as possible, leaving both you and the seller free to work out the details of the agreement. In most cases, if the seller accepts your offer and you change your mind, you forfeit your deposit, so offer as little as possible.

contract of sale: a contract that itemizes the terms and conditions of sale, usually of real estate; also called a purchase contract

The next step is to draw up a **contract of sale**, also called a purchase and sales agreement, or a contract of purchase. This contract protects both buyer and seller, because it clarifies the terms and the conditions that must be met. If one or more of the terms are not met, the contract can be canceled. And if the fault is not yours, the deposit or earnest money will be returned. Often, the binder and the contract of sale are combined, which speeds up the buying process, but that procedure leaves everything open for negotiation until the last minute. Here is a partial list of conditions that should be included in a purchase contract:

1. The name(s) and address(es) of the seller(s) and buyer(s)
2. A description of the property
3. The price of the house
4. The amount of the deposit (earnest money) and who holds it until the closing
5. The date and time of the closing
6. Where the closing will take place
7. A provision to extend the closing date
8. A provision for disposition of the deposit if something goes wrong
9. The amount of the broker's fee (if any)
10. The adjustments to be made at the closing (taxes already paid by the seller, fuel adjustments, points or extra service charges for a home loan paid by the seller or the buyer)
11. The details of what is included in the sale (carpeting, appliances, window coverings, light fixtures, and so forth)
12. Special conditions of the sale (for example, the seller will repair broken windows, pay for a termite inspection and treatment, and so forth)
13. Inspections the buyer can make before closing
14. Property easements

Blank purchase agreements can be obtained at stationery stores, sometimes from banks or savings and loan associations, or from attorneys, or they can be personally devised. Brokers provide these forms and complete them as part of their services. Changes can be made in the standard purchase agreement as long as the buyer and seller agree. Before you sign an agreement (1) make sure that all of the terms of the agreement are filled out properly, (2) add any special conditions you want included, and (3) delete any terms or conditions in the standard agreement that do not apply to you or that you do not want included.

An example of a condition you might include is a **defect clause**. This requires the seller to identify any existing defects that could serve as the basis of price negotiation. Such a clause might read: ''Seller promises Buyer that, except for these items listed below, the home will be delivered to Buyer free of major defects. The existing defects include _____.'' Another condition might be a termite inspection, or specific repairs, paid for by the buyer.

Once you have a deal, you are ready to choose a financing method.

Loans and mortgages. A **mortgage** is a claim against real property, that is, land and everything permanently fixed to it, such as buildings, fences, and so forth. A mortgage is given by the buyer (mortgagor) to the lender (mortgagee) as security for the money borrowed. The **mortgage note** is the written agreement the buyer signs with the lender to repay the loan. The money that the mortgagor borrows is secured by the value of the mortgaged property. If the borrower fails to make the monthly payments as agreed (that is, if the borrower **defaults** on the loan), the lender has the right to **foreclose** (to seize property and sell it to pay off the debt). For example, say that your neighbor was in a car accident and has been unable to work for several months and fallen behind in the house payment. The lender would have the right to evict your neighbor, auction off the house, and take the proceeds to pay off the loan. If any money is left after the loan is paid, it would go to your neighbor.

The mortgage note states the loan **principal**, which is the specific amount borrowed, the interest rate, and the specific details of the payment plan, which allows the mortgagor to reduce the debt gradually through monthly payments on the principal. This form of repayment is called **amortization**. The mortgage note also states whether there is a **prepayment penalty**, a charge for paying off the loan before it is due. Prepayment is often done when the house is sold to another person who has negotiated his or her own mortgage with a different lender. Some buyers assume the loan of the seller, that is, they accept all conditions and terms of the mortgage note and become responsible for its payment. Such **assumable loans** are often available at lower interest rates than prevail at a given time and so are an asset for both buyers and sellers. Even though the assumable rate might be as little as 1 percent lower than prevailing rates, that difference can be significant. For example, a difference in one percentage point on a 30-year, $80,000 loan could mean a $40,000 difference.

Now that we have given the basic vocabulary of mortgages, we can look at the terms and conditions of each type. Comparing types of mortgages requires all the skills you have developed in comparison shopping. You might want to consider help from a mortgage-reporting service. Although services and prices vary, they run about $20 and provide a computerized

mortgage: *a claim against real property given by the lender as security for money borrowed*

principal: *the amount of a debt or investment minus the interest*

amortization: *a payment plan that allows the mortgagor to reduce the debt gradually by monthly payments on the principal*

prepayment penalty: *a fee charged by the lender to the buyer for paying off a loan in advance, often as the result of selling property*

update on current rates and loan features available from lenders in a specific geographic area. Ask the local Board of Realtors which reporting services are appropriate for your region.

Fixed-payment mortgages. A **fixed-payment mortgage** has a payment and interest rate that stays at one level for the lifetime of the loan. Three types of fixed-payment mortgage loans are available. Although you may not be eligible for two of them, all three are availble from commercial banks, saving banks, and savings and loan associations, as well as from some credit unions and insurance companies.

Conventional loans can be arranged in any way that satisfies both parties. They may require down payments that range from 5 to 25 percent, with a larger "down" sometimes receiving a lower interest rate. Interest rates are established by the lender, within the limitations of state statutes, and they are affected by the forces of supply and demand in the national money market. For example, if the demand for money rises, the interest rate on conventional loans might rise from 11 percent to 14 to 15 percent or even higher. If the demand drops, lenders might offer conventional loans at a lower interest rate, perhaps 8 or 9 percent.

With most mortgages, the larger the down payment, the lower the interest rate. If you put at least 10 percent down, you will probably be able to negotiate a slightly lower interest rate than with only 5 percent down. If your down payment is less than 20 percent, lenders generally require that you have private **mortgage insurance** that protects the lender against loss by default on at least part of the loan.

Borrowers have another decision: on the length of time of the loan. Lenders offer a 15-year loan at a lower interest rate than the more common 30-year loan. Borrowers will find that their monthly payment might be only 20 percent higher than with the longer-term loan. Those who can afford the higher payment will appreciate the total savings and quicker build-up of equity. This comparison and evaluation is worth the time investment.

A second type of conventional loan is the **Veterans Administration (VA) loan guarantee.** The purpose of this loan is to ensure that an eligible member of the armed forces, a qualified veteran, or a widow or widower of a qualified veteran who died of a service-related cause, can obtain financing for home ownership. The interest rate is fixed by the federal government rather than by money availability, and it is usually slightly lower than the interest rate on a regular conventional loan. The Veterans Administration generally does not make loans, but it offers a guaranty against loss to private lending institutions. The government promises to repay a certain percentage of the loan (usually 60 percent), so the borrower needs no other mortgage insurance.

conventional loans (fixed-payment mortgages): fixed-payment loans for which interest rates are established by the lender as a result of supply and demand in the national money market

mortgage insurance: (1) a form of decreasing term insurance that protects the borrower in that the decrease in the value of the policy is small during the early years and then rapid in later years when the mortgage is being paid off; (2) insurance that protects the lender against loss by default of part of a mortgage, reducing the risk to the lender

Veterans Administration (VA) loan guarantee: a mortgage available to eligible veterans or veterans' widows at lower than prevailing fixed interest rates; mortgage insurance is provided by the federal government

To be eligible for a VA loan, the amount of the loan cannot exceed the VA's appraised value of the property. When you apply for a VA loan, a VA representative comes to the property to do an **appraisal**, an evaluation of what the property is worth, and to see whether, if you should default, the house can be resold for at least as much money as you paid for it. This guaranty of value makes VA loans safer for both borrowers and lenders. Because of this guaranty, VA loans (which are made for up to $100,000 for 30 years) have no prepayment penalty and a small down payment. During the 1970s, VA loans became available for mobile, or manufactured, homes and for mortgages on second homes, although under slightly different guaranty terms. All of these loan guaranties are available to veterans more than once if the previously guaranteed loan has been paid off and if the property has been transferred to another owner. Veterans are liable to the VA for loan losses if they default, until the VA releases them from this responsibility, usually at the time that the home is resold.

Federal Housing Administration (FHA) loan: This federal agency offers mortgages at lower-than-prevailing fixed interest rates, with lower down payments, and with mortgage insurance by the federal government

The Federal Housing Administration, established by Congress in 1934, insures home loans up to certain amounts ($101,250 in 1988) and for as long as 35 years. Anyone can apply for a **Federal Housing Administration (FHA) loan**, which can have a down payment as small as 5 percent of the appraised value of the house. This mortgage insurance was created to encourage and facilitate home ownership. As with VA loans, the maximum interest rate for FHA loans is usually below the prevailing market rate. It is set by the secretary of HUD.

Application forms for FHA mortgage insurance are normally available through lenders. If the lender approves the loan after reviewing the application, the lender notifies the FHA, which in turn assigns a private appraiser to investigate the value of the property. As with VA loans, this is done to affirm that, in case of default, resale of the house would pay off the loan. When this appraisal is completed, the report and the application are forwarded to the FHA for review and approval. As a result of this procedure, FHA loans take a bit longer to process. The result is that a seller who wishes to complete the transaction in a speedy way may not wish to sell to a buyer with FHA mortgage insurance.

discount points: a lump-sum payment to the lender to compensate the lender for offering a below-market interest rate

As we've shown, during the late 1970s, making a profit on a loan became less predictable as a result of meteoric interest rates. In response, lenders began to charge **discount points**, an advance interest charge that is paid in cash at the closing of the sale. One point is equal to 1 percent of the loan principal; for example, on a loan of $90,000, one point is equal to $900. Some mortgagees require four or five points, while other lenders offer similar mortgages with no points or loan fees. Paying fewer points, however, usually means paying more in interest during the term of the loan. It is the combination of the dollar costs of points and the dollar costs of interest that give you the real cost of a loan. Most lenders would prefer to quote just the interest rate in conversation and advertisements and ignore the costs of points, which could be $2,000 to $3,000 in cash. But since 1988, under the federal Truth-in-Lending laws, points must be included when a lender quotes its annual percentage rate (APR) for mortgages. Consumers would be wise to inquire and verify the APR when comparison shopping for loans.

Because VA/FHA mortgages are at interest rates below the prevailing market rate, they are less profitable to lenders. As a result, lenders usually charge points when they agree to lend money at the lower, less profitable rate. This practice increases their profit and still allows them to meet the interest rate allowed with VA/FHA loans. The amount of lump-sum fees depends on the amount of the loan and the prevailing interest rates. With VA/FHA loans, typically, two points are charged for each quarter of a percent difference between the interest rate available on conventional mortgages and the maximum rate of VA/FHA mortgages. For example, if the conventional rate is 10 percent and the ceiling rate on VA/FHA is 9 percent, you would pay eight points (two points times four quarters of a percent). On the $90,000 loan mentioned above, where one point is equal to $900, eight points would cost $7,200. With mortgages in general, points can be charged to the seller or the buyer, but both the FHA and VA only allow buyers to pay up to half these costs. As a result, if the seller agrees to a VA/FHA mortgage package, the costs of the seller's points are often passed on to the buyer in the form of a higher house price.

Because of the meteoric rise in housing prices and the decreased support for housing from the federal government during the 1980s (see Box 11.5), many cities and states have developed their own loan programs. These are aimed to assist low- and middle-income home buyers, particularly first-time buyers, to purchase housing. These programs feature below-market interest rates and often carry restrictions regarding quick resale, thus diminishing the risk of speculation. For details, prospective buyers should consult with the municipal government in the region in which they wish to purchase.

Floating payment mortgages. Up until the late 1970s fixed-rate, 30-year loans were the only type available and represented a constant level of expense in the family budget. Many families counted on the fact that as inflation and income increased, their mortgage payment would be easier to bear. But financial institutions were bearing the brunt of fast-rising interest rates. As a result, lenders experimented with ways to maintain their profits, including new types of mortgages in which the mortgage payment fluctuates.

Floating payment mortgages were created by savings and loan associations and adopted by other lenders in an effort to protect themselves

BOX 11.5   THE SEARCH FOR LOW—COST HOUSING AT CRISIS PROPORTIONS

The news is filled with stories of "the rich and famous" living in beautiful mansions, and Yuppies owning houses worth $250,000 and up. Yet recently the non-partisan League of Women Voters concluded that "not since the Depression has the housing crisis in America been so acute" (Redes, 1988). This conclusion resulted from 6,500 interviews with public and private social service administrators, caseworkers, hospital administrators, mayors and other public officials, and other service providers. The study indicated that only the wealthy had been untouched by the housing crunch, since housing costs have accelerated almost three times faster than income in the last 15 years. As a result the numbers of homeless individuals and families grew dramatically. Estimates of the homeless population range from 250,000 to 3 million, with no real way of being certain of the number. A Philadelphia official in 1986 reported that almost 50 percent of the homeless who sought shelter were families with children (Landers, 1987).

Even for low-income families that are not homeless, providing adequate shelter presents enormous challenges. Most low-income families are renters and pay more than 30 percent, some as much as 50 percent, of their income for housing. Affluent families who spend this much on housing may have to plan carefully, but for low-income families this is a real hardship. Spending 30 percent or more of income on housing means a deteriorating standard of living. It means having less money left for food, clothing, medical care, and other necessities.

Experts on this crisis point to many causes, mostly centered around availability and affordability of housing. Major depletion of low-income housing stock began in the 1970s with urban renewal, which destroyed inner-city housing and replaced it with commercial buildings and/or housing for the more affluent. *Gentrification*, the upgrading and remodeling of older, low-income housing into middle and upper-middle class housing, as well as the conversion of apartment buildings to condominiums also diminished the supply of low-cost housing.

During the 1980s federal housing assistance decreased dramatically. For example, in 1980 $30 billion was allotted to subsidized housing, but by 1987 that amount had been reduced by two-thirds to $10.7 billion. This occurred at a time when other social-welfare budgets (for food, medical care, etc.) were also being cut, placing many families in a disastrous financial dilemma.

Many cities and states have stepped into the void left by the federal government, and have attempted to make a dent in the low-cost housing shortage. They have created public/private partnerships to build or rehabilitate low-income rental housing. But the demand is so high that 17 out of 26 cities surveyed in 1987 had stopped adding names to the waiting lists for assisted housing. The survey also revealed that the average wait for such housing was two years (Reder, 1988). Other local solutions include issuing special housing bonds, assessing fees on commercial developments, and reallocating a larger portion of city or state budgets for construction and renovation. But many experts point out that even if the cities and states stretched themselves to their fiscal limits to raise housing funds, "the combined total would not fill the vacuum left by the federal government's retreat" (Dreier, *et al.*, 1988).

Phillip L. Clay of the Massachusetts Institute of Technology and author of *At Risk of Loss: The Endangered Future of Low-Income Rental Housing Resources* believes that the current crisis will only worsen, due to the convergence of three factors. First is the gradual expiration of existing federal contracts affecting a large portion of the 1.9 million privately owned, but federally assisted, low-income rental units. The expiration allows owners to rent for market rates, further reducing low-income rental housing stock. Secondly, the Tax Reform Act of 1986 eliminated most tax shelters, including accelerated depreciation, which had made investing in low-cost housing attractive to investors. Finally, there is a projected increase in the number of low-income families needing low-cost housing.

There is concurrence that if we do not do something about the gap between the demand for and supply of low-income housing that by the end of the century 18 million people in the United States will not have a place to live.

during periods of rapidly escalating interest rates. Historically, savings and loan institutions have been locked into long-term, fixed-rate mortgages, while trying to attract savings in a competitive market. As the overall demand for money has risen, they have had to offer higher interest rates to attract new money, or savings, to their business. This is done by raising the rates of new mortgages, creating a situation in which new borrowers are bearing the total burden of—in effect, subsidizing—older loans. Floating payment mortgages are an effort to make the lending side of the banking industry more responsive to changes in the supply and demand of money as it shifts some of the risk of rising interest rates to consumers.

Floating payment mortgages typically require lower than usual payments in the first few months or years of the contract in exchange for the possibility of higher payments in the future. This payment pattern may more closely fit the income pattern of many borrowers and so make home ownership possible for more people. Of the floating payment plans, the most used is the **adjustable-rate mortgage (ARM)**. With an ARM the interest rate charged for the loan can rise or fall according to the supply of and demand for money at a national level, resulting in an increase or decrease in the amount of a loan payment. There is great flexibility of terms in these types of loans, making comparison by consumers both a complex and an essential task.

In recent years the interest rate on ARMs has been 1 to 2 percent lower than conventional loans. In some areas where competition is fierce, lenders have resorted to offering low "teaser" rates, making loans 3 to 4 percent lower than conventional loans for the first six months to a year. At that point the rate is automatically scheduled to rise, typically two points, regardless of market conditions. The person who selects an ARM is betting against the bank that interest rates will not rise too high, and may even drop. If rates stay the same or don't climb too high, the borrower could reasonably anticipate making payments.

As home prices have risen, more and more buyers have turned to floating payment loans. Since the typical floating rate mortgage features a lower initial monthly payment, it has been a favorite choice for borrowers on a modest budget and is perhaps the only loan they could qualify for. Some critics point to the fact that if the cost of the house payment increases dramatically it may become too much of a burden for some households, as a small change in the mortgage rate can make a big difference in a family budget. For example, say the loan is for $100,000 for 30 years at an introductory, or "teaser," rate of 8 percent, making the monthly payment $718. For each one-point rise, about $80 would be added to the payment. If the interest rate is automatically scheduled to increase two points after the first year, (which is typical) to a 10 percent rate, the monthly payment will rise to $878. And if the market condi-

adjustable rate mortgage (ARM): a mortgage that allows the interest rate to rise and fall according to the supply and demand for money at a national level; sometimes called adjustable mortgage loan (AML)

tions should dictate an additional rise of 1 percent, the payment would be $958. This increase of $240 each month might be difficult for some families to manage, particularly if the family has variable interest rates on other types of loans, such as credit cards, auto loans, or a general line-of-credit debt. When market conditions cause the mortgage interest rate to rise, the rate on these other loans might increase as well, forcing the borrower to drastically curtail spending in other areas.

We will look at floating payment mortgage alternatives so that you can better understand what they could mean to you and your budget. First, we will consider the ARMs in detail, then graduated-payment mortgages, and finally the newer price level–adjusted mortgage.

Consumers can compare eight basic features of ARMs, all of which determine to what extent a monthly payment can change, how frequently the change can occur, and what total costs exist. Included are the following: (a) the index used to determine rate changes, (b) the frequency of the interest rate adjustment, (c) the payment adjustment period, (d) the amount of periodic rate change, (e) the maximum interest rate change permitted over the life of the loan, (f) restrictions regarding negative amortization, (g) "points," and (h) provisions for extending the term of the mortgage.

The first feature to compare is the *index used to determine the rate changes*. Lenders are required to use an index that is beyond their control, such as the rates paid on U.S. Treasury securities or the six-month Treasury Bill rate. If the index rises the lender can raise the interest rate on the loan. If the index drops, the lender *must* decrease the interest rate. A change in the interest rate affects the amount of money the borrower owes; therefore, the choice of index is critical. Borrowers should ask to see a ten-year history of the index used by the lender in order to estimate how the interest rate on the loan could change in the future. Short-term indexes tend to be more volatile, causing dramatic changes in a payment. The more volatile the indexes, such as the six-month Treasury Bill rate or the prime rate, the greater the potential for interest rate adjustment. Look for more stable indexes, such as the cost of funds index of the Federal Home Loan Bank Board (FHLBB).

A second feature is the *frequency of interest rate adjustment*. Some loans allow for adjustment annually, while a few feature monthly reviews. The *amount of periodic rate change* indicates how much the loan payment can rise in a review period (monthly or annually). Borrowers should look for a **periodic annual interest rate cap**, which limits the amount of annual increase. For example, a two-percentage-point annual rate cap would limit the interest rate to a 2 percent increase in one year. Borrowers also need to pay special attention to the maximum interest-rate change permitted over the life of the loan. An **overall interest rate cap** is required by the Competitive Equality Banking Act of 1987, but the federal regulation does not set limits on how high the ceiling can go. In many cases it might be wise to pass up a lower initial interest rate in order to get a better cap. For example with a 30-year ARM, the initial interest rate might be 9.75 percent with an annual adjustment and a 12.7 percent lifetime cap. Compare that to a loan with a 8.5 percent initial rate with an annual adjustment and a 14.5 percent lifetime cap. *Consumer Reports* conducted a survey and discovered that the average lifetime cap on ARMs was 6 percentage points, with an average annual cap of 2 percent (September 1988). Given this information, and all other factors being equal, the better choice of the two loans is the one with the lower overall interest cap. Remember that a rate cap is the main feature that holds the reins on the payment itself.

The *payment adjustment period* determines when the monthly payment is affected by all the changes. For most plans this occurs at the same time that the interest rate is adjusted. If however, the rate changes monthly but the payment is adjusted annually, borrowers would be making payments at the lower initial rate while the loan actually accrues interest at a higher rate. The additional interest is added to the loan balance, a practice which leads to **negative amortization**. If a loan is not fully amortizing, the monthly loan payment is not enough to pay off the loan in the specified time. Borrowers should look for *restrictions regarding negative amortization*. Upon sale of the house under negative amortization, a borrower may not be left with adequate funds for a down payment on a future home.

It is also important to compare the *points* being charged, since paying fewer points usually means paying more in interest, and since it is the combination of the dollar cost of points and the dollar costs of interest that give you the real cost of a loan. Be sure to verify the APR when comparison shopping. The final comparison feature is the *term of the mortgage*. As with other loans, the longer the term, the smaller the monthly payment but the greater the total cost.

One final word about ARMs: Some lenders offer the opportunity to convert from an adjustable rate to a fixed rate mortgage. The initial cost of this feature is an interest rate that is three-eighths to one-half a percentage point above an ARM that is not convertible. Again, you are betting against the lender that you can predict which direction interest rates will move. Many financial experts believe that the costs of convertibility are not worth the opportunity, and that it would be cheaper, if necessary, just to refinance the loan.

graduated-payment mortgage (GPM): a fixed-interest-rate loan for which monthly payments are low at first but increase each year for a stated time period, often causing negative amortization

A second type of floating payment mortgage is is the **graduated-payment mortgage (GPM)**. It features a fixed interest rate, and initial low monthly payments, which increase a specific amount each year for a stated time period, usually five to ten years. These loans are suitable for families whose income will rise steadily.

One disadvantage of GPMs is that a buyer pays more interest, because reducing the principal takes longer with smaller payments. At first glance, this may not matter to you if you do not plan to live in a home until the mortgage is paid off. But because the principal is not significantly reduced, your equity does not grow as quickly. And because of low payments in the early years, the principal may actually increase, causing negative amortization. All of this means you will get less cash when you sell, so you may not have enough for a down payment on your next house. It will, of course, depend on how quickly homes are appreciating in your area, as well as on the price of the next home you choose.

price-level adjusted mortgage (PLAM): a HUD program to aid in home purchasing, offering a mortgage with a very low initial interest rate; at specified times, the interest and payment do rise

In 1988 HUD initiated a loan program aimed at helping more people purchase homes. The new-style floating payment loan is called **price-level adjusted mortgage (PLAM)**. PLAMs begin with a very low initial interest rate, say 4 percent, at a time that fixed-rate loans are at 10 percent. This is possible because the rate does not include an inflation factor, just the cost of money to lenders. The lender recoups the cost of inflation in two ways: by increasing the loan balance through negative amortizations and by increasing the monthly payments as the loan matures.

For example, on a $100,000 mortgage the initial payments under a PLAM at 4 percent interest would begin at $477. (In comparison, payments on a fixed-rate loan would be about $878 if a 10 percent interest rate prevailed.) In five years, given a 6.5 percent annual inflation rate, the PLAM monthly payments would rise to $756. Simultaneously, the loan balance would rise to $144,000 resulting in negative amortization. After 15 years, the loan balance would begin to decline. Interest rate increases, and therefore payment increases, and indexed to the Consumer Price Index. This is a relatively volatile index, and the practice could cause payments to accelerate much faster in periods of rapid inflation.

Despite the volatility of the index and the negative amortization, PLAMs offer an alternative for young borrowers. PLAMS will be eligible for FHA mortgage insurance. The lower initial payments may allow homeownership to those who anticipate having an income that rises faster than inflation. However, anyone who chooses a PLAM needs to recognize the dangers of negative amortization and the possible lack of equity in the home.

Choosing a financing method. Choosing the mortgage or financing method you prefer is complex, because of the many options. Your choice of financing should be based on the willingness of a lender to offer the option, the monthly costs of the option, the total cost of the option, the prevailing rate and expected future interest rate, and your own goals.

To begin your decision making, be sure to compare the offerings of all types of lenders, such as savings and loan associations, banks, mortgage corporations, and credit unions. Find the best choice for fixed-rate mortgages in your area, and calculate your monthly payment. Then investigate the floating-rate mortgages available. With the lender's assistance, estimate how much the monthly payment would be during the second year, after the low introductory teaser rate expires. Could you afford the payment? How does it compare to the fixed-rate mortgage? Then, to avoid the basic pitfall of floating-rate loans, consider the worst scenario. That is, estimate the monthly payment if the mortgage rate were to climb to its highest point allowable. How would you manage to make the payment if that were to happen? Is the risk of losing your home and investment through foreclosure worth obligating yourself to a loan and a house that are too expensive for your budget?

Since 1988, the Federal Reserve Board requires lenders to provide potential borrowers with a 25-page booklet called *Consumer Handbook on Adjustable Rate Mortgages*, as well as a description of how your payments would have varied under historical interest rates and under a worst-case projection for the future. Use that information and this checklist to help you compare crucial features of loans:

1. The initial monthly payment and the highest monthly payment
2. The initial interest rate, cost of points, and the APR
3. How often the interest rate can change and what index is used to trigger these changes
4. The limits on interest rate changes
5. How often your monthly payment can change and how much notification you will be given
6. The limits, if any, on negative amortization
7. The term of the mortgage

Loan application. Once you have located the loan you want, you will be asked to supply personal information to prove that you are credit worthy. While you gather the data and they are being checked for accuracy, market conditions could change, causing interest rates to rise. To protect you from this, some lenders offer a lock-in, a guarantee that the mortgage terms will be available to you up to a specified period of time, say, 120 days. You can usually lock in both interest rate and points. A small fee may be charged for this service. However, if interest rates go down, you will still be charged the lock-in rate. If you decided on a lock-in, be sure to get all the terms of the mortgage and the lock-in in writing. Some lenders have been known to delay the loan-approval process, purposely allowing the grace period to expire, so many states have passed regulations prohibiting this practice. (Consult with your broker or the Board of Realtors regarding regulations in your state.) Also ask your lender for a copy of *A Consumer's Guide to Mortgage Lock-Ins*, prepared by the Federal Reserve Board.

In order to confirm your ability to make the mortgage payment, the lender will require bank account numbers, the address of your bank branch, your latest bank statement, recent pay stubs, and W-2 forms. Information about other debts, such as loan and credit card numbers, plus names and addresses of all creditors, must also be provided. The lender might also want evidence of your rental or current mortgage payments. In order to speed the loan-approval process, begin to gather this information as soon as possible and deliver it in a timely way to the lender.

Other financing. Although most people today use a fixed–interest rate loan or an ARM to finance housing, there are other alternatives. These include an assumable loan, sometimes used in conjunction with the buyer taking back a second mortgage, a shared equity loan, or a shared appreciation loan. We will briefly discuss each.

assumable loans: loans that transfer a mortgage and all its obligation from one person to another

An **assumable loan** is one that allows a new buyer to accept, or assume, all conditions and terms of the seller's mortgage note, including responsibility for its payment. This would be advantageous with a fixed–interest rate loan below market rates. Federal law allows lenders to make a mortgage nonassumable, so you will need to check with the seller's lender. If the loan is assumable, the lender may charge fees for credit check, processing, etc.

If a seller has accumulated a great deal of equity, the buyer may not have adequate down payment to make up the difference between the loan balance and the house price. A solution other than new financing is for the seller to *take back a second mortgage*. In this situation, the buyer makes a down payment, assumes the first loan, and accepts all of its terms and obligations. Then the seller lends the buyer the remaining balance. For example, say that the buyer agrees to pay $155,000 for the house and makes a down payment of $30,000. The seller's original loan was for $90,000 and is paid down to $85,000. The buyer still needs to finance $40,000.

Selling price	$155,000
minus down payment	−30,000
	125,000
minus assumable loan	−85,000
	40,000

The buyer and seller would establish mutually agreeable terms for the length of the loan, the interest rate, and therefore the monthly payment. This is attractive to sellers who do not need all the cash immediately from the house sale.

Two other ways to help prospective buyers include a shared-equity arrangement or a shared-appreciation mortgage. In a typical **shared-equity arrangement**, the buyer is paired with an investor, who provides the down payment. The buyer occupies the property and pays the mortgage, taxes, insurance, maintenance, and repairs. At some future point, the property is sold or refinanced, and the investor gets back the down payment money plus a share of any appreciation that has accrued. Tax deductions can be taken by the resident buyer or shared with the investor. With a **shared-appreciation mortgage (SAM)**, the lender or an investor provides a lower interest rate in return for sharing in the increase in value of the home when it is eventually sold or refinanced. It is particularly important that both parties get professional legal, tax, and real estate advice with these types of financing.

shared-appreciation mort-gages (SAMs): a mort-gage in which a lender pro-vides a lower interest in return for sharing in the in-creased value of a home when it is eventually sold or refinanced

Closing costs. Closing, or **settlement**, is the formal process by which ownership of real property transfers from seller to buyer. **Closing costs** for all services during this process are usually 3 to 4 percent of the total purchase price, and they are added to the down payment. In other words, you will need the amount of the closing costs in cash, besides the down payment. The 1976 revisions of the Real Estate Settlement Procedures Act (RESPA) require lenders to send you, within three business days after you apply for a loan, a booklet prepared by HUD that explains closing costs. Within the same period, the lender must provide you with a ''good faith'' written estimate of closings costs.

RESPA also requires the lender to identify any businesses or individuals from whom a buyer will be required to purchase services, such as appraisals or legal services. The law prohibits kickbacks, or ''under-the-table'' payments, from buyers or lenders to those involved in the real estate transaction (lenders, title insurers, or lawyers, for example). If the lender approves the loan, you must then be given a truth-in-lending statement that specifies the annual interest rate.

There are many fees that lenders charge to process or approve mortgage loans. A **title search** is usually required to review legal documents and public records to be sure no one else has a prior claim to the property. When a title search reveals that there are no prior claims to the property, usually title insurance is written to guarantee that if a flaw in the title is found later, the title company will defend the insured and pay all legal fees involved. Bear in mind that title insurance issued only to the lender does not protect the buyer. If you buy an owner's policy, it is usually much less expensive if it is purchased simultaneously with a lender policy, so ask the lender to include this. Other fees lenders charge include:

1. Loan origination fees—to cover the administrative cost of proces-sing the loan
2. Credit report fees—to show how the prospective borrower has handled other credit transactions (for instance, with credit cards or other loans)

3. Assumption fees — to pay for the costs of processing papers on a loan assumed by a new buyer
4. Appraisal fees — to pay for the costs of estimating the value of the house (paid by the buyer or the seller as specified in the sales contract)

A buyer may be required (on non-VA or non-FHA loans) to have mortgage or hazard insurance prepaid (for six months or one year) by the time of closing. Mortgage insurance protects the lender from loss caused by the borrower's default on payment of the loan. With conventional loans, this protection often allows the lender to permit a small down payment. It is not the same thing as mortgage life or disability insurance, which is designed to pay off a mortgage in the event of the physical disability or death of the borrower.

Hazard insurance protects the borrower and the lender against loss caused by fire, windstorm, and other natural hazards. It may be included in a homeowner's policy that insures against additional risks, such as personal liability and theft. However, hazard insurance or homeowner's policies might not protect the buyer against loss caused by flooding or earthquakes. In special flood-prone areas identified by HUD, a homeowner may be required by federal law to carry flood insurance on his or her home. Such insurance may be purchased at low, federally subsidized rates in participating communities under the National Flood Insurance Act. Earthquake insurance, on the other hand, is not subsidized but is available for those willing to pay the price.

Lenders use **escrow (impound) accounts** to hold funds in reserve to assure future payment for recurring items such as real estate taxes, mortgage or hazard insurance premiums, or annual assessments for municipal improvements like sidewalks and sewers. Homeowners' association fees might also be included. If an impound account is used, the total annual costs of the recurring expenses are prorated monthly by the lender and added to the monthly loan cost. The requirement for such an account may be negotiable, so feel free to discuss it with your lender. A few states require that this special account earn interest for the borrower, rather than for the lender. During the closing process, the buyer may need to make an initial deposit into this reserve account.

Box 11.6 provides a checklist of all the things that should be done before closing.

The closing process is the final step, and it is a simple one. Its purpose is to transfer the title, or ownership, from the seller to the buyer. A typical closing is a meeting between the buyer, the seller, a representative or agent for the lender, and a real estate broker. Here is the usual agenda:

1. The lender's agent will ask for the paid insurance policy (or binder) on the house.
2. The agent will list the adjustments (what is owed to the seller,

hazard insurance: insurance that is usually required for a mortgage; protects the borrower and the lender against loss from fire, windstorm, or other natural disasters

escrow (impound) accounts: accounts used by lenders to hold funds in reserve to ensure future payment for recurring items like real estate taxes and insurance premiums

BOX 11.6   WHAT TO DO BEFORE CLOSING: A CHECKLIST

1. Inspect the house one more time to make sure that everything is the way you expect it to be. If there has been any damage to the property, the seller must fix it before the closing. (Your purchase agreement should clearly state this.)
2. Make sure that the seller (and all his furnishings and trash) will be out of the house before your closing date. But remember, it is better not to let the house remain empty for too long.
3. Call your mover to confirm the moving date. Find out whether he needs a deposit, and make sure that you will have enough money to pay him.
4. Give your present landlord plenty of notice (at least 30 days).
5. Notify the gas, electric, phone, and fuel companies of your move so that they can shut off service in your present home and turn it on in your new one.

6. Check with the lender (or closing agent) to find out how much money you will need for closing costs. Federal law entitles you to know at least 24 hours before the closing what charges you will have to pay, including those that were not disclosed on your RESPA statement from the lender.

Be sure you have:

1. The right time, date, and place of the closing.
2. A paid insurance policy (or binder) for the house.
3. Receipts for other items you may have already paid for, such as the deposit on the house, mortgage application fees, and inspection fees.
4. Enough money in a certified check for all closing costs.

including the remainder of the down payment, prepaid taxes, and so forth, and what the seller owes the buyer, including unpaid taxes, prepaid rents, and so forth).
3. The buyer will sign the mortgage, or deed of trust (the legal document giving the lender the right to take back the property if the buyer fails to make his or her mortgage payments).
4. The buyer will also sign the mortgage note (the promise to repay the loan in regular monthly payments of a certain amount.)
5. The buyer will then be "loaned" the money to pay the seller for the house.
6. The title passes from the seller to the buyer, usually in the form of a deed (the document that transfers the title) signed by the seller.
7. The lender's agent will collect the closing costs from the buyer, usually in the form of a cashier's check, and will give the buyer a loan disclosure statement (a list of all the items the buyer has paid for).
8. The deed and mortgage will then be recorded (put on file) in the town or county registry of deeds.

THE FIFTH STEP: MOVING

Once you have selected a place to rent or purchase, you must prepare to move into it. Box 11.7 is a checklist of tasks that need to be done before

---

BOX 11.7 MOVING CHECKLIST

Have you:

1. Checked the condition of your new dwelling to make sure that all the previous resident's things are moved out and that it is swept and free of all trash (in the basement, the attic, and the yard)?
2. Given your landlord plenty of notice?
3. Cleaned your previous residence and had the landlord inspect it, if you were renting?
4. Returned your key to the landlord?
5. Arranged to get your security deposit back?
6. Notified all utility companies to shut off your present service and turn on service at the new address?
7. Notified your employer, the Department of Motor Vehicles, credit card companies, magazine companies, and so forth of your move?
8. Filled out change-of-address forms at the post office?
9. Notified your children's school or day care center?
10. Made arrangements for your children and pets during the move?
11. Checked with the moving company about the date of the move, the times of pickup and delivery, and the cost of the move (in a written estimate)?
12. Checked with the mover to make sure that all your belongings will be insured?
13. Checked with the rental company (if you plan to rent a truck or a van) about the date and the cost of the rental?
14. Arranged with family or friends to help you with the move?
15. Stocked up on plenty of boxes, cartons, rope, tape, and old newspapers?
16. Made a list of what items should be moved first (food, dishes, clothing, rugs) and where they should go in your new house?
17. Made a list of remaining items to be moved, boxed the items, and marked the contents on the boxes?
18. Made sure you have all the keys to your new house and that they work properly?

---

you move. Some, such as items 7 and 8, should be done as early as six weeks before the move.

If you have only a small number of possessions or if you are not moving too great a distance, you may find it more economical to rent a truck and move your things yourself. This is especially true if you have friends or family members to help you.

If you decide to hire a moving company, be aware that the federal government has specific requirements for movers:

1. The movers must come on the promised day. The company can be fined up to $500 if they fail to do so.
2. Price estimates must be based on the moving company's actual physical inspection of whatever you ask it to move.
3. Before moving day, a mover must give you an order for service that states the estimated price of the move and the mutually agreed on pickup and delivery dates.
4. Your property must be delivered and all services performed, with

charges due and payable on moving day no higher than the estimate plus 10 percent (because of an inaccurate estimate). You have 15 days to pay any amount over 110 percent of the written estimate.

5. The Interstate Commerce Commission (ICC) has established uniform charges for specific weights and mileage.

Do not postpone your move to the last minute. If you are rushed, possessions get damaged or broken, and people sometimes get hurt working too quickly. If you have decided to use a moving company, schedule it to come a few days before you must actually vacate. This allows for mistakes and emergencies. After all, you can get by without your furniture for a day or two.

To protect yourself when using a mover, be around during the loading and unloading of your goods. You should:

1. Make an inventory list of items to be moved.
2. Compare your inventory list with the mover's list of things loaded into the van to be sure nothing was left off the list.
3. Look at how the movers evaluate the condition of your furniture. Most movers use a code to indicate whether goods are scratched, marred, gouged, cracked, soiled, or whatever.
4. If you disagree with the evaluation of the condition, make sure it is changed. Because 25 percent of all moves end in a dispute over damages, this is important.
5. Observe the weighing of the empty truck and the loading, reweighing, and unloading of the truck to ensure that nothing is lost, stolen, or added to increase the loaded weight.
6. During the unloading, check off the items on your inventory sheet.
7. Do not sign the mover's inventory release sheet until you have had time to discover all possible damage or loss.

If damage or loss does occur, you will want to make a claim. If, after contacing the mover, you are not satisfied, call the nearest Interstate Commerce Commission office, listed in the telephone directory. If you are still not satisfied, you may want to go to small claims court (see Chapter 8).

THE SIXTH STEP: EVALUATING YOUR CHOICE

Your choice of whether to rent or buy depends on your values, goals, standards, budget, stage in the family life cycle, and economic conditions. Because these factors can change, you need to reevaluate your housing decision occasionally. We will briefly look at how economic conditions can affect your future decisions.

The demand for additional housing units is stronger than ever. Young adults now reaching the prime home-buying age of 25 to 40 compose an ever-increasing proportion of the population. A second group that affects the need for housing is composed of those aged 65 and over. Of the 20 million new households formed during the 1980s, more than 80 percent of them were single-person or two-person households. The shift toward smaller households increases the need for smaller housing units, particularly rentals. Providing suitable shelter for the unique needs and budgets of low-income households and smaller families is a major challenge in the 1990s. So what is your housing future?

Renting

Builders have shied away from construction of multifamily rental units in the past 15 years. The initial reason was the rising cost of construction. Changes in the tax laws in 1976 and again in 1986 reduced the tax deductions and diminished incentives to investing in rental housing. As indicated in Box 11.5, federal housing assistance was reduced by two-thirds in the 1980s. And in the next few years almost 2 million low-income rental units could convert to market-rate rentals. As a result, the supply of rental units is at a 40-year low, particularly for low-income households.

Renters will need to be clear about their rights and responsibilities as they face a national apartment vacancy rate (the amount of rental units empty at any one time) of 4.5—a figure that drops to 2 percent in major cities. As rents take an increasing portion of family budgets, renters may need to reevaluate their needs in relation to costs. Options to reduce costs include renting smaller spaces, sharing rentals with friends or family members, or returning to one's parents' home.

Buying

Homeowners of the 1990s will face rising interest rates and prices. They may have to wait longer than their parents did to purchase so that they can accumulate a down payment. They may need to choose smaller, less-luxurious housing that is more affordable. To reduce housing costs, for example, buyers might give up extra bedrooms, extra bathrooms, finished basements, and landscaping. Prospective buyers may need to be more flexible about their expectations and consider mobile homes and condominiums as well as traditional single-family homes. They may need to compromise on location, because the most affordable housing is often available in less-desirable neighborhoods or in distant suburbs.

Consumers should be alert to newer construction methods that can cut down expenses. One common cost cutter is building **modular homes**, which are made of factory-manufactured sections arranged in various ways on a permanent foundation on the building site. "Wet" modular units include plumbing, baths, heating, and kitchen equipment, and "dry" modular units include living, dining, and sleeping rooms. Using modular units saves one-third of the costs of traditional construction methods.

Buyers as well as renters should consider sharing their space with other individuals or family members. Part of the home could be rented, or two single individuals or families could buy the home jointly. Cooperation and flexibility of this sort allows needs and wants to be met despite economic restraints.

THE SEVENTH STEP: ACCEPTING RESPONSIBILITY

As with all decisions, a renter or a buyer has certain responsibilities. They include (a) keeping the property clean, (b) maintaining the property by making necessary repairs or by asking the landlord to do so, (c) refraining from causing damage to the property, and (d) making the rent or loan payment on time. By meeting these responsibilities, both renters and buyers can help keep down housing costs.

Doing maintenance and repair work oneself, rather than hiring someone to do it, can be a money saver for homeowners. Renters can offer to do such work in exchange for reduced rent. Before deciding to do it yourself, however, you should evaluate your skills, your abilities, and how much time the task will take in light of the cost of hiring a specialist. Owners who do repairs themselves save the labor cost of hiring someone else, and they also save income taxes on that money. For example, let us say that your home needs a new roof. You investigate and find that the average bid for the labor portion of the job is $3,000. How much do you have to earn to have $3,000 after taxes? That, of course, depends on what tax bracket you are in. If you are in the 28 percent tax bracket, you would have to earn about $3,840 (28 percent of $3,000 is $840) to pay for that labor. So you could spend your time working to earn $3,840, give $3,000 to the roofer for his or her labor, and give $840 to the federal government, or you could spend your time reroofing your house yourself and avoid paying the $840 to the Internal Revenue Service. Your decision should be based on how long it would take you to reroof the house, compared to the time it would take you to earn $3,840, the time necessary to develop your skill at that particular task, and which job (nonmarket production or labor-market production) you prefer.

Both the renter and the homeowner need to pay their monthly obligations on time, but the homeowner has additional responsibilities and opportunities. For the homeowner, earlier in this chapter, we described budgeting for fixed-rate and floating-rate loans. It is the homeowner's responsibility to be alert to fluctuations in the economy that could present budgeting opportunities or dilemmas. We have warned about the challenges of increased mortgage payments due to rising interest rates and the potential for negative amortization; now we will discuss a possible opportunity for homeowners.

If your income rises faster than inflation, and particularly if you have a fixed-rate loan, you might want to increase or accelerate your payments in order to build equity and decrease the amount of total interest paid on the loan. The procedures for doing this are based upon the fact that for the majority of the life of the mortgage, the lion's share of each monthly payment is going for interest, and only a fraction of it is going to reduce your principal. The procedure can be established formally, with a bi-weekly mortgage, or informally by the borrower. In either case, thousands of dollars in interest can be saved.

Say that you have a 30-year, $100,000 mortgage, with 10 percent rate. If the procedure you select is established formally using a biweekly mortgage, approximately $65,000 in interest payments would be eliminated. This is how it works: With a biweekly mortgage, the borrower would make half the normal monthly payment every other week (26 times a year). Regardless of which day of the week or week of the year you begin, this results in two extra half-month payments in each year. The extra payment money is used to reduce the principal, which pays off the loan sooner, in 21 years in our example above, generating the interest savings.

A second way to save is to make a larger mortgage payment each month than required, again applying the excess to reduce the principal. Ask your lender to show you a listing of payoff schedules, or consult *Consumer Guide to Mortgage Payments*. Find the table that lists the size of your mortgage (say, $100,000) and the interest rate (say, 10 percent). Then, instead of using the 30-year payoff schedule and monthly payment figure of $878, look at a 20-year payoff, or a 15-year payoff. Could you handle the extra $200 to $350 each month required for a speedy mortgage payoff? If so, ask your lender about the preferred way for you to pay the extra amount. That is, will the lender accept the surplus each month, or does the lender prefer that you accumulate a full extra payment first? In either case, be faithful to your plan.

After you have owned your home for some time you will more than likely have accumulated equity in your home, that is, the amount of money your home is worth minus the outstanding mortgage. This will make you eligible for a **home equity loan**. You will be besieged by enticing advertisements encouraging you to use your equity for emergencies, for travel, and for clothes. Should you take advantage of this opportunity? In the past few years many homeowners have used a home equity loan to pay off credit cards and other consumer debt, to finance automobiles and vacations, and to pay for home improvements. They have even used their home equity to secure a revolving-credit line which has a variable interest rate and where interest is only charged on the part of the principal borrowed. These loans are so popular because they are relatively inexpensive. Compare credit card rates of 18 percent and personal loans at 15 percent to home equity loans of 10 to 11 percent, and you see the advantage. A second advantage comes in the fact that, within certain limits, the interest you pay on a home equity loan can be deducted on your federal tax return. However, it is important to understand why the interest rates on home equity loans are so low.

Interest rates are based on the cost of the service and the risk involved. As you may recall from Chapter 6, any loan secured by a tangible asset, such as your home or car, represents a lower risk for the lender, since in case of default the asset can be sold to satisfy the debt. *It is crucial that homeowners understand that they could lose their home if they are not able to make payments on the home equity loan.* Therefore, the decision to use a home equity loan should be made after careful deliberation and for serious reasons such as meeting major medical expenses, remodeling the house, or paying for a college education. A home equity loan is inappropriate for frivolous purposes or for short-term spending, for example, on recreation and clothes.

Home equity loans come with fixed or variable interest rates. The former is the common, no-frills second mortgage, where the borrower is lent a lump sum that is repaid in fixed monthly installments. The variable- or adjustable-interest-rate loan is similar to an ARM but is more complex. Federal law does not require an annual cap on the variable interest rate. Although the law requires a lifetime cap, or ceiling, it does not specify a limit. As a result, some loans have a lifetime cap of 20 percent, obviously too high to provide any protection. The index used by many lenders is the 90-day Treasury bill rate, which is quite volatile, resulting in frequent adjustments. Some lenders use an index that is in exclusive control of the bank itself. All of these terms of the loan should be thoroughly scrutinized, and thanks to the Home Equity Loan Consumer Protection Act of 1988, terms must be clearly stated. Prior to the law, the quoted annual percentage rate sometimes excluded bank setup fees, which could be as high as $1,500, along with additional annual fees as high as $100; and ads stressed low temporary, introductory interest rates. Now if a low introductory, or teaser, rate is offered, all advertisements for the loan must state "with equal prominence" the annual percentage rate (APR) the borrower will pay in the absence of the temporary discount.

Home equity loans that feature revolving credit sometimes only require repayment of a small percentage of the amount borrowed, resulting in a loan balance that grows, rather than diminishes. When the loan term expires, the borrower faces a large balloon payment. Lacking the cash, the borrower will need to refinance or sell his or her house in order to pay off the loan. Clearly, this type of loan is not for the undisciplined.

SUMMARY

Whether one rents or buys a home, the decision is an important one. It is not made very often, so its consequences will be with one for quite a while. Renting requires a relatively small initial cash outlay, allows for mobility, and requires fewer responsibilities, but it does not provide tax deductions or equity. Buying can be a profitable financial investment that can provide feelings of pride and security, but it can also strain family budgets and restrict mobility and leisure. To decide which is best for you, clarify the needs and goals of all family members and evaluate them in terms of the family budget.

Renters and buyers will find housing options ranging from single-family homes to condominiums to manufactured housing. Whether renting or buying, it pays to investigate various locations and to inspect physical construction. Consumers should be aware that it is illegal to discriminate in renting or buying because of race, religion, sex, color, or national origin.

Renters need to know the rights and responsibilities that relate to rental agreements, deposits, and the implied warranty of habitability. Buyers have a more complex task: to understand how to shop for a home, negotiate a deal, select a mortgage, and close the sale. Moving involves choosing between doing the moving yourself or hiring a specialist.

The housing decisions that one makes represent a substantial portion of a family budget, perhaps 30 percent or more. They should be made carefully, following the decision-making model, reflecting one's values and standards and satisfying one's goals within the constraints of one's budget.

QUESTIONS

1. What purposes does housing serve for all families? What personal or individual needs might housing meet for you?
2. What alternatives to single-family houses exist in your community? What is your community doing in the areas of costruction methods and building codes to reduce the cost of housing?
3. Imagine that you are employed by a national firm that requires you to move every three years. Discuss the pros and cons of renting and of buying shelter under these circumstances. Consider also the pros and cons of purchasing a manufactured home under the same circumstances.
4. What specific characteristics of a particular location should be investigated when searching for a place to live?

5. What is an implied warranty of habitability? Of what use is it to consumers? How can it be enforced?
6. What specific information should be included in a purchase contract?
7. Define *mortgage note, principal, interest rate, amortization, prepayment penalty, loan assumption, closing, escrow (impound) account,* and *negative amortization.*
8. Describe why discount points are used and how they work.
9. What are the dangers of home equity loans? What is an appropriate use of them?
10. How would individual families be affected if homeowners could no longer deduct property taxes and mortgage interest from income taxes?

REFERENCES AND READINGS

"Banking: A Three Part Series." *Consumer Reports*, September 1988.

Bashinsky, Sloan. *Home Buyers: Lambs to the Slaughter?* Englewood Cliffs, N. J.: Prentice Hall, 1985.

Cooper, Mary H. "Suburban Homes" *Congressional Quarterly's Editorial Research Reports*, September 25, 1987.

Dolbeare, Cushing N. "Federal Housing Assistance: Who Needs It? Who Gets It?" A Policy Working Paper of the National League of Cities, 1986.

Dreier, Peter, Schwartz, David C., and Greiner, Ann. "What Every Business Can Do About Housing." *Harvard Business Review*, September–October 1988.

"Finding the Best Deals in Loans," *Consumer Reports*, September 1988.

Fleetwood, Blake, and Eichenwald, Kurt. "There's Nothing Liberal About Rent Control." *The Washington Monthly*, June 1986.

Giese, William. "How to Buy the House You Want." *Changing Times*, May 1988.

Klein, Robert J. "How to Hang on When Rates Rise." *Money*, October 1988.

Landers, Robert K. "Low-Income Housing." *Congressional Quarterly's Editorial Research Reports*, May 8, 1987.

Lown, Jean M. "Home Equity Loan: Mortgaging the Future?" *Journal of Home Economics*, Winter 1988.

National Association of Realtors. *Home Guide*, 1988.

Reder, Nancy. "The Search for Low-Cost Housing." *The National Voter*, August 1988.

Rothenbery, Henry H. *What You Should Know About Condominiums*. Radnor, Pa.: Chilton, 1974.

Schiffres, Manuel. "Personal Finance: Renting a Home May Be Wrong for You." *U.S. News & World Report*, March 10, 1986.

Scholen, Ken. *Home-made Money: Consumer's Guide to Home Equity Conversion*. American Association of Retired Persons (1901 K Street, N. W. Washington, D.C. 20049), 1987.

U.S. Department of Energy. "Tips for an Energy Efficient Apartment." Washington, D.C.: U.S. Government Printing Office, 1987.

U.S. Department of Housing and Urban Development. *Home Buyers' Information Package: A Guide for Buying and Owing a Home*. Washington, D.C.: U.S. Government Printing Office, 1979.

———. *Settlement Costs*. Consumer Information Center, Pueblo, Colo.: U.S. Government Printing Office, 1988.

U.S. Federal Reserve Board/Federal Home Loan Bank Board. *A Consumer's Guide to Mortgage Closings*. Consumer Information Center, Pueblo, Colo.: U.S. Government Printing Office, 1989.

———. *A Consumer's Guide to Mortgage Lock-Ins*. Consumer Information Center, Pueblo, Colo.: U.S. Government Printing Office, 1988.

———. *Consumer Handbook on Adjustable Rate Mortgages*. Consumer Information Center, Pueblo, Colo. 81002: U.S. Government Printing Office, 1988.

U.S. Federal Trade Commission. *How to Buy a Manufactured Home*. Consumer Information Center, Pueblo, Colo. 81002: U.S. Government Printing Office, 1986.

Chapter Twelve

THE AUTOMOBILE: WHEELS AND DEALS

☐ Basic Automobile Decisions
☐ The Costs of Automobile Ownership and Operation
☐ Shopping for a Car
☐ Automobile Repairs
☐ Automobile Insurance

DID YOU KNOW THAT ...

. . . with one phone call you can find out if your car has been the subject of a recall?

. . . the octane rating on a gasoline pump has nothing to do with how much energy the gasoline has or its quality?

. . . the price of extended service warranties includes very large sales commissions?

. . . it is a federal offense to tamper with an automobile's odometer?

. . . on an average day, Americans spend $55 million for automobile repairs that are unnecessary, faulty, or fraudulent?

. . . if you are a typical driver, you will be involved in two traffic accidents in the next eight years, and one of them will be your fault?

The automobile has become such an important part of our life-style that the make of car we choose to drive is a form of self-expression and status as well as a form of transportation. Try to imagine a Patrick Swayze look-alike telling his dancing partner that he drives a 1986 Yugo. But a car is more than a symbol; it is the most important form of private transportation in the United States. More than 87 percent of all American households own at least one car, many own two or more. Statistically, there is one car for every 1.8 of us. Compare this to the world average of 13 people per car. In a typical year, three times as many American households get new cars or pickup trucks delivered as have new babies.

Automobile-related expenditures also dominate personal budgets. An automobile is the second most expensive item an individual will ever purchase, ranking just below a house. And the purchase price of a car is just the beginning of your car expenses. The dollars you spend on fuel, general maintenance, repair, and insurance are all important expenses that continue as long as you own your car. Of course, these are not the only costs you bear as a car owner. In addition to these financial costs, car ownership saddles you with considerable time costs. Think of the time you lose looking for a parking space or trying to find a trustworthy mechanic.

Society as a whole also bears some of the cost of the care and feeding of your personal automobile. The air pollution your vehicle generates and the noise and traffic congestion produced by privately owned vehicles are just a few examples of the environmental costs we all bear because of the automobile. We will explore these society-wide costs in more detail in Chapter 13. This chapter is devoted to topics that help you in your role as an automobile consumer.

We begin this chapter with a discussion of your needs and consider various types of cars available, their characteristics, and how they might fit your needs. We then go on to explore the costs of ownership and operation. These costs far exceed monthly finance or leasing payments. Then we explore various shopping strategies and options, such as buying a used car or leasing a car rather than buying a new one. Regardless of the strategy you choose, you will need to know some of the information about auto repairs and warranties presented in the following sections. Finally, we look at the world of automobile insurance and its role in consumer affairs, and we offer some tips for getting better automboile insurance rates.

BASIC AUTOMOBILE DECISIONS

An automobile is a major consumer expenditure, and choosing one merits a greater degree of deliberation than does choosing a tube of toothpaste. Using a decision-making model like the one presented in Chapter 1 can help you avoid costly errors. This means taking some time to identify your reasons for getting a car. You will define the problem (step 1) by identifying

TABLE 12.1 Decision Matrix for Evaluating Auto Desirability

| | **Alternatives** | | | | | | |
Criteria	**New Car**	**Used Car**	**Lease**	**Buy**	**Subcompact Car**	**Midsize Car**	**Van**
Low initial cost	−	+	+	−	+	0	−
Low maintenance cost	+	−	+	−	+	0	−
Fuel economy	+	−	0	0	+	0	−
Comfort	+	−	0	0	−	+	0
Safety	+	0	0	0	−	0	+
Size	0	+	0	0	−	0	+
Multiuse	0	0	0	0	−	−	+
Reliability	+	−	0	0	0	0	0

your transportation needs. Maybe your old car needs some major repair work, or maybe your present car is not energy efficient and your gasoline bills are high. Or perhaps you are moving into a different stage in the life cycle and your present car is too big, too small, or too dumpy for your changing needs. Whatever the reasons, it is important to take some time to outline them.

There are many reasons for looking for another car, but their importance varies from one consumer to another, because no two consumers have identical values, goals, and standards (step 2). Table 12.1 lists some auto characteristics that could be important in an automobile consumer's decision-making process. Cost criteria, such as purchase price, mainte-nance costs and fuel economy, are listed along with comfort, safety, and reliability. The list is not exhaustive, but it should give you some idea of the considerations that affect a car-buying decision. The top row of the table lists various transportation alternatives. You could buy a used car, a new car, a large car, or a small car, or you could lease rather than buy. After establishing the relevant characteristics and alternatives, your next step is to collect information.

The information-gathering process (step 3) involves reading consumer and auto magazines, visiting car showrooms, and consulting knowledge-able people about their experience with particular cars or styles. These data can then be transformed into positive or negative reinforcements for choosing a particular alternative. In Table 12.1 a plus sign indicates an alternative has the positive characteristic listed at the left, a negative sign indicates that alternative does not have the characteristic, and a zero indicates that no definite judgment can be made. For example, the minus sign at the intersection of the "Low initial cost" and "New car" columns indicates that a new car does *not* have a low initial cost. The used car has a plus sign, which indicates that it is lower in cost than the other alternatives. The "Leasing" and "Subcompact cars" columns also have plus signs, because these alternatives are likely to involve low initial costs.

When you have filled in the table, you are ready for step 4, comparing the costs and benefits of the alternatives. Keep in mind that your evaluation is subjective and may not reflect another consumer's circumstances. For example, good fuel economy may not be as important to someone who drives infrequently as it is to someone who commutes 30 miles to work every day. Safety may be a more important issue to a carpool driver who takes young children to school than to a college student who skydives on weekends. The interior size of an automobile may be less important for someone living alone than for a big family or even for someone with a large pet.

When you have compared the costs and the benefits of various models and have seen how they stack up against your criteria, you are ready to make your decision (step 5). Recall from Chapter 1 that this is not the end of the decision-making process. You still must periodically review and evaluate your choice (step 6), and you must, of course, accept the responsibility for your action (step 7). But before you take the plunge, you ought to understand more about the basic costs of automobile ownership.

THE COSTS OF AUTOMOBILE OWNERSHIP AND OPERATION

As we mentioned earlier in this chapter, the decision to buy a car can be quite complex, and one consumer's rationale for buying might be quite different from another's. One person may be looking for basic transportation, whereas another wants considerably more than a good work car (perhaps he or she wants the car to reflect his or her personality or to project an image of prosperity). But regardless of whether one is looking for bare-bones economy or a car with "personality," a rational decision maker does not want to spend more than necessary. We have divided the expenses associated with automobile ownership into two basic kinds: fixed and variable. Both are important and should be estimated *before* you decide to purchase a car.

Fixed Costs

As you may recall from Chapter 4, **fixed costs** are expenses that do not change. They are costs that will be with you as long as you own your car, and they are not directly related to the number of miles you drive. They are the costs of ownership as opposed to the costs of driving. Fixed costs include depreciation, insurance, interest, taxes, and parking fees.

depreciation: (1) lessening of the value of a product because of age or use; (2) the decline in the market value of an asset

Depreciation. **Depreciation** is the loss in value of the vehicle during the time you own it. It can be measured by subtracting the current market value of your car from the purchase price. For example, if you paid $12,000 for your car three years ago and today you can sell it for $7,000, your car has depreciated $5,000. As soon as you drive a car out of a dealer's showroom, depreciation is at work, and it will, with few exceptions, continue to whittle away at the value of your car as long as you own it. Annual depreciation is most severe in the first year of ownership, when, according to the U.S. Department of Transportation, it equals about 25 percent of the purchase price.

Insurance costs. These costs are more closely related to the type of coverage you choose than to the number of miles traveled. We will explain this in more detail later in this chapter. In essence, buying auto insurance protects the consumer from having to pay the full cost of a variety of hazards that can befall an automobile owner.

Interest. Interest is another fixed cost that does not vary with the number of miles driven. If you choose to get a loan for your car, you will pay a finance charge each month for the privilege of using someone else's money. As we mentioned in Chapter 6, the size of this charge depends on the size of the loan, the length of the repayment period, and the interest rate. Table 12.2 illustrates some of the financing costs of car loans. If, for example, you borrow $10,000 and agree to repay it over five years in

TABLE 12.2 The Cost of Financing a Car

		Amount of the Loan					
		$8,000		**$10,000**			
APR	**Number of Months**	**Monthly Payment**	**Total Finance Cost**	**Monthly Payment**	**Total Finance Cost**	**Monthly Payment**	**Total Finance Cost**
10%	36	$258.14	$1,293.04	$322.68	$1,616.48	$387.21	$1,939.56
	48	202.91	1,739.68	253.63	2,174.24	304.36	2,609.28
	60	169.98	2,198.80	212.48	2,748.80	254.97	3,298.20
12%	36	265.72	1,565.92	332.15	1,957.40	398.58	2,348.88
	48	210.68	2,112.64	263.34	2,640.32	316.01	3,168.48
	60	177.96	2,677.60	222.45	3,347.00	266.94	4,016.40
15%	36	277.33	1,983.88	346.66	2,479.76	415.99	2,975.64
	48	222.65	2,687.20	278.31	3,358.88	333.97	4,030.56
	60	190.32	3,419.20	237.90	4,238.60	285.48	5,128.80
18%	36	289.21	2,411.56	361.52	3,014.72	433.83	3,617.64
	48	235.00	3,280.00	293.75	4,100.00	352.50	4,920.00
	60	203.14	4,188.40	253.93	5,235.80	304.72	6,282.96
22%	36	305.52	2,998.72	381.90	3,748.40	458.28	4,498.08
	48	252.04	4,097.92	315.06	5,122.88	378.07	6,147.36
	60	220.95	5,257.00	276.18	6,570.80	331.42	7,884.96

60 equal monthly installments at an APR of 10 percent, your monthly payment will be $212.48. This means that at the end of your payment period, you will have repaid the $10,000 plus $2,748.80 in finance charges. A 15 percent interest rate would raise finance costs on this loan to $4,238.60. If a difference of 5 percent in the APR can cost you almost $1,500, it pays to shop around for the lowest rate. So in addition to looking for the best car price, you should also look for the lowest-priced money. A review of loan sources discussed in Chapter 6 should help.

Worksheet 12.1 should also provide helpful information on the monthly cost of a loan. It will allow you to calculate your monthly payment for the most common auto loans. It also shows the monthly reduction in your car payment for each thousand-dollar increase in your down payment.

If you choose to pay cash for your car, there is still a cost: the interest you will lose by not leaving your money in a bank or in some other low-risk investment. This is the opportunity cost of paying for your car immediately. To calculate this cost, use the following formula:

$$V_f = V_p(1 + i)^n$$

where V_f = value of future savings

   V_p = value of present savings

   i = interest rate

   n = number of years

For example, $10,000 would grow to $12,624.76 if left in an account that paid 6 percent interest for four years:

$$V_f = \$10,000 \, (1 + 0.06)^4$$

$$V_f = \$10,000 \, (1.262476)$$

$$V_f = \$12,624.76$$

The interest on $10,000 would have amounted to $2,624.76 at the end of the four-year period ($12,264.76 − $10,000 = $2,624.76). If you compare the opportunity cost of using your money ($2,624.76) with the finance cost in Table 12.2, you will get a better idea which is cheaper. The finance charge on a $10,000 loan for four years at 15 percent interest is $3,358.88. This is more than your opportunity cost for lost interest on your savings in our example, which assumes you can get a 6 percent return on your savings. Thus, it is less expensive to use your own savings than to borrow. But if the interest on your savings declines, or if the dealer is offering loans with low finance charges, it may make better economic sense to borrow. The key is to compare your finance charge with the earnings on your savings, while you also keep in mind your personal ability to save.

WORKSHEET 12.1 FIGURING YOUR OWN CAR PAYMENT: MONTHLY COST PER $1,000 BORROWED FOR COMMON AUTO LOANS

APR	Length of Loan		
	3 years	4 years	5 years
5%	$29.98	$23.03	$18.88
6%	30.43	23.49	19.34
7%	30.88	23.95	19.81
8%	31.34	24.42	20.28
9%	31.80	24.89	20.76
10%	32.27	25.37	21.25
11%	32.74	25.85	21.75
12%	33.22	26.34	22.25
13%	33.70	26.83	22.76
14%	34.18	27.33	23.27
15%	34.67	27.84	23.79

blanks:

A. _(5 years)_____
B. _(10 percent)_____
C. _($15,000 ÷ 1000 = 15)_____

Now look at the table. Find the number in the 5 years column that is directly across on the 10% line; this is the cost per thousand dollars borrowed. In our example it equals $21.25. This means that for every thousand dollars you borrow at 10 percent interest for five years, you will pay $21.25 per month.

Now you are ready for the final step, calculating your total monthly payment. Multiply your cost per thousand dollars by 15. In our example:

$$15 \times \$21.25 = \$318.75$$

What would your payment have been for a three-year, 10 percent loan?

A. _____
B. _____
C. _____

The monthly payment would have been 15 × $32.27 = $484.05. Perhaps you now see why car loans are getting longer: to get the payment down to manageable size. But remember, nothing is free. If you stretch out your payments, your finance charges will be larger.

The table above can be helpful if you are planning to borrow money to buy a car. By using this table you can calculate your monthly payment, as long as you know three variables:

A. The length of the loan
B. The annual percentage rate of interest
C. The amount you wish to borrow, divided by 1,000

For example, let's suppose you wanted to borrow $15,000 and repay it in monthly installments over five years at 10 percent interest. Fill in the three

Taxes and licensing fees. These fees vary considerably among states, and they may include sales tax on the purchase, inspection and licensing fees, and property taxes.

Garage costs. These are simply the costs of parking. In a major urban area, garage fees can be a significant component of automobile ownership. In Manhattan for example, there are "car hops" who charge a monthly fee for finding safe street parking for cars. Why is this? Since urban mass transit is generally the most convenient way to get to work, a New Yorker's car often sits idle during most of the week, but street sweeping regulations often mandate that parked cars must be removed from certain residential streets during the day. So automobile owners often find it cheaper to pay car hops to move their vehicles during these times and thus avoid parking tickets and towing charges. These additional costs must be considered as part of the cost of ownership. They help explain why the car ownership rate for people living in Manhattan is only one-quarter of the national average.

Variable Costs

variable costs: expenses that vary directly with the amount of driving; the costs of operating a motor vehicle

Costs directly associated with the amount of driving are called **variable costs** (costs of operation). The two most significant costs in this category are those for maintenance and fuel.

Maintenance costs. These costs include everything from tune-ups and oil changes to replacing tires and paying for unexpected repairs. Paying attention to the owner's manual will reap dividends by getting better fuel economy and by helping to avoid major repair expenditures. Although most drivers know this, they seldom act on it. One study showed that fewer than one-third of all new-car buyers even bothered to read the manual, let alone follow the prescribed maintenance procedures. If you accept your responsibilities, you may well find that you will be like the car owners interviewed in *Money* magazine, all of whom went well over 100,000 miles in their cars. The one factor common to all of these car owners was not the type of car they owned or the kind of driving they did, but the fact they all met or exceeded the automobile manufacturers' maintenance requirements as stated in their owner's manual.

Fuel. Gasoline is a major expense for vehicles of all sizes, although the size and weight of the vehicle directly affects the cost of the fuel. It has been estimated that the difference in gasoline costs along between a full-size car and a subcompact amounts to $3,380 over the life of the two autos. One way to avoid some of the high cost of gasoline is to make sure that you do not buy a more expensive grade of gasoline than you need (see Box 12.1 for details on octane rating).

Evaluating Costs

Now you have a general idea about the kinds of costs involved in owning and driving a car. But before you can make a decision about buying or selling your car, you ought to have a more specific idea about costs. If you had to pay for each mile driven in your car, just as motorists pay for the right to drive on toll roads and turnpikes, how much would your car cost? Would 10 cents per mile be a reasonable estimate, or would the cost be 50 cents or more? Table 12.3 shows estimates of the costs per mile of owning

BOX 12.1 OCTANE RATINGS AND AUTOMOBILE
PERFORMANCE: DOES IT PAY TO BUY
PREMIUM GASOLINE?

Gasoline is a major expense, even for someone who owns a fuel-efficient automobile. But gasolines are not all the same. Some (the so-called premium gasolines) offer higher octane, whereas others have less octane and are called regular. There are no federal standards for the terms *premium* or *regular*. How do you know whether you are getting your money's worth? Should you buy higher-octane gas? Will you get better mileage?

First, you must understand that the octane rating of a gasoline is simply a measure of its resistance to engine knock. It is *not* a measure of power or quality. However, if your engine is designed for a higher-octane gasoline than you are now using, it will burn the gasoline unevenly and will thus be less efficient and less powerful. If a knock is loud and pesistent, it can severely damage your car's engine and require costly repairs. On the other hand, if you are using gasoline with too much octane, you are paying more than you need to.

Second, you should be aware that federal law requires all gasoline pumps to bear a bright yellow sticker showing the octane rating of the gas in each pump. With the help of this information you can save money, conserve energy, and protect your car's engine.

To determine whether your current gasoline has too much or too little octane, follow these steps:

1. Have your car tuned by a competent mechanic to exact factory specifications. Make sure that it is in good mechanical condition.

2. Wait until the gas is low; then fill up with regular. Drive a few miles until the engine is warmed up, come to a complete stop, then accelerate hard. If the engine knocks or pings on the gasoline with the recommended rating, use up the tank and refill with the next higher grade. Repeat the acceleration test. If the engine does not knock, this is the octane you need. If it does knock on this higher octane, see your mechanic. You have mechanical problems. If the engine does not knock or ping on the gasoline with the recommended octane rating, use up the tank and refill with the next lower grade, or octane. Repeat the acceleration test. If the engine knocks, the lower grade is inadequate for your car's needs. Go back to the higher octane. If the engine does not knock, you can probably use the lower grade safely.

and operating three types of vehicles that were purchased new and kept for four years while being driven 15,000 miles each year.

As you can see, the least expensive car to own is the compact model represented by a Ford Escort GL. It costs an average of 23.6 cents per mile to own if you keep it four years and average 15,000 miles of driving per year. A midsize vehicle like the Celebrity costs 28 cents per mile under similar conditions, while a full-size vehicle like a Chevrolet Caprice is the most expensive car to own, at 30.2 cents per mile.

Even though a large car costs 25 percent more to operate than a compact, is it irrational for consumers to buy large vehicles? Not necessarily. The benefits as well as the costs must enter into the decision. Some of the benefits of a large car are obvious, such as the passenger roominess and the

TABLE 12.3 Your Driving Costs

	1988 Ford Escort GL 4-cyl (114 CID) 4-door hatchback	1988 Chevrolet Celebrity 6-cyl (173 CID) 4-door sedan	1988 Chevrolet Caprice 6-cyl (262 CID) 4-door sedan	Average Cost
Variable Costs (per Mile)				
Gasoline and oil	4.0 cents	5.2 cents	5.7 cents	5.0 cents
Maintenance	1.4	1.6	1.7	1.6
Tires	0.7	0.8	0.9	0.8
	6.1 cents	7.6 cents	8.3 cents	7.4 cents
Fixed Costs ($ per Year)				
Insurance	$ 521	$ 573	$ 573	$ 556
License and taxes	110	139	144	131
Depreciation	1,568	1,784	1,982	1,778
Finance charge	427	565	577	523
Total fixed cost	$2,626	$3,061	$3,276	$2,988
Total Fixed and Variable Costs per Mile (Based on a 4-year/60,000-mile cycle)	23.6 cents	28.0 cents	30.2 cents	27.3 cents

SOURCE: American Automobile Association, *Your Driving Costs*, 1988 edition.

larger cargo area. Others, such as safety, are less obvious but could be very important. In a head-on collision between a Caprice and an Escort, the occupants of the larger car have a smaller risk of injury. And if you have ever carpooled or gone on a long vacation, you know that a larger car is usually more comfortable. But you must also consider the negative points

The size of your car is a matter of personal taste and income, but your decision also has an impact on others.

of a large car, such as finding a parking space and manuevering in traffic. You might also want to consider the greater environmental stress that a large car places on society in terms of pollution and energy use. All of these costs and benefits involve some subjective judgment that consumers must make based on their individual values and goals.

Once you have weighed the costs and benefits of alternative automobile models, you are ready to begin your search for a vehicle. In the sections that follow we explore ways of lowering your cost of transportation without diminishing your benefits. These topics include an application of the decision-making process to auto purchase as well as suggestions about finding a good mechanic and getting a better automobile insurance package.

SHOPPING FOR A CAR

The decision to buy a new car is rarely made solely because it would be cheaper to buy a new car than to buy a used one or to fix the one you already have. Depreciation on a new car in the first year alone will probably exceed the cost of repairs to any car with fewer than 100,000 miles on it. Nevertheless, in a typical year more than 10 million new cars are sold in the United States. Add to this the 17 million used cars that consumers purchase each year, and it is obvious that all consumers need to be better informed about the automobile selection process. In the following sections we review the three major choices: buying a new car, leasing a car, and buying a used car.

New-Car-Buying Strategies

Few experiences can be as traumatic as buying a new car. In most cases, there are only a few dealerships for any particular make, and their profit is directly related to the kind of bargain they can make with the consumer. There are various strategies that you should be aware of *before* you venture into the showroom full of sparkling clean, aromatic automobiles. Unfortunately, many consumers are unaware of these techniques and often wind up paying hundreds and perhaps thousands of dollars more than they have to for a car.

The first step in the buying process must involve a realistic assessment of what you are looking for in automotive transportation. Roominess, comfort, style, high performance, fuel economy, and reliability are only a few of the features to be considered. Obviously, there are trade-offs involved in getting a car that meets these standards. You may be forced to give up some acceleration performance in order to get better fuel economy. You may have to sacrifice style for roominess. These are decisions you should make well before you begin to talk seriously with an automobile salesman. If you don't, you may wind up with a car you never really wanted. If you are making a family decision, it is especially important that everyone involved have some input about these trade-offs.

Second, decide how much car you can afford. Place an upper limit on the monthly allocation for automotive needs that includes the monthly payment for a car loan and the costs of auto insurance, maintenance, parking, taxes, and gasoline. A general rule is that not more than 20 percent of your take-home pay should be devoted to transportation.

Third, get information about the types of cars you are considering. Much of this information can be obtained in consumer-oriented periodicals; for example, *Consumer Reports* publishes an annual *Buying Guide* issue and generally reports on all new cars in its April issue. Such periodicals describe and evaluate the newest models and report on the repair records of previous models. Another important piece of information is the wholesale price of the car, that is, the dealer cost. Newsstands generally carry several periodicals that list dealer costs for most models. If these are unavailable, you can generally estimate the dealer's cost by taking 12 percent off the manufacturer's sticker price. The average markup is a bit higher than this for larger cars and slightly lower for compacts, but this is a good general rule.

Given all of these information sources, it is little wonder that fewer than 10 percent of all new-car buyers actually pay the manufacturer's suggested price. So when the salesperson offers to lower the price, don't be surprised or feel any obligation. It is just good business.

Your homework assignment also includes finding out how much your present car is worth as a trade-in. Current used-car prices are published monthly in the *Official Used Car Guide* of the National Automobile Dealers Association (NADA) and in the *Kelley Blue Book Market Report*. Banks, credit unions, and libraries usually have the most recent issues. Ask to see them.

Two common practices you should be wary of when buying a new car are called low balling and high balling. When using the **low-ball technique**, a salesperson will quote a very low price on the car, perhaps 25 to 30 percent below the sticker price. But when you try to buy the car, you discover that the salesperson "made a mistake" and forgot to include some important costs. Or no mistake may be mentioned, but your trade-in car is appraised at half of its wholesale value. The **high-ball technique** is a deliberate overestimate of the value of your trade-in. You may get $500 to $1,000 over the wholesale value of your older car, but the dealer refuses to come down on the retail sticker price of the car or adds some extra charges into the final price. By obtaining good information and by knowing the wholesale value of your car and the dealer's cost of the model in question, you should be able to spot either of these techniques quickly.

Finally, as you saw in Table 12.2, interest rates can have a significant impact on the cost of financing an automobile. It is generally a good idea to

low-ball technique: *a sales strategy in which a salesperson quotes a low price for a new car and later discovers a "mistake" was made or simply offers a lower price on a trade-in*

high-ball technique: *a sales stategy in which a salesperson deliberately overestimates the value of a potential buyer's old car in order to make a sale and then overcharges for the new car*

shop for credit *before* you shop for a car. This allows you to determine the price of the car separately from the price of the financing. Auto dealers sometimes earn a significant return by getting their customers to use a particular finance company or bank. In essence, the dealer earns a fee for bringing in business. Having your financing arranged in advance also saves you the trouble of filling out the forms in the dealer showroom. These forms can provide the dealer with information that makes it more difficult for you to get the dealer to give you a discount from the sticker price. For example, if you live near a dealership, you might prefer to buy the car there rather than across town. If you fill out a credit application, the dealer will know where you live and may not offer you a price as low as would be offered to someone who lives farther away.

Now you are ready to enter the battleground—the dealer's showroom. Steel yourself against the urge to buy a car on the first visit. Take a test drive. Ask about the warranty. Get a feel for the car, and then leave. Look at the competing models and visit other dealerships before you decide to bargain. If you like a particular model but seem unable to strike a good price, consider purchasing its corporate twin. The Sable, sold by Mercury dealers, is essentially the same car as the Ford Taurus. The same is true for the Dodge Caravan and the Plymouth Voyager, as well as many models in the General Motors Buick, Chevrolet, Pontiac, and Oldsmobile divisions.

You may be unable or unwilling to bargain with your local new-car dealer. This should not deter you from looking over the cars and taking a test drive. You only need to indicate to the salesperson that you are considering a purchase but are not going to decide today. Then you can go to a car-buying service to complete the purchase. Some credit unions or automobile clubs like the American Automobile Association (AAA) can help you to get in touch with one of these services. Such services normally have agreements with one or two dealers of every automobile make sold in your area. For a fee, which varies from $150 to $500, the buying service will see that you get the car of your choice at factory cost. The factory warranties and even the rebates will be the same as if you had purchased the car directly from the dealer.

Leasing a New Car

Some consumers do not buy new cars; they rent them. This may not seem unusual; most of us know of two or three major car rental companies. But instead of renting cars for a day or a week, these consumers are now renting cars for up to five years. This rental arrangement, called a *lease*, has a number of advantages. First, a leased car is easier to obtain, partly because the buyer puts down a smaller amount of cash and partly because rules for computing a customer's financial eligibility are less strict. For example, a family could lease three cars, whereas it could only qualify to borrow enough money to buy one. Second, the leasing company may provide repairs and upkeep all in one neat package. Under such a "full-maintenance agreement," the driver need not make any outlay for the car other than the lease price and the cost of gasoline and oil. This means that the driver can budget exactly for the cost of driving. Finally, if the car is used for business purposes, leasing a car greatly simplifies record keeping for tax purposes. One simply adds up monthly leasing bills. Of course, the costs of using a personal car for business are also deductible, but figuring some of these expenses (especially depreciation) can be complex. If the car is used for business one-third of the time, it is easy to justify one-third of the leasing cost as a business expense, but it is more difficult to argue that one-third of the depreciation was related to business driving.

Of course, there are also disadvantages to leasing. Generally, there is a limit on the number of miles you are allowed to put on the car. There is also a penalty for ending the lease early. You are also responsible for the condition and maintenance of the vehicle. Any damage beyond normal wear and tear can be added to your bill. Even if the contract is fulfilled, you still do not own anything of value. Finally, if you choose to lease a new car rather than buy it, you are not protected by your state's **lemon laws**, which pertain to consumers who buy new cars that turn out to have serious, unrepairable defects, i.e., cars known commonly as lemons. In only 16 of the 43 states that have passed lemon laws do those laws apply to leased vehicles (*Consumer Reports*, 1988a.)

An open-end lease. In one type of lease, called the **open-end lease**, you are obligated to buy the car at the end of the lease period for a depreciated amount, the **residual value**. An advertisement might offer a brand new pickup truck for only $95.99 per month. The fine print must mention the length of the lease period, say 60 months, and the residual value ($1,812.42 in a recent ad). Some ads also mention a "capital-cost reduction payment" or "drive-off fee" ($1,690.00 in the pickup ad). This payment is often the equivalent of a down payment. It is included to allow the dealership to advertise a lower monthly lease price. The higher the drive-off fee, the lower the monthly payment. Some unscrupulous dealers have been known to advertise ridiculously low monthly payments just to get consumers into the showroom. When questioned about this, they simply point to their high drive-off fee.

Generally, the leasing company agrees to sell the car for the lessee if he or she decides not to pay the residual amount on an open-end lease. However, if it cannot get someone to pay this amount, then the consumer must come up with the difference. So, in addition to monthly payments, the consumer may have a large balloon payment at the end of the contract. In most cases, however, the Consumer Leasing Act of 1976 limits this end-of-lease payment to no more than three times the monthly lease amount. Of course, it is also conceivable that the car will be worth more

lemon laws: legislation, such as the Magnuson Moss Warranty Act of 1975, that is intended to help consumers who purchase new automobiles that are poorly built and need constant repairs

open-end lease: A conditional sales contract in which the consumer leases a car for a set period of time. At the end of the lease the consumer agrees either to buy the car outright or to pay the leasing company the difference between the actual market value of the car and the resale value that was stipulated in the original contract. If the resale value was overestimated, the consumer will have to make a large final payment.

than the anticipated residual value. In this case, a consumer with an open-end lease will actually get to keep the difference.

closed-end lease: an agreement to pay a monthly rental fee for a set period of time, usually 12 to 24 months; at the end of the lease the product is returned to the lessor

A closed-end lease. In the most common type of lease, called a **closed-end lease**, you pay a flat fee every month and then return the car at the end of the lease period. You owe nothing more as long as you have not damaged the car, or driven it more than the number of miles specified in the lease. This lease is generally a more expensive plan because the dealer assumes the risk associated with the depreciation of the car. If a car depreciates more rapidly than expected, it is the dealer who must take on this additional burden.

The decision to lease rather than buy should not be made before the costs and benefits of each are weighed. If you prefer not to argue with dealers over the price of a new car, and if you prefer to *know* how much car maintenance will cost, a closed-end, full-maintenance lease could be the best option. And with a closed-end lease, you don't have to worry about the residual-value problem of open-end leases. Of course, a closed-end, full-maintenance lease is also the most expensive monthly lease. Eliminating the full-maintenance lease will lower your cost, and opting for an open-end lease will lower your lease price, because you share some of the repair and depreciation risk. It's true that no matter what kind of lease you choose, you will still never "own" the car. If you buy a car and then hold onto it, you will be free of payments at about the same time that some long-term personal leases are up. If you hold a typical new car for ten years, you might be able to save enough in the nonpayment years to pay cash for your next car.

Buying a Used Car

Three out of every four cars sold for personal driving are used cars. In a typical year Americans spend about $85 billion to buy more than 17 million used cars (Federal Trade Commission, 1985). To understand why business is booming in the used-car industry, all you have to do is to walk into a new-car showroom and look at the sticker prices. In 1981, the average price of a new car broke the $10,000 mark for the first time, and prices have not fallen since then. Used cars have one major advantage over new cars: They are cheaper. Depreciation has taken its toll, and the changes in style may have further eroded the market value of older vehicles. In other words, you may be able to get more transportation value for your money from an older car. But there is always some risk.

There are four major outlets for used cars: new-car dealers, used-car dealers, rental car companies, and private owners.

Franchised new-car dealers. New-car dealers generally sell only the most marketable, late-model cars that they take in on trades. They have a service facility for repairing and maintaining cars, and they often provide a written guarantee that the used car will be free from defects for a specific time period or for a certain number of miles. This guarantee is called a **limited warranty**. New-car dealers will take your old car in trade (which is convenient for you), but you will probably net less money than if you sold it yourself. Given the kinds of cars and services offered at new-car dealerships, it is understandable that they sell almost 50 percent of all used cars, but they usually charge the highest price, too.

Used-car dealerships. Used-car dealers often have lower-priced cars on their lots, but they usually do not have their own service facilities, and they seldom sell cars that they take in trade. They buy their cars at wholesale auctions, sometimes in different states, or they purchase them from other dealers or fleet owners. They have been known to buy cars that will not pass inspection in one state and sell them in another that has different inspection laws. Taxis, police cars, and other late-model, high-mileage fleet vehicles often appear on these lots. In the past, some dealers rolled back odometers on high-mileage cars to make them appear less used. This happens less today, because it is a federal offense (see Box 12.2).

Rental cars as used cars. A small but growing segment of the used-car market involves purchases from large fleet owners, such as rental-car companies. In major cities, Hertz, Avis, Budget, and others are beginning to sell their cars directly to the public. They often provide some type of warranty, and you can usually see the maintenance record of any car you are considering—two advantages that few used-car dealers offer. But you

---

BOX 12.2   THE ODOMETER LAW

Federal law makes it illegal to do anything that would cause a vehicle's odometer to show the wrong mileage. No one, not even the vehicle's owner, is permitted to disconnect the odometer (except to perform necessary repairs). Federal law also requires that anyone who sells a vehicle or transfers ownership in some other way must provide the buyer with a signed statement indicating the mileage registered on the odometer at the time of the transfer. If the seller knows that the registered mileage is incorrect because the odometer was broken or previously tampered with, he or she must include a statement to that effect on the mileage disclosure form. When you purchase a vehicle, be certain that you receive a mileage disclosure statement before the transfer of title. Anyone who illegally tampers with an odometer or fails to provide the required mileage disclosure statement may be sued in a private civil action by the person wronged by the violation. A successful suit allows the plaintiff to recover $1,500 or three times the actual damages, whichever is greater. If you suspect an odometer has been tampered with, call the National Highway Traffic Safety Administration, 1–202–724–0670, or the Department of Justice, 1–202–724–6786.

will also get a car that has had 80 to 100 different drivers who had no vested interest in treating the car with care. These cars also have more miles on them than comparable cars owned by individuals, but many of these miles may have been relatively less demanding highway miles, rather than the strenuous stop-and-go traffic miles that wear out an engine faster. Selection is also more limited in the fleet-owner outlet, and fleet owners will not accept your old car in trade. Despite these drawbacks, the good reputation of the companies and the availability of a warranty and a maintenance record make this option worth consideration.

The private seller. This is the smallest segment of the used car market, accounting for about 20 percent of all vehicles. It is also the least regulated part of the market since private sellers are less likely to be prosecuted for violations of federal or state laws that were designed to protect consumers from shady businesses. When you deal with a private party, you are buying from another consumer, not from a business. Nevertheless, it is an important market to consider both when you are looking to buy a car, and when you are deciding whether to sell your car yourself.

If you buy from a private party, you should be able to negotiate a lower price than a dealer would charge for the same vehicle. After all, you are giving up some of the protection of the law and some of the convenience of shopping where they have a large selection. The average markup from the wholesale price on a used car is 22 percent, but it can be as high as 50 percent if the car is transported long distances or sold by one dealer to another. Use the same procedure we suggested earlier to find the value of a given used car—look at the *NADA Used Car Guide* or the *Kelley Blue Book* for help in appraising the list price of a given make and model. Scan the classified ads in your local newspaper, too, for the average price of a particular car model and year. Used-car prices rise in the spring and early summer as people begin to think about taking vacations and as the weather makes used-car buying less difficult. This means you should time your activity whenever possible. November is a good month to buy used cars, and spring and early summer are good times to sell.

Information and decision making in the used-car market. No matter which outlet you choose to buy from, there is always some risk involved in buying a used car. You could make the wrong decision and wind up with a lemon instead of the peach you thought you were getting. One way to lessen your risk is by obtaining information about the car you are considering. The FTC now requires all used-car dealers to place a large **buyer's guide window sticker** in the window of each vehicle they offer for sale. This sticker gives information concerning the type of warranty on the car and lists some of the major problems that may occur with any car. A more comprehensive FTC window sticker program was overruled by Congress in 1982.

More helpful information to get before buying a car includes evidence of the reliability of the car, proof of servicing, mechanics' records, and the like. Rental-car companies and private sellers will probably have such servicing records, and you should certainly ask for them. This kind of information will support assertions like "I just had the brakes relined" or "I just had the engine rebuilt" or "I always take the car in for servicing." In addition, records give you an idea of the costs of maintaining the car. These costs can be expected to rise as the car ages. Finally, general information about the frequency of repair records for most used cars can be found in the annual *Buying Guide* published by Consumers Union. The data in this publication are gathered from surveys of its members. These responses are then summarized by model and year. By looking up the record of a given used-car model, you can discover trouble spots to investigate before you buy, and you will have some indication of the reliability of the model you are considering.

In addition to seeking information, there are a number of general rules to follow when you are in the used-car market:

1. Never buy a car at night or when it is raining. Both conditions can obscure defects in the car and make it appear to be better maintained.

2. Avoid buying an "orphan," that is, a car that is no longer in production. Parts for such cars may be expensive and hard to get.

3. Be wary of used cars that are loaded with options such as power windows, power seats, power antennas, and the like. Cars seldom age gracefully, and they are less likely to do so if they are filled with technological contraptions that are waiting to cause trouble.

4. Never buy a car without taking it for a test drive. This should include some hard acceleration, emergency stops, and parking.

5. If you think you have found the car you want, have your mechanic look it over. A $50 investment may save you from making a much more costly error.

6. Check for recalls. Many vehicles have defects that are discovered after the cars are sold to the public. The owners of these cars are notified by the automobile company that their cars are being recalled and that the defect will be fixed at no charge. Since 1966 there have been 3,000 recalls involving 80 million vehicles, but not all of those recalled have been repaired. For example, in 1987 the National Highway Traffic Safety Administration (NHTSA) announced 175 recalls involving more than 8 million cars. According to Diane Steed, NHTSA administrator, only 54 percent of those cars were returned to dealerships for the necessary repairs (Gillis, 1988). While this may seem like a good record, it means that 46 percent of those recalled vehicles were *not* fixed. This makes it all the

more important to check for recalls on any used car you are considering purchasing. If you suspect a safety-related defect, phone the National Highway Traffic Safety hotline at 1–800–424–9393.

AUTOMOBILE REPAIRS

A recent study by Consumer and Corporate Affairs Canada found that of 24 potential areas of shopping problems, getting an automobile repaired was the area of most difficulty. When asked to indicate the problems encountered in getting their cars serviced or repaired, the respondents identified a bewildering array of 170 specific complaints that the authors of the study collected into six major problem areas:

- Lack of integrity on the part of repair shop
- Lack of competent mechanical service
- Failure to honor appointments and estimates
- Lack of personal concern for customers
- Inadequate warranties and guarantees
- Poor product design

These Canadian studies confirm reports by the NHTSA that 40 percent of the $50 billion spent each year on automobile repairs and service in the United States goes for shabby or unnecessary work. In this section, we cover some of the major factors involved in getting your car repaired: warranty coverage, service contracts, and selecting a mechanic.

Automobile Warranties

warranty: an assurance given by the seller that a product is in good working order and will provide good service for a period of time

secret warranty: extended protection sometimes provided, but not made public, by a manufacturer when a particular problem habitually develops in a specific model beyond the limited warranty period

According to Murphy's law, "If anything can go wrong, it will, and generally at the worst possible moment." Automobile breakdowns certainly follow this general principle. However, a knowledgeable consumer can be prepared and thus lessen the impact of these annoying incidents. This means knowing one's rights and responsibilities concerning the automobile. Research indicates that consumers are largely ignorant about warranties. And if your car breaks down, it may be important to understand just what your warranty covers.

As explained in Chapter 8, a **warranty** is an assurance that a product is in working order and will give good service for a reasonable period of time. If properly understood, a warranty can save thousands of dollars in repairs.

One type of warranty that has only recently come to light is the so-called **secret warranty**. This is a form of extended protection that is sometimes provided by the manufacturer when a particular problem habitually develops beyond the limited warranty period. It should not be confused with a recall, in which all owners are notified of a particular defect and are invited to have it repaired at an authorized dealer's expense. A secret warranty is never announced publicly; only the local dealers are notified, and then, at their discretion, repairs are made.

The Center for Automotive Safety, for example, uncovered a secret warranty program covering cracks in the floor pans on 1.2 million Mustangs and Mercury Capris built from 1979 to 1983. Under this plan, favored customers (or those who complained about the problem) had their floor pans repaired at no cost. But not all Ford owners were notified. It has been reported that General Motors has a similar program to repair power-steering problems in front-wheel-drive Chevrolets and Buicks from 1982 to 1984 (White, 1987).

Ford and General Motors have established a rather cumbersome procedure for assisting consumers in uncovering these secret warranties. You can call Ford (1–800–241–FORD) or GM (1–800–551–4123) on a toll-free complaint line and ask for their index of service bulletins. They will send you the index and you can check it to see if any of them apply to your car. If they do, you can write for the specific service bulletins you need, but there is a charge for each bulletin. Then, armed with a service bulletin from the manufacturer, you can march into your dealership and demand that they fix the defect. Sometimes they will.

Enforcing warranty rights. According to Clarence Ditlow, head of the Center for Auto Safety, ''There are two types of consumers who have a better than average chance in pressing their warranty claims. The first is the long-time customer of one dealership; the second is the obnoxious consumer.'' If you are a price-conscious consumer, you probably won't fall into the first category, so you may have to learn to be obnoxious. But you also need to follow the rules of the game.

In order to get the best results, you must keep good records and discuss your complaint with the dealer first. In many cases this will result in a satisfactory solution. If it does not, then call the manufacturer's representative in your area; the phone number should be in your owner's manual. If you are still unsatisfied, call corporate headquarters and ask for customer service. This exhausts your in-house complaint possibilities, but other remedies are available. There are more than 20 national Consumer Action Panels (Auto CAPs) for automobile problems. These panels help resolve disputes between consumers and the auto industry. After receiving your complaint, they will ask the manufacturer to reinvestigate the problem and report on the action taken. If the dispute still exists, they will sponsor a hearing and make a recommendation. Although the recommendation is not legally binding, most auto companies will follow it.

Forty-three states have passed **lemon laws** that cover buyers of new cars. According to most state laws, a new car is considered a ''lemon'' if it has been taken into the dealer for the repair of the same problem four times without success during the first year or 12,000 miles of service. The

BOX 12.3 LEMON AID

"I bought a lemon." This statement seldom refers to fruit; generally, it refers to a poorly made automobile that is continually breaking down. If you buy a lemon and cannot get satisfaction from the dealer or the auto maker, you can still do quite a bit before you have to hire a lawyer and go to court. The Maine Bureau of Consumer Protection has published the *Down-Easters Lemon Guide*, from which this list was adapted:

1. By law, all new cars have an implied warranty to provide safe, efficient, trouble-free transportation.

2. If something is wrong with your new car, you must give the dealer a reasonable number of chances to repair it.

3. If the dealer will not or cannot fix the defect within a reasonable time, and further, if the defect substantially impairs the car's value, you have a right to get a replacement or a refund. (Note: The problem must be major, not just a rattle or a clock that keeps poor time.)

4. To get a replacement or a refund, you must give the lemon back to the dealer. This procedure is called revocation of acceptance. This should include giving the dealer some reasons in writing and indicating that you are canceling your insurance and registration.

5. Do not forget to contact your lender and inform him or her of the situation and where the car may be found. You may wish to "play it safe" and continue to make payments to avoid the possibility of being sued for the outstanding debt balance.

6. This bold maneuver will generally result in a successful settlement. But if it does not, let the dealer know that you plan to hire an attorney. In most cases of this sort, the dealer or manufacturer will have to pay your attorney fees as part of the settlement.

If you do need an attorney, the *Lemon Guide* has a special section on law citations and the legal background of successful suits in which lemon victims got their money and expenses back. For $1.50, you can get the publication from the Maine Bureau of Consumer Protection, Augusta ME 04333. There is no charge for Maine residents.

prescribed remedy for a lemon is either another new car or a refund of the purchase price. If your state has not enacted such legislation, Box 12.3 may give you some ideas for additional sources of help.

Auto Service Contracts

A common practice among new-car and used-car dealers today is to offer the buyer a service contract that is sometimes called an **extended warranty plan**. As they often say, "For only a few pennies a day, you can have peace of mind." Recent estimates indicate that 67 percent of all new-car buyers purchase this additional protection against having to make automobile repairs. Are these consumers making a wise decision?

First, you should understand that there is a major difference between a warranty and a service contract. A warranty is provided by the manufacturer or seller at no extra cost. A **service contract** is an agreement in which the buyer agrees to pay a certain fee to a service contractor (who may be the auto manufacturer, the dealer, or some independent firm), who in turn agrees to maintain or repair the car for a given period of time. The service contract is purchased separately from the car, and you don't have to buy it from the dealer.

Second, you should be alerted to the fact that the price of the service contract is a negotiable item. This fact was revealed in a recent dispute between Nissan Motor Company and Adesco, the firm that provides Nissan's new-car dealers with extended service contracts. According to Adesco, only $131, or 16 percent of the $795 price for a typical Nissan Security-Plus extended warranty plan, goes to Adesco to pay for repairs. Nissan gets a $60 kickback and the dealer receives $555 as a commission for selling the extended warranty. Given the large dealer commission, you could very likely negotiate a reduced price for the service contract. (White, 1988).

If you decide to consider an extended service contract, you would do well to get answers to the following questions:

1. *Are there additional costs?* Even after you have negotiated the selling price, you may have other expenses. Service contracts, like insurance policies, often ask you to pay part of the cost of any problem that develops. Some contracts ask you to pay a fee for each unrelated repair, and some contracts ask for one fee each visit for all repairs. Frequently, contracts limit the amount paid for towing or rental-car expenses. You may also have to pay cancellation or transfer fees if you sell your car or wish to end the contract.

2. *What does the contract cover?* A service contract may cover repairs on all parts of your car or only major mechanical repairs. (For example, the car engine may be covered for major repairs, but you may have to pay for gaskets and seals.) Some contracts also pay for maintenance, towing, and rental-car expenses. Contracts may offer different coverage for different parts. Do not assume that something is covered if it is not written into the contract.

3. *What will my service contract give me that my warranty will not?* On a new car, your warranty coverage and your service contract coverage may overlap for a year or so. If they do, compare the coverages and decide whether you can justify the additional expenses for the added coverage you get from having a service contract.

4. *How will my repair bills be paid?* Your service contract company may pay the selling dealer or mechanic directly, or you may have to pay for the work and ask the service-contract company for reimbursement.

5. *Where can my car be serviced locally? What happens when I am traveling or when I move?* Under most service contracts, your car can be serviced only by the selling dealership. In some contracts, you may use any mechanic you choose. Manufacturers have dealerships nationwide, and service is available if you travel or move. Some service-contract companies

and dealers offer nationwide service, so you will get service if you travel or move. Other companies give you service only in a specific geographical area.

6. *What special requirements do I have to meet?* Some service contracts require you to use a certain brand of motor oil when you have your car serviced, or they may require you to get your car serviced at specific intervals.

Selecting a Mechanic

The average automobile consists of more than 15,000 parts, so it's understandable if you feel ill prepared to make an informed decision on your auto-repair problem. But even if you have the world's best automobile, you will eventually have to bring it in for repairs and servicing. When you do, you will face the problem of finding a good mechanic. Given the ratio of automobiles to mechanics in the United States (about 150 to 1), it is no surprise that you often have to schedule your appointment

As cars become more complex, regular maintenance becomes more important and often more expensive.

well in advance if you expect high-quality performance. Just as you wouldn't want a poorly trained doctor caring for your family, so, too, you wouldn't want an inept or unprincipled mechanic taking care of your car. The tight supply of mechanics compared to the demand for them makes it easier to understand why Americans spend so much on automobile repairs and servicing. The mystique that surrounds the servicing of a car (the strange-sounding names like "universal joint" and the odd procedures like "repacking the wheel bearings") leaves consumers easy prey to unscrupulous or incompetent mechanics. The $20 billion estimate cited earlier for unncecessary, faulty, or fraudulent auto repairs amounts to $55 million per day. To help avoid these unnecessary expenditures, you ought to spend some time selecting your repair shop.

Automobile repair shops come in all shapes and sizes, from the one-mechanic garage to the service station to the mass-marketing franchise shop, such as Tuneup Masters or Aamco, to department store auto-service departments, such as those in Sears stores. With such an array of sellers, it is often difficult to choose one (Watt, 1988). But there are some guidelines to follow:

1. Avoid garages that are located near highways and oriented toward transient business. These shops have the worst record for fraud, for a good reason: They expect their customers never to come back.

2. Find a local garage, especially one in which you can actually talk to the mechanic who is working on your car. Look for a mechanic who is familiar with your kind of car. This can be especially important if you have a foreign car. Ask friends or acquaintances who own similar cars to recommend someone.

3. Always get a written estimate for the repair work before anyone begins working on your car. After the work is completed, the mechanic should give you a detailed invoice of all work done and parts supplied. If the mechanic is unwilling or unable to do so, go somewhere else.

4. Ask if the mechanic has passed any of the voluntary testing programs. The most common are the tests administered by the National Institute of Automotive Service Excellence (NIASE).

5. Consider learning to do simple repairs and servicing yourself, possibly by taking a course in the fundamentals of auto repair. By being your own minor mechanic, you will save some money and learn more about how your car operates.

You can also provide yourself with some "consumer insurance" by paying for the work with a bank credit card like VISA or MasterCard. It will take about 30 days for this charge to show up on your statement, and in the meantime you will have an opportunity to see whether the repair was successful. If you are dissatisfied, you can return to the mechanic for an explanation. If you are still not satisfied, you can inform your bankcard company of the disagreement, and it will disallow the charge. As noted in Chapter 6, this is part of your consumer protection built into the Fair Credit Billing Act. Of course, the mechanic can challenge you in court, but the chances of your being troubled by a lawsuit are very slim if you are honestly dissatisfied with the repairs.

AUTOMOBILE INSURANCE

In a typical year there are more than 2 million traffic accidents in the United States. This means that we average one motor vehicle accident every 15 seconds. The odds are very good that you will be involved in an accident that ranges in severity from a fender-bender to a multiple-car collision in the next four years. The average motorist is involved in two accidents every eight years, and is judged to be at fault for one of them. With these kinds of odds, all drivers need some type of automobile insurance. In the sections that follow, we outline the basic insurance package and how to shop for it. We conclude with some ideas about no-fault insurance.

The Basic Insurance Package

Automobile insurance is just another form of **insurance**, which can be defined as an agreement between a consumer and an insurance firm, in which the consumer gives up a small fixed amount of money today in order to be protected from a potentially greater loss in the future.

Not all states require automobile insurance, but they all require that operators of motor vehicles be financially responsible for any damage that may be done by their vechicles. If you are involved in an accident in which someone is injured or in which there is significant property damage, you will be required to demonstrate that you are able to pay for a minimum

Tow trucks are a familiar sight for most of us. If recent trends continue, the average driver can expect to be involved in two auto accidents every eight years and be declared "at fault" for one of them.

level of damages. If you cannot, your driver's license will be suspended. For most people, financial responsibility is assured by having an automobile insurance policy. There are six forms of insurance in all insurance packages:

1. Bodily injury
2. Property damage
3. Collision
4. Comprehensive physical damage
5. Medical
6. Uninsured motorist

liability insurance: insurance that covers drivers for accidental damage to other persons and their property when drivers are judged to be at fault

Liability insurance. The first two categories are sometimes referred to as **liability insurance** because they are invoked only if the insured person is judged to be responsible (that is, liable) for the accident. The amount of the driver's liability is potentially unlimited, because he or she can be sued for any amount of money. But the amount that the insurance company is willing to pay is limited by the size of the protection stated on the insurance policy. You will frequently hear about or see figures like $100,000/$300,000 (simply, 100/300). These are the limits of the insurance company's guarantees in the event that you have an accident for which you are to blame. In the case of a 15/30 policy, the insurance company agrees to pay a maximum of $15,000 for a bodily injury claim to any person you may have hurt, provided the injury claims for all people who have been hurt do not exceed the $30,000 limit established under that policy. A 100/300 policy increases those limits to $100,000 for each person and $300,000 for the entire claim. If you have a 15/30 policy, have an accident that is your fault, and get claims of $50,000 against you, you are stuck with a $20,000 bill, even after the insurance company pays its share. Given the size of today's lawsuits, a 15/30 policy is hardly adequate, and yet it is the amount that most states accept as proof of financial responsibility.

Property damage liability insurance is always sold in the same package as bodily injury insurance, and it is only paid if the policyholder is judged to be at fault. It is invoked when the policyholder's car damages someone else's property, generally, another car, although it covers all property, including houses, telephone poles, shrubbery, and bicycles. The limit of this portion of an auto insurance policy varies depending on the desired level of protection, but $10,000 to $50,000 limits are most common. If you add a $10,000 property damage policy to your 15/30 bodily injury coverage, you will get a 15/30/10 policy. But if you are at all aware of the cost of repairs these days, you can easily see how a $10,000 property damage policy is hardly enough to protect you against someone else's claims. It is quite conceivable that a multiple-car collision could result in three or four times that amount of physical damage. And if you happen to hit a Porsche, your $10,000 property damage insurance will not help much.

Collision insurance. While liability insurance covers injuries and damages to other people, you may also need insurance to cover your personal losses and damages to your car. **Collision insurance** protects you when your car is damaged in an accident with another car or with an object like a tree or a telephone pole. The amount of this coverage is limited by the value of your car at the time of the accident. Because liability is not the most important question in such cases, your insurance company will generally appraise the damages and send you a check for the necessary repairs without regard to who was at fault. If another driver was involved and was judged to be at fault, your insurance company will collect from that driver.

collision insurance: insurance that covers the insured driver's car in the event of an accident

Another important provision of most collision insurance is the amount of damage that the policyholder is willing to pay for before the insurance company begins paying the claim. This is called the **deductible** amount, and it commonly varies from zero to $500. If you have collision coverage with a $100 deductible clause and you do $500 worth of damage to your car by backing it into a tree, the insurance company will only pay $400 to repair the damage, because the first $100 is deductible. The insured person's agreeing to assume some of the insurance risk is called **co-insurance**, and it is common to many types of insurance policies, such as health insurance and homeowner's insurance. The more the risk (and thus the larger the deductible), the lower the premium. A higher deductible amount reduces the number of small claims that must be processed by insurance companies, and part of the resulting reduction in administration is passed along to the consumer in the form of lower payments. Many insurance companies refuse to write zero-deductible policies, and even if they do, most insurance experts do not view zero deductible as a good deal (see Box 12.4). If your collision damage was someone else's fault, your insurance company will reimburse you for the deductible amount once it collects from the guilty party.

co-insurance: an insurance plan in which part of the loss is covered by the insured person; by agreeing to deduct some of the loss from the claim, the insured party can generally get a lower insurance rate

Collision insurance is optional. There are no state laws that require you to replace or repair your own car, but if you borrow money to buy a car, the lender generally requires collision insurance as a condition of the loan. In your decision-making process about whether or not to buy collision coverages, you have to weigh the costs of the coverage against the benefits. Many consumers misunderstand the benefits of collision coverage and the obligations of the insurance company. If you are involved in an accident and you have collision coverage, the insurance company is required only to restore your automobile to its previous condition; is is not required to buy a new car if your five-year-old Chevrolet is totaled in an accident. The collision insurance simply covers the average value of a five-year-old

BOX 12.4   HOW LARGE A DEDUCTIBLE?

You can reduce your automobile insurance premiums significantly by increasing the deductible, that is, the set amount of loss that you will pay before the insurance company has to honor its obligations. But how much should your deductible be? There are several alternatives for calculating this amount.

Some insurance experts recommend that the deductible amount equal about 5 percent of the value of the car. Thus, if a car is worth $10,000, a $500 deductible is about right under the 5 percent rule. These experts argue that the $100 deductible policies are a vestige of the past, when new cars cost about $2,000. Other experts recommend that the deductible equal one week's pay. This rule is probably better, because it more clearly reflects the size of the loss that could be absorbed. Thus, if you earn $20,000 a year, a $400 deductible would be appropriate. A third possibility uses a "payback method." This payback method focuses more

clearly on the costs and benefits of increasing the deductible. Ask your insurance agent how much the cost of an insurance premium would fall if you raised the deductible limit. This is a benefit. Divide this benefit into the proposed change in the deductible amount to see how many years it would take for you to accumulate the difference and in effect, insure yourself. For example, if you currently pay $300 for collision coverage with a $100 deductible amount and your premium would be reduced by $25 annually if you raised the deductible to $200, you would get a payback in four years:

$$\frac{\text{change in deductible}}{\text{reduction in premium}} = \frac{\$100}{\$25} = 4 \text{ years}$$

If you figure that you will not have a claim for the next four years, raising the deductible will save you money.

Chevrolet. As a general rule, it costs four times as much to repair a car as it does to build it from scratch. Thus, if 30 percent of your car is damaged, it is probably cheaper for the insurance company to pay you the estimated value of the car rather than to pay more to have it fixed. Given the rapid rate at which an automobile depreciates, the cost of collision insurance quickly exceeds the benefits. Once your car is worth less than (i.e., could be replaced for) $1,000, most experts agree that you should stop paying for collision coverage.

comprehensive insurance: insurance that protects the insured person's car against hazards other than collision with other automobiles; this generally includes protection against fire, theft, and vandalism, among others

Comprehensive physical damage insurance. Comprehensive insurance is also optional, but insurance companies frequently require you to purchase collision insurance before you are allowed to buy comprehensive insurance. This coverage provides protection against most hazards other than those from collision, including theft, fire, natural disasters, and vandalism. The insurance company may require a deductible of $50 or $100. If a deductible clause is not required, you may want to take it anyway to get lower rates.

Medical insurance. Medical insurance covers any medical expenses incurred as a result of a automobile accident, and it covers all members of the policyholder's immediate family, in the family car, in someone else's car, or as pedestrians. This policy also covers all other passengers in the insured vehicle. Coverage varies from $2,000 to $10,000, and payments are made regardless of who is at fault. If you already have good medical insurance, such coverage may be redundant for your family, but, of course, it need not be so for your passengers. Because the cost of such coverage is generally small, most drivers purchase medical insurance.

Uninsured motorist bodily injury insurance. What happens if you are injured by a hit-and-run driver or by someone who has no insurance? To protect yourself, you can get **uninsured motorist insurance** for yourself (the policyholder) and all family members, whether in someone else's car, in the insured automobile, or simply as an unlucky pedestrian. Such coverage is generally sold in amounts equal to the minimum financial responsibility laws of the state. In essence, uninsured motorist insurance sets up bodily injury liability insurance for the other party in case you are involved in an accident in which he or she is at fault but has no insurance and cannot pay. Suppose, for example, that you are driving through an intersection, and Frank, an uninsured motorist, runs the red light and hits your car, injuring you and your daughter. Because Frank has no insurance, your uninsured motorist coverage will pay for all your medical bills and for any additional claims that result from injury to you or to your daughter. If you are unable to work for two weeks, for example, you would be reimbursed by this coverage. Uninsured motorist insurance does not cover damage to your car, however; collision insurance covers that. And uninsured motorist insurance is limited to some amount usually equal to the minimum financial responsibility laws of the state.

Looking for Auto Insurance

Now that you understand the fundamentals of automobile insurance, you know what to look for in a policy. It may surprise you to learn that according to most surveys, only about one out of every four consumers shops around for auto insurance. Many people probably believe that the rates of various companies are all about the same, because companies are all regulated by the state. But in this case, state regulation does not mean uniform pricing. In a sample of 11 insurance companies in the Los Angeles area, the California Department of Insurance found that the average car owner can save between $100 and $400 per year by comparison shopping. Use Worksheet 12.2 to assist you in comparison shopping.

Before you go shopping, however, you would do well to consider your individual needs and to set some limits on the amount of coverage you want. The most important step is to determine how much liability insurance you need. In most cases, insurance experts recommend that

WORKSHEET 12.2 COMPARISON OF AUTO INSURANCE PRICES

Type of Insurance	Amount of Coverage	Company Name or Agent	
		Insurer 1	Insurer 2
Bodily injury liability (per person or accident)	_____	_____	_____
Property damage liability (per accident)	_____	_____	_____
Collision			
$100 deductible		_____	_____
$500 deductible		_____	_____
Comprehensive			
$100 deductible		_____	_____
$500 deductible		_____	_____
Medical (per accident)	_____	_____	_____
Uninsured motorist (per person or accident)	_____	_____	_____
Cost per year with $100 deductible		_____	_____
Cost per year with $500 deductible		_____	_____

As noted in the text, you must consider your own needs in establishing the insurance coverage you want. For this worksheet, however, we suggest you begin with the $100,000/$300,000 limits for bodily injury; $50,000 for property damage; $10,000 for medical payments; and the $15,000/$30,000 limits for uninsured motorist protection.

consumers opt for higher-coverage rather than the lower-coverage policies. Increasing liability coverage from 15/30/5 to 100/300/50 will cost only a few dollars more, and the extra security is generally worth the extra cost (*Consumer Reports*, 1988b).

Once you decide how much liability protection to buy, you must next decide whether to purchase collision and comprehensive insurance. If you get a loan to finance a car, you will not have the option to refuse these coverages. Creditors require this insurance as a condition of the loan.

As far as medical insurance and uninsured motorist protection are concerned, it is generally best to settle on a minimal but adequate amount of coverage and to get quotations from various insurers with this amount in mind. If you already have good medical coverage, you might consider omitting medical insurance from the agreement. But if you are part of a car pool, you should get medical coverage.

Most insurance agents are like other salespeople: They want to get your business. If they have to, they will offer you the best deal possible. You can help yourself by knowing what questions to ask and by demonstrating that you are a price-conscious consumer. In order to save yourself valuable time, first contact the insurance agent by telephone, telling the type of coverage you want and the model and year of the car you wish to insure. Keep the following tips in mind:

1. *Co-insurance means less costly insurance premiums.* If you are willing to accept a higher deductible amount on collision and comprehensive insurance, you will get a lower price. Ask about the rates for different levels of co-insurance.

2. *If you cannot afford the coverage you want, consider trading your collision and comprehensive coverage for better liability protection.* Remember, even if your car is stolen and never recovered, the cost to you will be only a few thousand dollars. On the other hand, if you get stuck with a large lawsuit, the cost could be hundreds of thousands of dollars. For example, if you were to do without collision coverage and were in an automobile accident that totally destroyed your 1987 Ford Mustang, the most you would lose would be a few thousand dollars. If the other motorist were at fault, his or her company would have to pay that sum. If you were to do without liability protection or were to buy a minimum ($30,000) policy and you permanently disabled someone in an accident that was your fault, you could face a $200,000 lawsuit. Which is potentially more damaging to your future, the loss of a car or the loss of $200,000?

3. *Look for discounts.* Some insurers provide discounts to nondrinkers, nonsmokers, people who have had driver training or have good driving records, and car-poolers. Sometimes, good students and small-car owners can also get discounts. The idea behind discounts (besides their being a sales gimmick) is that people with these characteristics tend to have fewer accidents and are better insurance risks. Nondrinkers never have their abilities impaired by alcohol, and nonsmokers do not take their eyes off the road to look for cigarettes or to light up on their way home.

4. *Consider insuring your car on your parents' insurance policy.* It is often cheaper to add another car to an established policy than to buy a new policy. This is especially true for young drivers who do not have established driving records. In 45 states—Hawaii, Massachusetts, Michigan, Montana, and North Carolina excepted—insurance companies can use sex and age as measure of risk. If a young male shares the driving of a car with a parent, insurance rates may drop 30 percent (*Changing Times*, 1988b).

5. *Drive the right car.* Insurance companies keep records of the claims they pay on different makes and models of vehicles. For example, State Farm Insurance reduced premiums on its policies on 1988 Toyota Tercel

station wagon based on their lower-than-average claims records but increased premiums on the Toyota Corolla GTS based on claims experience (*Consumer Reports*, 1988b). You can get information on different models by writing to the Insurance Institute for Highway Safety, Publications Department, Watergate 600, Suite 300, Washington, DC 20037.

6. *Don't get speeding tickets.* In other words, obey the law. Traffic citations make it more difficult to change insurance companies and more expensive to stay with a given company, because citations indicate a high-risk driver. If you cannot switch companies, your ability to comparison shop will be extremely limited.

7. *Never allow your current auto insurance coverage to lapse until you have an agreement with another company.* Insurers are skeptical of accepting a new driver who does not currently have an auto insurance policy. This means that your shopping should begin two or three months before your policy expires.

8. *Avoid duplication of coverage.* For example, if you already belong to an auto club, don't buy towing insurance. If your existing health insurance is adequate and you don't car-pool, you don't need medical coverage.

9. *Pay annually.* Many insurance companies have a variety of payment plans, but if you can pay once a year, you will avoid extra finance and handling charges. In addition, you will avoid the six-month rate hikes that can occur with shorter policies.

10. *Do not drive to work.* If your car is used only for pleasure and not to commute to work, you can save substantially. Bicycling, using mass transit, and ridesharing offer great promise in reducing insurance costs. If you can cut your weekly commuting distance to less than 30 miles roundtrip, you can save 10 to 25 percent on your insurance premium.

Even though you have obtained price quotations from various insurance agents, your task is still not complete. You must consider three other factors: ease of claim settlement, company cancellation policies, and the financial reliability of the company. No company enjoys paying claims, but some are more difficult to deal with than others. Check the most recent issue of the *Consumer Reports Buying Guide* for its recommendations of companies that settle claims easily, and talk to the agent about the process . You should also inquire about a company's cancellation policy. If a company makes no pledge about renewing a policy, you could wind up paying higher premiums in the future while you cast about, looking for another insurer. Finally, you should consult *Best's Insurance Reports* (available in your library) for information about the financial conditions of various insurance companies. Nothing would be more upsetting than to find yourself insured by a company that could not meet its obligations to you in the event of a major accident. In short, you must weigh the quality of the insurer, as well as the quality of the insurance offered.

No-Fault Insurance

When consumers buy insurance policies, most of them realize that a portion of their premium pays for expenses other than claims. Sales commissions to insurance agents is one obvious expense. But most consumers do not know the extent to which expenses other than claims payments eat into their insurance dollar. Less than half, and in some cases less than a third, of every premium dollar finds its way back to a claimant. This low payout ratio is partly caused by the expenses of elaborate trial procedures and other legal expenses associated with arguing in court over who was at fault and how much the injured party should receive. In an effort to limit this cost, some states have instituted a plan called no-fault insurance that applies to the bodily injury liability section of auto insurance policies.

no-fault insurance: an insurance system in which the injured parties collect from their own companies, regardless of who is at fault

No-fault insurance is a system of insurance that allows the injured parties to collect directly from their own insurance companies regardless of who is to blame for the accident. Instead of spending weeks and sometimes years trying to determine who bumped whom, the injured parties are reimbursed by their own companies within a few days for medical care and lost wages. It is still possible to go to court if large judgments against the offending party seem warranted, but claims below a stipulated amount, or "threshold level," are normally settled quickly, without an elaborate courtroom battle. By avoiding protracted litigation, insurance companies should be able to provide better claims service at lower cost. At least that is the theory behind the movement toward no-fault auto insurance.

Currently, almost half of the states have enacted some form of no-fault insurance (see Figure 12.1), but the results seem to depend on whom

FIGURE 12.1
Twenty-two states and Puerto Rico and the District of Columbia have no-fault auto insurance: Arkansas, Colorado, Connecticut, Delaware, Florida, Georgia, Hawaii, Kansas, Kentucky, Maryland, Massachusetts, Michigan, Minnesota, New Jersey, New York, North Dakota, Oregon, Pennsylvania, South Carolina, Texas, Utah, and Washington.
(SOURCE: *Motorland*, July/August 1988.)

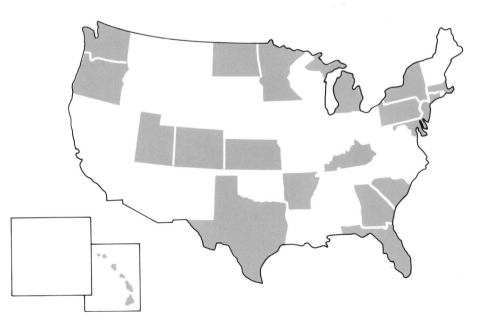

you ask. The American Trial Lawyers Association sees no-fault as a disaster. It argues that everyone deserves compensation from the person responsible for an injury, so no-fault is unfair. Other observers believe that lawyers oppose no-fault insurance because it tends to decrease the number of lawsuits and thus results in lower demand for lawyers' services (*Changing Times*, 1989).

In states where no-fault has not been successful, the problems seem to involve the size of the threshold level that triggers court cases. No-fault procedures are no longer followed once the threshold level is reached, and a low threshold level leads to most injury cases being treated in the traditional "fault system." In Nevada, for example, where the threshold level was set low ($750), the no-fault system never had a fair chance to operate. Things became so chaotic that the state legislature actually repealed the no-fault law and went back to the fault system. In New Jersey, the original no-fault law was simply grafted onto the existing system. It allowed people to sue if their damages exceeded $200. Thus, people involved in accidents in New Jersey had unlimited medical benefits plus the right to sue for additional compensation for what turned out to be very minor injuries. This system has given New Jersey the worst of both worlds, and the highest auto insurance premiums in the country (*Consumer Reports*, 1988b).

In states in which the threshold level was set higher, most impartial observers argue that no-fault insurance has resulted in lower premiums and better service. In Massachusetts, for example, during the first four years of no-fault operation, the cost of liability insurance dropped by more than one-third. In Michigan, no-fault insurance has been praised for reducing spending on court costs and attorney fees to only 4 cents of every premium dollar, compared to a national average of 32 cents. The Michigan system has also reduced claim settlement time from 16 months to less than 30 days. These impressive results could be duplicated in other states.

The drive to create a nationwide no-fault insurance law seems to have been replaced by a movement to increase public regulation of the insurance industry. Californians passed an initiative (Proposition 103) in the 1988 elections that called for an immediate rollback of auto insurance rates and a repeal of standard rate-setting techniques (based, for example, on age, sex, and urban residence) and required the popular election of a state insurance commissioner to enforce these new regulations. The insurance industry spent millions of dollars on a campaign to defeat this law and pass a version of no-fault insurance, but Ralph Nader's support for Prop 103 played a major role in defeating the insurance initiative. At this time, the future direction of auto insurance legislation is uncertain, but it clearly will remain a controversial area in consumer studies for the next few years.

SUMMARY

In the United States, dependence on automobiles is a way of life. Consumers are more likely to drive a car than they are to exercise their right to vote. Getting from place to place has become so important to most of us that we might add transportation costs to the traditional list of necessities like food, clothing, and shelter. In fact, we spent more on our automobiles than on our clothing. We have become so used to the automobile that we almost take these expenditures for granted, as a fact of life.

In this chapter we have emphasized that automobile expenditures should be subject to the same decision-making process as other important expenses, and that there are many areas in which wise decision making can lead to greater satisfaction and also save money. The major areas of decision making are identifying the kind of car desired, evaluating the costs of ownership and operation, shopping for a car, getting auto repairs, and shopping for automobile insurance.

Consumers should outline the major qualities they want in a car and then compare various options so that they can select the car that suits them best. The costs of an automobile can be divided into the costs of ownership (fixed costs) and the costs of operation (variable costs). Depreciation is one of the most important of the fixed costs, and it falls most heavily on consumers who buy new cars and trade them frequently. The cost of financing a car is another fixed cost, and it may be just as economical to borrow money to buy the car as it is to pay cash, as long as the opportunity cost of using one's own money is included. Gasoline and oil are the most expensive variable costs, but they vary depending on the size and the gas mileage of the vehicle: A new full-size car driven for four years and 60,000 miles costs its owner an average of 30.2 cents per mile; a compact costs an average of 23.6 cents per mile driven.

Used cars are an important alternative to new cars. Almost three-quarters of all cars purchased per year in the United States are used. Leasing is another alternative that has grown in importance as the prices of new cars rise. Leases come in many varieties, and consumers should understand all the terms before choosing this option.

Whether consumers buy new or used cars or even undertake lease plans, they should understand warranty rights. They should also learn how to find a good mechanic, since 40 percent of all auto-repair work is estimated to be unnecessary, poorly done, or outright fraudulent.

Automobile insurance is the final area in which consumers should know their rights and compare prices. By raising deductible limits and by increasing liability insurance coverage, consumers can generally improve their protection without paying more.

QUESTIONS

1. Explain why the automobile has become such an important component of the American life-style.
2. What are the two major kinds of costs of owning an automobile? Give two examples of each.
3. Discuss how consumers can lower their per-mile costs of driving.
4. How can you estimate the dealer cost for most new car models? How can you estimate the value of the car you own? How does this information help in buying a new car?
5. What are the advantages and disadvantages of leasing a new automobile? Do these depend on the kind of lease you get? Explain.
6. What are the four major outlets for used cars? Which is generally the most expensive? Which is the riskiest?
7. Summarize the guidelines that consumers should follow when they find that they have purchased a lemon.
8. What are the six essential elements in all auto insurance packages?
9. Explain the difference between liability insurance and collision insurance.
10. What part of your insurance package is most affected by no-fault, as opposed to fault, insurance? What are the advantages and disadvantages of the no-fault system?

REFERENCES AND READINGS

"A Breakdown in Auto Safety." *Consumer Reports*, February 1989.

"Buying a Used Car." *Facts for Consumers from the Federal Trade Commission*. May 1985.

"The Compelling Case for No-fault Insurance." *Changing Times*, July 1989.

Crandall, Robert, et al. *Regulating the Automobile*. Washington D.C.: The Brookings Institution, 1986.

Federal Trade Commission. *A Consumer Guide to Vehicle Leasing*. Washington, D.C.: U.S. Government Printing Office, May 1985.

Gillis, Jack. "Special Report: Warranty Wars." *Consumers Digest*, May/June 1988.

———. *The Car Book*. New York: Harper & Row, 1986.

"Need for No-Fault." *Motorland*, July/August 1988.

"New Car Buying Guide." *Facts for Consumers from the Federal Trade Commission*, February 1988.

"Should You Lease Your Next Car?" *Consumer Reports*, April 1988a.

"Special Report: Auto Insurance." *Consumer Reports*, October 1988b.

"Ten Ways to Cut the Cost of Car Insurance." *Changing Times*, October 1988.

U.S. Department of Energy. *Gas Mileage Guide*. Annual issues. Washington D.C.: U.S. Government Printing Office.

Watt, Walter. "Finding a Good Auto Repair Shop." *Consumers' Research*, December 1988.

White, Joseph. "Automobiles." *Wall Street Journal*, April 8, 1988.

———. "Detroit's Secret Warranties." *Wall Street Journal*, December 8, 1987.

Chapter Thirteen

ENERGY, THE ENVIRONMENT, AND THE CONSUMER

DID YOU KNOW THAT...

... the United States has 5 percent of the world's population and consumes 30 percent of the world's energy?

... the automobile is used for 98 percent of all urban transportation?

... you can increase your car's mileage by 20 percent without incurring any major expenses?

... an electric water heater is the most energy-expensive electric appliance an average family can own?

... of the entire world's supply of water, only about 0.003 percent is usable for drinking or agricultural or industrial use?

... of all the water consumed within the home, about 30 percent of it is used in flush toilets?

Until the early 1970s energy sources like gasoline and heating oil were cheap and plentiful, so consumers were not overly concerned with their energy expenditures. They bought cars with powerful engines and big homes with relatively little insulation, and they purchased home appliances with no thought to energy-related operating costs. Given the energy prices of the times, these decisions seemed to make good sense. There was even some talk about eliminating electricity meters because the use of cheap, nuclear-based electricity would have made it uneconomical for a utility to pay someone to read a meter. It was thought that electricity bills would become like the charges for trash pickup in most communities—one would pay a flat monthly fee and use as much service as one wanted.

The realities of the 1990s are vastly different from those of the 1970s, however. The prices of conventional sources of energy, such as oil, natural gas, and even coal, have risen dramatically, and nuclear power has not demonstrated the ability to provide safe, cheap, trouble-free electric power. Much of our oil and natural gas is imported, with prices dependent upon global economics and politics. Economists point out that the rising prices of petroleum products helped to fuel the double-digit inflation experienced in the late 1970s, and we do not want to repeat that experience. Today, consumers realize that higher energy prices make it worthwhile to allocate more time to energy decision making. (Many manufacturers of transportation and household products, utility companies, and construction firms employ energy specialists to help consumers with decision making; that job might interest you after you have read this chapter.)

Another concern of some consumers is the impact of their energy consumption on the natural environment and worldwide energy demand. They are more "eco-conscious" than other consumers and are interested in minimizing their energy demands to reduce the depletion of natural resources. They see **energy conservation** as having social as well as economic value. These consumers point to the voracious energy appetite of the U.S. economy and say that we cannot continue to use up a disproportionate share of the world's resources. Currently, the United States has about 5 percent of the world's population and consumes about 30 percent of its annual world production of energy. In doing so, we produce 21 percent of all global goods and services, simultaneously creating one-third of the pollution (Miller, 1988, 10). In a typical year, 241 million people in the United States use more energy to cool their homes and businesses than 1.05 billion Chinese use for all purposes (Miller, 1988, 337).

From a global perspective, it may be difficult to maintain our current share of the energy pie because other nations are beginning to demand a

energy conservation: *the practice of extending the useful life of the earth's energy resources through wise and efficient management*

larger share as their economies begin to produce more (see Chapter 18). Worldwide energy demand is going to increase well into the twenty-first century. Given the fact that technological breakthroughs take time and are unpredictable, we are going to have to learn to cope with rising energy prices. This means increasing our knowledge about energy as well as becoming better decision makers with regard to energy expenditures and energy conservation. The first section in this chapter outlines energy use in the United States, discussing the nature of energy, the amount we are using, our major energy sources, and the energy consumers. The next two sections single out the two most cost-effective areas for personal energy savings: transportation and housing. In the fourth section we look at hidden energy use in regard to water and trash. In the final section we explore the costs and consequences of energy and water consumption. Throughout the chapter we focus on what you can do in your home and your community to improve the quality of your life while still meeting your energy needs.

ENERGY USE: HOW MUCH, WHAT FORMS, BY WHOM?

energy: the ability to do work and overcome resistance

Whenever you eat dinner, bicycle to school, turn on a light, or start your car, you are using energy. **Energy** is the ability to do work or to cause a heat transfer from one object to another. At the most basic level, people need energy from food to keep their hearts pumping, and to warm and cool their bodies. A typical well-fed consumer in the United States uses about as much energy each day as a 100-watt light bulb uses in 24 hours (Hayes, 1977). But our energy consumption goes far beyond food; it includes the energy used to provide us with our entire way of life: the energy to plow fields, transport people and goods, provide shelter, and so forth. It reduces drudgery, makes our climate more hospitable, and can substitute for scarce resources. Energy permits us to replace copper with aluminium, wood with iron and time with speed.

If we measure energy as many scientists do, in **kilocalories** (the amount of heat energy needed to raise the temperature of one kilogram of water by one degree Celsius), we find that an average person needs about 2,000 kilocalories per day in food energy to survive. (A kilocalorie and a calorie are the same.)

In order to provide for the most basic needs of their people, early agricultural societies used about 12,000 total kilocalories of energy per day per person. Early industrial societies that had power machinery (eighteenth-century England, for example) averaged 60,000 kilocalories in daily energy use for each inhabitant. In the United States today, the per capita energy consumption has reached 250,000 kilocalories per day, with only 2,000 derived from food.

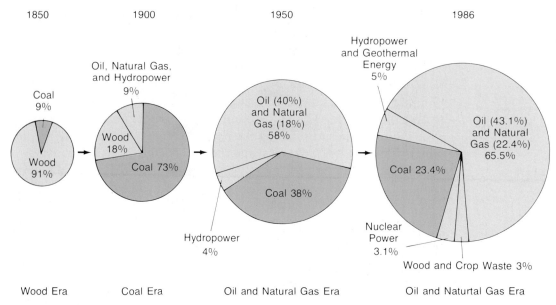

FIGURE 13.1

Changes in the uses of energy resources in the United States, 1850–1986. (SOURCES: U.S. Bureau of the Census, *Resources for the Future*; U.S. Energy Information Administration, *Annual Energy Review*)

As we approach the twenty-first century, life in America has become energy dependent. For example, many of us live many miles from where we work. This means we must commute long distances, creating a significant energy expenditure, since a gallon of gasoline contains about 30,000 kilocalories. The electricity we use in our homes is also a significant part of our increased energy use; during each kilowatt hour, 1,160 kilocalories are used. If all the energy that the average American consumer uses daily were derived from coal, each of us would need about 78 pounds of coal per day to supply our needs.

Certainly we don't power our cars with coal, so what actually are our energy sources? Figure 13.1 compares the sources of energy in the United States in 1850 and the present. In the mid-nineteenth century the United States depended primarily on wood for energy. By 1900, however, the United States emerged as an industrial civilization largely dependent on coal, oil, and natural gas. These sources of energy are often called **fossil fuels**, because they are the remains (fossils) of plants and animals that died millions of years ago. In order to understand the significance of this change, we need to know more about natural resources in general.

A **natural resource** is usually defined as anything obtained from the environment to meet human needs. There are three types: nonrenewable, renewable, and perpetual. A **nonrenewable natural resource** is one that exists in a fixed amount and that generally is not replenished by natural processes.

fossil fuels: the remains (fossils) of dead plants and animals that can be burned to release energy; they generally come in the form of coal, natural gas, or oil

natural resource: a form of matter or energy obtained from the environment that meets human needs

nonrenewable natural resource: resource that is not replaced by natural processes or for which the rate of replacement is slower than its rate of use

Fossil fuels like crude oil are currently our most valuable energy source. As demand has grown, we have discovered oil in more hazardous environments like the North Sea and Prudhoe Bay. This increases the cost of oil and its potential for creating environmental damage.

renewable resource: a resource that normally will be replaced by natural processes, such as trees, groundwater, and fertile soil

Examples include fossil fuels like coal, oil, and natural gas, which were converted from decayed plants and animals by heat and pressure over hundreds of millions of years. During 1986 these one-time deposits provided 82 percent of the energy used in the world for electricity, heating, cooling, transportation, and manufacturing (Miller, 1988, p. 10). A **renewable resource** is one that can be depleted in the short run if used too rapidly, but will normally be replaced through natural processes. Examples include trees in forests, deposits of groundwater, fresh air, and fertile soil. A **perpetual resource** is one that comes from an essentially inexhaustible source, and so would be available in a relatively constant supply. The most pertinent example of a perpetual resource is solar energy, which will be available for the remaining lifetime of the sun, estimated to be at least 5 billion years. Other perpetual resources as a result of direct solar energy input include wind energy, tidal energy, and flowing water.

Considering the three types of natural resources, take another look at Figure 13.1. You will discover that when we industrialized, we also became dependent upon nonrenewable energy resources. It is estimated that affordable supplies of oil will only be available for a few more decades. This is because most of the easily available deposits of fossil fuels have already been tapped. Extraction costs for remaining deposits are high, making the diminishing supplies ever more valuable. Indisputably, one of our greatest challenges is to find ways to meet our future energy needs in light of the imminent loss of traditional sources.

It certainly is not solely the responsibility of consumers to solve America's energy dilemma. The various levels of government and industry must also play important roles, but consumers can do much to help. And in the process of adjusting our individual energy budgets, we have the added satisfaction of knowing that we are contributing an important part of the overall solution. Imagine that our energy problem is a jigsaw puzzle with millions of pieces, many of which belong to consumers. If consumers neglect to put their pieces in their proper places, no effort by industry or government will be able to reconstruct the whole puzzle.

As Figure 13.2 shows, industry accounts for 39.2 percent of total energy use, firms engaged in commercial activity (banks and retail stores, for example), together with private residences, consume 35.5 percent, and various forms of transportation consume 25.3 percent. Consumers have a limited voice in how commercial and industrial sectors use energy, but they have a major impact on residential and transportation uses. By examining our consumer roles in these two areas, we can save ourselves money and also contribute to conserving more of the world's energy for the future. Informed decision making about transportation use can pay handsome dividends for us and for those around us. We turn now to some specific opportunities for saving energy and money.

FIGURE 13.2
Uses of energy in the United States, by sector. (SOURCE: U.S. Energy Information Administration, *Annual Energy Review*.)

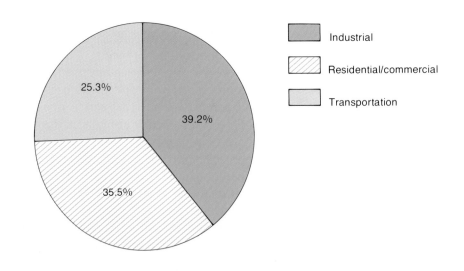

ENERGY AND TRANSPORTATION

In Chapter 12 we discussed one major form of transportation, the automobile, as a consumable good. Here, we discuss the automobile as an energy-intensive transportation choice and look at alternatives. We will review different forms of personal transportation, from the automobile to the scooter, as well as mass-transit alternatives like trains and buses.

The Automobile

At present there are more than 131 million cars in America, about half of all the cars in the world. The car is used for 98 percent of all urban transportation and 85 percent of all travel between cities (Miller, 1988). One-fourth of U.S. energy consumption is for transportation, and as Figure 13.3 shows, a majority of that energy goes to power automobiles (urban automobile and intercity automobile use). In addition, each year more than 70 percent of the rubber, 30 percent of the zinc, and almost 20 percent of the aluminium produced in the United States are used to produce new automobiles, which are eventually discarded at the rate of about 6 million a year.

No other form of transportation provides the privacy, security, and freedom of automobiles. But there is a growing awareness that these advantages come at a cost. Besides the personal monetary costs discussed in Chapter 12, consumers are becoming more alert to the time and environmental costs of traffic congestion, the loss of large areas of land to highways and parking lots, and injuries and deaths from auto collisions. Despite these costs, we believe that most U.S. residents will continue to use autos as their primary form of transportation in the foreseeable future. So we want to focus in this section on how to improve the energy efficiency

FIGURE 13.3 Transportation uses of energy in the United States. (SOURCE: Daniel D. Chiras, *Environmental Science: A Framework for Decision Making*, 2d ed. [Menlo Park, Calif.: Benjamin/Cummings, 1988], p. 234.)

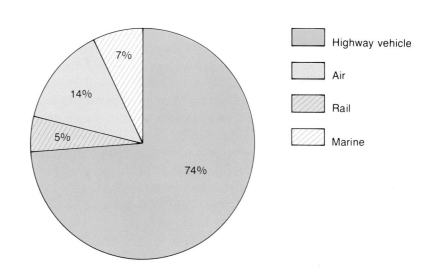

Highway vehicle

Air

Rail

Marine

TABLE 13.1 Sources of Increased Energy Efficiency for Automobiles

Sources	Estimated Percentage Increase in Fuel Economy
No Costs	
Changing driving habits	5.0–10.0
Cruising at 50 mph rather than at 70 mph	20.0
Correcting tire pressures	5.0
Minor Costs	
Getting regular tuneups	6.0–12.0
Using synthetic oil	2.0
Installing radial tires	3.0–5.0
Major Costs	
Installing manual transmission	10.0
Eliminating air conditioning	5.0–12.0
Getting a lighter car (by 100 pounds)	2.8

of automobiles. First, we will look at personal driving habits and then we will consider ridesharing.

Personal driving habits. With rising resource costs and with the average price of a new car exceeding $15,000, we could expect consumers to reevaluate their past consumption habits in relation to autos and gasoline. As you read Chapter 12, perhaps you weighed the advantages of purchasing a new car and those of repairing your old one. New cars are more energy efficient than older ones, but does the fuel savings justify an investment in a newer model? You may decide in favor of your old car if you elect to implement some of the suggestions presented here.

Although there are outside influences on your car's fuel consumption, many are under your control. Table 13.1 suggests three categories of owner/driver fuel savings: those involving no costs, minor costs, and major costs. As we have stressed before, any decision depends on more than explicit dollar costs. In considering fuel consumption, you need to consider the impact of your decision on the global conservation effort, as well as the implicit opportunity costs (time costs). On the other hand, conservation often entails a cost in time and a change in habits and customs. For most of us, driving is almost second nature. We seldom observe or analyze our behavior. At least initially, conservation requires a conscious change in the way we drive and even in our attitude toward driving. Whether you choose to adopt any or all of these conservation tips depends on your values and customs, along with the opportunity costs and dollar costs for you. If you follow all the tips, you can increase your fuel economy by as much as 50 percent. But before you can weigh the costs and benefits of fuel conservation, you need information.

Better mileage with no dollar outlay. Driving habits include a variety of behaviors. The way you accelerate from a stop, the way you behave in traffic, the number of trips you take, the average distances you drive, and even the way you start your car all affect the mileage you get from a gallon of gasoline.

You will recognize the impact of personal driving habits on fuel efficiency, if you consider the fact that every time you accelerate, you spend energy to overcome friction, and every time you brake, you use friction to negate the energy you spent to accelerate. So, for example, you can save gasoline by avoiding sharp accelerations, or "jackrabbit starts." You can also save gasoline (as well as time and personal energy) by consolidating short trips or running errands on the way to and from work. One final tip on driving habits concerns idling your car's engine: Many consumers believe they need to warm their engines before they can drive off, but this is no longer true; as long as you begin at a moderate speed, there is no need to let the engine idle after starting the car.

Decreasing speed also saves fuel. Cruising at 50 miles per hour rather than at 70 miles per hour can increase fuel economy from 12 to 35 percent, depending on auto design and wind resistance. Of course, it takes longer to get where you are going; time is the opportunity cost of the lower speed and needs to be included in your cost–benefit analysis. Table 13.2 provides a comparison of fuel and time costs. The information is based on the assumption that driving at 50 miles per hour gives about 20 percent better gas mileage and saves about four gallons of gasoline during a 350-mile trip; on the other hand, the trip takes two hours longer at the slower speed. If gasoline cost $1.00 per gallon, the $4.00 savings would not be very impressive, compared to two hours of the driver's time. Very few consumers consider their time worth so little. But as resources become scarcer, their cost rises. If the price of gasoline should reach $5 per gallon, the savings for the trip would be $20, or $10 per hour. Clearly, this is a more powerful incentive for conservation. As an aside, note that lower speeds also save lives. In a study by the National Academy of Sciences, the national 55-mph speed limit in force in 1985 saved between 2,000 and 4,000 lives and prevented 4,500 serious injuries. The lower speeds

TABLE 13.2 Comparison of Fuel and Time Costs at Different Automobile Speeds

Speed	Miles per Gallon	Distance (miles)	Driving Time (hours)	Gallons of Fuel Needed
50	20	350	7	17.5
70	16	350	5	21.8

reduced accidents and thus saved consumers $65 million in medical and insurance costs (Miller, 1988).

Routine inspection of tire pressure offers another opportunity to save energy. Keeping tires as hard as the owner's manual allows minimizes friction and thus raises gas mileage. The five minutes it takes to check the tires can save between $1 and $2 per fill-up. If you save $1 per five-minute check, you will have an after-tax saving of $12 per hour.

Fuel savings involving small dollar costs. The majority of the suggestions found in Table 13.1 require some financial investment, either minor or major. Whether the savings justify the additional costs depends on fuel savings and the size of the cost differential. To make the cost–benefit analysis, you need to know how many miles you drive each year and the average miles per gallon your car gets; then you can determine how many gallons of gas you consume in a year. For example, say that you drive the typical 12,000 miles per year; dividing this figure by 18 mpg (the 1989 average), you find your consumption to be 667 gallons of gasoline annually.

$$\text{miles driven per year} \div \text{miles per gallon} = \text{annual consumption}$$

$$12,000 \div 18 = 667$$

For a cost–benefit analysis, you must determine how many gallons of gas you would save by implementing a conservation tip. For example, a motor tuneup is probably the best way to increase a car's mileage. Generally tuneups should be done about once a year. According to the U.S. Environmental Protection Agency, keeping an automobile tuned up can improve fuel economy 6 percent on the average, and other estimates double this figure. Assume that you average 8 percent better mileage as a result of the tuneup. If you use 667 gallons per year at your pretune-up mileage, an 8 percent mileage increase saves you 53 gallons ($0.08 \times 667 = 53$). Multiply the average cost of a gallon of gasoline by the number of gallons saved to find the value of the fuel savings:

$$\text{price of gasoline, per gallon} \times \text{gallons saved} = \text{fuel conservation savings}$$

$$\$1.50 \times 53 = \$79.50$$

If a tuneup costs $150, fuel conservation does not make the work worthwhile. At less than $75, a tuneup represents financial savings. Of course, fuel conservation is only one reason to have a tuneup. Other reasons include prolonging the life of the engine, ensuring the safety and dependability of your major form of transportation, and decreasing your contribution to the air pollution problem. These issues are more difficult to quantify but still fit into the decision-making process.

retrofit: increasing the energy efficiency of an existing system by installing improved components

Another way to increase fuel efficiency is to **retrofit** your car. This means replacing less-energy-efficient parts with more-energy-efficient ones. Most retrofit techniques work by reducing friction. Recently developed synthetic oils, for example, are more slippery and thus lubricate better than traditional motor oils. Less friction within the engine allows the motor to expend less energy on moving its internal parts and more on propelling the car. Radial tires also lower a car's fuel consumption by lessening the friction between the tire and the road; they can increase miles per gallon by 3 to 5 percent. Does such a saving justify the additional cost of a set of radial tires? The answer depends on fuel savings and the size of the cost differential. By now you should be able to compute them and arrive at your own conclusion. But most calculations favor a radial retrofit only if you are already in the market for a new set of tires. In this case, the only cost of retrofitting your car with radials is the *difference* between the price of a set of conventional tires and the cost of radials.

Major expenditures and fuel efficiency. The conservation suggestions discussed above can all be used with your current automobile. On a new car, you can also apply all of these techniques, and you can choose other optional equipment that will further improve its efficiency. For example, if you choose a manual transmission (preferably one with five forward gears) you can expect to get 10 percent better mileage than with a similar car having automatic transmission. If your new car weighs less than your old car, you can add another 2.8 percent to your fuel economy for every 100 pounds. This can result in a 25 percent improvement in fuel economy if your new car weighs 900 pounds less than your old one. (Box 13.1 discusses the fuel economy that has been achieved in newer cars primarily by making them lighter—and according to some experts, less safe.) If you can do without air conditioning, you may save another 5 to 12 percent, although recent studies show that such a saving is almost nil at highway speeds if you have to leave your windows open to cool off. The additional wind resistance (friction) negates the fuel economy gained by eliminating air conditioning.

It is highly unlikely that fuel savings alone will pay for the expenses involved in purchasing a new car. Of course, circumstances differ among individuals. For example, a consumer who uses his or her car sparingly and drives only 4,000 miles a year will be less likely to consider fuel efficiency an important criterion of getting another car. On the other hand, a salesperson who drives 35,000 miles a year will have an entirely different cost–benefit calculation.

Ridesharing: a personal alternative. Almost two thirds of all working Americans travel to work alone each day in their own cars. Obviously, much fuel could be saved by ridesharing, or carpooling. **Ridesharing** combines the convenience, safety, and assurance of personal transit with

BOX 13.1   CAFE: WHAT ARE THE TRADE-OFFS?

Imagine driving 45 miles on one gallon of gas . . . not on a motorcycle but in an automobile. Could this goal be achieved in your car today? Perhaps, if you followed all our energy conservation suggestions—or if you've invested in a Geo Metro, which consistently records at least 53 miles per gallon in the city and 59 on the highway. Several foreign auto manufacturers have tested high-performance cars that get from 67 to 121 miles per gallon. According to the U.S. Office of Technology Assessment, all American-made autos could easily achieve 45 mpg at the turn of the century, halving our consumption of gasoline for transportation (Miller, 1988, p. 390). Just a pipe dream? Perhaps. But we have been on the road to that goal thanks to congressional legislation passed in 1975.

In that year the average automobile in the United States achieved 13.53 miles per gallon. Then Congress, in conjunction with the Department of Transportation, created the **Corporate Average Fuel Economy (CAFE)** standards, effective in 1977, which requires car makers to meet a government-mandated miles-per-gallon standard for their entire fleet of cars sold in America. That is, the average fuel economy for all autos manufactured in the United States has to meet the miles-per-gallon standard, which rises, on the average, 1.5 miles per gallon each year. Foreign manufacturers need to meet the standards as well for those cars imported to this country. As a result, fuel economy standards of 25.3 gallons were met in 1984.

By 1985, however, Chrysler met the CAFE standards by spending billions of dollars in redesign and retooling in order to produce lighter-weight, fuel-conserving autos. (All of this from a company that had been on the verge of bankruptcy a few years before.) Imported cars continued to meet the standards, although Ford and General Motors failed to meet the standards, not due to inadequate technology, but because they sold more large-sized (and higher-priced) cars demanded by consumers who had grown complacent because of relatively low gas prices.

The automakers were granted a lower standard for 1986 (26 mpg), and they requested a reprieve again in 1987, avoiding in both years the $50-per-car fine (approximately $1.2 billion in total) for not meeting the original standards. At the same time, CAFE regulations continud to impose a gas-guzzler tax, paid by consumers on new cars with poor mileage. The tax per car in 1986 ranged from $500 for cars that achieved an average mileage between 21.5 and 22.5 to $3,850 for cars averaging less than 12.5 miles per gallon.

By 1988 the standard of 26.5 mpg was all but forgotten as the Department of Transportation announced it would abolish the industry standards entirely. Critics say that CAFE forced U.S. manufacturers to build their cars overseas, exporting jobs. Transportation Secretary James H. Burnley was quoted as saying that the abolition of the CAFE standards would be the "greatest contribution the Department of Transportation can make to the automobile industry, to keep jobs in the states and to making domestic auto industry competitive on a worldwide basis . . ." (*Consumers' Research*, 1988.) Other critics say that CAFE standards, in encouraging the building of lighter-weight cars, have increased automobile fatalities as much as 10 percent (*Wall Street Journal*, 1988).

Do you agree with Secretary Burnley? What factors would need to be considered in a cost–benefit analysis of this situation? (As we go to press, President George Bush has announced the reinstatement of CAFE standards.)

Ridesharing is a way for consumers to conserve energy and save money.

the lower cost and energy-saving qualities of mass transit. Under this arrangement, commuters who live and work near one another share driving, and usually the expenses of commuting, by taking only one vehicle. When they take turns driving, they belong to what is called a *shared-driving-car pool*. Although carpool drivers should carry additional automobile insurance, most insurance companies offer a 10 percent discount for reduced commuter work mileage. If only one car or van is used with one regular driver, it is called a *shared-riding car pool*. This results in even greater savings because of further reduced insurance costs for nondrivers.

The American Automobile Association estimated that the national per-mile cost of driving averaged 32.2 cents in 1988, when gasoline was about $1 per gallon. Using that estimate, a person commuting 10,000 miles each year would spend about $3,220. A two-person car pool would save on gasoline, oil, maintenance, wear, and depreciation on tires and the car itself, allowing carpoolers to save at least $1,000 each year.

Commuters sometimes cite difficulty in locating ridesharing companions. Many companies now provide a matching service to help employees identify fellow employees who might be potential ridesharers. Many cities and counties promote ridesharing by setting aside special lanes for carpoolers and by providing free telephone service for matching drivers and riders. Louisville, Kentucky, has been particularly successful in its ridesharing program. The California Department of Transportation is using the Commuter Computer developed by ARCO oil company to help match ridesharers. This saves California commuters an estimated 2 million gallons of gasoline a year. Call your local mass-transit system or air-quality management district for assistance in joining ride-sharing or carpooling in your community.

Other Forms of Personal Transportation

For many of us, it is difficult to remember that the automobile is not the only form of personal transportation. People use everything from roller skates and skateboards to private planes to get them from one place to another. The range of choices is quite large, but we will focus on the bicycle, motorcycle, scooter, and moped, all of which offer attractive energy-saving alternatives to the automobile.

The bicycle. Bicycling is not only more efficient than using mopeds or motorcycles, it is even more efficient than walking, because of the mechanical advantage of gears and wheels. A bicyclist traveling at 10 miles per hour uses only 25 kilocalories per mile, whereas a pedestrian walking at 2.5 miles per hour uses five times that amount per mile, although traveling only one-quarter as fast. Because a gallon of gasoline contains 30,000 kilocalories, the bicyclist obtains the energy equivalent of more than 1,000 miles per gallon—considerably more miles per gallon than a Toyota or a Ford (Hayes, 1977). And the bicyclist uses food, a renewable resource, rather than petroleum for energy (and also improves his or her physical fitness). You can appreciate the bicycle's value even more if you consider that 43 percent of all urban driving involves trips of fewer than five miles (Miller, 1988) and that, in traffic, cars and bicycles both travel at the same average speed: 13 mph.

If the bicycle is such a great invention, why doesn't everyone ride one? In Holland almost everyone does. Holland has 12 million bicycles and 14 million people. And Holland is not alone: For decades the bicycle has been a major means of transportation throughout Europe and Asia. An emphasis on bicycling could be achieved in the United States. More than 10 million bicycles are sold here every year. We are estimated to have more than 100 million bikes nationwide. One city that provides leadership in promoting this mode of transportation is Davis, in northern California, which established more than 40 miles of bike lanes and paths and provided city employees with bikes. As a result one-fourth of all transportation within the city is by bicycle.

Until recently most bicycles used for short trips or commuting were the lightweight, ten-speed touring style. But when such a bike ventured onto city streets, tires could easily be punctured by small bits of broken glass, and a pothole could send the passenger into orbit. Now a new breed of bicycle blends the old-fashioned street bike with the standard touring components. The odd-looking hybrid, called a mountain bike, has a large seat, rear derailleur shifters, and fat, knobby tires for tractability.

Handlebars can be set in an upright position, which makes traffic watching easier.

Even though some people have found bicycles viable for short trips, there are several factors that limit their use:

1. *Comfort.* Bicycles, like their two-wheel cousins, the motorcycle and the moped, have no roofs. As anyone who has done it can tell you, bicycling during a rainstorm can be miserable. And in cold weather or in snow storms, bicycling is extremely difficult.

2. *Safety.* A bicycle takes only one-thirtieth of the space of an automobile, which is good if you want to reduce congestion or are looking for a parking space, but bad if you want to be seen. Small vehicles and bikes are frequently overlooked by motorists, with tragic results for the cyclist. And if you have a touring bicycle rather than a mountain bike, brakes may be unreliable in wet weather, an important reason for not counting on the bicycle to commute to work daily.

3. *Poor facilities.* A major complaint of bike riders is the inadequacy of safe bike paths and lanes. Many bicycle owners would commute to work or run errands if this problem could be corrected. Bike owners also incur difficulty finding secure parking facilities. Where can you put your bike once you are at work? Another problem is that of perspiration. If showers were readily available at the workplace, more commuters would probably be willing to ride their bikes during the warm summer months.

4. *Health.* There is evidence that moderate exercise of the kind that bicycling provides can help stimulate the heart and the circulation, promoting physical fitness. However when a bicyclist is caught in heavy traffic, where the air is rich in lead, hydrocarbons, and carbon monoxide from the exhausts of the idling autos, there may be unhealthful effects on the bicyclist.

5. *Time.* The opportunity cost of the potential cyclist's time must also be considered. Although autos and bikes average identical speeds in heavy urban traffic, their speeds differ radically as traffic lightens. At 10 miles per hour, a bicyclist can commute 20 miles in two hours, but the same distance can be covered in only 30 minutes in a car, which can average 40 mph. This time cost can be balanced if the cyclist considers the commute part of a regular exercise program, however.

The moped. Some consumers neglect the bicycle because of the basic muscle power it requires. For these folks, and for the fainthearted who prefer motored transportation, the moped may be an option. The moped can be operated like a standard bicycle, because it has pedals and gears, but it also has a small one- or two-horsepower engine capable of powering the vehicle up to 30 miles per hour. This hybrid is very popular in Europe, and it has worldwide distribution of almost 45 million. Moped prices range from $500 to $1,500; the moped gets more than 100 miles per gallon and has a better safety record than its better-known cousin, the motorcycle.

With all of these advantages, it is little wonder that ownership of mopeds in the United States has risen dramatically in recent years. Because the vehicle is a cross between a bicycle and a motorcycle, some states have chosen to view it as similar to a bicycle and impose few regulations. Other states have opted to treat it more like a motorcycle and require the operator to be licensed and to register the vehicle. For example, in Ohio a moped driver must be at least 14 years old, any driver under age 18 must wear a helmet, and no passengers are allowed on mopeds. As a result of these 1985 regulations the number of hospital admissions for moped accidents decreased dramatically.

Motorcycles and scooters. Motorcycles and scooters are more energy efficient than cars, but they are less efficient than mopeds or bicycles. Some smaller motorcycles and scooters may weigh less than 300 pounds and have modest engine sizes (generally less than 200 cubic centimeters). The small motorcycles can get up to 70 miles per gallon and cost between $900 and $2,500, while scooters may get as much as 150 miles per gallon and can be found for less than $2,000. Larger motorcycles can have engines that rival those of small cars, as does the 1,340-cubic-centimeter engines in the huge Harley-Davidson that many police officers ride. As with most cars, the larger the engine, the lower the gas mileage. Besides having higher energy costs, larger cycles are priced two to three times higher.

Insurance is another cost that must be considered before deciding to buy a motorcycle or scooter. A basic insurance package for a scooter or motorcycle that weighs less than 300 pounds costs about 50 percent more than that for a car. For big motorcycles (those more than 300 pounds), insurance rates may be three times the basic automobile insurance rate.

Many of the factors that limit bicycle use also pertain to motorcycles. Most people find a scooter more comfortable and easier to mount than a motorcycle; most scooter models also have a front splash guard. Safety, parking facilities, and health are also considerations, as is one's physical ability to handle a 300- or 500-pound machine. Most adults have little problem with a 30-pound bicycle or a moped that weighs less than 100 pounds. But could you pick up a 400-pound motorcycle if it toppled to the ground?

Mass Transit

Transportation is a necessity, but personal transportation is a luxury. In our society most people insist on mobility, but going it alone is not best for energy conservation. Kenneth Boulding, an economist at the

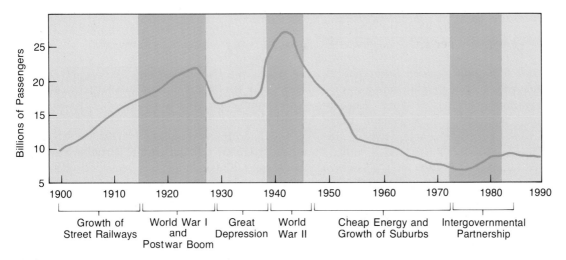

FIGURE 13.4
Major trends of transit ridership. Transit ridership has gone through six major cycles of growth and decline during the twentieth century, influenced by social and economic forces external to transit. From 1900 to 1929 transit ridership grew steadily — first, because of technical innovation and investment opportunities during the early development of street railways and then because of the economic boom of World War I and the postwar period. The Great Depression caused a steep decline in ridership between 1929 and 1939 as people made fewer work trips and often could not afford to take pleasure trips. A new federal law limiting utilities, ability to subsidize transit, as had been normal practice, led to a decline in transit capital facilities. World War II caused motor fuel rationing and an economic boom that led to a new rapid growth cycle in transit ridership. Ridership quickly declined from artificially high war levels as people fled to suburbs, spurred on by cheap fuel and government policy favoring low-density suburban growth. In 1973 the ridership cycle reversed again and transit began a modest growth based on a partnership of local, state, and federal government committed to improving America's transporation infrastructure. (SOURCE: Adapted from American Public Transit Association, "APTA Transit Fact Book," 1988.)

University of Colorado, once remarked that if the United States were to be visited by intelligent beings from outer space, their initial impression would probably be that the dominant form of life here consists of hard-shelled creatures with soft pulpy insides, who are propelled by wheels, although the creatures are capable of sluggish motion on their own when not encased in their natural external skeletons (Heilbroner, 1975). Because urban cars carry an average of 1.4 persons at a time, Boulding's characterization does not seem so farfetched.

Figure 13.4 illustrates the number of passengers using mass transit from 1900 to the present. Notice that the peak was achieved in 1945, at the end of World War II. From then until 1973, a steady decline took place. The decline resulted from decision making by individual consumers, and it eventually led to some massive transportation problems

BOX 13.2   DID ROGER RABBIT FRAME GM?

A recent hit film, *Who Framed Roger Rabbit*, may have seemed like nothing more than a special-effects extravaganza. Roger is a "Toon," an animated cartoon figure in a make-believe 1940s Hollywood, where cartoon characters live side-by-side with human beings. Roger and a private detective try to clear the Toon of a charge of murder. In their investigations they uncover a conspiracy to wreck southern California's mass-transportation system and replace it with a system of freeways. Many viewers probably didn't give much thought to the identity of the evil company that buys out the regional streetcar company in order to close it down. But filmgoers in southern California hissed and howled, being familiar with the facts and rumors underpinning the fiction.

First, the facts: Southern California once had an efficient, inexpensive mass transit system, the Pacific Electric Company, which operated trolleys known as Red Cars. By the 1920s there was 1,100 miles of track in four counties, carrying people from the foothills of Pasadena to the ocean at Long Beach to the inland empire of Riverside.

Now the myth: In the 1940s it was alleged that General Motors (GM), along with local tire and oil companies, bought the Pacific Electric Company in order to put the Red Cars out of business. They replaced the trolleys with buses, paving the way (so to speak) for the automobile. When left with inadequate bus transportation the southern Californian had no choice but to purchase a car and take to the freeways.

And the truth: As is typical of myths, there is a bit of truth in them. GM did acquire partial interest in Los Angeles transit companies, replacing what was once the largest electric interurban system in the world with diesel-powered buses. This occurred in cities other than Los Angeles, with the help of a consortium of auto, tire, oil, truck, and bus companies. The *inefficiency of the buses* that replaced the streetcars contributed to the demise of many once-healthy public transportation networks.

If this sounds simply like a conspiracy, however, we must remind our readers that the public played a role in the demise of the Red Car and other, similar systems. For after World War II, consumers, hungry for new goods and gadgets and with unprecedented prosperity, chose to buy new homes in the suburbs and new cars to wheel around in, abandoning public transportation.

The moral of the story: We learn as much from our failures as our successes. We need to develop a historical perspective, and consider the long-range effects as much as the immediate gains. Or as another Toon, named Pogo, once said, "We have met the enemy, and he is us."

and congestion. After World War II, consumer incomes began to rise steadily. Good low-cost housing became available on the outskirts of most major cities, and the real price of gasoline began to decline. Higher incomes, lower-density housing in the suburbs, cheaper gasoline, and the construction of new highways and freeways all weighted the consumer's cost–benefit calculations away from mass transit and toward personal transit (see Box 13.2). As we've mentioned, the private car has always had several advantages not available in a bus or trolley. The car is available at a moment's notice and offers door-to-door service and privacy. These benefits were significant in motivating people to buy cars. And once people bought cars, once it became normal to have a car, the cost calculations became loaded against mass transit.

The average cost of owning an automobile is quite high, as we demonstrated in Chapter 12, but once you have a car, the marginal cost of a particular trip is considerably lower than the average cost of ownership. The marginal cost of a trip is the cost of getting in the car and going somewhere. In essence, this is the price of gasoline, which varies between 3 and 10 cents per mile. A four-mile commute might result in an out-of-pocket expense of 40 cents. Private bus companies, on the other hand, must charge enough to cover their average cost, which includes maintenance, wear and tear on the equipment, and insurance, in addition to the cost of gasoline and wages. This marginal-versus-average cost dilemma is at the heart of the decline in bus ridership. Because the automobile is almost always more convenient, bus fares have to be equal to, and preferably lower than, the marginal cost of driving. Private bus companies in most urban areas simply cannot meet the competition. As mass transit costs rise, companies raise fares or lower service, which results in fewer riders, lower revenues, and increased fares once again.

During the 1970s the downward trend in mass transit ridership began to reverse due to the rollercoaster prices of oil. During the 1980s, consumers, hit with the high prices of housing, relocated further into the suburbs and experienced longer commutes and increasing traffic congestion. These pressures encouraged increased governmental subsidies to mass transit and led many consumers to reevaluate their cost–benefit calculations for transportation. As a result, depending upon the community, consumers can choose between four variations of mass transit: heavy-rail, light-rail, buses, and paratransit.

Heavy-rail mass transit. Heavy-rail mass transit is a fixed-rail system, including trains and subways, often in combination. Prominent examples include the METRO system in Washington, D.C., and BART in San Francisco. Although these systems have been criticized because of cost-overruns and financial losses, many cities, including Atlanta, Baltimore, and Pittsburgh have found their fixed-rail systems have steadily gained in riders, renewed interest in central city business, and helped reduce air pollution.

Light-rail. Many cities have installed an up-dated version of the streetcar system using fixed-rail trolleys. You might have been on the **light-rail** system in San Diego, California; Portland, Oregon; Buffalo, New York; or Toronto, Canada, and discovered that they are quieter and cleaner than buses. Although they are initially more expensive to build than heavy-rail systems, the investment is a wise one in the long run, as operating costs are much lower. This explains why more than a dozen U.S. cities are in the midst of building trolley systems.

With the rise in the price of fuel, consumers have begun to explore more energy-efficient forms of mass transit, like the railroad.

Buses. An obvious advantage of buses over fixed-rail systems is the flexibility of routing. They also require a lower initial investment, since no rails or tunnels must be installed. But due to the need to pass the average cost of a trip onto the rider, buses are only cost-effective when full. This explains why European governments subsidize bus transit by making up the difference between operating costs and receipts. They justify this expenditure by recognizing the result is decreased autos on European roads, a need for fewer multilane highways, and (of equal importance) decreased air pollution.

Paratransit. In areas where population is dispersed throughout a large geographic area, **paratransit** options like minibuses and dial-a-ride present attractive alternatives to the personal auto. Minivans or mini-buses, called *jitneys* in some countries, follow relatively fixed routes and stop upon demand, much like a taxi. *Dial-a-ride* systems provide door-to-destination service initiated by a telephone call. Many systems incorporate two-way radios and computerized routing, making them more efficient. Both systems attempt to provide the personalized service of a taxi for the price of a trolley ride, and expand a consumer's transportation options.

ENERGY USE IN THE HOME

The second most important area in which consumers can personally affect their energy demand is in home energy use, which accounts for 22 percent of American's total energy use. Government agencies, public utilities, and universities have all sponsored studies to test various home energy-saving strategies. Some strategies can immediately be implemented without cost, some entail moderate cost, and others are available only to the new home buyer. In sections that follow we present the results of these studies, offer some ideas on how to conserve residential energy use, and describe energy-saving systems available in new homes. Of course, you will choose to adopt strategies based on your evaluation of the costs and the benefits. But there is a wider dimension to this analysis than an individual's satisfaction. On a society-wide level, if Americans conserve energy, there will be an overall decrease in the demand followed by a decline, or at least by a more modest rise, in the real price of energy. From both these developments, consumers would get more money to spend (or save) than they would if they did not conserve energy. Moreover, conservation will help to keep inflation under control and contribute to a cleaner environment.

Measuring Home Energy Use

Home energy costs differ among households for a variety of reasons. Geographic location, size of the family, type of residence, and sources of available energy are among the most important. Figure 13.5 cuts across all these factors and develops a profile of total residential energy use in the United States. Most home energy use (59 percent) is devoted to creating a comfortable temperature around us. In fact, the vast majority of the energy we use in our homes is aimed at either heating or cooling something. For example, water heating uses 15 percent of our domestic energy, and refrigerator/freezers use 10 percent. That only leaves 16 percent for cooking our food, lighting our homes, and running other appliances, such as televisions and computers. As a result of research, the Energy Conservation Coalition estimates that in the next 20 years we

FIGURE 13.5 Residential uses of energy in the United States. (SOURCE: U.S. Energy Information Administration, *Annual Energy Review.*)

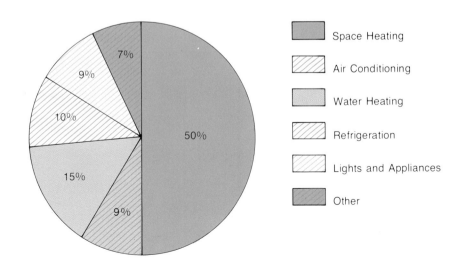

Space Heating

Air Conditioning

Water Heating

Refrigeration

Lights and Appliances

Other

FIGURE 13.6
How to read your gas meter. Read the large dials only. (The small dials at the top are for test purposes.) On each dial, a hand points between two numbers. Write down the smaller of these numbers. Read the larger dials from left to right. For example, the reading in this illustration is 6084. (SOURCE: Adapted from "Answer Book" [Anaheim, Calif.: Southern California Gas Company, 1981].)

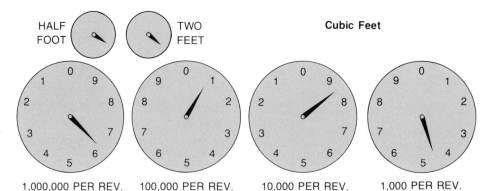

HALF FOOT   TWO FEET   Cubic Feet

1,000,000 PER REV.   100,000 PER REV.   10,000 PER REV.   1,000 PER REV.

could avoid building 100 large power plants if households and commercial buildings were outfitted with the most energy-efficient appliances on the market (National Wildlife, 1984). Figure 13.5 is based on national data, so in order to estimate your personal potential payoff from home energy conservation, you need some information about how much energy you are currently using, what kind of energy it is, and where it is being used.

For most consumers, monitoring energy use in the home should be no more difficult than calculating a car's miles per gallon. All homes and most apartments have meters conveniently located so the gas and electric company can determine the energy usage over a period of time, usually a month. Company meter readers perform this task, but you can be your own meter reader once you understand the basics of the system. (See Figures 13.6 and 13.7.)

Additional meter monitoring. Utility companies list on the bill the amount of energy consumed for a month, in kilowatt-hours for electricity or in therms for gas. Recently, many companies have begun to include comparative figures for present and past years, both by month and by daily average. If your daily average in August was 15.8 kwh this year and 20.2 kwh last year, it could mean, for example, that it was cooler this year

FIGURE 13.7
How to read your electric meter. The dials are like watch faces lined in a row (every other dial moves counterclockwise). The reading for a five-dial meter is 16,064. The reading for a four-dial meter is 6,064. When the pointer seems to be directly on a number, look at the dial to the right; if the pointer on the right-side dial has not passed 0, write down the lower number on the first dial. (SOURCE: Used by permission of Southern California Edison Company.)

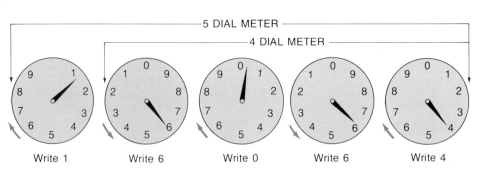

5 DIAL METER
4 DIAL METER

Write 1   Write 6   Write 0   Write 6   Write 4

FIGURE 13.8
Load management programs are designed to shift some of the uses of electricity from periods of peak demand to periods of lesser demand. Utilities must always be prepared to generate the amount of electricity needed at a peak-demand time in the geographic area they serve. The peak-demand time usually occurs between 12 noon and 6 P.M., often during a particularly cold or warm spell, and may occur only 10 to 20 days a year. By shifting some energy consumption to another time of the day, demand is kept from exceeding generating capacity.

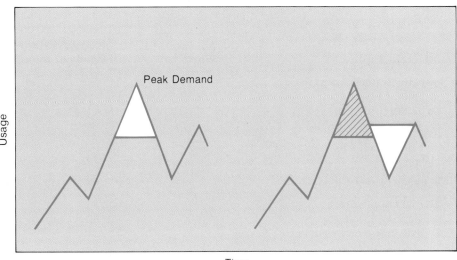

and so you used less air conditioning, that you have been conserving by setting the thermostat higher, or both. It is for you to determine. But with information like this on the bill, you get an indication of what your habits save you or cost you.

Another habit that may soon become economically wise is **load management** (Figure 13.8). This refers to shifting electrical use from periods of peak or high demand to periods of lesser demand. Peak-demand periods generally occur between the hours of 12 noon and 6:00 P.M. on week days. This is the time that more businesses and manufacturing firms are using electricity for production while maintaining temperature control and meeting lighting demands for employees. Utility companies have encouraged these commercial and industrial firms to shift power use wherever possible by selling power to them at a lower cost during low-demand time periods. Reducing the growth of peak demand can help postpone the need for building more power plants. Since building more power plants, regardless of type, is exceedingly expensive, some power companies choose to charge residential users, as well as commercial users, a higher rate for electricity consumed during peak-demand periods. Therefore, it would be wise for consumers to develop the habit of shifting electrical usage to early mornings, evenings, or weekends whenever possible. This will help maintain the cost of electrical service and postpone the need for expensive power plants.

Saving Energy in the Home

With the help of your local public utility company and with a few lessons on meter reading, you can begin to get a better idea of how much energy you consume at home. The next step is to put yourself and your home on

TABLE 13.3 Average Energy Use of Electric Appliances

Electric Appliance	Average Wattage[a]	Kilowatt Hours Used per Month	Average Use
Air conditioner (room)			
6,000 Btu	850	0.9[a]	Per hour of operation[b]
12,000 Btu	1,380	1.4[a]	Per hour of operation[b]
Freezer, 15 cu. ft.			
Manual defrost		100	Continuous
Frost free		147	Continuous
Furnace blower $\frac{1}{3}$ h.p.		60	5 hours per day, winter
Refrigerator/freezer			
Manual, 12 cu. ft.		61	Continuous
Frost free (energy efficient)			
16 cu. ft.		78	Continuous
Frost free (energy efficient)			
20 cu. ft.		95	Continuous
Frost free, 16 cu. ft.		150	Continuous
Frost free, 20 cu. ft.		185	Continuous
Swimming pool pump, 1 h.p.		1.4[b]	Per hour of operation[b]
Water heater (elec.)	4,475	400	Continuous
Water bed heater	450	105	Continuous
Clothes dryer	4,850	79	26 loads per month
Clothes washer	510	9	26 loads per month
Microwave oven	1,450	16	18 minutes per day
Range (cooking top and oven)	12,200	62	3 meals per day
Television			
Black and white, solid state	55	10	6 hours per day
Color, solid state	200	37	6 hours per day
Clock	2	1	Continuous
Iron	1100	5	2 hours per week
Radio	70	7	3 hours per day
Stereo with phonograph	110	9	3 hours per day
Curling Iron	15	1	$\frac{1}{2}$ hour per day

[a] Average wattage can be taken from the nameplate of the appliance.

[b] Hours of use vary widely for these appliances. To figure the cost for your household, estimate the number of hours used monthly and multiply by the cost per hour.

Determine the current cost per kilowatt-hour (kwh) for electricity by looking at the "billing detail" section at the bottom of your electric bill or by calling your local utility office. Round off the price per kwh to the closest half cent.

SOURCE: Southern California Edison, "Energy and You, for a Bright Tomorrow."

an energy diet. Instead of counting calories, you will count kilowatts. Table 13.3 presents the average monthly energy consumption of most electric appliances. As you can see, unplugging your electric clock or even permanently abandoning your television set will do little to reduce your energy bill. The major users of electrical energy are appliances that heat or cool. Water heaters, air conditioners, refrigerators, freezers, ranges, and clothes dryers head the list of energy users. Together, they account for most home electricity costs. Have you ever returned home after an extended vacation expecting your electric bill to reflect your absence, only to discover that your utility bill was just about the same? The reason is simple. The water heater, the refrigerator, and the freezer continue to operate in your absence. If you vacationed during the hot summer months, the refrigerator and freezer may have worked even longer to overcome the additional house heat.

Reducing your personal energy budget throughout the year calls for several strategies. There is no simple cure-all. We divide these strategies into three parts, as we did for transportation: (1) cheap techniques, (2) minor expense-saving strategies, and (3) major expense-saving plans. Consumers will not be able to employ all these techniques (some of which you may already know), but energy decisions will certainly improve if they get better information about the alternatives.

Cheap techniques. The single most effective quick-fix conservation technique is regulating your home thermostat. At one time, 72 degrees was considered the optimal temperature for a home, and most thermostats were set at that temperature. If you are willing to deviate from that norm by 6 degrees (78 degrees in the summer and 66 degrees in winter), you will save an estimated 15 percent on your energy bill. Larger savings can be achieved, of course, if you are willing to change the temperature even more. Other simple conservation practices include closing your drapes or blinds at night during the winter, washing and drying only full loads, turning your water-heater thermostat to a lower setting, cooking with a microwave oven, avoiding preheating your oven, matching the stove's burner to the size of your pots and pans, and lighting only work areas rather than entire rooms. Worksheet 13.1 lists these and other simple energy-saving tips.

Minor cash outlays: Retrofitting techniques. Turning down the thermostat during the winter to save energy is similar to changing driving habits to get more miles per gallon. There is no direct cost, but you will have to change your habits and adjust to a different life-style. Other changes in energy consumption involve more than a simple change in behavior; they require investments in energy-saving equipment. Buying and installing new equipment (retrofitting), for example, upgrades the

WORKSHEET 13.1   ENERGY CONSERVATION TIPS

Review the following list to determine what you are already doing to conserve energy. Then go back to see what additional steps you can and will take to save energy as well as money.

	Doing Now	Will Do
Home Heating		
Keep room temperature at 65 degrees or lower. Turn control down at night or when you are away from home. Consider installing a thermostat with a setback feature that does this automatically.	_____	_____
Draw draperies at night to limit heat loss. Open them on sunny days to let heat in.	_____	_____
Close damper when fireplace is not in use.	_____	_____
Check the furnace filter monthly. Replace when dirty.	_____	_____
Check heater filter. Hold it to the light: if light does not pass through readily, replace filter. Cleaning is not recommended (unless heater has a permanent filter).	_____	_____
Turn off furnace pilot at end of heating season, but *only* if you are capable of relighting it.	_____	_____
Laundry		
Wash and dry full loads of clothes. Adjust water level for the size of the load.	_____	_____
Wash clothes in warm or cold water.	_____	_____
Don't overdry clothes. Follow manufacturer's instructions for drying time.	_____	_____
Remove lint from dryer filter before each load.	_____	_____
Remove accumulated material from dryer moisture exhaust.	_____	_____
Consider drying laundry outdoors. Let solar energy do the job.	_____	_____
Lighting		
Keep bulbs and fixtures clean. Accumulations of dust can lower lighting levels.	_____	_____
Turn off unnecessary lights.	_____	_____
Use reflective, light-colored interior decor whenever possible.	_____	_____
Natural lighting should be used whenever it does not interfere with air conditioning.	_____	_____
Water Heating		
Take fast showers.	_____	_____
Repair leaky faucets.	_____	_____
Install water-saving showerheads that restrict water flow.	_____	_____
Operate dishwashers only for full loads.	_____	_____
Set water heater thermostat below normal. Turn to "pilot" position when you are away for extended periods of time (one week or longer).	_____	_____
Use cold water for operating garbage disposal and for prerinsing dishes.	_____	_____
When handwashing dishes, avoid rinsing under continuous hot running water.	_____	_____

Cooking

Do not preheat gas oven. Preheat electric oven only for baked goods requiring precise temperatures at the start of the cooking cycle.

Keep pots and pans covered.

Adjust top burner flame to fit pans.

Reduce burner flame to "simmer" after cooking starts.

Cook by time and temperature. Avoid opening oven door while food is cooking.

Do one-place cooking. Prepare an entire meal using only the oven, the broiler, or the top burner.

Turn all burners off when not in use.

Use a steamer or a pressure cooker to cook several foods at the same time.

Use a microwave oven.

Air Conditioning

Hang a thermometer on the wall and check it to see that room temperature stays above 78 degrees.

Investigate an energy-saving unit. Before buying a room air conditioner, compare the energy efficiency ratios. The higher the number, the more cooling you get from the electricity.

Cut down the use of heat-producing equipment by restricting the use of major appliances (dishwashers and dryers) to early morning or evening. Turn off unused lights.

Clean or replace filters. Clogged filters make your air conditioner work harder and less efficiently.

Shield outdoor air conditioners from sunlight. Be sure that you don't shield the air flow. Plants or lattices are excellent sunscreens.

Keep units clean. Dust or dirt particles can block air flow and waste energy.

Set thermostat higher if you are away from home for most of the day, or install a thermostat with a timer.

Locate thermostats away from heat sources.

Turn thermostat off when you are away from home for 24 hours or more, unless you live in a climate in which air conditioning is needed to prevent damage to furniture or paintings.

Do not overcool. Maintain as warm a temperature as comfort permits to minimize cooling costs and equipment use.

The size of your air-conditioning system is vitally important. An oversized system turns on and off too often, decreasing the efficiency of the unit. An undersized unit operates almost continuously on hot days. Either way, you'll waste energy.

Shade window areas from direct sunlight with window awnings or plants.

Refrigerators and Freezers

Allow food to cool before refrigerating. Your refrigerator has to work harder to cool hot food.

Check your refrigerator door seals occasionally. A misaligned door or a buildup of soil around the gaskets lets cold air out. To test the seal, close the refrigerator door with a dollar bill between the gaskets. If there's resistance as you pull the bill out, the seal is tight.

If refrigerator frost becomes more than a half-inch thick, it acts as an insulator and makes your refrigerator work harder. Defrost frequently, but never use an ice pick or a knife. You could puncture cooling tubes or seriously damage freezer walls.

Keep condenser coils clean (bottom or rear of the refrigerator). If they accumulate dust and dirt, operation will be impaired and cold temperatures cannot be maintained.

Open refrigerator doors only when necessary. Loss of cold air results in unnecessary cycling of the compressor, increasing the amount of electricity used.

Set refrigerators at warmer temperatures during vacations, and leave them fairly empty. When unused for longer periods, refrigerators and freezers should be unplugged, cleaned, and left open.

energy efficiency of an energy-using system by changing some of its components.

Because retrofitting a building or a home costs money, you should estimate the benefits *before* you spend your money. One commonly used way to estimate the usefulness of a particular retrofit is to calculate the **payback period**, the time it takes to get back your investment as a result of lower energy expenditures. The shorter payback period, the more profitable the retrofit.

payback period: the time it takes to recoup a dollar investment

To calculate the payback period, divide the cost of the retrofit by the annual energy saving. For example, if a new furnace costs $3,000 and is 20 percent more efficient than your old one, the payback period can be calculated once you are able to estimate how much money you are saving as a result of the 20 percent decrease in fuel consumption. If the 20 percent decrease in your annual heating bill is $200, then the payback period is 15 years (3,000 ÷ 200 = 15). This is a long payback period, but if fuel costs were to double, so would fuel savings, with the result that the payback period would be cut in half. Here are some suggestions for energy conservation techniques that offer short payback periods:

1. *Insulation* is high on everyone's list of conservation techniques. About one-third of all American homes were built before 1940, when there

**FIGURE 13.9
Recommended
insulation standards
for climate zones of the
United States.** (SOURCE:
U.S. Department of
Energy, Technical
Information Center,
"Insulation Fact Sheet.")

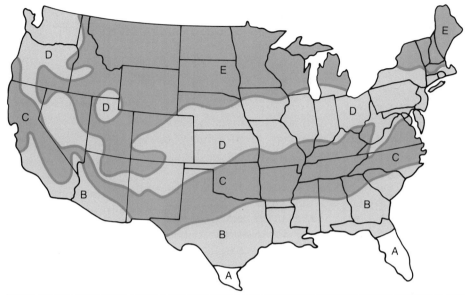

Feature	Zone A	Zone B	Zone C	Zone D	Zone E
1. Ceiling Insulation	R-19	R-19	R-26	R-30	R-38
2. Wall Insulation	R-11	R-11	R-13	R-13	R-19
3. Floors Over Unheated spaces	none	none	R-11	R-11	R-19

were few or no standard requirements for insulation. By some estimates, about 30 percent of the residences in the United States are completely uninsulated, and another one-third are underinsulated (Stobaugh and Yergin, 1979). When standard insulation was installed in a test house in Washington, D.C., the annual energy consumption decreased by 25 percent. In a three-year study conducted in Portland, Seattle, and Spokane, a $981 investment reduced fuel consumption by 50 percent, with a payback period of less than four years (Tsongas, 1977).

The amount of insulation that is most energy efficient and economically justifiable is determined by the climate in a particular area. Figure 13.9 shows the recommended insulation standards for ceilings, walls, and floors in different regions. Generally speaking, the milder the weather, the lower the recommendations. Notice, too, that the standards are listed as **R-values**. The *R* stands for resistance to heat transfer from the outside of the house to the inside of the house. R-values are more accurate than inches as a means of measuring the performance of insulation. The higher the R-value, the greater the resistance to heat flow. For more details on selecting the most cost-effective insulation, see Box 13.3.

2. *Caulking and weather stripping* are two additional energy-saving devices that are simple, cheap, and efficient. Caulking is a puttylike

*R-values: measures of an
insulation's ability to resist
the flow of heat from a
warmer area to a cooler one;
the higher the R-value, the
greater the insulating power
of a given material*

BOX 13.3   CHOOSING THE MOST COST-EFFECTIVE HOME INSULATION

Two homes stand side by side in Mount Airy, Maryland, 40 miles northwest of Baltimore. The homes are identical in almost every respect: size, age, floor plan, and method of heating (all electric). Even the families that occupy the two homes are similar: married couples with two young children. However, one of the houses has utility bills that are 50 percent lower than the other's. Both homes are part of a government study on the economic effects of conservation techniques in the home. The study has found that one of the most cost-effective forms of household energy conservation is insulation.

A few years ago, it was common to recommend a certain number of inches of insulating material to achieve a given level of energy conservation. But today, there are so many different types of insulation material, from mineral to wool to foam, and so many different ways of applying the insulation, from rolling it on to blowing it in, that an inch of one material may not have the same energy-conserving effect as an inch of another. This is the basic reason for the creation of the R-value, which measures the ability of a given insulating material to resist heat transfer.

All stores that sell insulation are required to have the manufacturer's R-value fact sheet for each type of insulation sold. These sheets identify the type of insulation, the manufacturer, the R-value, and the coverage capability. Given these facts and the price

of different insulation materials, here is how to decide which one to buy.

1. Find out what R-value you need. This varies with the part of the house you are insulating and the climate (see Figure 13.9).

2. Decide what kind of insulation to install. Do you want to use a loose fill and blow in the insulation, or do you prefer a blanket type of insulation? You should consult with a building supply house (or two) to see which method suits your need.

3. Measure the area you are going to insulate. Multiplying the length by the width gives you the area in square feet. Check the R-value fact sheet to see how much insulation you need to get the desired R-value. If you install more insulation than you need, you will waste money.

4. Shop for the best deal. To find the lowest cost, compare the dollar cost per unit of R-value. Here is an FTC-recommended way of calculating cost:

$$\frac{\text{price of}}{\text{the}} \div \frac{\text{square feet}}{\text{of insulation}} \div \frac{\text{the}}{\text{R-value}} = \frac{\text{cost per}}{\text{unit of}}$$
$$\text{package} \quad \text{needed for a} \quad \text{number} \quad \text{R-value}$$
$$\text{given R-value}$$

The smaller the number, the more economical the package of insulation.

---

substance that can be squeezed into cracks and crevices where outside air might seep into the house. Weather-stripping performs the same function, but it comes in strips made of felt, foam rubber, vinyl, or interlocking metal. Plugging air leaks can lower home heating and cooling costs by as much as 10 percent, and given the low price of the materials, the payback period may be less than one year.

3. *Doors and windows* play an important role in energy conservation. Storm doors and windows can be purchased in cold climates for about $35 per window and provide energy savings of up to 15 percent. If you are renting a home or an apartment, an investment in storm windows would

not be cost effective, because the payback period is not short enough. But you might tape a sheet of clear plastic reflective film to the inside of the windows. This has been shown to be nearly as effective as exterior storm windows, and the price is exceptionally low. If you own your home you need to know about "low-emissivity," or low-E, windows, which have a nearly invisible layer of metal that lets through only visible light and reflects heat back toward the source. This means that the heat from your fireplace stays inside in the winter and the heat from the sun stays outside in the summer. If you cannot afford to replace all your windows at one time, consider mounting low-E windows on the cold side of your house, where they will do the most good.

4. *Lighting* your home is another area in which some minor changes could lead to long-term savings. First, remove light bulbs or lower their wattage in areas where bright light is not needed. Second, wherever possible, replace incandescent light bulb fixtures with fluorescent ones. Flourescent lights last 20 times longer and produce more light per watt. A 40-watt fluorescent lamp, for example, will produce more light than a 100-watt incandescent bulb. The wattage rating measures electricity used, not light given off. Engineers measure light in units called **lumens**. A bulb that gives off 900 lumens is twice as bright as one that emits 450 lumens. Higher-wattage bulbs tend to give off more lumens and thus are more efficient than a combination of lower-wattage bulbs. A 100-watt bulb might be rated at 1,750 lumens, whereas two 60-watt blubs together might have only 1,740 lumens. The new long-life bulbs last longer partly because they deliver less light (lumens). This, coupled with their higher price, makes them a poor buy, unless you are lighting an area where the bulb is difficult to replace. If you follow these tips, you can save electricity costs.

5. *Other indoor energy savings* can be achieved with a variety of retrofits. Insulating your water heater with a wraparound blanket and installing reduced-flow shower heads that conserve hot water can reduce your energy bill up to 5 percent. Replacing oven and furnace pilot lights with electric ignition devices may seem like a small change, but oven pilot lights account for more than 40 percent of the fuel that ovens consume.

6. *Exterior energy conservation* can also be an important part of a retrofit program. Trees planted on the southern side of a house give pleasant cooling shade during the summer months and do not interfere with the winter sun's rays, because they conveniently shed their leaves in fall. This type of energy conservation is known as a **passive solar technique**, because it uses the sun's energy and doesn't require a mechanism with moving parts. Large, south-facing windows under an overhanging roof are also examples of passive solar design; they allow the sun's rays to penetrate and warm the home's exterior when the sun is low in winter, and they block rays in the summer when the sun is high overhead.

passive solar techniques: designs that take advantage of the sun's energy without using moving parts

Major expenditures on energy conservation. Consumers have many opportunities to try low-cost and no-cost energy-conservation strategies but few chances to make major expenditures for energy conservation. But major conservation strategies are just as important. A family may buy only three refrigerators over its entire life cycle, but it will have to live with each decision for an average of 15 years. A poor energy choice will cost hundreds of dollars over the life of the purchase, whereas an energy-efficient choice will pay dividends over the life of the purchase. A similar argument can be made for buying, building, or renovating a home. The size of the total expenditure coupled with the infrequency of the expense requires that consumers spend more time gathering information and investigating energy options.

solar energy: direct sunlight or indirect forms of energy (such as wind or falling water) that are produced by the interaction of sunlight and the earth

One of the most interesting energy options available today is **solar energy**. We mentioned passive solar techniques above, but in this section we focus on **active solar systems**, which use the sun's energy but also require mechanical parts.

A primary example of active solar technology is the solar water heater. Such heaters consist of panels, each about three by seven feet, which are bolted on the roof facing south. The panels, generally made of aluminum, glass, plastic, and copper, catch and concentrate the sun's rays, which in turn heat the water or air that flows through pipes in the panel. Fans or pumps then circulate the heated air or water through a heat exchanger, which transfers the solar heat to a storage tank. Cool water is returned to the solar panel, and the water in the storage tank is generally hot enough to be used in the house. Three panels are enough to satisfy the hot-water needs of an average house, and it is estimated that one-third of all American houses are suitable for this type of conversion (Maidique, 1979).

Contrary to popular belief, solar water heating is not a new idea. It has been available to American consumers since the early part of the twentieth century. Twenty-five percent of the homes in Pasadena, California, had solar water heaters in 1920. Miami, Florida, had more than 50,000 solar water heaters still in place in 1950; most were more than 20 years old. Americans abandoned their solar water heaters for a very good reason: cost. Natural gas was so much cheaper to use, when it was readily available, that people turned their backs on active solar technology. Now, with rising energy costs, many people are reconsidering solar power. Many new housing developments, such as those in Davis, California, are having solar water heating and space heating built in before the homes are sold. The world's largest solar-heated building, a 325,000-square-foot athletic field, is in the heart of oil country, Tabuk, Saudi Arabia.

If there are solar facilities in Saudi Arabia, it is probably worth your while to consider solar heating. But for the choice to make economic sense, you must consider the costs and the benefits. Suppose, for example, that

Solar water heaters are good examples of an active solar system, but shrubs and trees are also ways of conserving energy through passive solar techniques.

for $2,400 you could buy a solar water-heating system that would satisfy 75 percent of your hot-water needs each year. If you owned an average electric water heater, you might be using 500 kwh per month (see Table 13.3), and at 8 cents per kilowatt-hour, this amounts to $40 per month, or $480 per year. With a solar water heater, you would save $360 per year (0.75 × $480), and your payback period would be 6.7 years ($2,400 ÷ $360). This would justify going solar, and you would have two added benefits: (1) you would be protected against a further rise in the cost of electricity, and (2) the solar system would increase the value of your house. Of course, if you had a natural-gas water heater, the energy costs of which are generally a third of electricity costs, the payback period would be tripled (almost 20 years), so the system would not be justifiable on purely economic grounds.

Consumers also make large investments in refrigerators and air conditioners. The FTC requires that all large electrical appliances be rated for energy efficiency. The standard measure is called the **energy efficiency ratio (EER)**. The EER typically ranges from 4.0 to 12.0. The higher the EER, the greater the energy efficiency of the unit. An air conditioner with an EER of 4.0 costs three times as much to operate as one with an EER of 12.0. The EER is computed by dividing the cooling power of the appliance (rated in **British thermal units [Btu]**) by the watts consumed. For example, a unit that produces 8,500 Btu per hour and uses 1,000 watts per hour has an EER of 8.5. You may find another model that produces the same output (8,500 Btu) but uses only 900 watts per hour. The second unit has an EER of 9.4 (8,500 ÷ 900). Because it uses less, it has a higher EER, which can be translated into an energy saving of 100 watts per hour, or 0.1 kilowatt (1 kilowatt equals 1,000 watts).

To determine your annual energy saving, multiply the hourly energy saving by the number of summer cooling hours in your area. In Bangor, Maine, which averages 360 summer cooling hours annually, the air conditioner with a 9.4 EER would save 36 kwh each year (0.1 × 360). To determine dollars saved, multiply the annual kilowatt saving by the cost of a kilowatt. At 5 cents per kilowatt-hour, the more efficient unit would save a Maine family $1.80. But in New Orleans, for which the FTC estimates 2,090 cooling hours, the saving would be $9.95. So a $10 difference in the cost of the two units would be paid back in the first year in New Orleans but would take almost six years to pay back in Maine.

Your local electric company can tell you the average number of cooling days in your area, if you wish to make the comparison yourself. The FTC now requires that all literature that accompanies air conditioners list the **seasonal energy efficiency rating (SEER)** and the expected average cost of the energy the air conditioner will use. Although this allows consumers to make some rough comparisons between models, it does not give them a precise indication of the cost, because seasonal cooling hours vary from place to place (from 40 hours in Anchorage to 3,950 in Honolulu) and because the price of a kilowatt-hour of electricity varies from 2 to 14 cents. To make an informal comparison between two units with the same cooling power (Btu rating), obtain the information needed to use the following formula:

$$\frac{\text{difference in watts}}{1,000} \times \frac{\text{summer cooling}}{\text{hours}} \times \frac{\text{cost per}}{\text{kilowatt-hour}}$$

Suppose the comparison is between two 9,000-Btu air conditioners: unit A, which uses 860 watts per hour and has an EER of 10.5, and

energy efficiency ratio (EER):
A measure of the ability of an appliance to economize on the use of electricity; for a cooling appliance, it is calculated by dividing the unit's cooling output (measured in Btu's) by the watts needed. The higher the EER, the less the unit costs to operate.

unit B, which uses 1,100 watts per hour and has an EER of 8.2. The difference in watts is 240. Let us also assume that the local utility company says that there is an average summer cooling load of 2,000 hours and that the price of electriciy is 8 cents per kilowatt-hour. How much would the more energy-efficient unit save each year?

$$\frac{240}{1,000} \times 2,000 \text{ hours} \times \$0.08 = \$38.40$$

The difference in wattage per kilowatt times the number of summer cooling hours times the price per kilowatt-hour gives the answer: $38.40. Of course, if the cost of electricity rises, the saving from the more efficient unit also rises. In the 1970s, electricity could generally be purchased for 4 cents per kilowatt-hour. In the 1990s, 9 cents per kilowatt-hour is closer to the average price. The increase doubles energy savings and cuts payback time in half.

Energy-Saving Systems in New Homes

According to the National Association of Home Builders, 69 percent of new home buyers have placed energy efficiency at the top of their shopping list (Howard, 1987). Many home builders have taken heed of this desire, and are utilizing energy conservation research and incorporating new techniques to create houses that are 25 percent more efficient than in the 1980s. Many experts look forward to a time when homes can actually produce energy rather than consume it. The basis of this optimism is the adaptation of construction techniques and designs to the regional climate demands; insulation of attic, roof, and walls; utilization of double-glazed, triple-glazed, or low-E windows; use of higher-efficiency heating, ventilation, and air-conditioning equipment; and installation of passive solar systems when appropriate.

Incorporating these features does increase the initial cost of the home. However, owners of energy-efficient homes will have lower costs for heating and cooling and often for hot water. Potential home buyers can seek more information from the National Association of Home Builders, Technical Services Department, 15th and M Streets, N.W., Washington DC 20002. Inquire about the Thermal Performance Guidelines (TPGs) for your region.

WATER, THE ENVIRONMENT, AND THE CONSUMER

Another natural resource that is increasingly of concern for consumers— and rightly so—is water. Although there is more water on the planet than any other commodity, there are times when enough is not available. We need water for our morning coffee, to wash our cars, and to bathe ourselves and our dogs. Of course, on a grander scale we need water to create our food supply, including fruits, vegetables, bread, milk and meat. Many of us need water on the job in order to create a product or provide a service. This section will explore the seemingly endless supply of water, discuss the implications of water supply on consumer budgets, and look at household water conservation.

Water Supply: So Much, Yet So Little

groundwater: water that sinks into the soil, where it is stored and can be slowly renewed in underground reservoirs

Your body is about 70 percent water. Water is the major component of all animals and plants on earth. In our environment we are surrounded by water in the oceans, lakes, and streams. But about 97 percent of the earth's total water is found in the oceans and is too salty for drinking, agriculture, and most industrial uses. The remaining 3 percent is fresh water, but it is mostly unavailable for use. About five-sixths of it is too far underground or is tied up in glaciers, polar ice caps, or the atmosphere. Of the remaining water found in lakes, streams, or recoverable underground deposits, called **groundwater**, much of it is too expensive to tap or is polluted. The remaining usable supply amounts to about 0.003 percent of the world's supply, still a very respectable 232,000 gallons for each person on earth (Miller, 1988, p. 209). And this is a renewable resource, as long as we don't use up or pollute the water supply faster than it can replace or purify itself via rain percolating through the soil.

If there is so much water, why the concern? First, water is often in the wrong place at the wrong time. In some areas of the world, there is too much rain all at once, causing massive flooding, death, and destruction. Other areas suffer from inadequate and irregular precipitation. This reduced precipitation usually triggers a drought (this has been the situation in parts of Asia and Africa in recent years). To get water, women and children in such areas often need to walk 10 to 15 miles each day, carrying home heavy water-filled containers. Even after these efforts, the water may not be safe to drink; three out of five people in developing countries do not have access to clean, disease-free drinking water. The World Health Organization estimates that 80 percent of all disease in these countries can be traced to the water that people drink and in which they bathe.

The availability of water to *you*, as well as its cost, depends on where you live. Much of the eastern half of the United States has adequate water supply and sometimes suffers from floods. It also has increasing difficulty in supplying nonpolluted drinking water due to contamination from industrial wastes, leaking septic tanks, and landfills. The central and western states, which produce much of the nation's food supply, generally have too little precipitation. As a result, farmers and cities are drawing out groundwater at increasing rates, risking water depletion and sinking of the ground, a situation that will only be exacerbated as more people and industries move to the West.

We will now look at the ways that safe water can be made available to consumers, with an eye to economics and household budgets.

Managing Our Water Supplies

In the early years of our country's growth, water supply was generally not a problem as people tended to locate their towns and villages near a lake or stream. As the westward movement began in earnest, so did the search for groundwater. In the twentieth century, as towns and cities grew beyond their water supplies, they sent engineers in search of this precious commodity, to transport it back to the needy communities to water the crops and supply factories and kitchens. Rather than paying for the cost of exploration for and the transportation of water in their water bill, users paid for it in municipal taxes. Soon, tunnels and canals stretched like a maze across the country, diverting water from lakes and streams from one community to another. As you might expect, this caused resentment at the very least, and all-out war in some cases. Today, land developers and energy companies often find themselves at odds with farmers. Environmentalists often disagree with those who love certain water sports. Negotiations in and out of court have been the result. Many western states have negotiated with each other over water rights, as has northern California with southern California, and the United States with Mexico.

As Figure 13.10 shows, municipal water users, such as residents, restaurant owners, and libraries, consume relatively little water. The biggest user is agriculture, followed by industry. But it is in the best interest of consumers to understand water usage, since they pay for it not only in the utility bill, but also in the cost of products. For example it takes 3,200 gallons of water each day to grow the food for a family of four. It takes 50,000 gallons of water to create the nylon carpet in a typical house, and 4,500 gallons to produce the steel in a washing machine (Chiras, 1988).

So, we pay the water bill directly and indirectly in the cost of goods and services, as well as in city, state, and federal taxes. The methods

**FIGURE 13.10
National water use.**
(SOURCE: U.S. Geological Survey, *Estimated Use of Water in the United States.*)

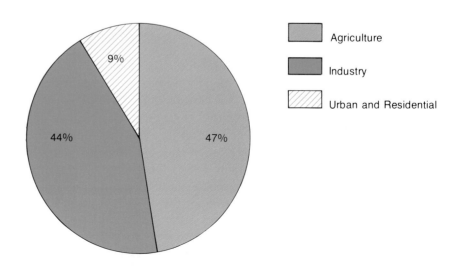

Agriculture

Industry

Urban and Residential

9%

44%

47%

for providing a safe, adequate water supply are numerous but are not without costs, both financial and environmental. Here, we will explore options that can be chosen by local, state and federal agencies, including tapping groundwater, building dams and reservoirs, water diversion projects, desalination, and conservation and recycling. (In the next section we will look at conservation from the residential perspective.) The choices that your governing bodies make will depend upon your input and will affect the price you pay for water, the quality of the water, and the impact of the decision on the environment.

Tapping groundwater. About half of all drinking water (96 percent in rural areas and 20 percent in urban areas) and 40 percent of all irrigation water is withdrawn from underground water supplies. This water is found in **aquifers**, layers of sand, gravel, and porous rock under the earth's crust. The porous rock filters the water and removes suspended particles and bacteria, creating excellent-quality water. The rate of recharging, or replacing this groundwater is very slow, however. Between 1950 and 1985 the rate of withdrawals of groundwater supplies tripled. Four problems can occur if withdrawal of groundwater is excessive.

1. *Aquifer depletion, or overdraft.* This occurs when water is withdrawn at a rate faster than it is recharged. Presently, there is a particular problem with the Ogallala Aquifer, which supplies water to the farm-belt region located between northern Nebraska and northeastern Texas.

2. *Subsidence, or sinking.* When water is withdrawn without being replaced, the soil in the aquifer compacts, creating a sunken area. This has occurred in the San Joaquin Valley of California and in Phoenix and is a potential problem in Houston and New Orleans.

3. *Salt-water intrusion.* In coastal areas where groundwater is not adequately replenished, salt water seeps into the soil to replace the fresh water. Intrusion now threatens drinking water of towns and cities along the Atlantic and Gulf coasts. Once intrusion occurs, it is difficult to reverse.

4. *Groundwater contamination.* Agricultural and industrial activities that chemically pollute the lakes, rivers, streams and air also gradually pollute the aquifers. It may take hundreds to thousands of years for contaminated groundwater to cleanse itself. Of particular concern is the public revelation in 1988 that since the early 1950s, tons of radioactive materials were released into our water supply by U.S. weapons plants (Magnuson, 1988). Groundwater contamination is a problem in hundreds of communities around the nation and may be a causal factor in some forms of cancer.

Dams and reservoirs. Once the local groundwater seems inadequate for agricultural, industrial, and urban needs, a search by local and state leaders for other sources of water usually commences. Snowmelt and rainfall can be captured by dams on rivers and stored in reservoirs behind the dams. The result is increased water supply, generation of inexpensive electricity, flood control for areas below the dam, and the creation of some forms of recreation, such as boating and swimming. The economic costs of these water projects are usually shared by the state and federal government.

The benefits just described must be weighed against the high cost of dam and reservoir construction and the changed environment. The permanent flooding behind the dams to form reservoirs displaces people from their homes and communities and alters valuable agricultural land, wildlife habitat, and natural scenic beauty. Good farmland below the dam that depended upon the natural flow of nutrient-rich sediment often must be abandoned or heavily fertilized. Dams interfere with the natural migration of fish to spawning grounds and reduce the flow of nutrients to estuaries. An **estuary** is a coastal region or wetland, for example, at the mouth of a river or inlet, where salt and fresh water mix. Two-thirds of all fish and shellfish depend on estuaries during some part of their life cycle. As nutrients to estuaries decrease, so does our food supply. As for recreational activities, a dam replaces white-water rafting and canoeing, kayaking, and stream fishing, with sailboating and lake fishing. And a dam is not forever. Depending upon the local climate and land-use practices, a dam will fill with silt in 20 to 200 years, if it doesn't come apart first. In 1986 the Federal Emergency Management Agency reported that the United States has 1,900 unsafe dams in populated areas due to weak state laws regulating construction and inspection and budget cuts preventing repairs.

Since the economic and environmental costs of dams are so high, consumers are reminded that they have a responsibility to study dam and reservoir proposals that appear on the ballot, to do their own cost–benefit analysis, and act accordingly.

Water diversion projects. Moving water from a water-rich region to a water-poor region is the most popular solution to the shortage problem. Frequently, water is moved from a rural, less-populated area to an urban, densely populated, and politically powerful region. Los Angeles, Phoenix, Denver, and New York benefit from extensive water-diversion projects. Because up to 80 percent of the annual run-off of some streams may be taken, the environment can be changed dramatically

For example, diversion of clean, high mountain snowmelt from the Colorado River to western states via the Central Arizona Project ultimately diminishes the quality of the water flow in the Colorado River. The lower sections of the river carry less water, along with a heavy amount of sediment and concentration of dissolved salt. Salt concentration is 40 parts per million (ppm) at the headwaters of the Colorado, but by the time the water reaches Mexico it can have over 800 ppm, violating a U.S.–Mexican treaty. (Drinking water is considered acceptable with 500 ppm, while the agricultural limit is 700 ppm.) In order to improve the situation, in 1973 Congress authorized the construction of three desalination plants along the river for the necessary removal of 400,000 tons of salt annually.

Desalination. Removing salt from ocean or groundwater has a definite appeal. The basic problem with the methods used for this process is that they require large amounts of energy, making water obtained by desalination four to ten times more expensive than water from other sources. Additional expenditures of energy would be necessary to pump desalted water uphill and from the coasts to inland water-short locations. Thus, this option is one of the least viable for meeting our water needs.

Conservation and recycling. As noted, agriculture and industry are the major users of water. Agricultural specialists at university extension offices around the country, in conjunction with the USDA and local state and county governments, have studied water conservation. As a result of their research and information dissemination, farmers are beginning to switch from open, dirt-lined irrigation ditches to plastic-lined ditches or pipe and from overhead sprinklers to drip or trickle irrigation. Some farmers are also employing computers to detect water leaks and set water flow rates according to soil moisture and weather conditions.

Industry can design processes that use less water or recycle water. More than 80 percent of all water used in U.S. manufacturing is in four industries: paper, chemicals, petroleum, and primary metals. During a 20-year period, from 1968 to 1988, these four industries increased their recycling by more than 400 percent, but much more could still be done. For example, to produce a ton of paper, a paper mill in Hadera, Israel, uses only one-tenth the water used in a typical U.S. mill (Miller, 1988, p. 229).

The results of water management decisions will be born by consumers today as well as by generations to come. Consumers have a responsibility to be alert to municipal and federal policies and provide decision-making input. They can help decide if conservation should be voluntary or mandatory. Since U.S. taxpayers pay for water management projects, such as dams, diversion projects, and desalination plants, agriculture and industry have little incentive to conserve or recycle. This is particularly true of industry where water may only account for about 3 percent of manufacturing costs.

As water shortages worsen and the awareness levels of government, business, and consumer leaders heighten, recycling wastewater may become more common. We may emulate the Mitsubishi leaders in Tokyo

FIGURE 13.11
Daily water use in the home. Anywhere from 75 to 100 gallons of water are used inside the home by each individual each day. This amount does not include water used outside for garden and lawn care, washing cars, and so on. Household use will vary with size of family and water use habits.
(SOURCE: U.S. Geological Survey, *Estimated Use of Water in the United States.*)

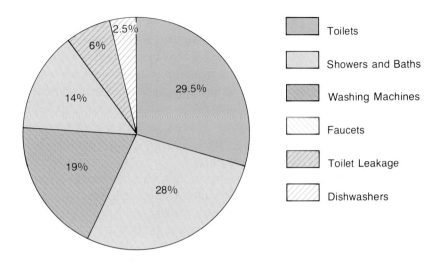

Legend:
- Toilets
- Showers and Baths
- Washing Machines
- Faucets
- Toilet Leakage
- Dishwashers

whose 60-story office building has a fully automated recycling system that purifies all of the building's wastewater, making it safe to drink.

Water Conservation in the Home

As more communities find that they have inadequate water for their needs, consumers are being asked to conserve water, and are even offered financial incentives to do so. Much conservation can be accomplished in the home. When water meters were introduced in Boulder, Colorado, and people were charged according to consumption, rather than given a flat service rate, water consumption dropped by one-third. Some water districts award a rebate to owners of new homes for having a minimal lawn, or for using **xeriscape**, that is, landscaping with plants that require only rainwater for survival. This could provide double benefits if you reside in a water district that charges a premium price for water used during warm, summer months. Other financial incentives go to those who install ultra-low flush toilets. As Larry Farwell, Conservation Program director for Goleta, California, explained: "We've found that to develop more water supply through toilets costs us about $200 per acre-foot . . . [including the rebate program, which compares favorably] to $500 per acre foot to build a new reservoir, $900 to connect to the state water system, and $2,200 per acre-foot to desalinate ocean water" (Johnston, 1988). And this from a community located on the ocean, just north to Santa Barbara.

xeriscape: landscaping with plants that require only rainwater for survival

Before you know what conservation measures will be best for you, a bit of information about residential water usage will be necessary. Figure 13.11 shows how a typical resident in the Los Angeles Basin consumes water within the home, excluding lawn and garden care. Notice that 29.5 percent of the water is used to flush toilets. With each flush, a typical toilet in the United States turns five gallons of drinking-quality water into wastewater. Another 6 percent of household consumption is lost to toilet leakage. A large chunk, 28 percent, is used for showers and baths; hence the recommendation during a drought to "shower with a friend." The water your family uses will depend upon your family size and usage habits, but chances are you can benefit by making some changes. As with previous conservation tips, we present those that require little or no monetary investment, a minor cash outlay, and major expenditures.

Cheap techniques. Many water districts provide customers with water-saving flow restrictors free of charge; these can easily be installed on all faucets and shower heads. A flow restrictor can also be purchased for about $1. Since toilets are heavy users of water, some municipalities also provide plastic bags for use in toilet tanks; you fill these with water, reducing the amount of water per flush by displacement. In lieu of this, use a tall plastic bottle, filled with water, weighted with stones, and sealed. Bricks also work, but eventually they disintegrate and muck up the water. (And consider the hint found on a bathroom wall in a drought-stricken area: "If it's yellow, let it mellow; if it's brown, flush it down.")

Other water conservation tips relate to changing old habits or establishing new ones. Don't keep water running unnecessarily for brushing teeth, shaving, washing, or showering. Keep a jug of drinking water in the refrigerator to eliminate running tap water until it's cold enough. While waiting for the faucet water to get hot enough, catch the cool water in a pan or pitcher for cooking or watering plants. Avoid using a garbage disposal. Run automatic dish and clothes washers only with full loads, using the appropriate water temperatures and shortest cycles. For outdoor tasks, sweep walks and driveways instead of hosing them off. Reduce water evaporation by watering lawns and plants in the early morning or later in the evening. Do not use water-intensive ornamental plants. Wash your car less frequently, using a bucket of soapy water, saving the hose for rinsing.

Minor outlays. Check for toilet, shower, and sink leaks, and repair them immediately, as a pinhole leak in the household water system can cost up to $25 a month in excess water and electricity charges, and a fast leak can cost even more. Outdoors, use drip irrigation and mulch for plants. Landscape with pebbles, wood chips, and drought-tolerant plants.

Major expenditures. Replace your toilet with a low-flow (3.5 gallons per flush) or ultralow-flow (1.6 gallons per flush) model or, where health codes permit, a waterless or composting toilet. Some communities offer rebates to consumers or landlords who replace toilets, since this not only saves water but places a lesser strain on sewer systems. Replace your current lawn and landscaping with xeriscape. Conservation and recycling of water around the home can make an important contribution to water management efforts, as well as play a role in keeping water affordable. New laws and codes can help reduce water consumption by requiring water-conserving toilets and shower heads. Local communities could also encourage the implementation of special systems to reuse wastewater for lawns and gardens or systems that purify and completely recycle wastewater.

COSTS AND CONSEQUENCES OF ENERGY AND WATER USE

To this point, we have been exploring energy and water use and have suggested many ways to control consumption and hence the impact on family budgets. Now we will go a step further, showing some of the societal costs of consuming energy, paid for by consumers in gas, electric, water, sewage, and trash bills, local and federal taxes, and a diminished environment.

People who study systems, whether economic, political, or environmental, recognize that all parts of a system are interconnected and interrelated. If a change occurs in one part of the system, a commensurate change occurs in another part of the system. For example, say the system is your family budget and there is a change in the cost of energy, specifically an increase in energy prices, including gasoline, electricity, and natural gas; you will make a commensurate change in your spending, consciously or unconsciously. What the change *is* depends upon your decision making, but options include spending less money for food or recreation or increasing your income; otherwise, you will go into debt. As a nation, and despite conservation efforts, we are consuming more and more energy each year. The change, or consequence, has been depletion of nonrenewable resources and rising energy prices. Other changes, or consequences, have been polluted water, polluted air, and increasing amounts of **urban solid waste**, commonly thought of by consumers as trash. Awareness of these environmental problems has gradually been developing over the past two decades. The direct impact on family budgets, however, has been ignored by most of us, and yet it is very real. In this next section we explore the interrelationships among energy consumption, pure water, waste disposal clean air, and your money.

urban solid waste: typically called trash, any unwanted or discarded material that is not liquid or gas

Is It Safe to Drink?

We have explained the sources of household water and explored how communities have ensured an adequate water supply. Here, we are concerned with the quality of the water, an issue that has led about one out of every 20 of us to drink bottled water at an average cost of $1 per gallon. Some people have even gone to the expense of installing activated-charcoal filter units under their home sinks. These units, which may cost from $500 to $2,500, filter most toxic synthetic chemicals but do not filter out toxic metals. All of this is done to ensure safe drinking water, something that most of us believe to be our right and many of us think we are already getting.

We assume that you would prefer not to have the additional expense of bottled water for cooking and drinking. Nor would you wish to go to the added expense of adding a water-purifying system to your home or spend the time to change the filter frequently. We are also sure that you do not want to worry about the safety of the water you swim in or wonder if there are toxic chemicals in the fish you eat. To avoid unnecessary expenditures and worry, you need to know what is being done nationally to ensure water safety. Armed with this background, you need to investigate your local situation and draw your own conclusions about your local water supply.

Historically, water contamination has afflicted many civilizations. The recognition of the link between water supplies and disease first led to filtration and then to chlorination; three-fourths of U.S. water is now treated. But chlorine is powerless against agricultural or industrial chemicals that run off or are dumped into lakes, rivers, or streams. Only in the past 20 years have we had the technology to detect minute quantities of pollutants. As a result of the 1974 Safe Drinking Water Act, which was amended in 1986, the Environmental Protection Agency (EPA) issued maximum contaminant levels for bacteria, radioactivity, ten inorganic chemicals (including lead), and ten organic chemicals (such as the weed killer 2,4-D, which makes up 50 percent of the infamous product known as Agent Orange used during the Vietnam war.) The law leaves about 700 other chemicals unregulated, although the 1986 amendment required the EPA to set standards for another 83 contaminates by 1989 and 25 more by 1991.

Following the passage of the Safe Drinking Water Act, the EPA surveyed the water supplies of 80 cities and found that all of them contained at least one of the six potentially harmful chemicals investigated (Carey, 1984). By 1985 the situation had improved; the EPA reported that 87 percent of the 59,000 municipal water systems were in compliance with the Safe Drinking Water Act. Water from private wells is not required to meet the standards, primarily because the cost of individual testing exceeds $1,000 per well. A study by Cornell University indicated, however, that two out of three U.S. rural residents were drinking water from wells that did not meet the federal standards for one or more pollutants (Miller, 1988, p. 483).

Recognizing that safe drinking water is partially dependent upon unpolluted surface water, Congress passed the Federal Water Pollution Act of 1972 and the Clean Water Act of 1977 (with amendments in 1981 and

1987), with the goal of making surface waterways, such as lakes and streams, safe for swimming and fishing. Prior to this legislation, many communities were using their waterways as sewers, killing fish and making the water unsuitable, if not unsafe, for swimming. By 1986 more than $45 billion dollars was spent by the federal government, primarily for sewage treatment plants, to remedy this situation. However, many large cities still purposely release billions of gallons of untreated sewage into their harbors, lakes, and the ocean, so much remains to be done.

As mentioned earlier, parts of systems are interconnected and interrelated. This is definitely true of our global water system, perhaps our most important renewable resource. Recognizing this, consumers need to be as concerned about where their wastewater goes as they are about where their fresh water comes from. Dumping wastewater into the headwaters of a river will negatively affect the quality of the water downriver. If we swim in harbors and bays where sewage has been dumped or eat fish caught in these waters, some scientists believe we are increasing our chances of contracting cancer. For these reasons, we need to know where waterborne waste goes in our communities after we flush the toilet or run the garbage disposal.

Down the Drain

raw sewage: waterborne wastes from homes, factories, and perhaps streets that has received no mechanical or chemical treatment

In urban areas waterborne wastes from homes, factories, and streets flow through a series of sewer pipes to a sewage treatment plant. Most urban areas have separate pipes for sewage and for storm runoff. Some cities, particularly in the East, have one system because initial construction is cheaper. Unfortunately, during heavy rains, the total volume of water can increase a hundred-fold, causing the system to overflow and discharge **raw sewage**, untreated, into surface waters, creating an obvious health problem.

When sewage reaches the treatment plant, it undergoes various levels of purification. **Primary sewage treatment** is a mechanical process that filters out debris, such as sticks and stones, and then provides for a settling time, removing about 60 percent of suspended solids from the water. **Secondary sewage treatment** is a biological process that uses aerobic bacteria to remove biodegradable organic wastes and then allows for sedimentation. The remaining suspended solids settle out as **sludge**. This process removes three times as much oxygen-demanding wastes as primary treatment, as well as most suspended solids. The final step in either process is to disinfect the water, usually with chlorine gas, which kills disease-carrying bacteria and some, but not all, viruses. The water is then discharged into surface water, such as harbor or river. In the case of secondary treatment, the sludge can be converted to fertilizer or buried in a landfill. The Clean Water Act mandated that all communities served by sewage treatment plants must use secondary treatment, but to date not all communities have complied. Consumers have been paying for these treatment plants, and will continue to do so, through local and federal taxes.

After the passage of the water protection regulation in the 1970s, the EPA discovered that as pollution in the surface waters was halted or decreased, pollution in the groundwater increased. It was deduced that since pollutants could not be discharged into rivers, they were being dumped on the land, and percolating into wells and aquifers. As noted previously, the soil and porous rocks under the ground do filter harmful bacteria but are virtually helpless against many artificial organic chemicals.

The United States has no comprehensive legislation, goals, or funding to protect its precious groundwater supply. There is a clear connection between what we put into our water supply and the quality of our drinking water. We can do our part at home and on the job by being sensitive to the problem. Toxic chemicals are found in many common products, such as automotive waste oil, antifreeze, insecticides, herbicides, paints, lacquers, and cleaning products. These products should never be poured down a sink, toilet, or street drain. Call the local health, water, or trash department for proper disposal methods.

Waste Disposal: Where Is "Away"?

Ironically, as water quality and air quality have improved, or at least not worsened, despite population growth, in the past 20 years, waste disposal has become an enormous problem. Any useless or unwanted material that is not a liquid or a gas is classified as solid waste. This includes the things consumers typically call trash, such as junk mail, newspapers, empty jars and cans, grass clippings, broken appliances, and worn-out sofas. It also includes sludge from sewer treatment plants, fly ash removed from smokestack exhaust, and mining, manufacturing, and agricultural waste. Much of this waste is recycled, particularly by agriculture. Urban solid waste produced by homes and businesses makes up only 3 percent of all of the solid waste in the United States, about four pounds per person per day. Because much of the waste is generated in densely populated areas, it needs to be removed quickly and effectively before it poses a health hazard.

Most people, perhaps even readers of this text, don't care where their waste goes, as long as it disappears, with no traces of flies, rodents, or odors. But this service can be costly. In 1986, for example, we spent $10 billion to have urban waste removed and deposited out of our sight. In the past decade these fees doubled as older sites for disposal became filled and needed to be replaced by more sophisticated types, as we became more knowledgeable of the ecological consequences of past disposal methods.

Before the passage of the Resource Conservation and Recovery Act (RCRA) in 1976 most urban solid waste was literally dumped on the ground at predetermined locations. These **open dumps** were unsightly and a health hazard due to insects and rodents. As we have since discovered they also introduced toxic substances to our groundwater and surface water through leaching or run-off. The RCRA banned the creation of new open dumps, and required that all open dumps be closed or updated as sanitary landfills.

sanitary landfill: land waste disposal site that is located to minimize water pollution from runoff and where waste deposits are covered and compacted daily

More than 80 percent of urban solid waste is deposited in **sanitary landfills**. These waste disposal sites are located geologically and prepared to minimize water pollution from run-off. Solid waste is transported to the site and immediately compacted and covered with dirt. Years later, when the space is filled, it can be used as a green belt or for recreation, but not for building, as the land will subside, or sink, over time. Some landfills generate energy by collecting the methane gas produced by the anaerobic decomposition of organic waste. The gas is then used for heating fuel or for generating electricity.

A major difficulty facing sanitary landfills today is the "nimby" syndrome. **Nimby**, the acronym for *"not in my backyard,"* expresses how most people feel about sanitary landfills. People object to the traffic, noise, dust, and, indeed, just to the idea of living near a landfill. Because of this opposition, the increasing amounts of solid waste, and the lack of environmentally acceptable sites, more than half the cities in the United States have run out of acceptable landfill sites. This means increasing costs as local government leaders search for an acceptable place to throw away our trash.

An obvious piece of the puzzle is to generate less trash. Here consumers have an important role to play at home and on the job, where waste materials can be separated and recycled. Typical categories include glass, paper, metals, food scraps, and lawn clippings. City collectors, private haulers, volunteer groups, or a combination of these can collect the segregated wastes and sell them to scrap dealers, compost plants, and manufacturers. Studies have shown that **source separation** takes only 16 minutes per week for the average family. This low-technology approach to waste management produces little air and water pollution and has low start-up costs and moderate operating costs. For example, it costs an average of $30 a ton to recycle solid waste, while it costs $50 a ton to place it in a landfill and $65 to $75 a ton to incinerate it. If source separation were implemented nationally, it could save 5 percent of U.S. energy consumption, which is more than the energy generated by all U.S. nuclear power plants, at perhaps one-hundredth of the cost (Miller, 1988, p. 498).

source separation: The separation at the point of use of resources like glass, aluminium, and papers for the purpose of recycling

It is estimated that recycling and reuse of products by households and businesses could eliminate 30 to 40 percent of urban solid waste. Did you know that almost three-fourths of the U.S. consumption of paper goods ends up in the trash, most of it in the form of newspapers? That's a lot of trees! Newspapers are easy to recycle and/or can be shared. Another way to decrease solid waste is to change some consumption habits. Avoid overconsumption; buy only what you really need. Buy products that last longer, and take good care of them. Avoid products that are overpackaged, as packaging just adds to the product cost. Give away products you no longer want; numerous charities and religious groups can help you locate those in need. In other words, be an environmentally and economically wise consumer.

On a Clear Day You Can See Forever

As noted above, everything in a system is interconnected and interrelated. For example, when we reduce energy consumption, we also contribute to reducing air pollution. This is certainly desirable, since transportation and industrial fuel combustion are the major sources of air pollutants in the United States (see Figure 13.12). On the other hand, some of the ways we solve our waste management problems increase air pollution. In this section we will briefly explore the connection between energy consumption, air pollution, and your wallet.

Most urban areas have some type and some degree of **air pollution**. An air pollutant is any chemical that is added to or forms in the air, causing harm to humans, other animals, vegetation, or metals and other materials. Most air pollutants come from motor vehicles (49 percent) or fuel combustion from stationary sources, such as power plants, and then are emitted into the air. We recognize air pollution by its grayish haze and by our decreased visibility and burning eyes. Groups particularly sensitive to air pollution include the very young, the elderly, and those with heart or lung disorders, chronic nasal congestions, colds, or allergies.

**FIGURE 13.12
Air pollutants: where they come from.** (SOURCE: Environmental Protection Agency.)

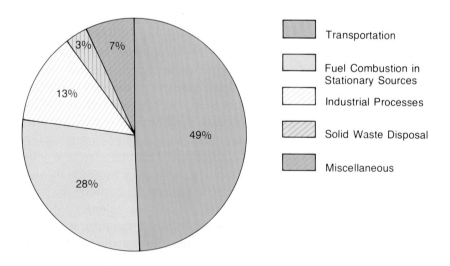

Transportation

Fuel Combustion in Stationary Sources

Industrial Processes

Solid Waste Disposal

Miscellaneous

Health effects of air pollution include burning eyes, breathing difficulties, and dizziness. Persistent exposure to air pollution, particularly if coupled with smoking, can lead to chronic bronchitis, emphysema, lung cancer, and eventually suffocation or heart failure. Air pollution robs us of our health, costing an estimated $11 billion annually in respiratory-related medical expenses. Naturally, damage is not confined to humans, but affects plants, trees, animals, lakes, buildings, and monuments. Again, the costs in damage and lost crops, farm animals, and wildlife is high. Finally, research affirms the role that air pollution plays in the greenhouse effect, an apparent warming of the planet, and the loss of ozone, which protects people and other animals from the harmful ultraviolet radiation from the sun. These last two matters will be explored more fully in Chapter 18.

It certainly is in our best interests, then, to decrease air pollution across the country. Accordingly, Congress passed the Clean Air Act of 1970 and 1977, which required the EPA to establish maximum allowable levels of seven specific categories of air pollutants. The country was divided into 247 air quality control regions, each of which is required to have a plan aimed at achieving air quality. If a region does not have a plan or does not meet the federal air quality standard, the EPA has the authority to prevent new construction of manufacturing plants or the expansion of existing ones, and it can cut off federal funds for highway construction. This law also required a reduction in motor vehicle emisssions of carbon monoxide, hydrocarbons, and nitrogen oxides.

In response to this law, state and local governments passed regulations that affected consumers, consumer goods, and manufacturing methods. New jobs were created in research, product development, marketing, and environmental control, and new products were introduced, such as electric vans, methanol buses, and paint coatings that dry without releasing pollutants. Many states now require periodic inspections of motor vehicles in order to maintain emission standards. Residents of four smog-plagued counties in California (Los Angeles, Orange, San Bernadino, and Riverside) can report smoking vehicles and other air-pollution offenses by calling 1–800–CUT SMOG. In the first two months of operation more than 13,000 observed violations were reported. After reviewing this impressive list, you will note that most of these efforts focus on control of pollutants once they have entered the environment. There is another approach, however.

The most effective and least costly way to reduce air, water, and soil pollution is to prevent pollutants from being generated in the first place. This means we need to reduce energy use; practice energy conservation; switch from fossil fuels to energy from the sun, wind, and water; reduce waste by reusing and recycling; and design products so they will last longer and can be repaired easily. Additionally, we must control population growth, for as we said at the beginning of this chapter, people in the United states represent 5 percent of the world population, consume 30 percent of its resources, and create 33 pecent of its pollution. The choices we make have an impressive impact on the quality of life for everyone on the planet.

SUMMARY

This chapter has explored the sources and uses of energy for transportation and in the home. It has shown how the natural resources available to us in our environment help us meet our needs. And perhaps it has given you an idea for a career.

Until the 1970s, U.S. energy costs were relatively low and were getting even lower. New discoveries of oil, coal, and natural gas expanded energy supplies and kept prices very affordable. Over the first three-quarters of the twentieth century the American economy became heavily dependent on these nonrenewable resources. When the price of oil was abruptly raised in 1974, and again in 1978–79, consumers and producers alike began to look for ways to decrease this dependence. Although prices for fossil fuels remained moderate in the 1980s, there was a gradual shift toward conservation and the use of energy from renewable sources, a wise strategy for consumers and the nation.

Since the automobile is a major user of energy and the major source of air pollution, it offers consumers great potential for conserving energy and saving money. All changes, however, involve opportunity costs, and some changes, such as trading one's car for a newer model, are quite expensive. If one is willing to use another form of personal transportation, such as a bicycle or scooter, savings can be great. Mass transit offers the greatest savings, although the benefits depend upon its availability and one's values.

The greatest opportunities for cutting home energy costs are in heating and cooling systems, which account for the majority of the average home's energy bill. Minor expenditures, such as weather stripping, and major expenditures, such as installing a solar water heater, should be analyzed by the payback method, estimating the time it will take to pay off the investment in energy conservation.

Water is a natural resource we have tended to take for granted. Although it is renewable, the replacement and purification process may take hundreds of years to occur, if it occurs at all. In an effort to harness and transport adequate water for food-growing, manufacturing, and household needs, we often consume fossil fuels. Therefore, when we conserve water we also conserve energy, and vice versa. The prime method for water conservation in the home is minimizing water used to flush toilets. This can be done by displacing water in the toilet tank, fixing toilet leaks, and installing low-flow toilets. Further attention needs to be paid to water use habits and landscaping.

We place our precious water supply at risk from contamination from heat, toxic chemicals, and air pollution. We generate urban waste as we purify the water and air. And we consume energy doing all of this, proving that within a system, everything is interconnected and interrelated. Thus, consumers are challenged with making wise decisions about personal and governmental expenditures, energy, and the environment. Individual choices will in the aggregate make a difference in the future of our planet.

QUESTIONS

1. Describe the general changes in the uses of energy in the United States from 1850 to the present. Rank American energy sources in order of importance in 1850, in 1900, and today.

2. How much of the American energy transportation budget is used for automobiles? For buses? For planes?

3. List four ways to improve a car's energy efficiency.

4. What does the term *retrofit* mean, and how does it apply to energy conservation in transportation?

5. Give an illustration of the relationship between fuel costs and time costs. How does this explain the speeding behavior of certain drivers?

6. If you were choosing between a bike, a moped, and a motorcycle, what criteria would you use to help you decide? List the benefits and drawbacks of each form of transportation. Which would you choose? Which would you have chosen if you were five years younger or 25 years older?

7. Describe the pattern of mass-transit ridership since World War II. Why did people abandon mass transit in the 1950s and 1960s? What could make mass transit a better competitor to personal transportation?

8. Here are two meter readings:

	June 20	July 20
Electricity (kwh)	97,640	98,481
Natural gas (cu. ft.)	1,310	1,340

a. How many kilowatt-hours were used by this household?

b. If the cost of electricity is 9 cents per kilowatt-hour, how much would the electric bill be?

c. Many gas companies charge by the therm, not by the cubic foot. If a therm costs 70 cents and there are 1.1 therms in a cubic foot of gas, how much is the gas bill?

9. What is the difference between passive solar strategies and active solar strategies? How would you classify the following solar strategies?

a. Planting a tree.

b. Building a greenhouse.

c. Installing a solar water-heating system with an electric backup unit.

10. The yearly energy consumption of an electrical appliance depends on the climate, the EER, and factors like the time of day and the thermostat setting. Here is an example of the consumption of two room air conditioners:

	Unit I	Unit II
Size (Btu/hr)	10,000	10,000
Watts	860	1,800
Operating hours	600	600

Calculate the following:

a. The EER of both

b. The annual amount of electricity used for each in kilowatt-hours

c. The annual energy savings of the more efficient model, assuming a 5-cent-per-kilowatt-hour cost

d. The approximate payback period if a more efficient air conditioner costs $100 more

e. The change in the length of the payback period if electricity costs 2 cents per kilowatt-hour or 10 cents per kilowatt-hour

11. What is the connection between water consumption and energy consumption? How does our accumulation of solid waste affect water quality?

12. Most urban areas use a combination of groundwater and surface water; what does your community do? What difference does this combination make in terms of quality and safety?

13. What is the difference between primary sewage treatment and secondary sewage treatment? Has your community complied with the EPA regulations for sewage treatment? If so, where does it take the resulting sludge?

14. What will happen if no one takes action to protect the environment? What is the value of protecting the environment? Who should bear the cost of a clean environment? Should there be penalties for damaging the environment? Who should decide what ''damage'' is?

REFERENCES AND READINGS

''CAFE's Costs,'' *Wall Street Journal*, September 1, 1988.

Carey, John. ''Is It Safe to Drink?'' *National Wildlife*, Special Report, February/March 1984.

Chiras, Daniel D. *Environmental Science: A Framework for Decision Making*, 2d ed. Menlo Park, Calif. Benjamin/Cummings, 1988.

''Dateline Washington: CAFE Away.'' *Consumers' Research*, March 1988.

Egan, Richard. ''Carless in America.'' *Road and Track*, November 1987.

''Energy and You, for a Bright Tomorrow.'' Southern California Edison, 1987.

Gever, John, Kaufmann, Robert, Skole, David, and Vorosmarty. *Beyond Oil: The Threat to Food and Fuel in the Coming Decades*. Cambridge, MA: Ballinger, 1988.

Haldeman, Virginia A., Peters, Jeanne M., and Tripple, Patricia A. ''Measuring a Consumer Energy Conservation Ethic: An Analysis of Components.'' *The Journal of Consumer Affairs*, Summer 1987.

Hayes, Denis. *Rays of Hope*. New York: Norton, 1977.

Hayes, Jack. ''Windows with a View to the Future.'' *The Saturday Evening Post*, October 1987.

Heilbroner, Robert. *The Making of Economic Society*. Englewood Cliffs, N.J.: Prentice-Hall, 1975.

Hirsch, Werner Z. *Urban Economics*. New York: Macmillan, 1984.

Howard, Bion. ''What's In an Energy Efficient Home.'' *Consumers' Research*, March 1987a.

Hutterrauch, Roland. ''Environmental Considerations and the Assessment of Quality.'' *The Frontier of Research in the Consumer Interest*. Columbia, Mo.: American Council on Consumer Interests, 1988.

Johnston, David. ''Down the Drain,'' *Los Angeles Times*, February 2, 1988, Part V, page 1.

''Keeping Warm Within'' *Consumers' Research*, December 1987b.

Lovins, Amory, Lovins, L. Hunter, and Zucherman, Seth. *Energy Unbound: A Fable for America's Future*. San Francisco: Sierra Club, 1986.

Magnuson, Ed. ''They Lied to Us.'' *Time*, October 31, 1988.

Maidique, Modesto A. ''Solar America.'' In Stobaugh and Yergin (1979), pp. 183–215.

Miller, G. Tyler, Jr. *Living in the Environment*, 5th ed. Belmont, Calif.: Wadsworth, 1988.

''1984 Environmental Quality Index: 15 Years Later.'' *National Wildlife*, February/March 1984.

''Planet of the Year.'' *Time*, January 2, 1989.

ReVelle, Charles, and ReVelle, Penelope. *The Environment: Issues and Choices for Society*, 3d ed. Boston: Jones and Bartlett, 1988.

Rice, Faye. ''Where Will We Put All That Garbage?'' *Fortune*, April 11, 1988.

Shea, Cynthia Pollock. *Worldwatch Paper 81: Renewable Energy: Today's Contribution, Tomorrow's Promise*. Worldwatch Institute, 1988. Washington, DC.

Stobaugh, Robert, and Yergin, Daniel, eds. *Energy Future: Report of the Energy Project at the Harvard*

Business School. New York: Random House, 1979.

Tsongas, George A. *Home Energy Conservation Demonstration Project: Final Report for Chevron, USA.* August 1977.

U.S. Department of Energy. "Your Keys to Energy Efficiency." Washington, D.C.: U.S. Government Printing Office, 1984.

————. "Tips for an Energy Efficient Apartment." Washington, D.C.: U.S. Government Printing Office, 1986.

————, Technical Information Center. "Insulation Fact Sheet," Washington D.C.: U.S. Government Printing Office.

U.S. Department of Housing and Urban Development. *The Energy Wise Home Buyer.* Washington, D.C.: U.S. Government Printing Office, 1979.

"Your Driving Costs." Falls Church, Va.: American Automobile Association, 1988.

Chapter Fourteen

HEALTH CARE: WHAT HAPPENS WHEN YOU GET SICK?

- ☐ Health Care in the United States
- ☐ The Cost of Health Care
- ☐ The Demand for Health Care
- ☐ The Supply of Health Care
- ☐ Prescription Drugs
- ☐ Health Insurance: Private Plans
- ☐ The Health Maintenance Organization
- ☐ Alternative Health Care Systems: Is There a Better Way?
- ☐ Staying Healthy: The Best Way to Avoid the High Cost of Health Care

DID YOU KNOW THAT . . .

. . . the United States is not among the top ten countries with the highest life expectancies or the lowest infant mortality rates?

. . . health care expenditures in the United States amount to $2,500 per person per year?

. . . most prescription drugs are produced by more than one company, and many are much cheaper when purchased under generic names?

. . . between 20 and 30 percent of all medical testing is either unnecessary or inappropriate?

. . . the American Medical Association estimates that 15 percent of all medical costs are "defensive medicine," i.e., caused by fear of litigation rather than by illness?

. . . one-third of the government's entire Medicare budget is spent on patients' last year of life?

. . . there are 400 counties in the United States that have no doctors?

. . . nine million children in the United States lack routine medical care?

. . . taking ampicillin, a commonly prescribed antibiotic, increases the chance of pregnancy for a woman using birth-control pills?

. . . chemicals in ordinary food like bananas, dairy products, and citrus juices can produce unwanted side effects when they are taken with commonly prescribed medications?

. . . about two-thirds of all personal health care expenditures today are financed indirectly through third parties, such as private insurance companies or the government?

. . . your habits and your personal life-style have a much larger impact on your health than the amount of medical care you buy?

The first sound you hear in the morning is the shrill pitch from your alarm clock. Your eyes open somewhat unwillingly. As you try to silence your mechanical tormentor, you become aware of a soreness in your throat. Once you arise, you become increasingly aware that you simply don't feel well. Your throat hurts, your head throbs, and suddenly you know that this is not going to be a routine day. This is one of those sick days. What should you do?

Most of us do not immediately reach for the phone to call a physician. Nor do we rush to the hospital. Most of us try to stick it out; we can beat or treat the illness by ourselves or with a little help from our friends. Why don't we seek medical aid immediately? One reason is very simple: the cost of such care can be rather high, both in money and time.

Despite our natural inclination to avoid buying medical care, it is one of the most important components of a consumer's budget. As such, it merits considerable study, both from society's view and from an individual standpoint. As a society, we must once again realize that there is no free lunch. If we choose to provide more medical resources, we must subtract resources from housing, transportation, national defense, or another sector. As consumers, we must also know that paying the high cost of health care will cause our insurance premiums and taxes to rise. As a result, we will have less income to spend on other consumer goods or less to save and invest. There is no cure-all for these problems, but after studying this chapter you should have a greater appreciation for the origins of the problem and be better able to minimize your individual health care costs while maximizing your benefits.

We begin with an overview of the state of health care in the United States. How does our system compare with those of other nations? How much do we spend on health care? Where does the health care dollar go? Then we look at the demand for and the supply of health care. Government-sponsored programs like Medicare and Medicaid, coupled with the growth of the health insurance industry, have lowered the price of medical care for some consumers and thus increased the amount they demand. Meanwhile, the supply of health care facilities and personnel has not always kept pace with the increases in demand, which means higher prices.

Of course, there are ways that wise decision making can limit your health care expenditures. Selecting your doctor, getting a second opinion on surgery, asking for generic drugs, and understanding your health insurance program are a few of the ways that information can lead you to make most cost-effective decisions concerning your health care dollar. Today, there are more alternatives than the traditional fee-for-service plan. Health maintenance organizations that stress preventive medicine are available in many areas. Moreover, many studies indicate that by following some commonsense guides on eating and exercising, you can improve your chances of staying healthy.

HEALTH CARE IN THE UNITED STATES

Any way you look at it, health care is a big business in the United States. One out of every 20 employed persons is working in some area of health care, which means that more people work to keep us healthy than work to grow the food we eat. Health care is the third largest industry in the country. But how good is it? Is big always best? And more to the point, is health care efficient as well as effective?

From the consumer's standpoint, one of the best ways to judge the effectiveness of America's health care industry is by the output— health—rather than by inputs, such as money, the number of workers, or other resources. Of course, this means that we must define and then measure health. Like singing while swimming under water, these can be difficult to do at the same time. The preamble of the charter of the World Health Organization (WHO) defines **health** as "a state of complete physical, mental and social well-being, not merely the absence of distress or infirmity." Such an ambitious definition makes it nearly impossible for any society to reach the goal of perfect health for its members. Nevertheless, it is possible to compare the state of health in the United States by looking at how we are doing compared to other nations.

health: *a state of complete physical, mental, and social well-being, not merely the absence of distress or infirmity*

Health care does not always have to be painful, but the bill for the care often is.

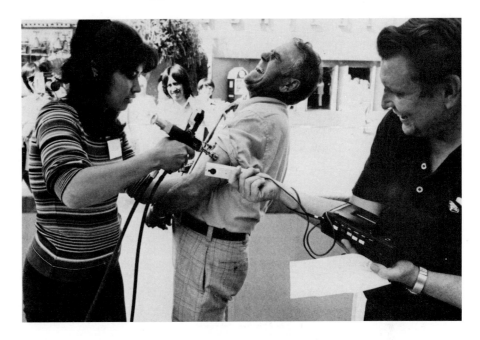

life expectancy: the number of additional years a person can expect to live given the current death rate; can be calculated for a person of any age

Life expectancy at birth (that is, the number of years that a newborn child can expect to live) is an important measure of health care. Comparing international life expectancies can be a tricky business, because differences between nations may reflect factors other than the quality of health care. Life-styles, socioeconomic conditions, and the distribution of income can also play important roles. For example, the Japanese diet emphasizes fish and rice but not meat or dairy products. As a result, studies have shown a much lower level of saturated fat, serum cholesterol, and heart disease in Japanese than in similar populations in the United States, where heart disease is the leading cause of death (Twaddle and Hessler, 1987). Even so, you might have expected the United States to rank among the top ten nations in life expectancy, but it does not. The United States consistently ranks between tenth and twentieth in life expectancy.

Another important indicator of health care is the **infant mortality rate**. It indicates for every thousand babies born, how many die before their first birthday (see Figure 14.1). In the United States, out of each thousand babies born, ten do not live to see their first birthday. As you can see, the United States is not among the ten best nations in the category; our rate is almost twice as high as the world's leader, Japan. Part of the reason for our relatively poor showing in infant mortality statistics reflects the startlingly high infant mortality rate for black children born in the United States. Their mortality rate is twice as high as that of white babies, but, of course, this does not take into account other factors, such as prenatal care, access to physicians and hospitals, and income levels, all of which serve to increase the difference in infant birth rates.

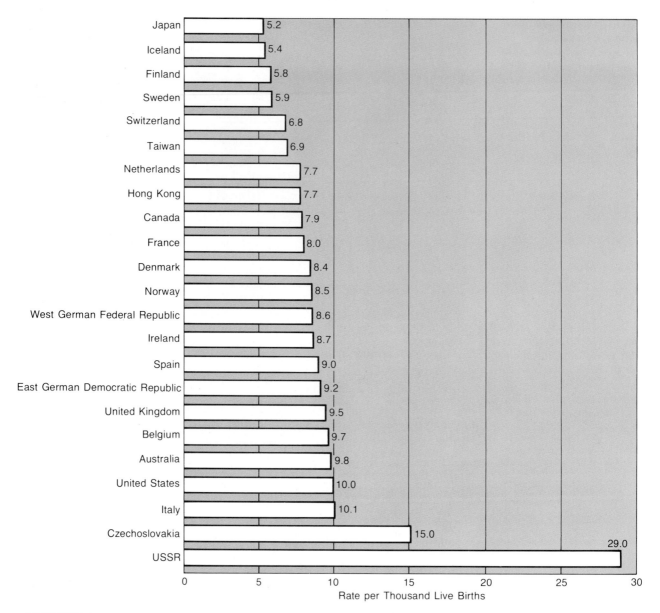

FIGURE 14.1
Infant mortality rates for selected countries (deaths per thousand live births).
(SOURCE: Population Reference Bureau, *World Fact Sheet 1988.*)

Another reason for our higher rates is the accessibility and availability of health care in the United States. Many people living in rural areas or small towns do not have access to physicians or health care facilities. The distribution of the population of the United States over a much larger geographical area than that of Sweden, Japan, or Iceland makes

TABLE 14.1 Gains in Life Expectancies for Americans of Various Ages

Age	Sex	Life Expectancy Remaining		Life Expectancy Gain (percent)
		1939	**1983**	
0	Male	62.8	71.7	14.2
	Female	67.3	78.7	16.9
20	Male	47.8	53.1	11.1
	Female	51.4	59.8	16.3
40	Male	30.0	34.6	15.3
	Female	33.3	40.4	21.3
50	Male	22.0	25.7	16.8
	Female	24.7	31.2	26.3

SOURCE: *Statistical Abstract of the United States* (Washington, DC: U.S. Government Printing Office, 1987).

the logistics of supplying health care much more difficult. This geographic disadvantage weighs especially heavily on newborn infants who are delivered far from the nearest hospital.

We have clearly established that the U.S. health care system is not the unparalleled leader in delivering quality care to its citizens. However, we should not leave you with the impression that our system is an unmitigated disaster. Although we are not first in health care, we are among the leaders, and the differences are not huge when one realizes that the life expectancy at birth in many nations is still less than 50 years and that every year infant mortality rates in some countries exceed 100 per 1,000 births.

If you are curious about how well the American health system has done in recent years, look at Table 14.1, which compares life expectancies for average Americans at various ages based on data from 1939–1941 and 1983. Notice that over this period, all age groups experienced significant gains in the number of years they could expect to live. In 1939, a 20-year-old man could expect to live nearly 48 more years, whereas by 1983 he could expect to live 53 more years—a gain of more than five years. A woman of the same age gained eight years: A woman who was 20 in 1983 could expect to live to see her seventy-ninth birthday.

THE COST OF HEALTH CARE

How have we managed to increase our life expectancies over this century? One of the ways is by devoting a larger proportion of our national income to the health industry. Figure 14.2 shows the overall rise in national health expenditures since 1950. As you can see, we have spent substantially

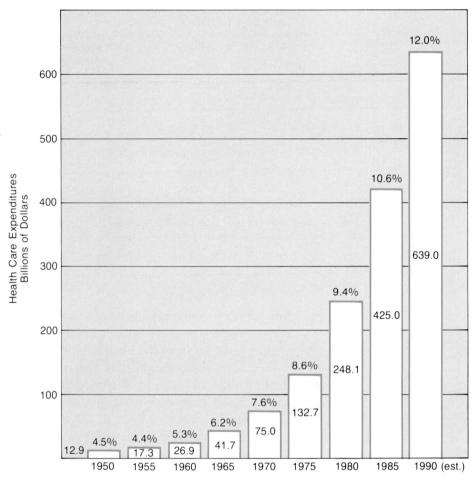

FIGURE 14.2
National health-care expenditures and percentage of GNP, selected years, 1950–1990. (SOURCES: Data from Health Care Financing Administration and Department of Commerce, Bureau of Economic Analysis, *Statistical Abstract of the United States*.)

more, and a bigger proportion, of our national income on health care. In 1950, expenditures were about $16 billion, only 4.5 percent of our GNP (the value of all final goods and services produced in the United States during that year). By 1985 we were spending $425 billion, or 10.6 percent of the GNP. This amounted to spending $1,700 per person every year, as opposed to $107 in 1950. This upward trend is continuing. According to the Health Care Financing Administration, at the start of the 1990s we are spending $639.6 billion on health care. This represents about 12 percent of GNP, or $2,500 per person per year.

How did health care become so expensive? More importantly, how can consumers avoid the high price of medical care? We cannot answer the second question until we give you a better understanding of the first. To do that, we need to look more closely at the most important components of demand and supply.

THE DEMAND FOR HEALTH CARE

The demand for medical care is not quite the same as the demand for automobiles or housing, although there are some similarities. The law of demand states that as the price of a commodity rises, consumers will buy less of it. This fits consumer behavior fairly well when it comes to cars, and even when it comes to housing. If some automobile producers raise their prices, you can shop around for a better deal or simply postpone the purchase. This is not the case with health care. It is much more difficult to shop around for a lower-priced surgeon to take out your appendix, especially when delaying the operation can be fatal. Even if you could comparison shop, how could you judge quality? Consumer health information is often difficult or expensive to obtain, so it is difficult to be a rational decision maker.

The rise in our national health care bill cannot be laid solely to the lack of informed consumers. Other demographic, personal, and institutional factors are at work. In the sections that follow we list the five most important variables: age distribution, income, third party payments, medical malpractice, and government programs.

Age Distribution: A Demanding Variable

Age is a major factor in the demand for health care. Whereas personal health care spending averages less than $500 per year for people under the age of 19, the average for those 65 and older is more than $4,000. The oldest one-tenth of the population uses one-third of the health care.

BOX 14.1   WHERE DOES YOUR HEALTH CARE DOLLAR GO?

In the text we discuss the causes of the rise in the cost of health care. But you may be curious about who gets what proportion of those health care dollars. The chart gives a breakdown of an average dollar spent on health care in the United States. The largest piece of the pie, 41 cents of every dollar, goes to pay for hospital care. The second most important slice pays for physicians' services. Together, these two components account for almost two-thirds of every health care dollar, with the rest going to pay for nursing homes, drugs, dental services, and administration costs.

If expenditures on research were reported separately they would amount to less than 2 percent of our national health care expenditures. In an era when diseases like AIDS threaten to reach epidemic proportions, it seems odd that we spend so little on research.

Dentists' services	6.7%
Other personal health care	3.1%
Drugs and medical sundries	7.0%
Nursing home care	8.7%
Administration, prepayment, public health activity, research and construction	13.1%
Physicians' services	20.3%
Hospital care	41.0%

SOURCE: U.S. Department of Health and Human Services, *Health Care Financing Notes*, Sept. 1986.

Thus, we can expect increased demand for health care as our nation's population ages. By the year 2000, some demographers estimate, the over 65 age group will constitute 14 percent of America's population. Of even greater concern is the age composition of those over 65. It is now understood that this group is not homogeneous. The greatest risk of disabling disease does not occur until a person reaches his or her midseventies. By the year 2000, one-half of the elderly people in this country will be over 75, which will put additional demands on our health care delivery system.

Income: The Ability to Pay

Income also affects the demand for medical care. As incomes rise, people tend to buy more of some things and less of others. We touched on this phenomenon in Chapter 1 when we discussed the concepts of normal and inferior goods. Medical care is a normal good; as our incomes rise, we tend to purchase more of it. One of the hallmarks of U.S. economic history has been the slow but steady rise in real incomes and consumer purchasing power. A good example of the interaction of income and health care expenditures is in the increased demand for orthodontics, the dental specialty that deals with straightening teeth and improving the bite. In 1950 having crooked teeth may have been considered an unfortunate attribute, but they were rarely corrected. Today, the proportion of the population that has had braces is much higher. It is rare to find a class of college students in which fewer than 10 percent have had braces. A large part of the reason is simply that families have more real income and can thus afford to have their children's teeth straightened. The child who grows to adulthood with "buck teeth" is a real exception. And more than likely, he or she will choose to have the orthodontia done as an adult.

Third-Party Payments

Another problem with applying traditional demand analysis to the health care market is that there are few economic incentives for spending time locating lower-priced health care. For medical care and hospitalization, the recipient of that care rarely pays the full price.

To use our earlier automobile analogy, if you shop around and bargain hard in the car market (as we suggested in Chapter 12), you will pay a lower price and get a better deal; thus, there is an economic incentive for practicing comparison-buying strategies. But for medical care and hospitalization, the recipient of the health care service would not benefit as much from a lower price, because a large portion of the bill is generally paid by someone else—an insurance company or a government agency. These outside sources of payment are called **third-party payers**.

Today about 72 percent of all personal health care expenditures are financed by third parties. The rest is paid directly by patients. Of the 72 cents of every health care dollar that third parties pay, private insur-

FIGURE 14.3
The proportion of medical care costs paid directly by patients for 1950 and 1985. (SOURCE: Adapted from Robert M. Gibson and Daniel R. Waldo, "National Health Expenditures," *Health Care Financing Review*, September 1986.)

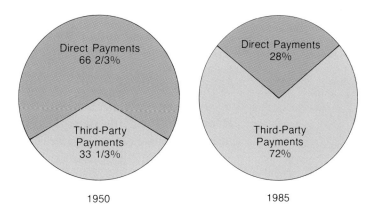

ance companies account for 29 cents, and government programs at the local, state, or federal level pay 43 cents. This distribution of the health care cost burden has not remained constant over the past 30 years. As Figure 14.3 shows, the importance of third-party payments has increased dramatically since 1950. In that year, the proportions of direct payment versus third-party payment were reversed from what they are today. Because patients in 1950 paid two-thirds of their bill directly, they had a greater incentive to economize. This incentive still exists in areas like dental services and prescription drugs, in which patients continue to pay more than two-thirds of their bills directly. In the health care industry, inflation correlates directly with the proportion of third-party payments. Hospital room charges, for instance, are most often paid for by third parties, and they have risen the most rapidly, followed by physicians' fees. Dentist fees and drug costs, however, have risen more slowly, because patients bear a larger share of the costs directly.

Malpractice and Demand for Medical Care

malpractice suits: lawsuits in which patients claim they have been harmed by a trained professional, such as a doctor or a nurse, because accepted medical procedures were not followed

A few years ago there was a popular television series called "Marcus Welby, M.D." Robert Young, the actor who portrayed Dr. Welby, played a kind, gray-haired authority figure who always had the patient's best interest at heart. Most physicians could easily visualize themselves in this role as health care adviser and healer. But the realities of the courtroom have driven a wedge between the physician's concern for patients' well-being, and the physician's own. In particular the threat of being sued for improper medical procedures, called **malpractice suits**, has caused many doctors to change the way they practice medicine, with an increased demand for tests, diagnoses, drugs, and even surgical operations.

Many doctors are now practicing **defensive medicine**, which can be defined as using medical procedures to avoid lawsuits rather than to benefit the patient. According to the American Medical Association, 15 percent of all medical costs (about $68 billion) stem directly from doctors' fear of litigation. As Arnold Relman, editor of the *New England Journal of Medicine*, has said: "The threat of a lawsuit is always there. It's powerful motivation. Doctors get the message that if they don't cover all the bases, they could be sued" (*U.S. News & World Report*, 1987).

Defensive medicine takes many forms, but additional testing is certainly one of the most common. It is estimated that between 20 and 30 percent of all medical tests in the United States are either unnecessary or inappropriate. One study found that American doctors order eight times more x-rays than do British doctors for patients with high blood pressure.

Additional testing is only one way that medical practice has been affected by the concern over the courtroom in the operating room. Twenty percent of all general practitioners now refuse to deliver babies because of the increased insurance hazards. In 1987 the average insurance premium for obstetricians was $37,000 per year. As a result of the increase in lawsuits over delivering babies, the number of cesarean sections has increased dramatically. In 1970 only 6 percent of all babies were delivered this way. By 1987, 24 percent of all children were delivered by cesarean. The U.S. Department of Health and Human Services projects that if the insurance liability problem continues, obstetricians will choose to deliver 40 percent of all American babies by cesarean section in 2000. Keep in mind that the cost of a normal birth is about half the cost of a cesarean birth. These trends lead to an increase in the cost of health care without a commensurate rise in quality. As Dr. Sidney Wolfe, head of Ralph Nader's Health Research Group has said: "Reducing the number of procedures like cesarean sections could save money, provide better care, and reduce death" (*Newsweek*, 1989).

Government Intervention

A discussion of the demand for health care would not be complete without exploring the most important reason for an increase in the demand, namely, government programs. In 1988 the federal government spent $124 billion on health programs, an increase of 11 percent over the previous year's expenditures, making health the third largest category after national defense and social security. When these federal moneys are combined with state and local health expenditures, government programs account for more than 40 percent of all personal health care spending. Moreover, their impact on demand has been even greater, because they aim at those groups that have historically had unfilled health needs: the poor, the elderly, and the disadvantaged. Once the government began to subsidize their health care, these groups began to use more health services. This increased demand to some extent resulted in higher prices. Two-thirds of all government health care expenditures are spent in two programs: Medicare and Medicaid.

Medicare: aid for the elderly. The **Medicare** program was established under Title XVIII of the Social Security Act, and it went into effect on July 1, 1966. It was originally designed as a federal insurance program to protect those age 65 and over from the high cost of hospital and physicians' services. On July 1, 1973, permanently disabled workers and their dependents and persons in need of kidney dialysis machines were added to the program. Nevertheless, 90 percent of those on Medicare are age 65 or over. In 1988 Medicare expenditures were almost $80 billion.

Once the Medicare program began, hospital admission rates for persons covered by the program rose markedly. In 1967 short-stay hospital admission rates were 260 per 1,000 patients. By 1978 this rate had risen to 350 per 1,000, an increase of about 33 percent. So Medicare was successful in making hospital care more affordable for the elderly, but it had the undesirable side effect of increasing the cost of such care on a national basis. Another quirk in the program was the schedule of fees for doctors, which provided for larger payments to physicians if their patients were in hospitals. This may be part of the reason that more elderly patients were put in the hospital.

Medicare: the federal health insurance program that serves Americans aged 65 and over; it has two parts: hospital insurance that pays for inpatient care and medical insurance that helps pay for doctors' services, outpatient hospital services, and many other medical services not covered under standard policies

Medicaid: health care for the poor. Another program that created an increase in the demand for medical services was **Medicaid**, a joint federal–state program that provides health care funding to low-income persons. This program provides medical assistance to people who are eligible to receive cash assistance under one of the existing welfare programs, such as Aid to Families with Dependent Children (AFDC), Supplemental Security Income (SSI) for the aged, blind, and disabled, or unemployment compensation. In 1985, Medicaid paid $40 billion in benefits. By reducing the cost of medical care to segments of the American population that need it but often are unable to obtain it, this program increased demand and thus pushed prices higher. Together with Medicare, Medicaid accounted for one-third of the growth in personal health care expenditures since 1970. Taxes pay for the costs of these progams, but other users of medical service must also bear the burden of higher prices brought on by increased demand. Nevertheless, no one can deny that medical care is more available to the poor and the elderly today as a result of government programs.

Health care policy: examining the limits of life. Some critics of Medicaid and Medicare point out that they are vastly inadequate to handle the health problems of poor people in the United States. Despite the good intentions of Medicaid, it is estimated that more than half of all people living below the poverty line remain outside the program. In some states a family of four with an annual income of more than $4,248 is no longer eligible for benefits (*Newsweek*, 1989). Even the budget of the program has been accused of bias against the young and the poor. For example, 50 percent of the Medicaid budget is spent on long-term care for the aged. In 1986 Medicare spent $25 billion—one third of its budget—on people who died that year. Most of this expenditure ($20 billion) paid for medical expenses incurred in a patient's last *month* of life. Heroic measures are being taken to prolong a teminally ill patient's life by a few weeks.

While our system seems bent on prolonging the last weeks of life, it does not adequately address the cost and benefits of that choice. As Judith Walker, Chicago's Commissioner of Human Services has said, "It costs approximately $10 to give a baby a series of immunizations as opposed to $500,000 to $1,000,000 for a lifetime of institutional care for a child left retarded by the measles. But less than half of all poor children in the U.S. are immunized against preventable diseases" (*L.A. Times*, 1985). These are real-world examples of the estimated 9 million children who lack routine access to medical care.

Can Medicare continue to subsidize organ transplants, heart bypasses and kidney dialysis for the aged, while ignoring the health needs of the young? The situation will worsen as we approach the year 2000 when one-half of the elderly people in this country will be over 75 years of age. Daniel Callahan, the medical philosopher who wrote *Setting Limits: Medical Goals in an Aging Society*, complains that Americans have an insatiable appetite for a longer life. He argues that we ought to give up our relentless drive to extend the life of the aged and emphasize the quality of life over the simple quantity of years. He says that in many cases the elderly are being saved from a natural death only to fall victim to a chronic illness, such as Alzheimer's disease, where they eventually lose all forms of memory and enter a vegetative state.

Obviously, there is no simple resolution to the health care dilemma. Nevertheless, we can enhance our understanding of the problem by exploring the determinants of the supply of medical care in the United States.

THE SUPPLY OF HEALTH CARE

Trying to understand changes in the demand for medical care is like hearing only half of a good story. You can never be sure that you know what will happen until you hear the second half. In this section, the supply of medical care represents the second half of the story. As we said earlier, the two most important components of supply in the health care industry are physicians and hospitals, which account for almost two-thirds of all health care costs in the United States. In the next few sections, we explore how changes in these basic health care deliveries can affect the prices you pay for health care. We will look at the supply of physicians and the use of other health care personnel. Then we will explore the rising costs of hospital care and a federal cost containment plan.

Physicians

According to the U.S. Department of Health and Human Services, we had more than 500,000 active physicians in 1985. That number was expected to rise to 588,000 by 1990 as the nation's 142 medical schools graduated more than 17,000 new doctors each year. Is this adequate to fill our needs? The answer depends on who is asking the question.

A presidential commission, the Graduate Medical National Advisory Committee, predicted in its 1980 report that by 1990 there would be a *surplus* of doctors. It argued that the United States would have a surplus of 70,000 doctors by 1990 and a surplus of 145,000 by the year 2000. According to the report, such an oversupply would increase rather than decrease the cost of health care because of the third-party payment system in our nation. The commission believed that physicians have a certain target level of income, and if each doctor has fewer patients, he or she will simply raise his or her fees in order to meet the level of expected income. This increase in fees will then be passed along to insurance companies or the government and will thus be reflected in higher health care costs for the general public. The committee's solution was to cut back on the number of new medical graduates and restrict the number of foreign medical graduates allowed to practice in the United States. In short, the report said that cutting back on the supply would cause doctors to have more patients and thus be able to make their projected incomes, even though they charged less.

The "oversupply" of doctors is an issue that bears more analysis, because it contradicts standard economic theory. Contrary to the assertion by the AMA and other spokespersons for the industry that a surplus of physicians exists, there is evidence of a shortage of physicians in many parts of the United States. Table 14.2 shows the distribution of medical doctors by state. In Alabama, there are 142 doctors per 100,000 people, whereas in the District of Columbia there are 552 doctors per 100,000 residents. Mississippi has the fewest doctors relative to its population: 117 per 100,000 compared to a national average of 199 per 100,000 people. If there were a cutback in the number of graduates, would we be better off? More importantly, these figures do not begin to indicate the paucity of physicians in rural areas, where it is estimated that 400 counties do not have even one medical doctor. Even California, a state that appears to have more than its share of doctors, has hundreds of small towns with no doctors at all. How would a cutback in the number of new physicians help these towns?

TABLE 14.2 Number and Rate of Active U.S. Physicians, per 100,000 Population

State	Number	Rate
Alabama	5,653	142
Alaska	634	127
Arizona	5,804	184
Arkansas	3,202	136
California	61,267	235
Colorado	6,243	196
Connecticut	8,685	275
Delaware	1,141	185
District of Columbia	3,415	552
Florida	21,474	191
Georgia	9,399	159
Hawaii	2,116	212
Idaho	1,174	118
Illinois	22,921	199
Indiana	7,823	142
Iowa	3,929	136
Kansas	3,916	162
Kentucky	5,500	149
Louisiana	7,698	173
Maine	1,904	165
Maryland	13,163	303
Massachusetts	17,396	300
Michigan	15,805	174
Minnesota	8,506	203
Mississippi	3,022	117
Missouri	8,982	179
Montana	1,121	136
Nebraska	2,481	156
Nevada	1,431	155
New Hampshire	1,774	179
New Jersey	16,486	219
New Mexico	2,302	161
New York	50,943	287
North Carolina	10,320	168
North Dakota	1,055	157
Ohio	19,555	182
Oklahoma	4,502	138
Oregon	5,073	189
Pennsylvania	25,324	214
Rhode Island	2,144	223
South Carolina	4,812	146
South Dakota	910	130
Tennessee	8,318	176
Texas	25,952	194
Utah	2,805	171
Vermont	1,239	232
Virginia	10,752	194
Washington	8,526	196
West Virginia	3,018	156
Wisconsin	8,186	172
Wyoming	633	125
Total	470,434	199

Other Health Care Personnel

physician assistant: a para-medic; an individual with medical training who can augment the health-care services of a doctor

It seems clear that a partial solution to the problem of too few physicians is to expand the number of people who deliver health care services. One way to do so is to encourage doctors to use **physician assistants** in their practice. Just as medics augment the supply of health care services in the armed forces, physician assistants could help with medical services to patients on the home front. One study has shown that using paramedics could increase a physician's productivity by 74 percent (Golladay, 1973). An efficient medical practice could deal with 147 patients per week, but the use of paramedics could increase that figure to 265, with no loss of quality. After all, is a shot given by a paramedic any less effective than the same treatment administered by a physician?

In general, the quality of care delivered by physician assistants and nurses has been found to be the equal of that of medical doctors for routine procedures. These midlevel practitioners can handle the majority of patients without consulting a physician (Twaddle and Hessler, 1987). In areas lacking doctors they can improve health care dramatically. For example, a health project in rural California demonstrated how effective **nurse-midwives** can be in reducing the infant death rate. During the first 18 months of the project, the death rate for newborn infants fell from 23.9 to 10.3 per 1,000 live births. Considering our nation's record for infant mortality, such a program merits expansion.

Hospitals

The cost of all components of health care is rising, but none is rising as rapidly as the cost of hospital care. The average daily cost of staying in the hospital rose from $15.62 in 1950 to more than $500 in 1988. Such a dramatic rise in the price has led some people to remark that it would be cheaper to move into a first-class hotel with room service than go to a hospital. In fact, a new type of health facility called the recovery care center has begun to offer patients an alternative to standard hospitals. These centers, which provide medical services for up to three days following surgery, look more like hotels than hospitals. They even offer gourmet meals and private rooms for about $300 per day. Hospitals may get some competition from these centers, but it is unlikely to cause them to lower their prices because third parties pay 90 percent of all hospital bills.

The third-party payment system, coupled with the malpractice penalties for omitting a test or failing to take every precaution, helps explain why thousands of people are hospitalized each year for treatment that they could obtain as outpatients at a hospital or a clinic and why others are given expensive tests or surgery that they do not need. According to some estimates, as many as one-half of all surgeries are unnecessary. For example, based on recent surgical records, someone living in Ohio is three times as likely to have surgery as a Pennsylvanian, but only half as

Part of the high cost of hospital care can be attributed to the fact that hospitals often spare no expense in trying to attract doctors and patients. As a result, many modern hospitals look more like hotels than health-care facilities.

likely as a resident of New Jersey. Do people in New Jersey really need six times more surgery than their Pennsylvania neighbors? The possibility of unnecessary surgery seems very real. To counteract this, some insurance companies are now encouraging their policyholders to seek second and third opinions *before* they submit to surgery (see Box 14.2). Medicare and Medicaid *always* pay for a second opinion when nonemergency surgery is recommended.

Community Hospitals

If we are seeking the basic causes of the increase in the cost of hospital care, we must look at the structure of the hospital itself. **Community hospitals** are nonfederal, short-term, general and special hospitals that provide care to the public. They account for 90 percent of all hospital admissions, with most other admissions going to federal veterans hospitals. These institutions are overwhelmingly nonprofit undertakings that were started from community fund raising, gifts from wealthy patrons, or by religious groups. Their original purpose was primarily to provide charitable care for the poor and the terminally ill, but after their founding, they quickly came to serve the nonpoor as well. In return for being able to bring their patients to the hospital for treatment, physicians normally donated their services for the poor, who occupied the majority of the hospital beds.

BOX 14.2 GETTING A SECOND OPINION *BEFORE* SURGERY

At one time, it was almost unheard of for patients to question their doctor's opinion, especially with regard to having an operation. But you should be aware that even doctors may disagree about the best way to handle a medical problem. Because all surgery costs both time and money and because there are certain risks no matter how minor the surgery, it is a good idea to have a second opinion. A second opinion should *not* be used to delay an emergency operation like an appendectomy, but when there is time, a second opinion will often give one additional information so that one can make an informed choice about whether surgery is the best alternative. Operations that are usually not emergencies include tonsillectomies, gall bladder operations, hysterectomies, and some cataract operations.

The Department of Health and Human Services suggests that one find the answers to the following questions before agreeing to nonemergency surgery:

1. What is the doctor's diagnosis?
2. What operation does the doctor plan to do?
3. What are the likely benefits of the operation?
4. What are the risks of the surgery, and how likely are they to occur?
5. How long would the recovery period be, and what is involved?
6. What are the costs of the operation? Will your insurance cover all of these costs?
7. What will happen if you do not have the operation?
8. Are there other ways to treat your condition?

There are several ways to get a second opinion. One is to ask your physician to recommend someone. A second way is to contact your local medical society or medical schools for names of local doctors who specialize in the relevant field. Or you can call the government's toll-free number, 1–800–638–6833 (in Maryland, 1–800–492–6603), to locate a specialist near you.

There are a number of advantages to telling your doctor that you want a second opinion, not the least of which is that you can have a copy of your records sent to the second physician. In any event, be sure that you know the names of the recommended surgical procedure and the tests you have had. If the second doctor agrees with the surgical plan, he or she will normally refer you to the original doctor for surgery. If there is disagreement, at least you will have some facts to discuss with your first doctor. Do not be afraid to assert yourself, because it is *you* who will be undergoing the surgery.

With the institution of federal and state programs for the poor, the number of charity cases in community hospitals has diminished, but the essential feature of the doctor–patient referral scheme has not. Because the physician brings patients to the hospital, the hospital must cater to the physician, not the patient. This scheme is like the relationship between a travel agent and a resort hotel. The hotel does not, under any circumstances, want to alienate the person responsible for booking its customers. This point explains why patients often feel like second-class citizens. As Herman Somers (1969) put it, "The doctors make a special point that the hospital cannot practice medicine, that the patient is the doctor's, not the hospital's—a precious distinction which strikes at the unity and authority of the hospital.''

This need to satisfy physicians leads to a number of problems. Because they want to assure doctors that their patients will always have a bed, hospitals may add new wings or renovate old ones. This expansion, coupled with shorter hospital stays has led to a decline in occcupancy rates, from 84.6 percent in 1960 to about 75 percent today. In Los Angeles alone, an estimated 10,000 beds are empty every day. In the Los Angeles area, some private hospitals have been accused of offering kickbacks to physicians who send patients to their facilities.

In addition to guaranteeing enough bed space, hospitals are under pressure to provide the most modern technological equipment, even if this equipment is not used often enough to justify its cost. Hospitals fear that physicians will simply move their patients to hospitals that do have more sophisticated facilities. According to the American Council of Life Insurance Institute, the rapid growth in use of the CAT scanner, a sophisticated diagnostic tool using an x-ray scanner and a computer, is a case in point. According to the institute, these machines, which cost over $500,000, are so popular that there are enough CAT scanners in southern California hospitals to fill the needs of *all* the hospitals west of the Mississippi River. As a result, they are underused, and a portion of their cost is redistributed in the form of room charges or other fees.

The Federal Hospital Cost Containment Plan

The rising cost of Medicare spurred the federal government to seek new ways to reduce health care costs. As part of the Social Security Amendments of 1983, Congress replaced the traditional system of paying for hospital care. Instead of allowing hospitals to determine their charges after service has been performed, the new legislation sets a flat fee for hospital services to Medicare patients, based on the ailment covered, not on the actual services rendered.

The new program uses a system that puts thousands of possible disorders into categories called **diagnosis related groups (DRGs)**. The government then establishes a standard price and a set number of days that a patient may stay and still qualify for these fees. For a tonsillectomy, for example, the hospital might be permitted to charge $837.50, with an allowable length of stay of two to five days. If a patient spends fewer than two days or more than five days in the hospital, the fees are adjusted; otherwise, the flat fee holds. The advantages of the system are a more uniform set of charges and an added financial incentive to the hospital to get someone well as quickly as possible (and thus pocket the difference between costs and charges).

One disadvantage that could develop among hospital staff would be a "get-em-up, get-em-out" attitude that could put patients through a revolving door of admission, surgery, and quick discharge. A recent study published in the *New England Journal of Medicine* found evidence that Medicare patients with hip fractures were victims of this syndrome. They were discharged earlier than non-Medicare patients, and were three times more likely to enter nursing homes (*Newsweek*, 1989).

The DRG system itself needs some refinements, because any plan to narrow all ailments into 400 categories results in some miscellaneous categories. Julie Micheletti, the DRG coordinator for the Freehold Area Hospital in Freehold, New Jersey, is not completely sold on the idea. According to her, some DRGs are just "dumpster categories." A headache, for example, is classified under DRG 333, and it could cost $1,982.16, because it is an "ill-defined indication of disease" (Larson, 1980).

Another problem that has developed from the use of the DRG system is the **cost-shifting** phenomenon. Hospitals claim that the government has deliberately underestimated the actual cost of Medicare patients. As a result, the shortfall between actual cost and government reimbursal is made up by charging the other patients more. The Health Insurance Association of America estimates that non-Medicare patients' bills would be almost 13 percent *lower* if the DRG system were abandoned.

Hospital cost containment has proved to be a difficult task, but the prescription drug industry is one where a combination of increased competition and better consumer information can lead to better prices for health care buyers. In the section that follows, we cite some ways that consumers can lower their health care costs by making more-informed decisions.

cost shifting: results from the federal government's reimbursing hospitals an inadequate sum of money for a specific medical service; as a result, the shortfall between actual cost and reimbursement is made up by charging other patients more

PRESCRIPTION DRUGS

Until 1980 the prescription drug industry was the one area of medical care that we could point to when we were looking for an example of price restraint. Since 1980, however, drug prices have risen 50 percent faster than consumer prices in general. If you want to avoid some of this inflationary pinch, you need to become familiar with **generic drugs**, that is non-brand-name drugs. In 1988 generics had 35 percent of the market, compared with only 7 percent in 1980. By the early 1990s, some experts expect, they will command 50 percent of the marketplace, giving consumers a considerable price benefit.

generic drugs: nonbrand-name drugs that contain the same ingredients as their better-known rivals; they are usually less expensive

Generic Drugs: A Bargain for the Consumer

When a new drug is developed, it is usually patented and sold exclusively under a single brand name. Such patents last for 17 years, after which any firm can manufacture the drug and sell it under the drug's generic, or "official," name. The generic name usually describes the chemical composition of the drug, often some unpronounceable name, such as chlordiazepoxide hydrochloride (the trade name of this chemical compound is Librium; it is a drug often prescribed to relieve anxiety or tension). Ampicillin is the generic name for a drug that fights infections. Some of the common trade names given by various producers of this drug are Amcill, Omnipen, Polycillin, and Principen. They are all ampicillin; they just have different trade names because different companies produce them.

If you are familiar with wines, you know that the term *generic* is sometimes applied to a wine made from a specific grape, like Cabernet Sauvignon or Chardonnay. But unlike the production of generic wines, the production of generic drugs must proceed under strict supervision, so that no matter who manufactures them, the end result is precisely the same. The FDA, which we discussed in Chapters 8 and 10, monitors all prescription drugs, both brand-name and generic, and tests them for purity and strength.

The FDA has a list of the more than 5,000 prescription drugs approved for sale in the United States. About half of these drugs are available from more than one manufacturer, and the FDA has certified them as "therapeutically equivalent" to other brands of the same strength and dosage form (liquid, tablet, or capsule). They do not necessarily look or taste the same, but you can be sure that they are all equally safe and effective and that the body will absorb their active ingredients at the same rate.

Prices of prescription and over-the-counter medications vary among pharmacies and brand names.

TABLE 14.3 The 14 Most Prescribed Drugs with Their Generic Equivalents

Generic name	**Commonly Prescribed Brand Names**	**Purpose of Drug**
Ampicillin	Amcill Omnipen Polycillin Principen	To fight infection (antibiotic)
Tetracycline	Achromycin V Panmycin Sumycin Tetracyn	To fight infection (antibiotic)
Acetaminophen/codeine	Tylenol with Codeine	To relieve pain, fever, and cough
Hydrochlorothiazide	Esidrix HydroDIURIL Oretic	For hypertension and edema (diuretic)
Penicillin V-K	Pen-Vee K V-Cillin K Veetids	To fight infection (antibiotic)
Chlordiazepoxide hydrochloride	Librium	To relieve anxiety and tension
Propoxyphene hydrochloride, aspirin phenacetin, and caffeine	Darvon Compound-65	To relieve pain (analgesic)
Erythromycin stearate	Erythrocin Stearate	To fight infection (antibiotic)
Amitriptyline hydrochloride	Elavil Endep	To relieve symptoms of depression
Diphenhydramine hydrochloride	Benadryl	Antihistamine (also for motion sickness and parkinsonism)
Diphenoxylate hydrochloride with atropine sulfate	Lomotil	To help control diarrhea
Meclizine hydrochloride	Antivert	To convert nausea and vomiting, and dizziness from motion sickness
Chlorothiazide	Diuril	For hypertension and edema (diuretic)
Erythromycin ethyl succinate	E.E.S.	To fight infection (antibiotic)

SOURCE: "Generic Drugs: How Good are They?" *FDA Consumer* (Washington, D.C.: U.S. Government Printing Office, 1980).

Table 14.3 lists the 14 most often prescribed drugs available generically. If you or someone you know is taking one of these drugs under a brand name, you can probably save money by asking your physician to write a generic prescription instead. Of course, this is only a partial list, but the six most popular generic antibiotics account for over 60 million prescriptions each year. Keep this list in a handy place; it could save you hundreds of dollars.

FIGURE 14.4
New York's Generic Drug Law requires that patients receive prescriptions on slips containing two lines for doctors' signatures. Substitutions are forbidden when doctors sign on the left-hand side over the statement "Dispense as Written."

R℞

JOHN DOE, M.D.
MEDICAL BUILDING
OAK STREET
ANYTOWN, NEW YORK 00000

Jane Doe April 8, 1990

50 Tablets — Ampicilin

John Doe, M.D.

'DISPENSE AS WRITTEN   SUBSTITUTION PERMISSIBLE

More than 40 states have passed generic substitution laws that either allow or require pharmacists to substitute generic for brand-name drugs, if the prescribing physician has no objection. In 1978 the New York State legislature passed its Generic Drug Law, which provided for a standard format (see Figure 14.4) for all prescriptions written in that state. The placement of a doctor's signature on the right-hand side of the prescription slip signifies that the doctor has no objection to generic substitution. As a result, pharmacists are required to use the lower-cost generic drug. You might wonder why pharmacists must be *required* to use the lower-cost generic. This procedure has the added advantage of making it easy for physicians to prescribe generic drugs, even if they are not familiar with the generic name. Unfortunately, a 1979 study by the New York Public Interest Research Group (NYPIRG) found that 98 percent of the pharmacists surveyed were violating one or more provisions of the state law. According to NYPIRG (1980), "more than half of the pharmacists refused to dispense generic drugs even when the doctor had requested it." Largely because of this consumer survey, the New York Pharmacy Board fined 50 drugstores for noncompliance with the state law. Legislation is only half the battle. Consumers must also remain active to assure that such laws are enforced.

Over-the-Counter Drugs

Not all drugs require a prescription. Many of our most common drugstore purchases are for standard problems like headaches or sore throats. If one

**BOX 14.3   DRUG INTERACTIONS AND POTENTIAL
HEALTH THREATS**

Being a good decision maker in the area of health care expenditures can be difficult because of the high cost of information. In the text we outline some of the ways you can save money on prescription drugs by comparison shopping and by asking for generic drugs rather than their more expensive brand-name rivals. The effectiveness of the drug you take is a second area of concern that is just as important as saving money. Once again, information is important but often difficult to obtain.

An article by a pharmacologist presents some information about the interactions between drugs and commonly ingested foods (Romankiewicz, 1981). For example, citrus fruit can reduce the absorption of penicillin into the bloodstream. Thus, if you take ampicillin with orange juice, you will reduce the drug's ability to fight or control infection. Milk has a similar effect on tetracycline, another commonly prescribed antibiotic.

One of the most hazardous food–drug interactions is the one between monoamine oxidase (MAO) inhibitors, drugs often prescribed for depression and high blood pressure, and such common foods as bananas, chocolate, aged cheese (Parmesan, for example), red wine, yeast and yogurt. MAO inhibitors can react with a substance called tyramine in the foods and force blood pressure to dangerous levels, causing severe headaches, brain hemorrhage, and even death.

One reaction that women who take contraceptives should be especially alert to is the effect that ampicillin (an antibiotic prescribed to fight infection) can have on the effectiveness of birth-control pills. In some cases, ampicillin has been shown to counteract the effects of birth-control pills, and the result may be an unwanted pregnancy.

Alcohol is another potent reactor with certain drugs. Antihistamines can interact with alcohol to produce pronounced drowsiness. This may be a minor side effect if you are trying to rest, but it could be dangerous if you need to be alert to drive a car. Alcohol will also impair the effectiveness of most antibiotics. Bleeding from the stomach could result if alcohol is taken with aspirin.

were to judge one's needs by viewing television commercials, the number-one health problem in the United States would seem to be the common headache or loose dentures. As far as headaches are concerned, there are really only three forms of over-the-counter medication; acetylsalicylic acid (aspirin), acetaminophen, and ibuprofen. Bayer Aspirin is the largest-selling acetylsalicylic acid, Tylenol is the best-known acetaminophen, and Advil is the most popular ibuprofen brand.

Extensive tests have established that the only physician difference between various brands of aspirin is the size of the cotton plug in the bottle. The same analysis holds for other pain relievers (Liska, 1988). The smart consumer compares prices, chooses the least expensive variety, and disregards those clever commercials that help drive up the cost of the advertised brands, but do nothing to enhance their therapeutic value. A more important concern, as Box 14.3 shows, should be the potential hazards of drug interactions.

HEALTH INSURANCE: PRIVATE PLANS

health insurance: insurance designed to help cover expenses arising from sickness or injury and in some cases to provide income during disability

Now that you have some idea of the components of supply and demand for health care, we will explore health insurance, one of the most important ways to minimize your personal health costs. **Health insurance** is insurance designed to help cover expenses arising from sickness, injury, or disability. Because a prolonged illness can wipe out a family's savings, put tremendous debt on household members, and ruin the most carefully planned family budget, most people choose to pay for some form of health insurance.

In 1985 more than 180 million Americans—about 77 percent of the population—had some form of private health insurance. This broad base of support makes it possible for health insurance companies to spread the risk over millions of families; thus, the healthy subsidize the sick. This is the same principle that automobile insurance companies use to spread the risk of loss caused by accidents (see Chapter 12). The premiums from healthy, insured consumers help to pay for those who become ill. This "share-the-risk" principle is basic to all types of insurance.

The private insurance industry is highly competitive, with more than 1,200 companies writing policies for hundreds of millions of people. Some of these companies, such as Mutual of Omaha, Prudential, and Occidental, are set up like any other profit-oriented corporations. Their goal is to maximize their profits for the benefit of their stockholders, who expect a return on their investment. The average profit-making insurance firm pays about 80 percent of its premium income in claims. For the other major kind of insurance company, the nonprofit membership corporation, such as Blue Cross and Blue Shield, the goal is to charge a premium high enough to pay the health care bills of its members and cover the costs of administering its plans. Blue Cross and Blue Shield plans cover almost half of all health insurance holders, and they pay out almost 95 percent of their premium income in claims.

Based on the payment ratio of nonprofit plans, one might think that nonprofit plans are the best choice. This may be so. Before you are ready to make an intelligent decision about which health-insurance company to choose, you need to know something about the general provisions of health insurance policies. Almost every company offers a wide variety of plans. Some will be better suited to your needs than others. There is no way that we can cover a majority of these plans here, but we can lay out the basic categories of health insurance and what they do and do not cover. In many respects, the sections that follow parallel the sections on automobile insurance presented in Chapter 12. The concepts of co-insurance and the deductible also apply to health insurance, but there is seldom any problem with who is at fault. If you become ill, the health insurance company pays for all covered expenses; it does not try to assess blame. But what does your policy cover?

The health insurance industry is undergoing dramatic change because the costs of health care (and insurance premiums) are rising faster than the general inflation rate. This has led many companies to restructure their sales techniques, benefits, and programs. Nevertheless, you can still divide health care insurance into these categories:

1. Basic coverage, which includes protection against the cost of ordinary, short-term hospital care, surgery, and doctors' services for nonsurgical care
2. Major medical coverage, which provides broad protection against the costs of serious or prolonged illness
3. Disability insurance, which provides income for people who are unable to work because of sickness or injury
4. Dental insurance, which provides coverage for the costs of dental services

Basic Coverage

Basic coverage is insurance that covers the costs of ordinary hospital care, surgery, and doctor's services. Before the days of spiraling health care costs, basic coverage and disability insurance were the only kinds of health insurance offered. Depending on the policy, basic coverage benefits usually last a year or less, and they often have a stipulated maximum payment. These benefits are geared to the normal, everyday medical needs that many people experience, from hospital visits because of pregnancy or a broken leg to having one's tonsils removed or simply visiting a doctor because of illness. If your insurance plan has a basic coverage provision, it probably includes hospital-expense insurance, surgical-expense insurance, and physician-expense insurance. But in many plans, it is possible to purchase these coverages separately.

Hospital-expense insurance. If a person has any health insurance coverage at all, it is most likely hospital-expense insurance, because it is the most widely held type. **Hospital-expense insurance** provides specific benefits for daily hospital room and board and for routine nursing care. It also provides for other hospital services, such as laboratory tests, x-rays, anesthesia, the use of an operating room, drugs and medications, and even local ambulance service.

With hospital-expense insurance, as with all insurance policies, the benefits received, the number of days covered by the plan, and the value of the insurance depend on how much coverage a policy allows. These are always stated in terms of daily charges. For example, if the room-and-board benefit is $200 per day and the additional covered services are eight times that amount, one would be covered for $1,800 in charges for each day in the hospital.

Blue Cross uses a service-benefit approach when paying the room-and-board charges for the hospital confinement of one of its policyholders. With **service-benefit insurance**, the insurance carrier pays the full cost of a semiprivate room, without regard to the specific dollar cost. The hospital bills Blue Cross and receives its payment directly from Blue Cross; the patient does not receive a check or pay the bill directly. A possible problem with this plan for Blue Cross policyholders is that they must make sure that the hospital qualifies for the plan and is considered a participating hospital. Otherwise, all charges may not be covered.

Another frequently purchased form of hospital-expense insurance is **hospital indemnity coverage**; it pays a fixed amount of money (indemnity) directly to the patient for every day that he or she spends in the hospital. The amount of money paid to the patient is unrelated to actual hospital expenses. Hospital-expense policies that use the indemnity approach are sometimes sold through the mail or with television ad campaigns. Insurance companies that sell hospital indemnity coverage often border on being disreputable. Remember, with rising hospital costs, $150 a day does not go far in paying medical bills. These kinds of policies should be viewed only as supplements to other health insurance plans. A ten-day hospital stay for which charges average $500 per day leaves a patient with a hospital bill of $3,500, even after a daily indemnity of $150 is paid. One point to check *before* signing up for indemnity coverage is the manner in which insurance companies deal with preexisting ailments, that is, illness that a patient was treated for before subscribing to the insurance plan. If preexisting ailments are broadly defined, this clause can be used to deny payment. A final question to ask of these companies is what proportion of a policyholder's premiums are repaid to insured patients. This can be determined by looking up the company in the *Argus Chart of Health Insurance*, which should be available at your college or public library. If an insurance company is returning less than 65 percent of its premiums to its hospitalized policyholders, its policies are probably a poor buy.

Surgical-expense insurance. As the name implies, **surgical-expense insurance** provides benefits for the costs of surgical procedures performed as a result of accident or illness, but not for cosmetic procedures, such as a face lift. Benefits under this type of policy can follow either the indemnity or the service-benefit approach. Under the indemnity approach, an insurance company pays up to a certain amount, according to a price schedule of surgical procedures. But Blue Shield and an increasing number of other insurance companies are now moving to the service-benefit approach, in which they agree to pay for all surgical costs, as long as the charges are "usual, customary and reasonable" (UCR). The UCR reimbursement system is based on how much other physicians in the area charge for similar operations. For a participating Blue Shield physician, as long as his or her fee is below the ninetieth percentile (not in the top ten percent for the same operation), it is paid in full. For example, if 90 percent of all the physicians in a given area charge $600 for a tonsillectomy, then the insurance company would consider a bill of up to $600 reasonable, but it probably would not pay a doctor $650 for the operation, unless there were some unusual circumstances. Surgeons do not get bonuses for charging less. But because next year's UCR fees depend on this year's fees, some critics have argued that the system has a built-in upward bias.

Physician-expense insurance. Physician-expense insurance provides benefits that help pay doctor's fees for nonsurgical care in the hospital, the home, or the office. This insurance does not cover routine checkups, eye examinations, or immunizations, probably because preventive medical care is not a high priority for most insurance companies. Payments are usually made by the indemnity approach, with a limit on the number of doctor visits allowed per year. Some consumer advocates believe that this type of insurance is not very useful, because the risk of major expense is slight and the indemnity payments are low. Thus, the consumer can achieve the same level of protection by holding a financial reserve, a form of self-insurance. The nice part of holding a financial reserve is that it becomes a regular part of savings and can pay interest, rather than earning money for an insurance company.

Major Medical-Expense Insurance

The three categories of insurance detailed above (hospital-, surgical-, and physician-expense) are basic coverage. **Major medical-expense insurance** is a backup plan that protects the policyholder from large, unpredictable medical expenses. It was introduced nationally in 1951, and its growth has been rapid. Today, more than 160 million people are covered by major medical-expense insurance (Health Insurance Association of America). It generally covers a much broader number of accidents and illnesses, including mental illness and sometimes alcoholism. In 1986, 90 percent of those covered by this kind of plan had maximum benefits of $1 million or more; a third of these had unlimited benefits.

A good major medical plan normally has a deductible amount that limits minor claims and thus keeps administrative costs lower. It also has a co-insurance provision that requires a policyholder to pay a percentage, often 20 percent of the major medical expenses. Beyond this, however, the only limit is the maximum stated in the policy. In order to protect oneself against catastrophic illness, under no circumstances should this maximum be less than $100,000, and it should preferably be $1 million. Oddly enough, major medical insurance is usually the least expensive form of

TABLE 14.4 Basic and Major Medical Coverage

Expense	Total Charges	Basic Coverage	Major Medical Coverage
Hospital room and board			
10 days of intensive care at $800 per day	$ 8,000	$ 6,000	$ 2,000
40 days of room and board at $400 per day	16,000	8,000	8,000
Other charges: laboratory, blood tests, drugs, medicines	4,500	3,000	1,500
Registered nurse's fees:			
10 days at $150 per day	1,500		1,500
Physicians' fees	4,100	2,700	1,400
Totals	$34,100	$19,700	$14,400
Less deductible of $1,000			− 1,000
Balance subject to co-insurance			$13,400
Less co-insurance at 20 percent			− 2,680
Amount paid by major medical insurance			$10,720

private health insurance, and when the size of the risk is considered, it is a very good buy.

Table 14.4 shows how major medical coverage supplements basic coverage and considerably reduces an insured person's costs. For example, suppose Frank Jones develops a severe case of hepatitis, has to be hospitalized for a long time, and needs ten days of nursing care after he is discharged. Basic coverage pays $19,700 of the total bill, but because it has certain maximum limits on how much it covers, it does not pay all of the bills for this illness. If Frank did not have major medical coverage, he would still owe $14,400 to hospitals, doctors, and nurses. It is in cases like this that the backup coverage of major medical insurance is so important. Of the $14,400 in additional costs, major medical insurance pays $10,720. The rest, $3,680, Frank owes, because of the $1,000 deductible and 20 percent co-insurance provisions in his policy. Nevertheless, it would be a lot easier to pay $3,680 than the $14,400 left over after basic coverage has paid its share.

Disability Income Protection

In addition to the problem of rising medical bills, one has the problem of being unable to work and thus not receiving a paycheck to help pay other bills. **Disability income insurance** provides an income if one is unable to work because of sickness or injury. In 1985, 28 million workers had some form of disability income coverage.

Not all disability policies are alike. Cash benefits usually range from one-half to two-thirds of one's regular gross income, depending on the policy selected. The total amount of benefits paid also varies, based on the extent of the disability and on whether the policy is short or long term. Short-term policies pay an insured person for two years or less. Long-term policies can last an indefinite period, but they rarely go beyond retirement age, generally assumed to be 65. In addition to these conditions, most plans also have a **waiting period**, an amount of time between the onset of the disability and the beginning of the payments. This waiting period is like the deductible amount in other health insurance policies; it lowers

As the cost of dental care has increased, more consumers have enrolled in dental insurance plans.

the claims and also the size of the premiums. But be careful, do not accept a policy for which the waiting period may exceed your ability to maintain your household financially. A one-month waiting period is optimal for most families; it balances the advantages of lower premiums against the risk of a prolonged loss of income.

Dental-Expense Insurance

Dental-expense insurance is the most rapidly expanding form of health insurance. In 1967, fewer than 5 million persons were covered, but by 1985 there were more than 100 million people with some form of dental insurance. Unlike the other forms of private health insurance, dental insurance emphasizes preventive as well as remedial care. Most policies reimburse clients for routine oral examinations, including x-rays and cleaning, fillings, extractions, inlays, and dentures, as well as for oral surgery and orthodontics. The major problems with dental insurance are twofold. First, unless one belongs to a labor union or works for a large corporation or the government, dental insurance is difficult to get, because most insurance companies offer it only to large groups. Second, even if one is able to obtain dental insurance, the maximum payment to any policyholder in one year is generally low, rarely exceeding $1,500.

THE HEALTH MAINTENANCE ORGANIZATION

health maintenance organization (HMO): an organization that provides comprehensive health-care services for a fixed payment

The difficulty in controlling health care costs led some health care specialists to create a different form of health care delivery called a **health maintenance organization (HMO)**. An HMO offers its members comprehensive, coordinated medical services and hospitalization for a prepaid monthly or yearly fee. This plan eliminates the sometimes arbitrary distinctions between basic coverage and major medical-expense insurance. It also eliminates the deductible expense for insurance claims. In fact, once you are enrolled, you rarely have to fill out any claim forms or burdensome paperwork. There may be a small charge ($5 to $10) for office visits, just to discourage indiscriminate use of health care. But once you pay this fee and present your HMO card, you can be assured that the HMO will do the rest.

Although the first HMOs began in the United States in the 1930s, they grew very slowly. By 1970 there were fewer then 50. Congress gave HMOs a big push when it passed the Health Maintenance Organization Act in 1973, requiring all businesses with more than 25 employees to offer an HMO alternative to standard health insurance. By 1986 there were more than 626 HMOs serving almost 28 million consumers.

There are several variations of HMO. The classic HMO is the Kaiser Permanente Plan, which began in 1933. Under this model the HMO employs a staff of doctors at its hospital, where all patient care is centralized. Another version of an HMO involves a group of independent physicians who agree to supply their services under contract to an HMO. Members of the local HMO choose one of these doctors to be their "primary care physician" and they must go to this doctor first, before being referred to specialists. This plan allows the doctors to see private patients as well as HMO patients. It also gives patients the most latitude in retaining a family physician. But it can prove more inconvenient if extensive testing or referrals are required. Only HMO-related laboratories and specialists are covered under this plan. If a patient insists on seeing a doctor outside the contract, the fee will probably not be reimbursed.

HMOs are not the best solution for everyone. They can offer services only in a given geographical area, and they are limited by the specialties of their staff doctors. A member who becomes ill outside the HMO's area is covered only if the illness or accident is a genuine emergency. Otherwise, the member is expected to return home for treatment. Another problem with some of these plans is that members are not allowed to choose a particular physician. They are treated by whoever is on call when they arrive.

On the other hand, there are many advantages to belonging to an HMO. Unlike most private insurers, HMOs often stress preventive care and encourage periodic check-ups and routine immunizations. Partly because of the emphasis on prevention, persons covered by these prepaid plans tend to make more doctor visits per year than those covered by fee-for-service plans. However, a study conducted by the U.S. Department of Health and Human Services showed that the HMO group had fewer and shorter hospital stays. In addition, there may be a certain peace of mind in knowing that whatever the ailment, however long the treatment, and no matter what drugs are prescribed, the patient will never have any medical bills over and above the monthly HMO fee.

The success of the HMO has led to a hybrid between a standard health insurance plan and the HMO. The new health care plan is called a **Preferred Provider Organization (PPO)**. Since the first PPO was established in Denver, Colorado, in 1980, a flurry of new groups have spread to all parts of the United States. A PPO is a group of physicians and hospitals that agrees to offer health care at a discount to members of a health insurance plan. A PPO is a traditional health insurance plan with a "preferred staff" of health care professionals who charge less to PPO members than to their other patients. If PPO members choose one of these "preferred providers" they know they will incur little or no expense. If a member chooses to go outside this list, then the plan pays for those services as if it were a standard health insurance contract. Thus, unlike the HMO, the PPO gives the patient a greater choice, but its costs are often higher as well.

preferred provider organization (PPO): a hybrid between a standard health insurance plan and an HMO; it provides an opportunity for the consumer to choose a physician or hospital that in turn has agreed to offer health care at a discount to members of that health insurance plan

ALTERNATIVE HEALTH CARE SYSTEMS: IS THERE A BETTER WAY?

The U.S. health care system has been described as a crazy patchwork quilt of programs. Many health care professionals argue that the health insurance system in our country needs a major overhaul. But what direction should we take?

Socialized Medicine

socialized medicine: *a term that generally means that a large fraction of all medical facilities are run by the government; in addition, most medical personnel are government employees who receive a salary and do not charge patients for treatment*

Some nations, such as the United Kingdom and Sweden, have overhauled their health care delivery systems and instituted a program of **socialized medicine**. Under this plan, many doctors, dentists, and other health care specialists became government employees. Their salaries are paid by taxes in much the same way that American police, teachers, and civil servants are paid. Anyone in need of their services can obtain them without charge. This system does not provide "free" medical care, because someone has to pay for the resources used by patients. For Sweden and the United Kingdom, this has meant massive governmental intervention in health care: paying bills from tax revenues, setting salaries for physicians, dentists, and other health care personnel, and establishing regulations about the quality and quantity of care, in addition to deciding who qualifies. The record of socialized medicine has been neither all bad nor all good. As mentioned previously, the Swedish infant mortality rate is one of the best in the world—a strong indication of a good medical system. On the other hand, Sweden has a tremendous shortage of dentists and general practitioners, partly because of government interference. In the United States, there have already been so many complaints and even scandals involving our more limited Medicare and Medicaid programs that the idea of having the federal government take over the wholesale provisioning of health care seems unlikely in the next decade. However, there is a program that might be a middle ground between our current health care system and socialized medicine. It is called national health insurance.

National Health Insurance

Most people in the United States have some form of health insurance, but a sizeable minority does not. Estimates of the number of Americans without health care coverage vary, but most indicate that about 17 percent of the U.S. population, or 37 million people, remain uncovered by either government or private health insurance (Malloy, 1988). Who are these people? Would they gain from a national health insurance program?

A breakdown of the uninsured population has some surprises as well as some obvious generalizations. People who are young, nonwhite, poor, less educated, or living in rural areas are more likely to be uninsured. These categories all make sense, given the lower incomes of these groups. It is perhaps less obvious that almost half of the uninsured people under age 65 have a full- or part-time job. It is this statistical generalization that has led to a proposal for a new patch on our health care quilt.

Senator Edward Kennedy has introduced a bill that would require employers to pay 80 percent of health care insurance premiums for any employee who works 17.5 hours or more per week. A similar proposal that taxes employers who refused to comply will take effect in Massachusetts in 1992. Kennedy's plan would also create regional insurance associations to make it easier and cheaper for small firms to buy health insurance. The Congressional Budget Office estimates that Kennedy's bill would cost employers an additional $25 billion in health insurance premiums. It does have the advantage of not raising taxes or government expenditures; however, it places an additional health care burden on employers, who will ultimately try to pass this cost along to consumers. Chrysler Corporation estimated that its employee health care benefits add $600 to the price of each car it sells (Kilpatrick, 1983).

| The Canadian System: Universal Health Insurance | In 1960 Canada spent slightly more of its GNP on its health care system than the United States did; today, it spends significantly less. Under the Canadian system the provincial governments provide health insurance but do not directly employ health care personnel. Every citizen is automatically insured. Canadians are free to choose any physician or hospital in Canada, and the provincial insurance plan pays all the charges. The big difference is that the provinces negotiate mandatory fee schedules with local physician groups—fees that are much lower than in the United States. Canadian doctors earn about 70 percent as much as U.S. doctors, and these savings are passed along. Similar cost controls are in effect with hospitals that are heavily subsidized by provincial governments. As the vice-chairman of Toronto-based Crown Life Insurance said about the Canadian and U.S. health care systems, "In Canada, the costs are a lot less because the government is controlling them. In the U.S., nobody is controlling them" (Malloy, 1988). If the Canadian system continues to perform well in the 1990s, even the U.S. may turn to a universal health insurance system. |

The Canadian System: Universal Health Insurance

In 1960 Canada spent slightly more of its GNP on its health care system than the United States did; today, it spends significantly less. Under the Canadian system the provincial governments provide health insurance but do not directly employ health care personnel. Every citizen is automatically insured. Canadians are free to choose any physician or hospital in Canada, and the provincial insurance plan pays all the charges. The big difference is that the provinces negotiate mandatory fee schedules with local physician groups—fees that are much lower than in the United States. Canadian doctors earn about 70 percent as much as U.S. doctors, and these savings are passed along. Similar cost controls are in effect with hospitals that are heavily subsidized by provincial governments. As the vice-chairman of Toronto-based Crown Life Insurance said about the Canadian and U.S. health care systems, "In Canada, the costs are a lot less because the government is controlling them. In the U.S., nobody is controlling them" (Malloy, 1988). If the Canadian system continues to perform well in the 1990s, even the U.S. may turn to a universal health insurance system.

STAYING HEALTHY: THE BEST WAY TO AVOID THE HIGH COST OF HEALTH CARE

Research on the economics of health care has come to a startling conclusion. Habits and life-style have a much larger impact on health than does the amount of medical care purchased. In other words, if people have good diets, exercise sensibly, and ingest few substances like alcohol, or tobacco, they will be considerably healthier.

There is already some evidence that shows the healthy impact of the movement away from smoking. Figure 14.5 shows the proportion of men

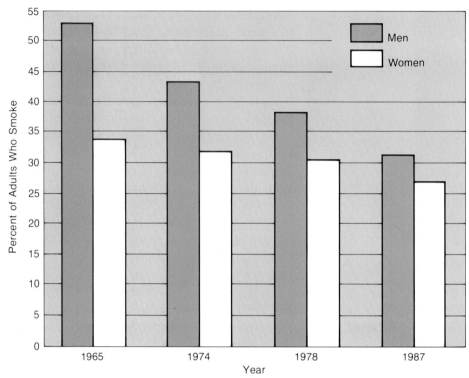

and women who smoke tobacco. The precipitous decline in the proportion
of men who smoke has already had an important impact on their mortality
patterns and in their rate of hospitalization. Women do not show such a
marked decrease in cigarette smoking, which has led to an annual age-
adjusted increase in lung cancer of 7.7 percent for white women. As one
observer noted, "The figures speak for themselves. Insofar as the rate of
cancer deaths in this country is rising, the single largest factor is the vast
increase in cigarette smoking by white women over the past generation"
(Schwartz, 1980). If men and women ever reach equality in their smoking,
we will probably see a much more equal life expectancy as well.

Regular exercise is another important ingredient in maintaining health.
Some of us are fortunate enough to have occupations that fulfill the need to
exercise, but most of us are products of the postindustrial revolution: We
buy machines or pay other people to do the tasks that require muscle
power. We are left with sedentary mental tasks that may pay better but
are not really as healthful. One of the most interesting studies done on
the impact of occupational exercise on health was a time-series study
on the bus drivers and ticket takers on London's double-decker buses.
These men (there were no women) were issued uniforms by the company,
and over the years records were kept of their sizes. The ticket takers
(called squirrels), who went up and down the stairs hundreds of times

each day, stayed slim and healthy. The drivers, because they were sitting most of the time, got heavier with age, and their medical records showed a much higher incidence of heart attacks and other illnesses.

SUMMARY

The health care industry in the United States is big business. It employs 5 percent of the workforce and costs well over $600 billion every year. It can also be called a growth industry, because it accounts for a larger proportion of the GNP today than it did 30 years ago. But with all this increased activity, there is still some question about its ability to produce adequate health care for all Americans. Certainly, death rates have fallen and life expectancies have risen, but the United States is still not in the forefront in many areas. Our infant mortality rates, for example, are still higher than those of many other developed nations, and our life expectancies are not the greatest in the world, either. But there are other factors involved in death rates besides medical care.

Health care expenditures have risen dramatically in recent years, largely because of inflation within the industry. These inflationary tendencies can be traced to changes in demand and supply. On the demand side, large segments of our population that had previously been excluded from the health care market have been brought in via the Medicare and Medicaid programs. Added to this factor is the increasing use of private insurers as third-party payers. The prevalence of third-party payments led to a decrease in the price consciousness of consumers, who felt little of the direct cost at the time of treatment. It was only when their insurance premiums rose or their taxes went up that they related the rise in health care costs to their personal budgets.

Changes in the supply of medical care have also played an important role in the pattern of health care costs. Recent increases in the supply of doctors have not been sufficient to increase access and lower prices to health care consumers. Training additional health care personnel, such as physician assistants and nurse-midwives, offers some hope, but it is certainly not a panacea.

Hospital cost containment is another area in which important strides can be taken to lessen inflation in health care costs. The Medicare DRG system, with fixed fees for certain treatments, offers some hope in this area, but some critics argue that this system simply shifts costs to other patients. Moreover, the basic doctor–hospital relationship makes it difficult for hospitals to avoid buying the latest equipment, even if it is expensive and underutilized.

Prescription drugs have recently experienced rapid inflation, despite the advent of generic drugs. Consumers can save significantly by learning to ask for generic drugs that have been classified by the FDA as therapeutically equivalent to their brand-name competitors.

Most consumers protect themselves against the potentially devastating costs of medical care by buying insurance. More than 1,200 private insurance companies sell insurance, but almost all offer basic and major medical coverage. Basic coverage takes care of ordinary, short-term hospital care and doctors' services. But for broader, long-term coverage consumers need major medical coverage. Disability income insurance is a form of health insurance that provides a cash grant while one is unable to work. Dental-expense insurance is the fastest-growing form of health insurance, but it is difficult to obtain without belonging to a labor union or working for a large firm.

HMOS offer an alternative to private insurance plans. They often stress preventive care, and according to recent studies, their members spend less time in hospitals than do privately insured consumers.

A number of alternative health care plans have been tried in other nations and have been suggested for trial in the United States. Socialized medicine is practiced in the United Kingdom and Sweden, with mixed results. National health insurance seems to be a more likely plan for the United States, because it requires less government intervention than does socialized medicine. The Canadian experience with universal health insurance may offer a model for a long-run solution to our health care dilemma of providing high-quality care at a reasonable cost.

The best way to improve your own health is to control what you eat and drink, to exercise frequently, and to avoid smoking. These personal habits are your responsibility, and they, more than your medical expenditures, tend to affect your health.

QUESTIONS

1. How successful has the U.S. health care industry been in maintaining Americans' health? What evidence could you use to point to the health industry's success? Is there any evidence of failure?

2. How is the average health care dollar spent? List the types of health expenditures in order of their importance. What proportion of the total do hospital care and physician services take?

3. What is a third-party payment system, and how is it related to the increase in health care costs?

4. Compare the Medicare and Medicaid programs. How are they funded? Who benefits from them?

5. Have you or anyone in your family ever had nonemergency surgery? Was a second opinion sought? If so, why? How would you go about seeking a second opinion? Explain.

6. Explain how an increase in the supply of physicians could cause a rise in prices, as predicted by the Graduate Medical Advisory Committee. Do you agree with its conclusion?

7. Why does the unique doctor–hospital relationship lead hospitals to buy expensive equipment that is already available and underused at nearby hospitals or to build new wings with additional rooms when other hospitals have high vacancy rates?

8. What is a generic drug and how does it benefit consumers?

9. What are the four basic types of health insur-

ance? If you could afford only one, which would it be? Why?

10. What are the characteristics of the typical uninsured consumer? Would socialized medicine or national health insurance benefit uninsured consumers? Who would bear the cost of these programs?

11. Is it a consumer's responsibility to take care of his or her health? How can you improve your health without spending more money? Are there any costs associated with such health improvement?

REFERENCES AND READINGS

"Are We Hooked on Tests?" *U.S. News & World Report*, November 23, 1987.

"Benefits Shock." *U.S. News & World Report*, March 28, 1988.

Callahan, Daniel. *Setting Limits: Medical Goals in an Aging Society*. New York: Simon & Schuster, 1987.

"Can You Afford to Get Sick?" *Newsweek*, January 30, 1989.

"For Health and Wealth." *U.S. News & World Report*, June 6, 1988.

Freed, Kenneth. "In Canada, Sick Never Turned Away." *L.A. Times*, May 19, 1986.

Fuchs, Victor. *The Health Economy*. Cambridge, Mass.. Harvard University Press, 1986.

"Generic Drugs: How Good Are They?" *FDA Consumer*, 1980.

Golladay, Frederick. "Allied Health Manpower Strategies." *Medical Care*, November/December 1973.

"Health Insurance: What You Need, What You Get." *Changing Times*, April 1988.

Health Insurance Association of America. *Sourcebook of Health Insurance Data*. Washington, D.C. Annual Editions.

"HMO Approach to Health Care." *Consumer Reports*, May 1982.

Kilpatrick, James K. "The High Cost of Health." *Nation's Business*, October 1983.

Larson, Erik. "Hospital Program to Charge by the Ailment." *Wall Street Journal*, November 11, 1980.

Lehman, Phyllis. "Food and Drug Interactions." *FDA Consumer*, September 1984 (revised).

Liska, Ken. *The Pharmacist's Guide to the Most Misused and Abused Drugs in America*. New York: Collier, 1988.

Luciano, Lani. "HMO, Yes or No?" *Money*, July 1988.

Malloy, Michael T. "Health, Canadian Style." *Wall Street Journal*, April 22, 1988a.

Romankiewicz, John A. "Don't Take Your Penicillin with Orange Juice." *Redbook*, May 1981.

Schwartz, Harry. "Looking at the Ways We Die." *Wall Street Journal*, December 9, 1980.

Somers, Herman M. "Economic Issues in Health Services." In Chamberlin, Neal W., *Contemporary Economic Issues* (Homewood, Ill.: Irwin, 1969).

Stipp, David. "The Tattered Safety Net." *Wall Street Journal*, April 22, 1988b.

Twaddle, Andrew C., and Richard M. Hessler. *A Sociology of Health*. New York: Macmillan, 1987.

U.S. Office of Consumer Affairs. *People Power: What Communities Are Doing to Counter Inflation*. Washington, D.C.. U.S. Government Printing Office, 1980.

"Who Can Afford a Nursing Home?" *Consumer Reports*, May 1988

Young, Frank E. "Questions About Your Medicine? Go Ahead—Ask." *FDA Consumer* October 1987.

Chapter Fifteen

GOVERNMENT SERVICES AND TAXATION: PAYING YOUR FAIR SHARE

DID YOU KNOW THAT . . .

. . . there are more than 80,000 governments in the United States?

. . . transfer payments to individuals make up the largest portion of the federal budget?

. . . taxes are about 20 percent lower in the United States than they are in other developed nations?

. . . the federal income tax on individual income provides almost half of the federal budget revenues, yet before 1913 the income tax was unconstitutional, and as late as 1939 less than 4 percent of the population had to pay income tax?

. . . there is a simple formula to help one compare an investment that offers a tax-free income with an investment offering a taxable yield?

. . . you can get a tax credit when you pay someone to care for your child while you work, and the size of this tax credit varies inversely with your income?

. . . tax evasion is punishable by fine or imprisonment, but the art of tax avoidance is rewarded by lower taxes and more spendable income?

. . . you can significantly lower the likelihood that your tax return will be audited?

. . . income tax rates and rules were dramatically changed in the 1980s?

Most consumers are aware of the importance of government both in providing services and in demanding payment for those services. In recent years we have witnessed an increase in this awareness, as consumers have fought to get the most from their tax dollars. In a sense, consumers' desire to get the most for their tax dollars is no different from their attempt to get the best clothing or housing for their money. However, unlike purchasing a new coat or a residence, it is difficult to invoke the principles of comparison shopping when paying taxes. One cannot decide to pay more for public hospitals and less for national defense. Our elected officials make these decisions collectively. Nevertheless, consumers are not powerless. They can affect the expenditure process through political action, by voting for those candidates who are closest to consumers' individual positions on various issues and by making their views known to those elected. And just as important, consumers can learn the fundamentals of the tax system and make sure that they are not bearing an unusually large share of the tax burden. An understanding of the tax laws and a conscious effort at tax planning can really pay off for an individual consumer.

We begin this chapter with an overview of two of the major functions of government: providing goods and services and transferring income. Then we move on to the main topic of this chapter: taxation. First, we look at the principles of taxation, and then we narrow our focus to the federal income tax. Our purpose is to help you to understand the most important sections of your income-tax forms and to give you some guidance on tax planning as well as in actually preparing the forms. For example, understanding the difference between marginal and average tax rates is essential to weighing the tax consequences of working overtime, taking a second job, or calculating your rate of return on an investment.

Tax laws change frequently, and even the most astute consumer may find it difficult to keep up. As a result, the sections on federal income tax are followed by some advice on how to find a professional tax preparer and what to do if you are called in for a tax audit. We conclude the chapter with a look at the fairness of the overall tax burden.

THE GOVERNMENT: AN OVERVIEW

How often have you heard someone talk about "the government"? In the United States, such a blanket term can have many meanings. There are more than 80,000 governments in the United States, ranging from small townships and villages to the massive federal bureaucracy. With such a large collection of agencies exercising varying degrees of control over our lives and money, it is little wonder that many people have the idea that government has grown too big and become unresponsive to taxpayers' needs. But the functions of government have not changed. It must still provide needed goods and services and transfer income from one group to another. An understanding of these functions is basic to an informed consumer's ability to live within the system. Let us start, then, with these functions and move to the more specific everyday realities of taxes and tax paying.

Providing Goods and Services

Regardless of how big government seems, almost everyone admits that a society needs a government to maintain order. Without a system of enforceable laws, society would rapidly deteriorate into anarchy, a situation in which "might makes right" and weaker members of society are terrorized by the strong. In order to avoid this, people have established laws to govern their behavior, and they have delegated the administration of these laws and their enforcement to the courts and the police. The resulting social and legal framework is like a giant rulebook. As long as people play by the rules, they can continue to function in society. If they violate these rules, they will be subject to a suitable punishment, which may vary from a small fine for a parking ticket to life imprisonment or even death for a serious crime.

All levels of government—local, state, and federal—participate in the basic law-and-order function. But in addition to ensuring the rule of law, government often provides other goods and services. On the local level, for example, government provides its citizens with fire protection and public schools. At the national level, the federal government maintains the armed forces. There is little debate over the necessity of spending tax dollars on fire protection, public education, and national defense, but there can be a heated debate over how much to spend and how best to achieve these ends. In the 1989 federal budget, for example, 27 percent of the expenditures were slated for national defense. Is this too much or too little?

public good: a good or a service with significant social benefit that cannot be denied to people who are unable to pay for it; public goods such as national defense, parks, and police and fire service are examples

Public goods. Justice, fire protection, public education, and national defense are examples of what economists call **public goods**. A public good is a good or service that the business sector would not produce in sufficient quantities, even though society as a whole would benefit. Why won't private firms produce an ample supply of public goods? The answer

Government provides consumers with many important services, like fire protection.

free-rider effect: a situation in which nonpaying members of society obtain the benefits of goods or services

is simple: There is not enough profit in it. Imagine the difficulty a company would have in trying to provide national defense and selling it to its customers. Many people would refuse to pay, yet they would still be protected once the public good was produced. In other words, the company could not count on a payoff from all those who used the good. The problem of being unable to exclude the nonpaying public from using a good or service is called the "nonexclusion principle," or the **free-rider effect**. In essence, the nonpaying public gets a free ride: It gets the service without paying for it. It is as if a company produced bread but only got paid for every tenth loaf, because it did not control the distribution of bread. Whenever the free-rider effect is important, you can be sure that the private sector will either underproduce the good or not produce it at all.

A second characteristic of public goods is "shared consumption." People who use a public good do not prevent others from enjoying that good. Consumers are not rivals. They can all share the public good. In the cases of national defense and the justice system, for example, one consumer's satisfaction is not reduced when another consumer utilizes them. If there were 300 million people in the United States instead of 250 million, your satisfaction from our national defense expenditure would not be reduced. By the same token, if you utilize the justice system, another's rights to that system are not diminished. The classic case of a public good that illustrates shared consumption is a lighthouse. Its beam of light can protect one or many ships without reducing their effectiveness.

In most cases, public goods must be provided by the government if they are to be produced at the required level. Private enterprise is simply not geared to providing such important services as national defense, lighthouses, and public parks, for which it is difficult to make all beneficiaries pay. Government can use its power to tax and thus can both provide goods and require the citizenry to pay for them. This is an important function of government and one that accounts for a significant share of total government expenditures.

Unemployment compensation is one form of government transfer payments. This entitlement program provides households with income and helps to counteract the business cycle.

Transferring Income

entitlement program: an umbrella term for social programs that provide transfer payments

Aside from providing certain goods and services, another major task of government is to oversee **transfer payments**, unearned payments made to individuals for social reasons. Transfer payments can take the form of direct money payments, such as those for Social Security, farm price supports, or veterans benefits, or they can be in-kind subsidies, such as food stamps, public housing, or free medical care. Whatever their form, they contribute the largest portion of the federal budget, 43 percent in 1989 (see Figure 15.1).

Most government transfer payments are part of so-called **entitlement programs**, in which anyone who meets the qualifications established by Congress is entitled to the benefits prescribed by law. The cost of these programs is not determined by a fixed dollar amount, but by the number of people who qualify. Thus, expenditures on entitlement programs is out of the hands of the current Congress, unless it changes the rules. Congress has changed the rules on these programs from time to time, but in general these changes have enhanced the benefits and enlarged the size of the group entitled to these benefits. One such example was the legislation that indexed Social Security retirement benefits to inflation. This analysis is consistent with Figure 15.2, which shows that government transfer payments to individuals have taken a larger share of the federal budget over time. The reason for this growth has been congressional legislation that has increased coverage of various entitlement programs in addition to increasing the size of the individual payment and, in some cases, indexing the payments to the inflation rate.

Many consumers find the tax law too difficult to interpret on their own, so they choose a professional tax-preparation service.

FIGURE 15.1
1989 Federal budget.
(SOURCE: *Budget of the United States Government, 1989.*)

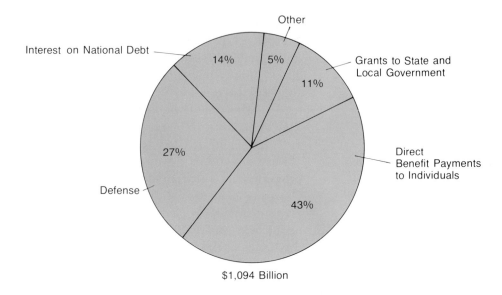

FIGURE 15.1
1989 Federal budget.
(SOURCE: *Budget of the United States Government, 1989.*)

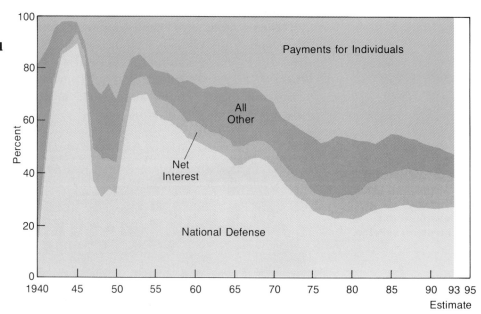

FIGURE 15.2
Percentage composition of federal government outlays.
(SOURCE: *Budget of the United States Government, 1989,* Historical Tables.)

The government provides transfer payments for a different reason than the one for which it oversees public goods. The free-rider problem does not apply here. The reason for transfer payments lies in our free-market economy. As we explained in Chapter 3, in a pure market economy, everyone is supposed to earn income by working. Some earn more than others. But if for some reason, such as age, infirmity, or disability, a person cannot work, the system will not reward him or her with income. In the past, retired or disabled citzens had to depend on private resources such as personal savings, insurance, or pensions. Failing this, they relied on charity. In this century Americans decided that government should see that all these groups have at least some income. Government, therefore, collects money from the income-earning members of society and transfers it to others.

Interest on the National Debt

The third largest expenditure on the federal level is net interest on the national debt. Every year since 1970 the federal government has spent significantly more than its annual revenues would finance. This has led it to borrow money to help finance the annual deficit.

Very few economists insist that the government balance its budget every year. Most economists agree that the health of the economy can sometimes be stimulated by budget deficits. But even fewer economists favor the large deficits that came to be commonplace in the 1980s. In less than a decade the **national debt**, i.e., the accumulation of all past annual surpluses and deficits, doubled. When President Reagan took office in 1981, our national debt stood at $1 trillion. When he left office that debt had more than doubled, reaching $2.2 trillion. The interest payments on that debt constituted 14 percent of all federal expenditures. This means that we paid about $140 billion each year to people who lent us money in the past. These payments severely limit our ability to finance programs needed in the 1990s. In addition, continued federal deficits tend to push interest rates up for consumers and business. When the federal government must borrow $100 billion to $200 billion annually, interest rates will naturally be affected due to the basic laws of supply and demand. By demanding huge loans, the federal government will bid up the cost of money (the interest rate). It remains to be seen if Congress and a new president will be able to resolve this serious macroeconomic problem. Most observers believe that the solution will involve a significant increase in taxation.

TAXATION

Justice Oliver Wendell Holmes once said that taxation is the price we pay for civilization. There is more than a grain of truth in this observation, because we cannot maintain our government without the income it gets from taxation. But are we paying more than is reasonable or just?

According to the Tax Foundation, the average U.S. worker spends two hours and 45 minutes of each working day paying for taxes. Of that, one hour and 50 minutes goes to Uncle Sam; the rest pays state and local taxes.

Economists at the Tax Foundation have also estimated how many days it would take you to pay all of your taxes if you decided to devote all of your earnings from January 1 onward to this task. The date that you would

**FIGURE 15.3
Tax Freedom Day,
selected years, 1950–
1988.** (SOURCE: Tax
Foundation, *Tax
Features*, April/May
1988.)

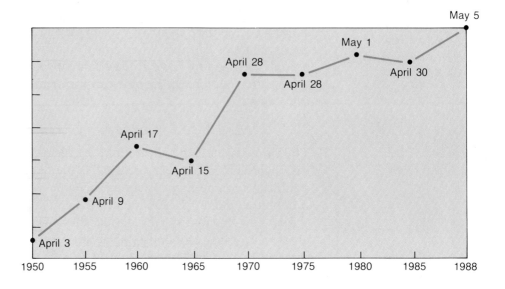

hypothetically be free from taxes is known as **Tax Freedom Day**. As Figure 15.3 shows, Tax Freedom Day has been getting progressively later. In 1950 it was April 3, but by 1988 it came more than a month later.

Contrary to popular belief, Americans are not heavily taxed, compared with citizens in other industrialized nations. The Organization for Economic Cooperation and Development (OECD), an association of the most highly developed nations in the world, collected data of the relative tax burdens of industrialized nations. As Figure 15.4 shows, the United States tax burden is well below that of most other developed economies.

Accordingly to OECD data, total taxes are a little under 29 percent of total output (GNP) in the United States, whereas taxes average more than 37 percent of output in the other nations. Japan and Turkey are the only OECD nations in the survey with a tax burden lower than that of the United States. In Sweden, the leader in this category, tax collections average more 50 percent of its GNP; thus, in Sweden a typical taxpayer works for more than half a day just to pay taxes. In other words Tax Freedom Day would be around July 7 in Sweden.

Compared with citizens of other developed nations, Americans do not appear to be overtaxed. However, we should point out that all taxes are not alike, and in nations with high tax rates, such as Sweden, government services are also more abundant. By focusing on the overall tax burden, we are also ignoring the types of taxes and the manner in which they are collected. In some nations, taxes are more heavily weighted toward personal income; in others, sales taxes and property taxes may be more important. To understand how taxation works, then, we need to know more about the basic principles behind it.

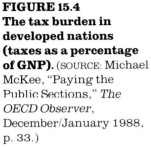

**FIGURE 15.4
The tax burden in developed nations (taxes as a percentage of GNP).** (SOURCE: Michael McKee, "Paying the Public Sections," *The OECD Observer*, December/January 1988, p. 33.)

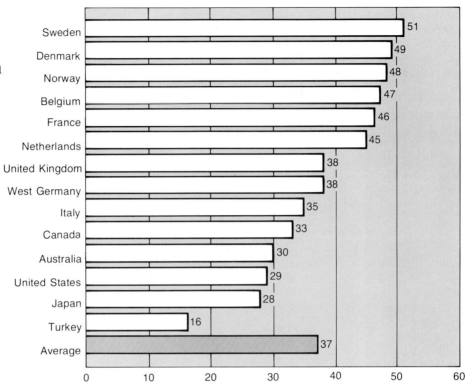

The Principles of Taxation

benefits-received principle: the principle of taxation which argues that whoever receives government services should pay for them

There are two basic views about deciding who should bear the burden of taxation. One school of thought argues that taxes should be levied on the **benefits-received principle**. This is a fairly straightforward approach, arguing that because taxes provide goods and services, the households and firms that receive these benefits should pay for them. Because many government expenditures produce public goods, such as national defense, highways, and street lights, it is sometimes difficult to apply this theory. Nevertheless, we do have some taxes based on this principle. The gasoline tax, for example, is typically earmarked for financing road construction and maintenance. The assumption is that those who use the highways should pay for them when they buy gasoline and other petroleum products. Automobile- and truck-licensing fees may also be classified as benefits-received taxes, because the owners of these vehicles have the right to use them on public highways. Even a public good like a lighthouse could be financed on a benefits-received principle if the cost of the lighthouse were paid out of a boat license fund. But for many public goods and for most transfer payments, the benefits-received principle cannot apply. How could welfare recipients pay for their benefits when they have little or no income?

ability-to-pay principle: the principle of taxation which argues that those most able to pay taxes should subsidize those who are less able to pay

Another approach to taxation is called the **ability-to-pay principle**. The idea here is that the burden of taxation should fall most heavily on the members of society who are most able to pay. In other words, citizens who have more income or greater wealth should be asked to pay a larger share of the cost of government.

There is a certain appeal to asking the better-off members of society to pay more for government. A $1,000 tax payment would not burden a household earning $100,000 per year as much as it would burden a household earning $10,000.

The economic concept of **diminishing marginal utility** has also been used to support levying higher taxes on the rich. In this context, diminishing marginal utility refers to the fact that at low levels of income, households buy goods and services that are essential and are thus more useful (have the most utility). At higher levels of income, consumers spend their dollars first on essentials and then more and more on less urgently needed goods or even on luxuries. The higher the income, then, the less usefulness or "utility" that is achieved from the last dollar spent. If marginal utilities can be compared among households (and not all economists agree that they can be), the last dollar spent by a household earning $100,000 will result in a smaller increase in utility than the last dollar spent by a household earning only $10,000. If this is true, then in order for all households to sacrifice equally, those with higher incomes must pay more money in taxes, because an equal dollar contribution would mean that the lower-income group would sacrifice more than its share.

Neither the ability-to-pay principle nor its corollary, the equal-sacrifice principle, gives us a guideline as to how much more higher-income groups should pay. If a tax rate were so high that no household was able to keep a portion of its increased income over some minimal amount, the tax system could destroy the incentive to work. In this case, tax rates would become **confiscatory tax rates**: All additional income would be confiscated, and as a result, the economic incentives to work more and thus earn more money would break down. Obviously, this can lead to chaos in the economy.

Progressive, Proportional, and Regressive Taxes

Now that you understand something about the benefits-received and ability-to-pay principles of taxation, you are ready to look at three basic types of taxes, which are all classified by their relationship to household income: progressive taxes, proportional taxes, and regressive taxes.

Progressive tax. Identifying the relationship between tax rates and household income is one of the most common ways to classify taxes. If a form of taxation takes a larger and larger fraction of a household's income as the family's income rises, it is called **progressive taxation**. Those who

TABLE 15.1   An Example of How a Progressive Income Tax Works

Taxable Income Bracket	Bracket Tax Rate (Marginal Tax Rate)	Tax Owed on Bracket Income	Total Tax Owed on All Income	Average Tax Rate
$2,000 or less	0%	$ 0	$ 0	0%
$2,001 to $3,000	5%	$ 50	$ 50	1.67%
$3,001 to $4,000	10%	$100	$150	3.75%
$4,001 to $5,000	20%	$200	$350	7.00%
$5,001 to $6,000	30%	$300	$650	10.83%

believe strongly in the ability-to-pay principle generally support the idea of a progressive tax. Under a progressive tax structure, high-income people pay more, both in absolute dollar amounts and in percentage. For example, a tax that takes $2,000 from a family that earns $20,000 and $10,000 from a family that earns $50,000 is a progressive tax, not because it takes more money from the higher-income family ($8,000 more to be precise), but because it takes a larger proportion (20 percent) from the higher-income family.

Understanding the structure of a progressive tax is especially important in planning your personal tax burden. Table 15.1 shows how a progressive income tax works. Taxpayers with different levels of income fall into different income brackets. According to the table, a person earning $4,000 would be subject to a 10 percent **marginal tax rate**, sometimes referred to as the "10 percent bracket." This does *not* mean that all of the $4,000 is subject to a 10 percent tax. Only the income from $3,001 to $4,000 is subject to the 10 percent rate; income in the $2,001 to $3,000 bracket is taxed at 5 percent, and the first $2,000 is not taxed at all according to Table 15.1. Thus, someone with a $4,000 income would owe a total of $150 in taxes ($0 on the first $2,000 plus $50 on the next $1,000 plus $100 on the last $1,000). This is a progressive tax because higher income brackets have higher taxes levied against them (see Figure 15.5.)

The **average tax rate** is computed by dividing the total tax owed by the total income earned. For someone earning $4,000 and subject to the marginal tax rates in Table 15.1, the average tax rate would be $150 divided by $4,000, or 3.75 percent. Notice that in a progressive tax system, the average tax rate and the marginal tax both increase as incomes rise, but they are not equal. The marginal tax rate applies only to a specific range of income, whereas the average tax rate combines a group of marginal rates. The relevant rate to consider in tax planning is the marginal rate, because this is the rate applied to the last dollar of income. Thus, someone earning $4,000 and able to reduce his or her taxable income by $100

FIGURE 15.5
The structure of a
progressive income tax.

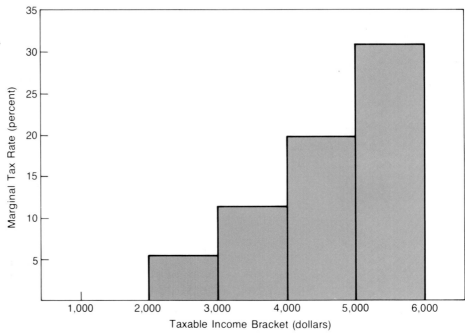

will reduce his or her taxes by $10 (marginal tax rate × taxable income reduction = 0.10 × $100). In this case, taxable income would be reduced to $3,900, and total tax owed would be $140. We will return to these concepts when we discuss the federal income tax in more detail.

Proportional tax. Proportional taxation takes the same proportion of household's income, regardless of the income level. When an income tax is proportional, more money is taken away from higher-income groups, but the percentage of income taxed is equal for all households. Thus, if two families earn incomes of $20,000 and $50,000, respectively, per year, under a proportional income tax they would pay different amounts in taxes ($2,000 and $5,000, respectively), but the same proportion, 10 percent. Milton Friedman, a Nobel Prize–winning economist, has suggested that the proportional tax is a more equitable and efficient way to tax income than a progressive income tax. He argues that a proportional tax with virtually no deductions or loopholes could generate the same revenue as the progressive tax and at lower rates, because the system would be so simple. If you can imagine a single-page tax form on which the only entries are questions about how much income you have earned, a box indicating the percent of taxation, and a line indicating how much tax is owed, you can understand the simplicity of the proposal.

The Tax Reform Act of 1986 was supposed to incorporate many of these ideas to simplify the forms and eliminate many of the deductions

BOX 15.1 FILLING OUT THESE SIMPLE TAX FORMS

The Internal Revenue Service is required by law to publish estimates of the average time taxpayers spend learning about filling out their income tax forms. According to the IRS it takes the average person about nine hours a year to comply with the law if he or she files a standard 1040 form with no additional schedules. We reproduce their estimates below. Most tax experts believe these estimates are low. But even using these optimistic data, the IRS believes that in a typical tax year we spend 5.3 billion hours poring over forms and keeping tax records.

Estimated Average Times Needed to Complete and File the Following Tax Forms

Form	Record Keeping	Learning About the Law or the Form	Preparing the Form	Copying, Assembling, and Sending the Form to IRS
1040	3 hr., 7 min.	2 hr., 22 min.	3 hr., 1 min.	35 min.
Sch. A (1040)	2 hr., 47 min.	26 min.	1 hr., 1 min.	20 min.
Sch. B (1040)	33 min.	8 min.	16 min.	20 min.
Sch. C (1040)	7 hr., 4 min.	1 hr., 11 min.	2 hr., 9 min.	25 min.
Sch. D (1040)	1 hr., 2 min.	45 min.	54 min.	35 min.
Sch. E (1040)	3 hr., 12 min.	1 hr., 2 min.	1 hr., 22 min.	35 min.
Sch. F (1040)	10 hr., 53 min.	2 hr., 2 min.	4 hr., 10 min.	35 min.
Sch. R (1040)	20 min.	16 min.	22 min.	35 min.
Sch. SE (1040)				
Short	20 min.	11 min.	13 min.	14 min.
Long	26 min.	22 min.	37 min.	20 min.

SOURCE: *Wall Street Journal*, September 1, 1988.

and tax loopholes. The compression of the progressive tax brackets from 14 to two is one example of Congress' attempt to follow these suggestions. Judging by the time it takes to fill out a tax return, the new Tax Act is far from fulfilling the goal of simplicity (see Box 15.1).

Regressive tax. If progressive taxation takes a higher percentage of income as income rises, then **regressive taxation** takes a lower percentage of income as income rises. Before you jump to the conclusion that a regressive tax is preferable because its impact declines as income rises, remember that the reverse is also true. A regressive tax takes a larger proportion of household income as income declines. According to the ability-to-pay principle, the regressive tax is the least preferred tax, because it places a disproportionate burden on the poorer segments of a community.

Examples of regressive taxes abound in most communities. Any tax that is not specifically indexed to a household's income level is a candidate for the regressive label. Take the almost universal state sales tax, existing in 45 states and providing almost one-third of state tax revenue. In 1987, 17 states applied this tax to consumer food purchases. A 5 percent tax on food sales might seem to be a proportional tax, because all consumers pay the same rate when buying food. However, the relevant rate is not the stated percentage of the sale item but the percentage of a household's income used to pay the tax. In the case of food, low-income families spend a much higher proportion of their budgets for this item. According to the Bureau of Labor Statistics, low-income families spend 22 percent of their income on food, whereas high-income families spend only 7 percent. Thus, a 5 percent food tax would be levied on 22 percent of a poor family's income but on only 7 percent of a well-to-do family's income.

The Social Security tax is also a regressive tax, because there is a limit on the amount of income subject to this tax. An employee earning less than $45,000 in 1988 paid 7.51 percent of that income in Social Security tax. Any amount earned over $45,000 was not subject to the tax. If a person earned $90,000, the average Social Security tax rate would

TABLE 15.2 Effective Tax Rates of Regressive Taxes by Family Income Class

Adjusted Family Income	Property Tax	Sales and Excise Tax	Social Security Payroll Tax	Personal Property and Motor Vehicle Taxes
$ 0– 5,000	7.9	19.5	16.7	0.3
5– 10,000	3.0	7.6	9.8	0.1
10– 15,000	2.4	6.1	8.5	0.1
15– 20,000	2.1	5.5	8.1	0.2
20– 25,000	2.1	5.2	7.9	0.2
25– 30,000	2.1	4.8	7.6	0.2
30– 50,000	2.2	4.4	7.0	0.3
50– 100,000	2.3	3.3	5.5	0.2
100– 500,000	2.2	1.6	2.4	0.1
500–1,000,000	2.2	0.8	0.8	0.1
1,000,000 +	2.3	0.6	0.4	0.0

SOURCE: Joseph A. Pechman, *Who Paid the Taxes, 1966–85?* (Washington, D.C.: Brookings Institution, 1985), Table 4-9, variant 3b.

have been only 3.75 percent, because half of the income would not have been subject to any Social Security taxes. Table 15.2 illustrates the regressive nature of many taxes levied on individuals.

THE FEDERAL BUDGET AND INCOME TAX

In the previous section we introduced the principles of taxation and the various classes of taxes. You now know the difference between regressive, proportional, and progressive taxes. In this section, we focus on federal taxes and apply some of the concepts learned. At the conclusion of this section you should know how the federal income tax works and be ready to proceed to the next section, filling out income tax forms.

Figure 15.6 illustrates the federal government's revenues for fiscal year 1989. Individual income-tax receipts account for 38 cents of every federal tax dollar collected. An additional 32 cents is collected in the form of the Social Security payroll tax, with the remainder coming from corporate income taxes (11 cents), excise taxes, such as specific taxes on tires, firearms, and air travel (see Box 15.2), and the public borrowing, which increases the national debt (12 cents). The federal income tax is obviously the most important source of revenue, although Social Security tax receipts are also important. The burden of these taxes falls directly on individuals.

The average taxpayer owes the government more than $5,000 in income taxes and another $2,000 in Social Security contributions (U.S. Bureau of the Census, 1988). Whenever you spend more than $7,000, you should take some time to evaluate your choices. Obviously, taxes are a necessity, because we could not have a civilized society without them.

FIGURE 15.6
Federal tax revenues,
1989. (SOURCE: *Budget of the United States Government, 1989,* pp. 1–2.)

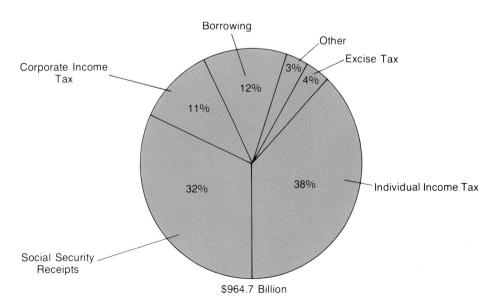

BOX 15.2   ADDITIONAL FEDERAL TAXES

Although the income tax is the most important federal tax, Americans are subject to a host of other federal taxes. Many of these taxes are categorized as **indirect taxes** because the businesses that send the tax revenue to the government are not the ones who ultimately pay the tax. The customers who buy their products are the ones who actually pay these taxes because the business firms raise their prices to compensate for the tax. Thus consumers pay these taxes "indirectly" to the government through higher prices charged by manufacturers. Would you classify these taxes as progressive, regressive, or proportional?

Type of Tax	Rate
Alcohol taxes	
1. Distilled spirits	$12.50 per proof gallon
2. Beer $9.00/barrel	$0.29 gallon
3. Wine:	
(a) Still wine	
14% alcohol or less	$0.17 per wine gallon
14% to 21%	$0.67 gallon
21% to 24%	$2.25/gallon
more than 24%	$12.50/gallon
(b) Sparkling wine or champagne	$3.40/wine gallon
artificially carbonated	$2.40/wine gallon
Tobacco taxes	
Cigarettes	$0.16/pack of 20
Miscellaneous taxes	
1. Telephone service	3.0%
2. Transportation by air	
(a) Domestic passenger tickets	8.0%
(b) International passenger tickets	$3.00
3. Tires, weighing	
40 lb. or less	No tax
41 lb. to 70 lb.	$0.15/lb. more than 40 lb.
71 lb. to 90 lb.	$4.50 + $0.30/lb. more than 70 lb.
more than 90 lb.	$10.50 + $0.50/lb. more than 90 lb.
4. Gasoline	$0.09/gallon
5. Diesel fuel	$0.15/gallon
6. Pistols and revolvers	10.0% of mfr. price
7. Other firearms, shells, and cartridges	11.0% of mfr. price
8. Fishing equipment	10.0% of mfr. price
9. Bows, arrows, etc.	11.0% of mfr. price

Type of Tax	Rate
10. Coal—underground mines	
11. Coal—surface mines	$1.10 ton
12. Gas guzzler tax	$0.55 ton
Purchase of automobiles, 1986 model with mileage ratings (per gallon) of	
22.5 or more	$ 0.
21.5 but less than 22.5	$ 500.
20.5 but less than 21.5	$ 650.
19.5 but less than 20.5	$ 850.
18.5 but less than 19.5	$1,050.
17.5 but less than 18.5	$1,300.
16.5 but less than 17.5	$1,500.
15.5 but less than 16.5	$1,850.
14.5 but less than 15.5	$2,250.
13.5 but less than 14.5	$2,700.
12.5 but less than 13.5	$3,200.
Less than 12.5	$3,850.

SOURCE: Advisory Commission on Intergovernmental Relations, *Significant Features of Fiscal Federalism*, 1988 ed. (Washington, D.C.: The Commission, 1988), p. 21.

Nevertheless, it makes good sense to try to limit your tax liability by developing good decision-making habits. This means calculating the tax impact of just about every major decision you make before you make it. Given that income tax is progressive, as you work and earn more, your income is taxed at a higher rate. The higher your tax bracket, the more the incentive you have for finding ways to reduce taxable income by looking for legitimate loopholes.

The Federal Income Tax

Under current law almost every American adult is required to file a tax return with the Internal Revenue Service (IRS). In a typical year, more than 190 million tax returns are prepared, 70 million refunds are paid, 3 million tax delinquency notices are served, and more than 2,500 people are convicted of tax crimes (Pechman, 1987).

Given the current importance of the income tax, it may surprise you to learn that before World War II very few Americans had to worry about filing a tax return. As late as 1939, fewer than 5 million Americans (about 4 percent of the population) paid any income tax. It was not until 1943 that the federal government began the policy of withholding a portion of income at the time it was earned. Before 1943, federal income taxes were paid in quarterly installments after the income was earned. In fact, it took the passage of the Sixteenth Amendment to the Constitution (1913) to make the federal income tax legal in the first place. Before that,

TABLE 15.3 Maximum Marginal Federal Income Tax Rate for Selected Years, 1961–1988

Year	Maximum Tax Rate (%)
1961	91
1964	77
1965	70
1980	70
1981	50
1987	38.5
1988	33

the Supreme Court had ruled that the federal government could not levy an income tax.

The early federal income tax forms were models of simplicity. There was a generous exemption for all families, so very few had to concern themselves with filling out the form. And the rates were low, varying from 1 percent to a top rate of 6 percent. Today's tax laws are far from simple, and the highest marginal tax rate for individuals is 33 percent rather then 6 percent.

A 33 percent tax may seem like a significant proportion of your income, and it is. But if you were to review the history of the income tax, you would discover that as recently as 1961 the tax code actually had a top rate of over 90 percent. Even as late as 1980, when President Reagan first took office, the income tax rate on nonwage income, such as interest on savings accounts, stock dividends, and royalties from textbooks, reached as high as 70 percent (see Table 15.3). These high rates were seen as a tribute to the ability-to-pay principle. Another term for this principle is **vertical equity**. In this context, equity is another word for "fairness." Vertical refers to your place on the income scale. According to this principle, the higher you are on the scale, the greater should be your tax burden. But is it fair to take away 70 percent of someone's earnings?

vertical equity: the economic principle that considers a tax to be fair only to the extent that those with higher incomes pay a greater amount of taxes

Tax loopholes were created by Congress in part to compensate for some of these very high rates. A **tax loophole** can be defined as a legal method of reducing your tax burden by engaging in a particular economic activity. For example, if you borrow money for a mortgage on your house, you are allowed to subtract the interest payment you pay from your taxable income. This reduces the taxes you will pay because, officially, that money is excluded from your tax base. The money escapes through a loophole. The home mortgage loophole is estimated to have cost the federal government $30.8 billion in fiscal 1989. (*Tax Features*, 1988). Table 15.4 lists the five tax loopholes that account for more than half of all taxes legally avoided by individuals in 1989.

TABLE 15.4 The Five Most Important Income Tax Loopholes for Individuals

Loophole	Cost to Government in Lost Taxes (billions of dollars)
Exclusion of pension contribution and earnings	45.6
Deduction of mortgage interest on homes	30.8
Exclusion of employer payments for medical insurance and care	27.6
Deduction of state–local property and income taxes	24.5
Exclusion of Social Security benefits	18.0

SOURCE: Tax Foundation, *Tax Features*, June 1988.

horizontal equity: *the economic principle that considers a tax to be fair only to the extent that those who receive the same income are also paying the same amount of taxes*

The presence of tax loopholes violates another fairness principle in taxation called **horizontal equity**. Horizontal equity means that equals should be treated equally. In other words, people with the same income should be treated equally and pay the same amount of tax. Loopholes violate this concept because they reward those people who are able to alter their behavior and take advantage of the tax laws. Renters have historically felt cheated by the mortgage and property tax loopholes given to homeowners. Workers in firms that provide good health and pension benefits get added tax advantages over those workers who must pay for these benefits out of their own pockets. People who earn interest on municipal bonds get a tax break, whereas people who earn interest from a savings account at a bank do not. These are all violations of the horizontal equity principle.

Incentives and the Tax Code

Another problem that many economists find with the tax code is its impact on economic incentives. Ideally, the government would like to collect taxes without affecting the behavior of its citizens. It certainly does not want to discourage its citizens from working hard and investing their savings. And yet strongly progressive taxes can do just that. If workers are allowed to keep smaller percentages of their incomes as they work more, then the government is providing a disincentive to work.

The relationship between the income tax rate and the taxpayers' willingness to work, save, and invest is at the heart of **supply-side economics**, discussed in Chapter 3. Supply-side economics stresses the importance of increasing production by using tax incentives to encourage savings, investment, and work effort. Supply-siders like economist Arthur

**FIGURE 15.7
Laffer Curve.**

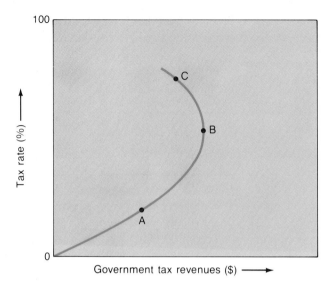

Laffer argue that high tax rates discourage work effort and investment by taking away too large a portion of workers', savers', and investors' incomes. Professor Laffer even argues that the disincentives from taxation can be so strong that they reduce government revenues.

The Laffer Curve (Figure 15.7) illustrates the potentially negative relationship between tax revenues and tax rates. As the graph shows, if tax rates are zero, revenues will also be zero. And as tax rates rise, tax revenues also rise, up to point *B*. But if tax rates rise higher than *B*, the curve bends backward, indicating that smaller government tax revenues are associated with higher and higher taxes.

Why would higher tax rates bring in less revenue? According to the supply-side economists, at some point people decide that the income they get to keep after they pay their taxes is not enough reward for them to work, save, or invest. For example, laborers refuse to work overtime, savers decide to spend their money rather than put it in the bank and pay tax on the interest, and businesses decide not to expand their plants, because increased profits would mean higher taxes. In addition, higher taxes make it more tempting to hide income or cheat on tax forms. As tax evasion becomes more commonplace, it is more difficult to catch, and tax revenues fall. The solution, according to supply-side theory, is to lower tax rates. This can move the economy from point *C* to point *B* and can increase tax revenues by giving people a greater incentive to work, save, and invest. As laborers begin to work overtime again, as the number of two-income families begins to grow, as savers begin taking advantage of their lower tax rates, and as businesses begin to earn tax credits with new investments, the GNP will rise and government will automatically get more revenue, because incomes in general are rising. This was the principle behind the 1981 tax bill, the largest tax cut in the history of the United States. Unfortunately, it did not generate the revenue that many supply-side economists had predicted. In fact, partly as a result of these tax cuts, the 1980s were a decade with large federal deficits (Lindsey, 1988).

The Tax Reform Act of 1986

The problems of vertical and horizontal equity combined with the supply-side arguments about economic incentives led the U.S. Congress to revise federal tax law significantly in the 1980s. The most significant revision was *The Tax Reform Act of 1986*. This Act was intended to satisfy many of the criticisms that had been leveled at previous tax legislation.

Table 15.5 illustrates the new tax rates established by the 1986 Act. The rate structure begins at 15 percent, rises to 28 percent, peaks at 33 percent, and then returns to 28 percent. This rather confusing set of rates exist because Congress chose to phase out the personal exemption and the advantages of the 15 percent bracket for people with higher incomes. Thus, in 1989 a single earner paid 33 percent on all income earned between $43,150 and $100,000. Beyond this point the maximum tax rate returned to 28 percent. For married couples the 33 percent rate begins later and lasts longer. This pattern of marginal tax rates rising from 15 to 28 to 33 and then falling back to 28 percent will continue through the 1990s or until the 1986 Tax Reform Act is changed.

Congress lowered the tax rates in a effort to spur work effort and capital accumulation. Congress also wanted investors to be less concerned with how tax rates would effect the return on investment (see Box 15.3). But these lower rates seemed to violate the vertical equity principle, so Congress increased the basic level of deductions that taxpayers could claim without retaining special records or receipts. The 1986 Act repealed or curtailed some significant deductions in an effort to reinforce the concept of horizontal equity. Additional tax legislation was passed in 1987 and 1988 to further modify the tax code. In the next section we will integrate the new tax laws into our discussion of your income tax return.

TABLE 15.5 1989 Federal Personal Income Tax Rates

Single Taxpayers		**Married Persons Filing Jointly**	
Taxable Income	**Rate (%)**	**Taxable Income**	**Rate (%)**
Up to $ 17,850	15	Up to $ 29,750	15
$17,850 to $ 43,150	28	$29,750 to $ 71,900	28
$43,150 to $100,760	33[a]	$71,900 to $171,650	33[a]
More than $100,760	28	More than $171,650	28

[a] Phase out 15 percent bracket and personal exemption.

BOX 15.3   WHAT IS TAX-FREE INCOME WORTH TO YOU?

The Tax Reform Act of 1986 significantly reduced the rates of income taxation, but it did not eliminate loopholes like the tax-free interest you can get by owning municipal bonds. How do you compare tax-free rates of return on your investment with taxable yields? The following formula can be used to calculate whether a tax-free investment gives a better return than a taxable investment:

$$\frac{\text{tax-free yield}}{(1 - \text{marginal tax rate})}$$
$$= \text{equivalent taxable yield}$$

For example, if a tax-free bond offers 8 percent annual return and your highest effective tax rate is 28 percent, you are getting more than an 11 percent return:

$$\frac{8\%}{(1 - 0.28)} = \frac{8\%}{0.72} = 11.11\%$$

If you know the taxable yield and want to calculate the after-tax yield, simply subtract your marginal tax rate from one and multiply the answer by the taxable yield. The formula is:

$$(1 - \text{marginal tax rate}) \times \text{taxable yield}$$
$$= \text{tax-free yield}$$

For example, someone in the 28 percent bracket who is considering an investment with a taxable yield of 10 percent would really only earn the equivalent of 7.2 percent after income taxes:

$$(1 - 0.28) \times 10\% = 0.72 \times 10\% = 7.2\%$$

Higher tax rates make tax-free yields much more important. Under the old 70 percent tax bracket for high income groups, a 10 percent taxable return was equal to a 3 percent after-tax yield. One of the reasons for lowering the maximum tax rate was to make the search for these tax-free investment shelters less important.

UNDERSTANDING THE FEDERAL INCOME TAX

Contrary to popular belief, the IRS is not trying to rob you blind. Its job is to enforce the tax laws so that the federal government receives enough money for its budget to provide the goods, services, and income transfers mandated by Congress. Congress, as the source of all federal tax law, is very much aware that we do not like to pay taxes and can pay only so much. It does not want to strangle the taxpayers. It also knows that changes in the tax law can encourage certain behaviors and discourage others. Congress often tries to use taxes as policy tools as well as revenue makers. By being aware of tax laws, consumers can save money by taking advantage of congressionally approved tax incentives.

Congress maintains some slack in the tax noose for many reasons. Some taxpayer expenditures, such as business or employment expenses, are given special treatment because they are seen as necessary costs of doing business and thus create income that will eventually be taxed. Other taxpayer expenditures, such as payments for medical care, alimony, and casualty losses, are tax deductible because they may involve financial hardship to the taxpayer (although alimony is taxable for the recipient).

Still other tax provisions, such as tax incentives to encourage consumers to purchase diesel-powered cars or to use gasohol may be included to encourage certain kinds of behavior. Finally, the tax laws have general provisions that allow all consumers to keep a certain amount of tax-free income, based on the size of the household or on special circumstances, such as blindness.

It should be clear by now that not every dollar one earns during the year is subject to income tax. The income earned from wages, interest, rents, dividends, or other sources may not be part of **taxable income**, the income that is subject to federal income tax. In the following sections, we will outline in some detail the various forms of exclusion, deductions, exemptions, and tax credits that can and will reduce your taxes. Understanding how the tax system works can lead to big savings if this understanding is coupled with good planning and decision making. Given the wide range of taxation, you need to anticipate the tax implications of every major decision you make, from buying a car to taking a vacation or getting your teeth fixed. And as your income rises, so does the value of tax planning. Knowledge and tax-planning strategies learned now will pay dividends now and even larger dividends in the future.

taxable income: the income that is subject to tax after deductions and exemptions have been subtracted

An Overview of Tax Calculations

Our objective in this section is to give a brief summary of what is involved in calculating the amount of federal income tax you owe, based on the amount of money you earn in a given year. Table 15.6 outlines all steps we will be discussing. Some of the forbidding and unfamiliar words and

TABLE 15.6 A Basic Outline for Calculating Income Tax

Your income
— Exclusions

Gross income
— Adjustment to income

Adjusted Gross Income
— Standard deduction or excess itemized deductions

Income before exemptions
— Exemptions

Taxable income
× Tax rates from tax table

Tax from tax table
— Tax credits

Taxes due

phrases, such as "exclusions," "standard deduction," and "adjusted gross income," may give many students an almost uncontrollable urge to shut their books at this point. For other students, the words on the page may begin to blur and run together. Do not be discouraged. No one expects you to look at Table 15.6 and instantly understand how the tax system works. Could someone from Mars know what a human being from earth looks like if the only clue were a human skeleton? A skeleton is an important part of the body, but we must put some flesh on those bones for aliens to get some idea about what humans look like. The same is true for our tax system. Table 15.6 presents the skeleton; the following sections supply the definitions and the examples to fill it out. But you may find it handy to refer back to this table after you have read each section, in order to see how the pieces fit together.

At the conclusion of these sections, you should review and understand the following terms:

exclusions
deductions
standard deduction
exemption
taxable income
tax credit

We begin our analysis with exclusions.

Exclusions: Tax-Exempt Income

As we have mentioned, not every dollar that a household receives is considered income. Certain forms of income are excluded from federal income taxation, and they are called **exclusions**. For example, life insurance proceeds paid to you on the death of an insured person are excluded from **gross income**, the income, minus exclusions, on which federal income tax is computed. Child-support payments received from a divorced spouse are also excluded from gross income. Even a federal income tax refund (but not a state refund) is excluded from gross income. Exclusions come and go, depending on the mood of Congress. For a complete list of the exclusions and other tax rules applicable to the current tax year, get a free copy of Internal Revenue Service Publication 17, *Your Federal Income Tax—For Individuals*. You can write to the IRS or simply call its toll-free number, 1–800–424–1040.

Look at Table 15.6 again. Once you have determined all of your exclusions, you are ready to report your gross income, which includes all income not specifically subject to exclusions. From here on, the only way to reduce your tax liability legally is through deductions, exemptions, or tax credits.

Deductions

deductions: taxpayer expenditures that may be subtracted from earnings before calculating income tax

Deductions are specific taxpayer expenses that can be subtracted from gross income or adjusted gross income before going on to calculate taxable income. Those deductions that are subtracted directly from gross income are called **adjustments to income**. The 1986 Tax Reform Act severely curtailed these adjustments in an effort to broaden the tax base. Nevertheless, they still include items like alimony and interest penalties paid on early withdrawal from a savings account. If you qualify for any of these deductions, the only way to receive them is to file for them specifically.

Other deductions apply to all individual taxpayers, and they are subtracted from the adjusted gross income. The government realizes that all households spend a portion of their income for goods and services that are legally deductible under the tax laws. As a result, they automatically provide a standard deduction for taxpayers who choose not to record their deductions separately. In essence they estimate your deductions for you. The automatic base level of deductions is called the **standard deduction**. In 1988, there were five standard deduction amounts, each linked to filing status:

Filing Status	Standard Deduction ($)
Married, filing jointly	5,000
Married, filing separately	2,500
Head of household	4,400
Qualifying widow(er)	5,000
Single	3,000

Additional standard deductions are provided for taxpayers who are blind and/or at least 65 years old. In 1988 these additional deductions ranged from $600 to $750, depending on filing status. After 1988 all standard deductions will be adjusted upward to account for inflation.

It is interesting to note that when two people marry, they give up a portion of their standard deduction. As single wage earners, people are entitled to take a $3,000 standard deduction, but once they marry, their combined standard deduction cannot exceed $5,000, regardless of whether they file jointly or separately. This phenomenon has been called the **marriage tax**, because it is a tax penalty applied only if you are married. Notice, however, that this applies only if you accept the standard deduction.

Many taxpayers find that their tax-deductible expenditures exceed the standard deduction established by the government. For them, the logical course of action is to file for the amount of itemized deductions they are entitled to. However, this means an increased burden in terms of record keeping and tax planning. It also means that taxpayers will have to fill out additional schedules and attach them to their 1040 tax form.

The decision to itemize your deductions may be a good one, but you should not make it until you have some idea about which expenditures are deductible. The IRS lists six general categories of deductible expenditures:

1. Medical and dental expense
2. Taxes
3. Interest deductions
4. Contributions
5. Casualty and theft losses
6. Miscellaneous deductions

We will not be able to go into great detail for any of these categories, but we will outline some of the most important ones. For more specific information, refer to the pamphlet mentioned earlier, IRS Publication 17, *Your Federal Income Tax—For Individuals*.

Medical and dental expenses. As we mentioned in Chapter 14, health care expenditures are some of our biggest and most important expenditures. Federal law allows people to deduct all of their medical, hospital, and dental expenses in excess of 7.5 percent of their adjusted gross income. This can include transportation expenses for obtaining medical care. Some other legitimate medical care deductions are payments for acupuncture, cosmetic surgery, eyeglasses, psychiatry, abortion, and vasectomies. Any prescribed medicines or drug expenses are also legitimate deductions. These include pharmaceuticals, birth control pills, vitamins, and even whiskey, if a physician advises a person to take a certain dosage. You cannot, however, deduct a medical expense for which you were reimbursed by your insurance company.

Other taxes. One of the most controversial changes in the 1986 Tax Reform Act was the repeal of the deduction for state and local sales taxes. Since 45 states have sales taxes, this meant a significant reduction in taxpayer deductions. At one point it looked as if Congress would also repeal the deduction for state and local income taxes, but that wasn't done. Thus, state and local income taxes, real estate, and personal property taxes are still deductible on your federal tax form.

Interest deductions. Under previous tax codes, the federal government subsidized borrowers by allowing them to deduct interest charges on personal loans. Thus, if you had outstanding balances on your credit cards, you could at least take some comfort knowing that every dollar you paid in interest or finance charges was deductible on your 1040. The 1986 Tax Reform Act changed this rather dramatically. It established a sched-

TABLE 15.7 Schedule for Phasing out Deductibility of Personal Interest
for Federal Income Tax

Year	Percentage Deductible
1986	100
1987	65
1988	40
1989	20
1990	10
1991 and later	0

ule to phase out the deductibility of personal interest charges, as shown in Table 15.7. For tax year 1991 and later, personal interest will no longer be allowed as a deduction.

Do not confuse personal interest with mortgage interest. The new tax law maintains the traditional deduction for interest payments on your primary residence, and on a second home as well. The Revenue Act of 1987 amended the 1986 Tax Reform Act to allow homeowners to deduct the interest on home equity loans up to a maximum loan of $100,000, regardless of the original purchase price or outstanding mortgage. By allowing this deduction, Congress opened the door to homeowners who want to finance the purchase of a consumer good like a car and still take a tax deduction for the interest payments. All they have to do is get a home equity loan and they transform the interest expenses into a deductible expenditure! There are risks, however. If you fail to meet the payments on that new car, you could end up losing your house. As George Barber, executive director of Consumer Financial Institute said, "Your most important tangible asset should not be frittered away on a depreciating asset such as a car" (*Money*, 1988). Even more ominous is a new phenomenon we discussed in Chapter 8: credit cards that tie into a home equity loan. Is transforming nondeductible interest into tax-deductible interest worth the risk of losing your home?

Charitable contributions. Donations of cash or property to recognized charitable, religious, or educational organizations are tax deductible. Your contribution can be made by check, in which case you automatically have a receipt, or it can be in the form of personal property, in which case you should have some proof of its fair market value and the date it was donated. For example, if you donate an old television set, you can only deduct the current market value of that set, not its original price. And it is a good idea to get the charitable organization to agree on the true value and give you a receipt. You may even deduct transportation expenses and the cost of meals and lodging incurred as a result of charitable activity. Suppose, for example, that you volunteer your time to help at a nonprofit school for the blind. Perhaps you take some of the children on field trips in your car and you pay all your own expenses, including some overnight lodging. All of your expenses are deductible, but you cannot deduct anything for the value of your time.

One area of confusion among taxpayers deals with benefits received from a charitable or nonprofit institution. If you donate $500 to a university, for example, and get a complimentary season ticket to its basketball games, you cannot legally deduct the entire $500 contribution. You can deduct only the amount in excess of the cost of a season ticket. If you could have purchased a season ticket for $150, then your tax deductible contribution is $350 ($500 − $150 = $350). Many taxpayers conveniently forget this rule until they are reminded of it by the IRS.

Casualty and theft losses. The federal government recognizes your right to deduct the value of anything stolen from you or destroyed as a result of an accident. So if you are burglarized, if your car is in an accident, or if a tornado destroys your house, you may be eligible for this deduction, provided that your insurance company does not reimburse you. This deduction can be taken even if you never replace or repair the item in question. You may also deduct any loss of deposits in a bankrupt financial institution. Once again, this cannot include any reimbursal you received from a federal or state insurance fund.

Miscellaneous deductions. This category is a catch-all that incorporates many diverse areas. Union dues, tax preparation fees, investment advisory fees, safe deposit box rental, and unreimbursed employee business expenses are all included.

The cost of additional job-related training is an example of a typical miscellaneous deduction. For example, if you are employed and you are required by your employer or by law to continue your education, you can deduct the cost of the necessary training. If there is not legal requirement but the training will maintain or improve the skills required to do your present work, you are also allowed to deduct the cost of the education. This provision in the tax law was intended to aid workers in maintaining their productivity. The Tax Reform Act of 1986 made it more difficult to take advantage of this and all the other miscellaneous deductions by insisting that these deductions must exceed 2 percent of a taxpayer's adjusted gross income before they can be subtracted from income. Thus, if your adjusted gross income is $30,000 the first $600 you spend on miscellaneous items cannot be deducted.

Exemptions

exemptions: specific amounts of money that are declared to be nontaxable

Once you have subtracted either your standard deduction or your excess itemized deductions from your adjusted gross income, you are ready to calculate your exemptions. (It might be a good idea to review Table 15.6, just to see where we are in the income tax calculation process.)

Exemptions are specific amounts of income that one is allowed to subtract from earned income before beginning to calculate taxes. The most important exemptions deal with the number of people in a household. In 1989 the federal government allowed a $2,000 income exemption for every member of a taxpayer's household. The rationale behind this exemption is that there is a basic level of income needed to support a household and the government should recognize this by not taxing this minimal amount. This means that a family of four filing one tax return could earn at least $13,000 before paying any federal income tax ($8,000 in exemptions plus $5,000 standard deduction).

The Tax Reform Act of 1986 increased the value of an exemption from $1,080 in 1986 to $2,000 in 1989. It also provided for an annual upward revision of this amount based on the rate of inflation. These changes significantly reduced the tax liabilities of all low-income households and removed an estimated 6 million of our poorest families from the tax rolls. Many observers have argued that this was one of the most significant aspects of the tax revision because it reinforced the concept of vertical equity.

After you have subtracted the value of your exemptions from your income, you need to look at the appropriate tax table to determine the amount of federal tax you owe. If your taxable income is less than $50,000 you will be able to find your tax liability in a table similar to Figure 15.8.

Tax Credits

tax credit: a dollar reduction in a person's tax bill that is subtracted after he or she computes taxes

After you have taken care of all your exemptions, have taken your itemized deductions (or the standard deduction), and have found your tax liability in the tax tables, you may further reduce your tax if you qualify for a **tax credit**, a dollar reduction, intended to encourage a behavior by making it less expensive. Unlike a deduction, tax credit returns the same number of dollars to taxpayers regardless of their marginal tax rate. For example, to a taxpayer in the 15 percent bracket, a $1,000 tax-deductible church contribution saves $150 in tax liability. To a taxpayer in the 28 percent tax bracket, the same $1,000 deduction saves $280 in tax liability. If, instead of giving taxpayers a dedcution for church contributions, the IRS gave them a 20 percent tax credit, both taxpayers would save $200 in tax liability from a $1,000 donation.

Under previous tax laws there were tax credits for residental energy conservation expenditures, political contributions, and investments in certain types of business-related equipment, such as computers. These

**FIGURE 15.8
A tax table.**

If line 37 (taxable income) is—		And you are—				
At least	But less than	Single	Married filing jointly *	Married filing separately	Head of a household	
			Your tax is—			
23,000						
23,000	23,050	4,127	3,454	4,513	3,454	
23,050	23,100	4,141	3,461	4,527	3,461	
23,100	23,150	4,155	3,469	4,541	3,469	
23,150	23,200	4,169	3,476	4,555	3,476	
23,200	23,250	4,183	3,484	4,569	3,484	
23,250	23,300	4,197	3,491	4,583	3,491	
23,300	23,350	4,211	3,499	4,597	3,499	
23,350	23,400	4,225	3,506	4,611	3,506	
23,400	23,450	4,239	3,514	4,625	3,514	
23,450	23,500	4,253	3,521	4,639	3,521	
23,500	23,550	4,267	3,529	4,653	3,529	
23,550	23,600	4,281	3,536	4,667	3,536	
23,600	23,650	4,295	3,544	4,681	3,544	
23,650	23,700	4,309	3,551	4,695	3,551	
23,700	23,750	4,323	3,559	4,709	3,559	
23,750	23,800	4,337	3,566	4,723	3,566	
23,800	23,850	4,351	3,574	4,737	3,574	
23,850	23,900	4,365	3,581	4,751	3,581	
23,900	23,950	4,379	3,589	4,765	3,592	
23,950	24,000	4,393	3,596	4,779	3,606	
24,000						
24,000	24,050	4,407	3,604	4,793	3,620	
24,050	24,100	4,421	3,611	4,807	3,634	
24,100	24,150	4,435	3,619	4,821	3,648	
24,150	24,200	4,449	3,626	4,835	3,662	
24,200	24,250	4,463	3,634	4,849	3,676	
24,250	24,300	4,477	3,641	4,863	3,690	
24,300	24,350	4,491	3,649	4,877	3,704	
24,350	24,400	4,505	3,656	4,891	3,718	
24,400	24,450	4,519	3,664	4,905	3,732	
24,450	24,500	4,533	3,671	4,919	3,746	
24,500	24,550	4,547	3,679	4,933	3,760	
24,550	24,600	4,561	3,686	4,947	3,774	
24,600	24,650	4,575	3,694	4,961	3,788	
24,650	24,700	4,589	3,701	4,975	3,802	
24,700	24,750	4,603	3,709	4,989	3,816	
24,750	24,800	4,617	3,716	5,003	3,830	
24,800	24,850	4,631	3,724	5,017	3,844	
24,850	24,900	4,645	3,731	5,031	3,858	
24,900	24,950	4,659	3,739	5,045	3,872	
24,950	25,000	4,673	3,746	5,059	3,886	

* This column must also be used by a qualifying widow(

particular credits have all been repealed, but the childcare credit provisions remain in effect.

Childcare. If you must pay someone to care for your child so that you can work, you are allowed to deduct a portion of that cost directly as a tax credit. The maximum allowable expense is $2,400 for one child and $4,800 for two or more. If your adjusted gross income is more than $28,000 per year, you are allowed to take 20 percent of your childcare costs as a tax credit, which means that you can subtract a maximum of $480 for one child or $960 if two or more are cared for while you work. Lower-income workers are allowed an even larger tax credit (up to 30 percent for families earning $10,000 or less). Thus, the maximum credit for a low-income family is $720 (0.3 × $2,400) for one child and $1,440 (0.3 × $4,800) for two or more.

Seeking Tax Advice:
Professional Tax
Preparers

tax evasion: an illegal at-
tempt to avoid paying taxes

tax avoidance: any legal
technique used to lessen a
person's tax liability

If the federal tax laws seem a bit complex, there is a reason. Tax laws are used for more than obtaining tax revenue. The government uses the tax code to encourage some activities and to discourage others. Your goal should be to minimize your personal tax liability by following the guidelines established by law. This does not mean evading your taxes. **Tax evasion** is an attempt to pay less than one is legally obligated to pay, and it is punishable by fine and/or imprisonment. However, it is perfectly legal to engage in **tax avoidance**, techniques for decreasing taxes by engaging in those activities that are undertaxed or not taxed at all. By getting a mortgage on a house, one can avoid paying taxes on the money spent to pay the interest on that mortgage. But how will you know whether such an activity is tax deductible, and how can you be sure that you will get the maximim tax refund? One of the easiest ways to handle this tax problem is to go to a professional tax preparer. This simple advice is not as easy as it may sound. In addition to the folks at the IRS, there are national tax preparation services such as H&R Block, local tax preparers, tax lawyers, and certified public accountants. All may be able to help you with your tax return, but their skills and level of expertise vary, and so will their prices.

If you have a simple return and plan to file the short form, the IRS will compute the tax for you. All you need to do is fill out the form, sign it, and enclose the wage form, called the W-2, sent by your employer. Most taxpayers are not keen on letting the IRS figure their taxes. The feeling is that there might be a conflict of interest, because the IRS is set up to collect money, not disburse it. Nevertheless, on a simple form there is little harm in letting the IRS do the work.

On a more complex form, especially when you plan to itemize your deductions rather than simply take the standard deduction, some professional advice could be worth the expense, and it is tax deductible. As a general rule, tax lawyers and certified public accountants are best able to deal with the thorny problems of tax law, but they are also the most expensive sources of advice. If your tax statement is not unduly complicated, a better buy might be a local tax preparer who is allowed to represent taxpayers at an IRS hearing. In order to be certified to practice before the IRS, such individuals must pass a series of stringent examinations administered by the U.S. Treasury. This is your assurance of the tax preparer's competence, and it may be of real comfort to you if your return is chosen for further scrutiny by the IRS.

THE TAX AUDIT

The U.S. tax system is built on voluntary compliance. There is no way that the IRS would be able to run the system if the majority of taxpayers either refused to pay or cheated. Nevertheless, the IRS estimates that between $75 and $100 billion of income goes unreported every year. If this is true, how is the system policed? The IRS uses several techniques, including a spot check of randomly selected tax returns and guidelines about the average amount of deductions for a given income. Tax returns that claim an exceptionally large amount for a particular deduction are suspect. These tax returns are subject to greater scrutiny and are more likely to undergo a personal examination, sometimes called a **tax audit**. The IRS collects an additional $2 billion each year as a result of these audits.

tax audit: an investigation of one's tax records by a representative of the IRS

Your chances of undergoing an audit are fairly small, because only about one in every 50 returns is selected each year. The odds range from one in 200 for those using the short form to one in ten for those using the long form and reporting more than $50,000 of income. However, if you are one of the unlucky ones, you will be notified by mail that your return is being examined. Frequently, a face-to-face meeting is arranged during which the IRS agent will ask some questions about your return. You will know the purpose of the audit in advance, so come prepared with all of your documentation. If the IRS is questioning the size of your charitable donations, for example, bring the canceled checks, as well as any supporting material, such as receipts for in-kind donations of clothing, appliances, or other goods. It is not necessary to bring receipts related to other areas of your return.

At the end of the meeting, the examiner will explain all proposed changes in your tax liability. If you accept this judgment, you sign an agreement. If you disagree, you may request an immediate meeting with the examiner's supervisor. After this, you must formally appeal the ruling if you disagree.

The IRS has only one appeal level, and cases are conducted as informally as possible. If you do not get satisfactory settlement at this level, your only alternative is to take your case to court. There are three courts available to you: the United States Tax Court, the Federal District Court, and the Claims Court. If you choose not to pay the disputed amount first, you may argue your case only in the Tax Court. If your case involves a dispute of $5,000 or less, the Tax Court provides the simplest form of redress. (You can write for a description of the procedures, free of charge, from the United States Tax Court, 400 Second Street N.W., Washington, DC 20217.) The Tax Court will travel to a convenient location near you to hear your case. There are only two catches here. First, you must file a petition with the Tax Court within 90 days of the formal IRS notice that you owe additional taxes. If you miss the deadline, you will have to pay the tax. Then your only recourse will be the Federal District Court or the Claims Court, for which you will need a tax lawyer. Second, if you have a small claim, the decision of the Tax Court cannot be appealed.

The IRS publishes its win–loss record of taxpayers' appeals each year. At all levels of appeal—the Tax Court, the Federal District Court, and the Claims Court—the IRS wins more than half of the cases. But its win–loss percentage has been lowest in the Claims Court, where it has won only 52 percent of the cases. Nevertheless, most tax experts agree that the Tax Court is the best place to appeal an IRS ruling if you have a strong case, because you do not need to retain counsel or pay the disputed tax, and the location of the hearing will be convenient. If your case is not strong legally but appeals to other taxpayers' sympathies, the experts recommend taking it to the U.S. District Court to be decided by a jury of your peers (*Money*, 1981). As with all decisions, you must weigh the costs and benefits. The costs include your time and psychological stress, as well as the cost of lawyers' fees and other fees.

Appealing a particular tax ruling raises the broader question of the fairness of the tax system. This transcends the federal income tax and opens up the entire tax system to investigation. Who bears the tax burden and who gets the benefits?

THE OVERALL TAX BURDEN: IS IT FAIR?

As we mentioned earlier, government covers a wide variety of agencies and levels. Thus far, we have generally focused on the federal government, but state and local governments are an important part of the picture as well. In 1987, state governments collected about 22 cents of every tax dollar, and local governments took about 15 cents. Figure 15.9 shows the combined tax revenues of state and local government. Notice that income taxes do not provide much of the total. State and local government depend more

**FIGURE 15.9
Total revenue, by major sources, for state and local governments. Total state and local revenue equals $783.2 billion.** (SOURCE: U.S. Bureau of the Census, *Government Finances, 1985–86* [Washington, D.C.: U.S. Government Printing Office, 1987].)

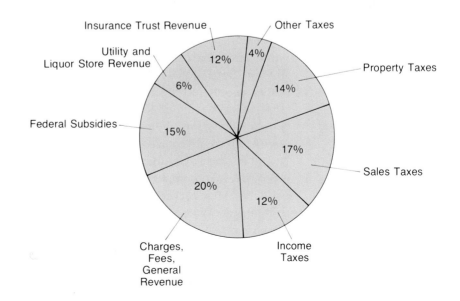

TABLE 15.8 Taxes and Transfer Payments as a Percentage of Income for Different Income Levels in the U.S. Population.

Population Decile	Approximate Family Income Range	All Taxes	Transfer Payments	Net Taxes Taxes Minus Transfers
Lowest	under $ 7,500	50.8	101.3	− 50.5
Second	$ 7,500–$11,999	28.3	54.7	− 26.4
Third	$ 12,000–$16,849	28.3	34.8	− 6.5
Fourth	$ 16,850–$21,654	28.4	23.7	4.7
Fifth	$ 21,655–$26,649	28.9	15.6	13.3
Sixth	$ 26,650–$31,749	28.6	10.5	18.1
Seventh	$ 31,750–$37,649	28.9	7.8	21.1
Eighth	$ 37,650–$45,799	29.8	5.5	24.3
Ninth	$ 45,700–$60,899	29.9	4.4	25.5
Highest	$ 60,900 and above	26.3	2.6	23.7
Top 5%	$ 80,500 +	25.0	2.1	22.9
Top 1%	$175,000 +	22.0	1.1	20.9
All classes		28.5	9.9	18.6

SOURCE: Joseph A. Pechman, *Who Paid the Taxes, 1966–85?* (Washington, D.C.: The Brookings Institution, 1985), Tables 4-5 and 4-7, Variant 3b.

heavily on sales and property taxes, whereas the federal government depends on income and payroll taxes.

The amounts of sales tax and property tax that a household pays is not directly linked to its income, as we saw earlier. Retired people, for example, often have only moderate incomes, and yet they may be liable for a high property tax on their homes. Low-income families tend to save very little, and many of their daily expenditures are subject to state sales taxes. As a consequence, people in higher income classes generally pay a smaller percentage of their incomes in sales taxes or property taxes. In general, state and local taxes can be labeled regressive, because they tax low-income households more heavily.

On the other hand, state and local governments provide goods and services that benefit low-income people as well as high-income people. Public education, welfare, and hospital care are only three of the many services provided at the state or local level that are open to everyone. If the value of these subsidies is compared to the recipient's income level, the system tends to appear more progressive.

Table 15.8 presents the results of a study that estimated the overall burden of taxation in the United States on taxpayers by income level (Pechman, 1985). This study also included the effect of cash transfers, such as Social Security and welfare benefits, but it excluded the impact of public goods like national defense. As you can see, by looking at the last column in the table, when taxes and transfers are considered together, the system emerges as mildly progressive. The lower-income groups get significant levels of transfers that offset their tax payments. Taxation is roughly proportional for most levels of income. However, since transfer payments decline as incomes rise, the system maintains its progressive nature until you reach the highest levels of income, where there appears to be a slight decline in tax rates. We should add, however, that Table 15.8 uses the least progressive estimates from Pechman's work. Other estimates would show slightly more progressivity at the highest income levels. Nevertheless, the conclusions remain the same: the U.S. system of taxation is roughly proportional for most income groups. When transfer payments are subtracted from taxes at each income level, the system emerges as mildly progressive.

SUMMARY

Because the tax system must balance so many conflicting objectives, it is little wonder that the U.S. Tax Code comprises more than 6,000 pages of exceedingly fine print, and it often takes an attorney to interpret its meaning. Given the complexity of the system, no one expects you to emerge as an expert simply because you have read this chapter. Nevertheless, you should have a better understanding of the American tax system and your part in it.

The original purpose of taxation was to provide revenue for the government so that it could maintain order. The basic law-and-order function of government remains, but many other public goods and services have been added. On the federal level, over 40 percent of the budget is devoted to programs that transfer income to individuals for social reasons. Despite the size and the rapid growth of these income transfers, Americans are among the least-taxed citizens of any highly developed nation.

Who bears the burden of taxation can be just as important as the size of the burden. Here, the benefits-received and the ability-to-pay principles can be used to justify different kinds of taxes. The ability-to-pay generally supports progressive taxes, which always take a higher proportion of income from those earning more. Two other classifications of taxes are those that take a higher percentage from lower-income consumers—regressive taxes—and those that take the same proportion from all income groups—proportional taxes. The federal budget depends heavily on the progressive income tax for its revenue, although regressive taxes like the Social Security payroll tax have become relatively more important in recent years.

Understanding how federal income tax works is important if you want to minimize your tax liabilities without going to jail. Taking advantage of your legitimate exclusions, deductions, exemptions, and tax credits can lower your taxes significantly. If you choose to itemize your deductions, you will need to keep good records with regard to medical expenses, state and local taxes, interest paid, charitable contributions, casualty and theft losses, and employment-related expenses. Otherwise, you can accept the government's estimate of these deductions, called the standard deduction.

If you have a great deal of income from a wide range of sources, professional tax advice is practically a necessity. But even if your tax return is not complex, it is often helpful to have someone review your form, particularly a tax preparer who is certified to practice before the U.S. Tax Court.

Random and selective tax audits are important enforcement tools of the IRS. If you are audited, you should be prepared with records to substantiate your case. If the IRS still disagrees with your deductions after seeing your evidence, you have the right to appeal your case.

Studies indicate that state and local taxes are largely regressive, whereas federal taxes are mildly progressive. When all taxes and income transfers are considered, net taxes are actually negative for the lowest-income groups, because their subsidies exceed their taxes. Overall, the system is progressive because transfer payments are heavily concentrated in the lower-income groups.

QUESTIONS

1. List four examples of public goods. Do they all have the free-rider problem? Could they be produced by the private sector, or must government always produce them? Explain.

2. The free-rider effect can apply to goods other than those produced by government. How does it apply to
   a. Educational television stations?
   b. Coffee available in offices?
   c. Fourth of July fireworks displays?

3. Classify the following taxes according to whether they are based on benefits received or ability to pay:
   a. Income tax
   b. Gasoline tax
   c. Fishing license fee

4. Many people argue that Americans are overtaxed. What comparative evidence do we have that seems to contradict this position? Is it still true?

5. What are the most important sources of revenue for the federal government? What are the most important expenditure categories? Did these categories dominate the federal budget 25 years ago? 50 years ago?

6. What is the difference between the average tax rate and the marginal tax rate? Can the marginal tax rate have a significant impact on consumer expenditure patterns? How?

7. If the federal income tax laws were rewritten overnight so that every citizen got a $2,000 personal exemption but no other exemptions, credits, or deductions, and if the rate were made strictly proportional, say 15 percent, what would the impact be on the demand for lawyers, accountants, IRS examiners, and tax preparers? How would consumer expenditure patterns change? Would the government lose any weapons in its economic arsenal? What is the possibility of such a change?

8. What is the standard deduction? What is its purpose? When does it make sense to keep tax records if you are not going to itemize your deductions?

9. What is the difference between a deduction and a tax credit? Which one favors high-income taxpayers?

10. What procedures can you follow to minimize the probability of having your tax return audited? If you are audited, what rights do you have? How can you appeal an IRS ruling?

REFERENCES AND READINGS

Advisory Commission on Intergovernmental Relations. *Significant Features of Fiscal Federalism, 1988 Edition.* Washington, D.C.: The Commission, 1988.

Browning, Edgar K., and Browning, Jacqueline M. *Public Finance and the Price System.* New York: Macmillan, 1987.

Internal Revenue Service. *Your Federal Income Tax.* Washington, D.C.: U.S. Government Printing Office, annual editions.

Laffer, Arthur B., and Seymour, Jan P., eds. *The Economics of the Tax Revolt.* New York: Harcourt Brace Jovanovich, 1979.

Lasser, J. K. *Your Income Tax.* New York: Simon & Schuster, annual editions.

Lindsey, Lawrence B. "Did ERTA Raise the Share of Taxes Paid by Upper-Income Taxpayers?" In Lawrence H. Summers, ed., *Tax Policy and the Economy.* Cambridge, Mass.: MIT Press, 1988.

McKee, Michael. "Paying the Public Sector's Bills," *OECD Observer,* December/January, 1988.

Pechman, Joseph A. *Who Paid the Taxes 1966–85?* Washington, D.C.: The Brookings Institution, 1985.

———. *Federal Tax Policy.* Washington, D.C.: The Brookings Institution, 1987.

"Special Report: Taxpayers' Revenge." *Money,* August 1988.

"Tax Audits: Improving Your Odds." *Consumer Reports,* March 1986.

U.S. Bureau of the Census. *Governmental Finances.* Washington, D.C.: Government Printing Office, 1988.

"You Versus the IRS." *Money,* July 1981.

"Your Taxes After Reform." *Consumer Reports,* March 1988.

"Your Tax Return: Deciphering the New Forms." *Changing Times,* February 1988.

Chapter Sixteen

PERSONAL INVESTMENTS: MANAGING YOUR MONEY

- ☐ Basic Concepts of Investment and Personal Finance
- ☐ Types of Investments: Creating an Investment Portfolio
- ☐ Comparing Various Investments

DID YOU KNOW THAT . . .

. . . You probably have an investment portfolio right now, even if you don't realize it?

. . . By mastering a set of personal finance terms, you can evaluate your portfolio and significantly improve your investments?

. . . There is a trade-off between financial risk and yield?

. . . Even if two banks advertise the same interest rate, they can pay different amounts of interest because of compounding or computing policies? The American Bankers Association estimates that there are 54 ways of computing interest on a savings account.

. . . The yield on U.S. Savings Bonds is a variable rate tied to the return on Treasury Notes?

. . . There are significant differences between common stocks and preferred stocks?

. . . Mutual funds without a sales charge (no-load funds) have been shown to perform as well as those that charge a sales commission?

. . . The average annual rate of return on an investment in a college education varies from 8 to 12 percent?

Many of us have fond memories of our first piggy bank and recall the implied parental message about the importance of saving. But as we grow up, we learn that stuffing money into a piggy bank is not the best way to save. For one thing, the money could be stolen, but more important, it is not doing anything for us. It is just sitting there. That's where the search for investments comes in. **Investments** are ways of using money in the present to create greater income in the future.

Interest, the income a lender earns for letting someone else borrow his or her money, is one kind of return on an investment. When you learned as a child that a bank would pay you interest for letting it keep your savings, it may have seemed like an "unearned bonus" for you, but it is certainly *not* unearned. It is a legitimate reward for allowing someone else to borrow purchasing power. There is a real opportunity cost involved, because you could be using that money for something else. The money could be used for a vacation, a quality stereo package, or some other investment.

Banks and other financial institutions are in the business of encouraging people to save a portion of their income so that other people and firms can borrow the money to increase their purchasing power. We discussed the demand of loans and credit from the borrower's perspective in Chapter 6. Borrowers want to minimize the interest they must pay to get this additional purchasing power. Savers, on the other hand, want to get as much interest as possible on their savings.

Inflation, changes in the tax laws, and the appearance of many alternative forms of investment mean that today, more than ever, consumers need to understand the principles of investment and personal finance if they are to make wise decisions regarding their money. In this chapter we begin with the fundamentals of investment, in order to give you a method for evaluating various types. We define and explain the concepts of yield, risk, and liquidity. We also emphasize the importance of planning for inflation and taxes when one makes investments. Then we move on to the sometimes confusing world of investments. Here, we apply our investment principles to a wide range of investments, from savings accounts to real estate and from the stock market to government bonds. Our objective is to give you information about each of these investment opportunities so that you can put them in perspective, understand the costs and benefits of each, and see how they could potentially fit into your investment strategy.

BASIC CONCEPTS OF INVESTMENT AND PERSONAL FINANCE

You would be hard pressed to find an area of business that is more confusing to the average consumer than the world of investment and personal finance. One of the most obvious reasons for this confusion is the jargon used by investors. It is so foreign to most of us that it could well be another language, "investese." Investment counselors, stockbrokers, bankers, and business professors seem quite at home when discussing "investment portfolios" and the problems of "liquidity," but many consumers are not. Many even avoid the concepts and the terminology. That, however, is not to their advantage. Without an understanding of the basic vocabulary and concepts of investment, consumers may cling to a few familiar kinds of investments or simply rely blindly on other people to make their decisions for them. Doing so limits both decision making and results. Taking the time to learn the vocabulary of investment will help you to evaluate alternative investment opportunities.

Yield

yield: the return on an investment

Have you ever played the psychological game of free association? In this game one is presented with a word, such as *white*, and is supposed to say the first thing that comes to mind. Perhaps you thought of the word *black*. What do you think of if you hear the word *yield*? If you are like most people, you probably think of the yellow and black traffic sign. But if you were an investment broker, you would think of a percent sign or a dollar sign, because in investment terms **yield** refers to the return on an investment, the amount of money that an investment returns. It is often expressed as a percentage of the cost of the original investment. The annual amount of interest a savings account earns, for example, can be translated into an annual yield by dividing the interest earned by the original amount deposited in the savings account. For example, if you left $100 in your savings account for one year and the bank gave you $5 interest, the annual yield would be 5 percent ($5 divided by $100). The annual yield on any investment is simply the additional income earned during the year, divided by the amount of the investment. The higher the yield, the better the return on the investment.

Risk

risk: the possibility of financial loss

Risk is the possibility that a financial investment may lose rather than earn money. Financial risk can take two forms: Either the yield on the investment will be less than expected when one decides to invest, or one may actually lose a portion (or all) of the investment. Investors want to limit their risk as much as possible for an obvious reason (no one wants to lose money). To some degree, one can lower the risk by gathering more information and becoming more informed about a potential investment, but ultimately, risk is directly correlated with yield. Higher-yielding investments almost always have a higher risk factor than do investments with lower yields, The reason is in the dynamics of the investments process and in the basic rationality of investors.

To see the logic of the relationship between yield and risk, we will look at a hypothetical example. Suppose that we offered you two investment opportunities, A and B. Option A involves a risky venture, such as drilling for oil. If you will invest $10,000 in the oil-drilling scheme and if we strike oil, we will give you your $10,000 back at the end of a year, plus $2,000 for your trouble—a potential yield of 20 percent. Under option B, we will accept your $10,000 investment and use it to help us build an addition to our steel mill, the largest and most productive of its kind in the world. At the end of the year, you can get your investment back with a 20 percent yield. Which option would you take? Both offer the same yields if everything goes right, but the oil scheme is much riskier, so if you are rational, you would invest in option B, the steel mill. Because almost anyone in his or her right mind would follow the same strategy, the yield on option A would have to be raised to attract investors. The dynamics of the market plus the rationality of investors make risk and yield move in the same direction. A higher risk necessarily must offer higher potential yield.

Capital Gains (and Losses)

capital gain: the increase in the value of an investment from the time it is bought until it is sold

The value of some investments, such as shares of stock in a corporation or a piece of undeveloped land, may change yearly, monthly, or even daily. If the value of an investment rises so that the income derived from its sale is greater than the original cost, the investor is said to have earned a **capital gain**. Of course, an investment sometimes loses value over time. For example, if you sell a house for less than you paid for it, you have sustained a **capital loss**.

Capital gains and losses are relevant only to those investments that can be sold to others. These investments are called **capital assets**, and they include any form of real or personal property other than those used in one's trade or business. Houses, stocks, bonds, paintings, old coins, and jewelry are some common forms of capital assets.

Liquidity

liquidity: the ease with which an investment can be turned into cash

Liquidity is an investment's ability to be converted into cash. If there is no difficulty in converting an asset into cash, it is said to be a highly liquid investment. On the other hand, if one has to wait for a buyer or if some prearranged agreement prohibits the sale for some time, then the investment is not liquid. Because investors would like to have their investment options open at all times, they prefer liquidity. No one wants to be locked into an investment when a better opportunity arises or when an emergency strikes. But once again, there is a trade-off among goals. Stuffing your mattress with cash gives you a great deal of liquidity;

however, the yield on your investment is zero, and the possibility for a capital gain is also nil. On the other hand, although buying a house has the potential to offer a significant capital gain, a house is not highly liquid. We will discuss this trade-off of goals and the evaluation of investments later in this chapter.

Inflation Hedges

Inflation can be a mortal enemy of investment. As we discussed in Chapter 3, an overall rise in the price level eats away at the purchasing power of money. In the later 1980s inflation was running at about 4 percent annually. The real yield on an investment with an 8 percent yield would have been cut in half, to a *real* gain of only 4 percent (8 percent minus 4 percent), but at least it would have been a positive 4 percent. A decade earlier, inflation reached double digits. For example, the 11 percent rise in the CPI during 1979 would have resulted in a 3 percent *negative* yield (8 percent minus 11 percent) on a similar investment. Given the realities of inflation, it is of critical importance to weigh an investment's ability to stay ahead of inflation. Investments whose values tend to rise with inflation are called **inflation hedges**.

inflation hedge: a purchase or investment that provides protection from loss caused by inflation

Table 16.1 shows the track record of ten well-known investments for three time periods. No particular investment ranks number one for all periods. Nevertheless, there are some lessons to be learned here. First, anyone considering an investment in U.S. farmland would do well to review its consistently poor showing over the past ten years. It is the only investment listed that failed to outpace inflation. Second, the change in

TABLE 16.1 The Ranking of Ten Popular Inflation Hedges by Their Compound Annual Rate of Return for Three Time Periods

	10 years		5 years		1 year	
Hedge Item	1977–1987 Increase	Rank	1982–1987 Increase	Rank	1987 Increase	Rank
U.S. coins	16.3	1	11.4	2	10.7	4
Stocks	13.9	2	24.1	1	20.6	3
Stamps	11.8	3	−1.3	9	0.5	9
Chinese ceramics	11.3	4	3.4	8	6.7	8
Old Master paintings	9.7	5	9.5	4	8.6	5
Silver	9.7	6	4.0	7	39.8	1
Gold	9.2	7	6.8	5	29.1	2
Diamonds	8.9	8	10.2	3	7.0	6
Residential housing	7.4	9	4.8	6	6.8	7
U.S. farmland	1.5	10	−7.8	10	−7.9	10
Consumer Prices	6.5		3.5		3.8	

SOURCE: Salomon Brothers. Adapted from *Changing Times*, November 1987.

the upper ranks of investments is an indication of the basic volatility of investment value. Over the past ten years the best inflation-hedge investments were U.S. coins and stocks. Does this mean that they will always be good inflation hedges? Prediction is difficult, but in October 1987 stock prices fell dramatically. Meanwhile concerns over inflation and liquidity pushed silver and gold prices up significantly in the most recently recorded one-year period (column three). But before you rush out to buy some precious metals, you should be alerted to the fact that between 1980 and 1982 the value of an ounce of gold fell from $800 to under $400, and the value of silver fell from $40 to less than $10. Their rapid decline points out the risk factor that is generally associated with any highly touted inflation hedge. By its very nature, an inflation hedge depends on investors' confidence in its ability to outpace inflation. If that confidence is shaken, large declines in price are possible. What goes up can also come down. And sometimes it can come down very quickly.

Information, Transaction, and Management Costs

By this time, you should begin to realize that cost involves more than the money paid to acquire an investment. Gathering information and making informed decisions involves time and monetary costs that may or may not result in deciding to undertake a specific investment. The greater the uncertainty about the quality of an investment, the more information one needs and the costlier it becomes. You may decide to subscribe to one of the investor newsletter services to get a better idea about the quality of various investments, or you may simply subscribe to an investment-oriented news source like *Money* magazine, or the *Wall Street Journal*. In

Some investments entail high information costs and require that the investor subscribe to a number of periodicals.

any case, the time and expense are part of the information costs, and they are tax deductible when used for investment purposes.

Some investments, such as stocks, bonds, real estate, and even diamonds, require brokers or dealers to help in acquiring or selling. Payments for such services are **transaction costs**, and they can significantly cut into returns. Day-to-day managing of investments may also involve costs. If the value of an investment fluctuates frequently, as do the prices of gold, silver, and stocks, one may have to devote some time each day to evaluating its progress (or decline). Other types of investments, such as rental property, may require management or paying someone else to see that they are maintained. These costs may seem burdensome to some investors, whereas other investors may actually enjoy them. Your particular mix of investments should reflect your attitudes toward these necessary expenditures of money and effort.

transaction costs: expenses related to the actual buying or selling of an asset; these could include commissions, appraisal fees, and licenses

Tax Status and Investment Strategies

Before you decide to make an investment, you ought to consider how this investment will affect your personal income taxes. The government often uses tax laws to encourage certain activities. For example, the government encourages home ownership by allowing all interest on home mortgages to be deducted from your income before calculating your income tax.

Tax-exempt **municipal bonds** can also help you avoid taxes. When cities and counties need to borrow money to construct a new facility like a hospital or a new highway, they often issue municipal bonds to attract money for these projects. A **bond** is a certificate of indebtedness for which the borrower agrees to pay a fixed amount of interest each year for the privilege of using the bondholder's money. At the end of the preset time period, generally from 10 to 30 years, the borrower agrees to redeem the bond at face value, that is, buy back the bond for a certain sum of money, generally printed on the front (face) of the bond. This description of a bond applies to corporate as well as municipal and federal bonds. However, interest paid on corporate and federal bonds is not exempt from federal income taxes. By the same token, interest earned on federal bonds is exempt from state and local income tax.

bond: A certificate of indebtedness that may be resold; an agreement whereby a borrower agrees to pay a fixed amount of interest each year for the right to use the bondholder's money. At the end of a specific time period, the borrower agrees to pay back the original debt.

Investment Trade-Offs and Your Comfort Zone

The ideal investment, like the ideal spouse, probably does not exist. If it did, it would have a high yield with no risk, it would be highly liquid with tremendous potential for capital gain, it would be an inflation hedge, and it would shelter those gains from taxes. If you can find something that has all these qualities and no significant transaction or management costs, invest in it.

The impossibility of finding the "perfect investment" points up the conflict that is inherent among the terms in our investment vocabulary.

Take the concepts of yield and risk, for example. All investors would like to maximize their return and minimize their risk, but some investors would be willing to accept a little more risk if the potential yield were higher. If the riskier investment did not offer a higher yield, no one would invest in it, as our earlier example about oil-drilling and steel mill investments showed. Thus, there is a trade-off between the variables, and there are different yields associated in systematic ways with their risks.

Individuals need to be especially sensitive to their feelings regarding the yield–risk trade-off. The goal is to identify your **comfort zone**, the amount of risk you feel is acceptable. If you select an investment that has an uncomfortably large risk, you could fall victim to a loss of confidence or even panic when you should be following your initial decision-making strategy. These panic attacks often result in an investor who ''buys high and sells low.'' To avoid this phenomenon, always consider your comfort zone when choosing an investment.

Figure 16.1 shows a hypothetical relationship between yield and risk, with some real-world examples to put it into perspective. For investors who dread financial risk, the least risky investment consists of lending money to the United States government. In more than 200 years, the federal government has never failed to pay its debts. And given its power to tax, there is no reason to assume that the government will ever be in a situation in which it is unable to pay its creditors. The unhappy side of this enviable credit record is that as a result of this zero-risk situation, the federal government offers investors a very low yield. Corporate

comfort zone: in investing, refers to the degree of risk a person finds acceptable

FIGURE 16.1
The relationship between yield and risk.

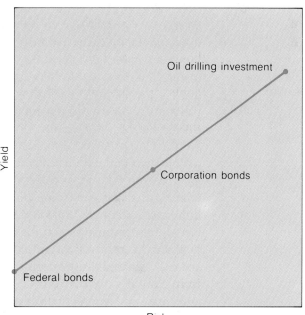

**FIGURE 16.2
The relationship
between yield and
liquidity.**

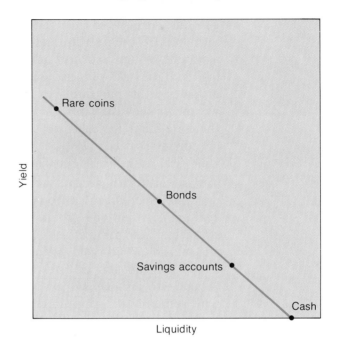

bonds cannot offer as much security as federal bonds, so corporations
have to offer higher yields to attract investors. Extremely risky ventures, such as drilling for oil, are often called speculative investments,
and they must offer even higher yields.

There are other trade-offs, of course. For example, what is the relationship between liquidity and yield? All other conditions being equal,
an investor would like to be able to earn a high yield and convert the
investment to cash instantly. Here again, because investments that
provide greater liquidity are preferred over illiquid ones, they can offer a
lower yield than those that are more difficult to convert to cash, as Figure 16.2 illustrates. According to Table 16.1, U.S. coins have offered a
good return on investment in the past decade. However, money invested
in rare coins is sometimes difficult to get back quickly; it is not very
liquid. Corporate bonds offer greater liquidity because they are easier
to sell than collectible coins, but their value can fluctuate, so investors
may have to take a loss to get their money back immediately. Savings accounts offer low yields but very good liquidity, except on weekends and
holidays. Even here, automatic teller machines are improving liquidity,
but still, nothing is as liquid as cash.

A similar trade-off often exists between investments offering a high
annual yield and those offering long-term capital gains. It is often true that
large capital gains can only be realized by reinvesting the profits of an
enterprise and paying little or no return to current investors. Corporations
often follow this strategy by paying their stockholders only a small

percentage of their profits in dividends and reinvesting the bulk of their profits in new equipment, plants, or research. If this investment is successful, the price of the stock will rise, because other potential investors will try to buy the stock in anticipation of larger future dividends to stockholders. As these new investors bid up the price of the stock, the stockholders earn capital gains by selling to them.

The best investment for an individual consumer depends largely on the importance of the various investment trade-offs. Some investors cannot sleep at night knowing that their investment involves some risk. Others are happy to accept a large degree of risk as long as the opportunity for a large capital gain or a high yield is in the offing. Some investors feel compelled to have as much information as possible before they make a decision. Others may simply be willing to accept the advice of a friend. The point is that one person's "ideal" investment may not be a good option for another person. Only you know your own comfort zone, for example. You must evaluate your own standards for acceptable levels of risk, yield, and capital gains before venturing into the investment world. You must also realize that these three factors are seldom present in all investments. In general, more of one factor can be obtained only by sacrificing another.

TYPES OF INVESTMENTS: CREATING AN INVESTMENT PORTFOLIO

investment portfolio: the mix of investments that an investor holds

Now that you understand terminology and trade-offs, you can evaluate some of the typical investments available in the U.S. economy. Remember, no single investment is perfect for everyone, and investment goals determine the forms and varieties of investments. The mixture of investments that you choose to hold is called your **investment portfolio**. By acquiring new investments and getting rid of old ones, you can change your portfolio so that it more closely reflects your investment goals.

As you review the following investment possibilities, try to keep in mind the major concepts we have discussed:

> Yield
> Risk
> Liquidity
> Inflation protection
> Information, transaction, and management costs
> Tax status

Savings Accounts

One of the best places to put your money to earn a safe yield is in a savings account at your local bank or savings and loan association. These institutions can offer more than 5 percent interest, and up to $100,000 of your savings is insured by a government-sponsored agency. (For details on insurance provisions for savings accounts, see Box 5.2 in Chapter 5). Of course, a 5 percent yield may not seem very large, considering the rate of inflation. Nevertheless, these accounts have certain advantages. They take almost no time to manage, information costs are virtually zero, and transaction costs involved in putting money in or taking it out are small. Savings accounts are highly liquid and virtually risk free, but before you decide to plunk your money into the most convenient bank, savings and loan association, or credit union, consider the rationale for saving.

Why consumers save. On a society-wide level, an economy needs to have some members who hold their consumption below their income (that is, who save) so that the other members can borrow that purchasing power and spend. But on an individual level, why do consumers save? The three main reasons are providing for an emergency, accumulating purchasing power for an expensive item, and providing for income in the long run. These reasons relate directly to budgeting and money management, the ways consumers define and achieve their financial goals. No matter what the reason for saving, one should be aware of some minor differences in bank interest procedures that could result in one's earning a lower return.

The importance of the three C's: compounding, computing, crediting. With a savings account, one not only earns interest on what one puts into it, but one earns interest on the interest itself, if it is left in the account. The concept of earning interest on previously paid interest is called **compounding**. Financial institutions have many different ways to compound interest. The simplest way is to do it once a year. A 6 percent interest rate that is paid annually will earn $60 interest on a savings account that has $1,000 in it for one year. Some banks advertise that they compound interest daily; their effective yield is higher. If 6 percent interest is compounded daily, for example, the earnings will be $61.83. One earns more because the interest earned on January 1 and on each succeeding day earns interest on itself. Table 16.2 shows the difference that compounding can make on a $1,000 savings account at various interest rates.

TABLE 16.2 Year-End Value of a $1,000 Savings Account, Using Various Compounding Techniques for One Year

	Nominal Annual Interest Rate				
Compound Technique	**6%**	**7%**	**8%**	**10%**	**12%**
Annual	1,060.00	1,070.00	1,080.00	1,100.00	1,120.00
Semiannual	1,060.90	1,071.20	1,081.60	1,102.50	1,123.60
Quarterly	1,061.36	1,071.86	1,082.43	1,103.81	1,125.51
Daily	1,061.83	1,072.50	1,083.36	1,105.22	1,129.40

Beside using various compounding techniques, banks and other financial institutions may also use various techniques in calculating interest. There are at least 54 ways to compute interest on savings accounts. We will not try to outline all of them, but the one most advantageous to consumers is the "day of deposit to day of withdrawal" method. Under this plan, a depositor begins earning interest on the day the money is deposited and continues to earn interest until the money is withdrawn. Some other, less favorable methods use the lowest monthly balance or offer interest only on money left on deposit for an entire quarter (three months). Still others penalize a depositor for making a withdrawal during the quarter or in the middle of an interest period.

A third factor to be considered is the procedure the bank has for crediting the interest to one's account. Some pay semiannually; some, quarterly; some, even monthly. The system of crediting interest can be very important for a retired person who may be using that interest for living expenses. It may also be an important convenience for a consumer who needs the interest to make a specific purchase.

Certificates of Deposit

Financial institutions have developed a series of ingenious ways to pay more interest in the hope that this will entice more people to save with their firms. The **certificate of deposit (CD)** is an example of this innovative spirit. A CD is an agreement between a bank and a depositor that the bank will pay a guaranteed rate of interest over a specific time period, as long as the depositor agrees to leave a certain amount of money in the bank over that same period. If you choose to withdraw your money early, you must pay an interest penalty. With a CD, the depositor gives up some liquidity in order to gain a specific yield for a certain period of time.

Government Securities

government securities: certificates of federal government debt, including savings bonds and Treasury bills, notes, and bonds

The federal government's debt is more than $2 trillion, much of it owed to private citizens. They finance this debt with a variety of debt instruments called **government securities**. The yields and restrictions on these securities can vary enormously depending on the length of the loan, the amount, and the state of general interest rates. Two investors could lend the government identical sums of money, and the more knowledgeable investor could earn a 50 percent higher return. To see how this might happen, we need to review the alternative forms of federal debt. We will begin with the best known (and lowest-yielding) government security, the U.S. Savings Bond, and then move on to Treasury bills, notes, and bonds.

Saving bonds. The name U.S. Savings Bond is as easily recognizable as the brand names Coca-Cola and McDonald's. However, if asked to explain what a savings bond is or how it works, many consumers would have a difficult, if not impossible, time doing so. All the posters, jingles, and television ads have conditioned us to accept U.S. Savings Bonds as a reasonable investment, but most of us do not know whether they are in fact a good one. In fact, only a few years ago one consumer group filed a protest with the FTC over the advertising of these bonds. They argued that the ads were false and misleading because the bonds were a poor investment. Since that time, the government has revamped the program and some financial advisers have even started to recommend them once again (*Changing Times*, 1988). What are savings bonds?

U.S. Savings Bonds are similar to all other bonds: They are certificates of indebtedness whereby the borrower agrees to pay a certain amount of interest for the privilege of using the bondholder's money. The most common savings bond, the EE series, can be defined as a contract showing that money has been loaned to the United States, which promises to repay it with interest when the bond is redeemed. Series EE bonds are issued at a 50 percent discount of the value printed on the front of the bond, the **face value**. The smallest face value on the EE series is $50, which means that you could buy one of these bonds for as little as $25. Most banks and savings institutions sell these bonds, but you may find it more convenient to order them by phone and charge them to your credit card. You can do this by calling a toll-free number, 1–800–US BONDS. The relatively small investment and the toll-free number are indications that the primary market for these bonds is the small investor. In fact, the federal government even limits your annual purchase of these bonds to $15,000 ($30,000 face value).

Legislation passed in 1982 requires that the yields on these bonds be periodically adjusted so that they equal 85 percent of the average yield on five-year Treasury Notes sold to large investors, or a minimum of 6 percent, whichever is greater. At this writing, the yield is 6.9 percent, but you can call the US BONDS number to get the current rate. Historically, savings bonds have not offered extremely high yields. Nevertheless, they do offer some advantages to the small investor. First, savings bonds offer a high degree of safety because they are backed by the taxing power of the government and because any bond that is lost, stolen, or accidentally destroyed will be replaced at no charge to the registered owner. Second, they are a convenient way to save. More than 40,000 employers nationwide offer automatic payroll deduction plans, purchasing bonds automatically at each pay period. This must be a powerful incentive, because about 60 percent of all savings bonds are purchased this way. Third, you never pay any fee or commission when buying or redeeming savings bonds. (By the way, the best time to redeem a savings bond is just after a six-month anniversary, because interest is credited only twice a year.) Finally, there are certain tax advantages. State and local governments are not permitted to tax the interest on these bonds, and even the federal government agrees to defer your tax bite until you redeem the bonds.

Treasury bills, notes, and bonds. Government securities are the least risky form of investment; therefore, they generally offer lower yields than those of corporate or municipal bonds. Once again, we see the trade-off between risk and yield. Nevertheless, the government must offer a competitive rate of return, or investors will not buy the bonds and help finance the federal budget. Savings bond yields, however, do not attract enough investors to finance our federal deficits, so other alternatives have been developed. The three most common ones are Treasury bills, Treasury notes, and Treasury bonds. In recent years these securities have offered twice the yield of an ordinary savings bond, along with most of the tax advantages. The simplest way to buy these securities is through a bank or a bond broker whose fees will be a tiny fraction of the total cost. However, they may be purchased directly from the Federal Reserve District Bank in your region (see Chapter 5, Figure 5.2).

The major differences among **Treasury bills** (often called **T-bills**), Treasury notes, and Treasury bonds come down to the size of the minimum purchase and the length of time before they can be redeemed. The minimum date for redemption is called the date of **maturity**. T-bills have the shortest maturities (anywhere from 30 days to one year), and the highest minimum denomination ($10,000). Treasury notes mature in one to ten years and come in minimum denominations of $5,000 for notes running for four years or less and denominations of $1,000 for longer terms. Treasury bonds cover a period of more than ten years and are available in $1,000 denominations.

Liquidity is not much of a problem for Treasury bonds because there is a large market for them and brokers are constantly buying and selling old as well as new issues. However, every time the services of a broker are used, a fee will be charged. Thus, transaction costs are higher for Treasury bonds than they are for savings bonds, which can be purchased and redeemed at any bank. As far as risk is concerned, you can be certain that the federal government will not default (refuse to pay its debt). And once a T-bill or T-bond is purchased, you know with certainty what the yield will be. However, a problem may occur if you try to sell the bond before it matures. In this case, the value of the bond depends on the yield you get versus the yield that another investor gets by buying a new bond. For example, if you purchased a 20-year bond several years ago at face value of $10,000 and receive $500 in interest annually, it is yielding 5 percent. But if new bonds are yielding 10 percent, the current market value of your old bond is really only $5,000 to someone who has a choice between buying your old bond or a new one.

FIGURE 16.3
Assets of money market mutual funds, in billions of dollars.
(SOURCES: Investment Company Institute, *Mutual Fund Fact Book* [Washington, D.C., 1989].)

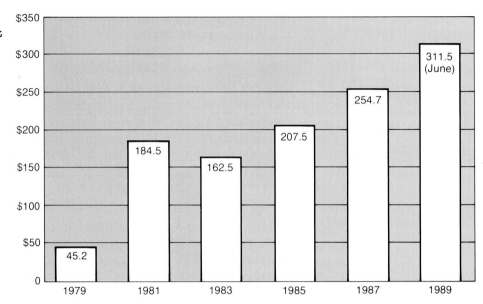

Money Market Mutual Funds

money market mutual fund: *an investment company whose primary aim is to pool investors' money and buy high-yield bonds; the income from the bonds is then passed on to the investors*

If you like the idea of earning more than the savings bond rate by buying larger government bonds but you do not have the $10,000 needed to buy a Treasury bill, you may be interested in a **money market mutual fund**. These funds, run by investment companies, pool small investors' money to buy jumbo bank CDs ($100,000 minimum), high-yielding government securities, and long-term corporate bonds. The funds require no day-to-day management on your part, and liquidity is almost as good as a regular checking account, subject only to a minimum withdrawal amount of about $500. These funds have had a good record as far as risk is concerned, but unlike the more traditional savings account, they are not insured. If the combination of higher yield, liquidity, and relative safety sounds good to you, you are not alone in your evaluation. When these funds began, they were not well accepted, but as Figure 16.3 shows, the assets in these funds rose dramatically in the 1980s. Today, their assets exceed $300 billion, accounting for about 10 percent of all consumer savings in the United States.

The Stock Market

Many people immediately associate the term *investments* with the stock market, and for good reason. Stocks have been a mainstay of investments for almost a century. Today it is impossible to watch a nightly news program or read a local newspaper without seeing a reference to the stock market. But what are stocks, and are they good investments for you?

To understand stocks it helps to look at them from a company's point of view. Whenever a company decides to expand its business or whenever a new company is being formed, it generally needs financial capital (money).

share of stock: a share that entitles the owner to an interest in the corporation and a share in its profits

There are many ways that a company could get this money, such as going to a bank and borrowing directly or selling bonds to the general public. However, both of these systems saddle the company with fixed periodic payments and interest on the debt. If the company is a corporation, it can raise money be selling stock, which entitles a buyer to an ownership interest in the corporation. To hold a **share of stock** is to own a piece, albeit a small piece, of the corporation itself. Once one becomes a stockholder, one has a right to a share in the profits of the corporation. However, unlike a bondholder, a stockholder is not a creditor of the corporation; he or she is an investor in the corporation. The reward paid to a stockholder is called a **dividend**, and it depends largely on the profitability of the corporation.

Types of shares. In the case of **preferred stock**, the size of the annual dividend is fixed by the corporation and never changes. In this regard, preferred stock is similar to a bond, but unlike bondholders, preferred stockholders cannot sue the corporation if their dividends are not paid because of the lack of profitability. Preferred stockholders definitely have an inferior position to bondholders. However, they are "preferred" over other stockholders in the sense that their dividends must be paid before other stockholders receive their dividends. On the other hand, preferred stockholders do not have a voice (vote) in who should run the company, because preferred stock is generally nonvoting stock.

Common stock is an investment in the ownership of a corporation that entitles the stockholder to share in the profits of the firm (if there are any) and also in the election of those who run the firm. Large corporations with publicly traded common stock have thousands of owners who seldom exercise their power to run the company. For example, if you owned 100 shares of IBM stock, you would own the equivalent of 0.00002 percent of the corporation. You would have 100 votes out of 583,900,000 potential share votes. If stockholders do not approve of a corporate policy, it is generally easier for them to sell their shares and invest elsewhere than to go to corporate headquarters and attempt to change things. Because the everyday buying and selling of these shares determines the price of the stock, dissatisfaction among the shareholders will drive the price of a stock down and act as an indirect, but effective, way of controlling corporate management. As the price of a stock falls, the company becomes vulnerable to a takeover by another firm (or by a few disgruntled stockholders) that would replace the top management people.

The appeal of common stocks as an investment lies in their potential for increased dividends and capital gains. Unlike the interest return on a bond or on the dividends paid to a preferred stockholder, dividends on common stock can be raised at any time. Dividends are usually paid every three months (quarterly), and they may take the form of a cash payment,

A common stock certificate indicates part ownership in a corporation.

additional shares of stock, or a combination of both. If a corporation is doing exceptionally well, it may even declare an extra dividend. Capital gains accrue to stockholders who sell their shares of stock for a higher price then they paid for them. Because common stocks have the greatest potential for increased dividends, they are also more likely than preferred stocks to show capital gains. If the price of a stock doubles or triples, many corporations will declare a **stock split**, in which every common stock shareholder will get additional shares based on the number of shares owned as of a certain date. For example, a two for one stock split for all shareholders of record on May 7, would credit someone who owned 100 shares of this corporation on May 7 with 200 shares.

One of the major reasons for a stock split is to make the shares more attractive to new investors. A stock split reduces the price per share by increasing the number of shares outstanding. (An increase in supply leads to a fall in the price). This in turn leads to a larger number of shareholders. Most large, publicly traded corporations would like as wide a distribution of their shares as possible for at least two reasons. First, this makes it more difficult for an unfriendly takeover by a small group of shareholders. Second, a broader distribution of a company's stock gives more consumers a sense of ownership and loyalty to the firm's products. This rationale is very similar to the one companies use when giving stock to their employees. They hope it will affect their attitudes and behavior with regard to the firm.

Buying stock. Investing in the stock market can be rewarding, but it can also be hazardous. For all publicly traded stocks, you need to find someone who is licensed to finalize the purchase or sale. This person is called a **stockbroker**. Stockbrokers are not difficult to find, but they charge for their services. Some brokers provide rather elaborate investment counseling and advice; others simply execute buy and sell orders. The kind of broker you choose depends on how much you are willing to pay and on how much advice you need. Large, well-known brokerage firms like Merrill Lynch, Dean Witter, and Prudential-Bache have extensive research departments to help you avoid bad buys and select good ones.

The problem with depending heavily on brokerage firms for investment advice is that too many experts may spoil the forecast. Because a large number of brokers are concentrating on learning everything they can about the companies on the major stock exchanges and then telling their clients everything they have learned, there are few surprises. No one can really get the jump on anyone else. It becomes difficult to follow the age-old dictum, "Buy low and sell high." In essence, many academic stock market researchers have come to believe that selecting a large number of stocks at random will give as good as a return as carefully selecting another set of stocks. This **random-walk theory** is based on the hypothesis that the current price of a stock already takes into account the present worth of a company and its future prospects as seen by the experts. In fact, according to this theory, the best strategy might be to buy and then hold a random selection of stocks for a long time. In this way you need not spend as much on sales commissions and should do as well as the market in general, which means that you can expect an 8 to 15 percent annual return on an investment over the long run. Otherwise, you risk buying high and selling low. See Box 16.1 for an overview of stock market behavior.

random walk theory: the hypothesis that no one can consistently outguess the stock market and make money by choosing the best stocks, because there is no secret information; thus, the best strategy for investing in the stock market is to choose a large number of randomly selected stocks and then hold on to them.

Equity Mutual Funds

The idea that randomly selected stocks perform as well as rationally, well-selected stocks is still not accepted by everyone. The presumption that the "experts" should outperform the individual investor lies behind **mutual funds**. These funds are run by companies that sell shares to individual investors and then pool this money to buy a range of carefully selected stocks that the investment fund managers believe will outperform the stock market in general. Because of the large number of investors in a given fund, each investor bears only a small part of the cost of hiring the best (highest-paid) financial advisers to run their investments. Investment fund managers do not readily accept the random-walk theory, because it strikes at the heart of one of their major selling points: expertise. Nevertheless, investment funds have other advantages. For example, they can limit the risk of loss to a small investor, because investment funds generally spread their ownership, or diversify, in

BOX 16.1 **MAKING A KILLING IN THE MARKET**

Watching the stock market can be a fascinating avocation. Prices change daily, and the connection to world and national events is so real and yet so mysterious that watching the market has all the ingredients of a good spy novel. But can you earn a living at it?

The answer depends on your skill and your luck. Certainly, large fortunes have been made and lost in the market. But first you need to understand that "the stock market" is really composed of several markets in which stocks can be exchanged. The largest and most famous one is the New York Stock Exchange. Most large, well-known corporations trade their stock on this exchange. But there are other national exchanges such as the American Stock Exchange as well as regional or local exchanges in which brokers can conduct stock sales without going through New York.

Because the overall health of the stock market is of considerable interest to investors, several averages have been developed to give a market overview. Two of the most frequently cited are the Dow Jones Industrial Average and the Standard and Poor's Composite Index. The Dow Jones Index mointors the progress of thirty U.S. corporations that are considered leaders in their fields. These are sometimes called *blue-chip* stocks, because they are supposed to be the best. The Standard and Poor's Index is a broader measure that includes the prices of 500 stocks. A rise in either index indicates that the average share prices of stocks are increasing.

Some experts take an increase in these indexes as a sign of the future prosperity of the economy. In fact, the government includes stock prices in its index of leading economic indicators. Whenever the market is rising, shareholders tend to be opti-

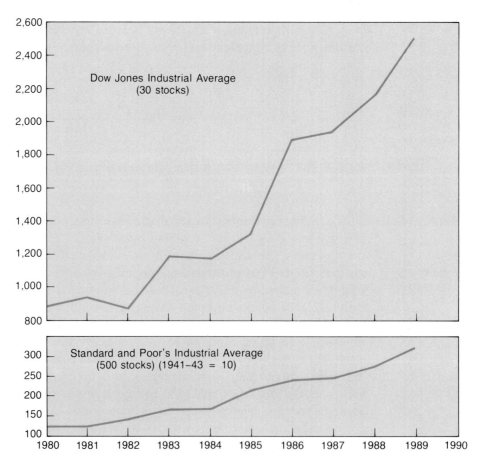

mistic and are said to be *bullish*. When the market declines or is expected to decline, a pessimism settles over investors and they are said to be *bearish*. Thus, a bull symbolizes an optimist, and a bear symbolizes a pessimist. In the figure on page 560, you can see waves of bullish and bearish behavior, as stock prices have risen and fallen in a wavelike pattern. Overall, the bulls seem to be winning.

Making money in the market requires good timing as well as good stock selection. If you are really going to do well, you must have a feel for forecasting the ups and downs of the market. Contrary to the opinion of many speculators, no one has yet demonstrated a consistent ability to do this. Some people have made themselves rich and famous by correctly predicting a turn in the stock market. But in the long haul, the evidence seems to indicate that the additional expense in sales commissions for the average investor is not compensated by higher profits. The buy-and-hold strategy, in which one buys high quality stocks and then holds on while the market averages follow a roller-coaster pattern, seems to promise greater returns.

hundreds of corporations in different industries. Thus, they avoid the small investor's dilemma of putting all of his or her eggs in one basket. If you like the idea of diversifying the risk but you don't believe that the high-paid investment advisers will be able to do better than the market average, you can buy an **index fund**, which mirrors the composition of the 500 stocks in the Standard and Poor's Index. Figure 16.4 illustrates the record for such investments over the past decade. Looking at that figure, you can certainly see the rationale for index funds.

Different investment funds may have different investment objectives. Some funds, such as "aggressive" or "growth-oriented" funds, try to invest in stocks that offer the greatest potential for capital gains. These funds are not concerned with earning high dividends in the present. They want to see the value of their investment grow in the future. Aggressive funds take higher risks than growth funds. Other investment funds seek to

FIGURE 16.4
Return on investment over a ten-year period: mutual funds versus random-walk. (SOURCE: Investment Company Institute, *Mutual Fund Fact Book* [Washington, D.C., 1989], p. 24.)

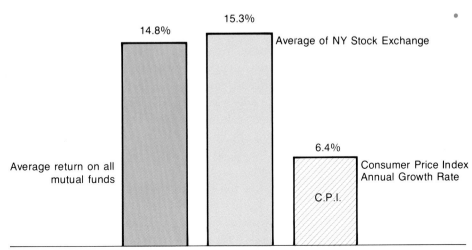

maximize current income rather than to invest in stocks that will rise in price in the future and provide big capital gains. The stress on current income causes these funds to look for preferred stocks and bonds that are offering higher dividends and interest. The remaining investment funds either try to balance the conflicting objectives of current income and long-term growth, or they seek to make high returns by specializing in a particular commodity like gold, chemicals, or foreign exchange.

Despite their wide variety of investment strategies, investment funds have only two major organizational forms: closed-end and open-end. **Closed-end mutual funds** sell a fixed number of shares and then go about their business of getting the highest possible return for their shareholders. Closed-end shares are traded in the same way that common stocks of any other publicly held firm are traded. **Open-end mutual funds**, often simply called mutual funds, issue shares on demand, and they will buy back any shares that someone wishes to sell. Some open-end mutual funds add a sales charge called a **load** whenever someone buys into the fund. Load mutual funds are usually sold through stockbrokers or mutual fund salespeople. Other open-end mutual funds are called **no-load mutual funds** because they do not have a sales charge added to the purchase price. Shares in these funds are generally bought directly from the investment company, either by mail or phone.

No-load mutual funds seem to offer the small investor a better deal because they put all of the investment into shares. Most research supports this hypothesis. A recent study of 542 equity mutual funds found that, on the average, no-load funds performed slightly better than load funds for the most recent one-, five-, and ten-year periods (Sebastian, 1986). Nevertheless, a particular no-load fund may not be the best investment if it buys the wrong stocks or has a different investment objective than yours. Before you decide to invest in one of the funds, always do some research on the past success of the fund, its current portfolio of investments, and its plan for the future. Most of this information will be contained in a brochure called a **prospectus**, available from the company. You can also consult the summaries of various funds published periodically in the financial section of your local newspaper, in weekly publications like *Barrons*, or in monthly magazines like *Money* or *Changing Times*.

The major advantages of investing in a mutual fund rather than directly in the stock market are the diversification and management services provided by the fund, not the chance for a big return. By buying into an investment portfolio that is managed by the experts, one is able to limit one's risk and management costs because one is leaving the task of watching the market to someone else. On the other hand, it is often difficult for large mutual funds to move quickly to take advantage of investment opportunities, whereas a small investor can get in, make a profit, and get out, without encountering the inertia that seems part and

prospectus: a brochure available from a company that describes its previous financial success or performance; necessary if one is to evaluate the risk of an investment

parcel of a large firm. Thus, one can expect one's lower risk to be reflected in lower potential yields. This trade-off should be weighed in a decision-making grid like the one for trade-offs among car size, fuel economy, and safety in Table 12.1. Remember, the decision-making model applies to investing just as it does to consuming.

Real Estate

Will Rogers, a famous comedian two generations back, offered this funny but true piece of investment advice: "Buy land. They ain't making any more of the stuff." The fact is that real estate can be a good and, in some cases, profitable investment, if one can accurately gauge the demand for land or buildings. People have to live and work somewhere, and real estate that is located in areas to which people are migrating is a better investment: Its value increases because the demand for it is growing. Unless investors have special information that others do not about demand in a particular area, for example, that a huge company is going to build its new plant in a certain city, they have the same problem investing in real estate that they have in buying stocks or mutual funds.

Investing in unimproved land has other drawbacks as well. Vacant land, unlike financial securities, does not provide an annual return. There are no dividends or interest payments to offset the investment costs or the taxes incurred while awaiting a prospective rise in land values. For example, if you used $10,000 of your own money to buy a vacant lot and then you sold it three years later for $13,000, did you make a good investment? Well, it looks like a 30 percent profit at first ($3,000 ÷ $10,000 = 30 percent), but do not forget the opportunity-cost concept. What was the next best alternative? If you had put your money in a savings account, you would not have earned such a return. However, CDs sometimes pay 10 percent interest; compounded annually, that comes to a 33 percent return over three years. Taxes and real estate commissions further complicate the comparison, but clearly, a simple increase in the value of your vacant land does not mean that you made a good investment.

The final characteristic to consider before you decide to invest in vacant land is liquidity. How easy is it to convert your ownership in that land into cash? Land is notoriously difficult to sell. If you are curious about this, simply call a real estate agent and mention that you are interested in underdeveloped property. You will get a list that will take months to go through, and much of the land will have been on the market for years.

Of course, vacant land is not the only form of real estate investment. As we mentioned earlier in this chapter, private housing has been shown to be a good investment. Buying your own home or condominium combines some nice tax advantages with long-term capital gain and short-term housing services. This kind of investment still suffers from some liquidity

FIGURE 16.5 Education and earnings. (SOURCE: U.S. Bureau of the Census, "Money Income of Households, Families, and Persons in the United States," *Current Population Reports*, F–60 series [Washington, D.C.: U.S. Government Printing Office, 1982].)

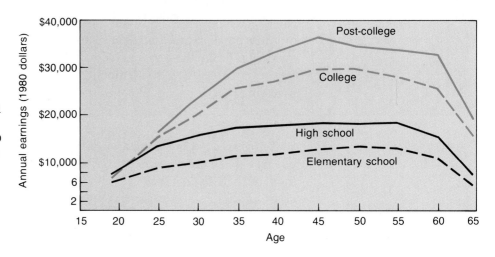

problems, but it is more liquid than other real estate ventures and certainly not as risky.

Human Capital

No discussion of alternative investments would be complete without mentioning one of the best investments available to everyone: oneself. It may seem odd to think of investing in yourself, but surely you and your parents have been doing just that. Your parents and you have been devoting resources to your education so that you will be a more productive member of society. In general, greater productivity leads to a higher income, which translates into a higher yield in investment terms (Putka, 1988). As Figure 16.5 shows, the average lifetime earnings of college graduates rise more rapidly and stay at higher levels than do the earnings of the less educated. Moreover, these data cannot quantify the psychological and life-enriching experiences that would be difficult and expensive to obtain elsewhere.

Of course, not all of the investment principles show a university education in such a favorable light. While there is not much risk, there is some. You are not guaranteed to earn more than a high school graduate. Liquidity is also very low, as anyone who has tried to turn his or her degree into cash is well aware. Finally, there are few tax advantages associated directly with a college degree, although some courses may help you to use the tax laws to your advantage.

COMPARING VARIOUS INVESTMENTS

Table 16.3 presents the investments we have just discussed and compares their strengths and weaknesses in seven major categories. As you can see, there is no "perfect" investment. All involve some trade-offs among goals.

TABLE 16.3 The Strengths and Weaknesses of Various Investments

Investment	Average Annual Yield	Risk	Possibility of Capital Gain and Long-Term Growth	Liquidity	Inflation Hedge	Information, Transaction, and Management Costs	Preferred Tax Status
Savings account	5%	None (up to $100,000)	None	High	Poor	Low	None
CDs	7–10%	None (up to $100,000)	None	Moderate	Moderate	None	None
U.S. Savings bonds	6–8%	None	None	Moderate	Poor	None	Moderate
Money market fund	6–9%	Low	Low	High	Moderate	Low	None or high (tax-exempt funds)
Common stocks	0–10%	Moderate to high	Moderate to high	Moderate	Moderate	Moderate to high	Low
Mutual funds	0–8%	Moderate	Low to moderate	Moderate	Moderate	Low to moderate	Low
Municipal bonds	4–6%	Low to moderate	Low	Moderate	Poor	Moderate	High
Real estate							
Unimproved land	0%	High	High	Low	High	High	Low
Housing	0–8%	Moderate	High	Low	High	Moderate	Moderate
College education	8–12%	Low	High	Low	Moderate	Moderate	Low
Cash	0%	Low	None	High	Poor	None	None

The investments that have the lowest risks are generally the ones that also have lower yields or fewer prospects for capital gains. Liquidity and hedging against inflation are two other characteristics that are subject to a major trade-off. Investments that tend to be highly liquid also seem to provide poor or, at best, moderate protection against inflation. Some forms of investment entail high management and transaction costs, whereas others can be ignored for long periods of time. Investing in common stocks is an example of the former, and buying a U.S. Savings Bond is an example of a "carefree" investment. Finally, the tax status of the return from an investment could be important in an overall investment strategy. As we stressed in Chapter 15, you can only spend after-tax dollars.

Given the variety of potential investments and their complementary, as well as conflicting, natures, you would be well advised to diversify your portfolio. This advice is very much like the proverb, "Don't put all of your eggs in one basket." By diversifying investments, you spread the risk of losing everything in the event of a catastrophe. On the other hand, by spreading the risk you also limit your gain if you guess correctly about the future direction of the economy. This quandary strikes at the heart of investment strategy. How bold should you be? There is no easy answer, but your life-style, comfort zone, and place in the life cycle all play a major role in your investment pattern.

Investment Choices and the Life-Cycle

No two people are exactly alike, but we all travel similar paths. One of the most important common paths is the life cycle outlined in Chapter 3. The regularity of life's requirements and opportunities that the life cycle represents can be used to fashion an intelligent investment strategy. For example, a young person with no dependents and a lifetime of work opportunities ahead might be well advised to engage in investments that involve lower current yields and even moderate to high risks, as long as the potential for long-term growth and capital gains is significant. A college education, as shown in Table 16.3, seems to fit this pattern rather well. A retired couple, on the other hand, should generally seek high-yield investments with little risk. Their concern is more with the immediate prospect of a return than with long-term growth and capital gains. Middle-aged investors in their peak earning years may be more concerned than other investors with tax advantages. They will probably seek to defer current income and look for capital gains or seek tax-exempt mutual funds to lessen their tax bite. Liquidity may not be as important to them as to the retired couple because their employment provides a steady cash flow.

These are only a few of the possible scenarios that could be developed to complement the varying needs of investors. The point is that no one knows your needs better than you do. Nor can anyone else estimate how much risk you are willing to assume. Now that you have an idea of how the investment world works, you can begin making some plans, setting some goals, saving, investing, and living with risk.

SUMMARY

Few areas are as confusing and yet as important to the average consumer as the world of investment and personal finance. Some of the essential concepts that you need to understand before making an investment decision are yield, risk, liquidity, inflation hedge, transaction costs, and tax status. As we stressed earlier, there is no such thing as a perfect investment, one that will outperform all others on all of these criteria. Some investments are better at providing high yields than at providing low risks. Others provide an inflation hedge, but at the cost of low liquidity. You need to gather enough information on a variety of investments so that you can accurately gauge the trade-offs involved in choosing among them.

Creating your own investment portfolio depends in large measure on your life-style, your place in the life cycle, and your ability to handle risk. If you are a risk taker, the potential gains from investments in common stocks or real estate will probably outweigh the fear of loss, the lack of liquidity, and the information, transaction, and management costs that accompany such ventures. If security is more important to you, bank CDs and U.S. Treasury bills offer a reasonable return with little chance of loss. For the small-scale investor who wants more liquidity, money market funds may prove to be a better investment. You can make these decisions yourself, or you can hire someone to make them for you, but in the final analysis, you must assume responsibility for those decisions, because you will bear the consequences.

QUESTIONS

1. What are the major reasons for saving? Give an example of each, and estimate how long it would take you to satisfy each goal.
2. Explain why a high-risk investment has to offer a better than average return in order for people to invest in it.
3. What is the most liquid kind of investment? How would such an investment fare in times of high inflation? How would it do in times of falling prices (deflation)?
4. Why is there no such thing as a perfect investment? How is this related to creating an investment portfolio?
5. Briefly explain the advantages of investing in U.S. Savings Bonds. What are the disadvantages? Would they be a good investment for you? Why?
6. What are the differences between T-bills, U.S. Treasury notes, and U.S. Treasury bonds? Would they be a better investment for you than U.S. Savings Bonds? Explain your answer.
7. What is a money market mutual fund and how does it compare to an equity mutual fund? Which one would you choose, and why?

REFERENCES AND READINGS

"CDs: These Once Dull Investments Now Offer Great Interest." *Money*, July 1988.

"Collectibles: What's Hot, What's Not." *Changing Times*, November 1987.

"A Dozen Painless Ways to Help a Nest Egg Grow." *U.S. News & World Report*, June 8, 1987.

Eisenberg, Richard. *How to Avoid A Mid-Life Financial Crisis*. New York: Penguin Books, 1988.

Investment Company Institute. *1988 Mutual Fund Fact Book*. Washington D.C.: The Institute, published annually.

Putka, Gary. Benefit of B.A. Is Greater Than Ever," *Wall Street Journal*, August 17, 1988.

Sebastian, Pamela. "Loaded Down: High Fund Charges Don't Always Mean High Returns." *Wall Street Journal*, December 1, 1986.

"What to Do with a Little Bit of Money." *Changing Times*, August 1988.

Chapter Seventeen

PLANNING FOR YOUR FUTURE: INSURANCE, RETIREMENT, AND BEYOND

☐ Life Insurance
☐ Retirement
☐ Making a Will
☐ Funeral and Burial Arrangements

DID YOU KNOW THAT...

... there are two basic types of insurance policies: term policies, which pay off only in case of death, and cash-value policies, which add a savings account to the death provision?

... insurance dividends on participating policies are nontaxable because they are considered refunds of an overcharge?

... group life insurance is generally the least expensive way to buy life insurance?

... insurance premiums for identical policies from two companies often vary by 100 percent and sometimes by as much as 400 percent?

... a study by the FTC showed that 20 percent of all new whole-life insurance policies were canceled by consumers in the first year and that even for those policies held for ten years, the average yield on the savings portion was less than 2 percent?

... Social Security automatically provides life insurance benefits based on one's contribution to the program?

. . . there is a straigthforward way to calculate how much life insurance one needs to provide income for dependents, including the value of Social Security benefits and inflation?

. . . by the time today's teenagers are ready to retire, the proportion of the U.S. population 65 and over will be 33 percent higher than it is today?

. . . company pension plans are regulated and guaranteed under federal law, and employees' pensions cannot be taken away once they are "vested"?

. . . even if you have never written a will, your state already has one prepared for you?

. . . misinformation and poor decision making lead most consumers to pay 50 percent more in funeral costs than they should, regardless of the type of funeral desired?

The information in this chapter is oriented toward helping you plan for your future. We begin with a discussion of life insurance, a subject about which many consumers make poor decisions because they are ignorant of its fundamentals. It is ironic that consumers are willing to spend more time shopping for a used car than shopping for life insurance. A poor decision about an automobile is fairly easy to identify and not terribly expensive to correct. But an error in a life insurance decision can cost a consumer thousands of dollars, and it may not be discovered until the family has to pay the consequences, 10, 20, or even 30 years after the policy is purchased. In our first major section, we will outline the principles behind life insurance and give you some insight into the kind and amount of life insurance that is right for you.

Life insurance can do more than provide death benefits to the survivors of an insured person; it can also provide retirement income. Our second major section looks at the retirement phase of the life cycle and goes beyond life insurance to compare various pensions plans, from Social Security to Individual Retirement Accounts and Keogh plans. There has been a great deal of recent legislation in the area of retirement plans and pension funds, and a little familiarity with your rights can pay off as you plan for your future.

Making a will is an integral part of planning for your future and for the disposition of your worldly possessions. It may surprise you to know that you already have a will, even if you have never drawn one up for yourself. We will outline your current will and suggest how you can change it.

Finally, we turn to the ultimate consumer expenditure: a funeral. You will undoubtedly be involved in a number of funerals during your lifetime, and some knowledge about what is involved and how to handle it should prove helpful to you and to others who may depend on you for support during such troubled times.

LIFE INSURANCE

premium: the amount paid for insurance of any type; can be paid in installments

In a typical year more than 30 million life insurance policies will be written for new or additional coverage. Today, there are more than 150 million life insurance policyholders who pay $160 billion annually for their policies. Obviously, the life insurance industry must be offering the American consumer something in return for this tremendous expenditure. But what are consumers getting in return? Are they paying too much?

Life insurance, like other types of insurance, such as auto, home, and health, is an agreement on a consumer's part to give up a small, definite amount of income in the present—a **premium**—in order to be protected from some uncertain but potentially greater loss in the future. It is a way of managing risk. In the case of homeowner's insurance, the probability that the homeowner will make a claim is not certain. One could go through life without a fire or a theft and thus never invoke one's right to payment. With life insurance, on the other hand, death is always a possibility, and at some point it is a certainty. Insurance companies are well aware that the laws of immortality apply only in the afterlife. Thus, at some point they will have to pay off. If this is so, how can they afford to offer a large payment in the event of the death of a policyholder? The answer lies in the regularity of mortality.

Figure 17.1 illustrates this regularity in a population whose average life expectancy at birth is 70. As you can see, the risk of death drops dramatically during the first few years of life and rises steadily thereafter. If a company insures a large number of people across the age spectrum, it

FIGURE 17.1
Death rate at various ages. (SOURCE: Based on United Nations, *Methods for Population Projections by Sex and Age* [New York: United Nations, 1956].)

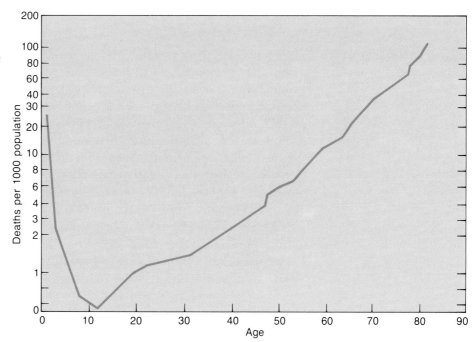

can spread this risk over a great number of policyholders. If hundreds of thousands of people are insured, the millions of dollars received in small premiums allow the companies to pay large claims to families of the relatively few unfortunate souls who die in any given year. In addition to taking advantage of this law of large numbers, insurance companies can adjust their charges to account for the particular age of the policyholder. For example, because a 60-year-old policyholder is twice as likely to die as a 50-year-old policyholder, the rates may be doubled to ensure that no age group subsidizes any other. Insurance employees who calculate these death probabilities are called **actuaries**, and they are good at what they do. They collect death probabilities based on the real-world behavior of death rates classified by age, sex, health, and sometimes life-style (for example, smoker, nonsmoker, drinker, nondrinker). These characteristics are then used to determine the risk of death and the cost of insuring someone against this risk. All this information is put into an **actuarial table**, which lists the probability that a person with certain characteristics will die in a given year.

actuaries: persons who compute insurance premiums according to probabilities based on historical risks for various age groups

In essence then, life insurance can be viewed in much the same way as any other wager. The odds are established by the actuarial tables produced by insurance actuaries. Given the odds, the policyholder bets that he or she will die, and the insurance company pays off only when the policyholder is correct. Given this situation, it is little wonder that insurance companies often support antismoking campaigns, jog-a-thons, and other sporting events that encourage fitness and longevity. They have a genuine interest in keeping people alive and healthy.

Types of Insurance Companies

Insurance companies take one of two forms; they are either stock insurance companies or mutual insurance companies. **Stock insurance companies** have a structure that mirrors those of all modern publicly held corporations. They are owned by shareholders who expect dividends as a return on their investment. More than 90 percent of all life insurance companies are stockholder owned, and they account for about 55 percent of the insurance in force. **Mutual insurance companies** compose a much smaller proportion of the industry, but they account for almost half of life insurance policies. These companies are technically owned and controlled by policyholders, who share in the profits of the company through dividends or reductions in their annual premiums. Insurance offered by mutual insurance companies is often called **participating life insurance**, because the policyholder gets to participate in voting for the company's board of directors and has the right to earn dividends on the policy. In reality, the voting power of any one policyholder is very slight, but the dividend rebate can be significant when one compares the relative costs of competing policies.

Because the dividend rate on a participating policy is never guaranteed by the insurance company, one does not know the exact amount of the annual rebate. However, in a study conducted by Consumers Union, participating policies were shown to be less expensive than nonparticipating policies in about 75 percent of the cases. Nevertheless, if one prefers to limit one's risk, a nonparticipating policy for which the cost is fixed and guaranteed might be preferable to a participating policy in which there is no assurance of a refund. For example, the annual premium for a $100,000 life insurance policy for a 35-year-old male might be $260 for a nonparticipating policy but $320 for a participating one. If the participating policy has been paying a 25 percent dividend, its annual premium will be only $240—$20 cheaper than the other policy. Dividends are never guaranteed, however, and they could decline, making the nonparticipating policy a better buy. Before you select a participating policy, you should ask for the insurance company's dividend record over several years, not just the previous year.

Four Ways to Buy Life Insurance

Life insurance is sometimes classified by how it is sold. You can buy life insurance from an agent in your own home, through your employer, or from a retailer who has just sold you a new car on credit. Life insurance companies also distinguish between insurance policies on the basis of *how* you pay—that is, whether you send in payments or an agent comes to collect them. The following sections describe four types of insurance: individual, group, credit, and industrial.

Individual life insurance. As Figure 17.2 shows, 37 percent of all life insurance policies are purchased by individuals through an insurance agent who issues a policy tailored to the particular needs of a consumer.

FIGURE 17.2
Life insurance policies by number and dollar value. (SOURCE: Data from American Council of Life Insurance, *Life Insurance Factbook* [1988], p. 16.)

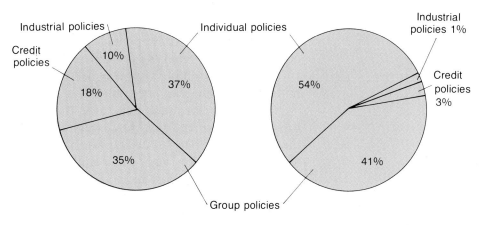

Share of the number of policies   Share in the dollar value of policies

Before the policy goes into effect, however, the insured person is generally required to undergo a physical examination so that the insurance company can more accurately estimate its risk. The poorer the health of the insured person, the higher the insurance premium.

Group life insurance. Members of a particular association or workers who have a common employer are often able to purchase life insurance as a group rather than on an individual basis. **Group life insurance** generally does not require a physical examination, because the group is large enough to allow premiums to be based on the life expectancies of people in that occupation or association. Often, there is no agent involved in the sale, and all correspondence is completed between the insurance company and the insured person. Because this type of insurance requires fewer intermediaries, it is often less expensive than individual life insurance, for which sales commissions have to be paid.

Another cost advantage is available to some consumers who belong to groups for which the life expectancy is better than average. College professors, for example, have exceptionally long lives and thus are often able to purchase group life insurance at lower rates than people in other occupations. Finally, because physical examinations are the exception rather than the rule, group insurance is a good buy for those in poor health.

Credit life insurance. As Figure 17.2 shows, 18 percent of all insurance policies—3 percent of the value of all life insurance—are categorized as **credit life insurance**. These policies are written to ensure prompt payment of a loan in the event of the borrower's death. In essence, credit life insurance is really loan death insurance. It is standard procedure among banks and finance companies to try to persuade their loan customers to insure themselves for the amount of the loan. Because these policies are for small amounts of money and because no physical examinations or, generally, adjustments for the life expectancy of the borrower are involved, these policies are usually quite expensive per dollar of insurance. This makes them a poor choice for the average consumer.

If credit life insurance is not a good buy, why were there more than 70 million credit life insurance policies in force in 1987? Part of the reason probably lies in consumer ignorance. Many consumers do not know that these policies are *optional*; they cannot be a requirement of a loan. Second, these policies *appear* to be inexpensive because they increase the cost of a loan payment by only a few dollars. But if those dollars were spent on additional individual or group life insurance, they could buy more insurance coverage. However, consumer ignorance does not explain all behavior concerning credit insurance. Some consumers are willing to pay higher premiums for the peace of mind that credit insurance gives them.

There is clearly a trade-off here. Obtaining credit insurance is easy and quick. Getting additional insurance on an individual or group basis takes time, and although it is cheaper, some consumers value their time more than they value the dollar saving.

Industrial life insurance. In 1900, when the United States life insurance industry was still in its infancy, the majority of insurance policies were industrial life policies. **Industrial life insurance** was sold on a door-to-door basis, largely to working-class Americans, who paid their premiums weekly to the agent who wrote the policy. They were fairly small policies, written for people whose death rates and incomes matched their dirty and dangerous jobs in early industrial America. Premiums were high for the coverage offered because they had to pay for the increasingly expensive weekly collection services and door-to-door sales techniques of the insurance agents. As the insurance industry grew, individual and group life insurance policies quickly emerged as lower-cost alternatives to industrial life policies. Nevertheless, these industrial policies and their descendants, more correctly described as **home-service life insurance policies**, continue to be purchased by a small but sizable number of consumers. Very few of these policies are issued for more than $2,000. In 1987 the average policy was worth $640.

About the only positive attribute of these policies is the convenience of having a salesperson come to your door to collect the weekly or monthly premium. But as Figure 17.2 shows, only about 1 percent of the value of all policies resides in home-service policies. These policies offer so little coverage and their overhead costs are so high that this category of insurance is practically useless for consumers.

As you may have realized by this point, the insurance industry has a vocabulary that could challenge even the investment counselor's for complexity. Individual life, group life, credit, and industrial life insurance are distinguished from one another based on *how* they are sold. In the following section, we introduce insurance policies that can be distinguished from one another on the basis of *why* they are bought. These policies have different objectives and suit different consumer needs. Some policies provide protection only in the event of death. Others incorporate a savings component with the death benefits. Still others are more closely related to some of the investment strategies we discussed in Chapter 16. These investment-oriented policies may stress tax advantages, retirement provisions, growth potential, or a combination. As we progress through the next few sections, you would do well to recall that there are only two major differences between these policies: one kind of policy pays off *only* in the case of death; the other kind of policy combines death insurance with a savings, or cash-value, component, so the policyholder can get money back if he or she lives.

Term Insurance

term insurance: life insurance payable to a beneficiary only if the insured person dies within a specified period; sometimes referred to as death insurance

Term insurance is the simplest form of life insurance. Under a **term insurance policy**, an individual's life is insured against death for a certain period of time (a term), which generally varies from one to five years. Term insurance also has a fixed price. Insurance agents frequently refer to term insurance as "death insurance" rather than "life insurance," because the policy pays off only in the event of the insured person's death. Thus, term insurance is similar to auto insurance (see Chapter 12) and health insurance (see Chapter 14): It pays off only in the event of a loss. But unlike auto or health insurance, a term life insurance policy pays the full amount of the policy in one lump sum, provided, of course, that none of the provisions of the policy are violated. For example, some policies do not cover death during warfare or while one is pursuing a dangerous activity such as skydiving or mountain climbing. However, if the insured person does not die during the term of the policy, all payments made to the company remain there. If no death occurs, the person holding a term insurance policy is just like a consumer with an automobile insurance policy and no accidents. No one gets paid.

Level term insurance. A common form of term insurance is **level term insurance**. It provides a constant level of protection throughout the term of the life insurance contract. Figure 17.3(a) shows the protection benefit of level term insurance. An important clause to look for in any level term insurance contract is its renewability. **Renewable term life insurance** differs from other term insurance in that it contains a clause that guarantees the insured person's right to renew the policy for another term, generally five years. Of course, as Figure 17.3(b) shows, the premium is higher because of the increased age of the insured person, but a physical examination is not required to continue the policy at the original death-benefit level. Most renewability clauses end at age 65 or 70 but some companies agree to renew policies to age 100. Because the death rates rise dramatically as one gets older, so do the annual premiums.

Decreasing term insurance. Term insurance is generally the cheapest per $1,000 of insurance because it provides only death protection; there is no cash value returned to a policyholder who survives. Figure 17.3(b) shows, however, that even the cost of maintaining a given term policy rises as an insured person ages. To counteract this rise in the cost of a policy, many companies offer **decreasing term insurance**. Under this policy, the total cost to the policyholder remains constant from year to year, but the amount of insurance protection decreases each year to take into account the higher risk of death. Thus, each year the same premium buys less coverage, as Figures 17.3(c) and (d) show. Another form of term insurance often taken out by homeowners when they buy a house is known as

**FIGURE 17.3
Protection versus cost
in various types of term
insurance.**

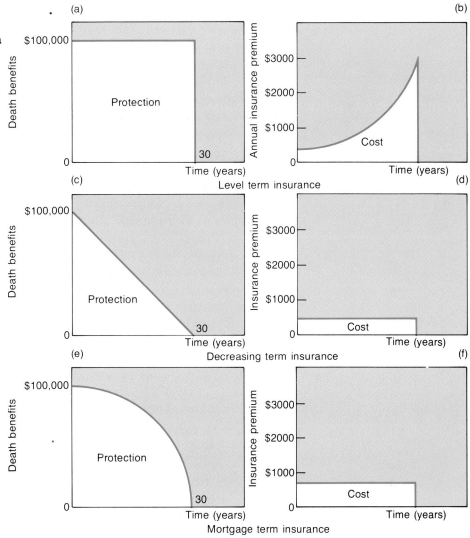

(a) Level term insurance

(c) (d) Decreasing term insurance

(e) (f) Mortgage term insurance

mortgage term insurance. Under this policy, insurance protection does not decrease at a uniform rate—see Figures 17.3(e) and (f). It remains high in the early years of the policy, when most of a homeowner's house payment goes to pay interest on the loan and does not reduce the mortgage principal by much. As the years pass, the mortgage payments reduce the indebtedness, so the amount owed to the bank remains about the same as the value of the insurance policy. In the event of death, the mortgage is paid off by such a policy. The same principle applies to credit insurance that some consumers buy when they finance a big purchase like a car or furniture.

The cost of term insurance. The cost of a term insurance policy depends on a number of variables. The age and sex of the insured person, the amount of type of coverage, the cost of administering the policy, and the insurance company's actuarial rates are some of the more important ones. Even though death rates are fairly predictable, insurance company premiums are not. It is common to find that some insurance companies charge twice as much as a competitor does for identical coverage. Some commentators have found price differences of almost 300 percent for similar policies (*Consumer Reports*, 1986a). Such price differences can continue only if consumer information is limited and consumer decision making is impaired. In such an environment it is worthwhile for most consumers to spend additional time seeking information and practicing the principles of decision making presented in Chapter 1. According to Barry Kaye (1981), ''Very simply, people are paying too much for life insurance because they won't stop, shop, and compare. Literally thousands of dollars can be saved through careful analysis of existing and new policies.''

It is obvious that many consumers are not making thoughtful decisions when it comes to buying life insurance. Many consumers are duped into buying outrageously expensive policies that provide inadequate coverage. One example involves television commercials for life insurance marketed to the elderly featuring some familiar and supposedly trustworthy personalities. In 1987 Tennessee Ernie Ford, Dick Van Dyke, Eddie Albert, Betty White, Gavin MacLeod, and Muhammad Ali were all charged by Florida's Department of Insurance with appearing in misleading TV ads for term insurance. Dick Van Dyke's ad was especially revealing. He said that a 45-year-old man could get up to $40,000 of protection for just 65 cents per day. What he did *not* say was that the insured man had to die in an *accident* to collect this sum. If this 45-year-old died of natural causes, the death benefit would be $9,600. And that innocuous 65¢ per day amounts to an annual premium of $237. That's enough to secure a $100,000 term life insurance policy from most reputable companies.

How much should you pay for term life insurance? Table 17.1 was developed by the National Insurance Consumer Organization to serve as a guideline for rates on renewable term insurance. Multiply the rate by each $1,000 of coverage that you want and then add $60 for a commission. This should give you a useful benchmark by which to compare policies. For example, a 35-year-old nonsmoking female who wants a $100,000 policy should be willing to pay about $134. That is $(100 \times \$0.74) + \$60 = \$134$. Notice that if she smoked, the same policy would be $190 because of her increased risk of death.

Evaluating term insurance. Term insurance is one of the most highly recommended forms of life insurance. Consumers Union, the nonprofit

TABLE 17.1 Benchmark Rates for the Annual Cost per $1,000 of Protection Using Low-Cost Term Life Insurance

Age	Nonsmokers		Smokers	
	Male	**Female**	**Male**	**Female**
18–30	$0.76	$0.68	$1.05	$1.01
35	0.80	0.74	1.36	1.26
40	1.03	0.95	2.06	1.65
45	1.45	1.20	2.95	2.30
50	2.60	1.76	4.16	3.30

SOURCES: National Consumer Insurance Organization (1–800–533–0777; 1–312–993–0355); *Changing Times*, 1988a.

organization mentioned in Chapter 9, has urged consumers to choose term insurance ever since its first study conducted in 1937 (*Consumer Reports*, 1986a). In addition to being the cheapest insurance, term insurance has the advantage of offering especially low premiums to households headed by younger adults. Families in the early stage of their life cycle can be especially hard hit if they lose their major source of income. Term insurance matches the life-cycle needs of most families because it is least expensive in the early years and more expensive later, when a family has additional purchasing power and decreasing obligations to children.

Term insurance can be subject to certain pitfalls, however. For example some insurance companies are willing to write term policies that have very low rates for the first year or two, but then rise dramatically. Other term insurers have begun to issue **revertible term policies**, which require policyholders to take a medical exam each time their policies are due to be renewed (*Consumer Reports*, 1988). Given your unknown medical future, this gamble is not worth the few dollars you may save now versus the coverage you stand to lose in the future. If you choose term insurance, you should insist on a renewability clause that disregards future health hazards.

The problem of renewability and escalating payments are alleviated by another life insurance product that combines death protection provisions with a savings plan. In the next section we will explain these cash-value policies.

Cash-Value Insurance Policies

There are a variety of **cash-value insurance policies**, but they all have some elements in common. In return for an annual premium that remains constant as long as the policy is in force, cash-value policies provide death insurance along with a savings account that increases in value throughout the life of the policy. If the policyholder dies while the policy is in force, only the death benefit is paid. In this case, a cash-value policy operates like a term policy. However, if the policyholder survives, the savings portion (cash value) of the policy builds, and the policyholder can elect to borrow part of it, use it to pay the premium, convert it into a retirement income, or take it all in a lump sum.

Whole life insurance: a savings-plus plan. The most popular form of cash-value insurance is called **whole life insurance**. Like term insurance, a whole life insurance policy pays a stipulated amount—the "face value"—in the event of the death of the insured person. But unlike term insurance policies, the annual cost of a whole life policy remains constant, even though the risk of death increases as the policyholder ages. The premium remains constant because the buildup of the cash value helps to reduce the insurance company's risk in that the company never pays more than the face value of the policy. The cash-value provision is much like a savings account. During the life of the policy, part of the insurance premium is set aside and invested by the insurance company. This reserve increases over time and earns interest at a predetermined fixed rate. In essence, then, someone who buys a whole life policy is buying death insurance plus a savings account for a fixed yearly fee. As you might suspect, however, this fee is significantly higher than the cost of term insurance during the early years of the policy.

As Figure 17.4 shows, the cash-value, or savings, portion of a whole life policy generally does not begin for a few years. In the early years of the

whole life: life insurance that combines term insurance with a cash value or "forced savings" plan; sometimes called straight life insurance or ordinary life insurance

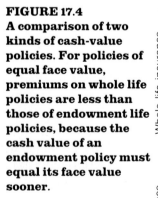

FIGURE 17.4
A comparison of two kinds of cash-value policies. For policies of equal face value, premiums on whole life policies are less than those of endowment life policies, because the cash value of an endowment policy must equal its face value sooner.

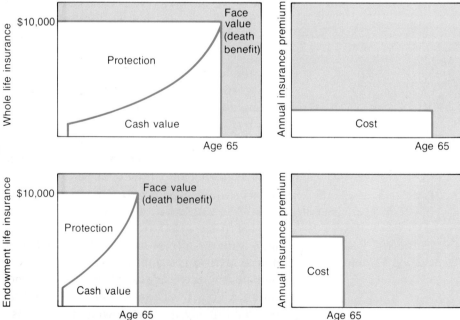

policy, administration costs and sales commissions take most of the funds not reserved for death benefits. In fact, one reason that life insurance salespeople are so eager to sell whole life policies is that the sales commission is eight times greater than that of comparable term insurance policies (Belth, 1985, p. 159). Given the heavy sales and administrative expenses during the early years of a policy, whole life insurance is an unrewarding way to save in the short term. An FTC study (1979) showed that 20 percent of all new whole life policies were dropped in the first year, resulting in consumer losses of more than $200 million. Even policies held for ten years returned less than a 2 percent yield on the savings component of whole life insurance. According to the FTC, 45 percent of whole life policyholders cancel within ten years and thus earn low and sometimes negative returns on the savings. Nevertheless, as shown in Figure 17.4, the cash values does eventually rise because the insurance company is collecting more than it needs to insure against the risk of the policyholder's death. This surplus is also growing because it is earning nontaxable interest as long as it remains in the insurance policy.

The insured person can withdraw this savings by cashing in the policy and thereby eliminating the death insurance provision, or he or she may continue paying the premium and borrow against the cash value at an interest rate that is generally well below the cost of credit elsewhere. However, the savings account and death insurance features do not pay off simultaneously. For example, in the event of the death of the insured person, the beneficiaries do not receive both the cash value of the policy and the face value of the insurance. Only the death-insurance provision applies in this case. And if any of the cash value was borrowed by the insured person, the face value is reduced by the amount of the loan plus interest owed.

Endowment life insurance. The savings element of whole life insurance is stressed in an **endowment life insurance** policy. This policy also provides some death benefits, but the real emphasis is on building a certain cash reserve in a given period of time, varying from 10 to 30 years or until the insured person reaches a specific age. At the end of the specific time period, the policy matures and the cash value, or "endowment," equals the face value of the policy, as illustrated in Figure 17.4. The insured person can elect to receive the value of the endowment in a lump sum or in annual installments over an extended period of time.

An endowment policy is designed for consumers who want a definite sum of money or income at some future date to supplement or replace their earnings. This income is often combined with other retirement income to ensure a comfortable level of living after a household's paychecks have stopped. The necessity of providing for one's retirement years is clear, but it is not clear that an endowment policy is the best way to do this.

endowment life: a form of whole life insurance that emphasizes the forced-savings feature so that the cash value of the policy builds rapidly

Traditional savings programs and the more recent tax-sheltered retirement programs discussed later in this chapter can offer the same cash values at significantly lower costs.

Single premium life insurance. A major investment advantage of life insurance is the tax-deferred status of the cash value in the policy. The IRS cannot tap the increase in your insurance policy's cash value unless you withdraw these earnings. In an ordinary whole life policy these tax-deferred interest earnings accumulate rather slowly at first because of the initial commissions and fees. It is only after 10 or 15 years that a significant amount of interest is credited to your account. But there are policies specifically designed to take advantage of the tax status of life insurance. One of these policies is called **single-premium life insurance (SPL)**. Like the endowment life insurance policies, SPL policies are aimed at achieving a certain cash value in a given period of time. Unlike the endowment policies, SPL does it all in one fell swoop. The policyholder makes one large payment, which can vary from $2,000 to $1 million. This payment buys a death benefit that depends on the policyholder's age and health. Two people depositing $50,000 in the same policy can obtain vastly different death benefits if one is much older than the other. But the purpose of SPL is not really insurance against the risk of death; rather, it is to build a tax-free investment account.

According to most financial planners this tax-free accumulation is most important to consumers in higher-income tax brackets. They recommend using SPL to finance a child's college education. Simply buy SPLs for your children and let the savings grow untaxed. The difference between ordinary savings and SPL tax shelters can be significant. On a $16,000 investment, for example, a policyholder could accumulate $7,000 more in interest by using an SPL than by putting the money in a bank CD.

Another advantage of SPL policies is their liquidity, i.e., ability to be turned into purchasing power. Once your SPL begins earning interest, you are free to get that interest back in the form of a tax-free loan. Under current IRS rules, you are borrowing against the policy and thus the loan is not taxable income. You can even borrow the principal back at rates around 3 percent. So you really still have some control over your purchasing power. The Congress and the IRS are considering some restrictions on SPL because of these tax advantages.

Universal life insurance. Another form of cash-value life insurance is **universal life insurance**; it differs from traditional whole life insurance in these areas: the interest rate on the cash-value portion of the life insurance policy is variable, not fixed; the policyholder can withdraw funds directly from the cash value without going through the usual borrowing pro-

single premium life: cash-value life insurance policies that require only one large payment that is made at the beginning of the policy period

universal life: similar to whole life insurance, except the cash value is variable, the face value can be changed without rewriting the policy, and cash may be withdrawn directly

cedures; and the face value of the policy can be changed without rewriting the policy.

The key to universal life policies is their variable interest rate. Given the comparatively low (but guaranteed) interest rates that whole life policies have paid in the past, many consumers switched to term insurance for basic protection and invested the money they saved in something that would yield a higher return. As a result, many insurance companies have begun to offer cash-value life insurance for which the interest rate paid on the cash value is tied either to the insurance company's earnings on their investments or to some easily monitored rate, such as the return on government Treasury Bills (see Chapter 16). Some companies also guarantee a minimum return on the cash value, in an effort to minimize the policyholder's risk in choosing a universal life policy over a whole life policy issued by the same company.

Because cash value can accumulate much more rapidly under a variable-rate plan, the amount of insurance protection and risk that the insurance company takes is lessened. As a result, the cost of the death-benefits package declines more rapidly than it does in whole life insurance. Insurance companies that offer universal life insurance deal with this problem in one of two ways. Either they automatically increase the death benefit, so that if the policyholder dies the policy pays more than its face value, or they agree, in the event of a policyholder's death, to add part of the cash value to the death benefit. Thus, universal life is the only kind of cash-value policy that offers to pay *both* the death benefit and part of the cash value.

Table 17.2 compares the growth in the cash values of (1) a universal life insurance policy for which the return is tied to the average performance of the stocks in the Standard and Poor's Index (discussed in Chapter 16), (2) a whole life policy with a 6 percent gross return, and (3) a savings account that yields 5 percent annually. The example assumes that the policyholder bought a $50,000 policy in 1947 at age 32 and paid an annual premium of $673.50 for 33 years until reaching the age of 65. The stock market experienced some significant ups and downs over this period and the policy actually *lost* value between 1956 and 1957 and between 1972 and 1977. Meanwhile the cash value in a standard whole life policy rose predictably, and the savings account continued to accumulate interest on the principal and on the $673.50 in new deposits every year. Despite the ups and downs of the stock market, the universal life insurance policy, based on its movements, would have returned significantly more ($17,369) than a similar investment in a savings account, and it would have provided death insurance besides. It outpaced the standard whole life policy by even *more*: $41,838. However, the future returns on investments in the stock market are certainly not guaranteed. If the stock market does

TABLE 17.2 Death Benefits, Cash Values, and Accumulated Premiums from Universal Life Insurance[a]

End of Policy Year	December 31 of	(1) Cash Value Assuming Hypothetical Gross Annual Investment Return Equal to Standard and Poor's 500 Common Stock Index	(2) Cash Value Assuming Hypothetical Gross Annual Investment Return of 6%	(3) Premiums Accumulated at 5% Interest per Annum[b]
1	1948	150	153	707
2	1949	705	627	1,450
3	1950	1,502	1,124	2,229
4	1951	2,400	1,646	3,048
5	1952	3,392	2,236	3,908
6	1953	3,786	2,855	4,810
7	1954	6,479	3,503	5,758
8	1955	9,084	4,181	6,753
9	1956	10,100	4,889	7,798
10	1957	9,329	5,628	8,895
15	1962	19,247	9,786	15,260
20	1967	34,955	14,777	23,383
25	1972	48,867	20,671	33,751
30	1977	45,763	27,535	46,984
33 (age 65)	1980	73,988	32,150	56,619

[a] Based on a $50,000 policy with $673.50 annual premium issued to a 32-year-old woman on December 31, 1947.
[b] Presents the amount the annual premium would accumulate to if it were deposited in a savings account.

poorly over the next 30 years (or suffers a crash just as one's policy is about to mature), one would do better with a different insurance policy.

Another problem with universal life policies is in trying to compare the costs and expected returns of policies issued by competing insurers. In a way, it is more like choosing an investment option rather than a life insurance policy. It is difficult to gauge which company offers a better return, because there are no guarantees about who will pay the highest return on the cash-value surplus. It may be helpful to ask how the insurance company plans to compute its variable return. Will it be based solely on the stock market or on the return from government bonds, or will it be an average return from the insurance company's investments? You should also ask whether there is a guaranteed minimum return of your cash value. This kind of information can limit your risk.

Which Form of Insurance Is Best for You?

Now that you understand the various types of insurance, you need to decide which one is best for you. The answer depends on your life-style, your life-cycle needs, and your goals and values. No one, not even the most observant and dedicated insurance agent, can tell you what you need. You must decide this for yourself.

Table 17.3 describes the major types of life insurance policies. As you can see, all forms of life insurance have advantages as well as disadvantages. As our earlier discussion indicated, term insurance is clearly the best low-cost alternative, but it is also the most limited in terms of its range of uses. There is no element of forced saving, no sheltering of interest from taxes, no loan provision, and no way to get your money back except by dying, which is not a very inviting idea for most of us. All forms of cash-value insurance have more to offer than the narrowly defined term insurance policies, but they are all more expensive if the object is simply to reduce the financial risk of death. If the objective is to set aside a cash reserve, the new universal life and single-premium life policies offer the greatest potential for yield, but as we learned in Chapter 16, higher yields are often associated with higher risks. However, as the yields cited in the FTC study showed, other forms of cash-value life insurance have not been shown to be good investments if held for less than ten years. Consumers who purchase life insurance policies to help them save also pay the insurance companies for administration and investment counseling. These fees are especially important during the early years of an insurance policy; thus, they reduce the yield more on policies cashed in early rather than on policies that mature.

An additional problem with all insurance policies is the impact of inflation. For example, a person may struggle for 30 years to pay the premium on a whole life policy with a $50,000 death benefit only to discover that an annual inflation rate of 7 percent has reduced the real buying power of the policy to a little over $6,000. Many insurance policyholders have discovered the ravages of inflation much too late to do anything about them. Remember, 30 years from now, $50,000 is not going to give you the same protection that it does today. Before you agree to any policy, you ought to invoke the "rule of 70" for calculating the effects of inflation (see Chapter 3). According to this rule, you can determine how many years it will take for the value of a given sum of money to lose half of its buying power by dividing 70 by the inflation rate. Thus, if you expect a 7 percent inflation rate over the life of your insurance policy, the value of your death benefit (and cash value) will be cut in half every ten years ($70 \div 7 = 10$). So a $50,000 policy will have only $25,000 worth of buying power in 10 years, $12,500 in 20 years, and $6,250 in 30 years.

How Much Life Insurance Do You Need?

In calculating how much life insurance to purchase, there are really only two elements that need to be weighed: the financial losses associated with the death and the assets that can be used to offset those losses. The

TABLE 17.3 Types of Insurance Policies

Characteristics	Term	Whole Life	Single-Premium Life	Endowment Life	Universal Life
Period of premium payment	Specific period of time, such as 5, 10, or 20 years.	For the entire life of insured person.	One initial lump-sum payment.	Stated period of 10, 15, 20, or 30 years, or to age 60 or 65.	Flexible, but premiums can be made over the entire life of the insured person.
When policy matures	Payment made to beneficiary if insured person dies within the term period. After term expires, coverage ends.	At death of insured person.	At death of insured person.	At death of insured person or at the end of the period, if the insured person is still living.	At death of insured person.
Advantages	Maximum protection at minimum cost for stated period of time. Usually may be converted to life or endowment policy without medical examination.	Provides lifetime protection at a constant rate. Investment may be used as income. Insured person may borrow money on the policy.	No additional premiums. Lifetime protection provided. Larger cash and loan values than whole life.	Pays a definite sum of money at the end of the period. Gives insurance coverage while premiums are being paid.	Premium payments are flexible, both in timing and amount. Yield on cash value is variable and geared to market rates. Cash value can be withdrawn with no penalty. Can pay more than the face value at maturity.
Suitable for whom?	Persons with limited income who need a large amount of protection, especially temporary protection.	Persons who have small incomes and need a forced savings plan as well as long-term protection. Persons who want a policy with a cash and loan value.	Persons in high tax bracket who wish to shelter yield from taxes.	Persons who want to save for children's education or for future years or to prepare for retirement and still have insurance in the meantime.	Persons who are willing to try a new insurance approach and accept some risk with possibility of higher yield.
Disadvantages	Premiums rise as the insured person ages. Lasts only for a few years and then must be renewed.	More expensive per $1,000 of insurance than term policies. Inflation can reduce the real value of the policy.	More expensive than term or whole life premiums. Better suited as an investment than as insurance.	Does not pay as much interest as traditional savings accounts. Insured person pays insurance company for investment management. Inflation can reduce the buying power of the endowment.	Difficult to judge future return and cost of competing policies.

financial losses can be separated into two parts: immediate and long-run losses. The immediate financial losses include all bills that are due shortly after the funeral. These might include uninsured medical bills, funeral expenses, estate taxes, and probate costs. If you have health insurance coverage and a written will and you do not want to leave this world with a funeral tribute rivaling the Shah of Iran's, the total for these expenses will probably not exceed $10,000. Long-run financial loss is the real reason for buying life insurance. Presumably, you are concerned that your death may cause some hardship on your family and you would like your insurance to provide some security for family members. We all realize that nothing can replace you, but you want to be sure that the assets you leave behind will be sufficient to meet your dependents' needs.

By narrowing our focus to the financial hardship that your death may cause to others, we are disregarding the investment aspect of insurance. But as the previous sections have demonstrated, life insurance has not been shown to be a good investment. On the other hand, death insurance can be a valuable and even a necessary adjunct to any consumer's budget. However, we should warn you that there is no magic formula for determining the amount of life insurance that a person should have. In some cases, it may be perfectly rational to have no life insurance at all. In order to put this problem into perspective, we will select a few typical life-styles and then apply a simple analysis to delineate some guidelines for buying insurance.

Insurance and the single person. If you are a single parent caring for a child or if you are helping to support your parents or other dependents, then you should consider obtaining a sizable term life insurance policy. How large a policy depends on how much of a burden the loss of your income would place on those innocent bystanders. We will explore some guidelines for people with dependents in the next section. But if you are a single person with no dependents, is there any reason for you to have an insurance policy?

Insurance agents have an entire portfolio of reasons for convincing single people that they need insurance. One of the most frequently used arguments instills the fear of future uninsurability. "You may be healthy and a good risk now, but if you don't take advantage of your situation and buy insurance today, you may not be able to get it at a later date." The fear of deteriorating health is not a very compelling reason for most people to buy life insurance. Consumers Union reported that only 3 percent of all life insurance applicants are rejected for any reason, and only 5 percent are charged extra because of health conditions (*Consumer Reports*, 1980). Many insurance companies are willing to sell some coverage for which the buyer is not required to have a medical examination, unless the answers to certain questions on the insurance application indicate a need for a further check. So unless you have a hereditary disease that will impair your insurability in the future, your current health status is not a good reason to seek life insurance.

Another argument that insurance agents use is that the younger consumer can lock into a low premium rate by buying early, before the risk of death (and the premiums) rises. Obviously, this locked-in premium applies only to cash-value insurance, because term insurance costs more every time it is renewed. But it is true that a 25-year-old-man could buy a $10,000 whole life policy for a $129 annual premium, whereas the same policy might cost $175 at age 35. But if the 25-year-old policyholder does not need $10,000 worth of insurance over this period, why should he or she pay the insurance company $1,290 for the right to buy insurance at a later time when it *might* be needed? If the $129 annual payment were put into an investment that yielded a 7 percent return compounded annually, it would have risen to almost $2,000 in ten years. This more than compensates the policyholder for the additional $46 ($175 − $129) yearly cost that buying insurance at age 35 rather than age 25 entails.

Reducing economic hardship on others is about the only reason for single persons to buy life insurance. In some cases, the death of a young single person may put an undue strain on the finances of family or friends, either because of the costs associated with the funeral arrangements or because of outstanding debts that cannot be resolved by selling the assets of the estate. When a person's death could cause hardship to others, he or she often takes out a small term life insurance policy to lighten the economic burden. Of course, this decision depends on the values and goals of the consumer involved. And it should not be made unless adequate information is sought from other members of the family, as well as from insurance agents. After all, before you decide to minimize the financial strain that your demise might cause to your family, you ought to find out whether your parents or grandparents already have a policy on you. And before you agree to sign up for a new policy, you should do some comparison shopping among agents, because prices can easily vary by 100 percent.

Insurance for those with dependents. For a husband–wife household, especially one in which children are involved, or for a single-parent family, the death of an adult could bring real economic hardship in addition to psychological loss to other members of the family. The amount of life insurance in force should be in proportion to the degree of economic hardship that may be suffered.

Relating insurance needs to economic hardship can eliminate the rationale behind buying certain kinds of life insurance. For example, it makes little economic sense to insure the lives of children for any large amount. In crude terms, the absence of a child reduces the economic

**FIGURE 17.5
Distribution of
individual life
insurance purchases.**
(SOURCE: Data from
American Council of Life
Insurance, *Life Insurance
Factbook, 1987*
[Washington, D.C., 1987],
p. 8.)

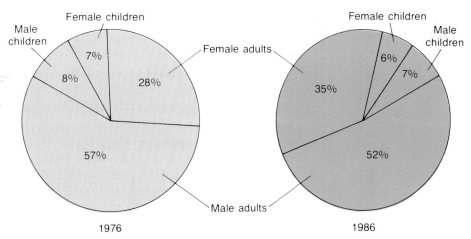

burden on a family. It does not increase the burden. Nevertheless, as Figure 17.5 shows, 13 percent of all individual life insurance policies in the United States in 1986 were issued to children under 15 years of age. Why do consumers take out such policies? Part of the reason is simply to cover the small but real burden that goes with any death in the family. But insurance agents often encourage parents to take out larger policies with the argument that the policy is building some cash value or that if the child becomes uninsurable later for health reasons, this policy can remain in force without a medical exam. The first reason is not very compelling in that inflation quickly reduces the real value of a given amount of insurance and the interest rate is low on such policies. The fear of deteriorating health is even less important for a child than for a college student. And as we pointed out earlier, few people are ever denied life insurance for health reasons.

What about the traditional family in which the wife does not work outside the home? Does it make good sense to insure the homemaker? Although there is no direct income generated by a spouse who stays home to run the household, it is obvious that if the many services performed by him or her were to be purchased in the marketplace, the cost would be quite high. If the death of a spouse would result in additional family expenses for childcare, housecleaning, meal preparation, and the like, it would make sense to provide sufficient life insurance to supply these services.

Clearly, the most urgent need for life insurance exists when the family wage earner dies. Because more than half of all married women are in the paid labor force, and because their earnings account for more than 30 percent of family income, life insurance policies for both husbands and their wives are often needed. As Figure 17.5 indicates, the growing importance of wives to family income has been reflected in their share of life insurance policies. In 1976, only 28 percent of all life insurance policies were written for women. By 1986 that share had risen to 35 percent. Families were responding to the growing importance of having two wage earners to maintain their levels of living by insuring them *both*.

Social Security: an automatic life insurance policy. The amount of life insurance you need to replace your share of the family income depends on the size of your earnings, your family composition, and the number of years you plan on providing for them. If you are a typical wage earner, you, like 90 percent of the labor force, are currently covered by Social Security. The abbreviation for this program is OASDHI, which stands for *Old Age, Survivors, Disability,* and *Health Insurance* program. The survivors program, is relevant here. Under this program, your spouse and dependents can expect to receive a monthly check from the government to supplement their income. The size of this income supplement varies, but in 1987 it could have amounted to $1,680 a month for a family of three. The amount is indexed for inflation; it increases as the CPI rises.

It is often difficult to determine just how much a family will receive from Social Security in the event of a wage earner's death. Life insurance agents have been known to ignore or grossly understate the size of these benefits, for obvious reasons. Consumers Union estimates that for a person who has consistently paid the maximum amount of Social Security taxes, the survivors' benefits equal an income stream worth more than $200,000 in term insurance. Table 17.4 presents the monthly income payable to various survivors of Social Security decedents. As you can see, these payments vary with income and family size.

How much income security should you provide beyond what Social Security supplies? To get a better idea of the additional insurance needed

TABLE 17.4 Monthly Benefits for Social Security Survivors

Earnings (Annual Gross Income)	Surviving Parent and One Child	Parent and Two Children	One Surviving Child
Federal minimum wage ($6,968)	$ 639	$ 651	$318
75% of average wage ($12,990)	806	960	403
Average wage ($17,321)	982	1,194	491
150% of average wage ($25,981)	1,270	1,479	635
Maximum wage covered ($45,000)	1,440	1,680	720

SOURCE: *Social Security Bulletin,* Annual Statistical Supplement, 1987, p. 31.

to offset the loss of income from your death, simply multiply your monthly take-home pay by 0.75 (75 percent). This should give you a rough idea of the monthly income loss that your family will need to absorb when your paycheck is no longer part of the family's budget. We use 0.75 rather than 1.00 (100 percent) because you consume a portion of the family's income, and this consumption will stop when you die. Once you arrive at the monthly income loss, subtract the monthly Social Security survivors' benefits to arrive at your net monthly loss. Multiply this figure by 12 to get the yearly income loss. Finally, multiply this yearly figure by the number of years you intend to provide for, and you have the total amount of your necessary insurance fund. The formula can be stated: $(0.75 \times$ monthly take-home pay$) - ($monthly Social Security$) \times 12 \times$ years of dependency = amount of insurance fund needed.

The rules regarding survivors' benefits have been revised and made more complex even as the basic benefits have been increased. Unmarried children of a deceased insured worker receive benefits until they are 18 (or until 19 if they are still full-time high school students). A surviving spouse who has children receives an additional supplement until the youngest child reaches 16. At that time, the spousal benefits are terminated, even though the child continues to qualify. The spouse will also lose Social Security Survivor benefits if he or she remarries. If remarriage occurs, the children continue to receive their benefits.

How much income security should you provide beyond basic Social Security? Ideally your family should be able to maintain its current standard of living. Call this base level of income your family's "target income"; most experts agree that this target level is about 75 percent of your current take-home pay. For a worker earning a take-home pay of $2,000 per month, the monthly target income would be $1,500 (0.75 × 2000). This income roughly corresponds to the 150 percent of average wage listed in Table 17.4. If a worker in this position were to die and leave a widow with a young child, the Social Security Administration would send a monthly check for $1,270 to the survivors. How much would this family receive if there were two young children instead of one? The payment would be $1,479. As you can see, these are significant amounts of income that will help offset the initial loss of purchasing power. (Use Worksheet 17.1 to calculate your life insurance needs.)

Can you expect Social Security to take care of all your life insurance needs? Probably not, but it is a good start. The problem with Social Security is that the large initial payments will be reduced as each child reaches 16, and then they will terminate as the children graduate from high school. Once the youngest child reaches 16, the surviving spouse will not receive any additional Social Security payments until reaching retirement age. This is the so-called blackout period, and it could be very traumatic for a middle-aged spouse with little job experience outside the

WORKSHEET 17.1   CALCULATING YOUR LIFE INSURANCE NEEDS

You can calculate your life insurance needs based on your monthly take-home pay and Social Security Survivor benefits by using the form below.

Step I. Calculate Your Target Income.
   0.75 × monthly take-home = target income
   0.75 × $ _____   = $ _____

Step II. Estimate Social Security Survivor benefits.
   (See Table 17.4 for benefits based on annual earnings.)
   Monthly Social Security benefit =
   A. $ _____ until youngest child is 16.
   B. $ _____ while youngest child is 16–17.

Step III. Calculate monthly shortfall.
   Target income minus Social Security payment = monthly shortfall
   A. Step I − Step II.A. = $ _____ until child is 16.
   B. Step I − Step II.B. = $ _____ while youngest is 17–18.

Step IV. Calculate insurance fund needed.
   Monthly Shortfall × 12 × years of dependency = insurance fund.

(Step III.A. × 12 × years) + (Step III.B. × 12 × years) = $ insurance fund
($ _____ × 12 × ____) + ($ _____ × 12 × 2)   = $ _____

home. Nevertheless, it does seem unrealistic in this world of increasing labor force participation rates for women that we should expect a widow to remain out of the workforce from the time her last child becomes 16 until she becomes 62. Thus, we would recommend that a fund be set aside to allow for education and retraining for a spouse who left the labor force to rear children. A reasonable estimate would be a sum of money equal to a four-year college scholarship for tuition, room, and board. If the surviving spouse held a good job as a partner in a two-income household, this fund may be disregarded.

The Cost of Life Insurance

Once you have established how much life insurance you feel you need, the next question—dear to most consumers' hearts—is: How much will this protection cost? The answer is not simple. Cost varies depending on age, employment, sex, and the type of policy, as well as the company one chooses to underwrite the policy. From our earlier discussion, you already know that group policies are generally less expensive than individual life policies because the sales costs are lower. It is also true that term insurance is less expensive than whole life because there is no forced savings plan

TABLE 17.5 Comparison of the Cash-Value Savings Aspect of a Typical Whole Life Insurance Policy with a Premium of $1,650 Annually and a Savings Account

Policy Year	Insurance Cash Value	Savings Account (5% Annual Returns)
5	$ 6,365	$ 9,544
10	15,156	21,724
15	25,521	37,271
20	37,487	57,113
25	51,067	82,436
30	63,441	107,647

included. And finally, we should note that paying your insurance premium on an annual rather than on a monthly or quarterly basis also reduces costs, because it is less expensive for the insurance company to administer.

Some insurance agents have been known to argue that insurance does not have to cost anything, if one buys the right kind of policy. These folks are often pushing orthodox whole life policies that incorporate the forced-savings feature we previously discussed. For example, a $100,000 whole life policy issued to a 35-year-old man might cost $1,650 per year. If he continues to pay every year until he is 65 (30 years later), his premiums would amount to $49,500 ($1,650 × 30 years). But each year the cash value continues to grow, as illustrated in Table 17.5. By the thirtieth year, the cash value is over $63,000, so if the policyholder wants to, he can cash the policy in and get a check for $63,441, that is, $13,941 more than he paid over those years. So the cost, according to some insurance agents, would be *negative*, because the policyholder took out more than he paid in. But these agents are not considering the opportunity cost. As Table 17.5 shows, if this man had saved $1,650 per year for 30 years in a savings account that paid only 5 percent interest, by age 65 he would have had over $107,000. So there is a *real* cost to the insurance—more than $44,000 in lost interest.

Comparing costs: the interest-adjusted cost index. You should realize by now that not all insurance policies are alike. Even policies that have identical death benefits and similar features often have widely different rates. In order to help consumers judge the real cost of competing policies, the National Association of Insurance Commissioners suggests that consumers use the **interest-adjusted cost (IAC) index**. This index compares the net cost of each insurance policy by applying an adjustment for the opportunity cost of a policyholder's money (the interest rate) to the annual premium, cash value, and dividends, if there are any. This index

interest-adjusted cost index: a method of comparing the relative costs of various insurance policies that takes the time-value cost of money into account

TABLE 17.6 Comparison of Insurance Costs

Quotes from the Services	First-Year Premium	Interest-Adjusted 10-Year Net Cost Index	Interest-Adjusted 20-Year Net Cost Index
Insurance Information (1−800−472−5800)			
American Mayflower Select GP5[a]	$165[b]	1.88	2.34
American International Life ART-87	97[c]	1.91	3.44
Life Quote (1−800−521−7873)			
American Mayflower Select GP5[a]	191[d]	2.27	3.22
Bankers Security Life			
5-year-renewable and convertible term	154	1.92	2.71
Select Quote (1−800−343−1985)			
Equitable Term	210	3.09	4.34
United Olympic Life 5-year term	154	1.92	2.71
Term Quote (1−800−444−TERM)			
First Colony Select 5 CRVT[a]	175	2.49	3.77
Provident Life 5-year term	154	1.92	2.71
Four Policies We Found			
Jackson National 10-year renewable term	176	1.76	1.92
Metropolitan 1-year term with premium adjustment	170	2.03	2.48
New York Savings Bank Life Group term	112	2.00	3.42
Northwestern Mutual Term-70	191	2.38	3.48

How to compare the quotes: The table shows the first-year premiums and 10 and 20-year interest-adjusted net cost indexes for $100,000 of coverage for a 42-year-old woman who doesn't smoke. Use the indexes to compare the average annual cost of similar types of life insurance policies. Listed are the highest- and lowest-cost policies recommended by the shopping services and quotes from four companies that had low-cost term policies in our insurance survey two years ago. (The indexes for policies from Insurance Information Inc. were supplied by the policy underwriters.)

[a] Revertible policy.
[b] Preferred rate.
[c] Insurance company quotes a premium of $87.50.
[d] Insurance company's standard rate. Company quotes a first-year premium of $204, a 10-year index of 2.44, and a 20-year index of 3.46.

SOURCE: Adapted from "Insurance Quote Services," *Consumer Reports*, June 1988.

can be computed for any number of years, but 10- and 20-year IAC indexes are the most common and useful. In many states insurance agents are legally required to furnish these data on request, but even if you are not in one of these states, it makes good sense to ask for the IAC index. And, as with all comparison shopping, you should compare policies from several companies before deciding to buy one. Table 17.6 illustrates these indexes for some term insurance policies obtained by *Consumer Reports*. Utilizing such secondary sources can lessen the time you spend on searching for the best rates.

RETIREMENT

If you survive the hazards of mortality during your working lifetime, you will then launch what could be an equally uncertain period known as the retirement years. Americans generally consider 65 the age of retirement, although many people retire sooner and some choose to work well beyond that age. Figure 17.6 shows the number of Americans over 65 in the United States from 1990 to 2050. As you can see, this segment of our population is projected to rise from 30 million in 1990 to more than 60 million in 2040, when today's teenagers will be retired. By then, almost 20 percent of our population will be over 65.

The dramatic demographic changes of the past 20 years mean that society will have to provide for a much higher proportion of retired people in the not-so-distant future. The consumer who wants to avoid sudden bone-wrenching decisions late in life should begin planning for retirement in the present. Given the magnitude of the society-wide aging problem, you cannot expect government to bail you out or absolve you from the responsibility of caring for yourself.

Besides adjusting to a new life-style when you quit work, your main concern will be whether you have enough income to maintain your level of living. This discussion is also pertinent to your parents' needs. As we discussed in Chapter 2, many of you will find yourselves responsible for the care of elderly parents. Therefore, it is in your best interest to review your parents' retirement plans as well as your own. In the sections that follow we will describe three major sources of retirement income: Social Security, company pensions, and personal pension plans.

Social Security and Retirement Income

As we have seen, the Social Security program is a massive undertaking that has health, disability, and life insurance facets, but no part of the Social Security system is more important than the retirement income program. Of the 40 million people receiving some form of Social Security

**FIGURE 17.6
Projected number and proportion of persons 65 and over in the U.S. population, 1990–2050.**
(SOURCE: Leon F. Bouvier, "America's Baby Boom Generation," *Population Bulletin* [April 1980], p. 29.)

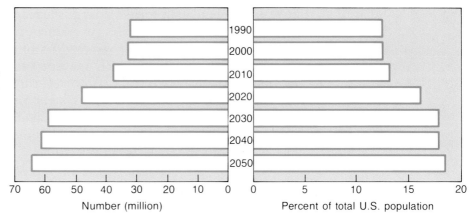

benefits today, more than two-thirds receive income under the retirement provisions of Social Security.

Your right to Social Security. The rules governing your right to Social Security retirement benefits are fairly straightforward. An individual's Social Security credit is measured in quarters (three-month periods of coverage), with a total of four quarters allowed for each year worked. In 1988, an employee or a self-employed person could earn one quarter of coverage for every three months in which he or she earned at least $470 that was subject to Social Security tax. The number of quarters needed to qualify for benefits depends on one's age. Anyone reaching 62 in 1991 or later will need 40 quarters (ten years) of tax payments to qualify for retirement benefits.

The level of benefits one earns also depends on one's average yearly earnings. Those who have higher incomes pay more into the program, so they can expect to receive more when they retire. However, all of us pay the same tax rate, up to a maximum income. In 1988, the Social Security tax rate was 7.51 percent of an employee's income up to $45,000 (the taxable wage base). The employer had to match the employee's contribution, so the maximum annual payment into the fund equaled $6,759. For 1990 and beyond, the tax is slated to be 7.65 percent of the taxable wage base for employed workers. The wage base will be adjusted upward annually based on the national inflation rate.

Politics and Social Security. How much can you expect to receive as a result of your forced savings? This depends again on how much and how long you have been active in the program, in addition to when you retire. But it also depends on the willingness of political leaders to maintain the program. Social Security does not operate in the same way as a private investment fund. It does not take your money and invest it in corporate stocks or real estate. Instead, the Social Security program takes tax money and distributes it to currently eligible participants. Any surplus is used to buy government bonds to help finance the federal deficit. As a result, the program more closely resembles government transfer payments than life insurance endowment funds. Some critics of Social Security say that it operates like a pyramid in which new entrants supply cash flow so that previous participants get paid. However, this is not really a fair comparison because the Social Security system, unlike fly-by-night pyramid schemes, has the support of the federal government behind it. In essence, it is our faith that the government will honor its commitment that ultimately supports the Social Security system.

Demography and Social Security. Detractors of the system do have a good point, however, in that it is going to be more and more difficult to

FIGURE 17.7
Number of persons paying Social Security taxes, per beneficiary aged 65 and over, United States, 1960–2050. (SOURCE: Leon F. Bouvier, "America's Baby Boom Generation," *Population Bulletin* [April 1980], p. 31.)

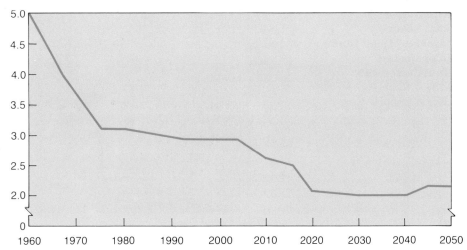

honor all of the commitments to people currently enrolled in the system. As Figure 17.7 shows, the number of persons paying Social Security payroll taxes per beneficiary has been falling. In 1960 there were five people paying Social Security taxes for every one receiving benefits. By 1980 the ratio of payers to beneficiaries had fallen to almost three to one. And by 2030 the ratio will be only two to one. The 1960 to 1980 decline necessitated a large increase in the tax rate and in the taxable wage base. This decline was coupled with a plan to index benefits to inflation and to offer a comprehensive medical plan for the elderly. All three events resulted in a large tax increase on workers. It remains to be seen whether workers in the twenty-first century will allow such burdens to be placed on them.

For the time being, however, the retirement funds portion of Social Security is building a cash surplus as the baby-boom generation moves through the workforce. In 1987, for example, Social Security's retirement and disability trust fund ran a $21.9 billion surplus. Annual surpluses are expected to raise the retirement trust fund until it peaks at $11.8 trillion in 2030 (see Figure 17.8). At that point the wave of baby-boomer retirees—80 million Americans born between 1946 and 1964—is expected to exceed the annual contributions of the workforce. This retirement wave will deplete the trust fund fairly rapidly. It is expected to be completely depleted by 2048.

Collecting your fair share. The assurance that Social Security is solvent through the middle of the twenty-first century should give you some hope of collecting some of your contributions to the program. How much can you expect to receive? Table 17.7 gives some examples of the amounts of Social Security retirement payments made to recently qualified retirees.

FIGURE 17.8
Social Security retirement trust funds and projected beneficiaries, 1985–2048. (SOURCE: *U.S. News & World Report*, June 13, 1988.)

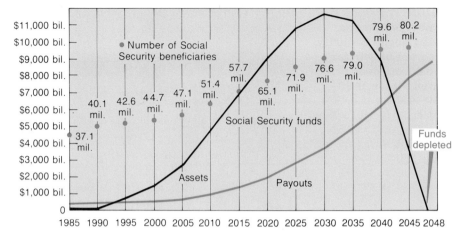

Note: Figures include year-end assets and beneficiaries of both Disability Insurance and Old Age and Survivors Insurance funds. Figures for 1988 through 2048 are projections. Asset projections assume an annual inflation rate of 4.0% and average annual wage increases of 5.4%.

The payments vary considerably based on your age and average income. Workers who earned an average monthly wage $1,403 in 1987 can expect to receive $655 each month if they retire at age 65. Retiring at 62 reduces their benefits by 20 percent, to $524. Clearly, Social Security is not meant to be your sole retirement fund.

The age at which full benefits are payable is set to rise from the current age, 65, to 66 in 2009 and 67 in 2027. Reduced benefits will still be available at 62, but the reduction will mean that a retiree at 62 will get only 70 percent of the pension of a 67 year old. These changes were all part of the systemwide revision to prepare for the retirement of the baby-boomers in the twenty-first century.

If you would like to get an official estimate of your future Social Security retirement check, you can request this information from the Social Security Administration. You can get Form SSA-7004 from your

TABLE 17.7   Examples of Monthly Social Security Retirement Payments for Workers Who Reach First Eligibility in 1987

	Average Indexed Monthly Earnings				
Recipient of Benefits	**$740**	**$1,052.00**	**$1,403.00**	**$1,900**	**$2,205**
Retired worker alone at 62	347.00	430.00	524.00	651.00	689.00
Retired worker and spouse at 62	509.00	631.00	769.00	956.00	1,012.00
Retired worker alone at 65	433.00	537.00	655.00	813.00	861.00
Retired worker and spouse at 65	564.00	699.00	851.00	1,058.00	1,120.00

SOURCE: *Social Security Bulletin*, Annual Statistical Supplement, 1987.

local Social Security office, or you can call the toll free number 1–800–937–2000. Their estimate will be calculated in current dollars, so the actual size of your check should be greater because future Social Security income will be adjusted upward based on the rate of inflation.

Restrictions on Social Security. Contrary to what some people think, one does not become mentally or physically incapacitated at 65. Many people choose to work beyond that age. For these people, Social Security offers two options. If they continue to work and choose to pay into the program, their benefits will increase by 0.25 percent for every month they work beyond age 65. This amounts to an annual increase in benefits of 3 percent, and it can be continued until age 70. The second option is to begin receiving Social Security retirement benefits at age 65 while continuing to work. Because Social Security checks are intended to replace part of the lost earnings occasioned by retirement, anyone who continues to work must pass what is called a **retirement test**, the maximum earnings that a Social Security retiree can receive without suffering any reduction in his or her Social Security check. In 1988 anyone retiring at age 65 could pass this test and suffer no reduction in his or her checks as long as the wages earned after retirement did not exceed $8,400. If someone received wages in excesss of $8,400, his or her benefits were reduced by $1 for every $2 of earnings above the retirement-test limit. Thus, a retiree who earned $10,000 in wages in 1988 would suffer an $800 reduction in Social Security payments.

The retirement-test doctrine has been quite controversial, although it is often misunderstood. In the first place, only wages are covered by the test. Income from interest on savings accounts, stock dividends, capital gains, inheritances, real estate income, royalties, or pensions are *not* included in the retirement test. Some people argue that excluding income from these sources biases the program against working-class people, who do not usually own large amounts of real estate or stock portfolios. As you might guess, one retired person could have thousands of dollars of income from these sources and still receive a full Social Security retirement check, whereas another person who takes a job and earns $10,000 to help supplement Social Security checks will have his or her benefits reduced. The misunderstanding is in trying to determine how much Social Security income will be lost by continuing to work. There is no reduction until wage income *exceeds* the retirement test. And even then, the marginal tax rate is 50 percent, not 100 percent, as is often assumed. After 1989 this tax will be reduced to 33 percent ($1 in benefits will be withheld for every $3 in earnings above the limit). As for anyone over 70, the retirement test is not applicable. One may earn as much as one likes without any reduction in benefits.

retirement test: the maximum wage earnings that someone receiving a Social Security retirement check can receive before suffering a reduction in benefits

**Company Pension
Plans**

The Social Security Plan was never intended to provide for all a person's retirement needs. When it was first introduced in 1935, it was seen as a supplement to other plans that could provide a minimal but important contribution to retirement. Since then, the program has expanded both in scope and benefits, but it still does not provide a complete retirement package. If you doubt this, look at Table 17.7 again and try to estimate how you would live if you had to depend on Social Security alone.

For the average retiree at age 65, Social Security will replace about 45 percent of his or her annual income. For those at the lower end of the scale, this replacement ratio is slightly higher. In any event, very few workers will be able to rely on Social Security to replace more than two-thirds of the income they need for retirement. This means that most retirees will need a plan to supplement Social Security.

One of the most common ways to supplement the Social Security program is a company pension plan provided by an employer. Such plans have been around for decades, but it was not until 1974, with the passage of the Employees Retirement Income Security Act (ERISA), that the federal government intervened in this vital and complex area. The problems with company pension plans prior to 1974 were in the qualifications for receiving benefits as well as insufficient funding to guarantee payments to retired workers. Before 1974, it was possible for a long-time employee to be fired and thus not qualify for retirement benefits, or for the company to go out of business and have the pension fund disappear with it. These abuses led Congress to pass ERISA, which set certain standards about employee participation and about the management of company retirement funds.

Under the rules established by ERISA, an employee is eligible to participate in the pension plan after one year of service, provided that he or she is at least 25 years old. Under most pension plans, both the employer and the employee make contributions to the retirement fund. The employee's contributions are treated like a savings account. An employee who is fired or quits can withdraw all of the employee contributions in the fund, but by doing so, he or she forfeits any contributions made by the employer. The employer's contributions are also regulated by ERISA. The question here is whether or not the employee has a right to any or all of these employer contributions. The process whereby an employee obtains a claim on the employer's contribution to the pension fund is called **vesting**. A vested right is a right that no one can take away. But one can give it up by quitting and taking one's money out of the pension plan. In plans in which employers make large contributions to the retirement fund, rules governing vesting can be important. It is possible for an employee to be fully vested or only partially vested, depending on whether all of the employer's contribution accrues to the benefit of the employee or only a portion remains with the employee if he or she changes employers.

vesting: the process by which an employee earns nonforfeitable rights over the employer's contributions into the employee's pension plan

If you get vested rights in a company pension plan, you will receive pension benefits based in part on your employer's contributions, even if you leave the company before retirement. But you have to leave your contributions in the pension fund. Nevertheless, vesting is an important right, and companies that offer pension plans must provide for full vesting (that is, 100 percent pension eligibility) after an employee has participated in the pension plan for ten years.

In addition to the problem of vesting, retired employees have sometimes been troubled by fund cutoffs caused by their former employer's mismanagement. Given the uncertainties of the marketplace, even an employee of a major company would like some assurance that the retirement program will still be there even if the company is not. When Congress passed ERISA, it set up a two-pronged approach to this thorny problem. First, all pension funds must be placed under the management of a trustee whose function is to oversee the fund, not to be involved with other company affairs. This trustee can be an insurance firm, a bank, or another organization, but it must follow a federal guideline known as the **prudent man rule**. This rule states that trustees should invest the funds "with care, skill, prudence and diligence . . . that a prudent man acting in a like capacity and familiar with such matters would use." Essentially, this means that the trustees are to avoid speculative or high-risk investments that might result in a loss of the pension funds. In practice, this may lead to a lower return on the fund, because some high-risk investment opportunities must be foregone. On the other hand, there is less chance for a total collapse of the fund.

In the event of a financial calamity for a pension fund, ERISA established the nonprofit Pension Benefit Guarantee Corporation, which provides benefits to retired workers whose pension funds prove inadequate. This corporation is financed by compulsory insurance premiums that come from companies with retirement programs.

Personal Pension Plans: IRA and Keogh

Not all companies offer their own retirement plans. Nor does everyone work for a company. To help people who do not have such plans provide for their retirement, Congress has created two strategies: Individual Retirement Accounts and Keogh plans.

IRA: retirement plans for employees whose employers do not have a company pension program; workers with lower incomes also qualify for a tax deduction of up to $2000 per year regardless of their company retirement benefits

Individual Retirement Accounts. One of the most popular forms of private pensions ever designed is the **Individual Retirement Account (IRA).** This plan allows single workers to invest up to $2,000 in a retirement account each year; $4,000 is allowed for a married couple if both work, and $2,250 for a joint husband–wife account when only one spouse is employed. The earnings on this investment are compounded in a tax-sheltered environment until they are withdrawn by the investor.

Another bonus for this retirement account is the tax deductibility of the investment if the worker is not covered by an employer-sponsored pension plan. Even if covered by a company pension plan, an employee who is a single worker may deduct a portion of this investment so long as his or her individual income does not exceed $35,000; couples filing joint tax returns are allowed $50,000. (Full deductibility remains for single workers with less than $25,000 income or for couples with less than $40,000.)

Regardless of the tax implication, you cannot withdraw any money from your IRA before you are $59\frac{1}{2}$ years old, and you must begin withdrawing money when you reach $70\frac{1}{2}$. If you take any money out of the fund before you reach $59\frac{1}{2}$, you must pay a penalty to the IRS of 10 percent of the withdrawal. IRAs are designed for retirement, not as emergency funds to be withdrawn as needed.

Keogh plans. Self-employed people or those who have outside self-employment income in addition to the income from their regular jobs can take advantage of a different tax-deferred pension account called a **Keogh plan**. Under a Keogh plan a self-employed person may contribute as much as 25 percent of his or her income, up to a maximum of $30,000 annually. There are no other major differences between an IRA and a Keogh account. The cutoff ages for beginning a withdrawal and for closing the account are basically the same.

Keogh: a tax-deferred pension account for self-employed people

MAKING A WILL

The theme of this chapter is planning for the future, and barring any last-minute miracle cures for mortality, the future has to end with death. Although this is not a pleasant subject, it is one that everyone must face at some point. The spiritual aspects of this topic are not relevant to consumer economics, but the material implications are. One of the most important is the preparation of a will.

It may surprise you to learn that almost 70 percent of all Americans die without preparing a **will**, which is a legal document that tells the living how one would like to see one's estate disposed of after one's death. Box 17.1 presents a typical case for someone who dies without a will. The first important advantage of drawing up a will, then, is the assurance that one's property will go to the people you want to receive it. A second important feature of many wills is the part that names a guardian for children. Obviously, one's spouse will assume this role if he or she survives. But what happens if both the husband and the wife die? This event, although rare, should be prepared for. Third, a will can minimize the costs of transferring one's estate by clearly naming the beneficiaries and what they should receive. This can limit lawsuit costs caused by arguments among heirs. Fourth, a carefully prepared will can

will: a legal document that allows the transfer of an estate based on the wishes of a deceased person

BOX 17.1   YOUR LAST WILL AND TESTAMENT

You already have a will—a last will and testament drawn up by the state in which you live. If you have not made out a will of your own, you must operate under the will as drawn by the legislature of the state.

Attorney James Leet furnished us with this will, which is based on California law.

FIRST, I direct that the Probate Court consider for appointment as administrator of my estate one or more of the following persons, in the order named:

1. My spouse or some competent person whom he or she may request to have appointed.

2. My children.

3. My grandchildren.

4. My parents.

5. My brothers and sisters.

6. The next of kin entitled to a place in the estate.

7. The relatives who are entitled to succeed.

8. Public administrator.

9. Creditors.

10. Any legally competent person.

SECOND, I direct that all of my debts be paid, including taxes, probate fees, administrator fees, and attorney fees. If necessary, the court shall order the sale of some of my assets in order to pay these debts.

THIRD, with the remaining property, I direct that all property that I acquired during marriage, excepting gifts or inheritance, be transferred to my wife/husband.

FOURTH, if only one child survives me, I direct that one-half of my property acquired before marriage or by gifts inherited during marriage be transferred to my spouse. If two or more children survive me, my spouse is to receive one-third instead of one-half of my property.

FIFTH, I direct that the remaining portion of my property acquired before marriage or by gift or inheritance be transferred to my child or to my children.

SIXTH, if my spouse does not survive me but my child or children do, I direct all my property to be transferred to my child or to my children equally.

SEVENTH, if my spouse survives me but I have no living children, I direct that one-half of the property that I acquired before marriage by gift or inheritance be transferred to my spouse. I direct that the remaining half of this property be transferred to my parents if living and if not, to my brothers and sisters and their heirs.

EIGHTH, if my spouse is the sole survivor of my family, including my children, parents, brothers, sisters, or their descendants, I direct that all my property go to my spouse.

NINTH, if I am not survived by any of the persons mentioned in article Eight, I direct the court to search for my nearest blood relative and to divide my estate among my closest blood relatives.

TENTH, if the probate court cannot locate any relative, I direct that all of my property be transferred to the state.

limit the tax liability of the heirs by taking advantage of the tax laws. Finally, writing a will allows one to name the person who is to be responsible for administering the will. This person, called an **executor** (male) or an **executrix** (female), should be a responsible, concerned, and capable administrator, because he or she is the one who must gather all records, pay debts, and satisfy the court that everything is in order before the decedent's wishes can be carried out.

The legal process for establishing the validity of a will and ensuring that it is properly executed is called **probate**. The purpose of a probate proceeding is to ensure an orderly and fair transfer of ownership from the decedent to the heirs. Nevertheless, because creditors will have to be notified and given time to respond and because tax authorities also need time to issue their blessing (and take their share), probate can last for more than a year. To limit the impact of this time loss on your heirs, you might consider placing some of your assets in **joint ownership**. This is most commonly done between husband and wife for possessions such as a house or a car. Any property held in joint ownership goes immediately to the surviving spouse without having to pass through the probate process.

probate: the legal process for establishing the validity of a will and for ensuring that its provisions are carried out

Whether or not property is jointly owned, it will be subject to estate tax because under federal law all property held jointly is assumed to belong to the person who dies first. However, the 1981 Tax Act gave surviving spouses an unlimited marital deduction so they will not have to pay estate taxes on anything they have inherited from their deceased husband or wife. In addition, according to the Act, all estates of $600,000 or less are exempt from federal tax.

It is generally a good idea to keep a will as simple as possible. Do not clutter it with interesting but irrelevant comments about the state of life or your opinions of relatives, friends, or how you would like to be buried. For these comments, a **letter of last instructions** should be drawn up. The whereabouts of this letter should be made known to your executor or executrix so that your final instructions can be carried out as efficiently as possible. The letter should contain information and instructions, as well as any personal messages. The information should include the location of your will, your insurance policies, and your bank accounts. Your instructions should include your desires concerning funeral and burial arrangements. We discuss this last point in the section that follows.

FUNERAL AND BURIAL ARRANGEMENTS

If you were to do a consumer survey and ask people to list the ten largest items they will purchase over a lifetime, very few would list a funeral. Nevertheless, this is a major purchase for almost everyone. According to the FTC, Americans arrange more than two million funerals for family and friends each year, at an average cost of $3,100. This is not very expensive when compared to housing costs, but it is almost twice the cost of delivering a child. Why does it cost more to leave the world than to enter it? And is there anything that consumers can do to limit the cost?

There are a variety of funeral and burial arrangements that can entail very low or very high costs, but many consumers are unaware of their choices.

Part of the reason for the high cost of dying lies in the nature of the buying process itself. Consumers are simply not in the best frame of mind when they must find a final resting place for their relatives or close friends. The emotional trauma of death is sometimes used by unscrupulous funeral directors to raise the cost of this final expenditure. However, if you understand the funeral and burial process, you can do much to limit the expense for your own funeral, and you can also be of great help to others in their time of bereavement.

The first thing to recognize is that the funeral business is just that: a business. More than that, it is a *big* business. Consumers spend more than $4 billion yearly to provide these services for their friends and relatives. As business people, funeral directors must tailor their services to meet public needs. But in the past, unlike many other firms, funeral homes have often refused to advertise their prices and sometimes offer more misinformation than information.

The FTC has long recognized that consumers are at a disadvantage when dealing with funeral arrangements. On April 30, 1984, the FTC promulgated a trade regulation concerning funeral industry practices. This rule insists that funeral directors provide price information over the telephone. They are also required to give you a general price list that itemizes the cost of each individual item and service offered. The objective of the Funeral Rule was to ensure that consumers received reliable and complete information about the cost of a funeral.

Another way to limit your funeral expense is to join a **memorial society**. These are nonprofit groups with the major goal ''to obtain dignity,

memorial society: a nonprofit organization whose function is to reduce the costs of funerals through preplanning arrangements

simplicity and economy in funeral arrangements by advance planning.'' Today there are more than 200 memorial societies in the United States, with more than one million members. For $50 or less, most consumers can obtain a family membership that provides them with information about the costs and types of funerals available and the names of local funeral homes who cooperate with the society. Most of these societies are affiliated with the Continental Association of Funeral and Memorial Societies, which estimates that a consumer can typically save 50 percent in funeral costs, regardless of the type of funeral desired.

SUMMARY

There are many types of decisions. Some have a relatively minor impact on your future, whereas others can have lasting consequences for yourself and your family. The topics covered in this chapter clearly fall into the latter category. The choices you make today concerning life insurance, retirement funds, and the final disposition of your estate may prove to be quite important in the not-so-distant future.

As we stressed in the first section of the chapter, a poorly conceived life insurance program could result in real hardship for people who depend on your income. Or it could result in your spending thousands of dollars more than you need to provide an adequate level of protection. But before you can make informed decisions about how much life insurance to buy or what kind of policy is best for you, you need to learn about the insurance industry itself. We explained that there are two kinds of insurance companies: stock companies and mutual insurance companies. Although mutual companies make up only 10 percent of the industry, they write almost half of all policies. We also reviewed various ways you can buy insurance, the two most important of which are through an individual agent (individual life insurance) or through a plan covering a large number of people (group insurance). Then we covered the great debate over which kind of insurance is best for you: Term insurance is strictly death insurance, because it pays off only if the policyholder dies during the one- to five-year term of the policy. The cost of term insurance rises as one ages—gradually at first, but much more sharply in later years. The cost of cash-value insurance remains constant throughout the life of the policy, and part of the premium is put into a savings account to grow and be reclaimed if the policyholder lives. But cash-value insurance is an expensive way to buy death insurance, and the savings feature yields a low return, especially if the policy is cashed in during the first ten years. However, there are some new cash-value insurance plans on the market, such as universal life insurance, that offer higher returns but involve a greater risk.

If you survive to retirement, as most Americans do, what can you expect in terms of income? As we demonstrated in the section on retirement, the twenty-first century is going to witness a dramatic increase in both the number and proportion of people 65 and older. Whether Social Security will continue to provide for the people on "pension mountain" will partly depend on political considerations, but there are ways to protect yourself through company and individual pension plans. All company pension plans are regulated and guaranteed by ERISA. If your company does not have a retirement plan, you can set up an IRA and make a $2,000 tax-deductible contribution to the account each year. If you are self-employed, you can established a Keogh account. But you cannot withdraw any money before you are $59\frac{1}{2}$ years old, and you must begin to make withdrawals by age $70\frac{1}{2}$.

Preparing for death is never pleasant; perhaps that is why almost 70 percent of all Americans die without preparing a will. Nevertheless, a well-written will and a letter of last instructions can lessen the burden on your dependents and assure you that your wishes will be carried out. If you choose not to make up a will, the state has one prepared for you, but it may not be to your liking.

You can limit the expenses of a funeral by taking some time to understand the basic features of the ceremony and by making preparations in advance, whenever possible. If you are able to dispel some of the misinformation about funerals, you can be of significant help to others during this difficult time.

QUESTIONS

1. What is the basic reason that consumers purchase insurance? Is it true that "you can never have too much insurance?" Explain.

2. What is a "participating life insurance policy," and how does it differ from a nonparticipating policy? Why are dividends on insurance policies nontaxable?

3. Compare and contrast the advantages and disadvantages of ordinary, group, credit, and industrial life insurance. Which types are most important to consumers today? Why?

4. Compare and contrast the characteristics of term insurance and cash-value insurance. Which generally has lower premiums per $1,000 of face-value insurance? Is it always a better buy? Explain.

5. What are some arguments that a good insurance salesperson might make in trying to sell life insurance to a young, unmarried college student? Under what circumstances would these arguments be valid?

6. What is the insurance industry's reasoning behind selling life insurance for children? Does it make good economic sense to insure children?

7. Calculate your insurance fund using the formula in Worksheet 17.1. How does it compare to the simple insurance-industry standard of multiplying one's annual income by seven?

8. The retirement provisions of the Social Security program have come under serious debate in the past decade. What are the major weaknesses of the program? What are its strengths? Do future recipients of the program's benefits have any cause for alarm?

9. What is the Social Security retirement test? Are

all forms of income counted in this test? Do people lose their Social Security benefits if they fail this test?

10. What are IRA and Keogh plans? How do they differ and what are their major advantages?

11. What is a will? What are the advantages of having one? What happens if someone dies without a will?

12. What is a memorial society? How can belonging to one help you plan for the future?

REFERENCES AND READINGS

American Council of Life Insurance. *Life Insurance Fact Book*. Washington, D.C.: The Council, published annually.

"Beating the High Cost of Probating a Will." *Changing Times*, May 1981.

Belth, Joseph M. *Life Insurance: A Consumer's Handbook*, 2d ed. Bloomington: Indiana University Press, 1985.

Bouvier, Leon F. "America's Baby Boom Generation: The Fateful Bulge." *Population Bulletin*, April 1980.

"Facts of Life Insurance." *Changing Times*, April 1988a.

Goodwin, David. "Dividends: Benefits or Overcharge?" *Consumers Digest*, November/December 1980.

Harmer, Ruth Mulvey. *The High Cost of Dying*. New York: Collier–Macmillan, 1963.

"Insurance Quote Services." *Consumer Reports*, June 1988.

Kaye, Barry. "Life Insurance: Don't Let the Cost Kill You!" *Consumers Digest*, July/August 1981.

Lieberman, Trudy. *Life Insurance: How to Buy the Right Policy from the Right Company at the Right Price*, Bridgeport, Conn.: Consumer Reports Books, 1988.

"Life Insurance: How to Protect Your Family, Part I—Term Life Insurance." *Consumer Reports*, June 1986a.

"Life Insurance: How to Protect Your Family, Part II—Whole Life Insurance." *Consumer Reports*, July 1986b.

"Life Insurance: A Special Two-Part Report." *Consumer Reports*, February 1980.

"Social Security: Should You Count on It?" *Changing Times*, October 1988b.

U.S. Department of Health and Human Services. *Social Security Bulletin* Washington D.C.: U.S. Government Printing Office, 1987.

———. *Your Social Security*. Washington, D.C.: U.S. Government Printing Office, 1980.

U.S. Federal Trade Commission. "Life Insurance and Savings," *Facts for Consumers*, September 28, 1979.

———. *Life Insurance Cost Disclosure*. Washington, D.C.: U.S. Government Printing Office, 1979a.

———. *Staff Report on Life Insurance Cost Disclosure*. Washington, D.C.: U.S. Government Printing Office, 1979b.

Chapter Eighteen

CONSUMER ECONOMICS FROM A GLOBAL PERSPECTIVE

- ☐ The Global Marketplace
- ☐ The Economics of International Trade
- ☐ A Sustainable Society
- ☐ Global Responsibility and the Quality of Life

DID YOU KNOW THAT...

... the United States is the world's largest importer and exporter?

... one out of every six U.S. manufacturing jobs and about 40 percent of our cropland are producing for the export market?

... when you buy Aquafresh toothpaste, Bantam books, Burger King hamburgers, Dove dishwashing liquid, Firestone tires, Keebler cookies, or Shell gasoline, you are patronizing U.S. firms that are owned by foreign multinational corporations?

... many large American corporations, such as IBM, Exxon, Dow, and Coca-Cola, derive more than half their sales revenues and profits outside the United States?

... while U.S. tariffs are among the lowest in the world, our nontariff barriers raise the cost of automobiles by $5.8 billion annually, and our trade restrictions on textiles cost consumers $27 billion a year?

. . . our global interdependence includes ecological as well as economic factors?

. . . the greenhouse effect threatens to raise global temperatures by 3 to 9 degrees Fahrenheit and raise the level of the world's oceans by 6 feet?

. . . each year approximately 20 million acres of tropical forestland are destroyed?

. . . manufactured chemicals are devouring the earth's ozone layer, which shields us from the sun's harmful ultraviolet radiation?

. . . the world's population has reached 5 billion and is expected to double before it stabilizes in the twenty-first century?

. . . as global citizens we will have to make responsible choices or suffer the consequences of a degraded environment on a strife-ridden planet?

We have stressed the importance of decision making throughout this text. But have you given much thought to the consequences that your everyday choices have on others? If you are like most consumers, you rarely consider the impact of your decisions on others. Nor are you overly concerned with the relationship between decisions made by others and the quality of your life. Nevertheless, there are important connections between your life-style, your future quality of life, and the well-being of other inhabitants of our planet. In this chapter we highlight the importance of developing a global perspective in order to see the importance of these relationships and adjust one's behavior accordingly.

In the first section of the chapter we describe the modern global marketplace. Our level of consumption is so great that it could only be sustained by importing large quantities of goods and services from practically every nation in the world. As we will show, it would be disastrous for us to pursue shortsighted policies aimed at closing our domestic market from foreign competition. Such policies would lower our level of living and cripple our ability to compete worldwide. In the second section of the chapter we outline the economics of international trade. This discussion includes the theory supporting free trade, as well as some of the costs of recent protectionist policies. In the third section we investigate some of the environmental problems that have arisen from the development of a global economy. We will review some of the evidence on the "greenhouse effect," deforestation, and the weakening of the earth's ozone layer. We conclude with some remarks about the importance of a global perspective if we are to preserve our quality of life.

THE GLOBAL MARKETPLACE

As consumers, we sometimes encounter slogans like "Buy American" or "Made in the U.S.A." These are attempts by certain groups to influence the buying patterns of American consumers. The general intention is to get you to give some additional consideration to goods that were produced in the United States. As you will see in the following sections, you would do well to classify these mottos as pure, unadulterated puffery.

We Are Global Consumers

Judging by the behavior of American consumers, we are giving less credence to patriotic advertising ploys. Americans seem more interested in the quality of the product and the relationship of quality to its price, rather than to its area of origin. In a typical year, the United States imports more than $400 billion in merchandise. A cursory examination of consumer purchases typically reveals cars from Japan, eyeglass frames from Italy, tennis shoes from Korea, coffee from Columbia, baseballs from Haiti, wines from France, and clothing from China. The American consumer's realistic appraisal of imports has helped make the United States the largest importing nation in the world.

Figure 18.1 shows the value, origins and destinations of U.S. imports and exports. Our trade with each region of the world amounts to billions of dollars each year. Of course, not all of our trade flows are equal. Canada is our most important trading partner, while Eastern Europe and the Soviet Union are least important. If you consider imports alone, Japan is our most important supplier. One other observation that should be emphasized is

**FIGURE 18.1
Map of U.S. trading patterns (in billions of dollars).** (SOURCE: *Statistical Abstract of the United States, 1989.*)

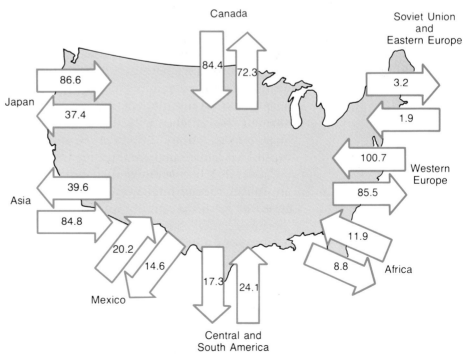

the orientation of U.S. trade to the Pacific Rim. Since the mid-1980s the value of our trade with Asia and Latin America has exceeded our trade with Europe. As we move into the twenty-first century, these regions are becoming even more important to our economic well-being.

We Are Global Producers

Figure 18.1 also illustrates that we are a leading exporting nation. The United States consistently ranks among the top exporting nations of the world. In 1988 we exported more than $300 billion in merchandise to other nations. American computers, aircraft, and agricultural products are known worldwide for their high quality and competitive prices. In an average year we will export more than 20 percent of our industrial output. This means that one of every six U.S. manufacturing jobs is a direct result of exports. Foreign trade plays an even more important role in U.S. agriculture, where 40 percent of our farmland produces for the export market. Our dependence on international markets is also apparent in our corporate boardrooms. Almost one-third of the profits of U.S. corporations are derived either from their exports or from earnings on their foreign investments (Bergsten, 1982).

The Role of Multinational Corporations

multinational corporation: a corporation that produces in two or more nations

It should be readily apparent from the preceding discussion that the U.S. economy is inextricably tied to the global marketplace. Even if we wanted to pursue a strictly nationalistic policy of buying only domestically produced goods and services, we would have great difficulty drawing the line to keep out foreigners. One rather dramatic example of foreign influence is the ubiquitous presence of **multinational corporations**. A multinational corporation can be defined as a stockholder-controlled business firm that produces in more than one nation. These firms may do business in foreign nations under their own well-established logo, for example, McDonald's with its "golden arches," or they may purchase a local corporation and continue its product line even though corporate control has been transferred outside the country.

Table 18.1 lists some well-known U.S. companies and products that are subsidiaries of foreign multinational corporations. You may be surprised to learn that profits earned on products as diverse as Aquafresh toothpaste and White-Westinghouse appliances are sent to foreign multinationals. In this example the relevant firms are Britain's Beecham and Sweden's Electrolux. Did you know that Carnation is owned by Nestlé which is a Swiss corporation? And it makes the Bridgestone Corporation (Japan) just as happy if you select four new Firestone tires instead of Bridgestone tires, because Bridgestone owns Firestone. Table 18.1 is a treasure trove of such corporate connections.

TABLE 18.1 Foreign Ownership of U.S. Corporations

U.S. Company	Foreign Owner	Nation
Allied Department Stores	Campeau	Canada
Aquafresh Toothpaste, Brylcreem, Geritol, and Sucrets	Beecham Group	United Kingdom
Bantam, Doubleday, and Dell Books	Bertelsmann	Germany
Baskin-Robbins	Grand Metropolitan	United Kingdom
Bayer Aspirin	Bayer	Germany
Carnation	Nestlé	Switzerland
Chesebrough-Ponds	Unilever	Netherlands
Citgo Petroleum	Petroleos de Venezuela	Venezuela
Firestone	Bridgestone	Japan
Freightliner Trucks	Daimler-Benz	Germany
General Tire	Continental	Germany
G. Heileman Brewing	Bond Corporation	Australia
Keebler	United Biscuits	United Kingdom
Lever Brothers	Unilever	Netherlands
Mack Trucks	Renault	France
Pillsbury, Green Giant, and Burger King	Grand Metropolitan	United Kingdom
Shell Oil	Royal Dutch Shell	Netherlands/U.K.
Timex Watches	Timex	Norway
Tropicana Products	Seagram Co.	Canada
White-Westinghouse Appliances	Electrolux	Sweden
White Trucks	Volvo	Sweden

SOURCE: "The 100 Largest Foreign Investments in the U.S.," *Forbes* July 25, 1988.

It is hardly unusual for an American consumer to encounter the domestic output of a foreign multinational in the marketplace. It is just as common for consumers in other nations to be employed by, or to purchase products made by local subsidiaries of U.S. multinational corporations. Table 18.2 lists some of the largest U.S. corporations and illustrates the importance of foreign sales and profits. The global spread of U.S. corporations has clearly been fostered by the profit motive. IBM, Exxon, Dow, and Coca-Cola, among many others, derive more than half their sales revenues and profits outside the United States.

This crisscross of multinational firms around the globe highlights the increasing global interdependence of consumers and producers. It also illustrates the futility of trying to close national borders. In a global age it is no longer possible to separate your economy from other nations'. As the prominent development economist Ralph Buultjens said about the importance of utilizing this phenomenon, "Third World countries are

TABLE 18.2 U.S. Multinational Corporations and the Importance of Foreign Markets

Corporation	Profit (billion $)	Foreign Profit as % of Total	Foreign Sales as % of All Sales
IBM	5.26	63.3	54.0
Exxon	4.84	68.2	75.1
Ford	4.63	25.6	32.8
Chevron	3.31	60.5	22.7
Dow Chemical	2.32	55.2	55.6
Eastman Kodak	2.13	38.2	39.6
Dupont	2.10	32.5	38.2
Coca-Cola	1.50	74.4	54.7
Johnson & Johnson	1.41	57.3	48.0
Pepsico	1.32	10.8	17.2
Goodyear	1.08	42.7	40.4
H. J. Heinz	0.59	37.1	40.1
Xerox	0.58	31.7	32.1
Gillette	0.54	63.9	63.2
Procter & Gamble	0.33	29.1	32.5

SOURCE: "The 100 largest U.S. Multinationals," *Forbes*, July 25, 1988.

increasingly realizing that multinationals are one of the few sources of capital, technology and management skills that can be introduced with speed and without bureaucracy into their own economic arena" (*Forbes*, 1988, p. 248).

THE ECONOMICS OF INTERNATIONAL TRADE

comparative advantage: *an economic principle which holds that nations should export those goods and services in which they have a lower opportunity cost*

free trade: *the idea that all nations will benefit by eliminating barriers to the international exchange of goods and services*

International trade has many benefits. More jobs, higher profits, and a greater range of consumer choices are some of the more important ones. Trade encourages individuals and nations to specialize in what they do best. In economics terminology the principle behind trade is called **comparative advantage**. It holds that nations should export those goods and services in which they have a lower opportunity cost. In other words, given their resource base, nations are better off if they produce an abundance of those goods that they can produce at comparatively lower cost than their trading partners and import those goods where they are at a comparative cost disadvantage.

Despite the unanimous support that economists have given the principle of comparative advantage and its **free trade** corollary, political controversy exists over how to implement real world policies. In the sections that follow we will briefly outline some of the arguments opposing free trade and highlight the U.S. experience with trade restrictions.

**The Case Against
Free Trade**

protectionist policies:
*policies that establish or en-
hance barriers to international trade*

Policies that establish or enhance barriers to international trade are called
protectionist policies. Given today's intellectual climate, however, most
supporters of protectionist policies argue that they are generally in favor
of free trade. It is only in a few specific industries that they favor protectionism. These specific cases, however, almost always hinge on their
self-interest. (See Box 18.1 for a famous historical example.)

Many U.S. protectionists argue that a particular industry is unable to
compete with imports because of the low wages paid to workers in other
nations. They go on to argue that by protecting this industry from foreign
competition we will be saving jobs for American workers. This argument

---

BOX 18.1   THE PETITION OF THE CANDLEMAKERS

The satire that follows was written by French
economist Frédéric Bastiat in 1845. He was ridicul-
ing the arguments for protectionism that were
routinely accepted by the French government. His
argument about the dangers of low-cost imports
destroying the candlemaking industry has made
this essay a classic defense of free trade principles.

To the Honorable Members of the Chamber of
Deputies:

We are subjected to the intolerable competition of a foreign rival, who enjoys, it would
seem, such superior facilities for the production of light, that he is enabled to inundate
our national market at so exceedingly reduced
a price, that, the moment he makes his appearance, he draws off all custom for us; and
thus an important branch of French industry,
with all its innumerable ramifications, is suddenly reduced to a state of complete stagna-
tion. This rival is no other than the sun.

Our petition is, that it would please your
honorable body to pass a law whereby shall be
directed the shutting up of all windows, dor-
mers, skylights, shutters, curtains, in a word,
all openings, holes, chinks, and fissures
through which the light of the sun is used to
penetrate into our dwellings, to the prejudice
of the profitable manufactures which we flatter ourselves we have been enabled to bestow
upon the country; which country cannot,

therefore, without ingratitude, leave us now to
struggle unprotected through so unequal a
contest.

We foresee your objections, gentlemen; but
there is not one that you can oppose to us
which you will not be obliged to gather from
the works of the partisans of free trade. We
dare challenge you to pronounce one word
against our petition, which is not equally opposed to your own practice and the principle
which guides your policy.

Do you tell us, that if we gain by this
protection, France will not gain because the
consumer must pay the price of it?

We answer you: You have no longer any
right to cite the interest of the consumer. For
whenever this has been found to compete with
that of the producer, you have invariably
sacrificed the first. You have done this to
encourage labor, to increase the demand for
labor. The same reason should now induce you
to act in the same manner.

You have yourselves already answered the
objection. When you were told, "The consumer is interested in the free introduction of
iron, coal, corn, wheat, cloths, etc.," your answer was, "Yes, but the producer is interested
in their exclusion." Thus, also, if the consumer is interested in the admission of light,
we, the producers, pray for its interdiction.

focuses on the cost of labor, but it ignores the productivity of labor and the cost of other resources like capital and raw materials. In general, workers earn high wages because they are highly productive. If a U.S. worker earns five times as much as a foreign worker, but the U.S. worker produces five times the output, then there is no rationale for protectionism. On the other hand, if the foreign workers are paid less and are nearly as productive as U.S. workers, then they will have a trade advantage. Does this mean it benefits the U.S. economy to continue producing goods that we could buy more cheaply from others? Who gains and who loses?

infant industry: the argument for protecting new domestic industries from foreign competition until they are more mature and able to compete

    Another argument sometimes used to favor protectionism is the **infant industry** argument. This holds that new industries have not yet developed enough to compete on a worldwide scale with older, well-established corporations in other nations. Thus, just as an infant must be nurtured and protected until it matures, so too must a young industry be protected from foreign competition. This protectionist argument may have some merit for firms in less-developed nations, where their labor force must be trained extensively before it will be productive enough to compete with the industrialized powers of the world. However, this line of reasoning can hardly be applied to developed nations like the United States. It would be difficult for us to argue that our automobile industry is an infant and needs protection until it matures. At its worst, many of our most protectionist industries seem to be suffering more from the characteristics of senility than of infancy.

The Case Against Protectionism: The U.S. Experience

tariff: a tax on imported goods

One of the basic forms of protectionism is a **tariff** which is simply a tax on imported goods. In nineteenth-century America, the debate on the appropriate level of the tariff was one of the most important issues in national politics. Northern politicians tended to favor higher tariffs to protect their local industries, while southern and western representatives tended to support lower tariffs in keeping with their largely agricultural electorate. Tariffs rose and fell based on who controlled the national government. Throughout most of the twentieth century, however, official U.S. policy has generally reduced tariffs. Figure 18.2 shows the average U.S. tariff rates on imports since 1900; with the exception of the infamous Smoot–Hawley tariff of 1930, our policy has generally lowered tariffs.

    In the case of tariffs our experience has mirrored that of other industrialized nations. In 1947 the United States helped to establish the General Agreement on Tariffs and Trade (GATT), which provided an organization for promoting free trade through simultaneous negotiations among all members. Today more than 80 percent of world trade is carried on by nations associated with GATT. The World Bank credits GATT with helping to reduce tariffs on manufactured goods from a world aver-

FIGURE 18.2
U.S. average tariff rates on dutiable imports, 1900–1985. Average tariff rates on dutiable imports in the United States ranged from the high of 59 percent reached in 1932 under the Smoot-Hawley Tariff Act of 1930 to less than 5 percent in 1985.
(SOURCE: Don R. Leet and John A. Shaw, *Economics: Concepts, Themes, Applications* [Belmont, Cal.: Wadsworth, 1980].)

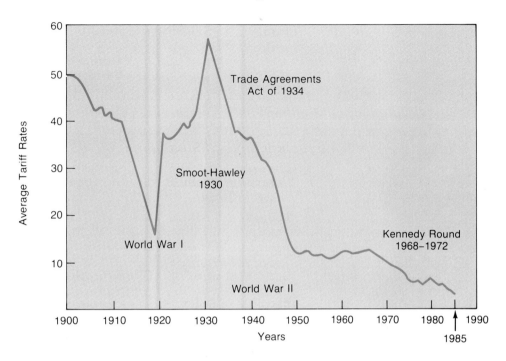

nontariff trade barrier: trade restrictions that limit the quantity of an import rather than taxing the import

age of 40 percent in 1947 to about 7 percent in 1974 and about 5 percent today (World Bank, 1987 pp. 134–36).

The large reductions in tariffs since 1947 contributed significantly to the growth in the world economy (Salvatore, 1987), but the past ten years have witnessed the rise of the newest protectionist devices, called **nontariff trade barriers (NTBs)**. Nontariff trade barriers are trade restrictions that do not involve a tax on imports. Their objective is more often an absolute limit on the quantity of goods imported. They can take a variety of forms, but one of the most common is called a **voluntary export restraint (VER)**. Under a VER an importing nation tells one of its trading partners to limit its exports to the importing nation "voluntarily," under the threat of even higher compulsory trade restrictions.

The new wave of protectionism in the United States has had a significant impact on our pocketbooks. Table 18.3 presents estimates of the annual costs of some of the more important NTBs to American consumers. Some of these are very old. The U.S. book manufacturing industry, for example, has been continuously protected since the passage of the International Copyright Act of 1891 (Hufbauer et al., 1986). Other NTBs, such as the voluntary export restraints on Japanese automobiles, did not begin until the 1980s. But regardless of the vintage of these NTBs, they are all very expensive to maintain. The costs range from $200 million

TABLE 18.3 Costs of Trade Barriers to U.S. Economy

Commodity	Annual Cost to U.S. Consumers (million $)	Annual Cost per Job Saved ($)
Automobiles	5,800	105,000
Book manufacturing	500	100,000
Carbon steel	6,800	750,000
Dairy products	5,500	220,000
Glassware	200	200,000
Maritime industries	3,000	270,000
Rubber footwear	230	30,000
Sugar	930	60,000
Textiles and apparel	27,000	42,000

SOURCE: Gary Clyde Hufbauer et al., *Trade Protection in the United States: 31 Case Studies* (Washington, D.C.: Institute for International Economics, 1986).

for glassware to $27 billion for textiles. Put on a more personal basis, a study by Brooking's economist Robert Crandall estimated that restrictions on the importation of Japanese automobiles in the 1980s added $2,500 to their cost and $750 to the price that American producers were able to charge for their vehicles (*U.S. News and World Report*, 1988a). The conclusion is clear: U.S. consumers pay higher prices and have fewer choices as a result of trade restrictions.

Most protectionists would agree that barriers to trade will drive up the cost to the consumer, at least in the short run. But many of them argue that while consumers pay a few dollars more, thousands of American jobs are saved. This is where the data in the last column of Table 18.3 are so important. The total cost to American consumers is divided by the number of jobs saved to arrive at the average cost of each job saved in the domestic industry. As you can see, the cost per job saved varied from a low of $30,000 in the rubber footwear (tennis shoe) industry to a high of $750,000 for each steel job protected. These are very high costs when compared with the wages earned by an average worker in these industries. Even in the footwear example, annual wages were less than half (about $14,000) of the $30,000 cost of job protection (Dardis, 1988).

As Table 18.3 shows, trade restrictions are a very inefficient way to preserve jobs. They deal only with the symptoms of the problem, not with the underlying economic forces that give one nation a comparative advantage over another. Examples of the inability of protectionism to prevent job loss can be found in the textile and the steel industries, which have been heavily protected in both the United States and the European Common Market. Despite massive trade protection from 1973 to 1984, the number of workers employed in these industries declined by 54 percent in the United States and by 46 percent in Europe. The failure of protectionist policies has led the World Bank to recommend a combination of financial compensation, retraining, and new job creation, rather than trade restrictions, when trying to limit the injury to workers whose jobs are lost to imports (World Bank, 1987).

Economic Interdependence

interdependence: the increased reliance on others that results from increased specialization

The preceding section illustrates the folly of protectionism. The United States and the world economy are clearly better off under free trade policies. By specializing in our comparative advantage areas we will produce more at a lower cost. It should be noted, however, that as we become more specialized, we also become more dependent on others, just as they become more dependent on us. This increasing reliance on others is **interdependence**. As world trade increases, the economic interdependence of nations increases.

Increased interdependence has both advantages and drawbacks. One of the obvious advantages is the increased output that results from each nation specializing and focusing its resources. Interdependence can also be an impetus to world peace. Nations that depend on one another for food or industrial goods are much less likely to try and destroy one another. On the other hand, we must also recognize that interdependence limits our course of action. We become less independent and are affected by actions taken by other governments thousands of miles away. The U.S. dependence on foreign oil is a good example of how our reliance on others leaves us vulnerable to sudden oil shortages or price increases that may result in an economy-wide recession or inflation. In the following section we move beyond economic interdependence to outline some of the consequences of our global ecological interdependence.

A SUSTAINABLE SOCIETY

We live in a global economy. Our well-being is dependent on other economic factors performing a multitude of tasks. The motivation for others to engage in this economic activity is usually individual self-interest. As Adam Smith wrote in *The Wealth of Nations*, published more than 200 years ago:

> It is not from the benevolence of the butcher, the brewer, or the baker that we expect our dinner, but from their regard of their self-interest. We address ourselves not to their humanity, but to their self-love, and never talk to them of our necessities, but of their advantages. (Quoted in Heilbroner, 1986, p. 55)

A world market driven by self-interest may indeed supply a cornucopia of goods and services; however, there may be serious environmental side

externality: unintended impacts of production or consumption on third parties

effects, or **externalities**, that harm others. A negative externality, or "external cost," is a side effect of production or consumption that harms innocent bystanders. If there are serious negative externalities associated with an industrial process, for example, making steel, then part of the cost of making steel will be borne by innocent bystanders. One negative externality discovered by environmentalists derived from the dangerous depletion of groundwater supplies and pollution of the Savannah River by a paper-bag plant owned by the Union Camp Corporation. The executive vice-president of the company replied to the accusation: "I had my lawyers in Virginia research that, and they told us that we could suck the state of Virginia out through a hole in the ground, and there was nothing anyone could do about it" (Passell and Ross, 1974, pp. 36–37). As we showed in Chapter 13, a body of federal legislation has been created to prevent such flagrant environmental abuses, but the attitude of many consumers is much like that of that corporate vice-president: Let the environment take care of itself.

sustainable society: a society that emphasizes conservation, recycling, and renewable resources in order to maintain the ecological balance of the earth's life-support system

Not all consumers or corporations are as callous as the Union Camp example might suggest. Many consumers and corporations support the concept of a **sustainable society**, which means that they support policies that will maintain the delicate ecological balance that has fostered human life on our planet. A sustainable society is one that emphasizes conservation, recycling, and renewable resources. It also requires a change in attitudes from the pure self-interest model of Adam Smith to a concern with the impact of one's life-style on others. One of the attributes of this change is a personal commitment to a simpler life-style. In Worksheet 18.1 we present a questionnaire that will help you assess your present attitude. We suggest you fill it out after you read the remaining sections of the chapter, which describe some of the more serious signs of ecological stress that are developing in our global environment. Our objective is to help you understand the importance of our global ecological interdependence and

WORKSHEET 18.1 VOLUNTARY SIMPLICITY AND A SUSTAINABLE SOCIETY

	Strongly Disagree	Mildly Disagree	No Opinion	Mildly Agree	Strongly Agree
1. I am concerned that what I buy will last a long time and need few repairs	1	3	4	5	7
2. I like the taste of food that has been home grown better than food from a grocery store.	1	3	4	5	7
3. More people should be involved in the protection of our environment.	1	3	4	5	7

4. I am concerned about human rights in other nations.	1	3	4	5	7
5. If I were to move, one important consideration would be the quality of air in the new area.	1	3	4	5	7
6. It is my responsibility to recycle used things.	1	3	4	5	7
7. The more buttons (or speeds) a blender has, the better it is.	1	3	4	5	7
8. If I had a choice, I would buy a new car rather than a used one.	1	3	4	5	7
9. I would rather drive my own car than depend on others for a ride.	1	3	4	5	7
10. Riding a bike or walking to school (work), rather than driving, is a good idea.	1	3	4	5	7
11. The more money I make this year, the happier I'll probably be.	1	3	4	5	7
12. Growing my own vegetables would be too much work.	1	3	4	5	7
13. If I had a choice, I would dry my clothes on a line rather than in a clothes dryer.	1	3	4	5	7
14. I feel better about myself when I wear new clothes.	1	3	4	5	7
15. I think collecting newspapers for recycling or reuse is a good idea.	1	3	4	5	7
16. I am willing to be paid for something with exchange of services instead of money.	1	3	4	5	7
17. To me, finding new uses for discarded things is not worth the trouble.	1	3	4	5	7
18. On a cold day, I would rather put on a sweater than turn up the heat.	1	3	4	5	7
19. I think it is important to drive within the speed limit to help conserve gasoline.	1	3	4	5	7
20. Canning and preserving my own foods would take up too much of my time.	1	3	4	5	7

Scoring: • Add together (a) your circled responses from items:1, 2, 3, 4, 5, 6, 10, 13, 15, 16, 18, 19.
• Add together (b) your circled responses from items: 7, 8, 9, 11, 12, 14, 17, 20.
• Subtract the total of (b) from the total of (a). The remainder is your score. The *higher the score, the greater your agreement* with a sustainable society.

SOURCE: *J. C. Penney Forum*, November 1983; adapted from Dr. Ruth E. Pestle, *Integrating Voluntary Simplicity of Lifestyle into Home Economics.*

to lay the groundwork for those actions we need to secure a sustainable society.

Global Warming: The Greenhouse Effect

The earth has nurtured life continuously for almost 4 billion years, but its ability to adjust to the human race is being severely tested. According to many scientists, we are unwittingly conducting a global experiment on the earth's climate control system. Our burning of fossil fuels—coal, oil, and natural gas—has dramatically increased the levels of carbon dioxide in the atmosphere. This gas helps to regulate the earth's temperature by trapping heat radiated from the planet's surface. Insufficient carbon dioxide would turn our planet into a frozen sphere in space, but too much carbon dioxide could raise the temperature to life-threatening levels. Scientists have established that concentrations of carbon dioxide have

We are all part of the global ecological system on a fragile planet in the midst of a hostile environment we call space.

increased 25 percent since 1958 (*Newsweek*, 1988). A rise of this magnitude will produce an increase in global temperatures of 3 to 9 degrees Fahrenheit within the next century. This is known as the **greenhouse effect** because the concentrations of carbon dioxide act to warm the planet just as a greenhouse warms plants.

greenhouse effect: an increase in average global temperatures over time that is associated with larger emissions of carbon dioxide from the burning of fossil fuels

The image of a greenhouse may not fill you with dread, but the greenhouse effect is a very serious problem. Global warming will cause a major shift in the weather patterns, with prolonged droughts in the American Midwest, decreased flow in U.S. rivers, and the enlarging of the tropics, bringing insect-borne diseases to formerly temperate zones. The oceans could also be expected to rise as much as six feet as portions of the polar icecaps melt; many low-lying islands and coastal areas would be swamped, and levees would have to be built to hold back the rising tides from important areas like Manhattan, New Orleans, and Oahu. These are only a few examples of global changes related to the greenhouse effect.

Deforestation: The Burning Jungle

deforestation: the destruction of large areas of forestland, especially tropical rainforests

Trees are one of our greatest allies in reducing the level of carbon dioxide in the atmosphere. Ironically, the internationalization of the world economy has created large economic incentives for destroying them, or **deforestation**. Some firms have made large profits by cutting down all the trees in Borneo and selling them to Japan or by clear cutting Central American rainforests to make pastures for beef cattle destined for American hamburgers. Unlike forests in temperate climates, the rainforests have very delicate soil that is protected by the trees. Once the forest is cut down, the topsoil begins to erode. In less than four years the soil loses its fertility and cattle ranchers have to clear new areas to provide pasture land. Thus, there must be repeated destruction.

Every year approximately 20 million acres of forest—an area the size of Pennsylvania—are destroyed. This has implications beyond the greenhouse effect because the tropical rainforests are home to more than half the plant and animal species on earth. There are far-ranging consequences to this mass destruction and disruption of ecological balance that are difficult to contemplate. But there are consequences for the human race that are clear, for example, the destruction of these forests, eliminating many species of plant and animal life, may impede research leading to cures for human diseases (see Box 18.2).

In order for this environmental devastation to cease, consumers will have to join with other organized groups to put political and economic pressure on those who currently benefit economically from destroying the rainforests. In Britain the Friends of the Earth helped establish a code of conduct for importers and retailers of tropical hardwood. In the United States the Rainforest Action Network has taken a leadership role in saving

BOX 18.2   THE INTERDEPENDENCE OF NATURE

Many people fail to make the connection between human existence and the presence of other species in nature. They often classify the attempts of scientists and conservationists to preserve species as "trivial." What these unthinking critics do not realize is that by clear cutting the rainforests of the world, we are destroying the habitat of untold numbers of species and thus committing the mass execution of other life forms on our planet. An estimated 20 percent of all species on earth may disappear over the next two decades. Gene pools are disappearing, never to reappear again.

The eradication of other plant and animal life is a serious problem because each species contains chemicals that are often unique to that species. These "natural products" allow a given species to fight disease, attract mates, or discourage predators. All of these chemicals are lost along with the species when the forest disappears. Previous scientific discoveries based on rainforest species have already established the importance of this research. For example, the most effective cure for childhood leukemia is derived from the Rosy Periwinkle, a plant found only in tropical rainforests. According to the National Cancer Institute, 70 percent of the most promising anticancer agents come from species found in these forests. And yet only a tiny fraction of the rainforest plants have been studied for their anticancer properties.

If we continue to devour the rainforest at present rates, there will not be any left by the middle of the twenty-first century. Thus, we will lose countless therapeutic chemicals before they can be discovered. Ironically, we have developed high-speed computers that enable us to identify, classify, and duplicate beneficial chemicals found in unique species, and yet we are rapidly destroying examples before they can be studied.

the forests. This group argues that most of the reduction in Central American rainforest is the result of transforming forest land into cattle ranches that export beef to the United States for processing into hamburger and pet food. In Costa Rica, for example, beef production has more than doubled over the past 20 years, and the forests have been destroyed. But since most of the output is exported, the average rural Costa Rican eats less beef today than 20 years ago—less, in fact, than the average American housecat. The Rainforest Action Network has organized demonstrations at fast food restaurants that use rainforest beef and urged a boycott of stores selling exotic designer hardwoods like teak. Pressure from environmental groups like these has led the World Bank to be more conscious of environmental factors when considering loans to fund development projects in Third World countries. And Brazil recently announced a reversal in its deforestation policy based on scientific evidence of the environmental consequences (*U.S. News & World Report*, 1988b).

The Ozone Layer: A Hole in the Sky

In 1928 a chemist working for the Frigidaire division of General Motors made an exciting discovery: **chlorofluorocarbons (CFCs)**. He was looking for a gas that could be used to chill refrigerators. Previous gases, such as

chlorofluorocarbons: an odorless, nonflammable, noncorrosive, nontoxic gas that is a very efficient refrigerant and can be used to make insulation; it destroys ozone

ammonia, sulfur dioxide, and methyl chloride, were either poisonous, flammable, or explosive. You can imagine his excitement when he discovered that CFCs were odorless, nonflammable, noncorrosive, nontoxic, and very efficient as refrigerants. Over the next 50 years CFC production grew into a worldwide business. CFCs were used in air conditioners, home insulation, aerosol sprays, solvents for cleaning electronic components, foam cushions, and even fast food containers (see Figure 18.3).

The widespread adoption of CFCs has dangerous consequences for the human population, however, because it is now clear that CFCs eventually find their way into the atmosphere and devour the earth's ozone layer. The **ozone layer** is a thin sheet of ozone molecules that shields our planet from much of the sun's harmful ultraviolet radiation. A study by the National Aeronautics and Space Administration (NASA) concluded that the amount of ozone over the northern hemisphere decreased by as much as 3 percent from 1969 to 1986. Each 1 percent reduction in the ozone layer could result in a 3 to 6 percent increase in skin cancer cases in the United States—potentially more than 30,000 new cases each year. A British team of scientists has reported that a hole about the size of the continental

FIGURE 18.3
Uses of chlorofluorocarbons in the United States. U.S. manufacturers produce more than 700 million pounds of chlorofluorocarbons a year for use in a wide range of products. Here is a breakdown of the main uses of the five major CFC compounds.
(SOURCE: "Ozone Warning: He Sounded the Alarm," *Los Angeles Times*, July 14, 1988, p. 18. Original data from Alliance for a Responsible CFC Policy, Rosslyn, Virginia.)

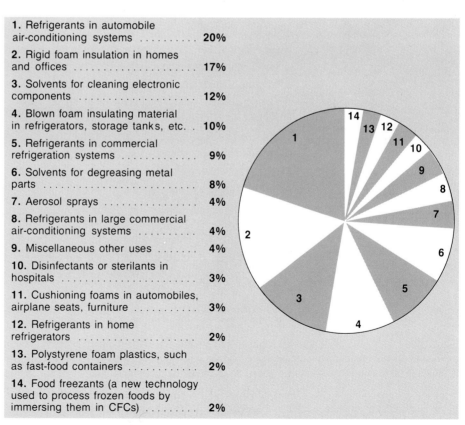

1. Refrigerants in automobile air-conditioning systems **20%**

2. Rigid foam insulation in homes and offices **17%**

3. Solvents for cleaning electronic components **12%**

4. Blown foam insulating material in refrigerators, storage tanks, etc. . **10%**

5. Refrigerants in commercial refrigeration systems **9%**

6. Solvents for degreasing metal parts **8%**

7. Aerosol sprays **4%**

8. Refrigerants in large commercial air-conditioning systems **4%**

9. Miscellaneous other uses **4%**

10. Disinfectants or sterilants in hospitals **3%**

11. Cushioning foams in automobiles, airplane seats, furniture **3%**

12. Refrigerants in home refrigerators **2%**

13. Polystyrene foam plastics, such as fast-food containers **2%**

14. Food freezants (a new technology used to process frozen foods by immersing them in CFCs) **2%**

United States has begun to appear in the ozone layer over the South Pole each spring. This hole disappears during the summer when winds change, but not until it disperses ozone-poor air throughout the southern hemisphere. There are some indications of a similar hole developing in the Arctic region and draining ozone from the northern hemisphere.

In 1978 the United States took the first steps toward a solution to the CFC problem by banning its use in nearly all aerosol sprays. At that time almost 55 percent of CFC production was used in this manner. But the problem today cannot be solved by unilateral action. In 1987 the United States and 33 other nations signed an international agreement to reduce global CFC production by 50 percent by the year 2000. DuPont Corporation, which produces about 25 percent of the world's CFC, has announced that it will phase out all production by 2000. The manufacturers of those plastic foam food containers have also agreed to replace CFCs in their products. In fact, there appear to be replacements for almost all CFC functions, but they are invariably more costly. Will consumers understand the necessity of such increased prices, or will they unwittingly accept a degraded environment for lower prices?

The Population Bomb

In 1968 Paul Ehrlich, a biologist at Stanford University, wrote a book entitled *The Population Bomb*. In it he argued that the single most important threat to continued human existence on our planet is our unwillingness to control the size of our population. Many critics labeled him a **neo-Malthusian**, meaning that he followed in the footsteps of the first population pessimist, the English economist Thomas Robert Malthus (1766–1812). Malthus had posed a similar proposition in his book. *An Essay on the Principle of Population*, first published in 1798. He said that whereas the best we could expect of agricultural output would be annual arithmetic increases (1, 2, 3, 4, 5 . . .), human population could increase at a compound (he said "geometric") rate (1, 2, 4, 8, 16 . . .). Thus, according to Malthus, humans' ability to reproduce themselves could very quickly outstrip the land's ability to feed them. The result of such a biological imbalance would be a rise in the death rate brought on by war, famine, pestilence, and plague. These dreary predictions by one of the earliest economists earned the entire economics profession the label "the dismal science."

Obviously Malthus was wrong, at least in the short run. Figure 18.4 shows that although the world's population has risen dramatically over the past 300 years, the food supply has generally kept pace. And while there have been many examples of the Malthusian checks to population growth, none has slowed population growth. It took about 200 years for world population to double from 500 million in 1650 to 1 billion in 1850. Just 80 years later, world population had reached 2 billion. From 1930 to

**FIGURE 18.4
Growth of the world's
population.** (SOURCE:
Population Reference
Bureau, World
Publication Growth,
1976.)

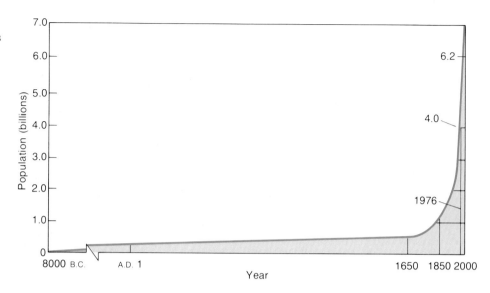

1976 it doubled again, to 4 billion. Today, the world population has passed
the 5 billion mark, and estimates are that it will peak around 10 billion
sometime in the next century (Weller and Bouvier, 1981, p. 33). About 90
percent of this population increase will occur in Third World nations,
since most developed nations have already achieved a balance between
their birth and death rates.

*demographic transition: the
model that describes the
change from high to low
birth and death rates among
the nations of the world*

Most experts believe world population will stabilize in the next century,
based on the historical pattern called the **demographic transition**, which
describes the changes over time in birth and death rates. Figure 18.5
illustrates the classic case for a nation passing through all three stages of

**FIGURE 18.5
The demographic
transition.**
(SOURCE: *Historical
Abstract of the United
States* [Washington, D.C.:
U.S. Government
Printing Office, 1972] and
*Statistical Abstract of the
United States*
[Washington, D.C.: U.S.
Government Printing
Office, 1987 and 1989] for
years since 1971.)

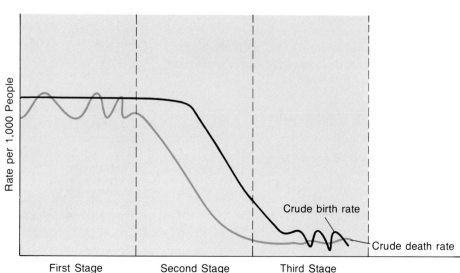

the transition. In the first stage birth and death rates are both high, resulting in very little population growth. This stage was typical of the human experience throughout most of its existence. The second stage begins with a decline in death rates, often caused by better diets, public health measures, and advances in medicine. Since birth rates do not fall immediately, there is generally a large population increase. As the economy develops, opportunities for women increase, along with the opportunity costs of rearing children. Lower death rates mean that fewer births are needed to ensure a family's survival, and the creation of national social security systems make children less important in supporting elderly parents. These economic and social changes slow and eventually stop population growth in the third stage.

However, although the Malthusian scenario of massive overpopulation has not come to pass, it is not clear that all preindustrial societies will be able to follow the traditional demographic transition. Some experts contend that the earth is already suffering from overpopulation (Brown, 1983). They argue that our present population of 5 billion has exceeded

---

BOX 18.3   U.S. CONSUMERS AND THEIR EFFLUENT SOCIETY

The Effluent Society

The global scale of the major environmental problems often obscures the fact they are the sum of billions of individual actions. Here are a few contributions made by the typical American consumer to the greenhouse effect (caused by increased levels of carbon dioxide, or CO_2, in the atmosphere) and depletion of the protective ozone shield (the result of chemicals known as CFCs):

Automobiles

Installed auto air conditioner	**2.5 lb. of CFC's**
Annual recharge of air conditioner	**1 lb. of CFC's**
Drive for one year	**5 tons of CO_2**

There are an estimated 90 to 95 million auto air conditioners in use in the U.S.

Hamburgers

Grazing land of tropical rain forest needed for $\frac{1}{4}$ lb. beef	**55 sq. ft.**
CO_2 emitted by clearing 55 sq. ft. of tropical rain forest	**500 lb.**

Some 138 million pounds of beef were imported from Central America last year.

Homes

One person's annual home electricity use	**4.5 tons of CO_2**
Heating one home with oil for a year	**6.5 tons of CO_2**
Foam insulation for a refrigerator	**2.5–3 lb. of CFC's**

Lighting accounts for 25 percent of U.S. electricity use; substituting a fluorescent light for a traditional bulb can keep a half-ton of carbon dioxide out of the atmosphere over the useful life of a bulb

SOURCE: Adapted from "Rediscovering Planet Earth," *U.S. News & World Report*, October 31, 1988, p. 68.

carrying capacity: the number of people who can be sustained by the earth's ecosystem

the **carrying capacity** of the earth, that is, the number of people who can be sustained by the ecosystem. As we have seen, the earth's environment has been placed under considerable stress around the globe. Each additional human inhabitant may add to that stress through his or her consumption and production of goods and services. If the objective of the poorer nations of the world is to emulate the development practices of their richer neighbors, the world's ecosystem may suffer irreparable damage. (See Box 18.3.)

GLOBAL RESPONSIBILITY AND THE QUALITY OF LIFE

Traditionally, consumer economics has focused on enhancing the well-being of the individual by stressing the importance of making informed decisions. By making better choices, we expect to achieve a higher level of satisfaction and avoid what Arthur Gish described as a major consumer problem, buying "things we don't want to impress people we don't like" (Gish, 1983, p. 21). Nevertheless, there is still the danger of confusing higher levels of consumption with higher levels of satisfaction. Some home economists have accused our consumer-oriented society of confusing the satisfaction of *being* with the satisfaction of *getting* (Frazier, 1983). Such confusion would inevitably lead to a lower rather than a higher quality of life.

Our life-style, dependent on consuming large quantities of energy-inefficient, nonbiodegradeable goods, has earned us the unflattering label, the "throw-away society." This inconsideration and wastefulness can seem merely selfish and uneconomical but innocent, causing others no harm. However, when our consumption habits leave a trail of CFCs in the atmosphere that destroy our razor-thin ozone layer, for example, we need to follow the decision-making process and reevaluate our behavior from a global perspective. Each year the average American consumes about as much wood in the form of paper as the average person in the Third World uses for cooking fuel. On average we each account for the production of five tons of the greenhouse-related carbon dioxide gas, while those in other nations average about one ton (Duke, 1988). Taken as a whole, the U.S. now consumes nearly 1.5 times more fossil energy annually than the total solar energy captured by all the plants in our forests and on our farms.

In an earlier era, when individual behavior could be isolated and thus had only limited impact on others, we might have been justified in ignoring the global implications of our consumer life-style. But as the nations of the world become increasingly interdependent, our actions can result in serious harm to others as well as ourselves. If we demand cheaper beef and are willing to get it from ranchers in Central America, then we share some of the responsibility for the destruction of the world's rainforests. If, on the other hand, we assist in the recycling of aluminum cans, we cut the release of nitrogen oxides and sulfur dioxides into the atmosphere by 95 percent. The point is that consumers need to consider the global implications of their behavior and act accordingly. If our consumer citizenry makes responsible choices, we will have gone a long way toward achieving our goal of a sustainable global society that will mean a better quality of life for all.

SUMMARY

We began this chapter with a description of the global economy and our role in it. Foreign trade and investment are vital to the continued survival of the U.S. economy. We are global consumers and producers. Many of the familiar brands that you buy are really wholly owned subsidiaries of foreign multinationals. Their profits are sent abroad. On the other hand, many of us produce for the export market. In fact, about one-third of the profits of our major corporations come from foreign sales revenues. This economic interdependence makes a mockery of the xenophobic solutions to our economic problems.

In the second section we investigated the case for and against free trade. Most protectionist policies are very expensive from the consumer standpoint and difficult to justify in economics terms. Ideally, nations should specialize in those areas where they have a comparative advantage and trade with other nations for goods they can buy more cheaply from others. On the whole, U.S. policies have followed this principle, but the exceptions have been costly.

Ecological interdependence has followed economic interdependence. As the nations of the world have learned the economic benefits of pursuing their respective comparative advantages, they have also discovered the environmental disadvantages of global trade. Central American rainforests are being destroyed by ranchers responding to the U.S. demand for cheaper beef. Chemicals that help cool our cars and insulate our homes have devastating effects on the earth's ozone layer. World population is expected to reach 10 billion by the next century, and it will be difficult if not impossible for these newcomers to imitate the American "effluent" life-style without wreaking havoc on the carrying capacity of our planet. These are just a few of the global environmental problems that will require multilateral cooperation from the nations of the world.

Finally, we explored the link between consumer responsibility and the quality of life on this planet. The economic and environmental challenges that face the current generation will require unprecedented global cooperation. Simple pursuit of self-interest will almost ensure a general deterioration in the quality of life for everyone. Many consumers may think that the tropical rainforests, the ozone layer, or the greenhouse effect are not their problems; they have the impression that these phenomena are too remote to have any real impact. But they are like a group of people in a lifeboat who refuse to worry about the appearance of a large hole below the waterline; after all, it is on the other side of the boat! Our planet is our lifeboat. If we make globally responsible choices, we can create a truly sustainable society. If we ignore the signs of ecological stress, we run the risk of damaging the global commons— and this might be damage that we and our future generations can never repair.

QUESTIONS

1. Using the data in Figure 18.1, list total U.S. trade (exports plus imports) with the following areas; then rank the regions in order of their importance to U.S. trade:
   a. Africa
   b. Asia (including Japan)
   c. Canada
   d. Eastern Europe and the USSR
   e. Latin America

2. How does the foreign ownership of U.S. firms affect people who simply want to "Buy American"? List five well-known consumer brands that are subsidiaries of foreign multinationals.

3. Some economists have argued that the "Made in the U.S.A." label in most clothing is really just a tax stamp. How could it be a tax? How much more do consumers spend annually on textiles and apparel because of U.S. trade barriers?

4. Protectionists sometimes argue that trade barriers save jobs for Americans. How much did it cost consumers for each job saved in the auto industry in the 1980s? How much did auto-mobile prices increase as a result of voluntary export restraints? Does this seem to be an efficient way to save jobs?

5. Answer the questionnaire in Worksheet 18.1. Administer the questionnaire to two other people. Are the results consistent with your consumption behavior?

6. What is the greenhouse effect? How would energy conservation affect it? How does the disappearance of the tropical rainforests worsen this effect?

7. What is the problem with continued use of CFCs, and what measures are being taken to eliminate this problem?

8. How large is the world population today, and what is the current projection for world population in the twenty-first century? Why is world population growing? Why do demographers expect it to stabilize in the next century?

9. List three actions you could personally take to illustrate that you are taking some responsibility for creating a sustainable global society.

REFERENCES AND READINGS

Bergsten, C. Fred. "The United States and the World Economy." In Finger, J. Michael, and Willet, Thomas D., eds., *The Internationalization of the American Economy.* Beverly Hills, Calif.: Sage, 1982.

Brown, Lester R. *Population Policies for a New Economic Era.* Washington D.C.: Worldwatch Institute, 1983.

Conklin, John E. *Sociology: An Introduction.* New York: Macmillan, 1987.

Dardis, Rachel. "International Trade: The Consumer's Stake." In E. Scott Maynes, ed., *The Frontier of Research in the Consumer Interest.* Columbia, Mo.: American Council on Consumer Interests, 1988.

Duke, James B. "A Greenworld or a Greenhouse?" *Earth Island Journal,* Summer 1988.

Ehrlich, Paul. *The Population Bomb*. New York: Ballantine Brooks, 1968.

Frazier, G. "The Global Importance of the Home Economics Teacher." *Illinois Teacher of Home Economics*, 1983.

Gish, A. G. *Beyond the Rat Race*. Scottsdale, Ariz.: Herald Press, 1983.

Heilbroner, Robert L. *The Worldly Philosophers*, 6th ed. New York: Simon & Schuster, 1986.

"A Hidden Tax on All Your Houses." *U.S. News & World Report*, March 21, 1988a.

Hufbauer, Gary Clyde, et al. *Trade Protection in the United States: 31 Case Studies*. Washington D.C.: Institute for International Economics, 1986.

"The 100 Largest Foreign Investments in the U.S." and "The 100 Largest U.S. Multinationals." *Forbes*, July 25, 1988.

"Ozone Warning: He Sounded the Alarm." *Los Angeles Times*, July 14, 1988.

Passell, Peter, and Ross, Leonard. *The Retreat from Riches*. New York: Viking Press, 1974.

"Rediscovering Planet Earth." *U.S. News & World Report*, October 31, 1988b.

Salvatore, Dominick. *International Economics*. New York: Macmillan, 1987.

"Special Report: The Greenhouse Effect." *Newsweek*, July 11, 1988.

Weller, Robert H., and Bouvier, Leon F. *Population: Demography and Policy*. New York: St. Martin's Press, 1981.

World Bank. *World Development Report*. New York: Oxford University Press, 1987.

Appendix

SEEKING HELP FOR CONSUMER PROBLEMS

This list of common consumer problems includes the names of appropriate agencies to assist you. The addresses and phone numbers of federal agencies and state consumer offices can be found in *The Consumer's Resource Handbook*, available from the Consumer Information Center, Pueblo, CO 81009.

Area	Problem	Agency to Contact
Advertising	*DECEPTIVE OR MISLEADING* Companies involving interstate commerce Companies in your state U.S. Mail involvement	Federal Trade Commission State Attorney General's Office U.S. Postal Inspector U.S. Postal Service
	Prescription drug ads Other drug ads	Food and Drug Administration Federal Trade Commission
	AUTOMOBILES Credit contracts (Truth in Lending) New-car sticker price Odometer alterations	Federal Trade Commission Federal Bureau of Investigation State Highway Patrol
Consumer information	General information; assistance in identifying the proper agency to help you	Federal Information Center
Communication	Radio and television broadcasting; mobile radio communications; interstate telephone and telegraph service	Federal Communications Commission
Credit	Deceptive, unlawful, or unfair financial practices; Truth in Lending, Fair Credit Reporting Act	Federal Trade Commission
	Unlawful practices of debt collection involving the mail	U.S. Postal Inspector
	Retail installment contract disclosure Credit bureaus (Insurance, obsolete credit ratings and reports)	State Attorney General's Office Federal Trade Commission
Debt collection practices	Collection agencies Private investigators Insurance adjusters Patrol service Repossession and harassment within your state	State Consumer Affairs Office or State Attorney General
	Interstate	Federal Trade Commission
Door-to-door sales	Deceptive practices Matters regarding recession (within states)	State Attorney General's Office Consumer Fraud Unit
	Interstate companies	Federal Trade Commission
Finance companies	Interstate and all Truth in Lending	Federal Trade Commission
Flammable fabrics	Carpeting, draperies, interior furnishing, and apparel	Consumer Product Safety Commission

Category	Problem	Where to Complain
Foods, drugs, cosmetics, and devices	Misbranding, contaminated foods, quality, labeling content, quack remedies, and drugs	Food and Drug Administration
	All foods, except meat and poultry Prescription and other drugs Medical devices	Food and Drug Administration (See "Advertising")
	Commercial weighing and measuring devices (scales, deceptive packaging and quantity labeling of consumer goods)	Department of Agriculture
Fraudulent schemes	Bunco schemes and other similar schemes	Local Police Department BUNCO Squad
	Forgery	Local Police Department BUNCO-Forgery Division
Home improvement	Licensed and unlicensed contractors, failure to complete contracts, and deceptive business practices	State Consumer Affairs Office
	Fraudulent sales practices	Attorney General's Office Consumer Fraud Unit
	Interstate	Federal Trade Commission
Investment fraud	Pyramid selling, chain schemes, franchises	Attorney General's Office Investment Fraud Unit
	Interstate	Federal Trade Commission
	U.S. mail involvement	U.S. Postal Inspector
Mail order complaints	Complaints, removal of names from "junk mail" lists	Consumer Relations Manager Direct Mail Advertising Association, Inc. 6 East 43rd Street New York, N.Y. 10017
Meat and poultry	False grading markings, interstate mismarking, mislabeling and false advertising	Compliance and Evaluation Staff, U.S. Department of Agriculture
	Inspection of meat at retail level for poor quality, adulteration, mislabeling, discloration	County Health Department
Mobile homes	Sales or warranties	Federal Trade Commission
Moving	Rail, bus, or truck carriers (complaints include overcharges, late deliveries, late pickups)	Interstate Commerce Commission
Product safety	Restricted to products for the home, school, farm, or recreation	Consumer Product Safety Commission
Toys	Dangerous	Consumer Product Safety Commission

GLOSSARY

ability-to-pay principle The principle of taxation that argues that those most able to pay taxes should subsidize those who are less able to pay.

acceleration clause A clause that requires a consumer to pay an entire debt in one lump sum if he or she fails to meet a single payment.

active solar systems Designs that take advantage of the sun's energy but require some moving parts, such as fans or pumps.

actuarial table A chart or list that shows the probability that a person with certain characteristics will have an accident or die in a given year; used to calculate insurance premiums.

actuaries Persons who compute insurance premiums according to probabilities based on historical risks for various age groups.

adjustable rate mortgage (ARM) A mortgage that allows the interest rate to rise and fall according to the supply and demand for money at a national level; sometimes called adjustable mortgage loan (AML).

adjusted balance method A method of computing finance charges in which creditors add finance charges only after subtracting all payments made during a billing period.

adjustments to income Deductions subtracted directly from gross income.

advocacy advertising Ads by a firm, an industry, or a special interest group that seeks to change public opinion on local or national issues.

affirmative action Preferential treatment of minorities and women in employment to rectify previous imbalance or discrimination.

age earning curve The gradual rise, leveling off, and perhaps reduction of income that occurs as a person ages.

amortization A payment plan that allows the mortgagor to reduce the debt gradually by monthly payments on the principal.

annual percentage rate (APR) The finance charge over a full year expressed as a percentage of the loan. The APR must reflect all the costs of the loan, as required by the Truth in Lending Act.

anorexia nervosa Self-denial of food.

appraisal A formal investigation of real property to estimate its value.

APR *See* annual percentage rate.

637

aquifers Permeable layers of underground rock or sand that hold or transmit groundwater below the water table.

arbitration Resolution of a dispute between a consumer and a merchant or tradesperson by an impartial person or board. Decision can be enforced by the courts.

ARM *See* adjustable rate mortgage.

asset 1. Something of value that can be sold to repay debt. 2. In financial terms, all forms of property owned by a person or a business.

assumable loans Loans that transfer a mortgage and all its obligation from one person to another.

ATM *See* automated teller machine.

automated teller machine (ATM) Conveniently located machine that allows electronic transfer of funds by the use of a debit card.

average daily balance method A billing method in which the outstanding balance is computed daily. The daily balances are then totaled, and the finance charge is based on this average.

average tax rate A tax rate that is computed by dividing the total tax owed by the total income earned.

bait and switch An illegal sales technique in which a merchant offers a product at a low price but then refuses to sell it and attempts to switch the consumer to a high-priced item.

bankruptcy A court action freeing a person of debt because of his or her inability to pay. Although most debts are discharged with this action, not all are dischargeable, and the assets of the debtor, with some exceptions, are turned over to the creditor in lieu of payment.

bank wire service Money is electronically transferred across country or to another country to another financial institution, where a cashier's check is issued.

barter Direct exchange of goods or services, involving no money.

base year period A selected period of time used as a comparison for price changes in later years. Econo-

mists give the base period a value of 100 so that changes from that period can be more easily understood.

basic coverage Hospital, surgical, and physician insurance that covers simple medical needs.

bearish Describes pessimists who believe that the average prices of stocks are going to fall.

benefits-received principle The principle of taxation that argues that whoever receives government services should pay for them.

bill consolidation loan A loan that combines several debts into one loan by providing the borrower with enough money to pay them off, with the new debt spread over a longer period of time.

binder *See* earnest agreement.

biomass Vegetable matter, such as wood, crops, or animal wastes, that can be burned to release energy.

blank endorsement Use of only the payee's name when endorsing the back of a check.

blended (reconstituted) family A family created by the marriage of two formerly married individuals who both bring children to the second marriage.

blue-chip stocks Shares of stock in corporations that have demonstrated their financial dependability by paying good dividends and maintaining leadership positions in their respective industries.

bond A certificate of indebtedness that may be resold; an agreement whereby a borrower agrees to pay a fixed amount of interest each year for the right to use the bondholder's money. At the end of a specific time period, the borrower agrees to pay back the original debt.

bottom-up theory The theory that fashions filter up from the young, particularly from lower-income groups.

British thermal unit (Btu) The amount of energy needed to raise the temperature of 1 pound of water by 1 degree Fahrenheit. A burning kitchen match gives off about 1 Btu.

budget A tool used for money management; a spending plan.

bulimia binging on food and then purging by vomiting or the use of laxatives.

bullish Describes optimists who feel that the stock-market averages are going to rise.

business cycles Irregular but recurring patterns of fluctuations in real GNP.

business firm An organization that combines resources and provides a service in order to earn a profit.

business sector See private sector.

buyer's broker An advocate for the buyer who can negotiate terms and price on the buyer's behalf.

buyer's guide window sticker A disclosure found on used cars that describes the warranty, if any. .

buying-process model A variation of the decision-making model; a step-by-step process that can be applied to the purchase of any consumer good.

calories Measurement of food energy, or heat, produced as a by-product of the utilization of food.

capital Goods produced to help make other goods and services.

capital asset For federal income tax purposes, any property not used in business, including stocks, bonds, real estate, consumer durables, and jewelry.

capital gain The increase in the value of an investment from the time it is bought until it is sold. It is a long-term gain if one owns the investment for more than 1 year.

capital loss The decrease in the value of an investment from the time it is bought until it is sold. It is a long-term loss if one owns the investment for more than 1 year.

carrying capacity The number of people who can be sustained by the earth's ecosystem.

cash advance An instant loan that can be charged to your credit card.

cash flow Typical monthly income and outgo.

cash-value insurance policy A policy that provides death insurance along with a savings account that increases in value throughout the life of the policy.

caveat emptor "Let the buyer beware;" that is, the producer is under no obligation to the consumer after a purchase has been made.

CD See certificate of deposit.

certificate of deposit (CD) An agreement between a financial institution and a depositor that the bank will pay a guarantied rate of interest as long as the depositor promises to leave a certain sum of money in the bank for a specified time.

certified check A personal check for which payment is guaranteed by the financial intermediary.

CFC See chlorofluorocarbon.

chapter 7 (straight) bankruptcy. See bankruptcy.

chapter 13 bankruptcy (wage-earner plan) A section of the Bankruptcy Act that restructures a consumer's debt without forcing a liquidation of all assets. Debts are not completely eliminated, and the debtor agrees to pay a regular sum each month to a court-appointed trustee.

characterizing ingredient The main ingredient of a food product, such as cherries in a cherry pie.

check Authorization or approval to withdraw money from a financial intermediary and give it to someone else.

chlorofluorocarbon (CFC) An odorless, nonflammable, noncorrosive, nontoxic gas that is a very efficient refrigerant and can be used to make insulation. It destroys ozone.

cholesterol Fatlike substances found in foods of animal origin; when consumed in excess, they increase the risk of heart disease.

circular flow model An economic roadmap of the economy that shows how households and firms interact.

classics Styles that endure and that are accepted over a long period of time.

clearing house In banking, a central location responsible for sorting checks and returning them to the appropriate financial institution and branch.

closed-end lease An agreement to pay a monthly rental fee for a set period of time, usually 12 to 24 months. At the end of the lease the product is returned to the lessor.

closed-end mutual funds   Investment funds that sell a fixed number of shares.

closing (settlement)   The formal process by which ownership of real property transfers from seller to buyer.

closing costs   Fees for services that effect the formal transfer of ownership of real property from seller to buyer.

co-insurance   An insurance plan in which part of the loss is covered by the insured person. By agreeing to deduct some of the loss from the claim, the insured party can generally get a lower insurance rate.

collateral   Anything of value pledged to ensure loan repayment and subject to seizure on default.

collision insurance   Insurance that covers the insured driver's car in the event of an accident.

coloring methods   Processes used on textiles to create color or design on fabrics for clothing or household use.

comfort zone   In investing, refers to the degree of risk a person finds acceptable.

command economy   An economic system in which the answers to the basic questions, what, how, and for whom to produce, are all predetermined by a central authority.

commercial bank   Chartered by the state or federal government, a financial intermediary that offers a full selection of services—savings, checking, loans, mortgages, and the like.

commission   A sum of money or a percentage of the selling price paid to an agent for his or her services.

common stock   An investment in the ownership of a corporation that entitles the stockholder to share in the profits of the firm and in the election of those who run the firm.

community hospital   A nonfederal, short-term, general, or special hospital that provides care to the public, most often on a nonprofit basis.

comparable worth   The application of the concept that employers should pay workers equally for jobs that are comparable but not identical in responsibility and required skills and training.

comparative advantage   An economic principle that holds that nations should export those goods and services in which they have a lower opportunity cost.

comparative advertising   An advertising strategy that compares the name-brand competitor(s) of the product being advertised.

compounding   Paying interest on previous interest. The period of compounding can vary from a year to a day, with the shorter period producing a higher effective interest rate.

comprehensive insurance   Insurance that protects the insured person's car against hazards other than collision with other automobiles. This generally includes protection against fire, theft, and vandalism, among others.

condominium   An individual housing unit to which the owner holds title plus a proportionate interest in common areas.

confiscatory tax rates   Extremely high tax rates that result in the government taking almost all the income earned by workers. Such rates discourage work effort and reduce total output in the economy.

conspicuous consumption   Purchasing goods or services because of the status associated with them rather than for a specific need.

consumer durable goods   Items that provide satisfaction to their owners over a longer period of time and, because of high cost, are often purchased with installment credit.

consumer economics   The study of personal decision making or maximizing well-being through rational economic choices.

consumer finance companies   Financial institutions that specialize in small consumer loans.

consumer price index (CPI)   Statistics that measure changes in the retail cost of a given set of goods and services purchased by the typical urban consumer.

The CPI is a common measure of the rate of inflation.

consumer sovereignty The doctrine that consumers hold ultimate power in determining what gets produced.

consumerism A movement whose goal is to ensure that individuals who buy and use products and services get what they pay for: fair value.

contract of sale A contract that itemizes the terms and conditions of sale, usually of real estate; also called a purchase contract.

conventional loans Fixed-payment loans for which interest rates are established by the lender as a result of supply and demand in the national money market.

cooling-off provision A time period (3 business days under an FTC ruling) during which a consumer is allowed to cancel a door-to-door installment sales contract.

cooperative A group of dwellings owned by a corporation whose stockholders are residents of the building.

corrective advertising Informal advertising that a company must undertake when the FTC rules that the firm's past advertising was false and misleading.

cost of living adjustment (COLA) A clause in many labor contracts that provides automatic increases in wages whenever the CPI rises (escalates); often called an escalator clause.

cost–push inflation A rise in the general level of prices caused by an increase in the cost of doing business.

cost shifting Shifting the cost of medical care for under insured patients to other patients who have full coverage. This often refers to Medicare and results from the federal government's reimbursing hospitals a set sum of money for a specific medical service, an amount that is lower than actual cost of the service. As a result, the shortfall between actual cost and reimbursal is made up by charging other patients more.

counterfeit goods Cheaply produced imitations of popular brand names that have been produced illegally and sold as if they were the original item.

CPI *See* Consumer Price Index.

creative financing Combining various mortgage instruments in order to sell real estate.

credit An arrangement to receive cash, goods, or services in the present in return for payment in the future.

credit bureau A firm that assembles credit information about consumers and then sells this information to other businesses.

credit history The record of how one has borrowed and repaid debts.

credit life insurance Life insurance issued through a lender to cover payment of a loan in the event of the death of the debtor.

credit union A cooperative financial institution that accepts deposits from and offers loans only to its members.

custom A societal value that conditions an individual's behavior in a particular situation.

debit card Similar in appearance to a credit card but used to identify a customer wishing to make a transaction at an automated teller machine or perhaps with a participating business.

deceptive advertising Any conscious attempt by a firm to mislead a consumer. This may take the form of false claims, free goods, high pressure, contests, or bait-and-switch tactics.

decreasing term insurance A form of term insurance in which premiums remain constant but the face value decreases as the probability of death increases.

deductible The amount of covered expenses that must be paid by the insured person before benefits become payable by the insurer.

deductions Taxpayer expenditures that may be subtracted from earnings before calculating income tax.

default Failure to make monthly payments on schedule as promised.

defect clause Can be incorporated in a home purchase agreement; requires the seller to identify any existing defects, which is an advantage to the buyer, who can then use this information as a basis of price negotiation.

defensive medicine   Using medical procedures to avoid lawsuits rather than to benefit the patient.

deflation   A decrease in the general level of prices.

deforestation   The destruction of large areas of forestland, especially tropical rainforests.

Delaney clause   A section of the 1958 Food Additives Amendments that prohibits the use of any chemical linked to cancer in people or animals.

demand–pull inflation   A rise in the general level of prices caused by an increase in total demand. This kind of inflation can be characterized as too much money chasing too few goods.

demographic transition   The model that describes the change from high to low birth and death rates among the nations of the world.

demography   The science of vital and social statistics of a population, for example, of births, marriages, and deaths; the number of people of certain ages in a population.

deposit   A set amount of money paid for security and to show good faith to obtain a service or a product; commonly required when renting equipment or an apartment or when buying a house.

deposit slip   Used to record the amount of cash and checks and to identify the checks that you deposit into your account.

depository intermediary   Financial institutions like commercial banks and thrifts, whose main function is to provide various accounts for holding funds for consumers and firms.

depreciation   1. A lessening of the value of a product because of age or use. 2. The decline in the market value of an asset.

depression   A severe recession.

deregulation   The removal of rules and laws governing the operation of a business or type of business, such as banking or air travel.

diagnosis related groups (DRGs)   A system of categories that classifies all ailments and thus allows hospitals to charge a flat-rate fee per disorder rather than individual fees for each service provided in treating a disorder.

diet (dietetic)   Label used to indicate a food is low calorie (less than 40 calories per serving) or reduced in calories (one-third lower in calories than when normally prepared).

diminishing marginal utility   An economic concept that states that the additional satisfaction a consumer gets from the last unit received will be less than the amount of satisfaction from the previous unit. For income, the utility of the last $1,000 earned is assumed to be less than that of the previous $1,000.

disability income insurance   A form of health insurance that provides periodic payments to replace income when the insured person is unable to work as a result of illness, injury, or disease.

discount points   A lump-sum payment to the lender to compensate the lender for offering a below-market interest rate.

discretionary income   1. Buying power that does not have to be spent on basic, life-supporting goods or services. 2. The money that is left after fixed expenses have been paid and allotments have been made for basic necessities.

disposable income   Take-home pay; the money available after deductions, such as taxes and Social Security; also called net income.

dividend   A sum of money paid to shareholders of a corporation out of earnings.

down payment   Cash paid at the time of purchase in installment or mortgage loans.

DRGs   *See* diagnosis related groups.

earnest agreement (binder)   A written offer to buy real property at a given price.

earnest money   A deposit to show one's intention to purchase real estate; also called a binder.

easement   Right to use land owned by another.

economic impact statement A statement in which the economic costs of a proposed regulation are measured against the prospective benefits.

economics The study of how societies and individuals cope with the problem of unlimited wants and limited resources.

economy A system by which a society mobilizes its resources to address the problem of scarcity.

EER *See* energy efficiency ratio.

EFT *See* electronic transfer of funds.

electronic transfer of funds (EFT) Uses automated teller machine, telephone, and computer for deposits, withdrawals, loan payments, and movement of money from one account to another.

emergency fund Money reserved to pay unexpected bills or living expenses during unemployment.

emotional advertising Ads with the major focus of persuading consumers to buy a product for psychological reasons, such as guilt, fear, or snobbery.

endorse To write your name on the back side of a check in preparation for cashing, depositing, or bill paying.

endowment life insurance A form of whole life insurance that emphasizes the forced-savings feature so that the cash value of the policy builds rapidly.

energy The ability to work and overcome resistance.

energy conservation The practice of extending the useful life of the earth's energy resources through wise and efficient management.

energy efficiency ratio (EER) A measure of the ability of an appliance to economize on the use of electricity; for a cooling appliance, it is calculated by dividing the unit's cooling output (measured in Btu's) by the watts needed. The higher the EER, the less the unit costs to operate.

enriched (fortified) Foods that have had small amounts of nutrients added to increase their nutritional level.

entitlement programs An umbrella term for social programs that provide transfer payments.

equity The dollar difference between the selling price and the mortgage payoff of real property.

escalator clause *See* cost of living adjustment.

escrow (impound) accounts Accounts used by lenders to hold funds in reserve to ensure future payment for recurring items like real estate taxes and insurance premiums.

estuary A narrow zone along a coastline where freshwater system(s) and river(s) meet and mix with a salty ocean.

exclusions Items or conditions not included; typically found in insurance policies and income tax.

executor A man who is responsbile for administering a will.

executrix A woman who is responsible for administering a will.

exemptions Specific amounts of money that are declared to be nontaxable.

expiration (use-by) date The date past which products do not perform their best and may not be safe.

export A domestically produced good or service sold to someone in another nation.

expressed warranty A written guarantee from the manufacturer that itemizes the rights and responsibilities of both the consumer and the manufacturer regarding product repair or replacement.

extended families Three generations living together in the same house.

extended warranty plan A competitive device used by retailers to add extra time to the manufacturer's warranty period, the cost of which is borne by the retailer.

externalities *See* spillover effects.

fabric construction A method used to form textiles from fibers or yarns, most frequently weaving or knitting.

face value The amount of money a bond can be redeemed for at maturity. This amount is generally printed on the front (face) of the bond.

factors of production The general term for the productive resources of an economy. They are often called *labor* (human resources), *land* (natural resources), and *capital* (man-made resources).

fad A short-lived fashion; often popular with smaller groups than those that adopt fashions.

family life cycle The identifiable stages that a family passes through, beginning with couples without children and progressing to the later years of retirement.

Fannie Mae *See* Federal National Mortgage Association.

fashion The prevailing or accepted style at a given time; the code language of status.

fashion cycle The stages through which an accepted style progresses, from introduction to rejection.

FDIC *See* Federal Deposit Insurance Corporation

Fed *See* Federal Reserve System.

Federal Deposit Insurance Corporation (FDIC) Insures deposits in commercial and mutual savings banks for up to $100,000 per depositor.

Federal Housing Administration (FHA) loan This federal agency offers mortgages at lower than prevailing fixed interest rates, with lower down payments, and with mortgage insurance by the federal government.

Federal National Mortgage Association (FNMA) One of two of the largest purchases of mortgages from banks and savings and loan associations; commonly called Fannie Mae.

Federal Reserve System (Fed) The central bank of the United States; regulates the supply of money and credit in our economy.

Federal Savings and Loan Insurance Corporation (FSLIC) Insures deposits in savings and loan associations for up to $100,000 per depositor.

fiat money Money not backed by gold or silver but having value due to the faith people have in the government that issued it.

fiber content The basic ingredient of textiles. Fibers may be natural (cotton, wool) or man-made (rayon, nylon).

finance charge The dollar cost of a loan. This includes the charges of administering the loan, as well as actual interest charges.

financial intermediary A business that acts as a go-between, taking lenders' funds and making them available to borrowers.

finishes Chemicals applied to textiles to improve durability, performance, or appearance.

firm A business organization that produces goods or services with the intention of earning a profit.

fixed expenses Large, regular, and predictable expenses established by a contract or an agreement.

fixed-payment mortgage A type of mortgage that has an interest rate and payments that stay level for the life of the loan; sometimes called a standard mortgage.

flat tax An income tax that takes the same percentage of your income no matter how much you earn. It is a type of proportional tax.

flexible expenses Daily living expenses that can be controlled by consumers, such as expenses for food, clothing, and entertainment.

float The time lapse between writing a check and debiting the account. With the advent of computers, this may be only a few hours.

floating-payment mortgage A mortgage for which a homeowner's payment may be flexible over the life of the loan, such as with an adjustable rate mortgage or an FLIP.

food additive A substance added to food as a result of processing, production, or packaging.

foreclose To seize property and sell it to pay off a debt.

fortified *See* enriched.

fossil fuels The remains (fossils) of dead plants and animals that can be burned to release energy. They generally come in the form of coal, natural gas, or oil.

Four Food Groups (Four Food Group Plan) A guide for wise food selection consisting of four food categories: milk and dairy foods, meat and other protein foods, fruits and vegetables, and bread and cereals.

fraud Deceit or trickery used to gain an unfair advantage.

free good Something that is so abundant that there is no cost to obtain it.

free-rider effect A situation in which nonpaying members of society obtain the benefits of goods or services.

free trade The idea that all nations will benefit by eliminating barriers to the international exchange of goods and services.

fringe benefits Nonsalary and thus nontaxable employer contributions to employees, for example, a fully paid employer-sponsored health plan.

FSLIC *See* Federal Savings and Loan Insurance Corporation.

full warranty A warranty that guarantees a consumer's right to full repair of a product in a timely manner at no cost to the consumer; may pay for incidental expenses incurred as a result of product breakdown.

generally recognized as safe (GRAS) Designates food additives that have been in use for a long time. Before 1968 many of these food additives had not been tested for safety.

generic drugs Non-brand-name drugs that contain the same ingredients as their better-known rivals. They are usually less expensive.

GNP *See* gross national product.

GNP deflator A price index measuring the real value of all goods and services produced in the United States. It does not count the cost of imports and is not available monthly like the CPI, but it is broader in scope than the CPI and is generally preferred by economists.

goal A result toward which some effort is directed.

government securities Certificates of federal government debt, including savings bonds and Treasury bills, notes, and bonds.

graduated-payment mortgage A fixed-interest-rate loan for which monthly payments are low at first but increase each year for a stated time period, often causing negative amortization.

GRAS *See* generally recognized as safe.

greenhouse effect An increase in average global temperatures over time that is associated with larger emissions of carbon dioxide from the burning of fossil fuels.

gross income The total of wages or salary before deductions for income taxes, Social Security, and so forth.

gross national product (GNP) The market value of an economy's annual output of final goods and services.

groundwater Water that sinks into the soil, where it is stored and can be slowly renewed in underground reservoirs.

group life insurance Insurance that is usually available from an employer; does not require a physical examination, and often is less expensive than other forms of life insurance.

hazard insurance Insurance that is often required for a mortgage; protects the borrower and the lender against loss from fire, windstorm, or other natural disasters.

health A state of complete physical, mental and social well-being, not merely the absence of distress or infirmity.

health foods An undefined and inherently deceptive term used to describe foods for special diets or foods used as nutrient supplements.

health insurance Insurance designed to help cover expenses arising from sickness or injury and in some cases to provide income during disability.

Health Maintenance Organization (HMO) An organization that provides comprehensive health care services for a fixed payment.

heavy-rail mass transit   Also known as subway or elevated trains. Electric vehicle fixed rail systems with the capacity for a heavy volume of traffic.

high-ball technique   A sales strategy in which a salesperson deliberately overestimates the value of a potential buyer's old car in order to make a sale and then overcharges for the new car.

HMO   *See* Health Maintenance Organization.

home equity loan   A loan that is secured by the difference between the current market value of your house and what you owe on your home mortgage.

home-service life insurance   A small life insurance policy sold door-to-door that features a small amount of coverage and weekly or monthly premiums; descended from industrial life insurance.

horizontal equity   The economic principle that considers a tax to be fair only to the extent that those who receive the same income are also paying the same amount of taxes. Equals should be treated equally.

hospital-expense insurance   Insurance that provides specific benefits for daily room and board, routine nursing care, and other hospital services.

hospital indemnity coverage   Insurance that pays a fixed amount of money (indemnity) directly to the patient for each day she or he spends in the hospital.

household   Any number of people voluntarily living together to form a decision-making unit.

human capital   Training or skills (mental or physical) that allow a person to perform services that he or she could not otherwise do.

identity standard   A food product with standard, well-known ingredients that is not required to have a content label.

implied warranty   An automatic guarantee by the producer that a product is usable and will not fall apart or break down under normal use.

implied warranty of habitability   A warranty that requires rental units to conform to building, safety, and sanitation codes.

import   A good or service produced in another nation and purchased domestically.

impound accounts   *See* escrow (impound) accounts.

income brackets   Divisions or levels of personal income used within the structure of a progressive tax system to determine tax obligation.

index fund   An investment fund that mirrors the composition of the 500 stocks in the Standard and Poor Index.

indexes   Measuring devices, such as the Consumer Price Index, used to follow the general level of prices.

indirect taxes   Taxes that are not levied directly on individuals but rather on products. Examples are sales and excise taxes.

Individual Retirement Accounts (IRAs)   Retirement plans for employees whose employers do not have a company pension program. Workers with lower incomes also qualify for a tax deduction of up to $2000 per year regardless of their company retirement benefits.

industrial-age values   Values that support the "more is better" philosophy. Consumers with such values tend to view the earth's resources as inexhaustible and believe that technological solutions will allow economic growth to continue indefinitely.

industrial life insurance   Life insurance issued in small amounts, usually less than $1,000, with weekly or monthly premiums collected at the home by an insurance agent. Also known as home-service life insurance.

infant industry   The argument for protecting new domestic industries from foreign competition until they are more mature and able to compete.

infant mortality rate   The number of children who die before reaching their first birthday for each thousand born.

inferior goods   Products or goods that are purchased less often by those with higher incomes than by those with lower incomes.

inflation   A sustained rise in the average level of prices.

inflation hedge A purchase or investment that provides protection from loss caused by inflation.

inflationary expectations Belief by consumers that inflation will continue, causing them to purchase goods in the present rather than in the future.

informative advertisement An advertisement that provides the consumer with specific, understandable, and verifiable claims about a product or service.

informative legislation Laws and regulations that require manufacturers and/or businesses to supply consumers with specific product information.

installment (closed-end) credit Loans that are set up to be repaid in set amounts at constant intervals over a period of time.

institutional advertisement An advertisement that associates a product with ideas and institutions that are valued by a majority of the consuming public.

insurance An agreement whereby one party agrees to give up a small, definite amount of money in the present in order to be shielded from some uncertain but potentially greater loss in the future.

interdependence The increased reliance on others that results from increased specialization.

interest The income that lenders earn for letting someone borrow their money.

interest-adjusted cost index (IAC) A method of comparing the relative costs of various insurance policies that takes the time-value of money into account.

investment A way of using current resources so that one will have a larger income in the future.

investment portfolio The mix of investment that an investor holds.

IRA *See* Individual Retirement Accounts.

item pricing The practice of marking a price on a product or package as opposed to marking the price only on a store shelf.

joint ownership A form of partnership in which two or more people own the same property. In the event of the death of one of the owners, the survivor(s) retain ownership.

Keogh Plan A tax-deferred pension account for self-employed people.

kilocalorie The amount of heat energy needed to raise the temperature of 1 kilogram of water 1 degree Celsius. Also known as a calorie.

labor Human resources, including mental as well as physical effort, that can be used to produce goods and services.

labor income The wage or salary paid to an individual in addition to paid benefits, such as pensions, medical and dental insurance, life insurance, paid vacation and sick days, and employees' Social Security contributions.

laissez-faire The absence of governmental control over the economy.

land All natural resources in an economy.

law of demand The law that states that consumers will buy more of a given product at lower prices than at higher prices.

lease A contract that conveys property to another for a specified time period for a specific fee.

legal clinic A group of lawyers who offer their services at reduced fees by using paraprofessionals and standardized forms, and by concentrating on common case types such as uncontested divorces and traffic citations.

legal tender A commodity that has been legally selected by the government for use in payment for all debts, including taxes.

leisure forgone The amount of time one gives up in order to work; time that is not now available for leisure.

leisure time Time not committed to income production or nonmarket home production.

lemon law Legislation, such as the Magnuson–Moss Warranty Act of 1975, that is intended to help consumers who purchase new automobiles that are poorly built and need constant repairs.

letter of last instructions A document that conveys the wishes of a deceased person to the survivors. It is not a substitute for a will and can be informal as well as informational.

level of living   The life-style and types of possessions that an individual income makes possible.

level term insurance   Insurance that provides a constant level of protection throughout the life of the insurance contract.

liabilities   1. In financial terms, all bills or loans owed by a person or business. 2. Legal responsibilities to repay debts.

liability insurance   Insurance that covers drivers for accidental damage to other persons and their property when drivers are judged to be at fault.

licensing   Minimum standards of safety and health set and enforced, usually by the state Department of Social Services. A major factor to consider when selecting childcare facilities.

life cycle   A series of identifiable stages of human growth that occur in a specific order.

life expectancy   The number of additional years a person can expect to live given the current death rate; can be calculated for a person of any age.

light rail mass transit   Trolleys or tramways.

limited warranty   A written guarantee in which the costs for product repair are shared with the consumer.

liquidity   The ease with which an investment can be turned into cash.

load   A sales fee charged to investors in open-end mutual funds.

lock-in   A guarantee that mortgage terms, such as interest rate and amount of points, will be available to a prospective buyer for a specified time, often 120 days.

low-ball technique   A sales strategy in which a salesperson quotes a low price for a new car and later discovers a "mistake" was made or simply offers a low price on a trade-in.

low-calorie   A food label indicating that the item has no more than 40 calories per serving.

low nutrient density   Describes foods that are low in nutrients and high in calorie content.

lumen   A measure of light.

macroeconomics   The study of problems that concern the entire economy.

magnetic ink character recognition (MICR)   A string of numbers or code printed in magnetic ink at the lower left bottom of a check, identifying your bank, branch, and account. It is used to debit your account.

major medical-expense insurance   Health insurance that pays the expense of major illness or injury; generally characterized by large benefit maximums and small deductible amounts.

malnutrition   faulty or inadequate nutrition; too few or too many nutrients.

malpractice suits   Lawsuits in which patients claim they have been harmed by a trained professional, such as a doctor or a nurse, because accepted medical procedures were not followed.

marginal cost   The additional cost of using a good that one already owns. For example, the marginal cost of driving across town to see a friend is the cost of gasoline used on the trip.

marginal tax rate   The percentage that taxes take of the last dollar earned.

market economy   An economic system that relies on individual decisions (for example, of firms and households) to produce and distribute the resources of society.

marriage tax   The increase in married couples' income taxes that results from a lower zero-bracket amount and a higher marginal tax rate.

mass-market theory   *See* trickle-across theory.

maturity   A minimum length of time before an investment, such as Treasury notes or bonds, can be redeemed.

medicaid   A joint federal–state program that provides health care funding to low-income people.

medicare   The federal health insurance program that serves Americans aged 65 and over. It has two parts:

hospital insurance that pays for inpatient care and medical insurance that helps pay for doctors' services, outpatient hospital services, and many other medical services not covered under standard policies.

medium of exchange Something that is widely accepted for the payment of debt as well as the purchase of goods and services.

memorial society A nonprofit organization whose function is to reduce the costs of funerals through preplanning arrangements.

mental human capital Skills and abilities obtained primarily through the application of education.

merchandise acceptance curve The graphic representation of a typical fashion cycle.

MICR *See* magnetic ink character recognition.

mineral An inorganic substance necessary for a healthy diet, such as iron and calcium.

mixed-market economy An economic system that is predominantly market oriented but allows government to have a substantial role as a producer, consumer and transfer agent.

mobile homes Factory-built units that are hauled to a semipermanent site, creating low-cost, minimum-upkeep housing alternatives.

modular homes Factory-manufactured living sections arranged in various ways on a permanent foundation on a building site.

monetarism A school of economic thought that argues that the size and growth of a nation's money supply is the chief determinant of inflation and output.

money Something that fulfills three basic functions: a medium of exchange, a store of value, and a unit of account.

money management A system of planning for spending based on expected income; also called budgeting.

money market mutual fund An investment company whose primary aim is to pool investors' money and buy high-yield bonds. The income on the bonds is then passed back to the investors.

money order A check made payable to a specific person for a specific amount of money, available at post offices, stores, and financial institutions.

monthly statement A record of checking or share draft account transactions.

month-to-month rental agreement A contract between a tenant and a landlord that identifies the amount of money charged to rent a living space for 1 month.

mortgage A claim against real property given by the buyer to the lender as security for money borrowed.

mortgage insurance 1. A form of decreasing term insurance that protects the borrower in that the decrease in the value of the policy is small during the early years and then rapid in later years when the mortgage is being paid off. 2. Insurance that protects the lender against loss by default of part of a mortgage, reducing the risk to the lender.

mortgage note A written agreement to repay a mortgage.

mortgage term insurance Insurance that pays off a home mortgage in the event of the death of the insured person.

multinational corporation A corporation that produces in two or more nations.

municipal bonds Bonds issued (sold) by a state or local government agency. Interest on these bonds is exempt from federal taxes.

mutual fund An investment company that sells shares and uses the money to buy stocks and bonds.

mutual insurance companies Insurance companies whose policyholders participate in company ownership and profits.

mutual savings bank State chartered, a financial intermediary that offers checking accounts and loans; offers dividend on savings rather than interest.

National Credit Union Association (NCUA) Insures deposit for credit unions, which pay for this service.

national debt The accumulation of all past annual surpluses and deficits created at the federal level.

natural food A food that contains no artificial preservatives, emulsifiers, or other additives.

natural resource A form of matter or energy obtained from the environment that meets human needs.

NCUA *See* National Credit Union Association.

necessities Goods or services that are essential to survival.

needs Goods or services, such as food, clothing, and shelter, that are required to sustain life.

negative amortization Can occur in a floating payment mortgage when a mortgagor owes more money than was originally borrowed.

negotiable order of withdrawal (NOW) A checking account that pays interest.

neo-Malthusian the opinion that the rise in world population is a potentially destructive element to the world's environment.

net income Take-home pay; wage or salary minus deductions for income taxes, Social Security, retirement, and so forth; also called disposable income.

net worth The mathematical difference between assets and liabilities for a person or a business.

new-home warranties Guarantees for materials, structure, and quality of workmanship that are now available from the National Association of Home Builders.

nimby Acronym for "not in my backyard," implying that the individual does not want the facility located near his or her home.

no-fault insurance An insurance system in which the injured parties collect from their own companies, regardless of who is at fault.

no-load mutual funds Mutual funds with no sales charge added to the purchase price.

nominal dollars Dollars measured by their face value, that is, not adjusted for inflation.

nonmarket home production Household tasks that include physical care for self, family, and possessions.

non-renewable resource Resource that is not replaced by natural process or for which the rate of replacement is slower than its rate of use.

nontariff trade barriers (NTBs) Trade restrictions that limit the absolute quantity of an import rather than taxing the import.

normal good A commodity that consumers buy more of as consumer incomes rise.

Not Sufficient Funds (NSF) Indication of an overdrawn account. There is a bank service fee for overdrawing.

NOW *See* negotiable order of withdrawal.

NSF *See* Not Sufficient Funds.

NTB *See* nontariff trade barriers.

nuclear family A family that consists of husband and wife, with dependent children, if any.

nurse-midwives Certified nurses who specialize in the care of pregnant women.

nutrients Substances contained in food that are essential for good health, specifically from six categories: carbohydrates, proteins, fats, vitamins, minerals, and water.

nutrition The process by which we take in and use the nutrients essential for good health.

obese Twenty percent or more above ideal body weight.

open dump Land disposal site where wastes are deposited and left uncovered.

open-end (revolving) credit A line of credit that may be used repeatedly up to some specified limit. There is no preestablished payment schedule, although there often is a required monthly minimum payment. There is no definite period of time for repaying the entire loan.

open-end lease A conditional sales contract in which the consumer leases a car for a set period of time. At the end of the lease the consumer agrees either to buy the car outright or to pay the leasing company the difference between the actual market value of the car and the resale value that was stipulated in the original contract. If the resale value was overestimated, the consumer will have to make a large final payment.

open-end mutual funds Investment funds that issue shares on demand and will buy back any shares that someone wishes to sell.

opportunity costs The value of whatever must be given up in order to get something else, that is, the value of all resources, including time.

organic food Food grown without artificial fertilizers or chemical pesticides.

outstanding check A check that has not been cleared or debited from an account.

overall interest rate cap In an adjustable rate mortgage, a limitation on the total interest rate increase allowed during the life of the loan.

overdraft protection A checking or share draft account feature that allows a customer to write checks for an amount greater than is in the account. Similar to a loan.

overdrawn Having too little money in an account to cover a check.

overregulation Government edicts whose social costs are greater than their benefits.

ozone layer A thin sheet of ozone molecules that shields our planet from much of the sun's harmful ultraviolet radiation.

Pack (packaging) date A date indicating the date of manufacture, appearing on many canned and packaged grocery items, although it is often in code.

Parkinson's law A theory that states that the amount of time spent doing a job expands to fit the amount of time available.

participating life insurance An insurance policy that can pay a dividend or a rebate to the policyholder based on the earnings of the company and the size of the policy.

passbook account A simple form of savings account that can be opened with a small amount of money and pays low interest rates.

passive solar techniques Designs that take advantage of the sun's energy without using moving parts.

payback period The time it takes to recoup a dollar investment, for installing energy conservation devices, for example.

periodic annual interest rate cap In an adjustable rate mortgage, a limitation on the amount of annual interest rate increase allowed during the life of the loan.

perpetual resource A resource that comes from an essentially inexhaustible source, and is available in a relatively constant supply, such as solar energy.

pesticides Chemicals that kill insects; used to prevent crop destruction.

photovoltaic cells (solar cells) Devices that convert the radiant energy from the sun directly into electrical energy.

physical human capital Skills and abilities that result primarily from strength and reflexes.

physician assistant A paramedic; an individual with medical training who can augment the health care services of a doctor.

physician-expense insurance Insurance that helps pay doctors' fees for nonsurgical care in the hospital, home, or office, usually on a fixed-fee basis.

PLAM *See* price-level adjusted mortgage.

post-industrial-age values Beliefs that support a conservationist attitude toward the environment. Consumers with such values tend to view the earth's resources as exhaustible, and they stress a go-slow approach to tampering with the environment.

PPO *See* Preferred Provider Organization.

Preferred Provider Organization (PPO) A hybrid between a standard health insurance plan and a HMO. Provides an opportunity for the consumer to choose a hospital or physician, who in turn has agreed to offer health care at a discount to members of that health insurance plan.

preferred stock A security that has some qualities of a corporate bond and some qualities of a common stock. Like a share of common stock it earns a return only if the firm earns a profit, but the size of this return is preset like the return on a bond. Like a bondholder, a preferred stockholder has no vote in corporate elections.

premium   The amount paid for insurance of any type; can be paid in installments.

prepayment penalty   A fee charged by the lender to the buyer for paying off a loan in advance, often as the result of selling property.

previous balance method   A billing method that charges interest on the full amount of the billing, regardless of payments made during the period.

price-level adjusted mortgage (PLAM)   A HUD program to aid in home purchasing, offering a mortgage with a very low initial interest rate. At specified times, the interest and payment do rise.

primary sewage treatment   Mechanical removal of large solids, such as large twigs, allowing the remaining suspended solids to settle out as sludge.

principal   The amount of a debt or investment minus the interest.

private (business) sector   The part of the economy composed of private business; not paid for by public funds.

probate   The legal process for establishing the validity of a will and for ensuring that it is carried out.

product construction   In determining performance of textile, four aspects are considered: style, supportive materials, construction details, and finishing details.

productivity   A measure of output per unit of input. Most often this index refers to the value of production per worker.

product pricing   Marking a product price on a package or product so that it is clearly visible to a consumer; a process required by many city and state laws.

product liability   Threat of lawsuits by users who claim to have been injured or died as a result of product use.

progressive income tax   1. A system of taxation in which an increasing tax rate is levied on each successive amount of taxable income. 2. A tax that takes a larger fraction of income as income rises.

proportional taxation   A system of taxation that takes a constant proportion of earnings regardless of one's income level.

prospectus   A brochure available from a company that describes its previous financial successs or performance. Necessary to evaluate the risk of an investment.

protectionist policies   Policies that establish or enhance barriers to international trade.

protective legislation   Regulations that force producers to alter the features or quality of their products or in some cases to discontinue production altogether.

prudent man rule   The federal regulation that stipulates that managers of pension funds must invest the funds in a manner that shows both care and diligence.

psychic income   Nonmonetary benefits of a job, such as feelings of satisfaction or pleasant working conditions.

public good   A good or a service with significant social benefit that cannot be denied to people who are unable to pay for it. Public goods such as national defense, parks, and police and fire service are examples.

public sector   The part of the economy composed of government services and paid for by public funds.

puffery   Advertising that provides only dubious or unverifiable assertions. Its major goal is to persuade rather than to inform the consumer. Appeals on the basis of emotion, trust, institutions, rigged comparisons with the competition, or half-truths are all forms of puffery.

random-walk theory   The hypothesis that no one can consistently outguess the stock market and make money by choosing the best stocks, because there is no secret information. Thus, the best strategy for investing in the stock market is to choose a large number of randomly selected stocks and then hold on to them.

raw sewage Waterborne wastes from homes, factories, and perhaps streets that has received no mechanical or chemical treatment.

RDAs *See* Recommended Dietary Allowances.

real dollars Nominal dollars adjusted for a change in their purchasing power over a specific period.

real estate broker Someone who has been licensed to sell real estate by the state as a result of passing a qualifying exam and as a result of job performance.

real income The number of goods and services one can purchase with labor income.

real interest rate The difference between the nominal rate of interest as stated on your loan and the inflation rate.

real property Land and everything permanently affixed to it.

recall The power to eliminate hazardous products from the marketplace.

recession A decline in real GNP that lasts for at least six months.

Recommended Dietary Allowances (RDAs) The adequate levels of intake of essential nutrients, such as vitamins, minerals, protein, that meet the known nutritional needs of most healthy people in America.

reconciliation statement A series of calculations performed to balance a checking account and make one's records agree with those of the financial institution.

reconstituted family *See* blended family.

recreation Leisure time used to refresh the mind, body, and spirit.

recurring costs The costs of shelter, such as those for rent or loan payments, taxes, insurance, utilities, and maintenance, that occur on a monthly basis.

reduced calorie A food label indicating that the food is one-third lower in calories than if prepared normally.

regressive taxation A system of taxation that takes a smaller proportion of one's earnings as income rises or, conversely, a larger proportion of one's earnings as income falls.

regular checking account Requires a minimum balance; otherwise, a service fee is charged. May include overdraft protection.

renewable resource A resource that normally will be replaced by natural processes, such as trees, groundwater, and fertile soil.

renewable term insurance Term insurance that a policyholder can renew at the end of a specific period of time, generally 1 or 5 years, without giving evidence of insurability.

rent control Laws that regulate the conditions under which rent can be increased and the percent increase allowable.

rental agreement An agreement that outlines the terms for renting living space, either from month to month or with a longer-term lease.

residual value The estimated resale value of a product, usually a car, at the end of the leasing period. This dollar value is always written into an open-end lease contract, and when the lease is over, the lessee guaranties that the lessor will receive this amount of money.

resources Anything that can be used to produce goods and services that satisfy our needs and wants.

restrictive endorsement Endorsement limiting the use of a check by stating a precise intention, such as "for deposit only."

retailer A firm that sells directly to the consumer

retirement test The maximum wage earnings that someone receiving a Social Security retirement check can receive before suffering a reduction in benefits.

retrofit Increasing the energy efficiency of an existing system by installing improved components.

revertible term policies Term life insurance policies that require policyholders to take a medical exam each time their policies are due to be renewed.

revolving credit (debt) *See* open-end credit.

ridesharing Car pooling as a means to energy conservation; car pooling by using a van provided for a fee and driven by members of the car pool.

risk The possibility of financial loss.

rule of 70 A simple way to discover how many years it will take for anything to double if it grows at a compound annual rate. Divide 70 by the annual rate to get the doubling time. For example, if prices are rising 7 percent annually, it will take 10 years (70 ÷ 7) for the price level to double.

rule of 78 A rule applied by creditors to one-year loans in order to determine the finance charge when the loans are paid off early.

R-values Measures of an insulation's ability to resist the flow of heat from a warmer area to a cooler one. The higher the R-value, the greater the insulating power of a given material.

SAM *See* shared-appreciation mortgage.

sandwich generation Refers to those currently in midlife who are caught between the needs of young adult children and those of elderly parents or relatives.

sanitary landfill Land waste disposal site that is located to minimize water pollution from runoff and where waste deposits are covered and compacted daily.

savings and loan associations A financial intermediary that offers checking accounts, mortgages, and other loans. Offers dividend on savings rather than interest. Also called thrifts.

scare resource A resource for which the demand exceeds the supply at a zero price.

scarcity A situation in which we do not have enough resources to satisfy all our wants.

seasonal energy efficiency rating (SEER) A rating found on appliances, such as air conditioners, that are used only part of the year. They are supplied to assist comparison shopping.

secondary sewage treatment A biological process that uses aerobic bacteria to remove biodegradable organic wastes, and then allows for sedimentation. The remaining suspended solids settle out as sludge.

secret warranty Extended protection sometimes provided, but not made public, by a manufacturer when a particular problem habitually develops in a specific model beyond the limited warranty period.

secured loan A loan agreement containing a provision that if the debt is not paid in full, certain pledged property may be claimed by the lender as payment.

SEER *See* seasonal energy efficiency rating.

sell-by (pull) date A date stamped on grocery products that indicates when they should be removed from sale for best performance and safety.

service-benefit insurance Insurance that makes benefit payments to the hospital or doctor to pay in full for the specific hospital or medical service rendered.

service contract A contract that covers the repair and servicing of consumer durables for a specific time period and for a flat fee when the warranty runs out.

service flow The amount of usage that a consumer receives from the entire lifespan of a product.

settlement *See* closing.

share of stock A share that entitles the owner to an interest in the corporation and a share in its profits.

shared-appreciation mortgage (SAM) A mortgage in which a lender provides a lower interest in return for sharing in the increased value of a home when it is eventually sold or refinanced.

shared-equity arrangements Arrangements in which an investor provides the down payment for a buyer who is responsible for the mortgage and other costs in exchange for a share of the increased value when the home is sold.

signature card Used for security purposes at a financial intermediary to identify your signature and the name you will use for a specific account.

single-premium life insurance (SPL) cash-value life insurance policies that require only one large payment that is made at the beginning of the policy period.

slack fill The practice of accepting empty space in a food container to allow for product settling.

sludge Solid matter that settles to the bottom of sedimentation tanks in a sewage treatment plant and must be disposed of by digestion or other methods of recycling to the land.

small claims court A court that handles disagreements between parties in which the sum involved is small, generally less than $1,500, and for which legal counsel is not necessary.

socialized medicine A term that generally means that a large fraction of all medical facilities are run by the government. In addition, most medical personnel are government employees who receive a salary and do not charge patients for treatment.

solar energy Direct sunlight or indirect forms of energy such as wind or falling water that are produced by the interaction of sunlight and the earth.

solid waste Typically called trash, any unwanted or discarded material that is not liquid or gas.

source separation The separation at the point of use of resources like glass, aluminium, and papers for the purpose of recycling.

special checking account No minimum deposit necessary; fees charged per check written. Appropriate for person who writes checks infrequently.

spillover effects (externalities) Unintended impacts of production or consumption on third parties.

SPL *See* single-premium life insurance.

standard deduction The dollar amount that taxpayers may subtract from their income before they compute their income tax. It is a benefit intended to reduce the need for every taxpayer to itemize actual deductible expenses like charitable contributions or medical expenses.

standard mortgage *See* fixed-payment mortgage

standards Qualitative or quantitative measures of performance that offer individuals a guidepost by which to measure progress toward a goal.

stereotyping A subtle form of discrimination by which people with certain roles, ideas, or values are identified, thereby restricting their behavior both individually and as a group.

stockbroker Someone licensed to buy or sell shares of stock.

stock insurance companies Insurance companies owned by their stockbrokers.

stock split A corporate procedure that gives every common-stock shareholder additional shares based on the number of shares owned at a certain date.

store of value The ability of a commodity to gather and put away the value of your productive activity, letting you spend it later.

straight bankruptcy *See* bankruptcy.

straight life insurance *See* whole life insurance

style A particular design or line having characteristics that do not change.

sunk costs Expenditures of resources that cannot be reclaimed or salvaged; also called fixed costs.

supply-side economics An economic theory that contends government should support policies designed to increase the productive capacity of the nation. More specifically, these policies often involve a reduction in tax rates and government regulation with the idea of stimulating work effort and private investment.

surgical-expense insurance Insurance that provides benefits for the cost of surgical procedures performed as a result of accident or illness.

sustainable society A society that emphasizes conservation, recycling, and renewable resources in order to maintain the ecological balance of the earth's life-support system.

take back a second An arrangement whereby a buyer makes a down payment on a house and assumes the responsibility of the seller's original loan and of a second loan that makes up the difference in the seller's equity and the selling price minus the down payment.

tariff A tax on imported goods.

tastes Consumer preferences about goods and services.

taxable income The income that is subject to tax after deductions and exemptions have been subtracted.

tax audit An investigation of one's tax records by a representative of the IRS.

tax avoidance   Any legal technique used to lessen a person's tax liability.

tax evasion   An illegal attempt to avoid paying taxes.

Tax Freedom Day   The hypothetical day in the year on which the average taxpayer would have paid all federal, state, and local taxes if all earnings from the beginning of the year had been devoted to paying taxes. It usually falls in May in the United States.

tax loophole   Special tax deductions that allow taxpayers to pay less in taxes.

T-bills   *See* Treasury bills.

technology   Society's pool of useful industrial knowledge that regulates the amount of production possible from a resource.

telegraphic transfer   A quick way to send a fixed amount of money to a specific individual or business, from one telegraphic office to another.

term insurance policy   Life insurance payable to a beneficiary only if the insured person dies within a specific period. This is sometimes referred to as death insurance.

testimonial advertisement   A positive recommendation about a good or service, often given by a famous person.

textiles   Fabrics that are constructed out of fibers or yarns, generally by means of weaving or knitting.

therm   The unit used to measure natural gas consumption in a home or business.

thrifts   *See* savings and loan associations

time cost   The direct cost, in time, of a decision; more generally, opportunity cost.

title search   A review of legal records and documents to determine whether there is a prior claim to real property.

trade-off   Another term for opportunity cost; what must be given up in order to get something else.

traditional economy   An economic system that relies on customs (traditions) to produce and distribute a society's output.

transaction costs   Expenses related to the actual buying or selling of an asset. These could include commissions, appraisal fees, and licenses.

transfer payment   An unearned payment generally made to individuals for social reasons. It can be made in money form, for example, Welfare or Social Security checks, or it can be an in-kind subsidy, such as food stamps or public housing.

transitional-age values   Beliefs that fall between the pro–economic growth values of industrial-age consumers and the conservationist beliefs of post-industrial-age consumers.

traveler's checks   Checks that can be purchased for face value and can then be used like cash. Can be replaced or totally refunded if lost or stolen.

treasury bills (T-bills)   Government bonds issued for up to 1 year in denominations of $10,000 or more. These bonds pay the market rate of interest.

trickle-across (mass-market) theory   A theory that suggests that a fashion can be accepted at all social levels simultaneously as a result of mass media.

trickle-down theory   A theory that suggests that a fashion is gradually accepted at progressively lower social levels.

truth to convey falsehood   Describes an ad that tells the truth but makes a product or service appear decidedly better than its competitors.

uninsured motorist insurance   Insurance that protects a policyholder and his or her family if they are injured by someone without insurance.

unit of account   An important characteristic of money that allows it to be used in a numbering system to count the size of wealth, debt, and everyday transactions. This characteristic means that money can measure the worth of goods and service.

unit pricing   Calculation of the price of a small unit of a food product, such as 1 ounce or 1 gram; usually appears on a shelf tag.

universal life insurance   Similar to whole life insurance, except the cash value is variable, the face value can be changed without rewriting the policy, and cash may be withdrawn directly.

universal product code (UPC) A grid of lines and bars printed on a product that can be read by an electronic scanner and that indicates the type of product, the size, and the manufacturer.

unsecured loan A loan that requires only a consumer's promise to repay and so is generally offered at a higher interest rate.

UPC *See* Universal Product Code.

use-by date *See* expiration (use-by) date.

U.S. recommended daily allowances (U.S. RDAs) Designed for use as a standard on food labels; expressed in a percentage, rather than as a unit of measurement, and applies to one serving size of a food product.

usury laws Legal constraints on how much interest can be charged on a loan. These ceilings have a tendency to contract the amount of money available to borrowers and to restrict the number of people who qualify for loans.

VA loan guarantee *See* Veterans Administration (VA) loan guarantee.

value judgment An opinion that is an outgrowth of a learned belief.

values Strongly held, learned beliefs that tend to arouse strong emotional, physical, and intellectual responses when they are challenged.

values clarification The process of search and choice that helps one understand one's values.

variable costs Expenses that are directly related to the amount of use.

variable costs Expenses that vary directly with the interest rate that can rise no more than $2\frac{1}{2}$ percent over the term of the mortgage, with no limit on the decrease.

VER *See* voluntary export restraint.

vertical equity The economic principle that considers a tax to be fair only to the extent that those with higher incomes pay a greater amount of taxes.

vesting The process by which an employee earns nonforfeitable rights over the employer's contributions into the employee's pension plan.

veterans administration (VA) loan guarantee A mortgage available to eligible veterans or veterans' widows at lower than prevailing fixed interest rates. Mortgage insurance is provided by the federal government.

vitamins Nutrients from food that are necessary for normal growth and health.

voluntary export restraint (VER) A common form of nontariff barrier under which an importing nation tells one of its trading partners to limit its exports "voluntarily" to the importing nation, under the threat of even higher compulsory trade restrictions.

wage-earner plan *See* Chapter 13 bankruptcy.

wage garnishment A court order that instructs an employer to set aside a portion of a consumer's wages until a debt is paid off.

waiting period The time between the onset of an insured person's disability and the start of the policy's income protection benefits.

wants Human desires that can be satisfied by consuming a good or service.

warranty An assurance given by the seller that a product is in good working order and will provide good service for a period of time.

weights and measure standards Guidelines accepted as a basis for comparing the quantity or quality of consumer goods.

whole life insurance Life insurance that combines term insurance with a cash value or "forced savings" plan; sometimes called straight life insurance or ordinary life insurance.

wholesaler A firm that sells to other firms, rather than directly to consumers.

will   A legal document that allows the transfer of an estate based on the wishes of the deceased person.

wraparound mortgage   A mortgage vehicle in which the seller loans the price of real property minus the down payment to the buyer, who in turn amortizes the loan directly to the seller. The seller retains the original mortgage obligation.

xeriscape   Landscaping with plants that only require rainwater for survival.

yield   The return on an investment.

zero-based budgeting   A concept under which all expenditures must be justified every year; no carry-overs are allowed from the previous year.

INDEX

A

Ability-to-pay principle, taxation, 514, 522
Acceleration clause, 147, 148
Actuarial table, 572
Actuaries, 572
Adjustable rate mortgages, 360–362
  adjustment examples, 360–361
  caps, 361–362
  consumer handbook on, 364
  features of, 361
  negative amortization, 362
Adjusted balance method, calculation of
    finance charges, 143
Advertising
  bait and switch method, 189–190
  benefits of, 190–194
  comparative advertising, 184–185
  contest method, 189
  corrective advertising, 187–188
  criticism of, 178
  deceptive advertising, 186
  door-to-door sales and, 188–189
  emotional advertising, 184
  expenditures/sales revenues of
    advertisers, 178–179
  false claims, 186–187
  federal regulation of, 180
  free goods sales strategy, 188
  historical view, 174–175
  influence on children, 185
  informative advertising, 180–181
  institutional advertising, 183
  now-or-never offer, 188–189
  professional advertising, 192–193
  puffery advertising, 181

  stereotyping and, 183–184
  testimonial advertising, 182–183
  top advertisers in U.S., 175–177
  truth to convey falsehood technique, 186
Affirmative action, 35
Age
  earning curve, 29–30
  income level and, 29–30
Age discrimination, credit related, 158
Aid to Families with Dependent Children,
    477
AIDS, 215, 239
Air pollution, 460–462
  approaches to, 461–462
  effects of, 460–461
American Chambre of Horrors (de Forest
    Lamb), 207
American economy. *See* Market economy
Amortization, loan, 355
Annual percentage rate (APR), 140–142
Anorexia nervosa, 286
Appliances
  average energy use, 436
  buying guidelines, 275
  energy efficiency ratings, 446–447
  energy saving, 439–440, 446–447
  service contract, 278–279
Appraisal, of property, 357
Aquifers, 450
Arbitration, 223
Assets, 103, 157, 164
Assumable loans, mortgages, 355, 365
Atwan, Robert, 184
Audit, tax audit, 535–537
Automated teller machines (ATM),
    126–127

Automobile
  costs related to, 380–387
  gasoline buying, 385
  leasing, 389–391
  new-care buying, process in, 387–389
  used car, 391–395
Automobile insurance
  buying guidelines, 405–409
  co-insurance, 403, 407
  collision insurance, 403–404
  comprehensive insurance, 404
  deductibles, 403, 404
  discounts, 407
  liability insurance, 402–403
  medical insurance, 404–405
  no-fault insurance, 409–410
  uninsured motorist insurance, 405
Automobile repairs
  lemon laws, 390, 396–397
  mechanic, selection of, 399–401
  service contracts, 397–399
  warranties, 395–397
Auto safety laws, 209, 214–215, 220
Average daily balance method, calculation
    of finance charges, 144

B

Baby boom, graphic representation, 42
Bait and switch method, advertising,
    189–190
Bankruptcy, 166–168
  Chapter 7, 168
  Chapter 13, 168
  exemption for debtor, 167–168
  filing, 166–167

ACKNOWLEDGMENTS

(Continued from copyright page.)

Worksheet 2.1 excerpted from *How to Get Control of Your Time and Your Life*, by Alan Lakein. Copyright © 1973 by Alan Lakein. Reprinted by permission of David McKay Co., a Division of Random House, Inc.

Worksheet 2.2 and Box 10.3 from *Today's Homemaker* by Dorothy Wenck. Cooperative Extension, Orange County, California.

Table 2.2 excerpted from *Journal of Home Economics*, Nancy H. Drennen and Carole J. Makela, ©1986 American Home Economics Association, Washington, D.C. Reprinted with permission.

Figure 5.1 courtesy of the Public Services Department, Federal Reserve Bank of Boston.

Table 6.2 adapted from "Methods of Computing Finance Charges," *Consumer Handbook*, reprinted with permission of the Board of Governors of the Federal Reserve System.

Figures 8.1 and 17.8 and Box 18.3 copyright February 11, 1980; June 13, 1988; and October 31, 1988, respectively, U.S. News & World Report.

Figure 8.2 adapted from *What's New in Home Economics*, September 1974, p. 87.

Box 10.1 adapted by permission from Vincent Hegarty, *Decisions in Nutrition*, St. Louis, 1988, Times Mirror/Mosby College Publishing.

Table 10.7 adapted from *The Fast Food Guide* by Michael Jacobson and Sarah Fritschner. Copyright © 1986 by The Center for Science in the Public Interest. Reprinted by permission of Workman Publishing Company, Inc. All rights reserved.

Figure 12.1 first appeared in *Motorland* (1988).

Table 12.3 adapted from *Your Driving Costs* (1988 Edition), reprinted with permission of the American Automobile Association.

Figure 13.3 from *Environmental Science*, Second Edition, copyright 1988, by Daniel Chiras. Reprinted with permission from Benjamin-Cummings Publishing Company.

Table 13.3 and Figure 13.7 adapted from "Energy and You for a Brighter Tomorrow." Reprinted with permission from Southern California Edison.

Tables 15.2 and 15.8 based on tables in *Who Paid the Taxes, 1966–85?* Reprinted with permission of The Brookings Institution.

Figure 15.3 adapted from *Tax Features*, April/May 1988, Tax Foundation.

Figure 15.4 adapted from data in Michael McKee, "Paying the Public Sector Bills," *The OECD Observer*, December/January 1988, p. 33.

Table 17.6 copyright 1988 by Consumer Union of United States, Inc., Mount Vernon, NY 10553. Reprinted by permission from *Consumer Reports*, June 1988.

Worksheet 18.1 ©1983 JCPenney Company, Inc. FORUM, "Voluntary Simplicity." Reprinted with permission. Originally adapted from a longer questionnaire developed by Dr. Ruth E. Pestle, Professor, College of Home Economics, The Florida State University, Tallahassee.

Tables 18.1 and 18.2 excerpted by permission of *Forbes* magazine, July 25, 1988. © Forbes Inc., 1988.

Table 18.3 ©1986 Institute for International Economics, Washington, D.C. Adapted with permission from *Trade Protection in the United States: 31 Case Studies* by Gary Clyde Hufbauer, Diane T. Berliner, and Kimberly Ann Elliott.

Figure 18.3 adapted from *Los Angeles Times* (July 14, 1988), p. 18. Original data from Alliance for a Responsible CFC Policy, Rosslyn, Virginia.

Figure 18.4 adapted from *World Population Growth* (1976), Population Reference Bureau.